Developments in Marketing Science: Proceedings of the Academy of Marketing Science

Developments in Marketing Science: Proceedings of the Academy of Marketing Science

Felipe Pantoja • Shuang Wu
Editors

From Micro to Macro: Dealing with Uncertainties in the Global Marketplace

Proceedings of the 2020 Academy of Marketing Science (AMS) Annual Conference

Springer

Editors
Felipe Pantoja
IESEG School of Management
Paris, France

Shuang Wu
Rohrer College of Business
Rowan University
Glassboro, NJ, USA

ISSN 2363-6165 ISSN 2363-6173 (electronic)
Developments in Marketing Science: Proceedings of the Academy of Marketing Science

ISBN 978-3-030-89882-3 ISBN 978-3-030-89883-0 (eBook)
https://doi.org/10.1007/978-3-030-89883-0

This Springer imprint is published by the registered company Springer Nature Switzerland AG
The registered company address is: Gewerbestrasse 11, 6330 Cham, Switzerland

2020 Academy of Marketing Science®
Annual Conference

From Micro to Macro:
Dealing with Uncertainties
in the Global Marketplace

Dec 14–19, 2020

Virtual Conference

AMS Officers (2020–2022)

AMS Board of Governors

2020 AMS Annual Conference

Co-Chairs

Pia A. Albinson
Appalachian State University, USA
Bidisha Burman, University of the Pacific, USA

2020 AMS Annual Conference

Tracks and Track Chairs

Advertising and IMC
Jean-Luc Herrmann, Université de Lorraine – IUT de Metz, France
John Ford, Old Dominion University, USA

B2B Marketing and Supply Chain Management
Dinesh S. Dave, Appalachian State University, USA
Jennifer Espinosa, Rowan University, USA

Big Data and Marketing Analytics
Haya Ajjan, Elon University, USA
Dana Harrison, East Tennessee State University, USA

Branding and Brand Management
Kate Pounders, University of Texas – Austin, USA
Bruna Jochims, SKEMA Business School, France

Consumer Behavior
Ruta Ruzeviciute, University of Amsterdam, The Netherlands
Annika Abell, University of Tennessee, Knoxville, USA

Digital and Social Media Marketing
Holly Syrdal, Texas State University, USA
Rebecca VanMeter, Ball State University, USA

Entrepreneurial Marketing and Entrepreneurship
Shawna Chen, Brock University, Canada

Ethics, Sustainability and CSR
B. Yasanthi Perera, Brock University, Canada
Sarita Ray Chaudhury, Humboldt State University, USA

Macromarketing
Aimee Huff, Oregon State University, USA
Kofi Dadzie, Georgia State University, USA

Marketing Pedagogy and Education
Kesha Coker, Ball State University, USA
Kevin Shanahan, Mississippi State University, USA

Marketing Strategy
G. David Shows, Appalachian State University, USA
Jeannette A. Mena, University of South Florida, USA

Innovations and New Product Development
Narongsak (Tek) Thongpapanl, Brock University, Canada
Adam Mills, Loyola University New Orleans, USA

Iberoamerican Marketing Studies
Juan Carlos Sosa Varela, Universidad Ana G. Méndez, Puerto Rico
Göran Svensson, Kristiania University College, Norway

International Marketing
Tarek T. Mady, University of Prince Edward Island, Canada
Sarah Mady, American University Washington DC, USA

Non-profit Marketing and Public Policy
Karen Hopkins, Auburn University, USA
Chris Hopkins, Auburn University, USA

Personal Selling and Sales Management
Mark Groza, University of Northern Illinois, USA

Sensory and Food/ Beverage Marketing
Dipayan Biswas, University of South Florida, USA
Claas Christian Germelmann, University of Bayreuth, Germany

Research Methods
Dennis Kopf, University of Wisconsin – Whitewater, USA
Maxwell K. Hsu, University of Wisconsin – Whitewater, USA

Retailing and Pricing
Monika Kukar-Kinney, University of Richmond, USA
Sara Hanson, University of Richmond, USA

Services, Tourism, and Hospitality Marketing
Courtney Szocs, Louisiana State University, USA
Felipe Pantoja, IÉSEG School of Management, France

Sports and Entertainment Marketing
Nina Krey, Rowan University, USA
Patricia Rossi, IÉSEG School of Management, France

Doctoral Colloquium
Altaf Merchant, University of Washington, Tacoma, USA
Mathieu Kacha, Cerefige – University of Lorraine, France

Mary Kay Inc. Doctoral Dissertation
Raj Agnihotri, Iowa State University, USA
Ritesh Saini, University of Texas Arlington, USA

Special Session Submission
Pia A. Albinsson, Appalachian State University, USA
Bidisha Burman, University of the Pacific, USA

Proceedings Editors
Felipe Pantoja, IÉSEG School of Management, France
Shuang Wu, Rowan University, USA

Director of Technology and Data Management
Dana Harrison, East Tennessee State University, USA

2020 AMS Annual Conference Reviewers

Thank you to all those who reviewed papers for the 2020 AMS Annual Conference. These people include:

Annika Abell	Michael Bimpeh	Benedetta Crisafulli
Zehra Abi	Samantha Bittner	Samantha Cross
Mohamed Akli Achabou	Ashley Blank	Ryan Cruz
Raj Agnihotri	Tim Boettger	Krista Cummings
Hee-Kyung Ahn	Victor Bohorquez	Vassilis Dalakas
Haya Ajjan	Stephen Bok	Derick Davis
M. Billur Akdeniz	Laura Boman	Vasileios Davvetas
Mohamed Didi Alaoui	Raghuram Bommaraju	Larissa Deikmann
Mohammed Didi Alaoui	Elsamari Botha	Ashley Deutsch
Levke Albertsen	Achilleas Boukis	Christian Dianoux
Pia A. Albinsson	Flávio Régio Brambilla	Radu Dimitriu
Anupama Ambika	Joël Brée	Diem Do
Lam An	Els Breugelmans	Virgin Dones
Elena Anastasiadou	Elten Briggs	Olivier Droulers
Kelley Anderson	Katja Brunk	Sherese Duncan
Thomas Anning-Dorson	Bidisha Burman	Marilyn Eastman
Denni Arli	Kyung-Ah Byun	Peter Ekman
Vikas Arya	Frank Cabano	Nada Elbishbishy
Ioannis Assiouras	Elke Cabooter	Leila Elgaaied-Gambier
Aslı Elif Aydın	Barbara Caemmerer	Maher Georges Elmashhara
Jessica Babin	Fanny Cambier	Maryam Farhang
Laurie Babin	Colin Campbell	Pablo Farías
Sophie Lacoste Badie	Ellen Campos Sousa	Manon Favier
Marat Bakpayev	Jeff Carlson	Hui Feng
Anjali Bal	Les Carlson	Bob Fennis
Silke Bambauer-Sachse	Grace Carson	Karen Fernandez
Amrita Bansal	Lina Ceballos	Caitlin Ferreira

Dovile Barauskaite	Julio Cervino	Carlos Ferro
Christian Barney	Nawar Chaker	Jose Flecha-Ortiz
Michelle Barnhart	Elena Chatzopoulou	Lura Forcum
Arne Baruca	Sarita Ray Chaudhury	John Ford
Nicole Beachum	Shawna Chen	Alexa Fox
Larissa Becker	Zixuan Cheng	Gary Frankwick
Gerald-Alexander Beese	Valeriia Chernikova	Ryan Freling
Mohammadali Koorank Beheshti	Raeesah Chohan	Pilar Rojas Gaviria
Mark Bender	Robert Ciuchita	Guanyu Geng
Ilgım Benoit	Pauline Claeys	Matthias Glaser
Subhalakshmi Bezbaruah	Mark Cleveland	Ashley Goreczny
Neeraj Bhardwaj	Zandereen Coetzee	Diana Gregory-Smith
Siddharth Bhatt	Kesha Coker	Merlyn Griffiths
	Andrew Crecelius	Christopher Groening
Reinhard Grohs	Moein Khanlari	Sudha Mani
Mark Groza	Adwait Khare	Babu Mariadoss
Abhijit Guha	Rae Yule Kim	Adam Marquardt
Aditya Gupta	Yeseul Kim	Percy Marquina
Brandon Gustafson	Eva Kipnis	Hannah Marriott
Tyler Hancock	Theresa Kirchner	Erick Mas
Sara Hanson	Sören Köcher	Ewa Maslowska
Jianyu Hao	Michalis Kokkoris	Anil Mathur
Haley Hardman	Mateja Kos Koklic	Lucy Matthews
Dana Harrison	Dennis Kopf	Mieszko Mazur
Mary Harrison	Elika Kordrostami	Elizabeth McDougal
Nathaniel Hartmann	Daniel Korschun	Brian McLeod
Jonathan Hasford	Alena Kostyk	Lisa McNeill
Ashley Hass	Nina Krey	R.G. Vishnu Menon
Heping He	Riley Krotz	Lars Meyer-Waarden
Xin He	Marc Kuhn	Joel Mier
Adam Hepworth	Monika Kukar-Kinney	Tyler Milfeld
Jean-Luc Herrmann	Atul Kulkarni	Chadwick Miller
Nico Heuvinck	Ankita Kumar	Adam Mills
Ganga Urumutta Hewage	Lauren Labrecque	Holly Milne
Bryan Hochstein	Russ Laczniak	Alex Milovic
Nancy Hodges	Guisell Larregui	Lisa Monahan
Stefan Hoffman	Kathy LaTour	Zachary Moore
Jenny Hong	Tommi Laukkanen	Masoud Moradi
Elisabeth Honka	Debbie Laverie	Julie Moulard
David Houghton	Thomas Leclercq	Jay Mulki
Ying Huang	Sarah Lefebvre	Ryan Mullins
Yu-Shan Sandy Huang	Donald Lehmann	Kavitha Nambisan
Verena Huettl	Jean-François Lemoine	Christopher Newman
Magnus Hultman	Shirley Li	Kevin Newman
Sajna Ibrahim	Yiyi Li	Marzena Nieroda

Subin Im	Marcel Lichters	Leila Marcano Nieves
Monika Imschloss	Luke Liska	Fabian Nindl
Chiharu Ishida	Dong Liu	William M. Northington
Anil Isisag	Yuping Liu-Thompkins	Edward Nowlin
Omar Itani	Jennifer Locander	Michael Obal
Mazen Jaber	Gautier Lombard	Obinna Obilo
Varsha Jain	Evelyn Lopez	Christina O'Connor
Melissa James	Jennifer Ramone Louis	Philippe Odou
Khalia Jenkins	Sandra Loureiro	Vanessa O'Neill
Bruna Jochims	Kate Loveland	Robert Opoku
Yannick Joye	Renaud Lunardo	Maribel Ortiz
Ashish Kalra	Andy Lynch	Carmen Otero-Neira
Harish Kapoor	Dominik Mahr	Tobias Otterbring
Brett Kazandjian	Suresh Malodia	Nil Özçağlar
April Kemp	Stephanie Mangus	Carmen Padin
Yue Pan	Camille Saintives	Daphane Tan
Nikolaos Panagopoulos	Laszlo Sajtos	Chuanyi Tang
Felipe Pantoja	Tina Saksida	Elina Tang
Karolos-Konstantinos Papadas	Roberto Saldivar	Andrea Tangari
Catherine Papetti	Leila Samii	Wayne Taylor
Andrew Park	Doreen Sams	Mohamed Sobhy Temerak
Young Park	Joaquin Sanchez-Herrera	Veronica Thomas
Janna Parker	Mirela Santos	Frauke Mattison Thompson
Michael Peasley	Roberto S. Santos	Steven Thompson
Fabien Pecot	Maria Santos-Corrada	Carina Thuerridl
Kiran Pedada	Hanieh Sardashti	Jose Saavedra Torres
Lou Pelton	Tobias Schaefers	Irina Toteva
Yasanthi Perera	Steffen Schmidt	Janell Townsend
Robert Peterson	Joachim Scholz	Gina Tran-Stafford
Maria Petrescu	Carsten D. Schultz	Ceren Turedi
Luca Petruzzellis	Christopher Schumacher	Serdar Turedi
Megan Phillips	Maximillian Schwing	Ebru Ulusoy
Christine Pitt	Barbara Seegebarth	Erbu Ulusoy
Kirk Plangger	Samuel Sekar	Nita Umashankar
Gordy Pleyers	Nuket Serin	Olga Unitlov
Anissa Pomies	Deepa Sethi	Elze Uzdavinyte
Randle Raggio	Marcos Severo	Alessandra Vecchi
Reza Rajabi	Kevin Shanahan	Valter Vieira
Peter Ralston	Anshuman Sharma	Udo Wagner
Nora Ramadan	Atul Shiva	Cindy Wang
Praneet Randhawa	Béatrice Siadou-Martin	Manxin Wang
Iman Raoofpanah	Josh Siegel	Ze Wang
Adam Rapp	Jeremy Sierra	Nathan Warren
Monika Rawal	Debika Sihi	Kittichai Watchravesringkan
Anouk De Regt	Rakesh Singh	Fei Weisstein

Brandon Reich	Ramendra Singh	Jutong Wen
Pavel Reyes	Jayati Sinha	Douglas West
Mary Rivera	Jose Ribamar Siqueira	Hillary Wiener
Jeandri Robertson	Stefan Sleep	David Woisetschläger
Rocio Rodriguez	Leah Smith	Yvette Woltman
Alexandra Rome	Michelle van Solt	Parker Woodroof
Marisabel Romero	Hyunsang Son	Lan Xia
Jimmie Röndell	Juan Carlos Sosa Varela	Guang-Xin Xie
José Rosa	Francesca Sotgiu	Linli Xu
Spencer Ross	Veasna Sou	Amy Yacus
Patricia Rossi	Arun Sreekumar	Amanda Yamim
Rajat Roy	Kristina Stuhler	Zhiyong Yang
Ruta Ruzeviciute	Sijie Sun	Jun Yao
Ouidade Sabri	Sarang Sunder	Beauty Yaoyuneyong
Raika Sadeghein	Göran Svensson	Atefeh Yazdanparast
Ritesh Saini	Zonaib Tahir	Chebli Youness
Max Yu	Jim Zemanek	Chongyang Zhou
Zhihao Yu	Junzhou Zhang	Fereshteh Zihagh
Alex Zablah	Zhuofan Zhang	Louis Zmich

Preface

The Academy of Marketing Science was founded in 1971, held its first Annual Conference in 1977, and has grown and prospered ever since. The relevancy of the Academy's mission and activities to our chosen target market of the marketing professoriate has been a key factor in attracting the discipline's best and brightest from all over the world.

The revised Articles of Association of the Academy, approved by the Board of Governors in the spring of 1984 and by the general membership in the fall of that year, define the mission of the Academy as follows:

1. Provide leadership in exploring the normative boundaries of marketing, while simultaneously seeking new ways of bringing theory and practice into practicable conjunction.
2. Further the science of marketing throughout the world by promoting the conduct of research and the dissemination of research results.
3. Provide a forum for the study and improvement of marketing as an economic, ethical, social, and political force and process.
4. Furnish, as appropriate and available, material and other resources for the solution of marketing problems, which confront particular firms and industries, on the one hand, and society at large on the other.
5. Provide publishing media and facilities for fellows of the Academy and reviewer assistance on the fellow's scholarly activities.
6. Sponsor one or more annual conferences to enable the fellows of the Academy to present research results; to learn by listening to other presentations and through interaction with other fellows and guests; to avail themselves of the placements process; to conduct discussion with book editors; and to exchange other relevant information.
7. Assist fellows in the better utilization of their professional marketing talents through redirection, reassignment, and relocation.
8. Provide educator fellows with insights and resources as may be available to aid them in the development of improved teaching methods, materials, devices, and directions.

9. Seek means for establishing student scholarships and professional university chairs in the field of marketing.
10. Offer fellows of the Academy status to business and institutional executives and organizations.
11. Modify the Academy's purpose and direction as the influence of time and appropriate constructive forces may dictate.

Paris, France
Glassboro, NJ, USA

Felipe Pantoja
Shuang Wu

Acknowledgments

This book contains the full proceedings of the 2020 Academy of Marketing Science Annual Conference held virtually for the first time. Appreciation and gratitude are extended to the organization committee for completing and handling a variety of tasks associated with an event of this scale particularly well.

Under the theme "From Micro to Macro: Dealing with Uncertainties in the Global Marketplace," this volume provides insights into topics related to the uncertainties resulting from emerging technologies and disruptive innovations. For example, some large privately held start-ups, specifically those created in the last decade have recently gone public to manage risks, with varied levels of success. Many of these are Hi-Tech companies that are leveraging artificial intelligence, machine learning, cloud computing, robotic automation, augmented reality, and other recent advancements. These digital technology companies are bringing incremental, as well as radical and disruptive innovations to the marketplace, sometimes challenging the status quo of long-standing incumbents and traditional industries and profoundly impacting consumer experiences. Hence, these challenges bring important discussions to the marketing practice that will be discussed during the 2020 AMS Annual conference.

The Academy of Marketing Science would like to acknowledge the individuals who have made the conference a success. Special recognition goes to the conference co-chairs, Pia A. Albinson and Bidisha Burman. An incredible commitment is necessary to coordinate and organize a conference of this measure in this new virtual environment. Further, track chairs were essential in encouraging submissions, managing the review process, and organizing session details. Gratitude is also extended to the AMS home office as well as all the volunteers who diligently work behind the scenes to ensure the success of the event.

Lastly, the Academy of Marketing Science extends sincere appreciation to all authors who submitted and presented their research, contributed as reviewers and discussion leaders, and all others who volunteered to ensure the success of the meeting. Thank you to all attendees from around the world who made this conference another special AMS event. The 2020 Academy of Marketing Science Annual

Conference would not have been possible without the support of all of these individuals.

Felipe Pantoja
Shuang Wu

Contents

The Essentials of Marketing Analytics: Teaching, Research and Practice—An Abstract

Dana E. Harrison, Haya Ajjan, Joe F. Hair Jr, Scott Ryan, Chris Myers, Peter Drewes, and William Disch

Abstract Marketing analytics encompasses data, statistics, mathematics and technology. In combination, these components facilitate decision making. We are witnessing companies across industries adopt marketing analytics to improve and expand decision making capabilities. Using marketing analytics is now within reach for most companies since advanced techniques and technologies have increased accessibility. Analytics applications are now becoming infused in everyday tasks. Marketing will continue to fundamentally change over the next few years as we witness increased digital and mobile infusion. As analytics techniques and technology advance, job opportunities and skills will see demand skyrocket. As a result, mar-

D. E. Harrison (✉)
East Tennessee State University, Johnson City, TN, USA
e-mail: harrisondl@etsu.edu

H. Ajjan
Elon University, Elon, NC, USA
e-mail: hajjan@elon.edu

J. F. HairJr
University of South Alabama, Mobile, AL, USA
e-mail: jhair@southalabama.edu

S. Ryan
Hanes Brands, Inc., Winston Salem, NC, USA
e-mail: scott.ryan@hanes.com

C. Myers
Texas A&M University, Commerce, TX, USA
e-mail: chris.myers@tamuc.edu

P. Drewes
Lockheed Martin, Ft Worth, TX, USA
e-mail: peter.drewes@lmco.com

W. Disch
DataRobot, Salem, CT, USA
e-mail: william.disch@datarobot.com

F. Pantoja, S. Wu (eds.), *From Micro to Macro: Dealing with Uncertainties in the Global Marketplace*, Developments in Marketing Science: Proceedings of the Academy of Marketing Science, https://doi.org/10.1007/978-3-030-89883-0_1

keting education must move to embed analytics using active learning techniques into existing courses and introduce students to emerging skills. The result will be a cohesively structured hands-on pedagogical framework which can focus on understanding domain elements when applied to business problems. Aligning analytics and domain knowledge will generate work-ready marketing analysts. Although teaching marketing analytics is crucial in producing work-ready graduates, research is also critical. Unfortunately, the inter-disciplinary lens required to accurately explore the interaction between marketing analytics and society is underdeveloped. As dependence in practice intensifies, industry and academic journals are increasingly searching for valid sources of information on marketing analytics.

The objective of this panel session is to discuss the transformation occurring in both academia and practice as a result of big data and data analytics. We will explore how marketing education and research can support the needs of practitioners. The panel will introduce curriculum and research ideas, as well as identify technologies and techniques most often used by practitioners. The panel session will include an introduction to marketing analytics, panel member insights for designing and implementing a marketing analytics curriculum, strategies for advancing research, followed by audience Q&A.

Keywords Marketing analytics · Marketing analytics education · Big data · Analytics tools

References Available Upon Request

Authenticity Goes Digital: A Big Data Analysis of the Influence of the Country of Origin and Authenticity Perceptions on TripAdvisor Ethnic Restaurant Reviews

Elena Chatzopoulou and Nicolas Travers

Abstract Authenticity perceptions are subjectively driven and rely on social constructions making the concept hard to be defined. The current study is following a big data approach to capture perceptions and beliefs concerning the authenticity of ethnic restaurants and also when online positive reviews are given about authenticity under the influence of a visit to the country of origin. The key idea of our method relies on the analysis of a 3-step characterization of a big data repository extracted from TripAdvisor. Step 0 concerns reviews made for Italian restaurants before consumers visit Italy, step 1 concerns the reviews made while consumers were in Italy and step 2 concerns reviews made after they visited Italy. This characterization exploits both sentiment analysis and graph data models. Our findings propose a depiction of authenticity for ethnic restaurants via e-word of mouth. With a big data analysis on TripAdvisor, we provided an analysis on both ratings and comments which showed the impact of authenticity. As such, consumers, after visiting the country of origin, were more critical while they provided lower ratings and they were also focusing more on authentic atmosphere and service, showing evolution of their online reviews.

Keywords TripAdvisor · Country of origin · Ethnic restaurants · Authenticity · Online reviews · Big data

---

E. Chatzopoulou (✉)
University of Kent, Canterbury, UK
e-mail: e.chatzopoulou@kent.ac.uk

N. Travers
École Supérieure d'Ingénieurs Léonard-de-Vinci, La Défense, France
e-mail: nicolas.travers@devinci.fr

F. Pantoja, S. Wu (eds.), *From Micro to Macro: Dealing with Uncertainties in the Global Marketplace*, Developments in Marketing Science: Proceedings of the Academy of Marketing Science, https://doi.org/10.1007/978-3-030-89883-0_2

Introduction

In quest of defining a successful restaurant, the existing literature focuses mostly on financial factors (Di Pietro et al. 2007; Harrison 2011; Susskind 2010). Another measure of success is customer loyalty and customer satisfaction (Han and Ryu 2009; Harrington et al. 2011). Nowadays, customer satisfaction is often expressed on online reviews and seems to influence potential customers to visit and dine in a restaurant. Restaurant owners should know that consumers' driving force for sharing their positive opinion online is food quality rather than discussions about prices (Jeong and Jang 2011).

Apart from positive online reviews, ethnic restaurant success and customer attraction can be also achieved by offering authentic and high-quality products and services (Bryla 2015; Muller 1999; Namkung and Jang 2007; Sulek and Hensley 2004; Tsai and Lu 2012). If consumers perceive an ethnic restaurant as authentic they are more than happy to spread positive word of mouth (Lu et al. 2013). As such, consumers' perceptions of authenticity need to be defined and especially how these are expressed nowadays in a digital global setting.

Marketers have defined authenticity as a social and commercial construction for differentiation and positioning (Becuţ 2011; Bryla 2015; Ebster and Guist 2005; Lu et al. 2015; Wood and Lego Muñoz 2007). In this study, authenticity is approached as a social projection which permits "*various versions of authenticities regarding the same object*" (Wang 1999, p. 352). This type of authenticity is not objectively defined but symbolically and personally constructed (Reisinger and Steiner 2006). Authenticity for the constructivists is a perception of cultures, which includes deeper meanings and different interpretations for every human (Lu et al. 2015). Personal experience and identity can additionally contribute to the characterisation of food as authentic or inauthentic (Chatzopoulou et al. 2019). Individuals are in an endless interaction with society, and so their personal experiences create the relations which may define authenticity. In our research, we explore the construction of authenticity meanings by the consumers of ethnic restaurants before vs. after visiting the country of origin of these restaurants. Moreover, we explore how consumers' visit to the country of origin affects their online reviews and what can restaurant owners learn from these reviews to improve their ethnic restaurant businesses.

We first propose a methodology to extract when positive reviews are made for ethnic restaurants and also to depict authenticity meanings through graph representations. Then, sentiment analysis of consumers' online reviews is outlined and so, the combination of those steps aids the exploration of ethnic authenticity perceptions and positive online reviews about it. As such, an innovative methodology is followed which integrated authenticity meanings extraction with a big data analysis.

Methodology

Modelling tourism data requires to take into account locations information, users' properties and their interactions. Data are based on a TripAdvisor extraction of locations, users and their reviews. In the *Neothentic* database, we propose a graph data model and data operators dedicated to authenticity extraction and consumers' reviews. Some studies focused on graphs to model trips with graphs (Brandes 2001; Sang-Hyun Lee et al. 2013; Shih 2006). Those analyzes focus on various centrality measurement methods on networks that are combined with maps. It proposes to identify interaction that can characterize tourism behaviors. We go one step beyond by characterizing authenticity paths in such graphs.

Our database is composed of geolocalized locations, restaurant reviews and users. Thus, a first filter is applied to locations in order to get only relevant ones. They are identified by *type* a cuisine type (a list of denominations such that ["Italian", "Pizza", "Sea Food"]), *l* a localization (lat, long) and *rat* a rating ($rat \in R \wedge rat \in [1.0, 5.0]$).

To simplify localization, each location has been aligned with administrative areas (GADM). Each location is then linked to an area if its geolocalization (*i.e.,* lat, long) is contained into the area's shape (*SpatialPolygon* function *SP*), such that $area = SP(l.\ lat, l.\ long)$. This area is composed of a country, a region, a department and a city: *area (country, region, department, city)*. Thus, each location *l* is identified by: $\boldsymbol{l} \in \mathcal{L}(\boldsymbol{type}, \boldsymbol{rat}, \boldsymbol{area})$.

A user *u* is identified by his nationality and age, $\boldsymbol{u} \in \mathcal{U}(\boldsymbol{country}, \boldsymbol{age})$.

A review is a note ($n \in N \wedge n \in [1,5]$) given by a user *u* on a location *l* at time *t* (*t* is in the discrete time domain $\mathcal{T}$). Each review is then defined by an event r_t such that: $\boldsymbol{r_t = (l, u, n)}$.

The stream of reviews $\mathcal{S}$ is a time serie of r_{t_i} events: $\boldsymbol{\mathcal{S}} = \left\{ \boldsymbol{r_{t_1}, r_{t_2}, r_{t_3}, \ldots r_{t_n}} \right\}$

Graph Data Model

In order to extract the authenticity experience of users in this time series, it is necessary to focus especially on users who have visited at least once the given destination (Italy) and have tested a "destination" restaurant in their country before and after the country of origin. To achieve this, we propose to model the time serie into a graph data model that represents the experience of each user corresponding to a given cuisine type (Italian).

Time Serie Specialization

Before producing a graph, we need to focus only on restaurants of a given cuisine type corresponding to the study. A filter $\sigma_{cuisine}$ on "destination" restaurants keeps only those which corresponds to the cuisine type parameter:

$$\mathcal{S}_{cuisine} = \sigma_{cuisine}(\mathcal{S}) \Leftrightarrow r_{t_i} \in \mathcal{S}_{\text{cuisine}} \Rightarrow \forall r_{t_i} \in \mathcal{S}\ cuisine \in r_{t_i}.l.type$$

We also need to keep specific localization of restaurants according to the protocol of our study. In fact, only restaurants located in the destination country, and those from the consumers' country are to be kept. Thus, the destination operator δ produces a new time serie $\mathcal{S}^{dest}$ that verifies users' country or review destination:

$$\mathcal{S}^{dest} = \delta_{dest}(\mathcal{S}) \Leftrightarrow r_{t_i} \in \mathcal{S}^{dest} \Rightarrow \forall r_{t_i} \in \mathcal{S}$$

$$r_{t_i}.u.country = r_{t_i}.l.area.country \vee r_{t_i}.l.area.country = dest$$

Finally, to produce the required time serie to produce the corresponding graph, we can combine both operators with the cuisine type and the destination. We can notice that the combination of operators can be permuted in order to optimize the process of extraction.

$$\mathcal{S}_{cuisine}^{dest} = \delta_{dest}\left(\sigma_{cuisine}(\mathcal{S})\right)$$

For instance, $\mathcal{S}_{Italian}^{Italy}$ denotes the serie of events where users reviewed Italian restaurants both in Italy and also in the consumers' country.

Online Reviews Analyzes Framework

We can manipulate more easily the sequence of nodes for each user or a group of users according to the required study. A query language *Cypher*[1] is available which allows manipulating the graph and to visualize how users behave on this graph.

We need to identify the experience before, during and after the user's experience on a cuisine type. For this, we can execute queries on $\mathcal{A}$ that extract the three sequences of circulation of users on the graph.

Table 1 proposes a query that extracts for each user the review sequence containing 3 paths in the graph. It specifies how sequences are extracted and filters that are applied on each of them. Three clauses are given: MATCH to give the pattern for paths, WHERE for the filters, RETURN to give the final result.

[1] Cypher: https://neo4j.com/developer/cypher-query-language/.

Table 1 Online reviews extraction in the Cypher query language

MATCH	p1 = (b1) -[*]- > (bn) -[u]- > (it1),
	p2 = (it1) -[*]- > (itn) -- > (a1),
	p3 = (a1) -[*]- > (an)
WHERE	ALL(r in *nodes*(p1) where r.country<>"Italy") AND
	ALL(r in *nodes*(p2) where r.country = "Italy") AND
	ALL(r in *nodes*(p3) where r.country<>"Italy") AND
	ALL(rev in *relationships*(p1,p2,p3) WHERE rev.user = u.user)
RETURN	u as **user**, AVG(p1.note) AS **before**, AVG(p2.note) AS **during**, AVG(p3.note) as **after**

Every edge is declared in the MATCH clause with a "-->" between nodes "()". Stars between brackets say that we accept any length of the path (from 0 edges to n). The red path p1 corresponds to all the edges that occur before getting to Italy (first restriction in the WHERE clause) from nodes (b1) to (bn). Path p2 corresponds to the reviews in Italy (second restriction) from nodes (it1) to (itn), and path p3 after Italy (third one) from nodes (a1) to (an). Notice that those three paths are linked together by linked nodes *it1* and *a1 at the end of paths p1 and p2*. Moreover, to specify that this long sequence of reviews is given by a single user, the fourth restriction in the WHERE clause says that all relationships are linked to user u (given at the end of path p1).

To finish with, the RETURN clause aggregates notes from reviews of each path in order to give the average rating *before*, *during* and *after* being in Italy. It will be called in the following the *authenticity vector*.

On top of that, we can refine queries by filtering the users' country. For instance, we can add in the WHERE clause that u must come from the UK (*u.user.country = "UK"*). Consequently, we will obtain the authenticity vectors from British citizens. The set of all authenticity vectors can be visualized to show the distribution of ratings for each step.

This final step will produce the 3-step vectors that will be used to extract both ratings evolution and comments extraction for sentiment analysis. The aggregation of such vectors helps to have a global understanding of customers' behavior on e-WoM.

Dataset

Global data were collected from TripAdvisor for the period 2010–2018 concerning reviews about 51,710 restaurants. The global study with the first filter ($S^{Italy}_{Italian}$) collected data from 786,896 users who have put at least one review on an Italian restaurant. We applied this filter to an initial source of over 54,572,165 users. As such, we got 16,901,269 corresponding reviews for analysis from an initial source of over 300,084,943 reviews.

Findings

From the above described procedure, USA and UK reviewers' comments have been collected from TripAdvisor platform concerning their experience in Italian restaurants. Their comments have been categorised in three different sections: before visiting Italy (step 0), during their visit to Italy (step 1) and after their visit to Italy (step 2). The purpose of doing so has been to explore whether food perceptions differ before the visit in the country of origin vs. after. The sentiment analysis was conducted with the use of NVIVO 12. First, we run a word frequency query for step 0, then for step 1 and finally for step 2. The most commonly words used per step are depicted on tree maps below. Secondly, a sentiment analysis of each and every word was conducted from consumers' reviews in order to depict how these commonly used words are perceived by the consumers.

The sentiment analysis has shown that during their visit to the country of origin (Italy) the words pizza, pasta, Italian and friendly were missing from the 20 most frequent words of reviewers' comments. The words appeared in the top 20 before they visited Italy. The words pizza, Italian and time appear only before the visit to Italy and again after their visit. The words: friendly, staff and excellent are missing from the top 20 most frequent words of reviewers' comments after the visit to Italy even if they appeared before the visit in the country of origin. The words excellent and staff appear only in the top 20 of reviewers' comments before and during the visit to Italy but, not after. As such, we may conclude that the country of origin affects perceptions of food quality and excellence making hard to give excellent reviews to an ethnic restaurant after visiting the country of origin. This is also evident by the less 5's of reviews after the visit to Italy.

As can be seen in Fig. 1, the distribution of customers' average ratings from authenticity vectors for UK and USA citizens is different from before to after visiting Italy. Their ratings are globally higher while dining in Italy. But we can notice that there are lower ratings after being in Italy as it tends to be more criticism between 4 and 5 average rating. As such, 57.14% of 4 s and more for USA users (resp. 43.48% for UK) before visiting Italy become 42.86% after their visit to Italy (resp. 39.13%). It means that US customers tend to be more criticism on ethnic

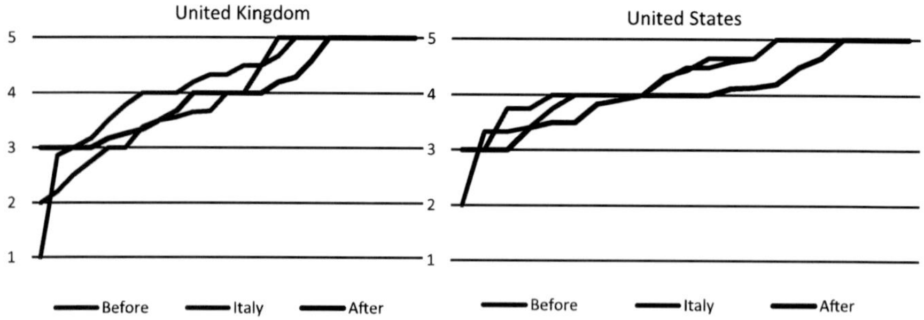

Fig. 1 Distribution of authenticity vectors from UK and USA citizens on Italian restaurants

authenticity after their visit than British citizen. Moreover, we can see that British customers leaved a better experience while being in Italy. Concerning the 5 s for UK users before vs. after visiting Italy were reduced by 7.2% while for USA users the number of 5 s witness a reduction of 5%.

Based on the analysis of all reviews the current study answers the question 'when are positive reviews made for ethnic restaurants'? In order to do so, we conducted a sentiment analysis of the reviews before visiting Italy vs. after the visit. As it can be seen on the tree maps of step 0 and 2, we may conclude that different perceptions exist about food aspects and the use of words good, great, pizza and restaurant. Concerning food, in step 0 there were no reviews about simplicity which is highlighted in steps 1 and 2 as a main characteristic of Italian cuisine. Moreover, only in step 2 is highlighted the value of real bread and not in step 0. Comments about nostalgia and how food reminded the country of origin can be seen only in step 2. Concerning the use of the word good, in step 0 the phrase good bread is missing whereas it has been pointed out in step 2. Moreover, the phrase "good flavoured dishes" is only used in step 2 but, not in step 0. Concerning the use of the word great, great location seems to concern consumers only in step 0 as it is missing from step 2. Consumers seem to care more about food aspects rather than the location. Concerning reviews about pizza, consumers seek for pizza variety only in step 0 but, not in step 2. They also tend to compare pizza with the country of origin only in step 2: "the best pizza outside Italia". Finally, when it comes to the use of the word restaurant, consumers make comparisons with Italy only in step 2: "reminds me of being in Italy", "I would call it more a good trattoria than a restaurant and don't get me wrong, this is a compliment".

Tree map analysis of step 0 (reviews on TripAdvisor before visiting Italy):

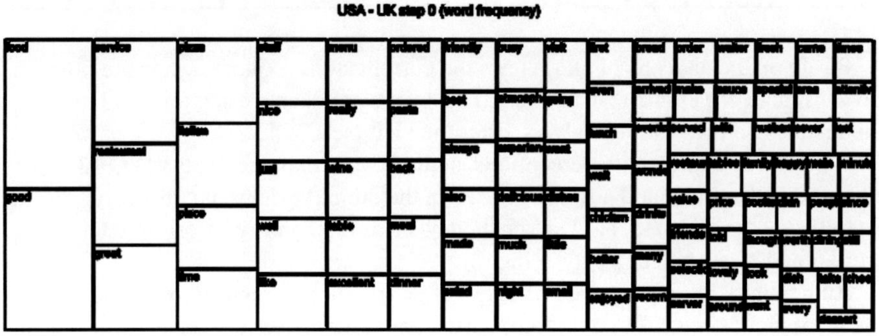

Tree map analysis of step 1 (reviews on TripAdvisor while visiting Italy):

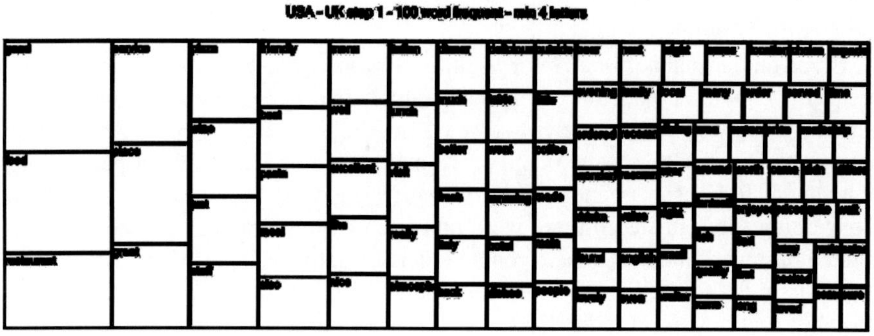

Tree map analysis of step 2 (reviews on TripAdvisor after visiting Italy):

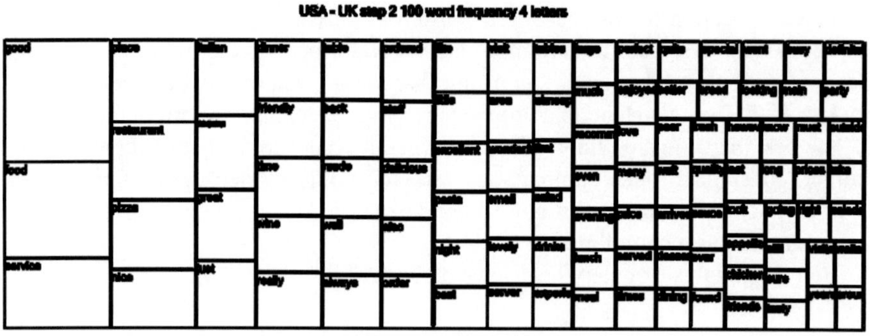

Based on the analysis of all reviews the current study explores when are positive reviews made for ethnic restaurants. To do so, we conducted a sentiment analysis of the reviews before visiting Italy vs. after the visit (see Table 2).

Concerning authenticity perceptions, a query was conducted in NVIVO 12 about the word authenticity and how this is used in the online reviews of consumers before (step 0) vs. during (step 1) vs. after their visit in the country of origin (step 2). A word cloud was created per step (Fig. 2).

Authenticity perceptions are affected after visiting the country of origin and so the word clouds are different before, during and after the visit to Italy. For instance, pizza is perceived as part of the Italian food authenticity and so the word is included in the word cloud of step 0. However, after visiting Italy consumers realized that Italian cuisine does not necessarily include pizza but rather other food options. As such, the word pizza is not included in the word cloud of step 2. Gelato on the contrary is an important aspect for Italians and so it is included as part of authenticity in step 2 but, not before visiting Italy, step 0.

Finally, authenticity relies much on the actual food menu and authentic atmosphere which are depicted in step 2 but, not in step 0. Step 0 is more about the staff, the service and to feel closer to the Italian-like character whereas, after visiting Italy consumers perceive the core of authenticity to rely on great food, simplicity and the traditional menu choices.

Table 2 Sentiment analysis – online reviews

Most commonly used words in the consumers online reviews of step 0	Analysis
Food	Good quality, cooked properly, well presented, tasty, warm plates have to arrive warm and not cold, price has to be reasonable in relation to food, fresh ingredients, authentic recipes, comparisons with Italian ancestors' cooking, sufficient food choices/range
Good	Food has to be good, good service, good staff (friendly is commonly used), good atmosphere, good price (value for money is commonly mentioned), good location, good menu, a restaurant to remain consistently good, good range of food, good portions
Excellent	Excellent: menu, service, staff, food, value for money, wine, special dishes, desserts
Great	Great: location, value, atmosphere, welcoming owners, staff, food, drinks, great range of dishes, great drinks selection, great food selection, bread, great time
Italian	Authentic, traditional food, wine, my own Italian mother's cooking, Italian experience, Italian staff, traditional Italian cuisine, pasta done properly-the Italian way, Italian chef, real Italian food, Italian atmosphere and decoration style, songs, products (imported)
Menu	They change the menu once every ice age so it just gets boring, good range of choices, lunchtime special menu, value for money, traditional, Italian food suppliers (imported)
Pizza	Well-cooked, cooked as it should: very thinly sliced and delicious, value for money, variety of pizza types, local ingredients, handmade, fresh, its taste and quality are stable over the years
Place	Cosy, pleasant, wonderful, well decorated, small/informal, friendly, quiet/for romantic meals, the place tries to give you an Italian experience, authentic
Restaurant	Recommended, tasty food, authentic Italian cuisine, busy restaurant is a good sign as long as the service is good, serves customers' favourite dishes, good location, good portions, nice decoration, not too loud music, independent is preferred (not chains), reasonable prices, keep the quality stable over the years, clean
Service	Low waiting time is a plus, efficient service, warm and friendly, polite staff, attentive staff but not too pushy, service with a smile, professional service (e.g. not part time students), knowledgeable staff, service charge normal (not too high)
Staff	Friendly, pleasant, attentive, helpful, welcoming, interested in customers' opinion/needs, Italian staff are preferred (perceived as a more authentic experience), well-trained staff, professional staff, quick/prompt, responsive to requests, able to explain each dish, not to bother too much the customers (e.g. interrupt their conversation)
Time	Low waiting time, visited the place several times (the restaurant and its food remain consistently good), allow time to customers to eat (not to kick them out quickly, avoid make them feel like fast-food), impress the customers since their first visit and make them regulars

(continued)

Table 2 (continued)

Wine	Take their time to enjoy the wine (not to feel rushed), house wine is much appreciated, variety of wine selection (thoughtful wine list not extensive though), Italian wine is expected to be in an Italian restaurant, the staff has to ask the customers to try the wine first before consuming it, good price, menu to be paired with wine suggestions helps customers to decide, wine decorations are liked by the consumers, if wine is served by knowledgeable staff is much appreciated, to be sustained properly otherwise it goes bad, to be served in clean and not too old glasses
Most commonly used words in the consumers online reviews of step 1	**Analysis**
Excellent	Service, wine and beer, fresh ingredients, food quality, food variety, location, service, atmosphere, staff (e.g. they could be city's ambassadors, friendly), bread, authentic meals, excellent value for money.
Food	Good quality, variety of food options, tasty food, good texture, good ingredients, value for money, tastier here than in their home country, care and effort put during food preparation, no photos of the food offered (as in touristic places), right portions (not too small neither too large), authentic Italian food, rustic, local food, well-cooked, well-presented, fresh (not microwave).
Good	Good drink choices (prosecco, beer, house wine), good coffee, good food quality, good desserts (tasty), good location, good service (good signs: no English menu, no fluent in English but, just enough to explain the dishes and make recommendations, locals are customers), good atmosphere and friendly, not stuffy atmosphere: just good, honest, traditional Italian.
Great	Great drink choices (wine, beers), great bread, great food (tasty, authentic, comes in good portions), great staff (friendly, helpful, treated customers with great care, knowledgeable, they make great recommendations for wine and specials), great place for dinner (atmosphere, view).
Menu	Comprehensive enough (choices for everyone, have options in order to return), menu is perceived as authentic if it is only in Italian (staff will do orally the translation), fresh ingredients.
Place	Busy but not noisy, nice setting, good location, good gelato place, clean, when owners run the place is much appreciated and is often characterised as personal and efficient service, relaxing place/cosy place, a place visited by locals is a good sign, from the outside the place seems inviting and traditional, value for money.
Restaurant	Cosy, convenient location, nice setting (not cheesy touristic), value for money, recommended by others (hotel reception recommendation, locals or eWOM), good service/efficient, friendly staff, nice atmosphere, good food quality, pasta made in the restaurant, fresh ingredients, good wine, traditional, family businesses are preferred, busy (good sign as long as the service is adequate), when locals are customers this is perceived as a good sign,
Service	Friendly, efficient, staff make suggestions when they are asked, attentive service (but not rushed), low waiting times, funny service (staff could be ambassador of the city).

(continued)

Table 2 (continued)

Staff	Staff with joy (e.g. the waiter sang, he joked, he took pictures, he was charming), friendly, welcoming, assisting/helpful (provide suggestions when they are asked-not annoying), when menu is in Italian only it is a good sign/ authenticity for the customers (staff is translating), knowledgeable (recommendations for wine pairing and the specials).
Wine	Sufficient choices, value for money, wine recommendations are made by the staff (knowledgeable staff is much appreciated), value for money, the dishes are accompanied with wine choices in the menu, house wine is much appreciated, local wine is preferred, high quality wine,
Most commonly used words in the consumers online reviews of step 2	**Analysis**
Food	Good quality, sufficient quantity, well-cooked, value for money, tasty, fresh ingredients, authentic (not just Italian style), arrive at the right temperature (hot), real bread, traditional recipes, give a dessert for a special occasion.
Good	Good service, good food, good atmosphere, good flavoured dishes, good value for money, packed place (which is a good sign), good selection of wine, good desserts, good bread, good ingredients, good portions, good fresh ingredients, good experience.
Great	Atmosphere, food, service, staff, atmosphere, value for money, coffee, pizza, taste, bread, great variety of wine.
Italian	Italian chains are not preferred (independent restaurants are preferred), homemade Italian cuisine, friendly waiters, good atmosphere, authentic Italian food, traditional Italian food, Italian gelato, staff speak Italian.
Menu	Variety of options, reasonably priced, to be renewed, authentic.
Pizza	Large-sufficient portions, oven pizza, not frozen, fresh ingredients, tasty, served quickly, value for money.
Place	Visit the place because of WOM, the place is popular which is a good sign, visited by locals, clean, friendly place, to have character (not to be tacky).
Restaurant	Nice décor (not dated), lovely feeling, fairly busy, authentic, clean, with good food, helpful staff/friendly.
Service	Quick, efficient, a smile from the staff helps, helpful service, friendly, attentive.
Time	Not spending too much time waiting for the meal, service on time, great time/great experience, to be seated on time if a reservation is made, if visiting the restaurant for the first time to have a good impression.
Wine	Wine pairing with food, variety of wine choices, good quality of wine, reasonably priced, clean wine glasses, wine barrels or bottles to decorate the place, price range for wine options.

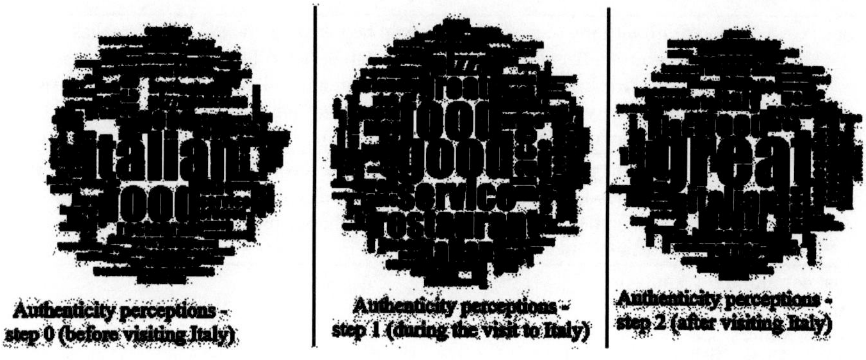

Fig. 2 Authenticity perceptions – word clouds before, during and after visiting the country of origin

References

Becuț, A. (2011). Apples, Quality Signs and Trademarks for Local Products. *international Review of Social Research, 1*(2), 65-83. doi: https://doi.org/10.1515/irsr-2011-0011

Brandes, U. (2001). A faster algorithm for betweenness centrality. *The Journal of Mathematical Sociology, 25*(2).

Bryla, P. (2015). The role of appeals to tradition in origin food marketing. A survey among Polish consumers. *Appetite, 91*, 302-310. doi: https://doi.org/10.1016/j.appet.2015.04.056

Chatzopoulou, E., Gorton, M., & Kuznesof, S. (2019). Understanding authentication processes and the role of conventions: a consideration of Greek ethnic restaurants. *Annals of Tourism Research, 77*, 128-140. doi: https://doi.org/10.1016/j.annals.2019.06.004

Di Pietro, R. B., Murphy, K. S., Rivera, M., & Muller, C. C. (2007). Multi-unit management key success factors in the casual dining restaurant industry. *International Journal of Contemporary Hospitality Management, 19*(7), 524-536. doi: https://doi.org/10.1108/09596110710818275

Ebster, C., & Guist, I. (2005). The Role of Authenticity in Ethnic Theme Restaurants. *Journal of Foodservice Business Research, 7*(2), 41-52. doi: https://doi.org/10.1300/J369v07n02_04

Han, H., & Ryu, K. (2009). The Roles of the Physical Environment, Price Perception, and Customer Satisfaction in Determining Customer Loyalty in the Restaurant Industry. *Journal of Hospitality & Tourism Research, 33*(4), 487-510. doi: https://doi.org/10.1177/1096348009344212

Harrington, R. J., Ottenbacher, M. C., & Kendall, K. W. (2011). Fine-Dining Restaurant Selection: Direct and Moderating Effects of Customer Attributes. *Journal of Foodservice Business Research, 14*(3), 272-289. doi: https://doi.org/10.1080/15378020.2011.594388

Harrison, J. P. (2011). Operating a successful restaurant. *3*(1). http://home.snu.edu/dept/tulsa/snuie/Harrison.pdf

Jeong, E., & Jang, S. (2011). Restaurant experiences triggering positive electronic word-of-mouth (eWOM) motivations. *International Journal of Hospitality Management, 30*(2), 356-366. doi: https://doi.org/10.1016/j.ijhm.2010.08.005

Lu, A., Gursoy, D., & Lu, C. Y. (2015). Authenticity perceptions, brand equity and brand choice intention: The case of ethnic restaurants. *International Journal of Hospitality Management, 50*, 36-45. doi: https://doi.org/10.1016/j.ijhm.2015.07.008

Lu, X. H., Ba, S. L., Huang, L. H., & Feng, Y. (2013). Promotional Marketing or Word-of-Mouth? Evidence from Online Restaurant Reviews. *Information Systems Research, 24*(3), 596-612. doi: https://doi.org/10.1287/isre.1120.0454

Muller, C. C. (1999). The business of restaurants: 2001 and beyond. *International Journal of Hospitality Management, 18*(4), 401-413. doi: https://doi.org/10.1016/s0278-4319(99)00045-6

Namkung, Y., & Jang, S. (2007). Does Food Quality Really Matter in Restaurants? Its Impact On Customer Satisfaction and Behavioral Intentions. *Journal of Hospitality & Tourism Research, 31*(3), 387-409. doi: https://doi.org/10.1177/1096348007299924

Reisinger, Y., & Steiner, C. J. (2006). Reconceptualizing object authenticity. *Annals of Tourism Research, 33*(1), 67. https://doi.org/10.1016/j.annals.2005.04.003

Sang-Hyun Lee, Jin-Yong Choi, Seung-Hwan Yoo, & Oh, Y.-G. (2013). Evaluating spatial centrality for integrated tourism management in rural areas using GIS and network analysis. *Tourism Management.*

Shih, H.-Y. (2006). Network characteristics of drive tourism destinations: An application of network analysis in tourism. *Tourism Management, 27*(5).

Sulek, J. M., & Hensley, R. L. (2004). The Relative Importance of Food, Atmosphere, and Fairness of Wait: The Case of a Full-service Restaurant. *Cornell Hotel and restaurant Administration Quarterly, 45*(3), 235-247. doi: https://doi.org/10.1177/0010880404265345

Susskind, A. M. (2010). Guest Service Management and Processes in Restaurants: What We Have Learned in Fifty Years. *Cornell Hospitality Quarterly, 51*(4), 479-482. doi: https://doi.org/10.1177/1938965510375028

Tsai, C. T., & Lu, P. H. (2012). Authentic dining experiences in ethnic theme restaurants. *International Journal of Hospitality Management, 31*(1), 304-306. doi: https://doi.org/10.1016/j.ijhm.2011.04.010

Wang, N. (1999). Rethinking authenticity in tourism experience. *Annals of Tourism Research, 26*(2), 349-370. doi: https://doi.org/10.1016/s0160-7383(98)00103-0

Wood, N. T., & Lego Muñoz, C. (2007). 'No rules, just right' or is it? The role of themed restaurants as cultural ambassadors. *Tourism and Hospitality Research, 7*(3-4), 242-255. doi: https://doi.org/10.1057/palgrave.thr.6050047

Conceptualization, Measurement and Effects of Suppliers' Perceived Control Over the Exchange on Multisided Platforms

Rémi Mencarelli, Renaud Lunardo, Cindy Lombart, and Ericka Henon

Abstract The sharing economy allows people to supply underutilized assets on multisided platforms (MSPs). Because MSPs must attract a sufficient number of suppliers – here, referring as people who aim to sell, lend or share products – to succeed, their design must provide feelings of protection from potential risks associated with the exchange with peers. In the same time, such MSPs are used by people who engage freely in the exchange and value the autonomy on the platform. In this context that combines risk perceptions and a need for autonomy, the perception of control within the exchange is likely to play a key role in explaining how people react to MSPs. Therefore, we here build on one qualitative and five quantitative studies to develop, refine and test a 12-item, three-dimensional scale of supplier's perceived control over the exchange. Results reveal sound psychometric properties of the scale, demonstrate its unique position in relation to key marketing constructs such as perceived value, satisfaction, trust and intention to re-use the platform and attest its stability across contexts. By applying the scale in their practices, MSPs managers can diagnose and improve suppliers' perceptions of control over the exchange and subsequently the attractiveness of their platforms.

Keywords Perceived control · Multisided platform · Supplier · Exchange

R. Mencarelli
University of Savoie Mont Blanc, Chambéry, France
e-mail: remi.mencarelli@univ-savoie.fr

R. Lunardo (✉)
Kegde Business School, Bordeaux, France
e-mail: renaud.lunardo@kedgebs.com

C. Lombart
Audencia Business School, Nantes, France
e-mail: clombart@audencia.com

E. Henon
Quali Test, Paris, France
e-mail: ericka.henon@u-bourgogne.fr

F. Pantoja, S. Wu (eds.), *From Micro to Macro: Dealing with Uncertainties in the Global Marketplace*, Developments in Marketing Science: Proceedings of the Academy of Marketing Science, https://doi.org/10.1007/978-3-030-89883-0_3

Introduction

The sharing economy has expanded with the emergence of peer-to-peer virtual platforms, such as Airbnb, Owners Direct, or Uber. Often described as multisided, due to their ability to facilitate interactions and get different sides of the market "on board" (Rochet and Tirole 2006), these platforms face a twofold problem: make contact with end-users while providing technological systems that facilitate interactions. Most research that investigates these multisided platforms (MSPs) focuses on their economic impact (Zervas et al. 2017) or their competitive landscape (Landsman and Stremersch 2011). Such considerations leave unexamined the reactions of end-users on platforms, and only a few studies adopt a micro-individual lens. Moreover, despite the reciprocal nature of MSPs, most research takes a customer view without addressing how suppliers – here, referring as people who aim to sell, lend or share products – on MSPs feel and behave. Such a lack of attention given to suppliers, who are yet at the origin of the exchange, appears problematic, because how individuals who act as suppliers on MSPs react to the design of a platform and are willing to exchange using that MSP could be explicative of their evaluation of, and their propensity to use, the platform.

Another reason for research on suppliers on MSPs lies in that these platforms usually provide options to appraise and share the quality of the service provider, but they offer less insight into the buyers. This lack of information might increase risk perceptions and prevent suppliers from developing a sense of control over the exchange. Nor are interactions on the platforms necessarily repeated (Sundararajan 2016), so suppliers cannot rely on their previous experience with specific customers to reduce those risk perceptions. Thus, perceptions of no sufficient control could arise and prevent suppliers from using the platform and managing the exchange. This threat represents a challenge for MSPs, which must find a way to ensure that suppliers feel in control and benefit from the experience.

Therefore, we posit that perceived control over the exchange (PCOE) provides an appealing theoretical foundation to predict suppliers' reactions. However, an examination of the role of perceived control is challenging, as a clear conceptualization of what perceived control means is lacking in marketing. A second issue stems from the lack of an existing measure of perceived control over an exchange. Hence, this research aims to: (1) provide a clear conceptualization of PCOE on MSPs, (2) develop and validating a specific measurement scale of PCOE on MSPs and (3) demonstrate that PCOE on MSPs predicts relevant marketing outcomes.

Conceptual Background

Characteristics of MSPs and the Role of Suppliers

MSPs are able to reintermediate fragmented markets and take a position in the center of the value chain that links user communities (Zervas et al. 2017). In these two- or multisided markets, these platforms present different characteristics depending on the nature of the activity (sharing, bartering, lending, trading, renting, swapping), the access to the platform (the degree of exclusivity) or the possession's status of the asset (permanently or temporarily transferred). However, such multi-sided markets have three main common characteristics (Rochet and Tirole 2006): (1) distinctive groups of actors can enter into mutually advantageous trades, (2) the exchanges generate network externalities among different groups of users, and (3) the platform can benefit from facilitating exchanges and internalizing externalities.

The success of a platform demands the presence of active suppliers. Hence, the lack of insight into suppliers' behavior represents a problem for MSPs, which face two critical challenges. First, they need to reduce risk perceptions associated with the exchanges, which mostly involve non-professional, individual users. Suppliers likely perceive substantial risk, because they have virtually no knowledge about the other party to the exchange (Hagiu 2014). Second, because MSPs cannot create value without users (Grönroos and Voima 2013), they need to ensure the actors' autonomy: suppliers engage in coproducing the exchange, from its initiation to its completion, and the platform functions as an intermediary, so the outcome depends mostly on the free will of the actors to engage and coordinate themselves (Roser et al. 2013). Therefore, the platform's ability to reduce risk perceptions and promote autonomy could affect the perception of individuals to be in control of the exchange.

Perceived Control Over the Exchange

Perceived control appears as a variable that explains intentions and behavior (Hui and Bateson 1991; Ward and Barnes, 2001). Yet this construct also suffers some limitations, stemming from its definition (Büttgen et al. 2012; Collier and Sherrell 2010). In particular, conceptualizations of perceived control regard it either as situation-dependent (Averill 1973) or as a stable personality trait. This latter view reflects locus of control theory (Rotter 1966), which cannot effectively explain people's reactions to specific stimuli. On the contrary, the former and more widely adopted approach builds on dominance theory (Mehrabian and Russell 1974). Yet, this unidimensional conceptualization ignores some of the theoretical complexity of the construct and assumes passive consumers, who perceive control because they do not sense any persuasive influence. Furthermore, some weak psychometric issues plague measures of dominance (Yani-de-Soriano and Foxall 2006).

An appealing alternative conceptualization proposes that perceived control is a combination of two beliefs, related to capacity and strategy (Skinner 1995). The capacity dimension suggests that people perceive control when they sense they have the ability to act in ways that will lead to the desired results in a specific environment. The strategy dimension instead implies that people feel in control when they believe that some means exist in the environment that can help them achieve the desired results. With this two-dimensional conceptualization, perceived control is no longer defined exclusively according to an intra-individual perspective, such that consumers feel either fully in control over their environment or else totally constrained. Instead, it includes consideration of how the environment can help them achieve their goals. Furthermore, its multidimensional nature offers an integrative conceptualization of perceived control. Relying on this conceptualization, we next develop a domain-specific scale for the measurement of perceived control on MSPs.

Developing and Testing the Scale: Method

We follow Churchill (1979) and conduct six empirical studies (one qualitative and five quantitative) to operationalize, validate the scale and demonstrate its position in relation to key marketing outcomes. The data for the qualitative study and the first four quantitative studies were collected from a second-hand market, which offers a widespread and economically important context, marked by varied actors and many MSPs (Guiot and Roux 2010). When replicating and providing evidence for the stability of the scale, we focus on a carpooling MSP in a fifth quantitative study. This context was retained according to similarity and variety criteria on MSPs. Indeed, if MSPs have common features, they also present some distinctive characteristics. In contrast with resale, the carpooling context offers some specificities in terms of activities (sharing *versus* trading) and access to the service (temporary access *versus* permanently transferred). If we show that in spite of these differences across the platforms the scale remains stable, then we offer evidence for its applicability to multiple types of MSPs.

Study 1: Item Generation and Face Validity

To determine if our conceptualization of perceived control reflects suppliers' actual perceptions of control, we started with a qualitative study, in which we conducted interviews with second-hand resellers who described the MSP they had used most recently (e.g., eBay, Le Bon Coin, Videdressing). In accordance with information saturation principles, we undertook 26 semi-directed interviews, averaging 40 min in length, with various consumers (16 women, 10 men; 17–75 years of age). The interviews took place in respondents' homes and included open questions to address three themes: most recent second-hand resale experience, transactions completed on MSPs, and how the transactions were conducted.

In line with previous research on perceived control, the content analysis reveals three dimensions. Reflecting the view that capacity beliefs are analogous to self-efficacy beliefs (Namasivayam 2004), the first dimension refers to individual self-efficacy, such that the actor believes in his/her ability to mobilize necessary skills to attain a given goal (Bandura 1997), including functioning well on the MSP. If self-efficacy beliefs are low, the person's actions may not have the desired effects; our respondents noted their need to feel capable of completing the transaction and able to guard against risk, unwanted free-riding, or information asymmetry with buyers, as well as the potential difficulty of assessing the monetary value of sold items.

Some respondents recognized their own sufficient competence to avoid risks, but others acknowledge difficulties in exchanges due to their lack of skills.

The other two dimensions that emerged from the interviews refer to the means provided by the platform to help users feel more in control. The first implies individual beliefs about security provided by the platform, reflecting their evaluations of the tools established by the MSP to reduce the risk of exchanging in a context of anonymity and lack of reputation. These different means established by the platform seek to secure the transaction financially, logistically, and/or legally. Finally, the respondents cited the platform's ability to provide partial or complete autonomy to users during service cocreation. Autonomy requires the presence of an appropriation process that enables the reseller to determine different options for the transaction (Denegri-Knott and Zwick 2012). These two platform-derived dimensions reflect strategy beliefs (Skinner 1995).

From this exploratory study, we generated 44 items that span three dimensions of perceived control. Five marketing professors evaluated the items, after receiving a presentation of the concept and definitions of its three dimensions, according to their degree of representation ("not appropriate at all to measure the concept" to "very appropriate to measure the concept") and clarity ("very ambiguous wording" to "very clear wording"), on seven-point Likert scales. We dropped several items that a majority of experts designated as not representative of the concept, ambiguous, or redundant (Churchill 1979). Thus, we emerged with a pool of 26 items for the scale purification phase.

Study 2: Purification of the Measurement Scale

In this first quantitative data collection, we used convenience sampling and solicited input from 295 respondents engaged in second-hand resales (69.2% women, 55.3% older than 25 years). In an online questionnaire, they recalled their most recent experience on an MSP and indicated their agreement with the 26 items (Likert scale, 1 = "Fully disagree" to 7 = "Fully agree"). The exploratory factor analysis with oblimin rotation revealed three dimensions, all with eigenvalues greater than 1 (Hair et al. 1998) and accounting for 66.2% of total variance, that paralleled the beliefs-based approach (Skinner 1995) and our qualitative study: a capacity belief in the form of self-efficacy and strategy beliefs related to security and autonomy.

To purify the measurement scale, we dropped items with unsatisfactory psychometric qualities, namely, those with factor loadings below 0.50 on their main dimension and cross-loading items (Hair et al. 1998). In terms of reliability, items with unsatisfactory alpha values also were eliminated, without lowering the face validity of the scale. We inspected the remaining items and removed those that were too redundant (i.e., exhibited strong correlations), after confirming that their removal did not change the meaning of the retained dimensions (Rossiter 2002). The Cronbach's alphas values – 0.79 (self-efficacy), 0.83 (security), and 0.84 (autonomy) – are satisfactory. The final 12 items all exhibit factor loadings greater than 0.70.

Study 3: Confirmation of the Measurement Scale

To confirm this three-dimensional, 12-item scale, we again used a convenience sampling and the same procedure as in Study 2 to gather data online from 278 respondents (68.3% women, 62.6% older than 25 years), with a questionnaire that asked them to recall their last resale experience on an MSP and rate their agreement with the 12 items. The confirmatory factor analysis (CFA) uses partial least squares (PLS; 5000 bootstraps; Hair et al. 2012). Reflecting our prediction that beliefs about self-efficacy, security, and autonomy combine to form a single construct (i.e., perceived control over the exchange), we test a second-order structure. The correlations across the dimensions, obtained from an exploratory factor analysis, support this approach. The links of the second-order factor (i.e., perceived control over the exchange) with self-efficacy ($\beta = 0.80$, $t = 22.25$), security ($\beta = 0.69$, $t = 12.63$), and autonomy ($\beta = 0.65$, $t = 14.38$) are all significant at 1%. The loadings are higher than 0.70 (the first one excepted, equal to 0.63) and statistically significant at 1%, making them satisfactory (Table 1).

To assess the reliability of the measures, we used Jöreskog' Rhô coefficient. The coefficients for self-efficacy (0.84), security (0.91), and autonomy (0.90) are all satisfactory, as is that of the second-order factor (0.76). With the Fornell and Larcker (1981) criterion, we conducted an initial assessment of the convergent and internal discriminant validities of the three dimensions. The dimensions share more than 50% of their variance with their measures, in support of the convergent validity of the measures; the convergent validity of the second-order factor is 0.52. We also confirm the internal discriminant validity of the variables, in that each latent variable shares more variance with its items than with the other latent variables.

Study 4: Scale Validation (Convergent and Discriminant Validities)

With Study 4, we test for convergent and discriminant validities. An online sample, recruited by a panelist, included 241 resellers (59.8% women, $M_{Age} = 41.86$ years, $SD_{Age} = 11.22$) who had used a MSP in the previous 6 months. The questionnaire contained the proposed 12-item perceived control scale, along with measures of some theoretically related constructs. Drawing on previous literature, we include a 3-item measure of dominance, which may constitute a form of perceived control (Hui and Bateson 1991; Van Rompay et al. 2008; Ward and Barnes 2001); a 3-item measure of general personal control (Cutright et al. 2013); and a 6-item measure of locus of control (LOC; Rotter 1966). As a test of the autonomy dimension, we also include a 6-item measure of empowerment (Fuchs et al. 2010). Finally, the presence of the security dimension in our perceived control scale led us to include a 3-item measure of perceived risk (Stone and Grønhaug 1993).

Table 1 Confirmatory factor analysis: item loadings, *t*-statistics, CR and AVE

Item	Study 3		Study 4		Study 5		Study 6	
Self-efficacy (CR; AVE): I have enough experience	(0.844; 0.576)		(0.949; 0.824)		(0.939; 0.793)		(0.870; 0.625)	
to resolve the situation in case of dispute	0.637	8.554	0.829	24.244	0.830	4.738	0.749	8.286
to not put myself at risk associated with the *exchange* (specific payment strategies, identity verification of the buyer)	0.714	14.989	0.939	38.269	0.917	52.765	0.756	7.251
to protect myself from scams (no payment, false bank transfer)	0.829	16.993	0.921	36.832	0.906	46.209	0.855	12.700
to overcome potential problems associated with the *exchange* (misleading description, frauds)	0.838	17.946	0.937	4.408	0.906	44.245	0.798	9.748
Security (CR; AVE): On this website,	(0.913; 0.723)		(0.956; 0.844)		(0.955; 0.842)		(0.905; 0.706)	
I have the guarantee to be paid	0.831	15.225	0.869	39.931	0.900	57.437	0.866	19.817
the honesty of the *buyer* is ensured	0.822	11.688	0.931	51.777	0.915	56.595	0.728	16.869
I am protected from the risk associated to the completion of the *exchange* (sell for less than market value, no payment)	0.852	16.604	0.934	49.408	0.929	6.782	0.886	22.227
I am preserved from scams that might arise during the *exchange* (no payment, false bank transfer)	0.894	18.475	0.939	47.938	0.925	57.710	0.873	25.654
Autonomy (CR; AVE): On this website,	(0.904; 0.703)		(0.938; 0.792)		(0.938; 0.790)		(0.894; 0.679)	
the completion of the *exchange* is in accordance with my terms (selling price, *delivery method*)	0.831	15.225	0.900	24.499	0.872	37.237	0.745	8.599
I feel free when I realize an *exchange*	0.822	11.688	0.915	17.218	0.901	4.340	0.848	13.173
the *exchange*'s progress depends mainly on me	0.852	16.604	0.855	2.526	0.880	38.594	0.838	14.341
I am independent during the completion of the *exchange*	0.894	18.475	0.889	22.321	0.902	46.415	0.861	13.289

Notes: CR = composite reliability; AVE = average variance extracted. All factor loadings and factor correlations are significant at $p < 0.001$. In each column, the loading appears on the left and the associated *t*-statistic is on the right. Italics indicate terms that can be adapted to reflect the focal exchanges on the platform (e.g., resale, rental, rides)

The CFA relied on PLS (5000 bootstraps). The composite reliability of the measures is satisfactory for both the perceived control scale (0.84) and its dimensions: self-efficacy = 0.94, security = 0.95, and autonomy = 0.93) (Table 1). With regard to convergent validity, we started with the average variance extracted (AVE) and find satisfactory values greater than 0.50 for the three dimensions, self-efficacy (0.82), security (0.84), and autonomy (0.79), and for the overall perceived control construct (0.65). Next, we tested for the external discriminant validity by considering the theoretically related constructs (dominance, LOC, personal control, empowerment, and perceived risk). We compared the squared correlation of all five constructs and the three dimensions of perceived control with their AVEs (Fornell and Larcker 1981). The AVEs for dominance (0.832), LOC (0.51), personal control (0.79), empowerment (0.74), and perceived risk (0.73) are all above their squared correlations with the dimensions of perceived control (self-efficacy, security, and autonomy) and the second-order construct. These results provide support for the convergent and discriminant validity of our 12-item measure of PCOE and its three dimensions.

Study 5: Scale Validation (Nomological Validity)

In Study 5, we develop a conceptual framework of PCOE on MSPs. From prior research in online contexts, we identify some antecedents and outcomes of suppliers' PCOE. Two main characteristics of MSPs likely affect perceived control over the exchange: customization and ease of use. Customization implies personalized tailoring of the website appearance and functionality, while ease of use refers to the layout, navigation sequence, and convenience associated with searching for a product or information (Rose et al. 2012), these two variables contributing to consumers' experience of a sense of being in control in website environments. Extending this rationale to MSPs, we argue that customization (H1) and ease of use (H2) when using an MSP enhance suppliers' PCOE.

We identify three main outcomes of PCOE on MSPs: experiential value, satisfaction, and online trust. Rose et al. (2012) underline that when perceived control increases, perceptions of difficulties decrease, leading to a more positive online experience. Hence, perceived control might increase experiential value. Turning to satisfaction, it results in a digital context from a customer's evaluation and impression of website performance on various attributes (Jin and Park 2006), suggesting that perceived control might increase satisfaction. Finally, trust in an online context may increase due to perceived control, which enhances confidence in e-retailing (Walczuch and Lundgren 2004). We therefore posit that PCOE can lead to a more valuable experience (H3), greater satisfaction (H4), and a belief that the MSP is trustworthy (H5).

These consequences also might affect one another, in that experiential value in a digital context is an antecedent of satisfaction and trust (Lin and Wang 2006).

Consumer satisfaction is a key driver of trust in digital contexts, as well as an antecedent of loyalty online (Jin et al. 2008; Rose et al. 2012). Finally, greater trust leads to stronger intentions to return to various online contexts (Jin et al. 2008; Rose et al. 2012). Therefore, the perceived value of the MSP may increase satisfaction (H6a) and trust toward the MSP (H6b). Further, satisfaction toward the MSP may have a positive impact on trust toward (Ha) and intentions to reuse the MSP (H7b). Finally, trust in the MSP may enhance intentions to reuse the MSP (H8).

To test these predictions, we recruited 508 resellers (50% women, $M_{Age} = 44$ years, $SD_{Age} = 12.90$) from an online panel. The MSP for this study is Le Bon Coin, which is popular in France where the study was conducted. Participants described their activity on the platform, and only active resellers (i.e., who had sold at least one item in the previous 6 months on the platform) were retained. They evaluated their PCOE using the proposed three-dimensional, 12-item scale, then completed two three-item measures of the perceived customization of the platform and its ease of use (Rose et al. 2012). They also rated the experiential value derived from the MSP on 19 items that span four second-order dimensions: return on investment (ROI), service excellence, playfulness, and aesthetic appeal (Mathwick et al. 2001). Next, participants rated their satisfaction with the MSP (Oliver 1997), trust (Lee and Turban 2001), and intentions to reuse the platform (Wu and Chang 2005).

For clarity, we present findings related to the second-order dimensions of the value construct. As we did previously (steps 3 and 4), we also present the results related to perceived control as a second-order construct (Table 2). As predicted by H1-H2, both customization (0.10, $p < 0.01$) and ease of use (0.56, $p < 0.001$) positively affect perceived control. Turning to the effects of perceived control, all those that relate to experiential value (H3) were positive, with aesthetic value (0.53, $p < 0.001$), playfulness (0.38, $p < 0.001$), customer ROI (0.59, $p < 0.001$), and excellence value (0.55, $p < 0.001$), supporting our predictions. The effects of perceived control on satisfaction (0.29, $p < 0.001$) and trust (0.234, $p < 0.001$) are also positive as predicted by H4–H5. Of note, the four second-order dimensions of experiential value— specifically, aesthetic value (0.17, $p < 0.001$), playfulness (−0.25, $p < 0.001$), customer ROI (0.468, $p < 0.001$), and excellence value (0.12, $p < 0.01$)—influence satisfaction (H6a). However, the effect of playfulness is here negative, indicating that consumers who use MSPs to resell products rather look for efficacy on the platform, as suggested by the positive effects of customer ROI and excellence value. The influence of playfulness on trust (0.09, $p < 0.001$) is however positive, as well as that of excellence value (0.26, $p < 0.001$), the other dimensions of value having no significant effect (H6b). Lastly, satisfaction positively affects trust (0.44, $p < 0.001$) (H7a) and re-use intentions (0.65, $p < 0.001$) (H7b) and trust has a positive impact on re-use intentions (0.23, $p < 0.001$) (H8). Thus, perceived control has an indirect positive influence on re-use intentions through its impacts on experiential value, satisfaction, and trust.

Table 2 Study 5: Results for the predictive validity

	Path Coefficient	*t*	R^2
Customization → Perceived control	0.107	2.289**	0.406
Ease-of-use → Perceived control	0.560	12.008***	
Perceived control → Aesthetic value	0.534	14.223***	0.286
Perceived control → Playfulness	0.384	9.345***	0.147
Perceived control → Customer ROI	0.598	16.792***	0.358
Perceived control → Excellence value	0.559	15.173***	0.313
Perceived control → Satisfaction	0.291	8.323***	0.637
Aesthetic value → Satisfaction	0.175	4.073***	
Playfulness → Satisfaction	−0.259	−7.013***	
Customer ROI → Satisfaction	0.468	10.642***	
Excellence value → Satisfaction	0.120	2.507**	
Perceived control → Trust	0.234	6.983***	0.709
Aesthetic value → Trust	0.016	n.s.	
Playfulness → Trust	0.094	2.703***	
Customer ROI → Trust	−0.038	n.s.	
Excellence value → Trust	0.267	6.206***	
Satisfaction → Trust	0.446	11.135***	
Satisfaction → Re-use intentions	0.650	17.860***	0.729
Trust → Re-use intentions	0.234	6.022***	
External GOF	0.999		
Internal GOF	0.916		

n.s: Non-significant
** $p < 0.01$
*** $p < 0.001$

Study 6: Generalization

With Study 6, we aim to replicate the factorial structure of the perceived control scale and evaluate its stability across contexts. We retained the context of carpooling and the MSP selected was Blablacar, a global leader among car-sharing MSPs. The common features of MSPs allowed us to test the stability of our construct (Rochet and Tirole 2006). However, this new context introduces different characteristics in terms of activities (sharing *versus* trading) and access to the service (temporary access *versus* transferred ownership).

A convenience sample of 139 users of BlaBlaCar included drivers who act as suppliers on the platform (64% women, $M_{Age} = 23.55$ years). They evaluated their PCOE on this car-sharing platform. We used the same measures but adapted the items to refer to the car-sharing MSP. The CFA of the perceived control scale with PLS (5000 bootstraps) revealed a factorial structure similar to that for Studies 2–5, with the same three dimensions. Results also confirmed the satisfactory composite reliability of the perceived control scale (0.83) and its dimensions (self-efficacy = 0.87, security = 0.90, autonomy = 0.89). The AVEs values for the perceived control scale (0.623) and its dimensions (self-efficacy = 0.625, security = 0.706, autonomy = 0.679) support its convergent validity. The results thus indicate the generalizability of the scale and its stability across different types of exchanges and MSPs.

General Discussion

Due to the importance of suppliers for MSPs and the lack of research on their reactions on those platforms, this research posited that PCOE offers a promising means to clarify of how actors interact on platforms. Facing the lack of sound measures of perceived control for the specific context of MSPs, we sought to conceptualize, develop, and test a new instrument to assess PCOE on MSPs. We proposed a more contextual, interactionist approach to perceived control, reflecting the conceptualization by Skinner (1995) that distinguishes strategy beliefs (i.e., beliefs that means exist to help produce desired outcomes) and capacity beliefs (i.e., beliefs about one's own ability to produce the desired results). With this distinction, we derive a 12-item scale with three underlying dimensions of perceived control on MSPs: self-efficacy, security, and autonomy. We tested this scale using data from multiple samples and platforms and provided solid empirical evidence of its reliability, validity, and robustness. Our theoretical reliance on Skinner's (1995) conceptualization and the encouraging psychometric properties of our three-dimensional scale suggest that our proposed interactionist, multidimensional measure of PCOE can elucidate users' behavior on MSPs.

In addition, our model of the effects of PCOE includes key marketing variables. Reflecting the well-established role of trust (Moorman et al. 1993), we specify this variable as being directly affected by perceived control, implying that our measure addresses important effects of marketing actions. Similarly, we identify perceived control as a key contributor to value creation in – and satisfaction toward – MSPs. The findings affirm the utility of the proposed scale for marketers who seek to enhance such customer responses. The results suggest that managers of MSPs should consider perceptions of control when designing their platforms, because it can establish a primary source of competitive advantage. The studies we report consistently support a three-dimensional structure, so managers might improve suppliers' perceptions of control by leveraging each dimension.

References

Averill, J.R. (1973). Personal control over aversive stimuli and its relationship to stress. *Psychological Bulletin*, *80*(4), 286.

Bandura, A. (1997). *Self-efficacy: The exercise of control*, New York: Freeman.

Büttgen, M., Schumann, J.H., & Ates, Z. (2012). Service locus of control and customer coproduction: The role of prior service experience and organizational socialization. *Journal of Service Research*, *15*(2), 166-181.

Churchill, Jr., G.A. (1979). A paradigm for developing better measures of marketing constructs. *Journal of Marketing Research, 16*(1), 64-73.

Collier, J.E., & Sherrell, D.L. (2010). Examining the influence of control and convenience in a self-service setting. *Journal of the Academy of Marketing Science, 38*(4), 490-509.

Cutright, K.M., Bettman, J.R., & Fitzsimons, G.J. (2013). Putting brands in their place: How a lack of control keeps brands contained. *Journal of Marketing Research, 50*(3), 365-377.

Denegri-Knott, J., & Zwick, D. (2012). Tracking prosumption work on eBay: Reproduction of desire and the challenge of slow re-McDonaldization. *American Behavioral Scientist. 56*(4). 439-458.

Fornell, C., & Larcker, D.F. (1981). Structural equation models with unobservable variables and measurement error: Algebra and statistics. *Journal of Marketing Research, 18*(3) 382-388.

Fuchs, C., Prandelli, E., & Schreier, M. (2010). The psychological effects of empowerment strategies on consumers' product demand. *Journal of Marketing, 74*(1), 65-79.

Grönroos, C., & Voima, P. (2013). Critical service logic: Making sense of value creation and co-creation. *Journal of the Academy of Marketing Science, 41*(2), 133-150.

Guiot, D., & Roux, D. (2010). A second-hand shoppers' motivation scale: Antecedents, consequences, and implications for retailers. *Journal of Retailing, 86*(4), 355-371.

Hagiu, A. (2014). Strategic decisions for multisided platforms. *MIT Sloan Management Review, 55*(2), 71.

Hair, J.F., Black, W.C., Babin, B.J., Anderson, R.E., & Tatham R.L. (1998). *Multivariate data analysis*, Upper Saddle River, NJ: Prentice hall.

Hair, J.F., Sarstedt, M., Ringle, C.M., & Mena, J. (2012). An assessment of the use of partial least squares structural equation modeling in marketing research, *Journal of the Academy of Marketing Science, 40*(3), 414-433.

Hui, M.K., & Bateson, J.E. (1991). Perceived control and the effects of crowding and consumer choice on the service experience. *Journal of Consumer Research, 18*(2), 174-184.

Jin, B., & Park, J.Y. (2006). The moderating effect of online purchase experience on the evaluation of online store attributes and the subsequent impact on market response outcomes. In Pechmann, C. and Price, L. (eds.), *Advances in Consumer Research vol. 33*, Duluth, MN: Association for Consumer Research, 203-211.

Jin, B., Park, J.Y., & Kim, J. (2008). Cross-cultural examination of the relationships among firm reputation, e-satisfaction, e-trust, and e-loyalty. *International Marketing Review, 25*(3), 324-337.

Landsman, V., & Stremersch, S. (2011). Multihoming in two-sided markets: An empirical inquiry in the video game console industry. *Journal of Marketing. 75*(6). 39-54.

Lee, M.K.O., & Turban, E. (2001). A trust model for consumer Internet shopping, *International Journal of Electronic Commerce, 6*(1), 75–91.

Lin, H.H., & Wang, Y.S. (2006). An examination of the determinants of customer loyalty in mobile commerce contexts. *Information & Management, 43*(3), 271-282.

Mathwick, C., Malhotra, N., & Rigdon, E. (2001). Experiential value: Conceptualization, measurement and application in the catalog and Internet shopping environment. *Journal of Retailing, 77*(1), 39–56.

Mehrabian, A., & Russell, J.A. (1974). *An approach to environmental psychology*. Cambridge, MA: The MIT Press.

Moorman, C., Deshpandé, R., & Zaltman, G. (1993). Factors affecting trust in market research relationships. *Journal of Marketing, 57*(1), 81–101.

Namasivayam, K. (2004). Action control. Proxy control and consumers' evaluations of the service exchange. *Psychology & Marketing, 21*(6), 463-480.

Oliver, R.L. (1997). *Satisfaction: A behavioral perspective on the customer*. New York: McGraw-Hill.

Rochet, J-C., & Tirole, J. (2006). Two-sided markets: A progress report. *RAND Journal of Economics, 37*(3). 645-667.

Rose, S., Clark, M., Samouel, P., & Hair N. (2012). Online customer experience in e-retailing: An empirical model of antecedents and outcomes. *Journal of Retailing*, *88*(2), 308-322.

Roser, T., DeFillippi, R., & Samson, A. (2013). Managing your co-creation mix: Co-creation ventures in distinctive contexts. *European Business Review*, *25*(1), 20-41.

Rossiter, John R. (2002). "The C-OAR-SE procedure for scale development in marketing." *International journal of research in marketing 19*(4,) 305–335.

Rotter, J.B. (1966). Generalized expectancies for internal versus external control of reinforcement. *Psychological Monographs: General and Applied*, *80*(1), 1–28.

Skinner, E.A. (1995). *Perceived control: Motivation and coping,* Thousand Oaks: Sage.

Stone, R.N., & Grønhaug, K. (1993). Perceived risk: Further considerations for the marketing discipline. *European Journal of Marketing, 27*(3) 39-50.

Sundararajan, A. (2016). *The sharing economy: The end of employment and the rise of crowd-based capitalism.* Cambridge, MA: The MIT Press.

Van Rompay, T.J., Galetzka, M., Pruyn, A.T., & Garcia, J.M. (2008). Human and spatial dimensions of retail density: Revisiting the role of perceived control. *Psychology & Marketing*, *25*(4), 319-335.

Walczuch, R., & Lundgren, H. (2004). Psychological antecedents of institution-based consumer trust in e-retailing. *Information & Management, 42*(1), 159-177.

Ward, J.C., & Barnes J.W. (2001). Control and affect: The influence of feeling in control of the retail environment on affect, involvement, attitude, and behavior. *Journal of Business Research*, *54*(2), 139-144.

Wu, J.J., & Chang, Y.S. (2005). Towards understanding members' interactivity, trust, and flow in online travel community. *Industrial Management & Data Systems*, *105*(7), 937-954.

Yani-de-Soriano, M.M., & Foxall, G.R. (2006). The emotional power of place: The fall and rise of dominance in retail research. *Journal of Retailing and Consumer Services*, *13*(6), 403-416.

Zervas, G., Proserpio, D., & Byers, J.W. (2017). The rise of the sharing economy: Estimating the impact of Airbnb on the hotel industry. *Journal of Marketing Research*, *54*(5), 687-705.

Guilty Red Food Packages: How the Color Red Affects Guilt through Negative Cognitive Associations for Vice Products: An Abstract

Renaud Lunardo, Camille Saintives, and Damien Chaney

Abstract Food companies frequently use color as a tool for easy identification, with for instance Coca-Cola being associated with the color red. Previous research supports this notion of colors as a powerful cue, colors being showed to influence emotional responses (Babin et al. 2003; Bellizzi and Hite 1992), but also brand evaluation (Labrecque and Milne 2012), price perception (Babin et al. 2003; Puccinelli et al. 2013), and purchase intentions (Gorn et al. 1997; Labrecque and Milne 2012). Given this role of cognitions following color exposure, it may be that cognitive inferences explain the mixed evidence found for one particular color: red. This color often carries positive meanings, as it is associated with love or energy, but also negative ones, priming, for example, the notions of danger, mistakes, ban, transgression, or war (Elliot et al. 2007). Surprisingly, however, no research to date has examined how the negative associations induced by the color red might negatively affect emotions and behavior. Therefore, the current research relies on recent studies highlighting the aforementioned importance of color for food products to examine the effect of the color red on consumers' responses to food packages. Specifically, because of its negative meanings and specifically its association with mistakes (Mehta and Zhu 2009), the color red may prompt negative feelings that are closely linked to transgression, more specifically guilt, an emotion that results from the transgression of moral or social standards (Baumeister et al. 1994).

To test this notion, this research builds on the S-O-R model and psychological literature on guilt to posit hypotheses about the relationship among red, negative

R. Lunardo (✉)
Kegde Business School, Bordeux, France
e-mail: renaud.lunardo@kedgebs.com

C. Saintives
INSEEC Business School, Bordeaux, France
e-mail: csaintives@inseec.com

D. Chaney
EM Normandie, Paris, France
e-mail: dchaney@em-normandie.fr

F. Pantoja, S. Wu (eds.), *From Micro to Macro: Dealing with Uncertainties in the Global Marketplace*, Developments in Marketing Science: Proceedings of the Academy of Marketing Science, https://doi.org/10.1007/978-3-030-89883-0_4

cognitive associations, and guilt. The research tests the hypotheses in a series of three studies. Because of the historical opposition between red and green (Nakshian 1964), A first study using chip packages as stimuli demonstrates the indirect effect of the color red (vs. green) on guilt through the mediating role of negative cognitive associations. Then, two additional studies using candies and cereal bar packages, respectively, replicate these effects and also demonstrate the role of the vice versus virtue product type. The results highlight the moderating role of perception of the product as a vice product, with the color red leading to stronger negative associations and guilt for such products. Implications for further research are discussed.

Keywords Color · Guilt · Negative associations · Vice · Food

References Available Upon Request

Variety-Seeking and Loyalty Points Redemption Behavior: An Abstract

Chen Li, Junhee Kim, Lawrence Duke, and Srinivasan Swaminathan

Abstract Loyalty programs are commonly used in a number of industries ranging from hotels to airlines to entice consumers to repurchase. One commonly practiced loyalty program is the award of points. Previous research has shown numerous benefits of point redemptions for retailers, such as improving customers' attitudes toward the retailer (Smith and Sparks 2009), boosting customers' spending (Taylor and Neslin 2005), and increasing shopping frequency (Henderson et al. 2011). However, researchers found that consumers tend to stockpile reward points in loyalty programs, and the majority of the loyalty points are unredeemed (Bijmolt et al. 2010). To encourage point redemption and cultivate customer loyalty through rewards, marketers use different types of promotion. These promotions include point-plus-cash promotions (PPC), which allow customers to combine their points with cash (Montoya and Flores 2019), and linear loyalty programs, which do not require a minimum amount in point redemption (Stourm et al. 2015). Stockpiling in these loyalty programs is not rewarding, and consumers have to forgo the time value of money for any delayed redemptions. Nonetheless, point stockpiling persists even in these programs (Stourm et al. 2015).

In this research, employing a dataset from a popular multi-vendor linear loyalty program in South Korea, we show that members in loyalty programs behave differently in their point stockpiling behavior. We identify four customer segments: (1) heavy purchasers with light point redemptions, (2) light purchasers with light point redemptions, (3) heavy purchasers with heavy point redemptions, and (4) light purchasers with heavy point redemptions. We find substantial heterogeneity in customer' point accumulation behavior among the four segments. This finding differs

C. Li (✉) · L. Duke · S. Swaminathan
Drexel University, Philadelphia, PA, USA
e-mail: cl3239@drexel.edu; lkd26@drexel.edu; swaminas@drexel.edu

J. Kim
California State University, Stanislaus, Turlock, CA, USA
e-mail: jkim28@csustan.edu

F. Pantoja, S. Wu (eds.), *From Micro to Macro: Dealing with Uncertainties in the Global Marketplace*, Developments in Marketing Science: Proceedings of the Academy of Marketing Science, https://doi.org/10.1007/978-3-030-89883-0_5

from the traditional view that point stockpiling behavior is common across the consumer population. Also, we find that the difference in customers' stockpiling behavior has a differential impact on their variety-seeking behavior. Specifically, members who redeem less often are more variety-seeking when they accumulate points than members who redeem more often. To marketing managers who consider introducing new products in the loyalty program, our finding is important because it provides insights into which customer groups are more accepting of new alternatives than other segments as the stock of their points increases.

Keywords Loyalty program · Point redemption · Variety-seeking · Sales promotion

References Available Upon Request

Consumers' Exposure to the Inexpedient Message: A Systematic Analysis to Evaluate the Consequences on Brand Reputation in Social Media

Matteo Napolitan, Eleonora Pantano, Nikolaos Stylos, and Michela de Pietro

Abstract The aim of this study is to evaluate consumers' moral judgements of the brand reputation of a luxury firm when exposed to wrongdoings in branded communications. A wealth of published research has shown that ill-prepared branding messages may cause confusion to consumers, misinterpretations on behalf of message receivers, generate negative perceptions to wider audiences and ultimately damage the firms' reputation. To this end, the case of Dolce and Gabbana 2019 campaign in China is analysed, drawing upon the basics of social media strategy, luxury market features and cross-cultural characteristics. The research evaluates consumers' Instagram posts and relevant reactions to the 2018 Dolce and Gabbana campaign in their effort to enter the Chinese market.

A systematic analysis is conducted about the extent to which luxury brand reputation is influenced by consumers' generated content in social media. Drawing on a comprehensive and unique dataset of unsolicited consumers' communications as response to a certain message, the study evaluates the immediate impact of the wrong message on the brand reputation. Results also show that after a negative message comes to light, firm reaction can hardly reduce or eliminate the negative consequences and restore the reputation.

Keywords Brand reputation · Luxury brands · Social media strategy · Cross-cultural communication · Systematic text analysis · Instagram

---

M. Napolitan
University of West London, London, UK
e-mail: 21364431@student.uwl.ac.uk

E. Pantano (✉) · N. Stylos
University of Bristol, Bristol, UK
e-mail: e.pantano@bristol.ac.uk; n.stylos@bristol.ac.uk

M. de Pietro
University of Calabria, Rende, Italy
e-mail: michela.depietro@unical.it

F. Pantoja, S. Wu (eds.), *From Micro to Macro: Dealing with Uncertainties in the Global Marketplace*, Developments in Marketing Science: Proceedings of the Academy of Marketing Science, https://doi.org/10.1007/978-3-030-89883-0_6

Introduction

The emergence of new media, with emphasis on social media, for communicating with consumers drives managers to revise their traditional strategies to include the adoption of these media. This is so, as they are able to support the corporate marketing communications by improving the diffusion of the marketing messages and their subsequent effectiveness (Floreddu et al. 2014; Reilly and Hynan 2014). In particular, social media offer a direct communication channel to interact with consumers (potential and existing) and stakeholders, by moving corporate communication to an interactive scenario (Floreddu et al. 2014). More precisely, social media provide a virtual space for knowledge sharing able to influence purchase decision (Sloan et al. 2015; Johnson et al. 2018). Indeed, consumers use social media to share their judgements about a firm. Therefore, social media can be considered as one of the most challenging and powerful force strengthening successful corporate marketing communication (Leeflang et al. 2014; Melewar and Nguyen 2014). For these reasons, past studies largely recognized the importance of social media marketing for promoting brands in general (Kang et al. 2014; De Vries et al. 2012; Hanson et al. 2019), and luxury brands in particular (Bian and Forsyte 2012; Dion and Arnould 2011; Godey et al. 2016). However, the role of social media in supporting luxury firms has still received little attention (Arrigo 2018). For this reason, scholars (Ko et al. 2019; Passavanti et al. 2020) call for new studies in the luxury brand management area, and in conjunction to social media.

Another issue related to social media influence on luxury goods is that they are particularly receiving the attention of public opinion with a great deal of online posts (Wiedmann et al. 2007), so their brand reputation seems to present a higher degree of exposure, and vulnerability as well, compared to other categories of retail products (Johnson et al. 2018). Thus, the aim of this study is to evaluate consumers' moral judgements of the brand reputation of a selected luxury firm when they get exposed to ill-advised online posts. Posting messages offhandedly on behalf of luxury firms might damage firms' reputation and generate huge negative consumer perceptions (potential and effective ones). Therefore, our findings identify (i) the conditions in which this damage to the firms' reputation might occur online, and (ii) the impact of the consequences. Drawing upon a comprehensive and unique dataset of unsolicited consumers' communications as response to a certain message, we provide a systematic analysis of the effects on consumers' judgements of the firm. To this end, we investigated the large luxury brand Dolce and Gabbana that has been damaged from their poorly prepared and released social media strategy, due to underestimating the effects of a particular online post. In fact, the message that was expected to be considered humorous or smart for an Italian or wider European audience (as the brand origin is) had been regarded as offensive, and with certain stereotypes of Chinese culture. This led social media influencers to share massively their reactions online, thus creating a largely negative impression to the vast majority of Chinese consumers, who in turn have also reacted, closing the loop of negative publicity for Dolce and Gabbana.

The remainder of this document is organized as follows: first, a comprehensive literature review on brand reputation and luxury brands, and on the social media strategy for luxury is presented, emphasizing the importance cultural differences when adopting international and global marketing communications strategies. Thereafter, the case research of Dolce and Gabbana is introduced, followed by the related methodology and analysis of results. Finally, the concluding section describes the extent to which firm reaction can somehow reduce or eliminate the negative consequences and restore the reputation when an unsuitable online communication is spread throughout social media. Some concluding possible guidelines to mitigate these consequences are further provided.

Literature Review

Brand Reputation and Luxury Brands

Brand reputation refers to what a firm's stakeholders (including consumers/customers) actually think about the firm (Varadarajan et al. 2006). In case of luxury brands, consumers attribute superior features to this type of products, which distinguish them from other products and brands (Amatulli et al. 2017). The literature on the three effects of conspicuous consumption, i.e., Veblen, snob and bandwagon effects, set the boundaries of luxury goods consumption (Tynan et al. 2010). Consumers create an impression of others on the basis of the (luxury) clothing brands they wear (Willems et al. 2012), through which they are able to evoke images of wealthy people who can support the cost of luxurious living in a sort of exclusive and inaccessible lifestyle (but highly desired) (Kapferer 2012). Indeed, luxury is more about what a brand represents, and not much about what are the technical product qualities are (Wiedmann et al. 2009). Thus, the consumption of luxury brands is driven by both social attributes such as self-expression and self-presentation, and the need to exhibit social standing (Bian and Forsythe 2012; Willems et al. 2012). Luxury products are considered to be symbols of personal and social individual identity (Tynan et al. 2010), while reflecting characteristics such as premium quality and price, heritage of craftsmanship, distinctiveness and recognizable style, superior quality, and uniqueness (defined by the intrinsic scarcity value), and global reputation (Bian and Forsythe 2012), which are the most important factors characterizing the luxury brand (Fionda and Morore 2009). Put differently, researchers realized that consumers choose luxury goods as various intangible benefits emerge, other than functional utility, including top quality and authenticity (Beverland 2019).

However, the high expectations towards luxury products might lead to high satisfaction or high disappointment (Wiedmann et al. 2007). Hence, consumers' response to luxury is always amplified due to their intrinsic features (Wiedmann et al. 2007). Thus, negative incidents might occur leading to extreme negative effects, such as brand hate (Bryson et al. 2013). In particular, the country of origin, consumer dissatisfaction with service, and negative stereotypes of luxury brand are the main influential factors of brand hate - as solicited especially by certain types of advertising) (Bryson et al. 2013). For instance, in February 2019 Burberry launched a collection for youth during the London Fashion Week with a hoodie with a noose around the neck, which has been criticized as it would recall the suicide (BBC News 2019). Thus, it has not been uncommon for luxury brands to propose controversial products not meeting all consumers' expectations. Similarly, in 2018 Gucci launched a woman's jumper which featured a cut-out at the mouth and red lips, which has been removed from the market immediately after the shoppers' complaints of "resembled blackface". This is why co-creation in branding is a very powerful concept, extending from building a new brand to creating effective marketing communications.

All in all, it is of utmost importance to carefully consider the interaction of luxury firms with existing and potentials consumers' communications in digital media, as users' input tends to amplify the effect of any unfortunate communication campaign elements (Quach and Thaichon 2017).

Social Media Strategy and Cross-Cultural Communication in Social Media

Social media offer particular features that companies/brands can use to improve their communication strategies: (i) interactivity; (ii) availability of large amount of free user-generated contents (contents developed directly by other users, rather than by professionals such as representatives of firms); and (iii) a greater emphasis on direct communication channels and community (Lindsey-Mullikin and Borin 2017; Athwal et al. 2019; Pentina et al. 2018). Social media are largely acknowledged in the relevant literature as a highly efficient instrument that can (i) reach millions of consumers, (ii) exploit consumers' (e)word-of-mouth communication (to spread information about products and services with limited investment), and (iii) influence consumers' decision-making processes and expanding the target audience (Hammick and Ju 2018). For these reasons, creating a page/profile on social media such as Facebook, Instagram and Twitter is now a common practice for many brands (Hammick and Ju 2018). However, the presence on the social networks does not necessarily imply they are used as interactive tools for engaging consumers, since they can also be used exclusively for advertising (largely informative) purposes (Black and Veloutsou 2017; Pantano et al. 2019). In case of luxury brands, any type of message in communications has in almost always a branded content to accompany the promotional efforts (Ghodeswar 2008).

As a consequence of consumers' abundant opportunities to freely share information, experiences, evaluations and opinions online, firms have limited control over the judgments shared online (Wiedmann et al. 2007), while the shared information includes both positive and negative statements. Concerning the negative judgments, scholars have suggested certain strategies to mitigate the negative e-word of mouth communications effects by interacting with dissatisfied consumers and revise their approaches accordingly, as well as encouraging the satisfied ones to share their positive experience, resulting in enthusiasm and loyalty towards the brand (He et al. 2014; Kaplan and Haenlein 2010; Johnson et al. 2018).

As reported, one of the main factors leading to luxury brand hate, conflicts and lack of trust is the adoption of negative stereotypes (as solicited especially by certain types of advertising) (Bryson et al. 2013; Moran and Youngdahl 2008). For example, in order to achieve a successful cross-cultural communication, as usually required by social media usage, marketers need to take into account the potential stereotypes usually involved in any culture (Moran and Youngdahl 2008). In particular, the cultural stereotypes formulated might impact positively but mainly negatively consumers based on ethnicity, gender or occupation (Moran and Youngdahl 2008). For instance, past studies indicated that successfully luxury marketing strategies in China should emphasize the social and emotional functions which consumers would consider as appealing and the accruing consequences of wearing luxury brands (Li et al. 2012). Other research showed the extent to which Chinese consumers prefer unique luxury goods while adopting conspicuous consumption behavior (Zhan and He 2012). In this vein, Luis Vuitton group (LVMH) representatives met Andrew Wu (President of Greater China) to discuss how to connect Chinese consumers to a set of brand values, since the potential LVMH consumers in China have differences compared to other market segments. Consequently, a major challenge luxury brands are facing in international marketplaces as the ones supported by social media is to identify and satisfy the needs and desires of global market segments, which requires a deeper understanding of local culture (Hofstede et al. 2012). When considering consumers segments across countries, the cultural data should be successfully adopted to better understand their behavior (Hofstede et al. 2012). On the other hand, a social media strategy spreading the wrong message (i.e., a message emphasizing negative stereotypes) might become a boomerang for luxury brands.

Methodology and Research Design

Case Study: Dolce and Gabbana

Dolce and Gabbana is an Italian luxury brand established in 1985 by Domenico Dolce and Stefano Gabbana, which rapidly achieved international audience. Nowadays, it is recognized as a symbol of Italian fashion, creativity and tradition around the world, considered as modern luxury, authentic and unconventional. The aim is to combine strong innovation with the Mediterranean value of Italian origin, with emphasis on Sicily Region in Southern Italy (the home region of founders) (Dolce and Gabbana 2019).

In 2018, Dolce and Gabbana launched a new campaign for promoting an event in Shanghai to enter the Chinese market on Instagram. To this end, the brand launched the specific hashtag #DGTheGreatShow. Unfortunately, the message communicated through this event solicited many negative reactions, due to the choice of featuring an Asian model attempting to eat Italian food (i.e., pizza, cannolo, and spaghetti with tomato sauce) with chopsticks (Fig. 1).[1]

Stefano Gabbana on his personal profile on Twitter mentioned "China ignorant dirty smelly mafia" (now removed from the social media). Influencers shared this comment to solicit more consumers' (negative) reactions. This first post in this sense got 58,025 likes (updated on the 13th of April, 2019) and 4591 comments (updated on the 13th of April 2019).

The comment of Stefano Gabbana generated even worse users' comments. To mitigate the negative impact of word-of-mouth communication, and limit the online sharing of negative opinions, the brand cancelled the event in Shanghai and shut down social media usage in China. The initial post of the brand launching the show has been cancelled by the Cultural Affairs Bureau of Shanghai. A subsequent post of influencers announcing the cancel of the show got 74,407 likes (updated on the 13th of April 2019) and 4,076 comments (updated on the 13th of April 2019). Finally, Stefano Dolce and Domenico Gabbana declared that their profiles have been hacked and provided official apologies (Haas 2018). However, Chinese e-commerce platforms (such as Kaola) and other luxury retailers (such as Secoo) removed Dolce and Gabbana products from their offer, as well as the international Yoox Net-a-Porter Group, Alibaba and JD.com, with negative consequences for

Fig. 1 Dolce and Gabbana new campaign for promoting an event in Shanghai to enter the Chinese market in 2018 (Source: Dolce and Gabbana official Instagram profile)

[1] Comments and users are covered for privacy issues.

sales and revenues. In particular, Alibaba and JD.com even canceled any reference to the brand pages in the main search. Moreover, the brand did not appeal to these decisions, thus accepting to being out of the Chinese retailing (offline and online) platform without any legal action. This showed the CEO's fear to lose even more clients with any further action. The video of Dolce and Gabbana is still available and freely accessible through a google search. Thus, the brand was not able so far to delete from internet and stop the sharing among consumers.

Data Collection and Procedure

In this paper, we follow the usual steps of automated text analysis for consumer research (Humphreys and Wang 2018), by using *WordStat* software to operationalize, analyse and validate the data. As suggested by Humphreys and Wang (2018), automated text analysis executed via computer would help quantifying constructs through new way of aggregating and displaying data to identify patterns that might not be obvious at the granular level. In particular, the analysis of spontaneous online communications among consumers allows determining how and how much certain concepts are mentioned and associated with (Walasek et al. 2018; Pantano and Stylos 2020). In this vein, *WordStat* largely supports the quantitative analysis of textual data consisting of the automatic extraction of the most important words from the tweets (text). This extraction leads to identify the thematic structures through executing a word frequency matrix. The subsequent factor analysis is conducted with Varimax rotation in order to recognize the most important factors (the most frequent phrases, all the phrases with factor loadings higher than a specific criterion are considered as part of the extracted factor). Drawing upon the frequency analysis, the phrases extraction tool further automatically identifies the common phrases. In this way, it is possible to discover the hidden thematic structure of a text collection by applying a combination of natural language processing and statistical analysis. To ensure the stability of the factoring solution, low-frequency items were excluded.

With this in mind, we used the automated text analysis to get insights on consumers evaluation of Dolce and Gabbana campaign through the large amount of posts on Instagram. In particular, we selected all the posts with the #DGTheGreatShow posted on Instagram in November 2019, then we limited the analysis to the ones with the highest number of shares/replies/likes, resulting in 653 posts.

In order to specifically analyse consumers' reactions to the luxury brand campaign, we conducted a frequency analysis (the analysis of number of word occurrences in the collected posts on Instagram), and a phrase extraction.

Since some words are more rare than others but more predictive, it is necessary to weight them more heavily, for this reason tf-idf corrects the infrequently occurring words as:

$$tf-idf\left(\text{word } w, \text{document } d, \text{corpus } D\right) = [1 + \log\left(\text{number of occurrences of } w \text{ in } d\right) \times \log\left(\frac{\text{total number of documents in } D}{\text{number of documents containing } w}\right)$$

Results

Table 1 summarizes the word frequency and the % of cases in which the single word is displayed, taking into account tf-idf per each word.

Drawing upon the frequency analysis, resulting in 9 most recurrent words, the subsequent phrase extraction provides a deeper understanding of consumers' sense of posts (Table 2). *WordStat* extracted 29 phrases, as shown below.

Discussion and Conclusion

Although luxury brands often launch controversial messages to solicit debates and increase visibility, firms have not the control of how these messages are perceived and shared. Across a systematic textual analysis of 653 posts related to the ad hoc event launched by Dolce and Gabbana to enter Chinese luxury market describing different consumers' judgements (all of them negative), we found that in the one hand the association of negative attributes with the brand (i.e., stupid, racist, and so on), in the other one the discouraging of purchasing this brand (i.e., "boycott Dolce and Gabbana"). Due to the huge amount of negative reaction, the brand was not able to further take action to mitigate the negative consequences. Thus, the brand had to turn down the expansion strategy in Chinese market. Therefore, the consequences are a damage in the both brand reputation and purchase intention. Our results show the extent to which Dolce and Gabbana campaign in 2018 shows a mismatch

Table 1 Frequency analysis of the most recurrent words

	Frequency	% Cases	TF • IDF
RACISM	125	15.95%	99.7
RACIST	85	10.28%	84.0
NOTME	46	7.06%	53.0
RESPECT	30	3.83%	42.5
DUMB	29	4.45%	39.2
LAME	29	4.45%	39.2
S**T[a]	24	3.37%	35.3
BOYCOTTDOLCE	18	2.61%	28.5
BOYCOTTDOLCEGABBANA	17	2.61%	26.9

[a]The word is not censored on the original posts

Table 2 Frequency analysis of the most recurrent phrases (phrases extraction)

	Frequency	% Cases	TF • IDF
RACISM DOLCEANDGABBANA	22	3.37%	32.4
LOVES CHINA	15	2.30%	24.6
EAT ITALIAN FOOD WITH CHOPSTICKS	10	1.53%	18.1
EATING WITH CHOPSTICKS	10	1.53%	18.1
RACISM CHINESE	9	1.38%	16.7
NOTME DOLCEGABBANA	8	1.23%	15.3
CULTUREAPPROPRIATION RACIST	7	1.07%	13.8
HASHTAG BOYCOTTDOLCE	7	1.07%	13.8
SHAME ON YOU DG RACISM ANTIRACISM RACIAL DISCRIMINATION	7	1.07%	13.8
CANCELLED DGTHEGREATSHOW	6	0.92%	12.2
CHOPSTICKS AS HAIR ORNAMENTS	6	0.92%	12.2
COMMENTS ABOUT CHINA AND CHINESE	6	0.92%	12.2
COUNTRY BEING CALLED SHIT BASICALLY	6	0.92%	12.2
FORCED TO CANCEL	6	0.92%	12.2
KIMONOS MISAPPROPRIATED AS CHINESE COSTUME	6	0.92%	12.2
RACISM DOLCE AND GABBANA STEFANO GABBANA	6	0.92%	12.2
RACIST REMARKS	6	0.92%	12.2
SHOW WAS CANCELED	6	0.77%	12.7
DG AD RACIST DOLCEGABBANA DEAD GONE STEFANOGABBANA	5	0.77%	10.6
NOT ME DGTHEGREATSHOW	5	0.77%	10.6
CULTURAL APPROPRIATION	4	0.61%	8.8
DOLCEANDGABBANA NOTME	4	0.61%	8.8
DOLCEANDGABBANA RACISM	4	0.61%	8.8
IGNORANT AND INSENSITIVE PEOPLE	4	0.61%	8.8
LOVE MY COUNTRY	4	0.61%	8.8
STUPID AND RACIST	4	0.61%	8.8
DISPLAY OF IMPERALIST TINGED RACISM	3	0.46%	7.0
DOLCEGABBANA IS A RACIST BRAND	3	0.46%	7.0
FASHION SCANDAL	3	0.46%	7.0

between the advertising chosen message and the culture of the entrance market, which lead to an unsuccessful marketing strategy emphasized by social media. Indeed, the company based the message on the European stereotype that Chinese in particular, and Asian in general always use chopsticks to eat. The luxury brand did not consider that the presence of the first forks have been found in archaeological sites in China dating back to the Bronze Age-Qijia culture (2400–1900 BC) (Needham 2000), which is much older than the first civilizations findings in Europe dating back to the Ancient Greece about the 6th century BC) (Iordanidis et al. 2009). Due to the high expectations towards luxury brands, which are always amplified due to their intrinsic features (Wiedmann et al. 2007), Dolce and Gabbana behavior generated high disappointment in consumers, which lead to the cancel of the show and ultimately no sales and revenues.

Our research contributes to a greater understanding of consumers' responses to negative stereotypes associated with luxury brands in the social media context. Previous research indicated that the adoption of negative stereotypes leads to luxury brand hate, conflicts and lack of trust (Bryson et al. 2013; Moran and Youngdahl 2008), while our study provides empirical evidence on what consumers say and do as reply. Thus, our research contributes empirically to a deeper understanding of consumers' judgements of the firms in response to negative stereotypes.

Through a systematic analysis of consumers unsolicited communications, our findings add new knowledge on the extent to which luxury brand reputation is influenced by consumers' generated contents in social media (He et al. 2014; Kaplan and Haenlein 2010; Johnson et al. 2018), by adding quantitative measures in terms of quantity and diversity of negative judgements and suggested future consumers' actions towards the brand. Thus, the study evaluates the immediate impact of the wrong message on the brand reputation.

Finally, it replies to the call of further investigations on social media management for luxury brands (Ko et al. 2019; Passavanti et al. 2020), by figuring out the new (negative) adjectives associated with the brand and the solicited consumers' behavior towards purchasing the brand in order to be able to take actions to stop the spreading of negative consequences.

From a managerial point of view, results also provide compelling evidence on the specific consequences of a luxury brand messages able to negative influence consumers at cognitive and behavioral level. Our research also provides brand managers with systematic tools of analysis to efficiently monitor social media. Finally, our results shed light on the consequences of a controversial message to enter a totally new market. In this case, deleting the message and apologies are not enough to support the entering, which has to be blocked and postponed. A similar research in the future might help the brand to identify the time to try to enter again the market with a different (and hopefully more appealing) message.

Our findings show the dramatic consequences of one controversial message on one luxury brand. However, the consequences might be even worse in the case of luxury brands with shareholders on the stock exchange like Tiffany, Ferrari, and LVM. Thus, further studies might develop some predictions on the effect of the image loss into economics values and shareholders.

The present research also considers only the data collected through unsolicited consumer's communications. Due to the word limit in the posts, triangulating the data with interviews with consumers might help achieving a deeper understanding of the consequences from consumers' perception point of view, and suggest more actions to recover the brand image. Similarly, additional analytics based on machine learning algorithms might further help to make more detailed prediction of consumer's attitudes towards the brand.

Finally, the present study further limits the analysis to one case in the luxury market, without comparing/contrasting with other not luxury brands, such fast fashion brand like HandM. For instance, this brand in 2018 chose a black child model with a jumper showing the slogan "coolest monkey in the jungle" that immediately reach negative eWOM. In particular, it was criticized by the famous NBA player LeBron James on his Instagram profile (his profile (@Kingjames) has more than 48.5 million of followers), through a post that got 1,233,498 likes and 30,415 comments (updated on the 13th of April 2019). The post consisted of a picture of the model wearing the jumper with a crown instead of the offensive sentence, specifying how much they (black Americans) have to work to be considered by others (white). In this case, the brand removed the jumpers and did not get further actions by consumers, in opposite with the Dolce and Gabbana 2018 campaign in China. Thus, a new line of inquiry might be related to the comparison of the consequences of the controversial message (through a commercial or a specific product) between the luxury and fast fashion brands.

References

Amatulli, C., Nataraajan, R., Capestro, M., Carvignese, M., and Guido, G. (2017). "Service" in luxury retailing in the twenty-first century: An exploratory look at the pleasure boating sector. *Psychology and Marketing*, *34*(5), 569-579.

Arrigo, E. (2018). Social media marketing in luxury brands: A systematic literature review and implications for management research. *Management Research Review, 41*(6), 657-679.

Athwal, N., Istanbulluoglu, D., and McCormack, S.E. (2019). The allure of luxury brands' social media activities: a uses and gratifications perspective. *Information Technology and People*, *32*(3), 603-626.

BBC News 2019. *Burberry sorry for "suicide" hoodie with noose around neck*. Retrieved April 13 2019, from https://www.bbc.co.uk/news/newsbeat-47302587.

Beverland, M. (2019). *Brand management: Co-creating meaningful brands*. Sage.

Bian, Q., and Forsythe, S. (2012). Purchase intention for luxury brands: A cross cultural comparison. *Journal of Business Research*, *65*(10) 1443-1451.

Black, I., and Veloutsou, C. (2017). Working consumers: Co-creation of brand identity, consumer identity and brand community identity. *Journal of Business Research*, *70*, 416-429.

Bryson, D., Atwal, G., and Hulten, P. (2013). Towards the conceptualisation of the antecedents of extreme negative affect towards luxury brands. *Qualitative Market Research 16*(4), 393-405.

Dion, D., and Arnould, E. (2011). Retail luxury strategy: assembling charisma through art and magic. *Journal of Retailing*, *87*(4), 502-520.

De Vries, L., Gensler, S., and Leeflang, P.S. (2012). Popularity of brand posts on brand fan pages: An investigation of the effects of social media marketing. *Journal of Interactive Marketing* *26*(2), 83-91.

Dolce and Gabbana 2019. *Dolce and Gabbana Corporate*. Retrieved April 11 2019 from https://www.dolcegabbana.com/corporate/en/history/main-stages.html.

Fionda, A.M., and Moore, C.M. (2009). The anatomy of the luxury fashion brand, *Journal of Brand Management 16*(5–6), 347–363.

Floreddu, P.B., Cabiddu, F., and Evaristo, R. 2014. Inside your social media ring: how to optimize online corporate reputation. *Business Horizons*, *57*(6), 737-745.

Ghodeswar, B. M. (2008). Building brand identity in competitive markets: a conceptual model. *Journal of Product and Brand Management 17*(1), 4-12.

Godey, B., Manthiou, A., Pederzoli, D., Rokka, J., Aiello, G., Donvito, R., and Singh, R. (2016). Social media marketing efforts of luxury brands: Influence on brand equity and consumer behavior. *Journal of Business Research*, *69*(12), 5833-5841.

Hammick, J.K., and Ju, I. (2018). Facebook fan page: the effect of perceived socialness in consumer–brand communication. *Journal of Marketing Communications 24*(7), 686-702.

Hanson, S., Jiang, L., and Dahl, D. (2019). Enhancing consumer engagement in an online brand community via user reputation signals: a multi-method analysis. *Journal of the Academy of Marketing Science, 47* (2), 349-367.

Haas, B. (2018). Chinese retail sites drop Dolce & Gabbana amid racist ad backlash. https://www.theguardian.com/world/2018/nov/23/dolce-gabbana-vanishes-from-chinese-retail-sites-amid-racist-ad-backlash.

He, W., Wang, F. K., & Zha, S. (2014). Enhancing social media competitiveness of small businesses: insights from small pizzerias. *New Review of Hypermedia and Multimedia, 20*(3), 225-250.

Hofstede, G., Hofstede, G.J., and Minkov, M. (2012). *Cultures and organizations: Software of the mind. Intercultural Cooperation and its Importance for Survival.* London: McGraw-Hill.

Humphreys, A., and Wang, R.J.-H. (2018). Automated text analysis for consumer research. *Journal of Consumer Research, 44* 1274-1306.

Iordanidis, A., Garcia-Guinea, J., and Karamitrou-Mentessidi, G. (2009). Analytical study of ancient pottery from the archaeological site of Aiani, northern Greece. *Materials Characterization, 60*(4) 292-302.

Johnson, A.R., Folkers, V.S., and Wang, J. (2018). When one bad apple spoils consumers' judgment of the brand: exposure to an employee's non-workplace transgression and potential remedies. *Journal of the Academy of Marketing Science, 46*(4), 725-743.

Kang, J., Tang, L., and Fiore, A.M. (2014). Enhancing consumer-brand relationships on restaurant Facebook fan pages: maximizing consumer benefits and increasing active participation. *International Journal of Hospitality Management, 36* 145-155.

Kapferer, J.-N. (2012). Abundant rarity: the key to luxury growth. *Business Horizons, 55*(5), 453-462.

Kaplan, A. M., & Haenlein, M. (2010). Users of the world, unite! The challenges and opportunities of Social Media. *Business horizons, 53*(1), 59-68.

Ko, E., Costello, J.P., and Taylor, C.R. (2019). What is a luxury brand? A new definition and review of the literature. *Journal of Business Research, 99*, 405-413.

Leeflang, P.S.H., Verhoef, P.C., Dahlstrom, P., and Freundt, T. (2014). Challenges and solutions for marketing in a digital era. *European Management Journal, 32*(1) 1-12.

Li, G., Li, G., and Kambele, Z. (2012). Luxury fashion consumers in China: perceived value, fashion lifestyle, and willingness to pay. *Journal of Business Research*, 65(10) 1516-1522.

Lindsey-Mullikin, J., and Borin, N. (2017). Why strategy is key for successful social media sales. *Business Horizons, 60*(4), 473-482.

Melewar, T.C., and Nguyen, B. (2014). Five areas to advance branding theory and practice. *Journal of Brand Management 21*(9), 758-769.

Moran, R.T., and Youngdahl, W.E. (2008). *Leading global projects: for professional and accidental project leaders*. Routledge.

Needham 2000. *Science and Civilisation in China. Volume 6: Biology and biological technology. Part V: Fermentations and food science.* Cambridge University Press (pp. 105–110).

Pantano, E., Giglio, S. and Dennis, C. (2019). Making sense of consumers' tweets: sentiment outcomes for fast fashion retailers through big data analytics. *International Journal of Retail and Distribution Management*, 47 (9), 915-927.

Pantano, E. and Stylos, N. (2020). The Cinderella moment: exploring consumers' motivation to engage with renting as collaborative luxury consumption mode. *Psychology and Marketing*, 37(5), 740-753.

Passavanti, R., Pantano, E., Priporas, C.-V., and Verteramo, S. (2020). The use of new technologies for corporate marketing communication in luxury retailing: preliminary findings. *Qualitative Market Research* 23(3), 503-521.

Pentina, I., Guilloux, V., and Micu, A.C. (2018). Exploring social media engagement behaviors in the context of luxury brands. *Journal of Advertising, 47*(1), 55-69.

Quach, S., and Thaichon, P. (2017). From connoisseur luxury to mass luxury: Value co-creation and co-destruction in the online environment. *Journal of Business Research, 81* 163-172.

Reilly, A.H., and Hynan, K.A. (2014). Corporate communication, sustainability, and social media: It's not easy (really) being green. *Business Horizons, 57*(6), 747-758.

Sloan, S., Bodey, K., and Gyrd-Jones, R. (2015). Knowledge sharing in online brand communities. *Qualitative Market Research: An International Journal 18*(3), 320-345.

Tynan, C., McKechnie, S., and Chhuon, C. (2010). Co-creating value for luxury brands. *Journal of Business Research, 63*(11) 1156-1163.

Varadarajan, R., DeFanti, M.P., and Busch, P.S. (2006). Brand portfolio, corporate image, and reputation: managing brand deletions. *Journal of the Academy of Marketing Science, 34* (2) 195-205.

Walasek, L., Bhatia, S., and Brown, G.D.A. (2018). Positional goods and the social rank hypothesis: income inequality affects online chatter about high and low-status brands on Twitter. *Journal of Consumer Psychology 28* (1) 138-148.

Wiedmann, K.P., Hennigs, N., and Siebels, A. (2009). Value-based segmentation of luxury consumption behavior. *Psychology and Marketing 26*(7), 625-651.

Wiedmann, K.P., Hennigs, N., and Siebels, A. (2007). Measuring consumers' luxury value perception: a cross-cultural framework. *Academy of Marketing Science Review 2007*(7) 1-21.

Willems, K., Janssens, W., Swinnen, G., Brengman, M., Streukens, S., Vancauteren, M. (2012). From Armani to Zara: impression formation based on fashion store patronage. *Journal of Business Research, 65*(10) 1487-1494.

Zhan, L., He, Y. (2012). Understanding luxury consumption in China: consumer perceptions of best-known brands. *Journal of Business Research, 65*(10) 1452-1460.

Exploring the Dark Side of Integrity-Impact of CEO Integrity on Firms' Entrepreneurial Orientation: An Abstract

Prachi Gala and Saim Kashmiri

Abstract The authors examine the effect of Chief executive officer (CEO) integrity on organizations' strategic orientation. The authors propose that CEOs who have high degrees of integrity tend to negatively influence their firms' degree of entrepreneurial orientation (EO) including each of the three core dimensions of EO — innovativeness, proactiveness, and risk-taking. They also argue that this impact of CEO integrity is likely to be stronger for overconfident CEOs and those with high power. Results from analyzing a sample of 741 firm-year observations of publicly traded American firms from 2014 to 2017 support the authors' hypotheses. Our findings lead us to conclude that organizations with CEOs who have high integrity tend to have lower levels of entrepreneurial orientation. Furthermore, these firms tend to have lower levels of the various sub-dimensions of EO. This negative effect of CEO integrity on firms' strategic orientation is strengthened when the CEO is overconfident and has more power. The authors add to prior work on CEO integrity in that they do not focus on the well-established positive aspects of CEO integrity.

This research has valuable implications for theory, board members, investors, managers, and researchers interested in understanding the antecedents of entrepreneurial orientation. We contribute to upper echelon theory literature by adding to the discussion of how business executives' psychological traits map onto firm behavior. Our findings suggest that future UET researchers need to pay attention to managers' integrity in order to understand and explain differences in firms' entrepreneurial decisions. We encourage future researchers to explore negative effects of other 'positive' traits in order to get a more nuanced understanding of the impact of such traits. We also highlight the relevance of CEO integrity as a hitherto ignored predictor of

P. Gala (✉)
Elon University, Elon, NC, USA
e-mail: pgala@elon.edu

S. Kashmiri
University of Mississippi, Oxford, MS, USA
e-mail: skasmhiri@bus.olemiss.edu

F. Pantoja, S. Wu (eds.), *From Micro to Macro: Dealing with Uncertainties in the Global Marketplace*, Developments in Marketing Science: Proceedings of the Academy of Marketing Science, https://doi.org/10.1007/978-3-030-89883-0_7

EO, with firms having high integrity CEOs likely to have significantly lower levels of EO. We reveal that it is advantageous for CEOs to understand that integrity is a double-edged sword.

Keywords CEO integrity · Entrepreneurial orientation · Proactiveness · Innovativeness · Risk taking · CEO power · CEO overconfidence · Duality

References Available Upon Request

Consumer Perceptions of Price Complexity, Manipulation and Fairness in the Context of Increasing Levels of Differential Pricing and Dynamic Pricing: An Abstract

Silke Bambauer-Sachse and Ashley Young

Abstract Dynamic pricing is gaining affluence as a differential pricing strategy in many services and the online retail of goods. Dynamic prices vary continuously based on multiple and opaque criteria, representing the most extreme form of differential prices. Previous research does not consider the whole spectrum of differential pricing that ranges from one criterion such as temporality, all the way to dynamic pricing. The literature on differential pricing mainly focuses on fairness perceptions (e.g., Haws and Bearden 2006). So far, none examines price complexity and manipulative intent perceptions, nor how the spectrum of differential pricing and increasing levels of price differentiation affects these variables. Price complexity is important as higher cognitive efforts and changing prices lead to a dilution of the reference price, which will influence purchase behaviour. The feeling of being manipulated by retailers will negatively impact product evaluations (Bambauer and Gierl 2008) and customer behaviour. Our study provides complementary insight to existing literature by observing the impact of increasing levels of differential pricing (one form of price differentiation; a combination of two forms of differential pricing; a combination of five forms; dynamic pricing, characterized by many opaque discriminatory criteria and ongoing price changes) on fairness, complexity, and manipulative intent perceptions.

We tested the various differential pricing strategies (temporal; temporal and demographic criteria combined; temporal, demographic, geographic, quality and quantity-based criteria combined; and dynamic pricing) and the test products (hotel room, rental car) with a sample of 114 respondents of an online questionnaire. The respondents read a scenario in which they were a price-disadvantaged customer

S. Bambauer-Sachse (✉) · A. Young
University of Fribourg, Fribourg, Switzerland
e-mail: silke.bambauer-sachse@unifr.ch; ashley.young@unifr.ch

F. Pantoja, S. Wu (eds.), *From Micro to Macro: Dealing with Uncertainties in the Global Marketplace*, Developments in Marketing Science: Proceedings of the Academy of Marketing Science, https://doi.org/10.1007/978-3-030-89883-0_8

learning that prices vary based on the previously mentioned criteria. We then measured price complexity, manipulative intent and price fairness perceptions.

The results show that with an increasing number of criteria used for differential pricing, including the extreme combination of many criteria (dynamic pricing), consumers see the price differences as increasingly complex and less fair, while all types of differential pricing lead to strong feelings of being manipulated. These results clearly show that consumers might accept simple forms of differential pricing, but that they react very negatively to differential pricing based on an increasing number of combined criteria. Therefore, there are very negative effects of differential pricing, and particularly of dynamic pricing, on existing customers in addition to the positive effects on profit that many marketers often only consider.

Keywords Dynamic pricing · Differential pricing · Price complexity · Price fairness · Manipulation

References Available Upon Request

The Effects of Matching Empty Ad Space Color to Featured Product's Color on Consumer Buying Impulse: An Abstract

Nazuk Sharma

Abstract This research investigates how matching an ad's empty space color specifically to that of the advertised product's color (instead of leaving it white) impacts consumers' product buying impulse. It tests two competing hypotheses, where the salience explanation proposes a positive effect of empty space-product color matching on product buying impulse, while the contrast account predicts an opposite effect.

Prior research suggests a positive link between stimulus-based salience and consumer urge to buy impulsively (Huang 2016), with a hedonic appraisal of the stimulus acting as a strong precursor to the buying impulse (Amos et al. 2014). Therefore, following the *Theory of Visceral Influences* which suggests that certain stimuli can narrow consumer attention to situational impulsivity, the salience explanation proposes that empty space-product color matching would increase overall ad salience due to an increased exposure to product color (an important sensory aspect) (Loewenstein 1996). This visceral sensory influence would then enhance the product's hedonic appraisal, in turn propelling consumers' product buying impulse (Monaco et al. 2003).

However, a traditional stream of research predicts more positive outcomes when there is a greater contrast between the ad elements (Schindler 1986; Moore et al. 2005; Pracejus et al. 2006; Olsen et al. 2012; Kim and Lakshmanan 2015). Greater contrast increases perceptual fluency, which creates a hedonically-marked, fluent processing experience (Reber et al., 1998; Reber et al. 2004). Therefore, it can be alternatively proposed that using a white (rather than product-colored) empty space in an ad increases contrast, which elevates the product's hedonic appeal due to an affect-laden fluent processing and that increases product buying impulse.

In testing these competing predictions (salience versus contrast), three experimentally-designed studies were conducted by soliciting participants from

N. Sharma (✉)
Fairfield University, Fairfield, CT, USA
e-mail: nsharma@fairfield.edu

F. Pantoja, S. Wu (eds.), *From Micro to Macro: Dealing with Uncertainties in the Global Marketplace*, Developments in Marketing Science: Proceedings of the Academy of Marketing Science, https://doi.org/10.1007/978-3-030-89883-0_9

Amazon's Mechanical Turk platform (Goodman et al. 2013). Findings from all studies support the salience rather than the contrast account across two product categories, three colors, and three online ad formats.

In addition to being the first to investigate the impact of using a product-colored empty space on consumer buying impulse as the focal outcome, the current work extends prior research studying stylistic visual cues (Peracchio and Meyers-Levy 2005; Yang et al. 2010). It also provides marketers with a systematic understanding of how making such a simple, cost-effective, stylistic change can not only increase their ad's noticeability in a competitively-cluttered digital ad environment, but also enhance their product's hedonic appeal.

Keywords Empty space · Salience · Contrast · Buying impulse

References Available Upon Request

Consumer Anger After Double Deviation: The Role of Failure Severity, Service Involvement, and Recovery Timing: An Abstract

Silke Bambauer-Sachse, Yannick Renaud-dit-Louis, and Ashley Young

Abstract When services fail, over half of the recovery attempts lead to double deviations (i.e. failed service recoveries) (Bitner et al. 1990). Double deviations lead to anger, but it is less clear whether consumers' anger is mainly due to the initial failure or the failed recovery because research on double deviations remains limited (Basso and Pizzutti 2016). Studies that simultaneously consider the effects of failure severity, involvement, and recovery timing on anger do not exist. Research on the severity of double deviations (e.g., Casado et al. 2011) does not always distinguish between the severity of the initial failure and the severity of the failed recovery although consumer reactions might differ depending on varying sequences of less (more) severe initial failures and more (less) severe failed recoveries. Moreover, previous research does not clearly answer the question of which effects an immediate (vs. delayed) compensation has in terms of reducing anger. As differences in consumer service involvement can determine consumer reactions to double deviations, it is important to also include involvement here. In our study, we analyse anger after experiencing a sequence of a less (more) severe initial failure and a more (less) severe failed recovery by considering consumer involvement and the timing of the service provider's final reaction.

The sample consisted of 497 respondents. We used a 2 (less severe initial failure, more severe failed recovery vs. more severe initial failure, less severe failed recovery) × 2 (involvement: moderate vs. high) × 2 (recovery timing: immediate vs. 6 days delayed) between-subjects design. We presented the respondents with scenarios (stay at a Spa Hotel) to implement the manipulations.

The results confirm that highly involved consumers show less anger when presented with an immediate recovery, independently of the failure severity combination. For moderately involved consumers, an immediate recovery better reduces anger if a more severe failure is followed by a less severe failed recovery. When a

S. Bambauer-Sachse (✉) · Y. Renaud-dit-Louis · A. Young
University of Fribourg, Fribourg, Switzerland
e-mail: silke.bambauer-sachse@unifr.ch; yannick.renaud@unifr.ch; ashley.young@unifr.ch

F. Pantoja, S. Wu (eds.), *From Micro to Macro: Dealing with Uncertainties in the Global Marketplace*, Developments in Marketing Science: Proceedings of the Academy of Marketing Science, https://doi.org/10.1007/978-3-030-89883-0_10

less severe failure is followed by a more severe recovery failure, the recovery timing has no effect on anger. Thus, service providers should encourage immediate recoveries after double deviations, especially for highly involved consumers and moderately involved consumers who experience more severe initial failures. Consumer anger after double deviations can be reduced if frontline employees have sufficient flexibility to handle such situations immediately. Only if less involved consumers experience double deviations with less severe initial failures, immediate vs. delayed compensation has no differential effect on anger.

Keywords Double deviation · Consumer anger · Failure severity · Recovery timing

References Available Upon Request

The Power of Consumers' Sustainable Product Purchasing: An Abstract

Barbara Seegebarth, Stefanie Sohn, and Ann-Kathrin Blankenberg

Abstract Socially and environmentally responsible business practices also aim to encourage sustainable consumer behavior (Kotler 2011; Olsen et al. 2014). However, it remains unclear to what extent purchasing of sustainable products as a form of sustainable consumer behavior indeed impacts the consumers' sustainable mindset. Although existing research provides comprehensive insights into both the determinants of sustainable consumer behavior (White et al. 2019) and the effects of sustainable business strategies (e.g., Olsen et al. 2014), extant research largely fails to study the consequences of consumer behavior (Pham 2015). In particular, knowledge is scarce on how sustainable consumer behavior and more specifically the purchasing of sustainable food affect the individual and more specifically the self-identity as a sustainable consumer. In other words, on the backdrop of the embodied cognition theory (Krueger 2013; Shapiro 2011), which states that bodily engagement (i.e., action) shapes both, the character and the content of consciousness, this article sheds light on how sustainable consumer behavior (i.e., organic and fair-trade food purchases) affects consumers' consciousness for sustainable consumption (CSC).

The findings of actual purchase data of both organic and fair-trade food products of 3,358 German households reveal that organic food purchases exert a positive effect on consumers' CSC while the fair-trade purchases do not. However, fair-trade purchases promote CSC with an increasing age. More specifically, seniors compare to young and middle-aged consumer consider fair-trade purchases to define their

B. Seegebarth (✉)
Technische Universität Braunschweig, Braunschweig, Germany
e-mail: b.seegebarth@tu-braunschweig.de

S. Sohn
University of Southern Denmark, Esbjerg, Denmark
e-mail: sohn@sam.sdu.dk

A.-K. Blankenberg
Georg-August Universität Göttingen, Göttingen, Germany
e-mail: ann-kathrin.blankenberg@wiwi.uni-goettingen.de

F. Pantoja, S. Wu (eds.), *From Micro to Macro: Dealing with Uncertainties in the Global Marketplace*, Developments in Marketing Science: Proceedings of the Academy of Marketing Science, https://doi.org/10.1007/978-3-030-89883-0_11

CSC. In addition, the positive relationship between organic food purchase and environmental CSC is significantly stronger for young than for middle-aged purchasers.

This work has significant implications for practitioners on how to improve consumers' CSC. Marketers on the one hand should therefore continue to promote and facilitate sustainable purchases (i.e., organic and fair-trade food purchases). Promoting this behavior should be realized in a targeted way. For instance, marketers should put further emphasis on the fair-trade food promotion for senior customers in order to activate CSC and therefore stimulating and amplifying the "foot in the door" strategy.

Keywords Sustainable food purchases · Consciousness · Sustainable consumption · Embodied cognition theory

References Available Upon Request

Can Memes Improve Online Survey Respondents' Engagement and Data Quality? An Abstract

Catherine A. Roster and Nick Flor

Abstract According to a recent international survey of market research firms (Macer and Wilson 2017), over 60% of all online surveys now rely on panel samples. Recently, market researchers have called for greater efforts on improving the online survey experience (Cooke 2011; Walker 2013). The benefits of such efforts are two-fold. First, data quality has been shown to be higher among respondents who are intrinsically as opposed to extrinsically motivated (Brüggen et al. 2011; Callegaro et al. 2015). Second, pleasant survey experiences help to assure marketers have access to a large, representative pool of panelists willing to repeatedly participate in online surveys.

Research has explored how graphics, visuals, and interactivity can be embedded into survey elements as a means of increasing respondents' engagement and enjoyment with the survey experience (e.g., Couper et al. 2004, Dolnicar et al. 2013; Downes-Le Guin et al. 2012; Gummer et al. 2020). More advanced approaches include incorporating elements of online gaming into survey contexts, called "gamification" (e.g., Pulleston 2012) or the similar notion of "surveytainment" (e.g., Krostyk et al. 2019), which adds entertainment-oriented features to the survey's design. A number of studies have reported minimal or no effects of these elements on quantitative measures of survey engagement, or worse, unintended bias or negative consequences such as lower response quality or higher administrative costs (e.g., Callegaro et al. 2015).

The study examined the effect of using Internet memes to improve online survey respondents' engagement and data quality. Field experiments were conducted with two different U.S. samples, one (n = 250) purchased from Prolific and another from Qualtrics (n = 935). Respondents answered a 13-minute survey about environmental attitudes. Half were randomly assigned to a control condition (no memes) and the other half saw memes of animals with motivating messages like "your opinions matter," or "we appreciate your help" at transitional points during the survey. We

C. A. Roster (✉) · N. Flor
University of New Mexico, Albuquerque, NM, USA
e-mail: roster@unm.edu; nickflor@unm.edu

F. Pantoja, S. Wu (eds.), *From Micro to Macro: Dealing with Uncertainties in the Global Marketplace*, Developments in Marketing Science: Proceedings of the Academy of Marketing Science, https://doi.org/10.1007/978-3-030-89883-0_12

assessed effectiveness using both behavioral and self-report measures of data quality and survey engagement

We found few statistically significant differences between conditions across both samples. There was no evidence that the memes impaired data quality or added to respondents' burden. Open-ended comments revealed that respondents found the memes to be motivating and engaging. In conclusion, it appears that memes are a relatively low-cost way to give respondents a cognitive break from answering questions and showing appreciation for their efforts.

Keywords Internet surveys · Memes · Survey engagement · Panels

References Available Upon Request

Schools' Evaluations and the Advocacy Roles of Students: An Abstract

Flávio Régio Brambilla and Bruno Morgado Ferreira

Abstract The importance of the evaluation for universities is fully recognized. Measuring student satisfaction with their higher education institution is not new. In several countries, some of these data are even mandatory and transversal to the institutions for the accreditation of their courses. They then contribute as indicators to compare and validate a position in national or international rankings. However, the validity of these data is sometimes questioned. In this study, we focus mainly on the influence of student advocacy roles on school evaluations. For this, since three academic years, in a higher school in Portugal, a team of teachers and researchers has set up the collection of data (as opinions for school evaluation) via one online survey distributed by email in each May, to their final year students of bachelor degrees. Until now, more than three hundred students freely participated. Among other information, this survey allows to collect students' opinion and judgment about their school by measuring the Net Promoter Score (NPS, known as the metrics of advocacy; Kotler et al. 2016) and also the SERVQUAL (known as the instrument to measure service quality, adapted to this specific context, with five dimensions: Tangibles, Reliability, Responsiveness, Assurance and Empathy; Parasuraman et al. 1988). The results show that all the dimensions of SERVQUAL show significant differences according to the profile of the student (as a detractor, as a neutral person or as a promoter). These findings confirm that it is very important and useful to compare all the results in more detail and, for that, according to the profile of NPS. This allows us to identify what is really most important to improve school management in the next school year in a specific way for each dimension of

F. R. Brambilla (✉)
Universidade de Santa Cruz do Sul, Santa Cruz do Sul, Brazil
e-mail: flaviobr@unisc.br

B. M. Ferreira
Polytechnic Institute of Viseu (IPV), Viseu, Portugal
e-mail: morgado.ferreira@estgv.ipv.pt

F. Pantoja, S. Wu (eds.), *From Micro to Macro: Dealing with Uncertainties in the Global Marketplace*, Developments in Marketing Science: Proceedings of the Academy of Marketing Science, https://doi.org/10.1007/978-3-030-89883-0_13

SERVQUAL. For future research, the question that arises is who should we trust and believe (promoters or detractors).

Keywords Net promoter score · Advocacy · SERVQUAL · Satisfaction

References Available Upon Request

Co-creation Design: A Theoretical Model of Design Management from the Service Dominant Logic of Marketing: An Abstract

Flávio Régio Brambilla, Silvia Bittencourt, and Ciro Eduardo Gusatti

Abstract This research seeks to concile the value co-creation with studies on design management in order to propose a theoretical model for co-creative design. Design management determines strategic role of the designer in the company. Such activities must be included in the company's marketing management at three levels: operational, tactical and strategic. Operational level is the first step to integrate design in the organization. Considers design as a product or project. Tactical level involves integrating activity to design company, focused on the planning, implementation and monitoring activities. The strategic level is the stage where design unites and transforms the vision of company. Vargo and Lusch (2004) Service-Dominant Logic focuses on the consumer as an active role in building value for the product and service. Prahalad and Ramaswamy (2004) DART: Dialogue, Access, Risk and Transparency for value co-creation actions, provides to the company and customer focus in the experience in full. From proposed Management Design defined by Mozota (2002) and Karjalainen (2012) and conditions for the viability, support and implementation of value co-creation processes, establishes a theoretical model for the Co-creative Design Management created by the authors of this research. **A Design Management in Co-Creative Strategic Level:** two enabling factors were identified (the organizational culture and management models/policies) The co-creative design depends on strategic planning that is consistent with a culturally willing company to new ideas and the participation of other in the creative process. **A Design Management in the Co-creative Tactical Level:** at the tactical level, the activities of design are linked to factors of resources of activity (human, physical, internal, external); skills to design; core competencies; training;

F. R. Brambilla (✉) · S. Bittencourt
Universidade de Santa Cruz do Sul, Santa Cruz do Sul, Brazil
e-mail: flaviobr@unisc.br; silvia@inovacomunicacao.art.br

C. E. Gusatti
Universidade de Passo Fundo, Passo Fundo, Brazil
e-mail: cirogusatti@upf.br

F. Pantoja, S. Wu (eds.), *From Micro to Macro: Dealing with Uncertainties in the Global Marketplace*, Developments in Marketing Science: Proceedings of the Academy of Marketing Science, https://doi.org/10.1007/978-3-030-89883-0_14

description of processes, standards and procedures for management of design and location, services and team goals responsible for design. These are the skills that will be able to motivate the public to effective participation in the design process. **A Design Management in the Co-creative Operational Level:** concerns the nature of issues related to processes and design projects; proposals; relationship management and project design team; selection of team members; documentation and control systems; implementation of solutions; evaluation of projects. Mozota (2002) argue that operational level promotes product differentiation and development. Product characteristics are essential to the viability or not of a co-creation model of shared value.

Keywords Co-creation design · Theoretical model · Design management · Service dominant logic

References Available Upon Request

How Facial Prominence Impacts Perception of Interaction Space and Consumer Response: An Abstract

Lam An, Ze Wang, Xia Wang, and Jonathan Hasford

Abstract Print ads, billboards, online banners, and product packaging frequently feature human faces, and both global brands and local service providers include human faces to increase the effectiveness of their persuasive appeals. While existing literature suggests that incorporating a face into marketing communications is beneficial, research has been surprisingly limited on issues related to the size of a face featured within a marketing message. The current research addresses this gap by examining how facial prominence in marketing communications affects consumer responses to various types of persuasive communications.

We define facial prominence as size of a source's face within a marketing communication relative to the overall size of a marketing message. Drawing from social communicative theories on facial perception (Fridlund 2017), we propose that facial prominence impacts interpersonal-level inferences about social interaction intentions that subsequently impact consumer reactions. While higher facial prominence is generally expected to have positive effects given its association with dominance and confidence, our findings counterintuitively suggest that less is more – that is, consumers respond more positively to marketing communications featuring lower facial prominence. This effect is driven by consumers' perceived social interaction intention with the endorser or spokesperson. These predictions were examined across four studies.

Study 1 looked at two accident lawyer advertisements with manipulated levels of facial prominence of the male spokesperson, and showed that the ad with lower facial prominence generated higher purchase intention. Study 2 generalized this

---

L. An (✉) · Z. Wang
University of Central Florida, Orlando, FL, USA
e-mail: lam.an@ucf.edu; ze.wang@ucf.edu

X. Wang
Renmin University of China, Beijing, China
e-mail: wangxia@ruc.edu.cn

J. Hasford
University of Tennessee—Knoxville, Knoxville, TN, USA
e-mail: jhasford@utk.edu

F. Pantoja, S. Wu (eds.), *From Micro to Macro: Dealing with Uncertainties in the Global Marketplace*, Developments in Marketing Science: Proceedings of the Academy of Marketing Science, https://doi.org/10.1007/978-3-030-89883-0_15

observation to a different product category (laptop) with a female spokesperson and provided support for interaction intention with the spokesperson as the underlying mechanism of the effect. Study 3 demonstrated that the effect went away when the spokesperson has a high level of similarity with the audience. Study 4 examined another boundary condition, showing that the effect reversed when the spokesperson was an aspirational individual such as a celebrity.

Four studies provided support for our hypothesis that higher facial prominence can have a negative impact on marketing-related outcomes. Our findings can be applied to improve the effectiveness of advertisements and layout of e-commerce websites that feature human faces.

Keywords Facial prominence · Nonverbal communication · Persuasion · Interaction intention

References Available Upon Request

Assessing the Perceived Environmental Friendliness of Different Packaging Materials: An Abstract

Jianyu Hao, Zixuan Cheng, and Anouk de Regt

Abstract In light of global environmental challenges such as climate change, sustainable consumption and production has been considered as a crucial issue by firms as a "triple bottom line" principle, which is balancing financial, social, and environmental performance (Pujari 2006; Dangelico 2016; Liu et al. 2016; Hussain et al. 2018). Among the ample means that corporations can take to achieve a higher environmental performance of their new products, an effective aspect, is to switch to materials that lead to fewer greenhouse gases emission during producing or more recyclable (Calantone et al. 2010; Dangelico and Pujari 2010).

Successful eco-innovative packages need elaborate understanding about how consumers recognise, perceive, consider, and purchase such products. This study intends to explore whether consumers perception towards packages has changed during these decades. An online survey is conducted in TurkPrime (Litman et al. 2017), in which 280 participants left (45.36% male; 87.5% is US citizens). Results indicate that, the perceived environmental friendliness of paper is higher than glass (t (279) = 6.82, $p < 0.001$), which is higher than metal can (t (279) = 7.36, $p < 0.001$) that is higher than plastic (t (279) = 10.97, $p < 0.001$). As for the shopping bags, the perceived environmental friendliness of cloth is higher than paper (t (279) = 8.72, $p < 0.001$), which is higher than plastic (t (279) = 18.81, $p < 0.001$). Consumers with higher environmental identity have higher WTP towards the paper cups ($\beta = 0.14$, $p = .009$; R2 = 0.344, $p = 0.002$).

Our findings of perceived environmental friendliness for beverage packages are different from Van Dam's (1996) result, in which he documents higher perceived environmental friendliness of glass than paper. This might be geographic effect or consumers changed their cognition towards these two kinds of packages in these two decades. The results have implications for marketing researchers and consumer psychologists. As it is shown, the perceived environmental friendliness in this study

J. Hao (✉) · Z. Cheng · A. de Regt
King's College London, London, UK
e-mail: jianyu.hao@kcl.ac.uk; zixuan.cheng@kcl.ac.uk; anouk.de_regt@kcl.ac.uk

F. Pantoja, S. Wu (eds.), *From Micro to Macro: Dealing with Uncertainties in the Global Marketplace*, Developments in Marketing Science: Proceedings of the Academy of Marketing Science, https://doi.org/10.1007/978-3-030-89883-0_16

is different from prior study. Some researchers may want to uncover the reasons for such changes. As for the implications for marketers, it is worth noting that for those brands who want to promote eco-innovative products, the packaging materials may impact how consumers perceive and how much they are likely to accept the eco-innovative image of the brands.

Keywords Sustainable consumption · Perceived environmental friendliness · Eco-friendly packing · Consumer perception

References Available Upon Request

Psychological Ownership and Consumer Happiness: An Abstract

Dan Li

Abstract The pursuit of happiness has received growing attention in consumer research over the past decade (van Boven and Gilovich 2003). Largely missing from this research stream on happiness, however, is attention to the idea of psychological ownership. This study introduces the concept of psychological ownership into consumer happiness research. Psychological ownership is the personal sense of possessing a consumer holds for a target (Pierce et al. 2001). According to self-determination theory, the author suggests that psychological ownership has an impact on happiness, because the routes to psychological ownership satisfy the basic psychological needs including competence, autonomy, and relatedness.

An online experiment was carried out to examine the effect of advertising message via a 2 (message framing: material vs. experiential) × 2 (product feature: smart vs. not smart) between-subjects experimental design. Participants were randomly assigned to one of four groups. In each group, the participants were exposed to an advertisement for a coffee mug that elicited psychological ownership, which ultimately influenced the reported happiness. The results demonstrate that people are more likely to perceive a product as theirs when it is featured in the advertisement as an experiential purchase. This increased psychological ownership ultimately influences consumers' happiness. Moreover, smart product features work as a moderator in this relationship. Emphasizing the smart features of a product in marketing messages could attenuate the effect of framing on anticipated happiness.

This study contributes to extant literature by distinguishing between the effects of psychological ownership and legal ownership. It enhances the understanding of consumer happiness. It also extended the endowment effect by introducing an antecedent and an emotional consequence into the psychological mechanism. The endowment effect argues that people ascribe greater value to things merely because they own them (Reb and Connolly 2007). This study demonstrates that psychologi-

D. Li (✉)
Widener University, Chester, PA, USA
e-mail: dli3@widener.edu

F. Pantoja, S. Wu (eds.), *From Micro to Macro: Dealing with Uncertainties in the Global Marketplace*, Developments in Marketing Science: Proceedings of the Academy of Marketing Science, https://doi.org/10.1007/978-3-030-89883-0_17

cal ownership could elicit the same endowment effect as legal ownership does. Furthermore, consumers might not only attach more values to the things they perceive as their possession, but also have more positive feelings towards those objects. Moreover, the findings have important managerial implications. Marketers could not only design persuasive marketing messages that elicit psychological ownership, but also facilitate the pursuit of intrinsic motivation throughout the entire buying process.

Keywords Psychological ownership · Happiness · Framing · Advertising · Smart products

References Available Upon Request

Signaling Product Quality with Virtual Reality? An Interpretation with Consumer-Perceived Marketing Media Innovativeness: An Abstract

Kelley Cours Anderson and Debra A. Laverie

Abstract The overabundance of new digital marketing media creates a challenge for marketing managers to identify effective options to differentiate and educate consumers about their offerings. Firms may use marketing tools to signal to consumers the quality of the offering. While literature conceptualizes that innovative marketing technology influences consumers' quality and value perceptions (Grewal et al. 2003; Parasuraman and Grewal 2000), empirical research is limited. Specifically, past research has not addressed how marketing can act as a signal simply because it is perceived as innovative by consumers. This study offers an explanation as to why the implementation of innovative marketing media may not always be successful in driving purchase intentions.

Conceptualizations of innovativeness vary, including firm innovativeness, brand innovativeness, product innovativeness, and consumer innovativeness (Calantone et al. 2006; Garcia and Calantone 2002; Kunz et al. 2011; Szymanski et al. 2007). This paper presents marketing media innovativeness (MMI) as a new conceptualization to expand our understanding of implementing optimal digital marketing. The following research question is addressed: How do consumer perceptions of an innovative marketing medium influence product perceptions and purchase intentions? The proposed model tests the influence of product promotion with virtual reality tours, an industry-perceived innovative marketing medium, and still-photography, a non-innovative marketing medium as a means to signal a product's quality to consumers.

Results from two studies support that while industry-perceived innovative marketing media may not positively influence product quality perceptions, consumers' perception of the innovativeness of marketing media can positively affect the product quality perceptions of the offering and increase purchase intentions. The study contributes to digital marketing (Lamberton and Stephen 2016; Yadav and Pavlou

K. C. Anderson (✉) · D. A. Laverie
Texas Tech University, Lubbock, TX, USA
e-mail: kelley.anderson@ttu.edu; debbie.laverie@ttu.edu

F. Pantoja, S. Wu (eds.), *From Micro to Macro: Dealing with Uncertainties in the Global Marketplace*, Developments in Marketing Science: Proceedings of the Academy of Marketing Science, https://doi.org/10.1007/978-3-030-89883-0_18

2014) and signaling theory literature (Biswas and Biswas 2004; Ho-Dac et al. 2013; Kozlenkova et al. 2017; Li et al. 2009; Mitra and Fay 2010; Wells et al. 2011) by offering a lens of consumer-perceived marketing media innovativeness. Furthermore, this study evaluates usage of innovative marketing media in consumers' purchase journey, providing a consumer-based strategic approach that has been called for in our literature (Dahl 2016; Deighton 2016; Hamilton 2016).

Keywords Digital marketing · Signaling theory · Innovative marketing · Virtual reality · Consumer-based strategy

References Available Upon Request

Special Session: How Do We Properly Quality Control Crowdsourced Data? A Round Table Discussion: An Abstract

Aaron D. Arndt, John B. Ford, Barry J. Babin, and David J. Ortinau

Abstract Marketing researchers, particularly in consumer behavior, rely increasingly on crowdsourcing and online panels as data sources. An examination of the top four journals in Marketing (Journal of Marketing, Journal of Marketing Research, Journal of Consumer Research and Journal of the Academy of Marketing Science) from 2014 to 2018 indicates that 360 out of 1101 articles (32.7%) utilized MTurk data. To date, researchers have focused on analyzing the validity and generalizability of data obtained through crowdsourcing and online panels. Yet given that crowdsourcing and online panels are being so relied upon, the panel will discuss ways of improving data quality rather than examining the question of whether academic researchers should use or avoid crowd-sourced data. We propose a special session to discuss how to increase the quality of online panel samples.

Screening and identification are important in setting up a sample. The presentation introduces a typology for classifying screening criteria that reflect the sampling goals of identifying respondents that (1) match the target population as much as possible and (2) provide honest, attentive responses. The presentation includes the results of a study testing screening criteria using Dynata, Qualtrics, three different MTurk panels, and students. The results show that screening criteria directly influences sample attention, honesty, and prevalence of VPNs to disguise physical location. Based on these results, we will discuss best practices for collecting high quality samples using online panels from the viewpoint of authors, reviewers, and journal editors. We will also allow time for a question and answer session. This special session will help researchers who use online sample improve the validity of their sam-

A. D. Arndt (✉) · J. B. Ford
Old Dominion University, Norfolk, VA, USA
e-mail: aarndt@odu.edu; jbford@odu.edu

B. J. Babin
University of Mississippi, University, MS, USA
e-mail: bjbabin@olemiss.edu

D. J. Ortinau
University of South Florida, Lakewood Ranch, FL, USA
e-mail: dortinau@usf.edu

F. Pantoja, S. Wu (eds.), *From Micro to Macro: Dealing with Uncertainties in the Global Marketplace*, Developments in Marketing Science: Proceedings of the Academy of Marketing Science, https://doi.org/10.1007/978-3-030-89883-0_19

ple and also help readers/reviewers evaluate the quality of online panel samples. The panel consists of researchers with considerable experience in marketing research and survey data methods.

Keywords Online samples · Sampling · MTurk · Screening · Data quality · Data integrity

References Available Upon Request

Brand Implications of Advertising Products with Their Reflections: An Abstract

Nazuk Sharma and Marisabel Romero

Abstract This research investigates the impact of advertising products with their reflections on important brand outcomes, such as purchase likelihood, brand trust, and consumer willingness to pay for the advertised product (Keller 1993; Chaudhuri and Holbrook 2001; van Doorn and Verhoef 2011; Anselmsson et al. 2014; Taute et al. 2017). Integrating literature on reflections from the fields of visual art, evolutionary and experimental psychology, visual cognition; together with *Signaling Theory* as the overarching theoretical framework, the current research documents that the visual cues of product reflections act as negative signals in brand advertising contexts and lower brand outcomes by increasing consumer uncertainty about the featured product's quality (Kirmani and Rao 2000; Bertamini et al. 2003; Cavanagh et al. 2008; Mamassian 2008; Dilks et al. 2011). This research also demonstrates how high ad spending information about the focal brand acts as a confidence signal that counters the negative effect of product reflection on brand trust (Kirmani and Wright 1989; Moorthy and Zhao 2000).

We test our hypotheses with the help of four experiments (Studies 1a, 1b, 2, and 3). Results evidence a replication of the negative effect of advertising a product with (vs. without) its reflection not only on a variety of brand outcomes (such as, purchase likelihood, brand trust, and consumer willingness to pay for the product), but also across three different product categories (multivitamins, energy-shots, and weight-loss products). Study 2 establishes product quality uncertainty as the underlying process. Finally, Study 3 demonstrates an attenuation of the negative effect of incorporating a product reflection in the ad on the outcome of brand trust when consumers are offered informational cues such as the focal brand's high ad spending that signals greater product quality (Kirmani and Wright 1989).

N. Sharma (✉)
Fairfield University, Fairfield, CT, USA
e-mail: nsharma@fairfield.edu

M. Romero
Colorado State University, Fort Collins, CO, USA
e-mail: mari.romero_lopez@colostate.edu

F. Pantoja, S. Wu (eds.), *From Micro to Macro: Dealing with Uncertainties in the Global Marketplace*, Developments in Marketing Science: Proceedings of the Academy of Marketing Science, https://doi.org/10.1007/978-3-030-89883-0_20

To the best of our knowledge, this inquiry is the first to systemically investigate brand-related implications of advertising products with their reflections. This research extends marketing research on visual cues by adding product reflections to the list of cues examined thus far. Counter to marketers' aesthetic intuitions behind this common advertising practice of featuring products with their reflections, the current research forwards that this practice can actually be detrimental for brands. Given that product reflections are used across many advertising channels (including digital platforms), the implications of the current findings span wide.

Keywords Product reflection · Brand trust · Product quality uncertainty · Signaling theory

References Available Upon Request

The Archetype of Bolsonaro Candidate in the Brazilian Presidential Election in the Perception of the Young Elector: An Abstract

Ciro Eduardo Gusatti, Flávio Régio Brambilla, and Daniela Prevedello

Abstract In the electoral period, politicians build an identity and image, have a positioning and seek for differentiation. In Brazil the communication strategy of the presidential candidate (the current president) Jair Messias Bolsonaro drew attention of experts, especially regarding the young people's public awareness capacity. This study aimed to identify the archetypal image of the candidate Bolsonaro and how it differed from other candidates' image among young public of Brazilian voters. Candidates Ciro Gomes and Fernando Haddad were also part of the research. In political context, Ribeiro (2002) compares the candidate with a product (using a brand as a way of promoting the person). Politician has a history, origin, position and must have a differentiation towards competitors. For the candidates be able to convince, they must work on positioning, image and identity. Image and identity are linked concepts, but also distinct. Identity refers to self-identification, and the image is about the way the public sees you. Images associations for Keller and Machado (2006) can be formed by consumer experiences or through representations by advertising or other communication actions. Archetypes are instincts that guide and shape behavior. Mark and Pearson (2001) found 12 frequent archetypes in commercial activity. These archetypes are: Innocent, Explorer, Wise, Hero, Outlaw, Wizard, Common Guy, Lover, Jester, Helpful, Creator and Governor. For data collection, a form was created for each of the three selected candidates with semantic scales associated with the personality of each of the brand archetypes indicated by Mark and Pearson. The equally divided sample totaled 450 young people aged between 18 and 24 years. Data collection took place during the electoral period, in the week preceding the first round of 2018 voting. Participants were students from 20 Universities in the south and southeast of Brazil. Data were analyzed statistically in

C. E. Gusatti · D. Prevedello
Universidade de Passo Fundo, Passo Fundo, Brazil
e-mail: cirogusatti@upf.br; prevedello@upf.br

F. R. Brambilla (✉)
Universidade de Santa Cruz do Sul, Santa Cruz do Sul, Brazil

F. Pantoja, S. Wu (eds.), *From Micro to Macro: Dealing with Uncertainties in the Global Marketplace*, Developments in Marketing Science: Proceedings of the Academy of Marketing Science, https://doi.org/10.1007/978-3-030-89883-0_21

order to recognize means of archetypes present in image. Variance Analysis (ANOVA) was performed. Outlaw Archetype obtained higher averages in the image of Bolsonaro compared to the other candidates. The average for Hero and Governor Archetypes were also higher for Bolsonaro. The Jester Archetype characterized the visions about Ciro Gomes. Bolsonaro obtained the highest average for Governor Archetype, which represents desire for security, stability, control and leadership.

Keywords Political Marketing · Archetypal images · Brand image · Candidate image

References Available Upon Request

Studying the Effects of Sponsorship Disclosure and Message Complexity on Consumers' Response Via Text Analysis: An Abstract

Lifeng Li, Zixuan (Mia) Cheng, Anouk de Regt, Jianyu Hao, and Matteo Montecchi

Abstract Influencer marketing utilizes influential online opinion leaders to disseminate brand related user-generated content and shape audience attitudes through social networking sites (Lim et al. 2017), is currently widely adopted by brands to effectively reach their target audiences (Evans et al. 2017). Despite many benefits of influencer marketing for brands, public policy concerns regarding the covert nature of paid brand endorsements that are masqueraded as unadulterated opinions have risen in the past years (Johnson et al. 2019). Sparking calls for transparency and disclosure of sponsorship information to facilitate the consumers' ability to differentiate sponsored content from authentic (i.e., non-sponsored) product reviews and editorial content (Veirman and Hudders 2019). Recent guidelines and (self-)regulatory initiatives (e.g., ASA 2018; FTC 2017; IAB 2016) prescribe the disclosure of any commercial relationship between the influencer and the brand in their social media posts.

Using automated text analysis (LIWC) on audio-visual branded content, this study explores the role and impact of sponsorship disclosure and message complexity on consumers' responses. Findings suggest that message complexity and sponsorship disclosure can significantly affect consumers' tone in their responses. Additionally, sponsorship disclosure significantly affects consumers' clout. The results also reveal that different levels of message complexity resulted in different levels of consumers' analytical thinking and clout when posts with or without sponsorship disclosure.

This study makes several contributions to the further understanding of the function of disclosures in sponsored Instagram posts as a type of native advertising. The disclosure of sponsorship would generate more confidence for consumers, as it pro-

L. Li · Z. (Mia) Cheng (✉) · A. de Regt · J. Hao · M. Montecchi
King's College London, London, UK
e-mail: lifeng.li@kcl.ac.uk; zixuan.cheng@kcl.ac.uk; anouk.de_regt@kcl.ac.uk; jianyu.hao@kcl.ac.uk; matteo.montecchi@kcl.ac.uk

F. Pantoja, S. Wu (eds.), *From Micro to Macro: Dealing with Uncertainties in the Global Marketplace*, Developments in Marketing Science: Proceedings of the Academy of Marketing Science, https://doi.org/10.1007/978-3-030-89883-0_22

vides information for consumers to arrive at causal explanations for events. However, disclosure of sponsored messages also generates feelings of suspicion and deception for consumers. Our finding further supports previous findings suggesting sponsorship disclosure helps consumer recognize sponsored posts as advertising, and in turn reduce the effectiveness of the persuasive (Evans et al. 2017; Boerman et al. 2017). Moreover, mediums with different levels of message complexity result in different clout levels. Consumers from video posts appeared to have more confidence and a sense of social status because compare with photos, videos provided involve them in a dynamic environment and provide more comprehensive storylines.

Keywords Influencer marketing · Sponsorship Disclosure · Message complexity · LIWC

References Available Upon Request

Making Sense of Meaningful Third Places: Effects of Servicescape, Place Meanings, and Emotions

Judy A. Siguaw and Xiaojing Sheng

Abstract This study advances the extant knowledge about consumer emotions and behavior within the context of place identity. Survey data from 348 community park visitors is analyzed using PLS-SEM. We confirm that individuals can develop emotional attachments for places as a result of the development of place meanings, addressing the need to broaden our understanding of the effects of this construct. These emotional attachments to physical locations that are personally and socially relevant lead to intentions to return to the location and to provide positive word-of-mouth. These findings add to the body of knowledge about emotions in an area not previously examined. The behavioral intentions elicited were somewhat strengthened by servicescape satisfaction's impact on satisfaction with the non-commercial venue. Emotional attachment was also found to heighten satisfaction with the community park venue. While the context of this study was an open community space, this work also increases our understanding of how attachment to a third place is developed, which can assist marketers in attracting more customers to a specific physical environment.

Keywords Place meanings · Servicescape satisfaction · Emotional attachment · Behavioral intentions

Introduction

Specific locations, outside of home and work, facilitate experiences and memories encapsulated in emotions that yield affective and cognitive attachments to a place (e.g., Marcu 2012; Simpson and Siguaw 2008). In turn, this "third place" may be

J. A. Siguaw (✉)
East Carolina University, Greenville, NC, USA
e-mail: siguawj@ecu.edu

X. Sheng
The University of Texas—Rio Grande Valley, Edinburg, TX, USA
e-mail: xiaojing.sheng@utrgv.edu

F. Pantoja, S. Wu (eds.), *From Micro to Macro: Dealing with Uncertainties in the Global Marketplace*, Developments in Marketing Science: Proceedings of the Academy of Marketing Science, https://doi.org/10.1007/978-3-030-89883-0_23

perceived as an essential part of one's self-concept (e.g., Hammitt et al. 2006). Following the lead of Oldenburg (1999), Hawkins and Ryan (2013, p. 192) describe third places as "sociable yet neutral spaces;" they note that the key to a third place is the social aspect. Understanding how attachment to a third place is formed can assist marketers in drawing more visitors to a location. Furthermore, generating emotional attachment to a third place is a key antecedent for place-related behaviors, such as "willingness to solve local problems, take over honorary posts or motivate others to do so" (Kalandides et al. 2012, p. 82).

Oldenburg (1991, 1999) pioneered the concept of third place theory and suggested that such places heighten individual wellbeing and improve ties to a community by creating a welcoming space for social connections. Third places, as envisioned by Oldenburg (1999), are inexpensive, accessible, and friendly physical environments with a casual ambiance that encourages a diversity of people to intermingle. These locations—including cafes, coffee shops, community centers, bookstores, bars, and hair salons—feel safe and their hallmark is the presence of "regulars," those who are frequent visitors (e.g., Oldenburg 1999; Slater and Koo 2010). Similar arguments have been made for open community spaces, such as parks and recreation areas. For example, Ujang et al. (2018) argue that public spaces provide a respite from home and work environments and offer opportunities where regular visitors can socialize with current friends and acquaintances, as well as strangers. Consequently, these experiences create memories and meanings for those visitors.

Although research concerning people-place relationships has grown in the last decade (e.g., Lewicka 2011; Meshram and O'Cass 2013; Rosenbaum 2006), research investigating the role of meanings and emotions towards public spaces and places that can be considered part of the identity and traditions of a community is largely absent in the marketing literature.

The objective of this study is to advance the extant knowledge about consumer emotions and behavior within the context of place identity. First, because attachment to branded products is associated with emotional dimensions and feelings (Malär et al. 2011), this research hypothesizes that people can also develop a similar emotional attachment to places that are personally and socially relevant to them. Community parks are among the types of locations where people spend memorable experiences, in a context where a commercial transaction is not the focal element of value as it is in business. Thus, this work adds to the body of knowledge about emotions by extending theoretical concepts into areas not previously studied in the field (Ladik and Stewart 2008; Whetten 1989). Second, prior research has noted that people's behavior is influenced by the atmosphere and environmental characteristics when visiting public areas and outdoor settings (Kim et al. 2003). Thus, this work examines the effect of public place servicescapes on other constructs. Finally, this investigation addresses the need to better understand the effects of place meanings on affective, cognitive, and conative outcomes in places of community recreation (Gustafson 2001; Stedman 2003; Phau et al. 2013).

Theoretical Background

Public recreational sites have long been recognized as places that provide valuable tangible and intangible benefits to people in a community, such as the opportunity to conduct leisure activities (Tinsley et al. 2002) and improve health and social well-being (Ho, et al. 2005; Mirotznik et al. 1995). However, the influence that such places have on people that visit them regularly is perhaps mostly reflected in their moods and emotions (Knez and Thorsson 2008; Krenichyn 2004).

Drawing from the theoretical perspective of environmental psychology (Mehrabian and Russell 1974; Russell 1980), this research examines the role of emotions on satisfaction and loyalty in the context of public parks. Based on the S-O-R (stimulus–organism–response) model outlined by Mehrabian and Russell (1974), and used by Baker et al. (1992) among others, this study hypothesizes that the attributes of public parks arouse the emotional states of people, which in turn affect loyalty responses toward the place.

In this investigation, we examine how perceptions of servicescape satisfaction affect perceptions of park satisfaction, which then affects loyalty intentions. We also examine how place meanings affect emotions, which in turn influence perceptions of park satisfaction and loyalty intentions (see Fig. 1).

Servicescape and Park Satisfaction

Building upon Bitner's (1992) seminal work on servicescape, Wakefield and Blodgett (1996) examine the impact of servicescapes on service quality evaluations, satisfaction, and loyalty behaviors in leisure service settings such as amusement parks, concert halls, and sporting events. They also highlight the need for research to offer insight on such servicescape settings because customers usually stay longer in those settings and therefore, experience the servicescapes to a greater extent. Such is the nature of the servicescape of community parks where community visitors are likely to stay for some time and to return with some frequency.

Using the law of image transference, Sheng et al. (2017) provide evidence of how satisfaction with a larger servicescape impacts satisfaction with another servicescape. Other studies also demonstrate that perceptions of one entity can affect perceptions of another, including the ability of an event's image to affect a destination's image or a company's reputation (Deng and Li 2014; Heslop et al. 2013) or the destination image's transference to products linked to the destination (Lim and Weaver 2012). Based on these works, we believe that satisfaction with the servicescape will enhance satisfaction with the community park. Thus, we investigate:

H1: Servicescape satisfaction positively and significantly affects park satisfaction.

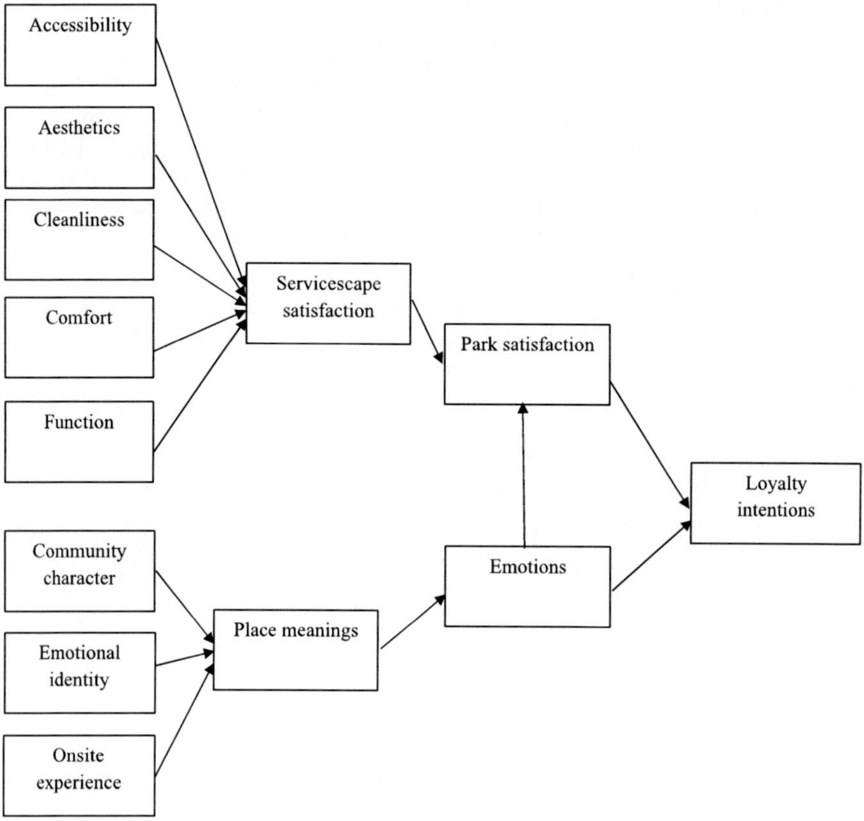

Fig. 1 Conceptual model of third place perceptions and emotions

Place Meanings and Emotions

Individuals' experiences at community parks can be related to the "leisure social worlds" described by Gahwiler and Havitz (1998, p. 1), which occur at places that encompass "people, organizations, activities, and practices in which participants have shared understandings of unique cultural elements." Place meanings such as those related to community life are linked to an array of emotions experienced at the location in question (Manzo 2005). Specifically, place meanings may be defined as representing "wide ranging characterizations of the personal and thus subjective attachments people use in the ways they construct meaning through experiencing" a locale, facility, or setting (Hutson et al. 2010, p. 418).

According to Williams et al. (1992), place meanings are derived from the life-enriching experiences people have, which induce a bonding to the place. As a result, relationships to places not only reflect people's psychological landscape and their particular way of "being-in-the-world" (Heidegger 1971) but also "convey the very sense of who we are" (Williams 2002, p. 353). Davenport et al. (2010) developed a scale where community character, emotional identity, onsite experiences, nature and natural processes, and economic dependence are key domains in the range of meanings that characterize people's connections with conservation and recreation areas and places. Community character involves how a certain place is tied to the historical past, economic efforts, and way of life of the community. Emotional identity involves how self-identification and family legacy are related to the place. Onsite experiences measure the degree to which a feeling of belonging is created by the place. Nature and natural processes include items tied to the regulatory ecosystem services natural settings provide such as wildlife habitat and clean air and water. Economic stability taps the extent to which local and regional economy is dependent on the place. For purposes of this study on community parks, we exclude nature and natural processes and economic stability due to their irrelevance to the study context and utilize three domains: community character, emotional identity, and onsite experiences. We expect that the deeper and more entrenched the meanings that individuals associate with the community park that they frequent, the stronger the emotions they have towards the park. Therefore:

H2: Place meanings evoked by the community park will increase the positive emotions concerning the park.

Emotions and Park Satisfaction

Emotional attachment has been shown to increase tourist satisfaction with a destination (Tsai 2015). Moreover, several others note that positive emotions improve satisfaction with visitor experiences (Bosque and Martin 2008; Chang 2008; Io 2017). Based on these findings, the effects from emotions on consumer satisfaction can also be expected in other contexts where places are important for people, such as community parks. Thus, we propose the following hypothesis:

H3: Positive emotions aroused by a community park will increase satisfaction with the park.

Emotions, Park Satisfaction, and Loyalty Intentions

Satisfaction and loyalty have been intricately linked in the marketing literature, although satisfaction alone may not be sufficient to guarantee loyalty (Kumar et al. 2013; Oliver 1999). Nonetheless, Tsai (2015) finds that emotional attachment and destination satisfaction affect repeat visits to a destination. Relatedly, Hosany and Whitam (2010) identify a relationship between place satisfaction and word-of-mouth. Furthermore, positive emotions have also been linked to behavioral and loyalty intentions in numerous contexts (Kühn and Bothma 2018; Muller et al. 1991; Razzaq et al. 2017). Hence:

H4: Park satisfaction will increase (a) intentions to return to the park and (b) positive word-of-mouth about the park.

H5: Positive emotions about the park will increase (a) intentions to return to the park and (b) positive word-of-mouth about the park.

Methodology

The target population for this study is people who visit community parks in a medium-sized urban area in the Southwest of the United States. A total of 348 subjects responded to a questionnaire while visiting any of three community parks selected for inclusion in the study. The average age of those respondents who provided demographic information is 49.6 years, 56.70 percent of the respondents were females, 47.5 percent were high school graduates, and 42.6 percent reported a household income between $30,000 and $99,000.

Building upon Wakefield and Blodgett's (1996) servicescape framework for leisure service settings, we conceptualize servicescape satisfaction toward a community park as a second-order formative construct comprising five, first-order reflective dimensions, including accessibility, aesthetics, cleanliness, seating comfort, and function. Measurement items for each dimension were newly developed for the current study. Place meanings is also modeled as a second-order formative construct comprising three, first-order reflective dimensions, including community character, emotional identity, and onsite experiences. Items for measuring each of these three dimensions were adapted from Davenport et al. (2010). Emotions are tapped with three items about feeling entertained, happy, and peaceful while in the park. These items are adapted from Bigné et al. (2005). Satisfaction towards the park is measured with one item evaluating overall satisfaction with the park and one item assessing customer service experiences at the park. Loyalty is assessed through recommendation and return intentions.

Results

We use PLS-SEM (SmartPLS, 3.2.4; Ringle et al. 2015) to test the proposed model and follow Hair Jr et al. (2016) guidelines by first assessing the measurement model and then the structural model.

Measurement Model

We adhere to Hair et al.'s (2017) specifications in evaluating both the formative and reflective measures. For reflective measures, as seen in Table 1, composite

Table 1 Measures and construct validity

Construct and measures	Factor loadings
Servicescape Satisfaction (second-order formative construct)	
How satisfied are you with the following park characteristics?	
Accessibility (Cronbach's $\alpha = 0.796$, CR = 0.903, AVE = 0.824)	
• Easy to find	0.866
• Appropriate information and signage	0.947
Aesthetics (Cronbach's $\alpha = 0.732$, CR = 0.88, AVE = 0.785)	
• Attractiveness	0.851
• Landscaping	0.920
Comfort (Cronbach's $\alpha = 0.899$, CR = 0.952, AVE = 0.908)	
• Comfortable places to visit	0.949
• Feels safe	0.958
Cleanliness	
• Clean and well-maintained	1
Function (Cronbach's $\alpha = 0.845$, CR = 0.896, AVE = 0.683)	
• Meeting place for friends and family	0.818
• Mix of activities	0.864
• Places to walk or run	0.768
• A place to exercise	0.853
Place Meanings (second-order formative construct)	
Do you agree or disagree with the following statements?	
Community character (Cronbach's $\alpha = 0.858$, CR = 0.934, AVE = 0.876)	
• This place contributes to the character of my community.	0.939
• This park is a special place for my family.	0.933
Emotional identity (Cronbach's $\alpha = 0.89$, CR = 0.948, AVE = 0.901)	
• Many important memories with family and friends are tied to this park.	0.948
• I feel like this park is a part of me.	0.950
Onsite experience (Cronbach's $\alpha = 0.916$, CR = 0.947, AVE = 0.856)	
• This park is the best place to do the things I enjoy.	0.941
• I feel a sense of pride in my heritage when I am here.	0.907
• I would prefer to spend more time here if I could.	0.928
Satisfaction with the Park (Cronbach's $\alpha = 0.604$, CR = 0.934, AVE = 0.876)	
Do you agree or disagree with the following statement?	
• Overall, I am very satisfied with this park.	0.939
How satisfied are you with the following park characteristic?	0.716
• Customer service experience	
Emotions about the Park (Cronbach's $\alpha = 0.\ 96$, CR = 0.974, AVE = 0.926)	
Do you agree or disagree with the following statements?	
• I am always entertained when I come to this park.	0.945
• Coming to this park makes me happy.	0.971
• I feel at peace when I come to this park.	0.97
Loyalty Intentions (Cronbach's $\alpha = 0.941$, CR = 0.971, AVE = 0.944)	
Do you agree or disagree with the following statements?	
• I would strongly recommend this park to friends or family.	0.972
• I will definitely come back with family and friends to this park.	0.971

reliability (CR) values range from 0.819 to 0.974, supporting the measures' internal consistency. Outer loadings are above 0.716, supporting indicator reliability. Average variance extracted (AVE) values are above 0.683, supporting convergent validity. Each reflective construct's AVE value is greater than the squared correlations between this construct and other first-order constructs in the measurement model.

For formative measures of servicescape satisfaction and place meanings, variance inflation factor (VIF) values are between 2.84 and 4.931, all below the critical threshold of 5, indicating no multicollinearity concerns. All formative dimensions significantly affect their respective second-order construct. Of the five formative dimensions of servicescape satisfaction, the function dimension has the largest impact, $\beta = 0.34$, $t = 17.818$, $p < 0.001$. In comparison to community character and emotional identity, the onsite experience dimension exhibits a stronger effect on place meanings, $\beta = 0.442$, $t = 44.679$, $p < 0.001$.

Structural Model

We next examine the structural model. As predicted, servicescape satisfaction positively affects satisfaction with the park ($\beta = 0.299$, $t = 6.01$, $p < 0.00$), and place meanings contribute to positive emotions ($\beta = 0.89$, $t = 30.044$, $p < 0.001$). Positive emotions further enhance park satisfaction ($\beta = 0.732$, $t = 14.134$, $p < 0.001$), and lead to greater intentions to return and recommend, ($\beta = 0.675$, $t = 5.138$, $p < 0.001$). However, park satisfaction has only a marginally significant effect on intentions ($\beta = 0.232$, $t = 1.824$, $p = 0.069$). The R-squared value is 0.781 for intentions, 0.793 for emotions, and 0.823 for park satisfaction.

General Discussion

This research examines the role of consumer emotions and behaviors as they relate to place identity. Consequently, this study contributes to a very small body of literature which examines how public spaces may impact the identity of a community. In this investigation, we confirm that individuals can develop emotional attachments for places as a result of the development of place meanings, addressing the need to broaden our understanding of the effects of place meanings as encouraged by Phau et al. (2013). These emotional attachments to physical locations that are personally and socially relevant lead to intentions to return to the location and to provide positive word-of-mouth. These findings add to the body of knowledge about emotions in an area not previously examined. The behavioral intentions elicited were somewhat strengthened by servicescape satisfaction's impact on satisfaction with the non-commercial venue. Emotional attachment was also found to heighten satisfaction with the non-commercial venue. While the context of this study was an open community space, this work also increases our understanding of how attachment to a third place is developed, which can assist marketers in attracting more customers to a specific physical environment.

The generalizability of this research is limited since three parks in one medium-sized city served as the focus of the study. Future research could test this model in other regions of the United States and vary the size of the cities in which the parks are located.

References

Baker, J., Levy, M., and Grewal, D. (1992). An experimental approach to making retail store environmental decisions. *Journal of Retailing,* 68(4), 445-460.

Bigné, J. E., Andreu, L., and Gnoth, J. (2005). The theme park experience: An analysis of pleasure, arousal and satisfaction. *Tourism Management* 26(6), 833-844.

Bitner, M. J. (1992). Servicescapes: The impact of physical surroundings on customers and employees. *Journal of Marketing*, 56(2), 57–71.

Bosque, I. R. D., and Martin, H. S. (2008). Tourist satisfaction: a cognitive-affective model. *Annals of Tourism Research,* 35(2), 551-573.

Chang, J. C. (2008). Tourists' satisfaction judgments: an investigation of emotion, equity, and attribution. *Journal of Hospitality and Tourism Research,* 32(1) 108-134.

Davenport, M. A., Baker, M. L., Leahy, J. E., and Anderson, D. H. (2010). Exploring multiple place meanings at an illinois state park. *Journal of Park and Recreation Administration* 28(1), 52-69.

Deng, Qian, and Mimi Li (2014). A model of event–destination image transfer. *Journal of Travel Research,* 53(1), 69-82.

Gahwiler, P., and Havitz, M. E. (1998). Towards and understanding of leisure social worlds, involvement, psychological commitment, and behavioral loyalty. *Leisure Sciences* 20(1) 1-23.

Gustafson, P. (2001). Meanings of place: Everyday experience and theoretical conceptualizations. *Journal of Environmental Psychology* 21(1), 5–16.

Hair Jr, J. F., Hult, G. T. M., Ringle, C., and Sarstedt, M. (2016). *A primer on partial least squares structural equation modeling (PLS-SEM).* Newbury Park, CA: Sage publications.

Hammitt, W. E., Erik, A., Backlund and Robert D. Bixler (2006). Place bonding for recreation places: Conceptual and empirical development. *Leisure Studies* 25(1) 17-41.

Hawkins, C. J., and Ryan, L. J. (2013). Festival spaces as third places. *Journal of Place Management and Development,* 6(3) 192-202.

Heidegger, M. (1971). *Poetry, language, thought* (translated by Albert Hofstadter). New York: Harper Colophon Books.

Heslop, L. A., John, N., Norm, O., and Anahit, A. (2013). Mega-event and country co-branding: Image shifts, transfers and reputational impacts. *Corporate Reputation Review* 16(1), 7-33.

Ho, C. H., Vinod, S., William, E., Fern, W. K., Alan, G., and Geoffrey, G. (2005). Gender and ethnic variations in urban park preferences, visitation, and perceived benefit. *Journal of Leisure Research,* 37(3) 281-306.

Hosany, S. and Whitam, M. (2010). Dimensions of cruisers' experiences, satisfaction and intention to recommend. *Journal of Travel Research,* 49(3), 351-64.

Hutson, G., Montgomery, D., and Caneday, L. (2010). Perceptions of outdoor recreation professionals toward place meanings in natural environments: A Q-method inquiry. *Journal of Leisure Research,* 42(3), 417-442.

Io, M. U. (2017). Understanding the effects of multi-dimensional tourism experiences on tourists' positive emotions and satisfaction in the context of casino hotels. *International Journal of Culture, Tourism and Hospitality Research 11*(2) 142-156.

Kalandides, A., Kavaratzis, M., Boisen, M., Mueller, A., and Schade, M. (2012). Symbols and place identity: A semiotic approach to internal place branding – case study Bremen (Germany). *Journal of Place Management and Development,* 5(1), 81-92.

Kim, S. S., Klenosky, D. B., and Lee, C.K. (2003). The influence of push and pull factors at Korean national parks. *Tourism Management* 24(2) 169–180.

Knez, I., and Thorsson, S. (2008). Thermal, emotional and perceptual evaluations of a park: Cross-cultural and environmental attitude comparisons. *Building and Environment,* 43(9) 1483-1490.

Krenichyn, K. (2004). Women and physical activity in an urban park: Enrichment and support through an ethic of care. *Journal of Environmental Psychology* 24(1) 117–130.

Kühn, S., and Bothma, M. (2018). The coffee shop dining experience and customer loyalty intentions: Brewing the perfect blend. *Management Dynamics* 27(4) 12-28.

Kumar, V., Pozza, I. D., and Ganesh, J. (2013). Revisiting the satisfaction-loyalty relationship: Empirical generalizations and directions for future research. *Journal of Retailing,* 89(3) 246-262.

Ladik, D. M., and Stewart, D. W. (2008). The Contribution continuum. *Journal of the Academy of Marketing Science,* 36(2) 157–165.

Lewicka, M. (2011). Place attachment: how far have we come in the last 40 years? *Journal of Environmental Psychology,* 31(3) 207-230.

Lim, Y., and Weaver, P.A. (2012). Customer-based brand equity for a destination: The effect of destination image on preference for products associated with a destination brand. *International Journal of Tourism Research* 16(3) 223-231.

Malär, L., Krohmer, H., Hoyer, W. D., and Nyffenegger, B. (2011). Emotional brand attachment and brand personality: The relative importance of the actual and the ideal self. *Journal of Marketing,* 75(4), 35-52.

Manzo, L. C. (2005). For better or worse: Exploring multiple dimensions of place meaning. *Journal of Environmental Psychology* 25(1), 67–86.

Marcu, S. (2012). Emotions on the move: Belonging, sense of place and feelings identities among young Romanian immigrants in Spain. *Journal of Youth Studies 15*(2) 207-223.

Mehrabian, A., and Russell, J. A. (1974). *An approach to environmental psychology.* Cambridge, MA: MIT Press.

Meshram, K. and O'Cass, A. (2013). Empowering senior citizens via third places: Research driven model development of seniors' empowerment and social engagement in social places. *Journal of Services Marketing* 27(2) 141-154.

Mirotznik, J., Feldman, L., and Stein, R. (1995). The health belief model and adherence with a community center-based, supervised coronary heart disease exercise program. *Journal of Community Health* 20(3) 233-247.

Muller, T.E., Tse, D.K., and Venkatasubramaniam, R. (1991). Post-consumption emotions: Exploring their emergence and determinants. *Journal of Consumer Satisfaction, Dissatisfaction and Complaining Behavior,* 4(1) 13-20.

Oldenburg, R. (1991). The great good place. Marlowe and Company, New York, NY.

Oldenburg, R. (1999). *The great good place: Cafes, coffee shops, bookstores, bars, hair salons, and other hangouts at the heart of a community.* New York: Marlowe and Company.

Oliver, R. L. (1999). Whence consumer loyalty? *Journal of Marketing,* 63(Special Issue), 33-44.

Phau, I., Lee, S., and Quintal, V. (2013). An investigation of push and pull motivations of visitors to private parks: The case of Araluen Botanic Park. *Journal of Vacation Marketing 19*(3) 269–284.

Razzaq, Z., Yousaf, S., and Zhao, H. (2017). The moderating impact of emotions on customer equity drivers and loyalty intentions. *Asia Pacific Journal of Marketing and Logistics* 29(2) 239-264.

Ringle, C. M., Wende, S., and Becker, J.M. 2015. SmartPLS 3. Boenningstedt: SmartPLS GmbH, http://www.smartpls.com.

Rosenbaum, M. S. (2006). Exploring the social supportive role of third places in consumers' lives. *Journal of Service Research*, 9(1), 59–72.

Russell, J. A. (1980). A circumplex model of affect. *Journal of Personality and Social Psychology*, 39(6) 1161-1178.

Sheng, X., Simpson, P. M., and Siguaw, J. A. (2017). Communities as nested servicescapes. *Journal of Service Research* 20(2) 171–187.

Simpson, P. M., and Siguaw, J. A. (2008). Destination word of mouth: The role of traveler type, residents, and identity salience. *Journal of Travel Research*, 47(2) 167–182.

Slater, A., and Koo, H.J. (2010). A new type of third place. *Journal of Place Management and Development,* 3(2), 99.

Stedman, R. C. (2003). Is it really just a social construction: The contribution of the physical environment to sense of place. *Society and Natural Resources: An International Journal 16*(8), 671–685.

Tinsley, H. E., Tinsley, D. J., and Croskeys, C. E. (2002). Park usage, social milieu, and psychosocial benefits of park use reported by older urban park users from four ethnic groups. *Leisure Sciences* 24(2) 199-218.

Tsai, C. (2015). The relationships among destination image, perceived quality, emotional place attachment, tourist satisfaction, and post-visiting behavior intentions. *Xing Xiao Ping Lun 12*(4), 455-479.

Ujang, N., Kozlowski, M., and Maulan, S. (2018). Linking place attachment and social interaction: Towards meaningful public places. *Journal of Place Management and Development* 11(1) 115-29.

Wakefield, K.L., and Blodgett, J.G. (1996). The effect of the servicescape on customers' behavioral intentions in leisure service settings. *Journal of Services Marketing 10*(6), 45-61.

Whetten, D. A. (1989). What constitutes a theoretical contribution? *Academy of Management Review 14*(4), 490-495.

Williams, D. R. (2002). Leisure identities, globalization, and the politics of place. *Journal of Leisure Research*, 34(4), 351-367.

Williams, D. R., Patterson, M. E., Roggenbuck, J. W., and Watson, A. E. (1992). Beyond the commodity metaphor: Examining emotional and symbolic attachment to place. *Leisure Sciences 14*(1) 29-46.

Me, Myself, and My Wine: (Over) Consumption of Wine as a Response to Narcissism, Social Attractiveness and Subjective Knowledge: An Abstract

Renaud Lunardo and Armando Maria Corsi

Abstract Is wine consumption the most rewarding experience? Although the question seems moot, one may recognize the quality of the wine experience. First, wine consumption is often described as an aesthetic experience (Charters and Pettigrew 2005). Second, because of its hedonic dimensions, wine consumption also represents a gratifying sensory experience (Holbrook and Hirschman 1982; Brakus et al. 2009). Third, such consumption is a social experience, as people associate wine with friendship (Mouret et al. 2013) and sometimes feel the need to drink wine to conform with the expectations of other people (Thompson and Vourvachis 1995). However, in spite of this positive—not to say romantic—view of wine consumption, one may acknowledge that wine, even if having health benefits (German and Walzem 2000), can reveal harmful when consumed irresponsibly (Guilford and Pezzuto 2011). While the question as to what individual variables could explain the tendency for people to engage in such irresponsible wine consumption—hereafter referred to as wine intoxication experience (Cornil et al. 2017)—is of primary interest for producers and policy makers, the marketing literature on this issue remains scarce, focusing mostly on the positive aspects of wine consumption (Ferrarini et al. 2010). In this research, we propose, test in a field study ($N = 654$), and demonstrate that because narcissism—or the individual inflated sense of self-importance (Brunell and Buelow 2017)—may prompt the belief that wine consumption enhances social attractiveness, it subsequently increases wine intoxication experience. We also show that this effect is stronger among people who exhibit a high (versus low) subjective wine knowledge. Finally, we discuss these results from both a managerial and public policy standpoints.

R. Lunardo (✉)
Kegde Business School, Bordeaux, France
e-mail: renaud.lunardo@kedgebs.com

A. M. Corsi
University of Adelaide, Adelaide, SA, Australia
e-mail: armando.corsi@adelaide.edu.au

F. Pantoja, S. Wu (eds.), *From Micro to Macro: Dealing with Uncertainties in the Global Marketplace*, Developments in Marketing Science: Proceedings of the Academy of Marketing Science, https://doi.org/10.1007/978-3-030-89883-0_24

Keywords Narcissism · Wine · Social attractiveness · Subjective knowledge

References Available Upon Request

The Future of Literature: Neuromarketing and Audio Books: A New Opportunity for Content Marketing

Manuel Quiñones

Abstract A good story can cause the brain to release dopamine, a neurotransmitter that can increase a person's blood pressure and heart rate. The growing importance of orality in communication and content consumption practices has made it more comfortable for many people to listen to a book instead of reading it. The main purpose of this study is to identify, if changing the way a story is presented, influences the emotional impact of the user. A sample of 120 people was considered, between 18 and 67 years of age. Research shows that audiobooks produced more consistent patterns of physiological change than movies or television clips, suggesting that the format can give authors better control of their listeners' emotional responses.

Keywords Oral narrative · Audiobooks · Neuromarketing · Galvanic response · Biosensors

Introduction

Our oldest narratives date back thousands of years and are prior to the advent of writing. In the vast majority of the extensive human tradition, stories are synonymous with oral tradition; the audience listened to a narrator who told a story. Humans did not evolve to read, so perhaps there is something primarily special in hearing a story.

The audiobook mode consists of the literal conversion of the paper book into audio format, but with a narrative voice that prints emotions to the text. Although it is not a new product, in recent years, the audiobook crossed the barrier of specialized niches, such as visually impaired populations or language teaching, and began a second life.

M. Quiñones (✉)
Universidad EAN, Bogotá, Colombia
e-mail: mquinones.d@universidadean.edu.co

F. Pantoja, S. Wu (eds.), *From Micro to Macro: Dealing with Uncertainties in the Global Marketplace*, Developments in Marketing Science: Proceedings of the Academy of Marketing Science, https://doi.org/10.1007/978-3-030-89883-0_25

There are three variables that have made it possible: the offer within the stores of applications for mobile or smart phones, a wide content and a model of consumption of platforms on demand (Schiffman 2011). The main purpose of this study is to identify whether changing the way a story is presented influences the emotional impact of users.

Theoretical Background

This research focused mainly on studying the emotional impact of the different content formats to which a user is exposed, through the formulation of a series of objectives and design of instruments that helped answer the following research question: Are audiobooks emotionally more attractive than movies or television?

Among the objectives pursued by this research are categorize the physiological reactions of users to the exposure of audio and video formats with different narrative genres, as well as measure heart rate and electrodermal activity with biometric sensors (Empathic E4) to reveal the cognitive processing and emotional subconscious of users, characterize the understanding of the narrative by the users and interpret the emotional commitment and attention focus of the participants through the measurement of BVP (Blood Volume Pulse), HR acceleration and temperature.

A Growing Industry

Despite looking like a recent industry in our country, the reality is that since 1975 Colombian writer David Sánchez Juliao started recording audiobooks in Colombia, making the format known. Today, in some applications for mobile devices, the audiobook of the Colombian literature nobel One Hundred Years of Solitude, Gabriel García Márquez, among other great works of Colombian and Latin American literature, is available for free.

Although the audiobook is a format already consolidated in the English-speaking market, because only in the North American market, it reached 2.5 billion dollars in sales in 2017, according to the latest studies (Storytel 2019), the audiobook is already imposed in Spain and Latin America: 50 percent of its subscribers in the region are between 35 and 50 years old, but about 35 percent are under 30 years old. This trend, called the new culture of listening, has ventured very rapidly into the so-called millennium generation in Latin America. Audiobooks already represent 10 percent of the total sales of publishers and it is estimated that, by about five years, that number will increase to 50 percent (Celaya 2019).

It goes without saying that the denominated millennial generation, millennial or Y generation, is now between 10 and 30 years old. However, as with the rest of the generations, the exact start and end dates of this generation vary among the different authors; mainly the limit of the end of the generation and the beginning of the Z or Centennials generation is discussed.

They grew up in a culture of protected and loved children (Zemke et al. 2013); characterized by the use of technology as an integral part of their lifestyle. His affinity for the digital world is one of the highlights of this group (PWC 2011). They have grown with the internet, smartphones, accelerated technological advances, social networks and, with these, instant information.

For them, technology is not surprising, it is obvious. According to this consulting firm, this is the first generation that enters the labor market with greater and better knowledge of business tools than its superiors. Currently in Colombia, the population between 10 and 30 years of age makes up about 40% of the population (DANE 2016), while worldwide they make up more than 40% of the population (United States Census Bureau 2016).

The Electronic Book Market

In this historical moment of the rise of audiobooks, there is a decrease in the format of electronic books worldwide, which after the year 2000 marked a revolution in the way in which the texts would be consumed. By the end of the first decade of the 21st century, the e-book market had grown by more than 1000 percent worldwide. The projections of the publishers affirmed that, for the first half of the second decade of this century, the sales of electronic books would exceed those of the printed ones. However, in 2016, this industry, led by Amazon and its physical reader Kindle, stagnated and decreased by 18 percent over the previous year, absorbed by the enthusiasm of audiobooks (Fig. 1).

According to the latest annual report of the digital book (Libranda 2018), Latin America was an exceptional case. The growth of the Spanish-language digital book in 2018 compared to 2017 is 10% worldwide and 8% in Spain (Fig. 2).

In 2018 there was an increase in e-book sales of 16 percent in the Andean region. The digital edition in Colombia is in a very relevant consolidation process, with higher levels of digital production (23.15%) and turnover (6.80%) in Latin America, and with strong increases in both indicators in the last two years.

Within the digital sale by subsectors we highlight the area of professional and university books as the most important segment (Celaya 2018). However, the trend in the continent, three years later, gives the reason to those who predicted that the digital format had its days counted. In fact, according to the data provided by the Colombian Chamber of Commerce of the Book (CCL 2018), 94.5 percent of books sold that year were in printed format (37 million copies per year).

According to the report Evolution of the electronic book in Latin America and Spain (Celaya 2018) ensures that audiobooks in Spanish exceed approximately 4000 titles. Its main consumers were under 35 years old (48 percent are men and 52 percent are women). According to the data of the Colombian Chamber of the book regarding ISBN Registries digital formats, the main thematic line is still education,

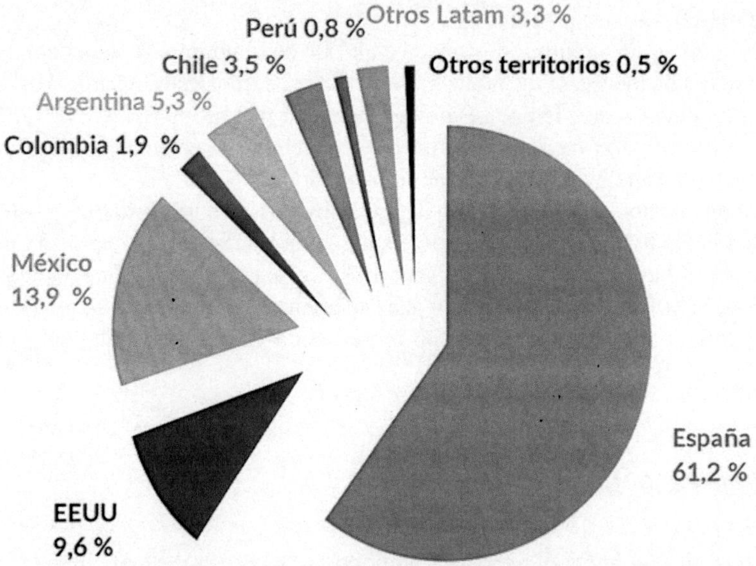

Fig. 1 Percentage distribution of the Spanish-language digital book market by territory in 2018 in units. Recovered from: https://libranda.com/wp-content/uploads/2019/05/Informe-Anual-Libro-digital-2018-online_online.pdf

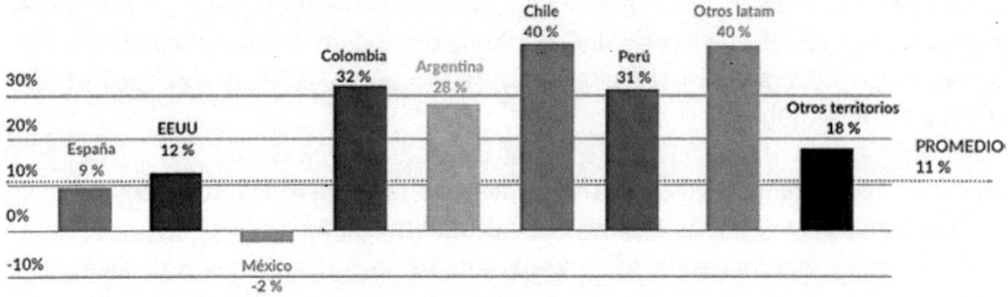

Fig. 2 Percentage distribution of the Spanish-language digital book market by territory in 2018 in units. Recovered from https://libranda.com/wp-content/uploads/2019/05/Informe-Anual-Libro-digital-2018-online_online.pdf

which went from 8 records in 2008 to 523 in 2017. Likewise, there is a boom in research topics related to the technology.

According to the author Francisco Ortega, the audiobook is a good alternative for those who do not have time, and should not be seen as an enemy, but as an ally and a complement to the book, just as the adaptation of a series is also (Ortega 2017). In this way we can contrast their statements, with the latest consumer behavior studies, collected in The Neuromarketing Yearbook 2019, which reinforce the hypothesis raised by the research question of this study.

However, it is interesting to return a few decades for an instant and review the words of Bill Gates (1995):

> Reading on a screen is still much lower than reading on paper. Even I have these expensive screens and I presume to be a pioneer of this "web" style of life, I print everything that exceeds more than 4 or 5 pages and I like to take it with me and write notes. Technology is still far from being able to offer that ease of handling (p.81).

The Neuroscience of the Stories

The so-called storytelling or storytelling, is the act of transmitting stories using the use of words and/or images, usually using improvisation and different stylistic ornaments (Gillett 2014), and that thanks to the advances of Neuromarketing has become in a great protagonist and shows that the brain is connected to the story. Opposing thumbs were a big step in human evolution, but stories were too. Our thumbs help us hold on, but stories tell us what to hold on to. Stories are a way of teaching and learning. When one is lost in a good story, it is not arbitrary, it is not pleasure for pleasure; It is totally biological, chemical, it is a survival mechanism (Cron 2013).

Stories help humans survive by acting as warning stories. For example, a Neanderthal, in the stone age, saw berries and wanted to eat them, but then remembered hearing about his neighbor who ate a handful of those same berries and died. The Neanderthal decided not to eat the berries and continued with his life. Without the story, he might not have survived.

A good story can cause the brain to release dopamine, a neurotransmitter that can increase a person's blood pressure and heart rate. Through the instruments used in this investigation, these variations were decisive to reach very valuable conclusions.

A powerful narrative can help readers gain empathy by relating to the protagonist. It allows readers to enter the protagonist's place and feel what they feel as they move forward in the story. It allows people to sympathize more with the situation. Depending on the emotions that the writer or reader places when reading or describing the situation, more empathy is generated with the story.

The story or narrative takes those great ideas, abstract concepts, raw facts and translates them into something very specific that we can experience and feel, and that is what tells us how we feel about it, what it means to us and that is what moves us to action.

Most audiobooks are now quite sophisticated, narrated by multiple actors and with wide sound effects. But even the audiobooks of a single narrator are, as this study showed, more cognitively and emotionally attractive than print, in part because a listener cannot slow down, as they can with a printed book.

Audio and Cognitive Activity

The increasing importance of orality in communication practices and content consumption, with the development of multitasking and with the role that the time variable plays in today's society has made many people more comfortable walking or transporting listening to a Podcast or an audiobook (Yuste 2019). The podcast consists of the distribution of multimedia files by means of a broadcast system that optionally allows subscribing and using a program that downloads it for the user to listen to (Badillo 2010).

But we also have an important group of society with some kind of special need that has found an unquestionable ally in digital devices. Older adults, to mention, with some difficulty accessing the printed text, and others with problems such as dyslexia among others.

When a person reads, he reaches a higher degree of concentration and therefore has a much slower heart rate; while when you listen, the emotional physiological reaction is greater. The body reacts physiologically to voices, music and sound effects, and that does not cause so much an introspective activity like reading (Rodero 2019).

Methodology

This research work was developed under a mixed modality, also using the qualitative approach, through the general approach to the problem posed. (Hernández et al. 2014). Considering that it is a little explored topic, a field and laboratory work was planned considering: the researcher's perspective, by his senses, by his experience, by his knowledge, by his professional motivations and by his multiple interrelations; It was also possible to deepen empirical generalizations, opinions, consultation of documents and experts, special studies that are binding on the research topic and the ability to grant meanings of how those involved in the research process subjectively perceive audios and videos.

A sample of 120 people was considered, between 18 and 67 years of age, belonging to stratum 3, 4 and 5 residents in the city of Bogotá, regardless of their places of origin. Methodologically speaking, there was also a phenomenological design whose main purpose was to explore, describe and understand the experiences of people with respect to a phenomenon and discover the common elements of such experiences. This design focuses on demonstrating the essence of the shared experience, the phenomenon is identified from the approach and can be as varied as the broad human experience (Hernández et al. 2014). In the development of the design, the phenomenon was first identified as described below and then the data of the people were summoned to the sensory experience, to finally develop a shared description of the essence of the experience for all participants, that they evidenced and how they did it (Hernández et al. 2014).

The information collection tools range from observation, to personal interviews, focus groups, with open, semi-structured and structured questions, review of all types of documents, audio and video recordings and even customized instruments (Hernández et al. 2014). Within the Phenomenological design there are two approaches to phenomenology: hermeneutical phenomenology and empirical phenomenology. The approach to be used in this paper will be the empirical approach in which it focuses less on the interpretation of the researcher and more on describing the experience of the participants.

The basic procedures for developing the empirical approach include: (a) determining and defining the problem or phenomenon to be studied, (b) collecting data on the experiences of various participants with respect to it, (c) analyzing personal behaviors and narratives to have an overview general of the experiences, (d) identify the units of meaning and generate categories, themes and patterns, detecting quotes or key units, (e) elaborate a genetic description of the experiences and their structure (conditions in which they occurred, the situations that surround them and the context) and (f) develop a narrative that combines the descriptions and structure in order to convey the essence of the experience regarding the phenomenon studied and the different assessments, assessments or opinions about it (Hernández et al. 2014).

Conscious responses from 119 participants were tracked (finally one of the participants after the test did not allow the use and dissemination of the results of their research), while listening and watching a series of audio and video clips of scenes loaded with emotions, to through a wrist biosensor that captures your heart rate, sweating and wrist temperature, and also measured heart rate and electro dermal activity with Empática E4 biometric sensors; two physiological signals that can reveal cognitive processing and the emotional subconscious (Fig. 3).

These clips were a mixture of audio and film extracts of eight fiction works, which included Harry Potter by J. K. Rowling, Dan Brown's Da Vinci Code and Game of Thrones by George R.R. Martin, among others. The order of the presentations, and if a particular story was presented as a video or as an audiobook extract, varied among the participants (Fig. 4).

Fig. 3 E4 sensor. Regulatory Compliance: CE Cert. No. 1876/MDD (93/42/EEC Directive, Medical Device class 2a) FCC CFR 47 Part 15b IC (Industry Canada) RoHS MIC Japan: BLE112 has type approval certification ID R 209-J00046. Recovery from: https://www.empatica.com/en-int/research/e4/

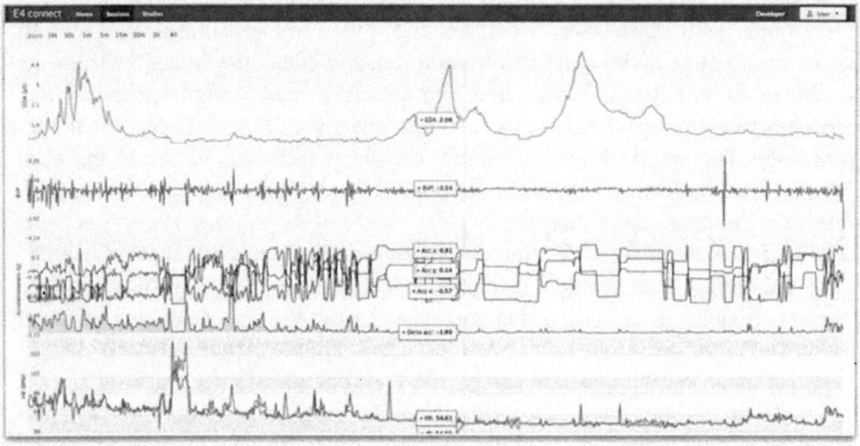

Fig. 4 Example of electrodermal activity (EDA) also known as galvanic skin response (GSR), blood volume pulse (BVP), acceleration, heart rate (HR) and temperature. Recovered from: https://www.empatica.com/en-int/research/e4/

At the end of each test, the participants completed a questionnaire that evaluated four aspects of their perceived participation in the story:

- Emotional commitment
- Understanding the narrative
- Attentional approach
- Narrative presence

In the latter, indicating the extent to which they agreed or disagreed with "Sometimes, history was closer to me than the real world," for example).

Results

Although participants reported feeling more involved with the videos, their heart rates, body temperatures and galvanic skin response readings through the biosensor were higher while listening to the audio.

The participants had approximately 2 degrees more body temperature (1.83 °C), and their skin conductance (EDA) was greater in 0.06 microsiemens when listening to audiobooks. During the measurement, cross-references of accelerometer data were made with the participants' heart rate data to rule out increased movement/restlessness as a possible explanation for higher heart rates while listening to audiobooks.

The increased heart rate was considered to indicate a greater cognitive effort (there were no differences in the levels of restlessness between the audio and video tests), especially given the other data: the conductance readings and skin temperature suggested that the participants were more emotionally involved when listening to audio, according to the data obtained.

Among the highlights of the study we can mention by way of summary, that the evidence showed with more than 99% certainty that the audiobooks produced a stronger emotional and physiological response than the visual means of narration.

This finding was consistent in different stories and different ages and demographics of the participants. The average heart rate of the participants was higher when they listened to audiobooks at approximately two beats per minute (mean difference = 1.82 bpm).

Likewise, participants who listened to audiobooks also had a higher maximum heart rate while listening to the story, of approximately 4 beats per minute (mean = 3.52 bpm).

General Discussion

Listening to a story told in an audiobook application such as Storytel, produces a greater emotional and physiological commitment than watching the scene on a screen, measured by both heart rate and electro dermal activity that the investigation of the selected sample showed.

The audio format enhances cognitive activity because it creates very vivid mental images of what is heard, at a level higher than any other modality.

Video offers more information than audio; While two participants listened to the story of a Game of Thrones chapter, they imagined quite different things despite being the same story (evocation of metaphors), while when they watched the video, it leaves little or practically nothing to the imagination. This is why we conclude that, oral stories could provoke more commitment, because the listener has to build a personalized interpretation of the narrative. But because audio is also more demanding than video, new questions arise around the possible risk that listeners may lose interest in the story.

The investigation also showed that audiobooks produced more consistent patterns of physiological change than movies or television clips, suggesting that the format can give authors better control of their listeners' emotional responses.

When they were surveyed, the participants stated that they were less committed to the story told in audio, but the biometric sensors indicated otherwise, as many times applying neuromarketing has happened. Without a doubt, it is the heart that really tells the story, as the results showed.

The research also contributed, that the spoken word excites, entertains, inspires and, most importantly, touches us like nothing else.

People are on a physiological level more emotionally committed to audio than watching movies, which is good news for novelists and writers in general. People love watching television dramas, but for people to get more involved in a story, the narrative in the form of a novel, whether printed or audio, would be the best.

Reading the printed text is essential for the development of adequate reading competence. It is important to raise both parents and teachers' awareness of the importance it has, to develop skills to execute the different forms of reading autonomously and critically, the training of readers runs important risks.

And although the rise of audiobooks among children can also reinforce the development of special reading functionalities, reading on paper for children is essential. The motor and neurological skills it provides are irreplaceable.

This new boom of the audiobook against electronic books and the printed format, invites you to wonder if the future of literature will not meet its farthest past: oral tradition.

Reading a book is associated with the exercise of immersing yourself in a story that is strictly text, whether on paper or digital media. Therefore, discovering a novel through an audiobook would not be reading, but it does allow you to know the story through other senses and unpublished resources.

Something is clear after this research is over; The printed book did not disappear with the arrival of the digital book and neither will it with the arrival of the audiobook.

References

Badillo, N. (2010). *¿Qué es un podcast?*. Recovery from: https://es.scribd.com/document/26858274/Que-es-un-podcast#scribd]

Cámara Colombiana del libro. (2018), *Informe anual de estadísticas del libro para el año 2017*. Recovery from: https://camlibro.com.co/estadisticas-sector-editorial-en-colombia-2017/

Celaya J. (2019). *La empresa en la web 2.0: el impacto de las nuevas redes sociales en la estrategia empresarial*. España: Gestión 2000.

Celaya, J. (2018). *Sociedad digital*. España. Aguilar.

Cron, L. (2013). *Wired for Story: The Writer's Guide to Using Brain Science to Hook Readers From the Very First Sentence*. USA. Ten Speed Press.

Departamento Administrativo Nacional de Estadística DANE. (2016) *Investigas. Estudios innovadores sobre economía, género e indicadores*. Recovery from: https://www.dane.gov.co/files/investigaciones/genero/publicaciones/INVESTIGAS_innova_estadisticas_genero.pdf

Gillett, R. (2014), *Why Our Brains Crave Storytelling in Marketing*. Fast Company. Recovery from: https://www.fastcompany.com/3031419/why-our-brains-crave-storytelling-in-marketing

Hernández, R., Fernández, C., & Baptista, M. d. (2014). *Metodología de la Investigación* (Sexta Edición ed.). México D.F., México: Mc Graw Hill. Education/Interamericana Editores, S.A.

Libranda (2018), *Informe Anual del LIBRO DIGITAL* 2018 Recovery from https://investors.storytel.com/en/wp-content/uploads/sites/2/2019/08/storytel-interim-report-january-june-2019-storytel-ab-publ-190813.pdf

Ortega, F. (2017), *Salisbury*. Santiago de Chile, Chile. Planeta.

Price Waterhouse Cooper, (2011). *Millennials at work Reshaping the workplace*. Recovery from: https://www.pwc.com/co/es/publicaciones/assets/millennials-at-work.pdf

Rodero, E. (2019), *Journal of Voice*, Volume 32, Issue 3, Pages 386. e11-386. e19. USA. Mosby.

Schiffman, L. G. (2011). *Comportamiento del consumidor*. México: Pearson educación.

Storytel (2019). *Interim Report January – June*. Recovery from: https://investors.storytel.com/en/wp-content/uploads/sites/2/2019/08/storytel-interim-report-january-june-2019-storytel-ab-publ-190813.pdf

United States Census Bureau 2016, *American Community Survey* (ACS) Recovery from: https://www.census.gov/programs-surveys/acs/guidance/comparing-acs-data/2016.html

Yuste, E. (2019). El cubo de rubik de la lectura. Recovery from: https://www.elisayuste.com/news/el-cubo-de-rubik-de-la-lectura/

Zemke, R, Raines, C., Filipczak, B. (2013). *Generations at Work: Managing the Clash of Boomers, Gen Xers, and Gen Yers in the workplace*, USA: AMACOM.

More Insights into the Role of Warm versus Cool Ambient Scents in Consumer Decision-making: An Abstract

Marcel Lichters, Susanne Adler, and Marko Sarstedt

Abstract Ambient scents often have fascinating effects on consumer behavior. The perceived scent temperature can, for example, affect purchase behavior (Biswas and Szocs 2019). Consumer researchers have recently started explaining these effects by exploring the causal chains triggering consumers' responses to ambient scents.

In this study, we extend prior research on ambient scent perceived temperature's effects. We employed a between-subject design with a peppermint scent in a cool scent and a vanilla caramel scent in the warm scent condition ($n = 124$). Participants answered—inter alia—questions on three dependent measures of premium product preferences (Madzharov et al. 2015), voting behavior in general elections, and relational perceptual focus (Ijzerman and Semin 2009). A pre-analysis's results did not show differences in the two scents' perceived properties, with the exception of temperature-related topics. The main analysis highlights the following:

First, we replicate prior research on warm vs. cool ambient scents' effects on premium product preferences. Extending these results to a FMCG product, namely coffee-to-go brands, we show that consumers under warm (vs. cool) ambient scents have a higher preference for the status-related premium brand (Starbucks) over the non-premium brand (Tchibo). Following previous explanatory approaches, we attribute this behavior to a power restoration motivation that results from warmth triggering a higher social density perception and, subsequently, a feeling of reduced control over the environment.

Second, we broaden the research scope to general election behavior. We show that warm (vs. cool) ambient scents nudge consumers to vote more often for more extreme, right wing parties. Following our previous line of reasoning, right wing parties might address power restoration motivations, as they traditionally promise to reduce social environmental threats and uncertainties (Swyngedouw 2001).

M. Lichters (✉)
Chemnitz University of Technology, Chemnitz, Germany
e-mail: marcel.lichters@wirtschaft.tu-chemnitz.de

S. Adler · M. Sarstedt
Otto-von-Guericke-University, Magdeburg, Germany
e-mail: susanne.adler@ovgu.de; marko.sarstedt@ovgu.de

F. Pantoja, S. Wu (eds.), *From Micro to Macro: Dealing with Uncertainties in the Global Marketplace*, Developments in Marketing Science: Proceedings of the Academy of Marketing Science, https://doi.org/10.1007/978-3-030-89883-0_26

Third, we replicate research on temperature's effects on relational foci. We find that warm (vs. cool) ambient scents lead to a more global relational focus than a local property focus in Kimchi-Palmer tasks (Kimchi and Palmer 1982). We attribute this behavior to an increased attention to social relationships under warm temperatures.

We identify each of these effects regardless of whether we filter our sample for conscious or non-conscious scent processing. This suggests that these effects function without consumers' conscious awareness. In summary, we strengthen and expand the previously established links between ambient scent temperature and premium product choice, expand research on temperature's effects on relational foci, and provide the first evidence of a link between perceived ambient scent temperature and voting behavior.

Keywords Ambient scent · Scent temperature · Branding · Premium · Elections · Perception · Relations

References Available Upon Request

Is Sharing Caring? Consumer Responsibility for Rented Products: An Abstract

Fabian Nindl and Cordula Cerha

Abstract In recent years, the sharing economy has challenged many traditional industries with several disruptive innovations. In 2018, access-based consumption moved into micromobility as E-Scooters instantly resonated with consumers. Revealing the dark side of sharing, consumer misbehavior in form of e.g., careless handling or vandalism is taking its toll on scooter companies and the public.

This study examines the constructs of responsibility and consumer misbehavior in access-based consumption in the context of E-scooter sharing. An exploratory observational study and 21 semi-structured interviews with moderate to high E-scooter users located in Vienna, Austria were conducted to uncover several dimensions why people engage in E-scooter sharing and to identify feelings of responsibility and potential misbehavior. Several reasons why people engage in E-scooter sharing were identified. Five striking dimensions represent the core why consumers rent E-scooters. Specifically, E-scooter usage varies along the dimensions of (1) temporality, (2) efficiency, (3) convenience, (4) responsibility, and (5) entertainment. Additionally, results uncover increasing potential for consumer misbehavior and hint at a reduced sense of responsibility for shared products. The conducted interviews highlight that consumers might feel less responsible for rented products and that subsequent misbehavior can moreover negatively affect other users. Although respondents denied personal misuse of products, the potential for non-responsible behavior was especially detected by interpreting statements via three different grounded theory coding techniques.

This research advances current understanding of access-based consumption by providing consumer motivations and by focusing on detrimental behavior. Although positive or neutral dimensions such as temporality, efficiency, convenience, and entertainment were identified, this research also highlights a reduced sense of responsibility. This in turn can lead to contagious misbehavior. While it is largely believed that access-based consumption represents a positive development, this

F. Nindl (✉) · C. Cerha
WU Vienna, Vienna, Austria
e-mail: fabian.nindl@wu.ac.at; cordula.cerha@wu.ac.at

F. Pantoja, S. Wu (eds.), *From Micro to Macro: Dealing with Uncertainties in the Global Marketplace*, Developments in Marketing Science: Proceedings of the Academy of Marketing Science, https://doi.org/10.1007/978-3-030-89883-0_27

research suggests that long-term market-mediated societal shifts typically also entail negative aspects, which require further investigation.

Keywords Sharing economy · Access based consumption · E-scooters · Customer interaction

References Available Upon Request

Complementary and Alternative Medicine: Exploratory Study of Provider Perspectives: An Abstract

Haeran Jae, Suzanne C. Makarem, and Bruce A. Huhmann

Abstract Complementary and alternative medicine consist of variety of health care approaches such as the use of natural products (e.g. dietary supplements and herbal medicine) or mind-body practices (e.g. acupuncture, chiropractic care) (NIH 2018). The 2012 National Health Interview Survey reveals that 30 percent of adults and 12 percent of children use nonconventional medical care; with Americans spending 30.2 billion U.S. dollars for adults and 1.9 billion U.S. dollars for children on complementary health care services (NIH 2016). Despite growing trends in CAM consumption, the extant marketing literature in the area is limited and narrowly focused on health claims, information processing, or consumer values (e.g. Bolton 2008; Homer and Mukherjee 2019; Mason and Scammon 2011).

The goal of the current research is to explore practitioner-based CAM offerings and their use by consumers from a provider's perspective. What benefits and value do CAM providers believe they are offering, compared to conventional medical services? What types of consumers do they target and how do they go about it? What insights can they provide about these consumers?

Exploratory expert interviews with prominent CAM providers in a mid-sized East Coast U.S. city offer preliminary answers to these questions. Based on CAM provider experiences and perceptions, patients seek CAM services because their needs are not being met by conventional medical services. These unmet needs are not only due to shortcomings related to interpersonal factors (communication, time with doctor) but also to technical shortcomings (undiagnosed or unsolved medical problems). CAM providers in this study describe their patients as proactive, engaged, well-informed, and having unmet needs. A new and surprising finding is that CAM providers cherry-pick patients who are likely to be compliant with recommendations of diagnostics, diets, exercise, and herbal supplements; and who can afford all these products and services, which are likely neither regulated nor tested for efficacy. Conventional healthcare providers seem to be failing at meeting the needs of a growing segment of consumers.

H. Jae (✉) · S. C. Makarem · B. A. Huhmann
Virginia Commonwealth University, Richmond, VA, USA
e-mail: hjae@vcu.edu; scmakarem@vcu.edu; bahuhmann@vcu.edu

F. Pantoja, S. Wu (eds.), *From Micro to Macro: Dealing with Uncertainties in the Global Marketplace*, Developments in Marketing Science: Proceedings of the Academy of Marketing Science, https://doi.org/10.1007/978-3-030-89883-0_28

Keywords Complementary and alternative medicine · Health Care Marketing · Targeted healthcare services · Alternative medicine patients

References Available Upon Request

Salesperson Attributes that Influence Consumer Perceptions: An Abstract

J. Ricky Ferguson, John T. Gironda, and Maria Petrescu

Abstract In recent years thousands of retail stores have announced closings and many major retail chains have declared bankruptcy, announcing dissolution of all their company stores. Facing increased competition from online retailers, the importance of high-quality interactions with salespeople has become more vital to gaining and maintaining a competitive advantage for brick-and-mortar stores (Cross et al. 2007; Cuevas 2018; Hoyle et al. 2020; Marshall et al. 2012). Salespeople can serve as a way for retailers to differentiate among one another as well as set themselves apart from online competitors (Boles et al. 1997; Zoltners et al. 2011). Furthermore, as a conduit for communicating information, building rapport, gleaning customer insights, and helping customers uncover unfelt or latent needs, retail salespeople remain an indispensable force in building customer relationships with stores, products, and brands, as well as fostering customer satisfaction and store loyalty (Dobrescu and Radu 2014; Homburg et al. 2011; Lee and Dubinsky 2003).

Customer satisfaction depends on how well the salesperson interaction matches customer expectations (Habel et al. 2020; Rippé et al. 2016). Salesperson attributes such as helpfulness, friendliness, responsiveness, expertise, knowledge of the firm's products, and ability to answer questions may also come into play when determining customer satisfaction (Tuk et al. 2009). Therefore, the objective of this paper is to assess how consumers prioritize salesperson attributes when evaluating their retail shopping experience and how these differ as a function of the shopping environment. The overarching goal of this research is two-fold: (1) Determine the sales-

J. R. Ferguson
Indiana State University, Terre Haute, IN, USA
e-mail: ricky.ferguson@indstate.edu

J. T. Gironda (✉)
University of North Carolina Wilmington, Wilmington, NC, USA
e-mail: girondaj@uncw.edu

M. Petrescu
International University of Monaco, Le Stella, Monaco
e-mail: mpetrescu@monaco.edu

F. Pantoja, S. Wu (eds.), *From Micro to Macro: Dealing with Uncertainties in the Global Marketplace*, Developments in Marketing Science: Proceedings of the Academy of Marketing Science, https://doi.org/10.1007/978-3-030-89883-0_29

person attributes consumers feel are most important in the salesperson-consumer interaction and (2) Develop an understanding of how these attributes impact feelings of satisfaction/dissatisfaction within a conceptual framework based on expectancy-disconfirmation theory.

To achieve these goals, two mixed-method studies were conducted analyzing how differences in consumer expectations regarding salesperson attributes affect consumer satisfaction. The results demonstrated that a variety of salesperson customer orientation attributes are essential for modern consumers, that the importance of these attributes differs as a function of context (retail, direct selling, service failure), and how various attributes contributed to the generation of digital word-of-mouth. The study of this topic should be beneficial for marketing research, as well as for marketing practitioners dealing with problems in attracting consumers to brick-and-mortar stores and facing issues related to the digital economy.

Keywords Salesperson attributes · Customer orientation · Word-of-mouth · Mixed methods

References Available Upon Request

Killing Two Birds with One Stone: Special Session on Marketing Research with Practical Relevance: An Abstract

Marc Kuhn, Francesca Bonetti, Vanessa Reit, Caroline Stern, and Benjamin Österle

Abstract Major outlets for marketing research specifically mention practical relevance as one of the main criteria for the publication of manuscripts, for example JM and JAMS. Yet despite this, a decreasing number of scholars are focused on practice (Jaworski 2018). With the introduction of the "Theory + Practice" section in AMS Review in 2018, the editorial team has specifically responded to this growing concern over many years, that "academic research in marketing is losing its managerial relevance" (Jaworski 2018, p. 1). This special session aims to strengthen the connection between marketing academia and practice, by showing that also while doing managerially relevant research, not "every paper is a consulting project" (Steenkamp 2018, p. 171). Within the special session, we discuss two exemplary projects, conducted in collaboration between academia and practice: One is located in the e-mobility/energy sector, focusing on the charging infrastructure of electric vehicles, the other is located in the fashion retail business, focusing on the drivers and barriers of the adoption of consumer-facing in-store technologies (CFIT). With these examples and the inclusion of marketing practitioners in the session, we want to show how researchers can start with asking "a CMO a simple question such as 'what are the most difficult issues that you are struggling with today?'" (Jaworski 2018, p. 2). Based on these examples, we show how research projects could be developed and designed in collaboration with practitioners, in order to conduct and disseminate research with both academic rigor and practical relevance.

M. Kuhn (✉) · V. Reit · B. Österle
Baden-Wuerttemberg Cooperative State University Stuttgart, Stuttgart, Germany
e-mail: marc.kuhn@dhbw-stuttgart.de; vanessa.reit@dhbw-stuttgart.de; benjamin.oesterle@dhbw-stuttgart.de

F. Bonetti
University of the Arts London, London, UK
e-mail: f.bonetti@fashion.arts.ac.uk

C. Stern
EnBW Energie Baden-Württemberg AG, Stuttgart, Germany
e-mail: c.stern@enbw.com

F. Pantoja, S. Wu (eds.), *From Micro to Macro: Dealing with Uncertainties in the Global Marketplace*, Developments in Marketing Science: Proceedings of the Academy of Marketing Science, https://doi.org/10.1007/978-3-030-89883-0_30

Keywords Marketing research · Relevance · Impact · Rigor · Industry collaboration

References Available Upon Request

Special Session: Killing Two Birds with One Stone: "All that Glitters is not Gold": Performance of EV-Charging Infrastructure from a European User Perspective: An Abstract

Marc Kuhn, Caroline Stern, Vanessa Reit, and Benjamin Österle

Abstract Is Europe ready for an "electric road revolution?" Particularly the charging infrastructure for electric vehicles is considered to play a significant role when it comes to technology acceptance by consumers. German energy provider EnBW, which also is a provider of charging infrastructure for e-mobility, was therefore asking themselves the following questions: How powerful is the charging infrastructure in Europe from the perspective of EV users today? How convenient is the charging process? How transparent are the charging costs? How do users evaluate more general environmental factors that are important to them, such as safety, lighting conditions, and traffic load at the charging station? To answer these research questions emerging from managerial practice, EnBW and Baden-Wuerttemberg Cooperative State University (DHBW) collaborated in a joint research project, in which EnBW acted as an 'integral partner'. Furthermore, the core research instrument, a survey-based checklist, was developed not only based on previous studies and theory, but adapted and extended through qualitative interviews with seven charging experts from the companies EnBW, ABB, Daimler, and Bosch. This instrument was subsequently used in a user experience study with 12 user teams evaluating 442 charging points from different providers in Germany, France, Austria, Italy and the Netherlands. Analyzing the data using cluster analysis, we take an exploratory look at which performance-types of charging services exist in European markets—with charging stations in one cluster already achieving quite satisfactory results on most

M. Kuhn (✉) · V. Reit · B. Österle
Baden-Wuerttemberg Cooperative State University Stuttgart, Stuttgart, Germany
e-mail: marc.kuhn@dhbw-stuttgart.de; vanessa.reit@dhbw-stuttgart.de; benjamin.oesterle@dhbw-stuttgart.de

C. Stern
EnBW Energie Baden-Württemberg AG, Stuttgart, Germany
e-mail: c.stern@enbw.com

F. Pantoja, S. Wu (eds.), *From Micro to Macro: Dealing with Uncertainties in the Global Marketplace*, Developments in Marketing Science: Proceedings of the Academy of Marketing Science, https://doi.org/10.1007/978-3-030-89883-0_31

factors, and room for improvement on the above-mentioned issues for charging stations in another cluster. The results of the study provides manufacturers of charging infrastructure as well as service providers such as EnBW with a reliable information base for improving the customer and user orientation of their offers, and contributes to further increase technology acceptance of electric vehicles.

Keywords E-mobility · Charging infrastructure · Technology acceptance · User experience · Industry impact · Relevance

References Available Upon Request

Early Adoption of Innovative Media into Digital Marketing Strategies: An Abstract

Kelley Cours Anderson and Kerry T. Manis

Abstract Integrated marketing communication (IMC) continues to evolve as new media emerge. To optimize digital marketing strategies, marketing managers need to understand the impact of integrating innovative, digital media into existing IMC strategies. Although prior literature investigates the incremental effect of multiple traditional offline media (e.g., Naik and Peters 2009; Olbrich and Schultz 2014; Wiesel et al. 2011) as well as the incremental impact of overlaying digital media (e.g., Edell and Keller 1989; Lemon and Nowlis 2002; Naik and Raman 2003), research investigating the effect of innovative digital media (IDM) when added to existing digital media is lacking.

This paper examines the impact of virtual reality (VR) as an IDM medium and its role as part of IMC. We define IDM as a novel application within the overall digital marketing strategy that is employed by marketing managers to proactively or reactively address market demands (Kleindl et al. 1996; O'Dwyer et al. 2009a, b). Recent advances in technology have improved VR to the point where it is a viable marketing medium. Due to its novelty, the effect of VR in IMC has not been fully studied. Utilizing secondary market data, we test the effects of VR in residential real estate using a quasi-experiment.

Results from this study support the strength of VR, an IDM, compared to existing traditional digital marketing (TDM). However, the results from this study also reveal a lack of an interaction effect, or 'cross-effect,' when adding VR to existing TDM. This paper answers calls for understanding the effect of innovative media, such as VR, (Hulland et al. 2019; Lamberton and Stephen 2016; Weingarden 2018; Yadav and Pavlou 2014). We contribute to the literature by evaluating the 'cross-effects' (Batra and Keller 2016) and advancing the knowledge of how the effect of TDM is impacted by the early entry of IDM. Limitations and managerial implications are discussed.

K. C. Anderson (✉) · K. T. Manis
Texas Tech University, Lubbock, TX, USA
e-mail: kelley.anderson@ttu.edu; kt.manis@ttu.edu

F. Pantoja, S. Wu (eds.), *From Micro to Macro: Dealing with Uncertainties in the Global Marketplace*, Developments in Marketing Science: Proceedings of the Academy of Marketing Science, https://doi.org/10.1007/978-3-030-89883-0_32

Keywords Digital media · Cross-effects · Virtual reality · Integrated marketing communication

References Available Upon Request

The Product Depth Effect: The Effect of Product Depth Size of a Brand on the Overall Impression of a Product: An Abstract

Samuel Sekar

Abstract This research investigates the effect of a number of product types sold by a brand on an individual product's overall impressions. The results suggest the influence of sensory property on overall impression depended upon the size of the product depth of a brand (i.e.) overall impression depended upon the number of products sold by a brand.

Product uncertainty is high for experience goods such as beer because any judgment about the sensory attributes can be made only after purchase (Smith et al. 2016). Therefore, when consumers buy experience goods, they rely heavily on other consumers' information (Smith et al. 2016). In this regard, the online ratings and reviews play a vital role in product evaluation and purchase as a result of their value in reducing product uncertainty during the decision-making process (Babić Rosario et al. 2016; Baker et al. 2016; Marchand et al. 2017; Mayzlin et al. 2014; You et al. 2015).

Small craft beer sellers with a single or fewer number of products in their portfolio are the brands with shallow product depth. Big brewers with a larger number of products in the portfolio are brands with deep product depth. Studies show that people prefer craft beers more than big national brewers (Aquilani et al. 2015), because consumers strongly believe that manufacturers with smaller product depth effectively produce authentic products due to their specialist identity (Carroll and Swaminathan 2000). Therefore, the research questions are as follows: "Does product depth affect the overall impression of a product sold by the brand?" and "Does sensory properties of a product influence the overall impression of a product?" Do sensory properties influence the overall impression of a product through the effect of product depth?

The beer rating dataset available from the www.beeradvocate.com website was used for testing the hypotheses. The beer rating data's hierarchical structure required

S. Sekar (✉)
University of South Florida, Tampa, FL, USA
e-mail: ssekar@usf.edu

F. Pantoja, S. Wu (eds.), *From Micro to Macro: Dealing with Uncertainties in the Global Marketplace*, Developments in Marketing Science: Proceedings of the Academy of Marketing Science, https://doi.org/10.1007/978-3-030-89883-0_33

a simple two-level HLM to investigate the effect of the brand's size of product-depth on the overall impression of a product. The interaction between the sensory property (level 1) and the size of product depth of a brand (level 2) was significant. The influence of sensory property on overall impression depended on the size of the product depth of a brand (i.e.) overall impression depended upon the number of products sold by a brand.

Keywords Product depth · Sensory attributes · Product impressions · Product authenticty

References Available Upon Request

Haptic Information Impacts Online Purchase Behavior: The Role of Price Framing and Consumer Characteristics: An Abstract

Monika Kukar-Kinney and Atefeh Yazdanparast

Abstract Haptic information can serve as an indicator of product quality and may be used to reduce consumer uncertainty about the product, its quality and value (Peck and Childers 2003). However, when other quality or value indicators are present, haptic information may not be as important, as the consumer may rely on other indicators to assess product quality and value. The way the selling price is framed—as a regular price or a discounted price—can serve as such an indicator, as it signals quality on one hand and influences perceptions of sacrifice on the other hand.

This research aims to identify how the effect of provided haptic product information (specifically, touch and feel) on consumer online perceptions and shopping behavior is moderated by the provided price/price discount information. Further, since consumers vary in terms of how important price/price discounts are to them and to what extent they actually utilize price-quality inferences when evaluating products, additional moderators studied include the extent of consumer sale proneness and consumer price-quality inferences.

We conducted an online experiment with a 2 (low regular price vs. discounted price) × 2 (haptic description present vs. absent) between-subjects design. The respondents evaluated a mock webpage listing a product (leather gloves), its description and price, and responded to questions about their perceptions of the product, shopping intentions towards the product, their general consumer and shopping characteristics, and demographics.

Structural equation modelling was used to test the proposed relationships. The results indicate that providing a touch and feel description for products with salient material properties can positively impact purchase intention of sale prone consum-

M. Kukar-Kinney
University of Richmond, Richmond, VA, USA
e-mail: mkukarki@richmond.edu

A. Yazdanparast (✉)
Clark University, Worcester, MA, USA
e-mail: ayazdanparast@clarku.edu

F. Pantoja, S. Wu (eds.), *From Micro to Macro: Dealing with Uncertainties in the Global Marketplace*, Developments in Marketing Science: Proceedings of the Academy of Marketing Science, https://doi.org/10.1007/978-3-030-89883-0_34

ers and/or those who make strong price-quality inferences, especially when products are offered at regular low prices. However, when products are discounted, the original price serves as a stronger quality signal, making product haptic description less useful for quality assessment. The results provide evidence that presenting product haptic descriptions can impact consumers' quality perceptions of the product, which in turn, result in higher purchase confidence and perceived acquisition value. Such perceptions then result in higher purchase intention for the product. These findings add specificity to extant knowledge on the relationship between quality perceptions and purchase intentions (Rodrigues et al. 2017) by identifying the underlying mechanism for this relationship and proposing individual characteristics (i.e., sale proneness and price-quality interference) and situational factors (discount framing and product information) that serve as boundary conditions.

Keywords Haptics · Price Framing · Online Shopping · Perceived Quality

References Available Upon Request

Data Here Today, Gone Tomorrow: A Longitudinal Study on the Delivery of Marketing Intelligence to Small Businesses: An Abstract

Christina O'Connor, Grace Carson, Holly Milne, and Denise Luethge

Abstract Typically, only larger businesses have been able to purchase Marketing Intelligence (MO), whilst small businesses have been unable to access and deploy data due to prohibitive costs and resource deficiencies. Despite these challenges faced by small businesses, research suggests that MI has a positive influence on the market orientation (MO) of small firms as it facilitates flexible market planning (Pelham and Wilson 1996; Donnelly et al. 2013). This paper questions what happens to the MO of small businesses when MI is provided, withdrawn and reinstated over a longitudinal period of ten years.

The MI at the centre of this paper is Dunnhumby data, also known as Tesco clubcard data. The 'Dunnhumby Project Northern Ireland' commenced in 2008 and acknowledged the lack of information flow and financial barriers constraining small agri-food businesses. The project ran for a 3-year period and intensively engaged 7 case firms. Despite firms acclimatizing to the continued exposure of MI over the 3-year period, the project ended, resulting in the automatic withdrawal of free data and interpretation support to all case firms in September 2011. In 2016, the researchers revisited the 7 case firms to explore the impact of this MI withdrawal. In the same year, however, funding was secured to reinstate the project and facilitate free access to MI for small agri-food businesses over the following 3 years. The research-

C. O'Connor (✉)
Maynooth University, Maynooth, Ireland
e-mail: christina.oconnor@mu.ie

G. Carson
Queen's University Belfast, Belfast, Northern Ireland
e-mail: grace.carson@qub.ac.uk

H. Milne
Ulster University, Belfast, Northern Ireland
e-mail: milne-h@ulster.ac.uk

D. Luethge
Northern Kentucky University, Highland Heights, KY, USA
e-mail: luethged1@nku.edu

F. Pantoja, S. Wu (eds.), *From Micro to Macro: Dealing with Uncertainties in the Global Marketplace*, Developments in Marketing Science: Proceedings of the Academy of Marketing Science, https://doi.org/10.1007/978-3-030-89883-0_35

ers returned to the case firms in 2019 to investigate developments in the firms during this period of data provision.

Overall, this study seeks to provide longitudinal insights into the 3 phases of this research, exploring whether these firms return to their old ways of marketing following MI withdrawal, or whether original exposure instils a market-oriented cultural change. The importance of free data and analytical support is evident, as at least 4 out of the 7 firms did largely revert back to their 'old' ways of marketing. The need for a sustainable delivery of MI is a necessity and must be facilitated in a format that is understandable to ensure that small businesses continue to derive long-term benefits, in a consistent and strategic manner.

Keywords Market intelligence · Market orientation · Data provision · Small businesses

References Available Upon Request

Managing Uncertainty in Consumer Research: Replicability and the Elephant in the Lab: An Abstract

Edward Rigdon, Marko Sarstedt, and Jan-Michael Becker

Abstract Research methods in the study of consumption and consumers, as across the social sciences, is dominated by a framework that emphasizes managing error—a framework borrowed from physical science (Borsboom 2005; Edgeworth 1888; Stigler 1985). Beginning in the late 1800s, social science pioneers adapted this framework for their research needs, in the process launching quantitative social science. By the late 1990s, physical sciences, including pure and applied chemistry, applied physics, and legal forensics, had recognized weaknesses in the error-centric framework (JCGM 2010; Vosk and Emery 2015). In response, metrologists within these various disciplines developed an alternative measurement framework that focused on uncertainty.

Uncertainty is quantified doubt, represented as the range of values that could plausibly be assigned to the measurand, consistent with the analysis (JCGM 2010; Vosk and Emery 2015). Uncertainty arises from many sources across the entire research process—from incomplete definition of the measurand, from an unstable measurand, and from limitations of the measuring instrument (Slaev et al. 2013). Most commonly, uncertainty comes from the human element brought to research activities by all of the participants (Bell 1999). For the metrologist, no measurement is complete without a statement of the uncertainty associated with the measurement (JCGM 2010). To construct that statement, the metrologist assembles an "uncertainty budget," a catalog of all material contributions to overall uncertainty (Tal 2011). Here the metrologist draws not only on statistical methods, which effectively address random sampling error and the influence of research design, but also on certifications from other sources, standard values, and expert judgment.

E. Rigdon (✉)
Georgia State University, Atlanta, GA, USA
e-mail: erigdon@gsu.edu

M. Sarstedt
Otto-von-Guericke University, Magdeburg, Germany
e-mail: marko.sarstedt@ovgu.ed

J.-M. Becker
BI Norwegian Business School, Oslo, Norway

F. Pantoja, S. Wu (eds.), *From Micro to Macro: Dealing with Uncertainties in the Global Marketplace*, Developments in Marketing Science: Proceedings of the Academy of Marketing Science, https://doi.org/10.1007/978-3-030-89883-0_36

Thoroughly tracking and quantifying all material sources of uncertainty affecting consumer research will involve immense efforts by individual researchers and research teams. Likewise, it will need contributions by the research community to develop standard measurement protocols, to help researchers control known sources of uncertainty. However, we also highlight several benefits of employing an uncertainty-centric research framework. One of them could be as large as providing a better approach for managing and overcoming the problem of poor replication rates across the social sciences. An uncertainty-centric research framework allows researchers to better predict the chance that an independent research team will successfully replicate a finding. The benefits from such a shift would be massive. The research community could consider the uncertainty disadvantage of working with proprietary, unshareable data, and non- random student samples. The development of more standardized lab procedures could lead to permanent reductions in uncertainty, ultimately making successful replication more the norm and less the exception.

Keywords Uncertainty · Replicability · Error · Measurement

References Available Upon Request

Texting and Driving: The Use of Specific Ad Elements for Attitude Change: An Abstract

Ilgım Dara Benoit, Elizabeth Miller, Elika Kordrostami, and Ceren Turedi

Abstract There are three types of driving distractions: visual (e.g. looking at the navigation system display), manual (e.g., eating since it requires the driver to take their hands off the wheel), and cognitive (e.g., talking to a passenger) (CDC 2013). While each distraction is dangerous in itself, due to the combination of visual (looking at the phone), manual (finding the phone, typing), and cognitive (reading and composing a message) distractions of texting, texting and driving is a major issue for public health concern (Sherin et al. 2014). Deaths due to texting and driving in the US have been steadily increasing, quickly reaching epidemic proportions (Darrow 2016). As a recent *Los Angeles Times* article noted "Texting—the most common cause of distracted driving accidents—is fast becoming the new drunk driving" (Wilson 2018). However, the majority of drivers do not think texting and driving is dangerous (Lardieri 2018), and over 50% admit to using their phone while driving (Darrow 2016). This suggests that a greater focus is needed on changing attitudes towards texting and driving in order to more effectively reduce this behavior. Accordingly, the purpose of this study is to find ways to increase the effectiveness of anti-texting and driving ads leading to changes in drivers' attitudes toward the texting and driving issue.

With use of an online survey, this paper studies multiple factors that change people's attitude toward the texting and driving problem, and lead them to think

I. D. Benoit (✉)
Appalachian State University, Boone, NC, USA
e-mail: benoitid@appstate.edu

E. Miller
University of Massachusetts Amherst, Amherst, MA, USA
e-mail: emiller@isenberg.umass.edu

E. Kordrostami
Rowan University, Glassboro, NJ, USA
e-mail: kordrostami@rowan.edu

C. Turedi
Purdue University Northwest, Hammond, IN, USA
e-mail: cturedi@purdue.edu

F. Pantoja, S. Wu (eds.), *From Micro to Macro: Dealing with Uncertainties in the Global Marketplace*, Developments in Marketing Science: Proceedings of the Academy of Marketing Science, https://doi.org/10.1007/978-3-030-89883-0_37

texting and driving is dangerous. The survey was conducted by using 162 real texting and driving advertisements. The findings show that while both rational and emotional appeals can change attitudes, emotional appeals tend to work better. The research also shows that the ads work better if the emotion is evoked via the image in the ad, rather than the text. In particular, fear evoked in the ad tends to change the attitude toward the issue the most –compared to other negative emotions such as disgust, anger, and guilt which are also commonly used in texting and driving ads. Finally, creativity of the advertisement effectively impacts attitude toward the issue as well. The findings of this research can be used by public policy makers and marketers in order to create more effective advertisements leading to a reduction in the texting and driving epidemic.

Keywords Texting and driving · Advertising · Emotional appeal · Fear · Creativity

References Available Upon Request

Time Flies: The Role of Desire to Stay at the Mall in Enhancing the Shopping Experience: An Abstract

Maher Georges Elmashhara and Ana Maria Soares

Abstract The desire to stay at the shopping area is one of the main approach behaviors in retailing (Bitner 1992). Previous research has shown that satisfaction predicts shoppers' desire to stay in shopping (Lloyd et al. 2014; Siu et al. 2012) and that the desire to stay is linked to other antecedents like service quality (De Nisco and Warnaby 2013), convenience (Lloyd et al. 2014), social (Martin and Turley 2004), emotional (Sherman et al. 1997), aesthetic, and environmental factors (Vukadin et al. 2018). These findings suggest two possible explanations: (1) higher levels of satisfaction lead to the desire to stay more in shopping, a link which has been investigated (Lloyd et al. 2014; Siu et al. 2012); (2) the desire to stay can be due to reasons other than satisfaction, including the surrounding environment. Based on that, we look at the impact of visual and sound atmospherics cues on the desire to stay in the mall, satisfaction, and patronage intentions. Then, we investigate whether the desire to stay contributes to enhancing the other retail outcomes of patronage intentions and positive Word of Mouth (WoM). Furthermore, we study the mediating role of shopper satisfaction in the relation between the desire to stay at the mall, positive WoM, and patronage intentions.

To test the proposed research model, we use Structural Equation Modeling (SEM) to analyze data collected from a convenience sample of mall shoppers. Results show that both color and music influence the desire to stay, while lighting does not. Moreover, there is a significant path between visual cues and satisfaction, while there is no significant path from any of the studied atmospherics to patronage intentions. Regarding the relation between desire to stay and shopping outcomes; results show that the desire to stay influences positive WoM directly, however, there is no such influence on patronage intentions. Finally, desire to stay impacts on both WoM and patronage intentions when considering the mediating role of satisfaction.

This paper contributes to the literature in several ways. First, it adds color and music to the antecedents of desire to stay at the mall. Second, to the authors' best knowledge, there is no prior research addressing the impact of desire to stay on

M. G. Elmashhara (✉) · A. M. Soares
University of Minho, Braga, Portugal
e-mail: maher@eeg.uminho.pt; amsoares@eeg.uminho.pt

F. Pantoja, S. Wu (eds.), *From Micro to Macro: Dealing with Uncertainties in the Global Marketplace*, Developments in Marketing Science: Proceedings of the Academy of Marketing Science, https://doi.org/10.1007/978-3-030-89883-0_38

positive WoM. Finally, previous research analyses the scenario of shoppers feeling satisfied then decided to stay more time in the mall. This research studies the opposite relationship, as a shopping trip can last longer due to different reasons other than satisfaction, and looks at how satisfaction mediates the role of desire to stay in driving shoppers to spend more money and refer positively to the shopping mall.

Keywords Visual and sound cues · Desire to stay · Shopper satisfaction · Word-of-Mouth · Patronage intentions · Shopping malls

References Available Upon Request

The Effects of Typicality and Novelty on Aesthetic Preference and Positive Emotions: An Abstract

Lina M. Ceballos, Nancy Hodges, and Kittichai Watchravesringkan

Abstract To better predict product preference, the *Most Advanced Yet Acceptable (MAYA) principle* has been introduced as a two-factor theory that explains why humans prefer a balanced mix of the aesthetic properties of typicality and novelty (Hekkert 2006; Hekkert et al. 2003; Lidwell et al. 2010). Limited studies examine both typicality and novelty in apparel products, as thus far studies have utilized other types of stimuli such as sanders, telephones, teakettles, medium-size cars (Hekkert et al. 2003), among others. Therefore, the overall purpose of this research was to examine the effects of aesthetic properties in apparel related to the MAYA principle. Based on the framework of consumer response to product form (Bloch 1995), the focus was on the effects of typicality and novelty on aesthetic preference and positive emotions, as well as on the moderating role of usage situation and the mediating role of aesthetic preference.

In Bloch's framework (1995), specific visual properties of the product form (e.g., the typicality and novelty of apparel products), engender psychological responses, which are cognitive (e.g., aesthetic preference) and affective reactions (e.g., positive emotions towards the product) within the organism (i.e., consumer) that are moderated by certain situational factors (e.g., usage situation). Appraisal theory links appraisals (e.g., aesthetic preference) with the affective response of emotions (Arnold 1960, p. 182), such as the positive emotions of pleasant surprise, fascination, desire, and joy (Desmet 2012). Drawing upon these relationships, this study proposed eight hypotheses (H_{1-8}) that were tested via a 2 (novelty: low vs. high) × 2 (typicality: low vs. high) × 3 (usage situation scenarios: professional oriented vs. non-professional oriented vs. neutral) between-subjects experimental design. After the selection of stimuli and a pre-test, a stimulus was selected for each of the four

L. M. Ceballos (✉)
Universidad EAFIT, Medellín, Colombia
e-mail: lceball4@eafit.edu.co

N. Hodges · K. Watchravesringkan
University of North Carolina at Greensboro, Greensboro, NC, USA
e-mail: njnelson@uncg.edu; k_watchr@uncg.edu

F. Pantoja, S. Wu (eds.), *From Micro to Macro: Dealing with Uncertainties in the Global Marketplace*, Developments in Marketing Science: Proceedings of the Academy of Marketing Science, https://doi.org/10.1007/978-3-030-89883-0_39

typicality/novelty cells and randomly included on a survey on Qualtrics distributed via TurkPrime. The data collection resulted in a total of 494 usable responses.

Results go beyond confirmation of what other studies (Hekker et al. 2003) have stated, such as that both factors; typicality and novelty, are jointly taken into account when explaining an individual's aesthetic preference for products. Findings extend theory and offer theoretical and practical contributions to academics as well as fashion industry marketers and designers to better understand typicality and novelty.

Keywords Aesthetics · Typicality · Novelty · Apparel · MAYA · Emotions

References Available Upon Request

The Negative Effects of Mobile Retail App Use: Dealing with Regrettable Escapism: An Abstract

Hannah R. Marriott, Graeme McLean, and Khalid Al Nabhani

Abstract The proliferation of smartphones and the continued advancement in technology has seen retailers adopt apps as a form of service delivery at an exhilarant rate (McLean 2018; Wang et al. 2015). Excessive time on mobile devices and mobile apps has prompted commentary and research on the addictive nature of smartphones (Barnes et al. 2019). With such high daily usage of mobile apps, the "always-on" consumer has been created whereby smartphones have become an extension of a persons' self.

Uses and Gratifications Theory explains the motivations of individuals to adopt and use technologies to satisfy their needs (Grellhesl et al. 2012). It proposes that individuals use certain technologies for precise purposes; in this circumstance, for the purposes of escaping. Escapism is defined as an escape from the self in both psychological and physiological levels. Although mobile apps often fulfil the needs of entertainment, stress relief, interest, or information searching (Wang et al. 2015), pursing gratification for the purpose of escapism can develop higher likelihoods developing smartphone addiction. Therefore, whilst those consumers addicted to smartphone use may hold positive perceptions of the technology, the negative consequences of addiction and immersion may affect important marketing outcomes.

Two studies were used to examine the role of branded mobile apps as a means for consumers to achieve utilitarian ("compatibility") and hedonic ("enjoyment" and "escapism") gratification goals. The quantitative results (Study 1) show that although respondents (n = 1410) reveal that compatibility and enjoyment significantly influences brand reputation, brand loyalty and app reuse intention, escapism negatively effects brand reputation, brand loyalty and future app reuse. Study 2 (n = 16) further shows that consumers seeking escapism can reflect the act to waste hours by using smartphone retail apps. Furthermore, experiencing escapism may

H. R. Marriott (✉)
University of Winchester, Winchester, UK
e-mail: hmarriott@cardiffmet.ac.uk

G. McLean · K. Al Nabhani
University of Strathclyde, Glasgow, UK
e-mail: greame.mclean@strath.ac.uk; khalid.al-nabhani@strath.ac.uk

F. Pantoja, S. Wu (eds.), *From Micro to Macro: Dealing with Uncertainties in the Global Marketplace*, Developments in Marketing Science: Proceedings of the Academy of Marketing Science, https://doi.org/10.1007/978-3-030-89883-0_40

lead consumers to be frustrated and realise that it was a waste of time, or in some instances "dangerous". Accordingly, this time wasting can cause sensations of "self-blaming" and promote negative feelings and reduced levels of personal well-being, to which we coin the term 'regrettable escapism'. Building upon the notions from literature, consumers may not value escaping from current reality to seek a better one when shopping through smartphone branded apps. Although consumers may experience escapism when using traditional retail smartphone branded apps, our findings illustrate that they may not like doing so as it causes them to spend more time than necessary using the retailer's app, resulting in feelings of guilt and regret.

Keywords Mobile apps · Escapism · Uses · Gratifications theory

References Available Upon Request

An Evaluation of Factors that Explain Delinquency in Credit Unions: Decision Implications for Credit Unions CEOs and Executives

Reginald A. Silver and Bryan B. Darden

Abstract Extant research in the financial services and banking domains has produced little in the way of managerial tactics for executives who oversee credit unions. Even less literature can be found regarding credit union service organizations (CUSOs). We propose a theoretical model that explores the relationship between CUSO investment, deposits, and earnings as predictors of delinquency. We analyzed publicly available data from the National Credit Union Administration's Credit Union and Corporate Call Report Data (n = 14,267). Although our model produced meager explanatory results for deposits (R^2 = 0.009) and earnings (R^2 = 0.012), our model explained nearly 75% of the variance observed in delinquency (R^2 = 0.748). The empirically tested model supports three of the five hypotheses that we proposed. CUSO investment is significantly associated with deposits (β = 0.097, t = 3.557) and earnings (β = 0.111, t = 2.074) but not delinquency. Deposits are significantly associated with delinquency (β = 0.922, t = 5.266). Earnings demonstrated no significant impact on delinquency. Credit union executives will be able to influence delinquency at their respective branches by focusing their attention on deposits and, to a lesser degree, on CUSO investment as a minor but still significant antecedent of deposits.

Keywords Credit unions · Delinquency · Data analytics · Transaction cost theory · PLS-SEM modeling

R. A. Silver · B. B. Darden (✉)
University of North Carolina at Charlotte, Charlotte, NC, USA
e-mail: rsilver5@uncc.edu; bdarden1@uncc.edu

F. Pantoja, S. Wu (eds.), *From Micro to Macro: Dealing with Uncertainties in the Global Marketplace*, Developments in Marketing Science: Proceedings of the Academy of Marketing Science, https://doi.org/10.1007/978-3-030-89883-0_41

Introduction

Credit Union Service Organizations (CUSOs) fill a niche within the banking industry. As extensions of federally insured and state-governed credit unions, CUSOs provide a range of services that help fill the void between the credit union banking experience and the banking experience associated with larger banks. CUSOs are typically wholly or partially owned subsidiaries of these credit unions, which offer an extended range of products and services. These services include investments, insurance services, and operational support through information technology infrastructure, compliance management, and a variety of other support services (Lueg et al. 2019). Because of the critical role that CUSOs play in providing services to members, it is crucial to understand the factors that play a role in the solvency of these organizations. The purpose of this research study is to investigate the association that CUSO investments may have with factors that may predict credit union delinquency as it pertains to the management of the organization.

CUSOs, in academic literature, are scarcely mentioned. In practice, however, CUSO benefits are becoming more widely known. Credit unions are continuously looking for income sources and ways to extend product offerings while also ensuring their overall financial solvency. CUSOs are a way to bring new members into a credit union to facilitate growth, much like their larger banking counterparts (Rubin et al. 2013) without having to merge with another institution (Akkus et al. 2015). Intuitively, this premise suggests that increasing credit union earnings and deposits vis-à-vis CUSO investment should lead to better managerial control over factors that influence delinquency. CUSO investment has, in practice, been viewed as a proxy for increased credit union membership. Our research seeks to inform researchers and practitioners about the extent to which CUSO investment might influence delinquency. We also explore whether CUSO investment might have a direct effect on deposits and earnings. Intuitively, one would expect to find that as CUSO investment increases, the resulting effects are increases in member deposits and increased earnings.

Our inquiry into the relationship between CUSO investment and delinquency leads us to five essential research questions:

RQ1. What role does CUSO investment play in explaining credit union delinquency?
RQ2. What role does CUSO investment play in explaining deposits?
RQ3. What role does CUSO investment play in explaining earnings?
RQ4. What role does the amount of deposits play in explaining credit union delinquency?
RQ5. What role does the amount of earnings play in explaining credit union delinquency?

Answering these research questions provides practical decision making (Cohen et al. 1981) and theoretical benefits to both academics and practitioners. In the practical setting, credit union executive managers and those involved with insolvency prevention can utilize this information to make decisions (Cohen et al. 1981) if investment in a CUSO is profitable. In an operations and risk context (Engemann and Miller 1992), the investment will require research and understanding of associated uncertainties (Kusy and Ziemba 1986). In theory, we will utilize transaction cost theory (Coase 1937), which suggests that firms must decide whether to invest in a new organization or build that which could be potentially hazardous (Williamson 1993). This holds for credit unions who are particularly interested in expanding while maintaining their fiscal strength. This work will help close the gap in the literature as it pertains to strategic decisions utilizing transaction cost theory and the utilization of investment as a vehicle to prevent insolvency.

To investigate these research questions, we first review existing literature on CUSOs and CUSO investment; we then propose our theoretical model and research hypotheses. Following these sections, we analyze and report the empirical results from our analysis. We close with a discussion of study limitations, implications for future results, and concluding thoughts.

Theoretical Background

CUSOs are vital because they give credit unions the ability to offer and implement products that have historically not been part of their repertoire (Fountain 2006). CUSOs have given credit unions the ability to venture into multiple realms that are traditionally not offered. This includes small business lending (Wilcox and Berkely 2011), and non-traditional services (Berger et al. 2016) which augment the financial services offerings (Sobek 2003), especially for lower-income households and those who may not have the ability to work with larger institutions (Barr 2004).

Credit unions provide an interesting lens through which to view how assets are described in the research literature. Literature about CUSO investment is divided in terms of assets size (Goddard et al. 2008) and performance (Fried et al. 1993). In the same vein, some credit unions are considered as "small" ($100 Million) (Thompson 2019) in comparison to larger credit unions who may have assets in the billions of dollars. Credit unions and CUSOs evaluate assets in terms of asset quality. For credit unions, asset quality is measured by the risk that an asset may not earn additional income, which could harm rates of return (Griffith et al. 2009). In contrast, credit unions and CUSOs with assets that are deemed to be of higher quality will tend to invest those assets into income-producing products and services (Pana et al. 2015). Overall, Jain and Lawrence (2014) found that credit unions, in comparison with Subchapter S banks have a higher asset quality, which tends to serve them well financially (Jain and Lawrence 2014).

Loan portfolios or the ability to lend money and increase income (Goddard et al. 2008) is an integral part of any financial institution, including credit unions (Black and Dugger 1981). Interestingly, credit unions have a more personal outlook on lending (Jones 2006) even while maintaining competitive rates against their banking competition (Feinberg and Rahman 2001) and managing risk (Elsinger et al. 2006). This outlook is built upon relationship lending which suggests that those who benefit from the institution will pay back those institutions at a rate higher than more traditional lending sources (Shimizu 2012) especially those with local bank branches and online banking resources (Xue et al. 2011). Traditionally, credit unions have participated in few lending products, as allowed by charter and law (Black and Dugger 1981) however, as time has progressed, credit unions have increased their lending portfolios to expand to small business lending (Ely and Robinson 2009) and even payday loans (Nembhard 2013) with the best interest of the member at heart (Carter et al. 2011). Lending is evolving for credit unions in order for them to remain competitive in the financial marketplace (Fried et al. 1993). Credit unions are important to members who need to obtain loan services for which they may not be eligible with larger financial intuitions.

Deposits, in the credit union context, were initially defined by Smith (1984), who described the competitiveness of credit union depository rates in comparison to the market (Smith 1984). Credit unions have historically had higher interest payouts than their larger banking counterparts due to the nature of their member-owner structures (Davis 2001). Credit union interest payouts have traditionally been higher than those of larger banks despite the inherently greater interest rate risk (Vuillemey 2019) they could encounter by offering these member-favorable rates.

Smith (1988) described how earnings are viewed in the credit union context. Smith found that credit unions often attributed earnings to the ability to make decisions under uncertain conditions to affect positive earnings (Smith 1988). This view of credit union earnings was further refined by Bauer et al. (2009) as an "annual percent change in equity" (Bauer et al. 2009). Credit union earnings are exempted from federal taxes under the Federal Credit Union Act, which allows credit unions to realize tax savings that result in lower operating expenses. Even though credit unions are exempt, they do have to ensure they are managing bank capital requirements (Fraisse et al. 2019).

To remain financially solvent and to sustain service levels to members, credit unions and CUSOs must manage revenues (De Vericourt and Lobo 2009) and delinquency. Delinquency is determined mainly by the amount of money tied up in loans to members. These loans are typically flagged as delinquent when they are two months past due. Loan delinquency appears to be especially problematic for smaller credit unions whose allowances for delinquent loans may be as much as 25% higher than that of larger credit unions (Sollenberger and Stanecki 2009). Credit union delinquency is also likely to be higher in credit unions that have a broader membership base because these credit unions typically experience more risk than those that maintain a more narrow membership base (Ely and Robinson 2009).

The relationship between the CUSO and the credit union is one that is especially unique because the CUSO is a wholly or partially owned subsidiary of the credit union. The utilization of the transaction cost theory as a lens to understand this relationship is critical because it provides evidence to support the notion that for businesses to expand, there must be a decision of cost between a joint venture or wholly or partially owned subsidiary (Makino and Neupert 2000). Sestu and Majocchi (2018) addressed this notion between family firms and subsidiaries in which the family firm would invest in a wholly-owned subsidiary is preferred (Sestu and Majocchi 2018). We would argue the same should be the case for these credit unions.

Transaction cost theory also explains how these entities form and evolve (Rindfleisch 2019). For credit unions, these changes evolve in a way that can control costs and builds alliances among organizations (Penney and Combs 2019). Following this idea and the transaction cost economics as part of a decision implication is the notion that cost weighs into the equation. Credit unions are no exception. To operate on a global scale, these entities must generate products and services that keep them competitive in the market. The decision to expand activities in house or invest is a crucial part of any business venture (Lioliou and Willcocks 2019); however, the ability to understand the risk is even more beneficial.

Methodology

We propose a theoretical model utilizing transaction cost theory that considers the influence that CUSO investment has on deposits and earnings. Our model also assumes that deposits and earnings have a direct impact on delinquency. We explore a direct relationship between CUSO investment and delinquency (Fig. 1).

For this research study, we measure CUSO Investment as the total dollar amount invested in CUSO services. We measure deposits as the total amount in shares (savings accounts), which is considered a "share" of stock in the credit union (this varies per credit union). This amount in members' share deposit accounts serves as a measure of ownership and active participation in the credit union. Earnings are measured as non-interest income. Delinquency is measured as the total dollar amount for delinquent accounts. We summarize the codification and mapping of these accounts with our model constructs in Table 1.

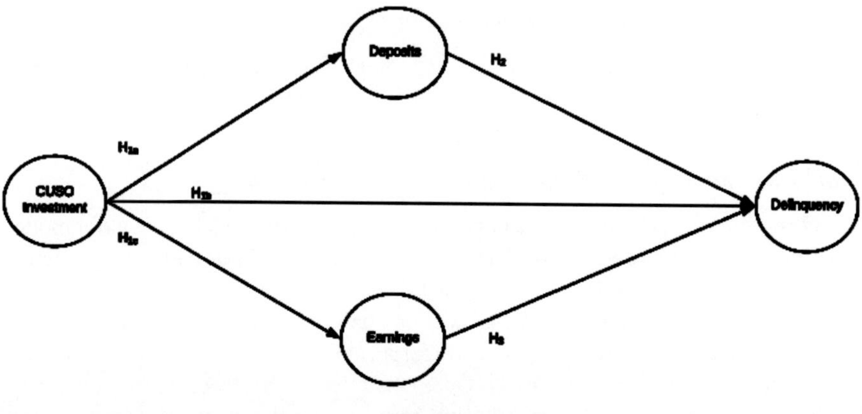

Fig. 1 Theoretical model of CUSO investment and delinquency

Table 1 Model constructs and account mappings from 5300 report

Model construct	5300 report account	Description
CUSO investment	ACCT_851	Total value of investment in CUSOs in dollars
Deposits	ACCT_013	Total share deposits in dollars
Earnings	ACCT_117	Total non-interest income in dollars
Delinquency	ACCT_041B	Total reportable delinquent loans in dollars

We anticipate that CUSO investment will indirectly influence delinquency through a direct association with deposits. We test a direct influence between CUSO investment and delinquency, which has not been widely studied in the existing literature. Under the theory of transaction costs, we expect that CUSO investment will indirectly influence delinquency through a direct association with earnings. This goes back to the theory that as CUSO investment increases, the ability to increase earnings will increase. This will influence the make vs. buy vs. ally decisions of the firm (Geyskens et al. 2006). For these reasons, we assume that when a credit union invests, which is a buy (investment) decision, the following will occur:

H_{1a}: *CUSO investment positively influences deposits*
H_{1b}: *CUSO investment negatively influences delinquency*
H_{1c}: *CUSO investment positively influences earnings*

We expect that our model will demonstrate a positive association between deposits and delinquency. These deposits are "shares," which measure direct ownership by members. We reason that more shares equate to more members who would potentially utilize credit union services and relationships. Intuitively, as deposits increase, we would expect delinquency to increase because of the relationship attribute of credit unions versus their banking counterparts. Since deposits should increase as CUSO activity increases, higher account balances in these accounts should translate to more risk being taken by the credit union to increase overall earnings.

H_2: *Higher deposit balances should affect lower delinquency amounts*

Earnings, which represent a cash in-flow and a form of income for the CUSO, should demonstrate a reduction in delinquency. We theorize that higher levels of CUSO earnings should, at least partially, reduce delinquency.

H_3: *Higher earnings should affect lower delinquency amounts*

In testing these hypotheses, we hope to identify relationships between our model constructs that might be used by CUSO executives to monitor and manage delinquency at the branch level.

We extracted a sample of CUSO account balances from the National Credit Union Administration Credit Union and Corporate Call Report (NCUA 5300 Call Report) for reporting institutions that demonstrated some level of investment in CUSO services. We tested the relationship between selected accounts, as illustrated in our theoretical model using PLS-SEM in SmartPLS®. From this, we derived an empirical model that we used to evaluate the R^2 values of the endogenous variables in our model. We also evaluated the path coefficients that demonstrate the degree of correlation between our model constructs. These path coefficients were also evaluated based on statistical significance by reviewing their associated t Statistics and p-values via bootstrapping with a bootstrapping sample of 500 iterations.

Results

Analysis

The mean, standard error, t statistics, and p-values were calculated in SmartPLS® as part of the initial run of the PLS algorithm. We found support for three of the five relationships that we explored in our model. Significant associations exist between CUSO Investment and Deposits between CUSO Investment and Earnings and between Deposits and Delinquency.

Our model demonstrated no support for relationships between Earnings and Delinquency or CUSO Investment and Delinquency. Intuitively, we had expected to find support for both of these relationships, but our model demonstrates a nonsignificant relationship between Earnings and Delinquency and CUSO Investment and Delinquency.

We assessed the discriminant validity of our model constructs by evaluating the heterotrait-monotrait (HTMT) ratios. We benchmarked each HTMT ratio against the long-established threshold of 90 (Gold et al. 2001). We did not observe any HTMT ratio greater than .90 for any of the constructs in our proposed model. Because of this finding, we assert that sufficient discriminant validity exists between our model constructs.

In addition to evaluating discriminant validity, we assessed the inner variation inflation factors (VIF) for our model. We note that none of the inner VIF values exceeded 5.0 (Hair et al. 2012). We can forego concerns about excessive multicollinearity between the constructs of our model.

Our PLS-SEM analysis allowed us to construct an empirical model that illustrates the relationships that we found between the constructs that we used in our model (Fig. 2). Our model explains nearly 75% of the variance observed in credit union delinquency ($R^2 = 0.7475$). This variance is explained primarily through an indirect effect from CUSO Investment → Deposits → Delinquency.

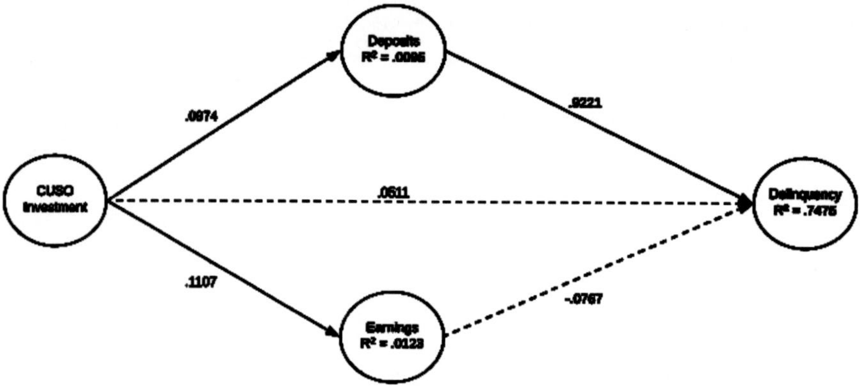

Fig. 2 Empirical model of CUSO investment and delinquency

General Discussion

The results from our analysis lend support to three of the five hypotheses that we tested. We found significant associations between CUSO Investment and Deposits and CUSO Investment and Earnings. There was a significant association between Deposits and Delinquency.

Our results did not support two hypotheses that we thought would have been supported (H_{1b}) and (H_3). There was no support for a meaningful association between CUSO Investment and Delinquency. Similarly, we did not find support for an association between Earnings and Delinquency.

RQ1. What Role Does CUSO Investment Play in Explaining Credit Union Delinquency?

CUSO Investment does not contribute to explaining delinquency by way of a direct association. As demonstrated by our empirical model, this association was nonsignificant ($\beta = 0.0511$, $t = 1.352$, $p = 0.177$). CUSO Investment, however, does serve to partially explain delinquency by contributing to the indirect effect, CUSO Investment → Deposits → Delinquency. This pathway in our model provided the only statistically significant link between CUSO Investment and Delinquency, again, an indirect effect.

RQ2. What Role Does CUSO Investment Play in Explaining Deposits?

CUSO Investment has a significant association with deposits ($\beta = 0.0974$, $t = 3.671$, $p < 0.001$). Although the amount of variation that is explained by the relationship between CUSO Investment and Deposits is small ($R^2 = 0.009$), the association between the two variables is positive, and it is statistically significant. We did, however, expect that CUSO Investment and Deposits would have been much more strongly associated, and the amount of variance in Deposits explained by CUSO Investment should have been much higher.

RQ3. What Role Does CUSO Investment Play in Explaining Earnings?

CUSO Investment appears to be significantly associated with Earnings. The amount of variation in Earnings that is explained by CUSO Investment is small ($R^2 = 0.0123$), however the association between CUSO Investment and Earnings is positive and statistically significant ($\beta = 0.1107$, $t = 2.116$, $p = 0.035$). Our findings suggest that CUSO Investment can have a positive effect on influencing Earnings. Still, there are several other variables that we did not explore in this paper that are likely to have a larger influence on earnings.

RQ4. What Role Does the Amount of Deposits Play in Explaining Credit Union Delinquency?

The strongest association in our model was found between Deposits and Credit Union Delinquency ($\beta = 0.927$, $t = 5.367$, $p < 0.001$). The practical implication of this association is that credit union executives can monitor the account balances of deposit accounts as one means of early detection for when delinquent account balances might be increasing as Credit Unions utilize the increased deposits to increase lending opportunities for income generation.

It would make sense that in our model, we expect deposits to increase as investment in CUSOs increase as this would drive more members; however, this would increase some risk to the organization and their delinquency as the organization would utilize those deposits for loans granted to their membership. Under transaction cost theory, this is critical for the decision implications because it could have an overwhelming adverse effect if the delinquency is too high or becomes out of control for the firm.

RQ5. What Role Does the Amount of Earnings Play in Explaining Credit Union Delinquency?

Earnings did not play a significant role in explaining Delinquency (β = −0.077, t = 0.410, $p = 0.682$). This finding contradicts our initial supposition that Earnings might play a factor in explaining Delinquency. The practical implication of this finding is that it informs credit union executives that Earnings, as measured by non-interest income, lack explanatory power for Delinquency.

Limitations

Our study was limited in that it did not include the asset size of the credit unions that comprised the data sample used. Asset size might be used in future research as a control variable to determine if the findings that we report in this paper will hold true across differently sized credit unions. Similarly, the inclusion of the number of members for each credit union might have strengthened the results that were realized in our analysis. Additional control variables might improve the explanatory power of our model as it related to the low R^2 values for Deposits and Earnings.

Our study was also limited in that we did not investigate any moderating or mediating effects. The addition of moderating variables to our model might serve to strengthen (or reduce) some of the associations that we observed in our model. For future research, we would consider the addition of possible moderators such as geographical setting (i.e., urban or rural), credit union type (i.e., state or federal), or credit union constituency (single membership category or multiple membership categories).

We explored the addition of mediating variables such as assets, other income streams aside from non-interest income and loans. The addition of these variables did not substantially improve our results, and, in some cases, the inclusion of these variables resulted in high degrees of multicollinearity. More sophisticated techniques can be employed in follow on research to address the issues with multicollinearity while simultaneously exploring the impact that the addition of mediating variables might have on our model.

Our research study focused exclusively on credit unions and CUSOs. While these institutions provide similar services to more substantial banking institutions, there could exist some unique credit union and CUSO features that limit the generalizability of our findings concerning larger banking institutions.

Overall, the limitations of this study unlock several future studies that can help further understand the credit union industry. One such future study might expand on a secondary analysis that we conducted using our model constructs in a multiple linear regression exercise. Until this point, our results have pointed to the use of CUSO Investment, Earnings, and Deposits as mechanisms to monitor and explain variation in Delinquency. Credit union executives might find utility in using these same constructs to attempt to predict Delinquency. We performed a multiple regression analysis in RStudio® and observed a moderate level of explanation of the variation in Delinquency when considering CUSO Investment, Earnings, and Deposits F(3,14,263) = 14,706, $p < 0.001$, $R^2 = 0.7475$, $R^2_{adj} = 0.7475$). The resulting multiple regression equation can be used to predict approximately 75% of the variation in Delinquency.

$$y = a + b_1x_1 + b_2x_{2+} b_3x_3 \ldots$$

(where a = intercept, b = regression coefficient, x = independent variable)

$$\text{Delinquency} \approx -243{,}960.01 + 0.20(\text{CUSO Investment}) + 0.01(\text{Deposits}) \\ -0.12(\text{Earnings})$$

or

$$\text{Delinquency} \approx -243{,}960.01 + 0.20(\text{CUSO Dollars invested}) \\ +0.01(\text{Total Shares}) - 0.12(\text{Non} - \text{interest Income})$$

The regression model demonstrates how the cumulative effect of CUSO Investment and Earnings will decrease Delinquency. Additionally, when factoring total shares, delinquency is positive and increased. Although seemingly counter intuitive, our findings support what the industry would suspect. When Credit Unions increase their deposit bases typically, they would increase their lending to maximize their profit. This makes sense because many Credit Unions will pay higher interest rates on their deposit-based accounts. To continue to pay these higher rates, these non-profits must maximize their earnings potential with the appropriate level of risk. This would explain their higher risk appetite to lend money on deposit and increase their delinquency ratio.

We note that this regression model is limited to only explaining approximately 75% of the variation in Delinquency. Still, we position this as a bookmark for a future research effort that could employ machine learning techniques to develop a more robust predictive model.

Conclusion

Our study suggests that credit union delinquency may be monitored by observing changes in account balances for CUSO Investment and Deposits. We also propose a predictive model that credit union executives might use to predict credit union delinquency. These contributions serve to expand the research literature about credit unions while concurrently providing a practical application for credit union executives. Credit union executives can refer to the findings from this research study to inform their decision processes when considering whether or not CUSO investment has a sound basis for their respective credit unions.

References

Akkus, O., Cookson, J. A., and Hortacsu, A. (2015). The determinants of bank mergers: A revealed preference analysis. *Management Science, 62*(8) 2241-2258.

Barr, M. S. (2004). Banking the poor. *Yale J. on Reg 21* 121.

Bauer, K. J., Miles, L. L., and Nishikawa, T. (2009). The effect of mergers on credit union performance. *Journal of Banking and Finance, 33*(12) 2267-2274.

Berger, A. N., El Ghoul, S., Guedhami, O., and Roman, R. A. (2016). Internationalization and bank risk. *Management Science, 63*(7) 2283-2301.

Black, H., and Dugger, R. H. (1981). Credit union structure, growth and regulatory problems. *The journal of Finance, 36*(2), 529-538.

Carter, S. P., Skiba, P. M., and Tobacman, J. (2011). Pecuniary mistakes? Payday borrowing by credit union members. *Financial literacy: implications for retirement security and the financial marketplace* 145-157.

Coase, R. H. (1937). The nature of the firm. *economica, 4*(16), 386-405.

Cohen, K. J., Maier, S. F., and Vander Weide, J. H. (1981). Recent developments in management science in banking. *Management Science 27*(10) 1097-1119.

Davis, K. (2001). Credit union governance and survival of the cooperative form. *Journal of Financial Services Research 19*(2-3) 197-210.

De Vericourt, F., and Lobo, M. S. (2009). Resource and revenue management in nonprofit operations. *Operations research, 57*(5) 1114-1128.

Elsinger, H., Lehar, A., and Summer, M. (2006). Risk assessment for banking systems. *Management Science, 52*(9) 1301-1314.

Ely, D. P., and Robinson, K. J. (2009). Credit unions and small business lending. *Journal of Financial Services Research, 35*(1), 53.

Engemann, K. J., and Miller, H. E. (1992). Operations risk management at a major bank. *Interfaces 22*(6) 140-149.

Feinberg, R. M., and Rahman, A. A. (2001). A causality test of the relationship between bank and credit union lending rates in local markets. *Economics Letters, 71*(2) 271-275.

Fountain, W. V. (2006). *The Credit Union World: Theory, Process, Practice: Cases and Application*: AuthorHouse.

Fraisse, H., Lé, M., and Thesmar, D. (2019). The real effects of bank capital requirements. *Management Science.*

Fried, H. O., Lovell, C. K., and Eeckaut, P. V. (1993). Evaluating the performance of US credit unions. *Journal of Banking and Finance 17*(2-3) 251-265.

Geyskens, I., Steenkamp, J.-B. E., and Kumar, N. (2006). Make, buy, or ally: A transaction cost theory meta-analysis. *Academy of management journal, 49*(3), 519-543.

Goddard, J., McKillop, D., and Wilson, J. O. (2008). The diversification and financial performance of US credit unions. *Journal of Banking and Finance, 32*(9) 1836-1849.

Gold, A. H., Malhotra, A., and Segars, A. H. (2001). Knowledge management: An organizational capabilities perspective. *Journal of management information systems 18*(1) 185-214.

Griffith, R., Waithe, K., Lorde, T., and Craigwell, R. (2009). The contribution of credit unions to the national development of Barbados.

Hair, J., Sarstedt, M., Ringle, C., and Mena, J. (2012). An assessment of the use of partial least squares structural equation modeling in marketing research. *Journal of the Academy of Marketing Science, 40*(3), 414-433. doi:https://doi.org/10.1007/s11747-011-0261-6

Jain, A., and Lawrence, E. R. (2014). Asset quality comparison of subchapter s banks and credit unions. *International Journal of Finance 26*(3).

Jones, P. A. (2006). Giving credit where it's due: Promoting financial inclusion through quality credit unions. *Local Economy 21*(1), 36-48.

Kusy, M. I., and Ziemba, W. T. (1986). A bank asset and liability management model. *Operations research, 34*(3), 356-376.

Lioliou, E., and Willcocks, L. P. (2019). The Transaction Cost Economics Discourse. In *Global Outsourcing Discourse* (pp. 185-219): Springer.

Lueg, R., Schmaltz, C., and Tomkus, M. (2019). Business Models in Banking: A Cluster Analysis Using Archival Data. *Trames 23*(1), 79-107.

Makino, S., and Neupert, K. E. (2000). National culture, transaction costs, and the choice between joint venture and wholly owned subsidiary. *Journal of International Business Studies, 31*(4), 705-713.

Nembhard, J. G. (2013). Community development credit unions: Securing and protecting assets in black communities. *The Review of Black Political Economy, 40*(4), 459-490.

Pana, E., Vitzthum, S., and Willis, D. (2015). The impact of internet-based services on credit unions: a propensity score matching approach. *Review of Quantitative Finance and Accounting, 44*(2), 329-352.

Penney, C. R., and Combs, J. G. (2019). A transaction cost perspective of alliance portfolio diversity. *Journal of Management Studies.*

Rindfleisch, A. (2019). Transaction cost theory: past, present and future. *AMS Review* 1-13.

Rubin, G., Overstreet, G., Beling, P., and Rajaratnam, K. (2013). A dynamic theory of the credit union. *Annals of Operations Research 205*(1) 29-53. doi:https://doi.org/10.1007/s10479-012-1246-7

Sestu, M. C., and Majocchi, A. (2018). Family firms and the choice between wholly owned subsidiaries and joint ventures: A transaction costs perspective. *Entrepreneurship Theory and Practice* 1042258718797925.

Shimizu, K. (2012). Bankruptcies of small firms and lending relationship. *Journal of Banking and Finance, 36*(3), 857-870.

Smith, D. J. (1984). A theoretic framework for the analysis of credit union decision making. *The journal of Finance, 39*(4) 1155-1168.

Smith, D. J. (1988). Credit union rate and earnings retention decisions under uncertainty and taxation. *Journal of Money, Credit and Banking 20*(1) 119-131.

Sobek, M. (2003). Methods and systems for facilitating investment transactions and accounting for banks and credit unions. In: Google Patents.

Sollenberger, H. M., and Stanecki, A. W. (2009). Credit union financial performance: the impact of asset size: bigness clearly gives a credit union advantages. *Bank Accounting and Finance 22*(3), 3-15.

Thompson, T. N. (2019). Merger, huh, what is it good for: the impacts of credit union mergers. *North Carolina Banking Institute 23*, 379.

Vuillemey, G. (2019). Bank interest rate risk management. *Management Science.*

Wilcox, J. A., and Berkely, U. (2011). The increasing importance of credit unions in small business lending. *Small Business Administration. Office of Advocacy. Washington, DC.*

Williamson, O. E. (1993). Opportunism and its critics. *Managerial and decision economics 14*(2), 97-107.

Xue, M., Hitt, L. M., and Chen, P.-Y. (2011). Determinants and outcomes of internet banking adoption. *Management Science, 57*(2) 291-307.

Do Birds of a Feather Flock Together? An Exploration of Why Consumers Follow Beauty Influencers on Social Media: An Abstract

Gina A. Tran, Atefeh Yazdanparast, and David Strutton

Abstract Influencers offer marketers a compelling combination of a large audience, a personable story that consumers often perceive as authentic, and the ability to reach across geographical boundaries. Specifically in the beauty industry, where products are less tangible, influencers easily bring products to life. This research aims to explore the nature of why individuals choose to follow certain influencers by investigating the beauty influencer industry and the connection between the follower and influencer.

The source credibility model may explain the phenomenal success of influencer marketing. The source credibility model relies on the source effect theory, with the influencer as the communication source (Erdogan 1999). In addition to the source credibility model and concept of normal attractiveness, social comparison theory may also explain why consumers follow specific beauty influencers. However, due to the lack of knowledge and limited literature about why consumers follow beauty influencers, an exploratory qualitative research design was deemed appropriate.

Following a grounded theory approach (Glaser and Strauss 1967), the responses to open-ended questions were first read in an attempt to acquire a feel for the data. Next, researchers interpreted the qualitative information and focused on coding the responses based on consistencies across participants' answers independently. Identified were verified and refined by checking the qualitative data and confirming the interpretations (Glaser and Strauss 1967). Analysis revealed four themes: authenticity, relatability, trustworthiness, and similarity. These concepts reflect the

G. A. Tran
Florida Gulf Coast University, Fort Myers, FL, USA
e-mail: gtran@fgcu.edu

A. Yazdanparast (✉)
Clark University, Worcester, MA, USA
e-mail: ayazdanparast@clarku.edu

D. Strutton
University of North Texas, Denton, TX, USA
e-mail: david.strutton@unt.edu

F. Pantoja, S. Wu (eds.), *From Micro to Macro: Dealing with Uncertainties in the Global Marketplace*, Developments in Marketing Science: Proceedings of the Academy of Marketing Science, https://doi.org/10.1007/978-3-030-89883-0_42

reasons why participants follow their favorite beauty influencers on social media. Defined as clear communication of the intent behind social media posts depicting influencers with branded products, authenticity is expected to impact trustworthiness as well. Relatability, defined as ease of establishing connection due to understanding, indicates the importance of sympathy in the social influencer-follower relationship. Trustworthiness refers to the belief that the influencers will be truthful and open. Similarity or perceived homophily between the influencer and his/her followers is the degree of resemblance (in beliefs, education, social status, etc.). Physical attractiveness was not an important factor for following beauty influencers. This finding provided indirect support for the importance of similarity with and relatability to the influencer, as most people do not meet the stringent, and often unrealistic, beauty standards depicted by media. Overall, the results contribute to the literature on source effectiveness and social media marketing by identifying factors that motivate social media users to follow others on social media.

Keywords Social media · Beauty influencers · Authenticity · Relatability

References Available Upon Request

The Multifaceted Interplay between Firms and the Financial Community: A Marketing Perspective: An Abstract

Hanieh Sardashti and Roger Calantone

Abstract We employ a scenario-based behavioral experiment to test the impact of customer-based brand equity disclosure and customer satisfaction on an analyst's stock price forecast. The results suggest that financial analysts favorably factor the increase in the value of customer-based brand equity information into their stock price forecasts. However, we do not find support for the effect of customer satisfaction on the stock price forecast analyzing the experimental data. Our results suggest that financial analysts consider brand equity a more robust leading indicator of economic performance than customer satisfaction, possibly because customer satisfaction captures customers' prior experiences with a brand. Previous research also shows that customer-based brand equity has a significant and massive impact on a firm's future financial performance (Mizik 2014). Moreover, we observe a synergistic interaction (positive/non-linear) effect of customer satisfaction and customer-based brand equity information on stock price forecast. These results indicate that analysts pay attention to customer satisfaction information when customer-based brand equity information is available and that both demonstrate a positive uptake in value.

This paper also includes an empirical test on customer-based brand equity's effect on the analyst's target price (i.e., a projected security price level over a 12-month horizon) and forecast accuracy, which refers to the absolute value of the forecast earnings error. This test uses analyst-level archival data, which tracks sell-side U. S.-based financial analysts who follow 147 mono-brand firms (i.e., firms in which a single brand embodies most of the firm's businesses) in 19 industries from 2007–2015. We find that customer-based brand equity reduces earnings forecast errors and is positively associated with the target price. As a proxy for skill, the analyst's experience moderates the relationship between customer-based brand

H. Sardashti (✉)
University of North Florida, Jacksonville, FL, USA
e-mail: h.sardashti@unf.edu

R. Calantone
Michigan State University, East Lansing, MI, USA
e-mail: rogercal@msu.edu

F. Pantoja, S. Wu (eds.), *From Micro to Macro: Dealing with Uncertainties in the Global Marketplace*, Developments in Marketing Science: Proceedings of the Academy of Marketing Science, https://doi.org/10.1007/978-3-030-89883-0_43

equity and the analyst's target price and forecast accuracy. Interestingly, the positive effect of brand equity on target price is weaker for more experienced analysts.

In summary, our findings suggest that firms can benefit from voluntary disclosure of customer-based brand equity beyond their traditional financial reporting. Increasing the quality of marketing information disclosure by including brand equity can redirect investors' attention to the firm, justify marketing costs, and improve its valuation.

Keywords Brand Equity · Customer satisfaction · Financial analysts · Marketing strategy

References Available Upon Request

Social Media Interactions and Offline Purchasing Decisions: Differences Between Products and Services

Maria Leticia Ribeiro Lousada, Paula Braz de Matos e Souza, and José Marcos Carvalho de Mesquita

Abstract Internet commerce continues to explore consumer behavior and their relationship with companies. In this context, special attention is given to the following drivers of purchasing intentions: social media advertising; bloggers or digital influencers; and electronic word-of-mouth (e-WOM). This research attempts to uncover the differences among the said factors regarding the purchase type—product or service. In particular, we studied the opinion of the social media users, who responded to a 20-item online questionnaire hosted by GoogleDocs. The study was conducted in Brazil and included two samples: one formed by customers of a clothing store and another formed by customers of an aesthetics center. Upon data analysis using ANOVA and Structural Equation Modeling, we identified significant differences between the two purchase types. We also observed the biggest influence of e-WOM in both cases. Digital Influencers represent the second most important factor. Finally, social media advertising is only the third factor which affects clothing purchasing decisions but not beauty service. The essential research contributions are: joint testing of the three communication forms; attesting the moderator effect of product type and evaluation of the usefulness of information from the interviewees' viewpoint.

Keywords Social media · e-WOM · Digital influencers · Consumer behavior

M. L. R. Lousada · P. B. de Matos e Souza · J. M. C. de Mesquita (✉)
FUMEC University, Belo Horizonte, Brazil
e-mail: maria.lousada@araujo.com.br; paulabraz@uit.br; jose.mesquita@fumec.br

F. Pantoja, S. Wu (eds.), *From Micro to Macro: Dealing with Uncertainties in the Global Marketplace*, Developments in Marketing Science: Proceedings of the Academy of Marketing Science, https://doi.org/10.1007/978-3-030-89883-0_44

Introduction

Internet potential and characteristics have made it an influential marketing channel, which affects consumer behavior and attitudes toward companies. Its expansion has promoted and spread social media as a significant element in the daily routine of a great part of the global population, even changing buying patterns (Ramanathan et al. 2017). Internet and, more specifically, social media represent an interesting option for companies to communicate and interact with their actual and potential customers (Vinerean et al. 2013), as they became important communication media, somewhat replacing traditional ones (Wang and Zhang 2012). Consequently, social media communication turned out an essential factor influencing various aspects of consumer behavior, such as awareness, information acquisition, opinions, attitudes, purchase, and post-purchase evaluation (Mangold and Faulds 2009). Several studies addressed the effects of social media interactions on customers related variables, such as purchase intention/decision (Vianna et al. 2016; Zhu and Zhang 2010), satisfaction and loyalty (Anderson and Srinivasan 2003; Srinivasan et al. 2002), trust (Chen and Dhillon 2003; Gefen and Straub 2004), or company's sales (Nunes and de Mesquita 2018; Tang et al. 2014; You et al. 2015).

In social media, three communication forms have prominence. The first, social media advertising, imposes on companies the need for adopting strategic postures consistent with the market trends. Increasingly connected, consumers base their buying decisions on comments and brand reputation on social media, which have become a powerful tool for companies to search consumers, their interests, desires, and pleasures (Arnaud et al. 2016).

Communication between companies and consumers is also affected by the power of digital influencers' opinion, the second factor, as bloggers became popular personalities in social media. These influencers generally have a large number of followers in their respective media and use this environment to generate content, share their opinions and personal feelings. They are considered influencers and opinion-makers because of their ability to affect followers' behavior and attitudes (Uzunoğlu and Kip 2014).

Consumer exposure and participation in the virtual environment, known as electronic word-of-mouth (e-WOM), is the third, where information and opinions about products and services are made available to other users. Its accessibility, due to its insertion in an easy-to-access environment, along with its reliability, as the messages are posted by customers, are the main factors strengthening the e-WOM relevance (You et al. 2015).

Although many advances have been achieved, consistently attesting the influence of social media on consumer behavior, there are some gaps still deserving more in-depth studies. The first gap is the moderating effect of the purchase type, good or service, which could play on distinct purchase conditions (Babić Rosario et al. 2016), or more specifically, the different importance consumers may attach to social media communication, regarding the product type. Seminal studies (e.g., Zeithaml 1981; Zeithaml et al. 2013) showed that consumers evaluate goods and services under distinct aspects, mainly because of the service intangibility, which prevents the quality assessment in a pre-purchase stage. Consequently, functional and financial risk increase and the information search focuses more on personal than institutional sources, because the former is considered trustworthy. In such cases, the referral gains importance. Even though the Internet reduced differences in the search process, by making all attributes searchable (Huang et al. 2009), this topic remains unclear in marketing literature.

The second gap concerns the commonly used metrics. Most papers evaluate parameters such as number or content of the reviews, comments, posts, and ads, and correlate them with either sales or purchase intention. However, only a few papers consider interviewees as information receivers and measure the usefulness of the received information on purchasing decisions (Zhang et al. 2010).

Facing the above, we attempt to answer the following research question: how different is the effect on consumer purchasing decisions respectively produced by social media advertising, digital influencers, and e-WOM, depending on the purchase type—product or service. To address the first gap, we interviewed Instagram followers of two brick-and-mortar retailers located in Brazil, one clothing store, specialized in female fashion, and one aesthetics center. To address the second gap, we used an unusual approach, by asking interviewees to evaluate the importance they attribute to the three social media communication concerning their purchase behavior.

Literature Review

Social Media Advertising

Organizations use social media as a communication tool to get closer to their clientele, aiming at gaining their engagement with content that arouses their attention. Therefore, companies use social media campaigns as facilitators of their contact with customers (Macnamara and Zerfass 2012).

Social media is a strategic channel for companies, in which it is possible to establish relationships with customers, perform calls, surveys, lead generation, sales promotion, delivery channels and paid advertising (Schmitt 2012). Regardless of the purpose, information about the advertised brand must be relevant, so that consumer gets involved. Social media tighten the relationship between companies and customers, who use this environment to find information about the desired product and service and brand information (Schivinski and Dabrowski 2014; Li and Bernoff 2011). The easy access to social media by organizations and users boosts its growing use as a communication tool and is recognized throughout the world as an essential communication media (Macnamara and Zerfass 2012).

In order to succeed in the virtual environment, companies need to develop and adjust their online marketing strategy constantly. Therefore, they need to be aware of behavioral changes and identify new values desired by consumers to achieve long-term success (Vinerean et al. 2013). Brazilian consumers greatly value the information made available on products and services on the web (Garcia 2012). Accordingly, Vianna et al. (2016) identified the positive influence viral marketing exerts on purchase intention and brand visibility.

Digital Influencers

In the virtual environment, digital influencers, who are bloggers with many followers, represent the new types of celebrity. These influencers are recognized as opinion-makers. There is a tendency on the part of companies to promote themselves using digital influencers in three different ways: by promoting their products or services, by offering discount coupons, and by asking for referrals (Korotina and Jargalsaikhan 2016).

In terms of market communications, digital influencers can play a key role in providing opportunities, particularly by introducing new products and services, and their opinion leader status is responsible for boosting sales (Cheung and Thadani 2012; Filieri and McLeay 2014). These opinion-makers have innovative behavior, are knowledgeable about particular products and services so that they can influence consumers (Van Eck et al. 2011).

Lyons and Henderson (2005) state that companies should seek partnerships with "online opinion leaders" because they are willing to share their knowledge with those who are less informed and who follow them. Online consumers tend to accept many bloggers' recommendations at face value, which becomes a crucial factor in making purchasing decisions (Hsu et al. 2013; Hsiao et al. 2010).

Electronic Word of Mouth

Berger (2014) mentions that people often share opinions and information with their social ties, and word of mouth has a major impact on consumer behavior. Zhang et al. (2010) and Elwalda et al. (2016) argue that comments can be very useful and persuasive to consumers. Chu and Choi (2011) argue that consumers have important potential to reach the global audience quickly and easily, and so understanding e-WOM in social media is crucial.

According to Tang et al. (2014), 92% of potential clients read comments from other consumers before making their purchases. These data indicate that positive communication created by users can influence other consumers' purchasing decisions, confirming that e-WOM influences buying behavior (Schivinski and Dabrowski 2014; Chen et al. 2011). Research conducted by the Internet Advertising Bureau points out that 90% of consumers will recommend a brand after an interaction in social networks, 80% will be more inclined to buy a brand after its promotion in social networks and 83% will be eager to try that brand's product (Glenday 2013; Zhang et al. 2010). These figures were confirmed by Tang et al. (2014), who found a direct relation between sales and positive comments (cars) or ratings (movies), and inverse relation with negative comments or ratings.

Differences Between Products and Services

Quality assessment involves different aspects, depending on the product type. As for goods, there are search attributes, which can be experienced or at least evaluated before the purchase, however, for services, there are only experience attributes, which can be tested only after the purchase. Furthermore, depending on service features, consumers do not have the knowledge to evaluate, in such situations, the credence attributes are the most relevant (Ali and Garg 2017; Zeithaml et al. 2013).

When evaluating a product in which technical results are dominant, consumers seek information from professional sources (e.g., expert reviews) that offer more impersonal information (Zhang et al. 2010). However, when evaluating a product in which interaction processes are dominant, such as services, consumers are more likely to consult the experiences of other consumers (e.g., e-WOM), relying on the reliability of personal experiences. Gefen and Straub (2004) showed that trust is an important predictor of purchase intentions, for products and services.

Hajli (2014) points out that online engagement, such as evaluations of products or services, are influenced by e-WOM and thus increase trust and reduce perceived risk. Babić Rosario et al. (2016) corroborate these findings stating that consumers use electronic word of mouth as a source of uncertainty reduction and help in choosing the best offer. A close related study was undertaken by Huang et al. (2009), by investigating differences between search and experience goods at the search stage and purchase behavior. Search goods are those for which the most important attributes to evaluate quality are discoverable before the consumption and experience goods are those for which the attributes are mostly discoverable during the interaction. Their results indicated the greater influence of consumer feedback on experience purchases than good acquisitions. Although not direct investigating differences between products and services, You et al. (2015) observed a greater influence of e-WOM on sales of products with low trialability, what is the case of services compared with products.

Thus, we hypothesize:

(H1): The effect of social media ads is greater on product purchases than service purchases.

(H2): The effect of digital influencers is greater on service purchases than product purchases.

(H3): The effect of e-WOM is greater on service purchases than product purchases.

Research Design

We used a quantitative approach to test the model. In particular, we studied the opinion of the social media users who responded to a 20-item online questionnaire hosted by GoogleDocs addressing: purchasing decisions (PD), do Patrocínio et al. (2015), Maclennan et al. (2014); social media advertising (SMA), Menegatti et al. (2017), Rosa (2010); e-WOM, do Patrocínio et al. (2015); digital influencers (DI), Korotina and Jargalsaikhan (2016), Hsu et al. (2013). The questionnaire also included questions concerning socio-demographic profile.

The study was conducted in Brazil and included two samples: one formed by customers of a clothing store and another formed by customers of an aesthetics center. All respondents were followers of the companies' Instagram Profile. Data were analyzed using ANOVA to measure the differences in evaluation of each indicator, and Structural Equation Modeling, Partial Least Square method, to measure the influence of social media communication on purchasing decisions.

Results

We received 520 responses, 204—from the aesthetics center clients and 316 from the clothing store customers. The sub-samples represent a similar pattern in gender and educational level, both composed mainly by women (about 90%), with high educational degrees (80% with college or graduate). The clothing store specializes in female fashion, so it is an expected result, but such a great number of women in the aesthetics center clientele is a surprising result. The subsamples have differences in the other three variables. In the clothing store sample, 50% are single and 44% are married, but in the aesthetics center sample, these numbers are 60% and 33%, respectively. 53% of the clothing store customers are between 25–34 years old and 20% below 24, whereas these proportions in the aesthetics center are 33% and 30%, respectively. Finally, 40% of the clothing store customers and 60% of the aesthetics center customers belong to the lower-income households.

The ANOVA results are presented in the appendix, separated by construct. Regarding purchasing decisions (PD), PD2 (I stopped buying something based on the opinions posted on social media) and PD4 (I choose to start relationships with companies that are highly recommended by friends on social media) showed significant differences, with higher values for services. So, opinions posted on social media and positive purchase experiences affect more purchasing decisions on services than products.

Concerning Social Media Advertising (SMA), SMA2 ("I get information and news from the brands I follow on social media") e SMA4 ("I purchase products/services based on company-provided information on social media") presented significant differences and higher grades for products. Thus, SMA has a greater importance for product purchasers than service purchasers.

As for Digital Influencers (DI), all indicators presented significant differences, with higher values attributed by product buyers. So, product purchasers consider DI's information more relevant than service purchasers. Results indicated significant differences for e-WOM1 ("the opinion of my friends posted on social media about companies, products and services is important for me"), e-WOM2 ("I consult my social media friends before purchasing a company's products or services for the first time"), and e-WOM3 ("before I buy, I check with my friends about the reputation they share on social media of a company, product, or service"). Service purchasers granted higher grades for all indicators. The results highlight the greater importance of personal references for service customers.

Regarding the structural model test, each sub-sample was evaluated separately. Variable PD2 was excluded, in clothing sample, due to insignificant load. Table 1 presents the reliability and validity tests. All Cronbach's Alpha and composite reliability were above 0.7, attesting the reliability and the AVE above 0.5 for all constructs confirms convergent validity.

Fornell-Larcker criterion (Table 2) confirmed discriminant validity, as the square root of AVE, displayed in the main diagonal, are greater than the correlation coefficients among constructs.

Table 3 presents the structural model results. Ads in social media exert a positive influence on clothing' purchasing decisions, but not for aesthetics services, and therefore H1 is confirmed. Consequently, the positive perception of fashion consumers about the ads performed by companies in social media was confirmed, which demonstrates consumers are open to companies that use Internet as a means of promotion and sales, in line with Schmitt (2012). As for aesthetics services, the relation is not significant, possibly because service evaluation depends on experiential qualities. This makes the ad information less trustworthy (Zeithaml et al. 2013) and reduces the influence of commercial ads.

Digital influencers exert a positive influence on purchasing decisions, for both products and services, as proposed by Korotina and Jargalsaikhan (2016), Lyons and Henderson (2005) and Uzunoğlu and Kip (2014). Opinion leaders express in social media reports and experiences of products and services they already used. Due to a large number of followers and their reliability in the transmitted messages, they influence the purchasing decisions of both products and services. Although the service coefficient is slightly higher, there is no statistically significant difference. Based on this, H2 is not confirmed.

Table 1 Reliability and validity tests

	Cronbach's alpha		CR		AVE	
	Clothing	Aesthetics	Clothing	Aesthetic	Clothing	Aesthetic
PD	0.821	0.819	0.875	0.871	0.584	0.533
SMA	0.769	0.794	0.844	0.855	0.521	0.543
DI	0.906	0.929	0.930	0.946	0.726	0.779
e-WOM	0.852	0.866	0.899	0.908	0.0691	0.711

Table 2 Discriminant validity

	Clothing				Aesthetics center			
	PD	SMA	DI	e-WOM	PD	SMA	DI	e-WOM
PD	**0.764**				**0.730**			
SMA	0.619	**0.722**			0.363	**0.737**		
DI	0.612	0.602	**0.852**		0.457	0.454	**0.883**	
e-WOM	0.694	0.621	0.596	**0.831**	0.615	0.458	0.384	**0.843**

Table 3 Structural model coefficients

	Clothing		Aesthetics center	
Variable	Coefficient	Significance	Coefficient	Significance
SMA	0.219	***	0.014	ns
DI	0.229	***	0.255	***
e-WOM	0.422	***	0.511	***
$\bar{R}^2$	0.564		0.435	

Significance level: *** 0.000%; *ns* non-significant

e-WOM is the one that most influences the purchasing decisions, for both products and services, in line with Zhang et al. (2010), Elwalda et al. (2016). So, we can say that consumers value the opinions posted online, and these views have considerable relevance in the purchasing decisions. The coefficient is higher in the aesthetics center estimation, in line with Babić Rosario et al. (2016) who identified the greater influence of e-WOM in sales of services and Huang et al. (2009) for whom consumers' feedbacks have greater influence in the case of experience goods. Therefore, H3 is confirmed, attesting the importance of personal information in services purchase. The considerable influence of e-WOM on the purchasing decisions of beauty services is highly related to the properties that surround services and the importance of consumer attributes in receiving the opinion of another user.

The explanation power is higher for clothing purchases, $\bar{R}2$ of .564, than for aesthetics services, $\bar{R}2$ of .435. This lower result should be attributed to the insignificance of SMA in services acquisitions. Summing up, we can observe the biggest influence of e-WOM in both cases. This is an expected outcome, as currently consumers search for information about products and services on social media and e-WOM is regarded as the most influential. The second most important factor is Digital Influencers, who became a very influent source of information. Social media communication is the third factor for clothing purchases and it is not significant for service acquisition. The third place was expected, as consumers search and trust more in referrals than the company's advertisement. However, the non-significance in the case of the aesthetics center is a surprising result. Maybe because of the personal characteristic this kind of service takes, the provider's trustworthiness remains in doubt unless good references are published on social media.

Regarding the research question, there are significant differences between the two purchase types. For aesthetics services, the e-WOM is higher, attesting the great importance of referrals as the intangibility increases. The digital influencers have similar importance, while social media advertising is important only for clothing customers.

General Discussion

The present study analyzed the current expansion of the Internet, a tool that consolidates itself as one of the most important means of global communication. In this environment, where the number of connected users grows considerably, e-commerce has led companies to be more present and more and more partaking in social media. Thus, we sought to evaluate the influence of social media on consumer purchasing decisions.

This work tested the combined effect of social media advertising (SMA), digital Influencers (DI) and electronic word-of-mouth (e-WOM) as purchasing decision drivers. All three are important in decisions about clothes and DI and e-WOM for aesthetics services purchases. In academic terms, the main contribution of this study is exactly testing the joined effect of the three antecedents. Likewise, we used an unusual approach by interviewing clients about the usefulness of social media communications and evaluate their importance on purchasing decisions. As this design is not very common in the academic literature, we consider it as a second contribution. Furthermore, we identified differences between product and service purchasing decisions, which is another academic contribution. Although this latter topic was proposed several years ago, the growth and current importance of social media on consumer behavior generate the need for new research specifically addressing this subject.

Speaking of the managerial implications, it can be pointed out that companies must be more and more active in social media in order to guarantee proximity to their consumers. Hence, they should improve their social media ads, invest in partnerships with DI and mainly encourage and monitor the feedback of their clients and followers. When it comes to fashion, companies should invest in daily posts of looks, pieces stories, promotion of their fashion products, answering and paying attention to all comments or searches posted on social media. Services demand another kind of ads, maybe highlighting trustworthiness. Investing in partnerships with digital influencers is also an important strategy as they positively influence the purchasing decisions. Online opinion leaders, or bloggers, are interesting alternatives to promote products and services.

However, the smartest strategy of all is to strengthen the attention to the online comments. In this way, the online opinions become increasingly valuable, exerting strong influence on consumers' attitudes and behavior. Any interaction with customers can be an opportunity to get more information about them. In the online environment, consumers are able to easily gather and share information related to a product with others, regardless of space or time perimeters.

Finally, limitations and suggestions should be addressed. The use of a convenience sample can be pointed out as one limitation, which prevents results generalization. Another limitation is that only one female fashion store and one aesthetics center were investigated, as other services or products may have different results. Furthermore, we had a result not confirmed, the non-influence of SMA on services purchase, which demands a deeper understanding. As suggestions for future research, it would be interesting to address other sectors such as financial or hospitality services or other types of products, maybe beauty products or electronics. It would also be interesting to develop research to understand the reasons of the non-importance of SMA in services with great interpersonal contact.

Appendix

	Questions	Clothing	Aesthetic	Sig
PD1	I prefer to buy something based on the opinions posted on social media	4.27	4.11	0.332
PD2	I stopped buying something based on the opinions posted on social media	4.47	3.44	0.000
PD3	I always come back to an establishment well-endorsed by my friends on social media	5.44	5.35	0.575
PD4	I choose to start relationships with companies that are highly recommended by friends on social media	5.29	5.44	0.331
PD5	I'd rather buy products or services from a company my friends recommend on social media than try new businesses	4.74	4.44	0.082
PD6	I prefer to buy products or services from companies with which my friends have had positive experiences and shared this insight on social media	5.70	5.40	0.040
SMA1	I consult the content produced by brands in social media	5.32	5.46	0.413
SMA2	I get information and news from the brands I follow on social media	4.58	5.10	0.003
SMA3	I opine about the content of brands that I follow on social media	3.47	3.48	0.950
SMA4	I purchase products/services based on company-provided information on social media	3.80	4.85	0.000
SMA5	I take part, via social media profile, in the process of building/improving a product or a brand process	3.30	3.22	0.685
DI1	I follow digital influencers in social media	4.26	5.08	0.000
DI2	I identify with the influencers I follow	3.68	4.31	0.002
DI3	Product/service referrals made by digital influencers influence my purchasing decisions	3.58	4.02	0.020
DI4	I trust the opinions posted by digital influencers	3.31	3.91	0.000
DI5	I believe that the digital influencers recommendations are really true	3.18	3.54	0.028
WOM1	The opinion of my friends posted on social media about companies, products and services is important for me	5.12	4.73	0.017
WOM2	I consult my social media friends before purchasing a company's products or services for the first time	4.71	3.93	0.000

	Questions	Clothing	Aesthetic	Sig
WOM3	Before I buy, I check with my friends about the reputation they share on social media of a company, product, or service	5.08	4.76	0.071
WOM4	I consider the opinion posted by my friends on social media about products, services or companies	5.18	4.86	0.049

References

Ali, I., & Garg, R. K. (2017). Marketing of Services: Challenges & Opportunities in Context of the Globalization of Business. *International Journal of Engineering and Management Research (IJEMR)*, 7(3), 522-526.

Anderson, R. E., & Srinivasan, S. S. (2003). E-satisfaction and e-loyalty: A contingency framework. *Psychology & marketing*, *20*(2), 123-138.

Arnaud, L., Mangini, E. R., Barros, T. F., & Urdan, A. T. (2016). A rede supermarket na era do marketing: um caso de mídias sociais. *Caderno Profissional de Administração da UNIMEP*, *6*(2), 118-135.

Babić Rosario, A., Sotgiu, F., De Valck, K., & Bijmolt, T. H. (2016). The effect of electronic word of mouth on sales: A meta-analytic review of platform, product, and metric factors. *Journal of Marketing Research*, *53*(3), 297-318.

Berger, J. (2014). Word of Mouth and Interpersonal Communication: A Functional View. *Journal of Consumer Psychology*.

Chen, S. C., & Dhillon, G. S. (2003). Interpreting dimensions of consumer trust in e-commerce. *Information Technology and Management*, *4*(2-3), 303-318.

Chen, Y., Fay, S., & Wang, Q. (2011). The role of marketing in social media: How online consumer reviews evolve. *Journal of Interactive Marketing*, 25(2), 85-94.

Cheung, C. M., & Thadani, D. R. (2012). The impact of electronic word-of-mouth communication: a literature analysis and integrative model. *Decision Support Systems*, *54*(1), 461-470.

Chu, S. C., & Choi, S. M. (2011). Electronic word-of-mouth in social networking sites: A cross-cultural study of the United States and China. *Journal of Global Marketing*, *24*(3), 263-281.

do Patrocínio, R. F., de Mesquita, J. M. C., & Dornas, K. B. H. (2015). Word of mouth communication and its effect on the affective commitment. In *Ideas in Marketing: Finding the New and Polishing the Old* (pp. 403-412). Springer, Cham.

Elwalda, A., Lü, K., & Ali, M. (2016). Perceived derived attributes of online customer reviews. *Computers in Human Behavior*, *56*, 306-319.

Filieri, R., & McLeay, F. (2014). E-WOM and accommodation: An analysis of the factors that influence travelers' adoption of information from online reviews. *Journal of Travel Research*, *53*(1), 44-57.

Garcia, B. (2012). Decisão de compra é cada vez mais baseada em comentários na web. Retrieved February 3rd, 2018 from: https://www.mundodomarketing.com.br/reportagens/comportamento-do-consumidor/25126/decisao-de-compra-e-cada-vez-mais-baseada-em-comentarios-na-web.html

Gefen, D., & Straub, D. W. (2004). Consumer trust in B2C e-Commerce and the importance of social presence: experiments in e-Products and e-Services. *Omega*, *32*(6), 407-424.

Glenday, J. (2013). 90% Of Customers Will Recommend Brands After Social Media Interactions. Retrieved February 3rd, 2018 from: http://www.businessinsider.com/90-of-customers-will-recommend-brands-after-social-media-interactions-2013-7.html

Hajli, M. N. (2014). A study of the impact of social media on consumers. *International Journal of Market Research*, *56*(3), 387-404.

Hsiao, K. L., Chuan-Chuan Lin, J., Wang, X. Y., Lu, H. P., & Yu, H. (2010). Antecedents and consequences of trust in online product recommendations: An empirical study in social shopping. *Online Information Review*, *34*(6), 935-953.
Hsu, C. L., Chuan-Chuan Lin, J., & Chiang, H. S. (2013). The effects of blogger recommendations on customers' online shopping intentions. *Internet Research*, *23*(1), 69-88.
Huang, P., Lurie, N. H., & Mitra, S. (2009). Searching for experience on the web: an empirical examination of consumer behavior for search and experience goods. *Journal of Marketing*, *73*(2), 55-69.
Korotina, A., & Jargalsaikhan, T. (2016). *Attitude towards Instagram micro-celebrities and their influence on consumers' purchasing decisions.*
Li, C., & Bernoff, J. (2011). *Groundswell: Winning in a World Transformed by Social Technologies.* Boston M.A.: Harvard Business Review Press.
Lyons, B., & Henderson, K. (2005). Opinion leadership in a computer-mediated environment, *Journal of Consumer Behaviour,* Vol. 4, N° 5, pp. 319-329.
Macnamara, J., & Zerfass, A. (2012). Social media communication in organizations: The challenges of balancing openness, strategy, and management. *International Journal of Strategic Communication*, 6(4), 287-308.
Maclennan, M. L. F., Lugoboni, L. F., Zittei, M. V. M., Tabata, R. Y., & Correa, H. L. (2014). Associação entre intensidade de uso de mídias sociais, credibilidade e decisão de compra. *Navus: Revista de Gestão e Tecnologia*, 4(2), pp. 65-77.
Mangold, W. G., & Faulds, D. J. (2009). *Social media: The new hybrid element of the promotion mix.* Business Horizons 52 (4), pp. 357–365.
Menegatti, M. S., Ribeiro, I., Meneghatti, M. R., & Serra, F. A. R. (2017). Decisão de Compras Pela Internet: Uma Análise a Partir do Tempo de Utilização de Mídias Sociais e da Interatividade com a Marca. *Revista Brasileira de Marketing,* 16(1), 41-54.
Nunes, R. P., & de Mesquita, J. M. C. (2018). Efeito da Comunicação Boca a Boca Eletrônica no Desempenho da Firma. *Anais do XXI Seminários de Administração*. São Paulo.
Ramanathan, U., Subramanian, N., & Parrott, G. (2017). Role of social media in retail network operations and marketing to enhance customer satisfaction. *International Journal of Operations & Production Management*, *37*(1), 105-123.
Rosa, N. G. H. D. (2010). *O impacto das redes sociais no marketing: perspectiva portuguesa* (Doctoral dissertation, Instituto Superior de Economia e Gestão).
Schivinski, B., & Dabrowski, D. (2014). The effect of social media communication on consumer perceptions of brands. *Journal of Marketing Communications*, 22(2):189-214.
Schmitt, B. (2012). The consumer psychology of brands. *Journal of Consumer Psychology*, *22*(1), 7-17.
Srinivasan, S. S., Anderson, R., & Ponnavolu, K. (2002). Customer loyalty in e-commerce: an exploration of its antecedents and consequences. *Journal of Retailing*, *78*(1), 41-50.
Tang, T., Fang, E., & Wang, F. (2014). Is neutral really neutral? The effects of neutral user-generated content on product sales. *Journal of Marketing*, *78*(4), 41-58.
Uzunoğlu, E., & Kip, S. M. (2014). Brand communication through digital influencers: Leveraging blogger engagement. *International Journal of Information Management*, *34*(5), 592-602.
Van Eck, P. S., Jager, W., & Leeflang, P. S. (2011). Opinion leaders' role in innovation diffusion: A simulation study. *Journal of Product Innovation Management*, *28*(2), 187-203.
Vianna, K. A., Mesquita, J. M. C. D., Linhares, M. R. S., & Moreira, P. D. C. G. (2016). The relationship between viral marketing, purchase intention, and brand visibility: Study with Brazilian customers. In Rediscovering the Essentiality of Marketing (pp. 229-241). Springer, Cham.
Vinerean, S., Cetina, I., Dumitrescu, L., & Tichindelean, M. (2013). The effects of social media marketing on online consumer behavior. *International Journal of Business and Management*, 8(14), 66.
Wang, C. & Zhang, P. 2012. The evolution of social commerce: the people, management, technology, and information dimensions. *Communications of the Association for Information Systems*. 31, 105–127.

You, Y., Vadakkepatt, G. G., & Joshi, A. M. (2015). A meta-analysis of electronic word-of-mouth elasticity. *Journal of Marketing*, 79(2), 19-39.

Zeithaml, V. A. (1981), "Encoding of Price Information by Consumers: An Empirical Test of the Levels of Processing Framework," in The Changing Marketing Environment: New Theories and Application. K. Bernhardt, et. al., eds., Chicago: American Marketing Association, 189-192.

Zeithaml, V. A., Bitner, M. J., & Gremler, D. G. Services Marketing: Integrating Customer Focus Across the Firm. 6th ed., McGraw-Hill, 2013.

Zhang, J. Q., Craciun, G., & Shin, D. (2010). When does electronic word-of-mouth matter? A study of consumer product reviews. *Journal of Business Research*, *63*(12), 1336-1341.

Zhu, F., & Zhang, X. (2010). Impact of online consumer reviews on sales: The moderating role of product and consumer characteristics. *Journal of Marketing*, *74*(2), 133-148.

Impact of Augmented Reality on Cross-Buying Intention at the Point of Sale: An Abstract

Björn Gorlas and Carsten D. Schultz

Abstract In view of the competitive pressure of online retailing, cross-buying behavior is increasingly important for stationary retailers (Ngobo 2004). Traditional approaches to increasing cross-buying at the point of sale, such as sales staff and product placement (Kamakura 2007), are limited. The use of new technology may overcome this limitation but has, so far, received little research attention. One such in-store technology are augmented reality application, so-called magic mirrors. Magic mirrors can provide consumers with cross-selling offers that match their originally chosen product and can be tried on virtually (Sjøbakk et al. 2017). Magic mirrors may also provide additional information to reduce the potential information deficit in comparison to online shopping.

This study examines the impact of augmented reality on consumers' cross-buying intention at the point of sale. Based on an experimental scenario setting, this study examines differences in cross-buying intention between a shopping situation with augmented reality and a shopping situation without augmented reality. The scenario specifically looks at the attractiveness of the cross-selling offer for the cross-buying intention. In this study, the attractiveness of the selling offer is formed by its perceived product benefits, price attractiveness, convenience, and fit (e.g., Maitzen 2016).

The empirical findings provide insights into the impact of augmented reality on cross-buying behavior. Beyond validating the underlying cross-buying model, the results demonstrate gender differences in cross-buying and the perception of the attractiveness of cross-selling offers whether augmented reality is present or not. The results indicate an increase of cross-buying intention for female consumers and a decrease for male consumers. Augmented reality can be used at the point of sale to create cross-selling potential, particularly at busy times in the store. As sales staff

B. Gorlas
FOM University of Applied Sciences, Dortmund, Germany
e-mail: bjoern.gorlas@fom-net.de

C. D. Schultz (✉)
University of Hagen, Hagen, Germany
e-mail: carsten.schultz@fernuni-hagen.de

F. Pantoja, S. Wu (eds.), *From Micro to Macro: Dealing with Uncertainties in the Global Marketplace*, Developments in Marketing Science: Proceedings of the Academy of Marketing Science, https://doi.org/10.1007/978-3-030-89883-0_45

can only serve a limited number of customers, retailers can combine sales staff and augmented reality technology to attend to more customers and create cross-selling offers for each customer.

The use of augmented reality increases the perception of price attractiveness and shopping convenience for women. The fit of the cross-selling offer likewise affects its attractiveness.

Additional information and functions via augmented reality can reduce consumers' information costs. Retailers may, for example, provide information on product availability, alternative sizes, and colors – especially in combination with virtual fitting. A primary challenge for such augmented reality technologies is how consumers perceive such recommendations. Do the recommendations provide additional value or are they perceived as promotional efforts and potentially intrusive?

Keywords Augmented reality · Cross-buying · Magic mirror · Magic fitting room · Point of sale · Price attractiveness · Product benefit · Product fit · Retailing · Shopping convenience

References Available Upon Request

User Acceptance of Information Technology Systems as a Driver of Innovation in the Colombian Fashion Industry: An Abstract

Lina M. Ceballos, Ana M. Ortega, Luis E. Torres, and Maria-Susana Jaramillo-Echeverri

Abstract Despite the key role innovation plays in determining competitiveness of organizations and regions (OECD 2015), there are still many challenges in the implementation of activities related to improving innovation, especially in the fashion industry (Godart et al. 2015). Based on the *Technology Acceptance Model* (TAM) (Davis 1986; Venkatesh and Davis 1996), this study proposes to examine the user acceptance of new information technology (IT) in the fashion industry in Colombia (South America) in relation to the firm's innovation performance. IT plays a major role in promoting innovation by reducing information costs and increasing inclusion (World Bank 2016). Multiple studies (e.g., Lyver and Lu 2018) confirm the influential role technology plays in the processes related to innovation. Moreover, even though TAM is highly popular among researchers, the majority of studies based on variations of TAM have been tested in the USA (Davis et al. 1992).

The original TAM posits that Perceived Usefulness (PU) and Perceived Ease of Use (PEOU) are the main beliefs influencing computer acceptance behaviors, and those beliefs are also determined by certain external variables (e.g., objective design characteristics of a system) (Davis et al. 1989). For this study, the IT considered will be of mandatory usage for employees. Consequently, the proposed model follows Venkatesh and Davis (1996), which is the original TAM with the addition of the Behavioral Intention (BI) construct and elimination of the attitude construct. Based

L. M. Ceballos
Universidad EAFIT, Medellín, Colombia
e-mail: lceball4@eafit.edu.co

A. M. Ortega · L. E. Torres (✉)
Georgia Gwinnett College, Lawrenceville, GA, USA
e-mail: aortega1@eafit.edu.co; ltorres1@ggc.edu

M.-S. Jaramillo-Echeverri
University of Memphis, Memphis, TN, USA
e-mail: mjchvrri@memphis.edu

F. Pantoja, S. Wu (eds.), *From Micro to Macro: Dealing with Uncertainties in the Global Marketplace*, Developments in Marketing Science: Proceedings of the Academy of Marketing Science, https://doi.org/10.1007/978-3-030-89883-0_46

on these relations adapted to the context of the fashion industry in Colombia, nine hypotheses were proposed (H1–9).

Survey research design was conducted to test the proposed model. Survey distribution was supported by Inexmoda through email invitations sent to all companies from the fashion system in Colombia (>5000 companies). Data analysis will be performed using Structural Equation Modeling. Results are not available at the time of submission. Findings will be useful for managers in the fashion industry aiming to increase innovation via the usage of newly implemented IT, as well as for academics by generating theoretical implications related to the proposed TAM extension.

Keywords TAM · Innovation · Fashion · Information technology

References Available Upon Request

Sustainability, Skepticism and Suspicion: What Do Consumers Think About Retailers? An Abstract

Laure Lavorata

Abstract Consumers are currently expressing new expectations and looking for new modes of consumption (degrowth, local products and organic products) and distribution (short circuits). In response to these new concerns, a significant increase in responsible practices by retail chains has been observed in recent years, including the development of private label and fair trade brands, the promotion of local products, and setting up partnerships with suppliers. The inclusion of sustainable products has accelerated in recent years, and these retailers are now developing specialized stores dedicated to organic products. Integrating sustainable development (SD) into practices can have consequences both for the image of brands and companies and for the behavior of consumers, who will shop in stores that reflect their values (Lavorata 2014).

However, these practices by retailers are encountering increased skepticism among consumers, who question their sincerity. McWilliams et al. (2006) point out that consumers often find it difficult to determine whether the company is really implementing a CSR policy. Even though Wal-Mart (US), Carrefour and Auchan (France) publish SD reports, consumers tend to think that this information is biased because it is communicated by the company's management and so gives rise to skepticism and suspicion. The present research thus proposes to analyze the perception that consumers have of retailers' SD practices and the consequences of such suspicion on the retailers' brand image and on their behavior (loyalty, word of mouth, etc.). A questionnaire was administered to 220 French consumers in December 2018. The sample was selected in accordance with the quota method (gender, age, and CSP) to be as representative as possible.

The findings highlight the importance of consumer suspicion and skepticism for the retailer's image, loyalty and recommendation. While studies of consumers have previously shown a general mistrust towards politicians and companies (only 28%

L. Lavorata (✉)
University of Reims Champagne Ardenne, Reims, France
e-mail: laure.lavorata@univ-reims.fr

F. Pantoja, S. Wu (eds.), *From Micro to Macro: Dealing with Uncertainties in the Global Marketplace*, Developments in Marketing Science: Proceedings of the Academy of Marketing Science, https://doi.org/10.1007/978-3-030-89883-0_47

of French people still trusted brands in 2018), no research to our knowledge has demonstrated the impact on these variables. This research shows that consumers' perceptions of retailers' SD practices are not influenced by suspicion, but there is nonetheless is a link between suspicion and skepticism, indicating that when consumers have a positive view of retailers' communication, the perception of their SD practices is also positive. This finding is interesting because it shows that communication by retailers can positively influence how they are perceived. Our research also has certain limitations. The concept of consumer suspicion could be deepened and supplemented with new items. It would also be appropriate to look at the factors giving rise to suspicion.

Keywords Skepticism · Consumers · Sustainable development · Retailers

References Available Upon **Request**

Internal City Branding: An Abstract

Rico Piehler, Michael Schade, Ayla Roessler, and Christoph Burmann

Abstract City branding involves the application of branding principles to cities, to help them achieve competitive advantages. The goal is to market the cities to residents as a place to live, to companies as a place to do business and to visitors as a place to visit. Among the target groups of city branding, residents are both an important internal target group of city branding efforts and a strategically valuable resource as co-creators in the city branding process. Although researchers have called for a consideration of internal branding for more than a decade, it has not been properly adapted to the city branding context. By integrating internal branding with place and city branding research, this study aims to develop a model for internal city branding which represents a concept for implementing the city brand in residents' minds (cognitively), emotions (affectively) and behaviors (behaviorally). Its goal is to retain and attract residents, companies and visitors, through efforts that enable residents to live the city brand and its identity, fulfil the city brand promise and strengthen the city brand through their behaviors.

The results of an online survey of 446 residents from the city of Bremen in Germany reveal that residents' city brand commitment and satisfaction both have positive effects on their intention to stay. Residents' city brand citizenship behavior is positively affected by their commitment, satisfaction and understanding. Residents' city brand satisfaction and understanding have positive effects on their commitment. Moreover, a positive relationship arises between residents' city brand understanding and their satisfaction. The quality of city brand communication as a brand management-related antecedent exerts positive effects on residents' city brand understanding and satisfaction, but not on their commitment. From a management perspective, residents' city brand understanding represents an important

R. Piehler (✉)
Macquarie University, Sydney, NSW, Australia
e-mail: rico.piehler@mq.edu.au

M. Schade · A. Roessler · C. Burmann
University of Bremen, Bremen, Germany
e-mail: mschade@uni-bremen.de; aroessler@uni-bremen.de; burmann@uni-bremen.de

F. Pantoja, S. Wu (eds.), *From Micro to Macro: Dealing with Uncertainties in the Global Marketplace*, Developments in Marketing Science: Proceedings of the Academy of Marketing Science, https://doi.org/10.1007/978-3-030-89883-0_48

objective for city brand managers that can be improved by ensuring that city brand communication is adequate, complete, credible, useful and clear.

Keywords Internal branding · City branding · Place branding · Residents · Brand communication

References Available Upon Request

An Item Analysis of an International Marketing Multiple-Choice Question Bank: An Abstract

John R. Dickinson

Abstract Item analysis is a cornerstone of the development of test questions (Aiken 1991, p. 73; Gregory 2011, p. 141). In light of the ubiquity of banks of multiple-choice questions–which accompany virtually all basic marketing and other business texts–relatively little item analysis of those questions has been published. Analyses that have been published include Dickinson (2011b, 2012a, b).

Publishing such analyses, of course, provides descriptions of the essential properties of the questions made available to instructors. Additionally, as such published descriptions accumulate, norms against which question banks can be evaluated would evolve. The purpose of the present study is to carry out a basic item analysis for a sample of questions from the multiple-choice question bank accompanying *International Marketing*, Seventeenth Edition by Cateora *et al.* (2016). The course in international marketing is typically taken by fourth-year undergraduate students.

A systematic random sample of 425 questions was drawn from the 1178 questions comprising the published bank. The mean number of potential answers per question, i.e., the mean number of students, is 39.26. The item criteria comprise:

- item difficulty operationalized as the proportion of students answering the item correctly, mean across 425 question equaling 0.8128,
- item discrimination operationalized as the point-biserial correlation between the dichotomy of answering correctly and overall exam score, mean across 388 questions equaling 0.4352, and
- item distractors operationalized as the distribution (*Intuit*) of incorrect answers across the distractor options, mean Intuit across 375 questions equaling 0.5312, and distractors attracting no responses, 38.24 percent of 1700 distractors.

Compared with Levy and Weitz (*Retailing Management*, Seventh Edition, 2009) and Solomon, Zaichkowski, and Polegato (*Consumer Behaviour*, Fourth Canadian Edition, 2008), the Cateora questions are far easier, have superior discrimination, about equal distributions of distractor responses, and a greater percentage of distractors that attract no responses.

J. R. Dickinson (✉)
University of Windsor, Windsor, ON, Canada

F. Pantoja, S. Wu (eds.), *From Micro to Macro: Dealing with Uncertainties in the Global Marketplace*, Developments in Marketing Science: Proceedings of the Academy of Marketing Science, https://doi.org/10.1007/978-3-030-89883-0_49

Keywords Multiple-choice questions · Item difficulty · Item discrimination · Item distractors · International marketing

References Available Upon Request

Understanding Service Innovation Strategies in Healthcare Organizations: A Preliminary Model: An Abstract

Michael Bimpeh and Robert A. Opoku

Abstract The slow progress with quality improvement in the healthcare industry is a sharp contrast to progress made in other industries like consumer electronics and automotive-manufacturing, which strive to improve service quality every year. The complexities and variabilities of specialized services in healthcare organizations; significant regulations creating the need to follow standard procedures with little tolerance for errors and ambiguity; wide variation in patients attended to; and large number of stakeholders, make it difficult to try innovations. Against this backdrop, not much is known about the nature of innovativeness in healthcare organizations and its relationship to performance, hence an evident need for a more detailed investigation of service innovation in this industry is compelling. Thus, this study is a starting point aiming to understand service innovation strategies adopted by innovative healthcare organizations and to attempt to construct a theory grounded in the data that to help explain best practices in designing and implementing service innovations for increased performance. The initial IMSIM framework developed around the six service innovation strategies could serve as an initial research framework to help enhance performance in IMD in healthcare organizations. Furthermore, the findings will be useful to healthcare practitioners who intend to design strategies and interventions to stimulate service innovations in their healthcare organizations. Practitioners outside healthcare industry could similarly use the findings. For example, wait time reduction and context diversity planning could be used in the banking and insurance sectors as service innovation strategies to help increase performance, and stimulate customer satisfaction. In terms of study limitations, this study was conducted in internal medicine department so the theoretical model is expected to apply best to this environment studies because healthcare departments perform specialized functions that make innovations department-specific. In the future,

M. Bimpeh (✉)
ASA College, New York, NY, USA
e-mail: mbimpeh@asa.edu

R. A. Opoku
Red Deer College, Red Deer, AB, Canada
e-mail: robert.opoku@rdc.ab.ca

F. Pantoja, S. Wu (eds.), *From Micro to Macro: Dealing with Uncertainties in the Global Marketplace*, Developments in Marketing Science: Proceedings of the Academy of Marketing Science, https://doi.org/10.1007/978-3-030-89883-0_50

researchers may use mixed design method (where quantitative approach is integrated with a quantitative one) to help support or disprove the qualitative findings of this study, which are inherently subjective in nature. Future researchers could replicate this study in a healthcare organization in a different geographical location and environment.

Keywords Healthcare · Service innovation · Grounded theory · New York City

References Available Upon Request

Special Session: Killing Two Birds with One Stone: The Retail Dilemma—Innovate or Die: An Abstract

Francesca Bonetti

Abstract Digitalization has revolutionized retailing and this has spurred retailers to adopt consumer-facing in-store technologies (CFIT), to enhance the shopping experience and for competitive advantage. CFIT are technologies that the consumer experiences directly whilst in-store, such as digital signage and interactive screens, AR and VR, Wi-Fi, virtual fitting rooms, etc. However, issues related to the strategic drivers and processes involved in technological change within a fashion retailing context are still open. This is a very current debate, both in academia and in the industry. The study adopts a qualitative approach to achieve deep understanding of rapidly-evolving managerial mindsets. Data was gathered through semi-structured face-to-face interviews with 67 senior industry informants drawn from fashion retailers, technology providers and strategists with fashion retail clients Thematic analysis of the data followed an inductive process. Findings suggest core issues revolving around levels of cultural change embracement for innovation, technology assimilation, and processes of technology integration. Results were fed back to the participants, via sharing reports, consulting and running workshops. Industry retail participants operating through more traditional point-of-sale formats in several instances used the comprehensive and up-to-date perspective provided from the research. This helped retail participants make informed decisions and overcome cultural transformational barriers, and map progress concerning issues of technological change with the implications deriving from them. Moreover, results helped technology providers understand the importance of providing a full coaching service to help them embrace change more holistically, where CFIT adoption comes as a consequence of more strategic cultural changes, and not as the adoption of the single piece of technology. Finally, start-ups could gain further details on implications for working with retail clients. This involves how to deal with systems integration and compatibility, and aspects such as successful communication to manage tech-related projects across the parties involved.

F. Bonetti (✉)
University of the Arts London, London, UK
e-mail: f.bonetti@fashion.arts.ac.uk

F. Pantoja, S. Wu (eds.), *From Micro to Macro: Dealing with Uncertainties in the Global Marketplace*, Developments in Marketing Science: Proceedings of the Academy of Marketing Science, https://doi.org/10.1007/978-3-030-89883-0_51

Keywords Fashion retail · Retail innovation · Industry impact · Consumer-facing in-store technology · Strategic drivers · Managerial processes

References Available Upon Request

Understanding the Uncertainty Using Sensitivity Analysis in Artificial Neural Networks

Li Eckart and Margit Enke

Abstract The uncertainty of outcomes with respect to the uncertain inputs is usually explored in sensitivity analysis. In particular, we address in this work the sensitivity assessment in artificial neural networks (ANNs) in terms of the investigation of black box models. ANNs have already proven its high prediction ability in various research domains. However, just few studies examined the explanatory potential of ANNs. This information reveals the relative importance of inputs, in other words, the relative influence of input perturbation on the final output. This explanatory perspective comprises both the ability to estimate the ranked importance of input variables and additionally, the robustness against changes in ANNs' structure, as proposed in this study. The second aspect is barely considered in such explanatory researches. Moreover, we compare different sensitivity criteria and exhibit their relationship. Furthermore, a new approach is introduced to analyze the sensitivity – norm approach, which shows the best overall performance in the empirical test. Those findings provide researchers a framework to select the appropriate method to conduct the sensitivity analysis in ANNs.

Keywords Black box model · Artificial neural network · Sensitivity analysis

Introduction

Understanding the contribution of input variables with respect to the final result is an important issue for researchers in a variety of research domains. Prior work has developed and empirically tested various approaches to reveal the robustness of the output referring to the input modifications. In this work, the sensitivity assessment is conducted in ANNs for following reasons:

L. Eckart (✉) · M. Enke
Freiberg University of Technology, Freiberg, Saxony, Germany
e-mail: li.eckart@bwl.tu-freiberg.de; margit.enke@bwl.tu-freiberg.de

F. Pantoja, S. Wu (eds.), *From Micro to Macro: Dealing with Uncertainties in the Global Marketplace*, Developments in Marketing Science: Proceedings of the Academy of Marketing Science, https://doi.org/10.1007/978-3-030-89883-0_52

1. Compared to traditional methods, ANNs are proven to exhibit remarkable predictive power. On the basis of ANNs' particular structure, they are considered universal approximators (Kolmogorov 1957). They enable us to scale the real-world tasks with high complexity, for instance, black box models, to find solutions to explain behavioral patterns and performances. The roots of ANNs can be found in computer science, engineering, mathematics, physics and astronomy, neuroscience and medicine (LeCun et al. 2015; Hochreiter and Schmidhuber 1997; Jones 1999; Rubinov and Sporns 2010; Hinton and Salakhutdinov 2006; Milo et al. 2002; Nielsen et al. 1997; Olden and Jackson 2002; Tu 1996).
2. In the most applications, the explanatory ability of ANNs is seldom demonstrated. ANNs are viewed as a predictive approach other than an approach that examines the robustness of a system across the range of inputs. In other words, sensitivity analysis in ANNs is rarely investigated.

The purpose of this paper is to answer the following research questions: (1) how can we use ANNs to assess the sensitivity? (2) how are the various classical sensitivity approaches in ANNs related to each other? (3) how is the performance of those approaches in terms of the robustness against the structural changes in ANNs?

This work is organized as following: Section "Background" sheds light on literature on theoretical background of ANNs. In section "Methodology", we introduce the classical approaches and compare them with a new method based on Euclidean norm to investigate the sensitivity analysis of ANNs. In addition, this comparison is carried out by means of empirical data.

Background

ANNs are viewed as a system of connected directed artificial neurons. In ANNs, the process of biological neural network will be reproduced with connected artificial neurons. Each network layer consists of artificial neurons and bias. The network signals will pass through various network layers and finally arrive the output layers. Mathematical functions (propagation function and activation function) represent the strengths of neural connections and activation levels of neurons. The connecting weights will be stored in the propagation function. The received signal will be transformed into network input using the activation function, also called transfer function. Bias can be seen as a weight whose input always equals 1. Using bias provides an affine transformation (nonlinear) instead of linear transformation. The application of bias prevents that a neuron without a bias will always transfer 0 when the network inputs are 0.

The magnitude and direction of the neural connections show the different contributions of inputs referring to the output. Inputs with larger connection weights possess greater intensities in the signal transfer process, compared to inputs with smaller connection weights. The connection directions can be inhibitory (negative) or excitatory (positive). The inhibitory connections reduce the intensity of the received signal and the excitatory connections, oppositely, will intense the received signal. It indicates that the connection weights can provide the insights into the relative importance of input variables of black box models. Therefore, the information about the weights can be used to assess the robustness of the observed system.

Based on the universal approximation theorem (Kolmogorov 1957), an ANN with one hidden layer can approximate any continuous function arbitrarily well, regardless of the activation function and the dimension of the input space (Hornik et al. 1989). ANNs with bias, a nonlinear and a linear output layer are capable of approximating any function with a finite number of discontinuities without any previous justification. This confirms the high predictive ability of ANNs and explains the widespread application of ANNs to black box models.

Given input and target data, ANNs can be trained in a so-called supervised learning process. In each learning step, the weights in propagation function will be adapted to minimize the learning errors (differences between outputs and targets). The adaptive changes of weights follow the learning rule determined by learning algorithms. Mean squared error (MSE) is usually applied to evaluate the learning results. The knowledge of the trained ANN stored in weights and bias can be used for further prediction.

Among different structures of ANNs, a multilayer feed-forward neural network (MFNN) consisting of three layers (input, hidden and output layer) is proposed in this paper for further explanation. The output layer comprises in our work one output neuron. An ANN with n (x_i, $i = 1, \cdots, n$) inputs is considered. $w_{i,j}$ implies the weights of the connections between input layer and the hidden layer, which consists of m neurons ($j = 1, \cdots, m$). b_j describes the bias of the neuron j. The network signal net_j is represented by the propagation function in terms of inputs, weights and bias, $net_j = \sum_{i=1}^{i=n} \left(x_i \cdot w_{i,j} + b_j\right)$. Depending on the activation level of neurons, the network signal is transmitted with the help of the activation function $a_j = f\left(net_j\right) = f\left(\sum_{i=1}^{i=n} \left(x_i \cdot w_{i,j} + b_j\right)\right)$. After the activation process, the signal a_j is passed to the output layer. The neuron in the output layer is y, $y = \sum_{j=1}^{m} w_{j,r} f\left(net_j\right) + b_r = \sum_{j=1}^{m} w_{j,r} f\left(\sum_{i=1}^{i=n} \left(x_i \cdot w_{i,j} + b_j\right)\right) + b_r$. b_r is the bias of the output neuron y. For convenience, we denote ANN-n-m-k as an ANN with n inputs, m neurons in the hidden layer and k neurons in the output layer.

Bevor detailing the methodology, it is important to point out the boundaries of this work. The aim of our paper is to examine whether the output of a system gives a robust or fragile response to the variation of inputs, not to estimate a structural model or to establish causal links.

Methodology

Introduction of Classical Approaches

There are some methods which are widely used to assess the relative importance of input variables within the framework of ANNs. We confine out attention to Garson's algorithm (Garson 1991), the connection weight approach (Olden et al. 2004) and the partial derivative approach (Dimopoulos et al. 1995, 1999), which are proven to perform reliably in many research fields (Garson 1991; Dimopoulos et al. 1995, 1999; Gevrey et al. 2003).

Garson's algorithm divides connection weights between the hidden and output layers into components in association with each input neuron using absolute values of connection weights (Garson 1991). Summed products of the absolute value of connection weights for each input neuron can be scaled relative to other inputs. The direction of the connections is not considered in this approach.

For each hidden neuron *j*, the relative importance of the input x_i for the hidden neuron *j* can be computed as:

$$Q_{i,j}^{Garson} = \frac{\# w_{i,j} \bullet w_{j,r} \#}{\sum_{i=1}^{i=n} \# w_{i,j} \bullet w_{j,r} \#}. \tag{1}$$

$w_{j,r}$ describes the connection weights between the hidden neuron *j* and output neuron *r*. The relative importance of the input x_i is viewed as the sum of the relative importance of the input x_i for every hidden neuron.

$$Q_i^{Garson} = \sum_{j=1}^{j=m} \frac{\# w_{i,j} \bullet w_{j,r} \#}{\sum_{i=1}^{i=n} \# w_{i,j} \bullet w_{j,r} \#}. \tag{2}$$

The connection weight approach is proposed by Olden, Joy and Death to quantify variable importance accurately. This approach calculates the sum of the products of connection weights. Both sign and absolute value are considered in this approach. The changes of sign of the connection weights are proposed to cause offset effect (Olden et al. 2004). The result differs from Garson's algorithm which just focuses on the absolute value of the connection weights.

The relative importance of the input variable x_i is expressed as:

$$Q_i^{cw} = \sum_{j=1}^{j=m} w_{i,j} \bullet w_{j,k}. \tag{3}$$

The determination of the partial derivatives reveals the system robustness, since they represent the link between the input perturbations and the changes in output. Dimopoulos proposed to examine the partial derivatives for ANNs with the logistic sigmoid activation function (Dimopoulos et al. 1995, 1999). The sensitivity can be estimated by the first and the second derivatives of the output in terms of the input variables. For more details, we refer the readers to (Dimopoulos et al. 1995, 1999). However, this approach requires high computing time, because both first and second derivatives of every input variable are exerted. In our work, a modified alternative is proposed to conduct the sensitivity analysis.

By holding other input variables constant, the partial derivative of x_i assesses the change of the function value with respect to changes in the input x_i. The partial derivatives of the output y in terms of the input x_i is defined as:

$$\frac{\partial y}{\partial x_i} = \sum_{j=1}^{m} w_{i,j} \cdot w_{j,k} \cdot \frac{\partial f}{\partial x_i}\left(\sum_{i=1}^{i=n}\left(x_i \cdot w_{i,j} + b_j\right)\right) \tag{4}$$

Equation (4) can also be written in vector form ($\bullet^T$ in formula (5) denotes the matrix transposition):

$$\underbrace{\begin{pmatrix} w_{i,1}\cdot w_{1,k} \\ w_{i,2}\cdot w_{2,k} \\ w_{i,3}\cdot w_{3,k} \\ \cdots \end{pmatrix}}_{W_{I,K}} \cdot \underbrace{\begin{pmatrix} \frac{\partial f}{\partial x_i}\left(\sum_{i=1}^{i=n} w_{i,1}\cdot x_i + b_1\right) \\ \frac{\partial f}{\partial x_i}\left(\sum_{i=1}^{i=n} w_{i,2}\cdot x_i + b_2\right) \\ \frac{\partial f}{\partial x_i}\left(\sum_{i=1}^{i=n} w_{i,3}\cdot x_i + b_3\right) \\ \cdots \end{pmatrix}^T}_{D^T} \tag{5}$$

In this work, the hyperbolic tangent sigmoid function:

$$f(z) = \frac{2}{1+e^{-2z}} - 1 = \frac{e^z - e^{-z}}{e^z + e^{-z}} = \frac{\sinh x}{\text{coshx}} \tag{6}$$

is chosen as the activation function due to the differentiability and the inclusion of both positive and negative domains (from −1 to 1). Note that the partial derivative of $f(z)$ is defined as:

$$\frac{\partial f(z)}{\partial z} = \frac{\partial \frac{\sinh z}{\text{coshz}}}{\partial z} = \frac{\frac{\partial}{\partial z}\sinh z * \cosh z - \frac{\partial}{\partial z}\cosh z * \sinh z}{\cosh^2 z} = \frac{\cosh^2 z - \sinh^2 z}{\cosh^2 z}$$
$$= 1 - \frac{\sinh^2 z}{\cosh^2 z} = 1 - f^2(z). \tag{7}$$

The domain of *f*(*z*) varies in range [−1,1]. It implies that the partial derivative in (7) is in the range between 0 and 1. Furthermore, all the components of the matrix D in formula (5) are between 0 and 1.

The partial derivative in vector form in formula (5) consists both magnitude and direction. Its magnitude can be seen as an indicator the relative importance of the input variables. The Euclidean norm enables us to calculate the magnitude of a vector, which is defined for a general vector $\boldsymbol{u}$ as following:

$$\| \boldsymbol{u} \| = \sqrt[2]{\sum_{h=1}^{h=t} u_h^2}. \tag{8}$$

Based on the submultiplicativity of the Euclidean norm and the value range of D, we obtain:

$$\| W_{I,K} \bullet D^T \|'' \| W_{I,K} \|' \| W_{I,K} \| \cdot \| D^T \| \tag{9}$$

For the purpose of reduction of the computational effort, we propose that $\| W_{I,K} \| = \sqrt[2]{\sum_{i=1}^{i=n} w_{i,j}^2 \bullet w_{j,k}^2}$ can be used as an upper bound of $\| W_{I,K} \cdot D^T \|$ in (5) to conduct the sensitivity analysis.

Comparison of Different Approaches

Based on the properties of the Euclidean norm and absolute value, we can obtain:

$$\| W_{I,K} \| \leq \sum_{i=1}^{i=n} w_{i,j} \bullet w_{j,k}, \quad \forall j = 1, \cdots, m \tag{10}$$

$$\sum_{i=1}^{i=n} w_{i,j} \bullet w_{j,k} \leq \sum_{i=1}^{i=n} w_{i,j} \bullet w_{j,k}, \quad \forall j = 1, \cdots, m. \tag{11}$$

(10) and (11) indicate respectively that the results of sensitivity analysis obtained from Garson algorithm is not smaller than the assessed sensitivity with the help of our norm approach and the connection weight approach. (9) and (10) imply together the following relationship:

$$\| W_{I,K} \bullet D^T \| \leq \| W_{I,K} \| \leq \sum_{i=1}^{i=n} w_{i,j} \bullet w_{j,k}, \quad \forall j = 1, \cdots, m. \tag{12}$$

Therefore, it can be postulated that the norm approach is a more accurate sensitivity analysis method than Garson algorithm.

The offset effect is not considered in Garson algorithm. The absolute value of the product of weights is summed to determine the relative importance. The application of Garson algorithm yields the potential overestimation of the actual influence of the input variables.

The relationship between $\left\| w_{i,j} \cdot w_{j,k} \right\|$ and $w_{i,j} \cdot w_{j,k}$ is determined by the sign of $\sum_{\substack{p,l=1 \\ p \neq l}}^{p,l=n} w_{p,j} \cdot w_{j,k} w_{l,j} \cdot w_{j,k}$:

$$\| W_{I,K} \| \leq \sum_{i=1}^{i=n} w_{i,j} \cdot w_{j,k},$$

$$\forall j = 1, \cdots, m, \ if \ \sum_{\substack{p,l=1 \\ p \neq l}}^{p,l=n} w_{p,j} \cdot w_{j,k} w_{l,j} \cdot w_{j,k} \geq 0 \tag{13}$$

or

$$\| W_{I,K} \| \geq \sum_{i=1}^{i=n} w_{i,j} \cdot w_{j,k},$$

$$\forall j = 1, \cdots, m, \ if \ \sum_{\substack{p,l=1 \\ p \neq l}}^{p,l=n} w_{p,j} \cdot w_{j,k} w_{l,j} \cdot w_{j,k} \leq 0 \tag{14}$$

The alternating direction of the links between the outturn of the norm approach and the connection weight approach suggests the poor robustness of the second one in terms of modifications of ANNs' structure.

As described in (9), the actual norm of partial derivatives $\| W_{I,K} \cdot D^T \|$ is smaller than $\| W_{I,K} \|$. In case of underestimation referring to (13), the connection weight approach may perform better than other approaches, which is in agreement with Olden, Joy and Death (Olden et al. 2004). However, the robustness of the connection weight approach against the structural changes in ANNs remains untouched in their work.

Our findings based on the mathematical properties can be briefly summarized that the norm approach is a more precise method to assess the relative importance of the inputs, compared with Garson algorithm. Additionally, it is more robust against the structural modification in ANNs in comparison with the connection weight approach.

Results and Discussion

We applied three methods of sensitivity assessments in the previous section on the data set of Gonzalez and Wu (Gonzalez and Wu 1999). They considered one of the typical situations of decision making under uncertainty - lotteries. The outputs of the decision alternatives are represented in monetary value and probability of occurrences. Within their framework, the perception of the probability can be assessed in the inverse-s-shaped probability weighting function and the perception of the value is identified to be an s-shaped value function. The data for the proposed nonparametric approach are obtained from a controlled experiment. The relative importance of the input variables, monetary value and probability, is however not explored.

To investigate this decision making process, two ANNs with following structures: 2–10–1, 2–5–1 with 2 inputs (also 2 input neurons), respectively 10 or 5 neurons in the hidden layer and 1 neuron in the output layer, are involved in the supervised learning process. Both of them performed very well for our black box model, with $r_{2-10-1} = 0.98805$ und $r_{2-5-1} = 0.98424$. The variation of the results from sensitivity assessments using different structured ANNs should be in a considerable small range. The modification caused by structural changes of ANNs indicates the robustness of the sensitivity analysis methods.

The data were computed in MATLAB® (for more details about weights and bias, see Appendix) and the results are shown in Table 1 (75 in the bracket is the number of observations in the experiment).

Both relative and absolute modification of the connection weights by applying different constructed ANNs are considered in Table 1. The result in Table 1 shows that the influences exerted by the two input variables are asymmetric. In ANN-2–10–1, the concordance can be identified among all the approaches: a slight to large alternations of the input variable, probability, can be identified in ANN-2–10–1 and ANN-2–5–1. As expected, the range modification of the connection weight approach is larger than norm approach. In our case, the largest variation due to structural changes can be even identified by using the connection weight method. In agreement with Olden, Joy and Death, Garson algorithm showed the fragileness in terms of sensitivity analysis (Olden et al. 2004). The ranking of relative importance of input variables is dependent on the ANN's structure. ANN-2–10–1 suggested that the perturbation of the input probability will cause larger changes in the output than the monetary value. However, ANN-2–5–1 proposed the opposite

Table 1 Results of sensitivity analysis

		Importance of input variables			
		Absolute		Relative	
Approach	ANN Architecture	Value	Probability	Value	Probability
Connection weight	2–10–1 (75)	0.547	6.912	0.073	0.927
	2–5–1 (75)	2.608	5.111	0.337	0.663
	Modification	376%	−26.1%	360%	−28.5%
Garson algorithm	2–10–1 (75)	4.379	5.621	0.438	0.562
	2–5–1 (75)	2.764	2.236	0.553	0.447
	Modification	−36.9%	−60.2%	26.2%	−20.4%
Norm approach	2–10–1 (75)	2.536	5.147	0.330	0.670
	2–5–1 (75)	2.204	4.884	0.311	0.689
	Modification	−13.1%	−5.1%	−5.8%	2.9%

ranking. The norm approach was found to exhibit the best performance compared to other methods in terms of the robustness against the structural change of ANNs.

Contribution and Limitation

Our study focuses on the explanatory capacity of ANNs for the investigation of black box models, not on the exhaustively studied predictive ability of ANNs. In addition to comparing the sensitivity approaches among each other, this paper acknowledges that the robustness against the structural changes of ANNs should also be considered in the sensitivity analysis.

We introduced a new norm approach to assess the sensitivity and addressed the criticism against the poor explanatory ability of the ANNs. The main findings of our study provide the researchers a framework for selection of approaches to conduct the sensitivity analysis in ANNs. Three different approaches are compared to analyze the relative contribution of input variables in ANNs theoretically and empirically. The relationship between those approaches is firstly verified based on their mathematical properties. Using the data set from Gonzalez and Wu, the relationship is also confirmed empirically. Our norm approach performs better in terms of robustness against the structural changes than the other two approaches. The application of the norm approach enables the determination of the relative contribution of input variables referring to the output. This can support the managers to make decisions involving uncertain factors.

However, this work contains some limitations to be addressed in future research. First, the ANNs applied in our study possess simple structures. We recommend to run similar tests in ANNs with high complexity. Second, our empirical comparison restricts the analysis to the data set of Gonzalez and Wu. Further research should examine their relationship using large-sized data sets of various black box models. Generally, larger sample size facilitates the supervised learning process of ANNs. Can we also expect that the larger sample size increases the performance of the sensitivity measurements? On the other hand, the computational effort will increase with the number of observations and the number of inputs and outputs (Simar and Wilson 1998). How can we find the balance between the accuracy of the sensitivity analysis and the appropriate computational effort? Moreover, our comparison just concludes three sensitivity approaches. Further research should determine the performance of the norm approach related to other sensitivity approaches considered in the work of Gevrey (Gevrey et al. 2003). Additionally, for the sake of simplicity, $||W_{I,K}||$ is proposed to estimate the magnitude of $W_{I,K} \cdot D^T$. Is there another upper bound with even greater accuracy than $||W_{I,K}||$?

Appendix

Weights and bias in ANN-2–10–1

	Hidden neurons									
	1	2	3	4	5	6	7	8	9	10
Input 1	−2.997	3.234	−1.540	4.691	4.822	−0.175	−3.600	3.805	3.929	−1.106
Input 2	−8.249	−13.070	−0.443	−10.483	3.386	6.280	−4.975	1.316	0.533	5.397
Bias in 1. hidden layer	7.717	−9.771	−0.546	−10.705	0.521	0.999	−1.184	3.055	0.617	−0.300
Output neuron	−0.649	−0.040	−0.689	−0.138	0.059	−0.061	0.017	−0.122	−0.306	0.066
Bias in output layer	−0.282									

Weights and bias in ANN-2–5–1

	Hidden neurons				
	1	2	3	4	5
Input 1	−1.671	2.790	1.170	2.475	3.994
Input 2	−5.570	−1.590	−1.293	2.802	0.202
Bias in 1. hidden layer	5.486	−3.156	−1.878	−0.138	2.512
Output neuron	−0.848	0.489	−0.723	0.072	0.122
Bias in output layer	−0.158				

References

Dimopoulos, I., Chronopoulos, J., Chronopoulou-Sereli, A., & Lek, S. (1999). Neural Network Models to Study Relationships between Lead Concentration in Grasses and Permanent Urban Descriptors in Athens City (Greece). *Ecological Modelling, 120*, 157–165.

Dimopoulos, Y., Bourret, P., & Lek, S. (1995). Use of Some Sensitivity Criteria for Choosing Networks with Good Generalization Ability. *Neural Processing Letters, 2*, 1–4.

Garson, G. D. (1991). Interpreting Neural-network Connection Weights. *Artificial Intelligence Expert, 6*(4), 46–51.

Gevrey, M., Dimopoulos, I., & Lek, S. (2003). Review and Comparison of Methods to Study the Contribution of Variables in Artificial Neural Network Models. *Ecological Modelling, 160*, 249–264.

Gonzalez, R., & Wu, G. (1999). On the Shape of the Probability Weighting Function. *Cognitive Psychology, 38*, 129–166.

Hinton, G. E., & Salakhutdinov, R. R. (2006). Reducing the Dimensionality of Data with Neural Networks. *Science, 313*, 504–507.

Hochreiter, S., & Schmidhuber, J. (1997). Long Short-Term Memory. *Neural Computation, 9*(8), 1735–1780.

Hornik, K., Stinchcombe, M., & White, H. (1989). Multilayer Feedforward Networks Are Universal Approximators. *Neural Networks, 2*(5), 359–366.

Jones, D. T. (1999). Protein Secondary Structure Prediction Based on Position-Specific Scoring Matrices. *Journal of Molecular biology, 292*(2), 195–202.

Kolmogorov, A. N. (1957). On the Representation of Continuous Functions of Many Variables by Superposition of Continuous Functions of One Variable and Addition. *Dokl. Akad. Nauk SSSR, 114*(5).

LeCun, Y., Bengio, Y., & Hinton, G. (2015). Deep learning. *Nature, 521*(7553), 436–444.

Milo, R., Shen-Orr, S. S., Itzkovitz, S., Kashtan, N., Chklovskii, D. M., & Alon, U. (2002). Network Motifs: Simple Building Blocks of Complex Networks. *Science, 298*, 824–827.

Nielsen, H., Engelbrecht, J., Brunak, S., & von Heijne, G. (1997). Identification of Prokaryotic and Eukaryotic Signal Peptides and Prediction of Their Cleavage Sites. *Protein Engineering Design and Selection, 10*, 1–6.

Olden, J. D., & Jackson, D. A. (2002). Illuminating the "Black Box": a Randomization Approach for Understanding Variable Contributions in Artificial Neural Networks. *Ecological Modelling, 154*, 135–150.

Olden, J. D., Joy, M. K., & Death, R. G. (2004). An Accurate Comparison of Methods for Quantifying Variable Importance in Artificial Neural Networks Using Simulated Data. *Ecological Modelling, 178*, 389–397.

Rubinov, M., & Sporns, O. (2010). Complex Network Measures of Brain Connectivity: Uses and Interpretations. *NeuroImage, 52*(3), 1059–1069.

Simar, L., & Wilson, P. W. (1998). Sensitivity Analysis of Efficiency Scores: How to Bootstrap in Nonparametric Frontier Models. *Management Science, 44*(1), 49–61.

Tu, J. V. (1996). Advantages and Disadvantages of Using Artificial Neural Networks versus Logistic Regression for Predicting Medical Outcomes. *Journal of Clinical Epidemiology, 49*(11), 1225–1231.

Can a Nudge Induce Inferences of Manipulative Intent? An Abstract

Soffien Bataoui, Jessica Gerard, and Pierre Valette-Florence

Abstract Thaler and Sunstein (2008) propose to encourage the implementation of public policies, particularly in the field of environment, based on nudges. Nudges aim to steer choices in specific directions by modifying individual's decision frameworks (Thaler and Sunstein, 2008). The mobilization of nudges by public authorities and companies is thus growing; many positive effects have been demonstrated (Pichert and Katsikopoulos 2008, Ferraro and Price 2013). However, manipulative behavior appears to be one of the most important critics of nudges (Hansen and Jespersen 2013, Wilkinson 2013) and the literature has not yet studied the effects of perceived manipulation on nudge adoption.

We conducted an *in situ* study using an ashtray nudge. The purpose of this ashtray is to encourage smokers to throw their cigarette butts in by answering a question. The following question was therefore chosen: "*You would rather go on vacation to*". The response modalities were "*the sea and the mountains*", both having a hole to throw the butt into. 75 responses were collected: 30 participants threw their cigarette butts into the nudge, and 45 on the ground. Our contribution is threefold. (1) Attitude towards the nudge appears to be positive, whether or not the respondents threw their cigarette butt into the nudge. (2) Smokers who threw their cigarette butts into the nudge reported a more positive attitude towards the nudge than those who threw it on the ground. (3) If an individual considered him/herself as being manipulated, he/she would unlikely adopt the behavior encouraged by the nudge. Thus inferences of manipulative intent play a role in the adoption (or not) of the behavior encouraged by the nudge.

This research has focused on better understanding nudge behaviors by using an underlying mechanism: inferences of manipulative intent. Practitioners wishing to mobilize a nudge will have to be aware of the role of the inferences of manipulative intent. Nudge is a tool that has proven its effectiveness but must complement educa-

S. Bataoui · J. Gerard (✉) · P. Valette-Florence
University of Grenoble-Alpes, Grenoble, France
e-mail: soffien.bataoui@univ-grenoble-alpes.fr; jessica.gerard@univ-grenoble-alpes.fr; pierre.valette-florence@univ-grenoble-alpes.fr

F. Pantoja, S. Wu (eds.), *From Micro to Macro: Dealing with Uncertainties in the Global Marketplace*, Developments in Marketing Science: Proceedings of the Academy of Marketing Science, https://doi.org/10.1007/978-3-030-89883-0_53

tional activities. Practitioners should also keep in mind the initial objective of a nudge, which is to promote more responsible behaviors and work for the public welfare.

Keywords Nudge · Environmental issues · Inferences of manipulative intent · Ecological behavior

References Available Upon Request

“As Different as Chalk and Cheese”: E-Mobility Acceptance from the Viewpoint of Users and Non-users

Marc Kuhn, Benjamin Österle, Vanessa Reit, and Viola Marquardt

Abstract Although governments and manufacturers are pushing the e-mobility branch, there are still large numbers of considerable reservations on the consumer side. Studies try to explain drivers' motivators and barriers for using electric vehicles (EV). However, there is a lack of knowledge on how different factors are influencing the acceptance and adoption intention of those cars. In order to develop segment-specific marketing strategies, companies still have to learn about the potential relationship between acceptance antecedents and the personal EV experience of individual drivers.

In this paper, we analyse the technology acceptance of e-mobility in two groups. We draw on the Customer Acceptance of Technology model (CAT). Conducting a field-study with standardized questionnaires, our sample contains 127 drivers owning an EV and 354 drivers owning a “classical” combustion car. Our findings reveal that there are differences in the antecedents and their effects on Adoption Intention between the groups. The total effect of Perceived Ease of Use on Adoption Intention is stronger for the non-driver group. Image benefits also contribute stronger to Relative Advantage of EVs for non-drivers. These key differences could have important implications for the acceptance of this, with respect to climate change and air pollution, potentially crucial technology.

Keywords E-mobility · Technology acceptance · CAT · Partial least squares

---

M. Kuhn (✉) · B. Österle · V. Reit
Baden-Wuerttemberg Cooperative State University, Stuttgart, Germany
e-mail: marc.kuhn@dhbw-stuttgart.de; benjamin.oesterle@dhbw-stuttgart.de; vanessa.reit@dhbw-stuttgart.de

V. Marquardt
Spiegel Institut Ingolstadt, Mannheim, Germany
e-mail: v.marquardt@spiegel-institut.de

F. Pantoja, S. Wu (eds.), *From Micro to Macro: Dealing with Uncertainties in the Global Marketplace*, Developments in Marketing Science: Proceedings of the Academy of Marketing Science, https://doi.org/10.1007/978-3-030-89883-0_54

Introduction

Tesla as an innovation pioneer. Chinese government as a volume driver. Europe as a lame duck. For years, it seemed unclear where the global e-mobility trajectory was heading for (Augenstein 2015; Peterson 2015). Recent developments show a significant positive change on the worldwide market for pure battery electric vehicles (BEV). Announcements of new e-car-platforms, founding programs and increasing license numbers might be influenced by climate change awareness and "diesel gate".

Several specifics differ EV's in comparison to "standard" combustion engine driven cars as there are reduced driving range, battery charging times, less driving noise, increased speed acceleration or negative influence of activated comfort functions like heating on driving range (Genuit 2013; Bures et al. 2013; Eschenbaecher et al. 2014). Based on these "consumer-perceivable" differences, there is a wide discussion on the potential motivators and demotivators of using EV's (Biresselioglu et al. 2018). While researchers already came up with a broad defined bench of those motivators and demotivators, there is still a lack in knowledge on the concrete influence on attitude and acceptance of the technology. As studies show experience related changes in acceptance drivers (Bühler et al. 2014; Kuhn et al. 2017) we apply a CAT technology acceptance model (Kulviwat et al. 2007) on two samples. Sample one contains EV owners, sample two contains Non-EV owners. Conducting standardized face-to-face questionnaires with both samples we compare the differences of influencing antecedents on the acceptance of electric vehicles between the two experience-groups. We want to provide insights to the question if marketers should address experienced EV-drivers in a different way compared to Non-EV-drivers in order to reach a maximum of technology acceptance in all customer groups.

Theoretical Background and State of Research

Potential emerges of electric mobility trajectories have been object of research activities since years (Dijk et al. 2013). Asking when and under which conditions electric mobility crosses a critical market threshold, this research object has to be reviewed consistently based on permanent change in technology developments, political frameworking and consumer attitudes (Kanger et al. 2019). Comprehensive contributions on motivators and barriers in decision making processes can already be found (Axsen et al. 2016; Barisa et al. 2016; Haddadian et al. 2015). Biresselioglu et al. conducted a meta-analysis on existing studies, mapping those motivators and barriers to formal categories "formal social units", "collective decision-making units" and "individual units" (Biresselioglu et al. 2018). On the individual level unit, they recognized the following main barriers to EV market acceptance: Lack of charging infrastructure, economic restrictions like price or battery replacement costs, technical restrictions like driving range and further individual aspects like lack of personal knowledge. EV motivators on the individual level have been: Environmental aspects like reduction of CO2 emissions, economic aspects like reduction of fuel costs or functional aspects like charging the EV at home (Biresselioglu et al. 2018).

Next to the identification of general driving and restraining factors of EV business, we found different types of research approaches dealing with the concrete influence of motivators and barriers on the acceptance of electric vehicles: (1) Some studies focus on the effect, single factors or factor groups have on the individual adoption and use of electric vehicles. Franke et al. investigated sustainable EV layouts and ergonomics as potential drivers for acceptance (Franke et al. 2018). Among others, they show that misleading EV ergonomics like invalid information about rest-range may result in “range-stress” and experienced discomfort potentially related to lower acceptance (Franke et al. 2018). Bühler et al. evaluated use patterns of electric vehicles as indicator for acceptance (Bühler et al. 2011; Krems et al. 2010). In a field study, 40 drivers experienced an EV for a longer period of time. Correlations between high usage intensity and positive attitudes have been found but significance was shown only on single isolated items (Bühler et al. 2011). While there seems to be an experience-depending increase of EV acceptance in general, Franke et al. recognize a slight acceptance-decrease after a first “honeymoon”-phase of using an EV (Bühler et al. 2011; Bühler et al. 2014; Schmalfuß et al. 2017). Günther et al. found out, that theoretical training on “how to use an EV” enhances drivers´ acceptance of the technology (Günther et al. 2019). Some contributions work on the detailed explanation of the antecedents of EV motivators and barriers. Franke et al. investigate the factors driving range preferences in electric vehicle users (Franke and Krems 2013). It could be shown that range preferences decrease with increasing practical EV experience (Franke and Krems 2013; Franke et al. 2012a, b). (2) Other studies outline a more comprehensive picture on how different antecedents influence EV acceptance and adoption intention. Ziefle et al. investigated a broad range of sociodemographic and personality factors and their influence on EV acceptance (Ziefle et al. 2014). Female users as well as aged persons and persons with higher environmental consciousness showed higher EV acceptance rates (Ziefle et al. 2014). Simsekoglu et al. looked at predictors of intention to directly buy an EV (Simsekoglu and Nayum 2019). Results show, that environmental aspects, personal subjective norms and the perceived behavioural control have positive influence on the buying intention (Simsekoglu and Nayum 2019; Schmalfuß et al. 2017). While most of the comprehensive studies do not relate on theoretical models of technology or innovation acceptance, Haustein et al. evaluate the factors of EV adoption referring on an extended Theory of Planned Behaviour (Haustein and Jensen 2018). Conducting an online survey with users and non-users of EVs in Denmark and Sweden, they investigated group related intentions to use/purchase an electric vehicle based on factors of the Theory of Planned Behaviour which is extended by personal norms, perceived mobility necessities and EV experience. Results show, that for users of combustion vehicles, symbolic attitudes related to EVs are the most important factor of intention to use an EV. In contradiction to other studies (Franke and Krems 2013; Franke et al. 2012a, b), functional barriers in terms of driving range are most relevant for EV users intention (Haustein and Jensen 2018).

Reviewing the broad range of existing studies, we still found a lack in knowledge on which factors and how they are driving pre-antecedents of adoption intention of

EVs like attitude towards adoption, perceived usefulness, perceived ease of use or concrete relative advantages of an EV compared to a combustion vehicle. Referring on such comprehensive, comparative evaluation in both groups of EV drivers and non-drivers, this knowledge would allow OEMs to conduct specific target group-oriented marketing for EV's. Marketers would be given a reference base on how different they should address potential customer groups of experienced and non-experienced EV drivers.

Research Approach and Methodology

We conducted two identic standardized face-to-face questionnaires in Europe. One with 127 owners of EV's, the other with 354 EV "non-owners" who had no experience using electric vehicles. The survey took place December 2018 to January 2019 in Germany, France, Austria, Italy, and the Netherlands. Our face-to-face surveys on e-mobility acceptance with users and non-users have been executed in the surroundings of charging points. The investigation teams addressed EV holders while charging their cars as well as pedestrians without an EV, again in the surroundings of charging points.

In both surveys we used an adapted version of the Consumer Acceptance of Technology model (CAT) (Kulviwat et al. 2007). This model is an extension of the Technology Acceptance Model (TAM) (Davis et al. 1989). The TAM identifies two central factors that influence the "Attitude Toward Adoption" (ATA), i.e. the attitude toward the use of the technology, and by the end the "Adoption Intention" (AI) of the technology: "Perceived Usefulness" (PU) and "Perceived Ease of Use" (PEU). PU refers to the degree to which a person believes that using a particular technology is helpful and enhances performance (Davis et al. 1989). PEoU is an individual assessment in terms of the effort required to use the technology (Davis et al. 1989). In addition to variables of TAM and Theory of Planned Behaviour which already has been applied in EV acceptance studies (Haustein and Jensen 2018), CAT adds the dimension of "Relative Advantage" (RA) of a new technology compared to the related "old" or "existing" technology. This dimension is highly fitting to the EV technology as users have the opportunity to directly compare the "classic" functionality and traits of a combustion vehicle with those of an electric vehicle. In other mobility innovation studies, e.g. on automated driving, the cognitive determinants of the CAT model showed high explanation of variance with regard to technology acceptance (Köpsel et al. 2018). Affective determinants didn't show any effects on the "Attitude Toward Adoption" (Köpsel et al. 2018). For that reason, we also reduced our EV investigation model to the cognitive part of CAT. Due to lack of academic contributions, the items of CAT acceptance determinants, shown in Table A1, have been derived of user related applied and industry related research contributions on electric vehicles (Schneider et al. 2014; Patergona et al. 2013; Emsenhuber 2012; Hoffmann et al. 2012; Götz et al. 2012). Table A1 shows the items used in the questionnaire for EV drivers. For the "non-EV drivers" the same items have been used, formulated in the subjunctive (Fig. 1).

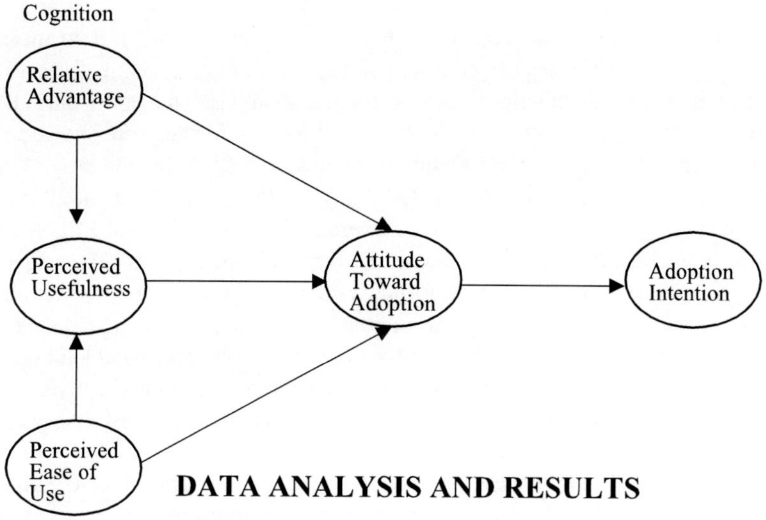

Fig. 1 Cognitive part of applied CAT model

Data Analysis and Results

Considering the "Relative Advantage" construct, this study draws on a second-order composite of common factors measurement model (van Riel et al. 2017), consisting of the lower order components "costs" (RA_C), "range & infrastructure" (RA_RI), "performance" (RA_P), and "image" (RA_I) (Schneider et al. 2014; Patergona et al. 2013; Hoffmann et al. 2012). All other constructs are conceptualized as common factors and measured reflectively. For this reason, we applied partial least squares structural (PLS) equation modeling (Henseler 2016; Henseler 2018) using ADANCO 2.1.1 (Henseler and Dijkstra 2015) to analyse our data. The consistent partial least squares algorithm (PLSc) implemented in the software allows for the consistent estimation of both composites and common factors (Dijkstra and Henseler 2015b), goodness of fit tests and inference statistics (Dijkstra and Henseler 2015a; Henseler et al. 2014), as well as the consistent estimation of second-order composites of common factors (van Riel et al. 2017). Our analysis followed the three-stage approach for investigating these second-order composites of common factors (van Riel et al. 2017) and confirmatory composite analysis (Schuberth et al. 2018). Due to the low amount of missing values of 7.5% across all observations, we used arithmetic mean imputation as missing value treatment, which only yields unsignificantly little biased path coefficients, mean loading estimates, and standard errors with PLS (Kock 2018).

After the removal of four indicators from the measurement model from both samples, and four additional indicators only from the non-driver-model due to their low loadings (see Table A1), all indicator loadings are significant and above the recommended minimum threshold of .4 (Hair et al. 2017). Since we removed two of the indicators of the "costs"-construct, this leaves us with a single item measurement, which we, with respect to content validity, deem fit to measure costs as total cost of ownership and therefore useable for our analysis (Hair et al. 2017). The assessment of the measurement model for all constructs furthermore showed satisfactory results for construct reliability (min. $\rho A > 0.65$, min. $\rho C > 0.64$, min. $\alpha > 0.64$) and discriminant validity (HTMT HI95 < .95) (Henseler et al. 2016). Yet, three constructs (RA_RI and RA_P for drivers and non-drivers, and PEU for non-drivers) showed an AVE slightly below the threshold of .5, indicating a lack of convergent validity. We therefore additionally conducted an exploratory factor analysis using principal axis factoring and the direct oblimin rotation. The goal was to test, whether there are other latent factors besides those constructs, that load strongly on their respective indicators. All first extracted factors accounted for more than 60% of the indicators' variances. Therefore, we could consider these constructs to exhibit convergent validity as well.

In the subsequent step of the three-stage-approach for composites of common factors (van Riel et al. 2017), we used confirmatory composite analysis (Schuberth et al. 2018) and a minimal composite model to statistically confirm our composite model for the "relative advantage" construct. Both for the drivers sample (SRMR = 0.0262 [HI95 = 0.0292]; duls = 0.0144 [HI95 = 0.0179]; dg = 0.0133 [HI95 = 0.0151]) and the non-drivers sample (SRMR = 0.0109 [HI95 = 0.0189]; duls = 0.0025 [HI95 = 0.0075]; dg = 0.0019 [HI95 = 0.0057]), the goodness of fit measures show excellent fit. Therefore, we conclude that we cannot reject our composite model of relative advantage (Schuberth et al. 2018).

Finally, looking at the full structural models, the drivers sample model shows acceptable fit (SRMR = 0.0805 [HI99 = 0.0785]; duls = 0.2334 [HI99 = 0.2217]; dg = 0.1450 [HI99 = 0.2073]), and the non-drivers sample model shows excellent fit (SRMR = 0.0449 [HI95 = 0.0595]; duls = 0.0725 [HI95 = 0.1277]; dg = 0.0899 [HI95 = 0.4893]) (Henseler et al. 2016). Path coefficients and their significance as well as R^2-values are shown in Fig. 2 for the driver-sample and in Fig. 3 for the non-driver sample. For both samples, the effect of Relative Advantage on Attitude Toward Adoption is fully mediated by Perceived Usefulness. Yet, an interesting difference between drivers and non-drivers can be seen when looking at the effect of Perceived Ease of Use on Attitude Toward Adoption. For the drivers, this effect is also fully mediated by Perceived Usefulness, whereas for the non-drivers, the effect of Perceived Ease of Use on Attitude Toward Adoption is only partially mediated by Perceived Usefulness. Additionally, the model explains more variance of the focal outcome constructs Attitude Toward Adoption ($R^2 = 0.792$) and Adoption Intention ($R^2 = 0.731$) for the non-driver sample, as it does for the driver sample (ATA: $R^2 = 0.635$, AI: $R^2 = 0.520$). Furthermore, Table 1 gives an overview of the total effects of the individual constructs on the target outcome construct of Adoption Intention. The results show, that Perceived Usefulness has the strongest total effect on Adoption Intention, followed by Perceived Ease of Use and Relative Advantage both for drivers as well as non-drivers of electric vehicles. The total effects on Adoption Intention are also quite similar for both groups for Relative Advantage and Perceived Usefulness yet a larger difference between the groups can be found for the total effect of Perceived Ease of Use on Adoption Intention. For the driver

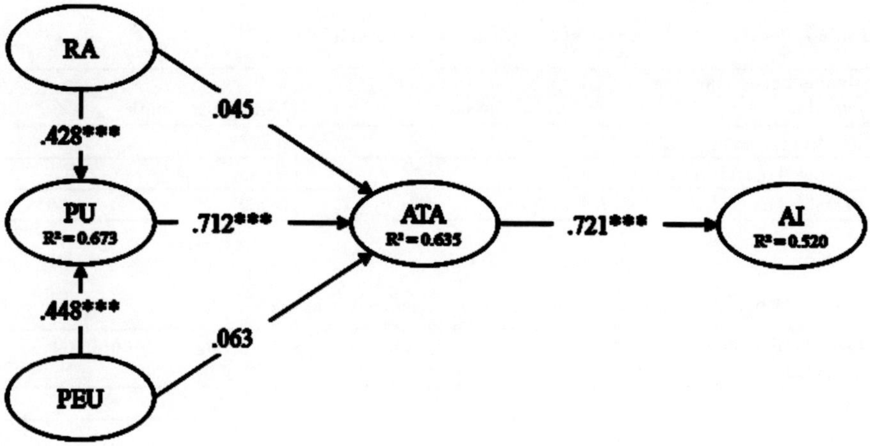

Fig. 2 Structural model for the driver sample. ***Significant at $p \leq 0.001$

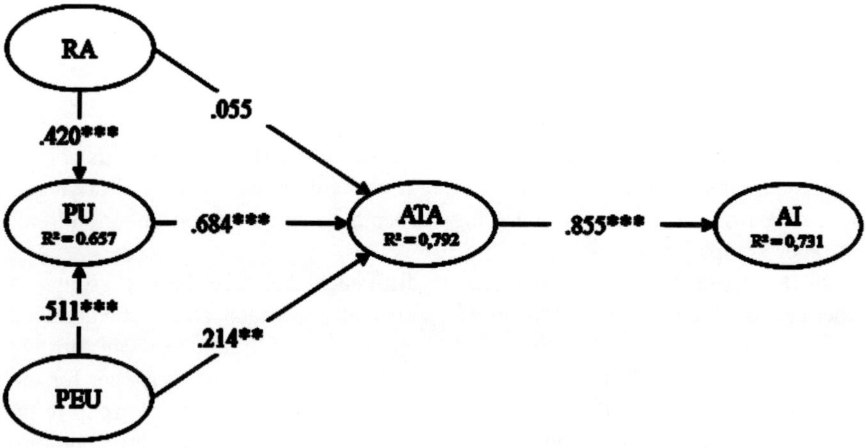

Fig. 3 Structural model for the non-driver sample. ***Significant at $p \leq 0.001$; **Significant at $p \leq 0.01$

sample, this effect only amounts to 0.276, while for the non-driver sample it is 0.482. Additionally, Table 2 displays the consistent weights of the lower-order components of the relative advantage composite. The weights of the lower-order components of the Relative Advantage construct also show some differences between the two groups. The cost component contributes most to Relative Advantage for drivers (w = 0.760) and non-drivers (w = 0.813), and the range & infrastructure component is the second most important (drivers: w = 0.233; non-drivers: w = 0.198). But for the driver sample, the performance component ranks third (w = 0.213), with image (w = 0.137) contributing the least to relative advantage, whereas for the non-driver sample, the image (w = 0.172) component contributes more to relative advantage, than the performance component does (w = 0.157).

Table 1 Total effect of antecedent constructs on Adoption Intention

Total effect on adoption intention	Driver sample	Non-driver sample
Relative advantage (RA)	0.252	0.293
Perceived usefulness (PU)	0.514	0.585
Perceived ease of use (PEU)	0.276	0.482

Table 2 Weights of lower-order components of Relative Advantage

Lower-order component of relative advantage (RA)	Weight *w* (driver sample)	Weight *w* (non-driver sample)
Costs (RA_C)	0.760	0.813
Range & Infrastructure (RA_RI)	0.233	0.198
Performance (RA_P)	0.213	0.157
Image (RA_I)	0.137	0.172

Discussion, Limitations and Future Research

The goal of this study was to provide insights to the question if marketers should address experienced EV-drivers in a different way compared to Non-EV drivers in order to reach a maximum of technology acceptance and adoption intention in all customer groups.

Our results clearly show that there are differences between the two groups of experienced EV-drivers and non-drivers. Especially the total effect of Perceived Ease of Use directly and indirectly through Perceived Usefulness on Attitude Towards Adoption and in the end on Adoption Intention is much stronger for the non-driver group (total effect PEU → AI = 0.482) than for the driver group (total effect PEU → AI = 0.276). Thus, targeting the group of non-drivers for technology adoption of electric vehicles, marketers should strive to increase the Ease of Use of their products in order to achieve this goal, and then also convey this ease of use stronger in their marketing communications. To strengthen the relative advantage of electric vehicles compared to combustion-powered cars, for both groups marketers first of all need to focus on the cost aspect, which contributes most to relative advantage. But also differences arise in the lower-order components of relative advantage. The results show that a stronger emphasis on the communication of image benefits of EVs could lead to a stronger relative advantage of EVs for non-drivers compared to the driver's sample. So, for targeting this group, marketers should change their communication strategy accordingly.

Within this study, we tried to overcome limitations by conducting our survey in five countries within Europe (Germany, France, the Netherlands, Italy, and Austria). All of them are highly different regarding governmental support for e-mobility and also technology adoption. During the analysis, we removed several items for statistical reasons, in order to improve reliability and discriminant validity, and also used single indicators. However, we are confident that all our measurements still exhibit content validity (Hair et al. 2017). Therefore, we are also confident that with its findings based on two solid samples for drivers and non-drivers and a rigorous analysis, this study makes an important contribution to academic literature on the technology acceptance of e-mobility and EVs.

With respect to future research, acceptance antecedents might not only differ between EV drivers and non-drivers, as also habituation effects within the EV user community could influence technology perception over longer timeframes. Future research could focus on longitudinal user experience of EVs in order to bring higher transparency in the adoption process of vehicle electrification. Considering such a dynamic "consumer-perception-lifecycle" could be at least a small step for European manufactures leaving the "lame duck" position and contribute to EV innovations in a significant way.

Table A1 Item summary–questionnaire for EV-drivers

Measurement / Indicator		Source
Relative Advantage		
Costs		Schneider et al. (2014)
ra_c_1	The possibility to save money by using an EV is...	
ra_c_2[a]	The purchase price of an EV is...[a]	
ra_c_3[a]	The maintenance costs of an EV are...[a]	
	7 point scale from "lower" to "higher"	
Range & Infrastructure		Patergona et al. (2013)
ra_ri_4	The driving range of an EV is...	
ra_ri_5	The charging/gas station infrastructure for EVs is...	
ra_ri_6	The confidence of the indicated range is...	
ra_ri_11[a]	The charging/refueling process of an EV is...[a]	
	7 point scale from "lower" to "higher" or 7 point scale from "worse" to "better"	
Performance		Hoffmann et al. (2012)
ra_p_7[b]	The acceleration performance of an EV is...[b]	
ra_p_8	The maximum speed of an EV is...	
ra_p_9	The driving pleasure is...	
ra_p_10	The driving comfort is...	
ra_p_12[a]	The driving noise is...[a]	
	7 point scale from "lower" to "higher" or 7 point scale from "worse" to "better"	

(continued)

Table A1 (continued)

Measurement / Indicator		Source
Image		Schneider et al. (2014)
ra_i_13	People's reaction when seeing an EV on the road is… *7 point scale from "worse" to "better"*	
Perceived Usefulness		Schneider et al. (2014)
pu_1	Using an EV increases the quality of my life	
pu_2	Using an EV is useful for me in everyday life	
pu_3	Using an EV is convenient for me	
pu_4	Using an EV is advantageous for me	
pu_5	I consider an EV a useful means of transport	
	7 point scale from "completely disagree" to "fully agree"	
Perceived Ease of Use		Emsenhuber (2012)
peu_1	An EV is easy for me to use	
peu_2[b]	Learning to operate an EV was easy to me[b]	
peu_3[b]	The operation of an EV is clear and understandable for me[b]	
peu_4[b]	Is was easy to become skillful at using an EV[b]	
peu_5	It is easy for me to schedule battery re-charging with my time planning	
peu_6	An EV is well-suited to carry out my daily tasks	
	7 point scale from "completely disagree" to "fully agree"	
Attitude Toward Adoption		Kulviwat et al. (2007)
	Overall, how would you describe your experience with the EV? For me, using an EV is…	
ata_1	… bad/good	
ata_2	… negative/positive	
ata_3	… unfavourable/favourable	
ata_4	… unpleasant/pleasant	
	7 point scale	
Adoption Intention		Emsenhuber (2012)
ai_1	I favour driving an EV rather than a traditional vehicle	
ai_2	I would recommend others to purchase an EV	
ai_3	There is a high probability that my next car will be an EV	
	7 point scale from "low probability" to "high probability"	

[a]Indicators removed for both samples due to low loadings
[b]Indicators removed for non-driver sample due to low loadings

References

Augenstein, K. (2015). Analyzing the potential for sustainable e-mobility—The case of Germany. *Environmental Innovation and Societal Transitions, 14(3)*, 101-115.

Axsen, J., Goldberg, S., & Bailey, J. (2016). How might potential future plug-in electric vehicle buyers differ from current "Pioneer" owners? *Transport. Res. Part D: Transp. Environ. 47(8)*, 357–370.

Barisa, A., Rosa, M., & Kisele, A. (2016). Introducing electric mobility in Latvian municipalities: results of a survey. *Energy Procedia, 95(9)*, 50–57.

Biresselioglu, M., Kaplan, M., & Yilmaz, B (2018). Electric mobility in Europe: A comprehensive review of motivators and barriers in decision making processes, *Transportation Research Part A: Policy and Practice, 109(3)*, 1-13.

Bühler, F., Cocron, P., Neumann, I., Franke, T., & Krems, J.F. (2014). Is EV experience related to EV acceptance? Results from a German field study. *Transportation Research Part F: Traffic Psychology and Behaviour, 25(7)*, Part A, 34-49.

Bühler, F., Franke, T., & Krems, J.F. (2011). Usage Patterns of Electric Vehicles as a Reliable Indicator for Acceptance? Findings from a German Field Study. *Transportation Research Board 90th Annual Meeting*. Washington DC.

Bures, T., de Rocco, N., Gerostathopoulos, I., Hoch, N., Kit, M., Koch, N., Monreale, G.V., Montanari, U., Pugliese, R., Serbedzija, N.; Wirsing, M., & Zambonelli, F. (2013). A Life Cycle for the Development of Autonomic Systems: The E-mobility Showcase. *2013 IEEE 7th International Conference on Self-Adaptation and Self-Organizing Systems Workshops*, Philadelphia.

Davis, F. D., Bagozzi, Richard P., & Warshaw, P. R. (1989). User Acceptance of Computer Technology: A Comparison of two theoretical models. *Management Science, 35(8)*, 982-1001.

Dijk, M., Orsato, R.J., & Kemp R. (2013). The emerge of an electric mobility trajectory. *Energy Policy 52(1)*, 135-145.

Dijkstra, T. K., & Henseler, J. (2015a). Consistent and asymptotically normal PLS estimators for linear structural equations. *Computational Statistics & Data Analysis 81*, 10–23.

Dijkstra, T. K., & Henseler, J. (2015b). Consistent Partial Least Squares Path Modeling. *MIS Quarterly, 39(2)*, 297–316.

Emsenhuber, E.M. (2012). Determinants of the acceptance of the acceptance of electric vehicles. Internal paper, Department of business administration, business and social sciences, Aarhus University 2012.

Eschenbaecher, J., Wiesner, S., & Thoben, K. D. (2014). Validation of Innovative Extended Product Concepts for E-Mobility. In Evolutionary Paths Towards the Mobility Patterns of the Fu-ture, Springer Berlin Heidelberg, pp. 131-152.

Franke, T., Bühler, F., Cocron, P., Neumann, I., & Krems, J.F. (2012a). Enhancing sustainability of electric vehicles: A field study approach to understanding user acceptance and behavior. In: Sullman, M., Dorn, L. (Eds.), *Advances in Traffic Psychology* (pp. 295-306). Farnham, UK: Ashgate

Franke, T., & Krems, J.F. (2013). What drives range preferences in electric vehicle users? *Transport Policy, 30(11)*, 56-62.

Franke, T., Neumann, I., Bühler, F., Cocron, P., & Krems J.F. (2012b). Experiencing Range in an Electric Vehicle: Understanding Psychological Barriers. *Applied Psychology: An International Review, 61(3)*, 368-391.

Franke T., Schmalfuß F., Rauh N. (2018) Human Factors and Ergonomics in the Individual Adoption and Use of Electric Vehicles. In: Thatcher A., Yeow P. (Eds.), *Ergonomics and Human Factors for a Sustainable Future*. Singapore: Palgrave Macmillan

Genuit, K. (2013). What will be the influence of e-mobility on soundscape? *19th ICA (International Congress on Acoustics) Conference.* Montreal, CA.

Götz, K., Sunderer, G., Birzle-Harder, B., & Deffner, J. (2012). Attraktivität und Akzeptanz von Elektroautos. *ISOE Studientexte*. Bundesministerium für Umwelt, Naturschutz und Reaktorsicherheit 2012.

Günther, M., Rauh, N., & Krems, J.F. (2019). How driving experience and consumption related information influences eco-driving with battery electric vehicles – Results from a field study. *Transportation Research Part F: Traffic Psychology and Behaviour, 62(4)*, 435-450.

Haddadian, G., Khodayar, M., & Shahidehpour, M. (2015). Accelerating the global adoption of electric vehicles: barriers and drivers. *The Electric Journal, 28(10)*, 53–68.

Hair, J. F., Hult, G. T. M., Ringle, C. M., & Sarstedt, M. (2017). *A primer on partial least squares structural equation modeling (PLS-SEM) (Second edition)*. Los Angeles, London, New Delhi, Singapore, Washington DC, Melbourne: Sage Publications.

Haustein, S., & Jensen, A.F. (2018). Factors of electric vehicle adoption: A comparison of conventional and electric car users based on an extended theory of planned behavior, *International Journal of Sustainable Transportation, 12(7)*, 484-496.

Henseler, J. (2016). New developments in PLS path modeling. *Industrial Management & Data Systems, 116(9)*, 1842–1848.

Henseler, J. (2018). Partial least squares path modeling: Quo vadis? *Quality & Quantity, 52(1)*, 1–8.

Henseler, J. & Dijkstra, T. K. (2015). *ADANCO 2.0*. Kleve, Germany: Composite Modeling.

Henseler, J., Dijkstra, T. K., Sarstedt, M., Ringle, C. M., Diamantopoulos, A., Straub, D. W., Calantone, R. J. (2014). Common Beliefs and Reality About PLS. *Organizational Research Methods, 17(2)*, 182–209.

Henseler, J., Hubona, G., & Ray, P. A. (2016). Using PLS path modeling in new technology research: Updated guidelines. *Industrial Management & Data Systems, 116*(1), 2–20.

Hoffmann, C., Graff, A., Kramer, S., Kuttler, T., Hendzlik, M., Scherf, C., & Wolter, F. (2012). Bewertung integrierter Mobilitätsdienste mit Elektrofahrzeugen aus Nutzerperspektive. *Final Report Projekt BeMobility – Berlin elektroMobil* 2012.

Kanger, L., F. W. Geels, Sovacool, B., & Schot, J. (2019). Technological diffusion as a process of societal embedding: Lessons from historical automobile transitions for future electric mobility. *Transportation Research Part D: Transport and Environment, 71(6)*, 47-66.

Kock, N. (2018). Single missing data imputation in PLS-based structural equation modeling. *Journal of Modern Applied Statistical Methods, 17(1)*.

Köpsel, A., Selinka, S., & Kuhn, M. (2018). Beaten Tracks? Application of existing innovation acceptance models on automated driving. *21st AMS (Academy of Marketing Science) World Marketing Congress*. Universidade Lusiada-Norte, Porto.

Krems, J.F., Franke, T., Neumann, I., & Cocron, P. (2010). Research methods to assess the acceptance of EVs – experience from an EV user study. *Smart Systems Integration: 4th European Conference & Exhibition on Integration Issues of Miniaturized Systems*. Como

Kuhn, M., Selinka, S., & de Jong, Natalie (2017). E-Mobility Marketing: Standardization or Specialization. *45st AMS (Academy of Marketing Science) Annual Conference*. San Diego, CA.

Kulviwat, S., Bruner, G., Kumar, A., Nasco, S., & Clark, T. (2007). Toward a Unified Theory of Consumer Acceptance Technology. *Psychology & Marketing, 24(12)*, 1059-1084.

Patergona, D, Pieper, N, Woisetschläger, D.M., Beuscher, G., Wachalski, T. (2013). Akzeptanz von Elektrofahrzeugen – Aussichtsloses Unterfangen oder große Chance? *Final Report Study P3 with Technical University Braunschweig* 2013. Braunschweig.

Peterson, B. (2015). *Vision Elektrofahrzeug – und warum es nicht weit kam. Eine empirische Untersuchung zur Non-Diffusion des Elektrofahrzeugs 1967 bis 2012*.

Schmalfuß, F., Mühl, K., & Krems, J.F. (2017). Direct experience with battery electric vehicles (BEVs) matters when evaluating vehicle attributes, attitude and purchase intention. *Transportation Research Part F: Traffic Psychology and Behaviour, 46(4)*, 47-69.

Schneider U., Dütschke E., Peters A. (2014) How Does the Actual Usage of Electric Vehicles Influence Consumer Acceptance? In: Hülsmann M., Fornahl D. (Eds.), *Evolutionary Paths Towards the Mobility Patterns of the Future. Lecture Notes in Mobility, pp.* 49-66). Berlin, Heidelberg: Springer

Schuberth, F., Henseler, J., & Dijkstra, T. K. (2018). Confirmatory Composite Analysis. *Frontiers in Psychology, 9:2541.*

Simsekoglu, Ö., & Nayum, A. (2019). Predictors of intention to buy a battery electric vehicle among conventional car drivers. *Transportation Research Part F: Traffic Psychology and Behaviour, 60*(1), 1-10.

van Riel, A. C.R., Henseler, J., Kemény, I., & Sasovova, Z. (2017). Estimating hierarchical constructs using consistent partial least squares: The case of second-order composites of common factors. *Industrial Management & Data Systems, 117*(3), 459–477.

Ziefle, M., Beul-Leusmann, S., Kasugai, K., & Schwalm, M. (2014). Public Perception and Acceptance of Electric Vehicles: Exploring Users' Perceived Benefits and Drawbacks. In: Marcus A. (Eds.), *Design, User Experience, and Usability. User Experience Design for Everyday Life Applications and Services* (628-639). DUXU 2014. Lecture Notes in Computer Science, Vol 8519. Cham: Springer.

Augmented Reality in Retail and E-commerce: A Literature Review: An Abstract

Virginie Lavoye, Joel Mero, and Anssi Tarkiainen

Abstract Driven by the rapid development of augmented reality (AR) in retail and e-commerce along with the unique ability of AR to add virtual content in a highly contextual and controllable manner, academic research has recently grown rapidly. This study is a systematic literature review and proposes a holistic view on the current knowledge on AR in retail and e-commerce, including the current state of the research and the factors influencing consumers responses.

We found that the topic is still scattered between various literature streams focusing on different marketing phenomena, such as consumer decision-making, consumer experience, self-brand connection and negative effects. The first research stream addresses decision making and involves research on AR as a decision-aid improving ease of decision in different ways depending on product types and consumers' characteristics (e.g., Heller et al. 2019). The second stream recognizes that in addition to utilitarian value, AR also creates hedonic and experiential value, which increase satisfaction and behavioral intentions (purchase, patronage and technology usage) (e.g., Dacko 2017; Poushneh 2018). The third stream is labeled self-brand connection and refers to the potential of the AR experience to trigger self-referencing and self-brand connection aspects, such as self-brand connection and self-brand congruity (e.g., Baek et al. 2018; Phua and Kim 2018). The fourth stream addresses the negative effects of AR that entail concepts closely related to privacy concerns, such as perceived intrusiveness, discomfort, and users' control of access to personal information, as well as a media irritation including issues about app quality (e.g., Poushneh 2018).

AR experience induces flow (Javornik 2016), which can create long-term relationships (Steinhoff et al. 2019). Although flow may be powerful to create or revive a long-term relationship, as it creates excitement it may divert consumers' attention.

V. Lavoye (✉) · A. Tarkiainen
LUT University, Lappeenranta, Finland
e-mail: virginie.lavoye@lut.fi; anssi.tarkiainen@lut.fi

J. Mero
University of Jyväskylä, Jyväskylä, Finland
e-mail: joel.j.mero@jyu.fi

F. Pantoja, S. Wu (eds.), *From Micro to Macro: Dealing with Uncertainties in the Global Marketplace*, Developments in Marketing Science: Proceedings of the Academy of Marketing Science, https://doi.org/10.1007/978-3-030-89883-0_55

Further research should address the differences in flow that arise through the consumer journey. In addition, AR intertwines self and brand by presenting them in a same view, in a believable manner and creates positive brand-related outcomes. Although, personalization could bring backlashes on the form of privacy concerns.

Keywords Augmented reality · Retail · Decision-Making · Experience · Self-referencing · Privacy

References Available Upon Request

Discovering Interdependent Digital Self: A Multidimensional Perspective: An Abstract

Varsha Jain, Russell Belk, Anupama Ambika, and Manisha Pathak-Shelat

Abstract The unraveling of the notions of self and the extended manifestations has immensely helped the scholars and practitioners alike, in deciphering the deeper meanings of consumption. However, while the basic tenets of the existing conceptualizations of self are still relevant, the possessions and expressions comprising the extended self-have been moving to new realms, owing to rapid transformations of the techno-socio-cultural spheres. As brands continuously unlock new digital avenues for interactions, interconnections, and self-expression among consumers, multiple layers are being added to the self in the digital space. In this paper, we adopt an interpretive approach to explore the evolving self in the digital space with the help of grounded theory. Through in-depth interviews with 20 main participants and 60 supplementary interviews with their friends and family, we identified the vital dimensions of self in the digital space. The study finds diverse, independent, narrative versions of self, which is co-developed through a dynamic collaboration with peers, technology affordances, and brands. The narratives fluctuate across platforms, conditional to the specific objectives, intended spectators, and affordances offered by technology. Further, we identified that the narrative self-alters itself with the wavering core-self, and also influence the actual behavior in tandem with the proteus effect. This study unraveled the specific acceptance and rejection criteria for people and technology in the digital narratives. Surprisingly, the insights discovered that the digital activities of the close & extended family are often unwelcome in the digital narrative of the young Asian consumers. The avoidance of family contradicts the western perspectives, where family cohesion is maintained through digital

V. Jain (✉) · A. Ambika · M. Pathak-Shelat
MICA, Ahmedabad, India
e-mail: varsha.jain@micamail.in; anupama_fpm18@micamail.in; manisha.shelat@micamail.in

R. Belk
York University, Toronto, ON, Canada
e-mail: rbelk@schulich.yorku.ca

F. Pantoja, S. Wu (eds.), *From Micro to Macro: Dealing with Uncertainties in the Global Marketplace*, Developments in Marketing Science: Proceedings of the Academy of Marketing Science, https://doi.org/10.1007/978-3-030-89883-0_56

intimacy. The participants of this study did not deem the family participation as a value-adding constituent of the narrative self. Moreover, the evasion also aids in escaping the moral and cultural barriers set by the family, prevalent in the interdependent cultural spheres. The findings have important theoretical and practical implications. This study extends the existing conceptualizations of self, by identifying the newer dimension, termed as narrative self along with the unique characteristics. Practically, we reveal opportunities for brands to be included in the consumer self-concept, by adding value to their narratives. Additionally, we highlight the need for an integrative approach to study multiple narratives of the consumers to understand them for academia and industry.

Keywords Digital · Self · Narrative · Self-Expression

References Available Upon Request

The Relevance of Demographical Similarity and Factuality in Social Influencer Marketing: An Abstract

Walter von Mettenheim and Klaus-Peter Wiedmann

Abstract This work aims to carve out differences on the success factors of social influencers in dependence of the consumers' consumption goal (hedonic vs. utilitarian). Nowadays, influencers are employed in a wider variety of fields, notably even B2B marketing, where product choices may occur for pure utilitarian reasons. Hypotheses on the differing relevance of demographic similarity of influencer and consumer as well as factuality of the influencer's communication style are developed. Thereby, we argue that demographic similarity is more important under hedonic consumption goal conditions, due to more heterogeneous hedonic customer needs. Factuality would be more relevant if the consumption goal is utilitarian, as utilitarian products include more tangible and rational attributes. The hypotheses are tested in two empirical studies, whose results are evaluated by means of structural equation modeling. As travel endorsement is an important but underexplored field of influencer marketing, the underlying scenario is a consumers' selection of a hotel for (1) a holiday (hedonic consumption goal) or (2) a professional/university seminar (utilitarian consumption goal). The results are to some extent surprising (Smith et al. 2005). Contrary to extant research (e. g. on customer reviews Smith et al. 2005; Grabner-Kräuter and Waiguny 2015) and perhaps human intuition, demographic similarity between influencer and consumer appears to be more important under utilitarian than hedonic conditions. A possible rationale for this finding may be, that also in a utilitarian context, consumer preferences may differ strongly. For example, when choosing a hotel for a professional or educational seminar, consumers may rely more strongly on influencers with an occupation similar to theirs. Moreover, there is no significant difference on the importance of factuality between hedonic and utilitarian conditions. A possible explanation for this finding may be that communication that is more factual could be perceived as more serious and reliable, for both product kinds. Finally, a negative moderating effect of

W. von Mettenheim (✉) · K.-P. Wiedmann
Leibniz University, Hannover, Germany
e-mail: vonmettenheim@m2.uni-hannover.de; wiedmann@m2.uni-hannover.de

F. Pantoja, S. Wu (eds.), *From Micro to Macro: Dealing with Uncertainties in the Global Marketplace*, Developments in Marketing Science: Proceedings of the Academy of Marketing Science, https://doi.org/10.1007/978-3-030-89883-0_57

demographic similarity on the impact of perceived factuality was found. This may be rooted in the fact that individuals are more accustomed to emotional encounters in relationships characterized by similarity (McPherson et al. 2001). Overall, the results show that findings from other research areas cannot be transferred one-to one to influencer marketing. This area rather seems to follow its own principles.

Keywords Social media marketing · Influencer marketing · Consumer behavior · Tourism marketing

References Available Upon Request

The Perceptions of Brand Co-appearance in Product Placement: An Abstract

Fanny Fong Yee Chan

Abstract Brand clutter has gradually extended from traditional advertising to less conventional marketing communication tools. La Ferle and Edwards (2006) reported that 27% of the visual and 23% of verbal brand placements analyzed had multiple brand occurrences while Bressoud, Lehu and Russell (2010) reported 28%. Marketers appear to be avoiding "brand clutter" in product placement, but the latest content analysis has revealed that about half of the brand appearances analyzed (544 out of 1225) contained more than one branded product at a time (Chan and Lowe 2016). Although brand co-appearance in media content is likely to continue to proliferate, little is known about the phenomenon and its effects. Building on research related to co-branding and comparative advertising, this study examined the moderating role of brand familiarity on the effectiveness of brand co-appearance on television programs.

When two products coappear in a television program, the products can come from one of the following conditions: (1) two unfamiliar brands, (2) one unfamiliar and one familiar brand and (3) two familiar brands. This study predicts that brand familiarity moderates the recall/recognition of, and attitudes and purchase intention toward the co-appeared products. Two pre-tests and a quasi-experimental study of 204 television viewers were conducted. It was found that brand familiarity has a significant impact on the recall and recognition of the coappeared products. It also moderates the attitudes toward the coappeared products though the effect on purchase intention is insignificant.

Acknowledgement: The work presented in this paper was supported by a grant from the Research Grants Council of the Hong Kong Special Administrative Region, China (Project Reference No.: UGC/FDS14/H15/17).

F. F. Y. Chan (✉)
The Hang Seng University of Hong Kong, Siu Lek Yuen, Hong Kong
e-mail: fannychan@hsu.edu.hk

F. Pantoja, S. Wu (eds.), *From Micro to Macro: Dealing with Uncertainties in the Global Marketplace*, Developments in Marketing Science: Proceedings of the Academy of Marketing Science, https://doi.org/10.1007/978-3-030-89883-0_58

The study develops a useful framework for understanding the effect of brand co-appearance in product placement which has significant theoretical implications for the field. The empirical results could also guide advertisers and communication practitioners to develop more effective brand placement strategies. Specifically, it provides strategic directions for brand owners in identifying the right co-appearing partners and shows the possible benefits to be gained. The theoretical and practical implications are discussed together with future research avenues.

Keywords Brand coappearance · Brand familiarity · Cognitive effect · Affective effect · Conative effect

References Available Upon Request

The Power of Touch for Degustation in Produce Retailing: An Abstract

Frauke Kühn and Marcel Lichters

Abstract The online retailing market has prospered tremendously (Statista 2019). Consumers are, nevertheless, unsure about buying fresh food online (Kühn et al. 2020). The low need for online grocery purchase is surprising, since consumers maintain that they perceive saving time and convenience as benefits of online shopping (e.g., Kühn et al. 2020). It is therefore important to understand what lies behind consumers' reluctance to purchase fresh food online, especially healthy produce. Consumer psychology provides an explanation by highlighting touch's pivotal role in consumer behavior (e.g., Peck and Shu 2009). When shopping online consumers do not have "the possibility of touching and feeling products before purchasing them to reduce uncertainty" (Herhausen et al. 2015, p. 311), resulting in negative expectations of online offered produce.

Our research shows that these negative expectations influence consumers' produce perception even after they have experienced such products (after tasting experience). A lab experiment allocated participants randomly to either an 'offline' or 'online' condition. In the offline condition, participants selected four apples (one of each presented type) from a basket mirroring a local supermarket context. These consumers believed, during a subsequent degustation, they were going to taste the chosen apple. We, however, served random tastings of each apple type. In the online condition, participants saw a fictive online shop on a computer and were told they were going to taste the apples shown. A local store's assortment served as the product pool in both conditions. The offline condition results show that participants rated their tasted produce better and were willing to pay more than those experiencing the online condition. The second lab experiment incorporates a third condition: online,

F. Kühn (✉)
Otto-von-Guericke-University, Magdeburg, Germany
e-mail: frauke.kuehn@ovgu.de

M. Lichters
Chemnitz University of Technology, Chemnitz, Germany
e-mail: marcel.lichters@wirtschaft.tu-chemnitz.de

F. Pantoja, S. Wu (eds.), *From Micro to Macro: Dealing with Uncertainties in the Global Marketplace*, Developments in Marketing Science: Proceedings of the Academy of Marketing Science, https://doi.org/10.1007/978-3-030-89883-0_59

using a direct touch interface (e.g., a tablet's touchscreen). This experiment replicated study 1's results but used tomatoes, ultimately resulting in higher produce consumption in the offline vs. the online condition. Further, study 2 offers online retailers a solution by addressing consumers' haptic experience. Using a direct touch interface during the online purchasing process compensates for online retailing's negative effects on consumers' product evaluation, taste, WTP, and consumption amount.

Results show that negative expectations impact product evaluation after product experience, as consumers do not learn from the degustation process. Online retailers should therefore not just use freebies to address consumers' negative expectation, but invest in strategies that increase their prepurchase expectations (e.g. image, reputation) (Biswas and Biswas 2004; Yazdanparast and Spears 2013). Online retailers could actively push direct touch usage via mobile apps to exploit direct touch interfaces' positive impact.

Keywords Degustation · Direct touch interface · Online retailing · Sensory marketing

References Available Upon Request

The Role of Alliance Portfolio Diversity in Sustainable Supply Chain Management: An Abstract

Tessa Tien Nguyen, Angelina Nhat Hanh Le, and Julian Ming Sung Cheng

Abstract Sustainable supply chain management (SSCM hereinafter) plays a significant role in the development of business strategies. Scholars and practitioners have thus devoted their effort to investigating the driving forces of SSCM and measures which serve to enhance its performance. A review of extant literature indicates that previous studies have focused on internal and external pressures as the main drivers of SSCM, while the crucial role of the diversity of the supply chain alliance system has not received sufficient attention. In view of such a literature gap, this research aims to explore the contribution of alliance portfolio diversity in sustainable supply chain practices and its impact on SSCM performance. Relevant diversity-related theories are applied to explain the mechanisms of alliance portfolio diversity and their effect on SSCM performance through several mediating roles. Furthermore, the current research framework is tested within contingencies, thereby providing better insight into the studied subject matter. A field study is conducted to examine the proposed framework and related hypotheses wherein survey data comprised from the participation of more than 300 manufacturing firms are collected and tested. An analysis of the findings confirms the significant role of alliance portfolio diversity in SSCM performance, in particular under contingencies. As a result of such findings, this current research not only provides field evidence for the applicability of applied theories, but also draws a set of theoretically grounded guidance criteria into SSCM policies for field practitioners to enhance supply chain performance within the scope of sustainability.

T. T. Nguyen · J. M. S. Cheng (✉)
National Central University, Taoyuan City, Taiwan
e-mail: 108481606@cc.ncu.edu.tw; jmscheng@ncu.edu.tw

A. N. H. Le
University of Economics Ho Chi Minh City, Ho-Chi-Minh City, Vietnam
e-mail: hanhln@ueh.edu.vn

F. Pantoja, S. Wu (eds.), *From Micro to Macro: Dealing with Uncertainties in the Global Marketplace*, Developments in Marketing Science: Proceedings of the Academy of Marketing Science, https://doi.org/10.1007/978-3-030-89883-0_60

Keywords Sustainability performance · Sustainable supply chain management · Diversity · Alliance portfolio

References Available Upon Request

Adopting Artificial Intelligence to Manage a Turbulent Environment: An Abstract

Jing Chen, Gary L. Frankwick, and Zhuofan Zhang

Abstract In a world where it is possible to collect data from credit card purchases, facebook sentiments, and customer returns on a minute to minute basis, marketing managers are inundated with data that may or may not have significant effects on their sales. To deal with this volume and velocity of data, companies are beginning to employ artificial intelligence (AI) to help. As the pace of technology change and as the amount of available market and competitor data increases, marketers are faced with the dilemma of managing this data to understand the changing market and competitive landscape.

This study explores potential antecedents and consequences of artificial intelligence (AI) adoption as a strategy to deal with this ever-increasing data. Based on the technology-organization-environment (TOE) framework and institutional theory, we examine four antecedents: technological opportunism, top management support, customer orientation, and normative pressure as potential influencers to AI adoption. AMOS SEM was employed to analyze responses from a survey of 225 marketing managers, product managers, and brand managers.

Our results suggest top management support is critical to adoption of AI along with a culture focusing on customers. These forces seem to get the firm to desire AI to meet customer needs. In addition, firms will likely adopt AI in industries already adopting AI or in environments where governments or suppliers are pushing AI adoption. The pressure from these outside entities seem to make management sensitive to the need to keep up with competition. The technological environment moderates these effects to the degree that possible higher risk from rapid and unpredictable technological change reduces the effect of top management support on AI adoption,

J. Chen (✉) · Z. Zhang
Texas A&M University Kingsville, Kingsville, TX, USA
e-mail: Jing.chen@tamuk.edu; Zhuofan.zhang@tamuk.edu

G. L. Frankwick
The University of Texas at El Paso, El Paso, TX, USA
e-mail: glfrankwick@utep.edu

F. Pantoja, S. Wu (eds.), *From Micro to Macro: Dealing with Uncertainties in the Global Marketplace*, Developments in Marketing Science: Proceedings of the Academy of Marketing Science, https://doi.org/10.1007/978-3-030-89883-0_61

while greater technological turbulence increases the effect of normative pressure on a firm's AI adoption as it tries to keep up with its competitors. Finally, our results suggest that adoption of AI should improve marketing performance.

Keywords Artificial intelligence · Marketing performance · Marketing strategy

References Available Upon Request

Antecedents and Consequences of Market Orientation in Micro Organisations: An Abstract

Barbara Caemmerer and Niki Hynes

Abstract The Market Orientation (MO) construct is fundamental to the marketing literature. The application of the MO concept to SME contexts is only slowly evolving, whereas its application in micro organizational contexts has been virtually neglected (Raju et al. 2011; Reijonen et al 2012). Micro firms are defined as having less than ten employees and often fall into the realm of the entrepreneurial literature. Investigating MO in micro organizational contexts is important as statistics suggest that a substantial amount of micro organizations fail within the first years in business. As Liberman-Yaconi, Hooper and Hutchings (2010) point out rightly, it is therefore critical to understand better if and how micro firms develop strategy, and how this impacts their success. In this context, research is required to explore to what extent MO as a strategic management tool applies to micro organizations and how it can contribute to their future performance and success in the market.

A mixed methods sequential exploratory study was undertaken over a two-year period in two stages through a pragmatic lens (Creswell 2002). In total 22 in-depth interviews with founders and principal managers of micro organisations were conducted. After thematic analysis of the interviews following the guidelines of Braun and Clark (2006), the themes were triangulated (Yin 2003) with extant research on MO and entrepreneurial motivations in order to develop measurement scales for the quantitative part of this study. On the basis of this triangulation, a questionnaire was developed. A total of 324 micro organisations responded.

This study contributes to the literature by exploring the nature of MO within micro firms, offering a better definition and understanding of the way in which MO

B. Caemmerer (✉)
ESSCA School of Management, Paris, France
e-mail: barbara.caemmerer@essca.fr

N. Hynes
University of Liverpool, Liverpool, UK
e-mail: niki.hynes@online.liverpool.ac.uk

F. Pantoja, S. Wu (eds.), *From Micro to Macro: Dealing with Uncertainties in the Global Marketplace*, Developments in Marketing Science: Proceedings of the Academy of Marketing Science, https://doi.org/10.1007/978-3-030-89883-0_62

is expressed. Second, this study identifies three main motivational groups of owner goals in micro firms, exploring the complexities of the motivations of owners and founders. Thirdly, we show the relationship between owners' goals for entrepreneurial activity and the way MO is implemented. Finally, we assess the MO-performance link in micro organizational contexts: Our findings suggest that customer orientation, cooperation with competitors and proactive product orientation are key to performance in micro firms. Small firm marketing can include networking with a range of stakeholders and is expressed through informal conversations internally and externally. The flexibility of the micro firm, together with the ability of the founder or key players to learn allows these tiny companies to react quickly to changes.

Keywords Market Orientation · Micro organizations · Entrepreneurial motivations · Performance

References Available Upon Request

Subtle Luxuries: Motivations for Consumption

Arthur J. Kover, William James, and Anil Mathur

Abstract Consumption of luxury goods is often associated with status and conspicuousness. However, a segment of luxury consumers do not wish their consumption to be too conspicuous. We can call this type of consumption to be subtle luxuries. In this research we explore what are subtle luxuries and why do some people consume them? These are luxuries used for some inner personal satisfaction and not to conspicuously broadcast their net worth. Depth interviews were conducted to elicit motivations for consuming luxury goods while avoiding broadcasting such consumption. This qualitative exploration suggested an underlying motivation: controlling to some extent contacts with other people. This could take the form of filtering access to or from others, passive exclusion, or hidden protest by differentiating themselves from people whose behavior they dislike.

Keywords Subtle luxuries · Consumption motivations · Personal interviews · Discreet consumption

Introduction

Most studies of luxuries approach them as insignia, as "bling," letting the often indifferent outside world know of the success or daring of the wearers. Similarly, the mass media tend to view luxuries as important bling. Thus, a recent *Wall Street Journal* article (Kapner 2015) worried about the economic consequences of

---

A. J. Kover
Fordham University, New York, NY, USA
e-mail: kover@fordham.edu

W. James · A. Mathur (✉)
Hofstra University, Hempstead, NY, USA
e-mail: william.james@hofstra.edu; anil.mathur@hofstra.edu

F. Pantoja, S. Wu (eds.), *From Micro to Macro: Dealing with Uncertainties in the Global Marketplace*, Developments in Marketing Science: Proceedings of the Academy of Marketing Science, https://doi.org/10.1007/978-3-030-89883-0_63

possibly changing consumer buying patterns of luxury handbags. Luxuries may even self-define the person as the consumer literature from marketing (Belk 1988; Belk and Pollay 1985), history (Berg 2005; Cohen 2006; Schama 1987), and economics (Carlsson et al. 2003; Dittmar 1992) has amply demonstrated.

But consider some luxuries also as masks behind which people hide, some because of fear, perhaps others who want to appear as somehow less than they are (Lavallee 2007), or others who do the modern version of shunning the world. Many of those luxuries are quiet and subtle.

Relatively little about such inconspicuous consumption appears in the marketing literature (with the exception of work about those who live simple lives). The more public (if rather highbrow) press, however, occasionally does cover this area. The Economist (2005) reported a turning away by the wealthy from overt displays but "...rather than abandoning status anxiety, the way the rich seek to display status may simply be getting more complex" (p. 67). More recently, Postrel (2008) noted a somewhat larger-scale movement away from but "bling" with a similar note about exclusiveness.

> The shift away from conspicuous consumption—from goods to services to experiences—can also make luxury more exclusive. Anyone with $6,000 can buy a limited edition...bag... or a Cartier watch. Or, for the same sum, you can register for [a] conference, four days in California hearing short talks by brainy innovators....But... the conference directors have to deem you interesting enough to merit one of the ...spots. It's the intellectual equivalent of a velvet rope. (p. 151)

As enticing as it might be to think of this as a general societal movement of the wealthy, this article examines other people, some wealthy, some not, who have personally chosen to consume different luxuries that are not flaunted. Here they are called "subtle luxuries."

People who consume subtle luxuries do so for many different reasons. In fact, at first it appeared as if there were as many reasons as there were people interviewed. Apparently, this is not a general social movement but is quite different from a general movement toward less conspicuous consumption.

Subtle Luxuries?

Initially, we defined subtle luxuries as consumer goods that appear to be of good quality but which do not broadcast their cost. Initial thoughts included jewelry of exquisite form and work but small in size, automobiles that seem ordinary but have sumptuous interiors and superb engines, plain wristwatches looking like throwaways but costing many thousands of dollars. However, this initial definition was too narrow. Participants had their own divergent definitions and examples of their subtle luxuries. This will be made clear in following sections.

Method

Consumers of subtle luxuries are not easy to find. In fact, it took almost two and one-half years to uncover fourteen. This was not surprising as most of these consumers keep their luxury consumption *very* quiet. They were contacted using a snowball method with the core consisting of four people who in turn suggested others. All of the participants lived in New York City or Boston with one exception.

The small size of this group, its northeastern United States location, and more particularly the manner of obtaining participants precluded making generalizations except for an interesting hypothesis finally generated, one that could be tested. Note also that about half of the sample was well off, with one exception all were white, and the youngest person in the group was in her mid-thirties. See Table 1 below for a profile of participants in the study. Note that the interviews represented both overt answers and, those elicited after considerable probing.

Interviewing generally took place either in participants' homes or, in three cases, places of work. Interviews were in person except that a letter supplemented one interview and two interviews were conducted by telephone. Each participant was interviewed at least once; most, two times. The first interview centered on subtle luxuries, what they were (examples), and what they meant. The second interview generally concerned the person's personal background, personal goals, and needs and how their subtle luxuries met those needs. Participants were promised anonymity. The initial interviews were relatively free form. Three basic questions were asked in the first interview:

1. What, in your opinion, is a luxury? Your luxuries appear to be rather subtle, rather 'quiet'. Tell me more of what they are.
2. Why do you have these rather than other luxuries?
3. What do they bring to you and your needs?

The interviews were not voice recorded. Because of the sensitive nature of the interviews and their locations, responses were written. Almost immediately after each interview, the notes were fleshed out and transcribed within two days. This is in line with the Notes and Queries guidelines for anthropological reporting (Briggs 1986; British Association for the Advancement of Science 1874); although it is considered out of date by contemporary anthropologists, it seemed to give good results.

Following this, the interviews were analyzed using Tinderbox, a program designed to help cluster similar sets of meanings. From this, several core reasons were adduced for this general consumption pattern. Early in the process, four additional interviews were conducted with purveyors of subtle luxuries: a London bespoke tailor, a New York store selling expensive and high quality but unmarked leather goods, a U.S. manufacturer of handmade shotguns, and a major outlet for fine watches. The interviews provided some background for the interviews with consuming participants.

Luxuries and Subtle Luxuries

In general, the participants agreed that luxuries were of high quality:

I need some things for my life and work. They could be serviceable or better than serviceable. It is that "better than serviceable" that could make them luxuries. [9]

But that quality must be only for items that a person wants, that fit their needs or tastes:

... my family ... only buys American cars; foreign cars are tacky. One would never see any of us own a Mercedes. We own Cadillacs or Lincolns. We do not own sports cars; we own cars we do not need to drive. [7]

[My wife] wanted a gas fireplace. I was appalled. The real luxury was the logs and the fire, a natural event. And looking into that fire was a kind of primeval luxury. [6]

You may think that this apartment is pretty grand. It is, but the real luxury for me is that most of it is cozy and warm. [4]

Luxury is something you don't really need, in part because of the expense. It might be something that caught my eye and would personalize. [Personalize?] Well, if I got it, it would be to fit my own needs to say something to other people. But I don't usually like to do that. [13]

It is not our purpose to review the various meanings of "luxury goods." That has been covered at length elsewhere. More interesting for our purposes was to review what has been said or written about subtle luxuries and then determine how these participants fit within these definitions or changed them.

Subtle luxuries: Obviously, what is defined as a subtle luxury has to do with attribution of value. Boudon (2001, 2004), following Max Weber, would say that people who acquire and use such luxuries are making rational choices. "Rational" means attributing values that are personally important to that person. This is done, of course, within recognizable limits; it is, however, quite different from Bourdieu's (1984) idea of cultural capital and its imposition by the upper classes. Subtle luxuries are more a matter of individual choice or else lie within the boundaries formed by some rather restricted group, real or imagined. As a result, that choice may also have to do with "good taste" and permanent values rather than living the grand style of the day. In Bayley's (1992) words, "There is a tension [that] arises from the conflict between my observation that taste changes, that values are fugitive, and my personal conviction that there are certain forms, shapes and ideas which transcend time and have a special, permanent value." (p. 108).

There may be some feeling that subtle luxuries are reserved for the well-to-do or well-born. "Your only hope is to approach what [my wife] calls 'the lucky sperm club'" (Conversation with Arthur Meranus, a retired advertising creative director, 2007). And, looking at some people who participated in this research, it may seem so. However, there are some indications that other kinds of people might desire subtle goods. Patagonia, a well-known line of sporting clothing, often features an almost hidden logo on its shirts; it is the word, "Patagonia," embroidered in tiny letters in thread matching the color of the shirt. Sports such as fly fishing, in which all sorts of people participate, almost demands shabby clothing. Even if one wears expensive gear, "there's a very clear reverse snobbism in effect in which old, patched waders trump brand new ones, 10-year-old Filson flannel shirts that look like they come from Wal-Mart are super-desirable. And the most expensive, hand-made reels look a little scruffy, as if they're 60 years old" (e-mail from Stephen Feinberg, an advertising executive, 2005).

Subtle luxuries have invaded the teenagers' shoe market. Some makers have introduced very expensive sneakers for young men. They can be distinguished from lesser products only by tiny marks. As one shoe marketer said: "If you know where to look and you are interested, you can find [the marks]" (Lehrer 2006).

That may be the key. Subtle luxuries communicate something. But what? Looking at the responses of the participants, we can begin to examine the complexity of what is communicated.

As [5] noted:

> These things I like? They have quality but it's unidentified [?] Not a label but some people know it when they see it. Not a Rolex. But Paul Stewart vs. Armani. Even jeans. Jeans: I didn't want a label. I want very good ones but not with that stitching on the back pockets. It is the difference between branded luxuries and those that don't show off externally. The quiet ones are the real luxuries. And other people can tell if they want to and know enough.

What Sorts of Subtle Luxuries do These People Consume?

First, note that the "luxuries" consumed might not be things at all. Subtle luxuries can be performances: giving money to charity [2], going on camping trips (important because they are central to the life of the participant). They can be the absence of something. Two participants noted that they work hard to have free time, time to do anything or nothing.

What is defined as "subtle" depends in part on the social situation of the person. One participant called his wife's ten-carat diamond ring a subtle luxury, considering the super consumer groups in which she moves. For others, the luxuries may be collections but they are subtle because they are known only to a few. And for one participant, his luxury was an obligation, to preserve family artifacts for the next generation. Of course, there were the usual suspects as well: fountain pens, watches, bespoke clothing and shoes, jewelry. These were used, however, for purposes other than communication.

In brief, what are defined as "luxuries" may not be things or activities that marketers sell *as luxuries* through advertising or word of mouth. But, for all participants, their subtle luxuries have important meaning for defining themselves (Sirgy 1982).

Motivations to Consume Subtle Luxuries

Examining the responses of the participants, three general clusters of reasons emerged: filtering access to or from others, passive exclusion, protest against others (usually hidden).

Filter Access to or from Others

Quiet invitation for inclusion by perceived superiors: Several participants thought that the understated sumptuousness of their consumption might entitle them to acceptance to (perceived) social or intellectual superiors.

> Look at this apartment. Rugs, paintings, painting of the walls. All very good but they don't shriek at you. Like the furniture. A mix of important and not important. But not that anyone would notice. It's taste, not style.... You can join an elite if you have taste even if you don't have all that much money. It's an entry in New York. You can attract the attention of certain other people. [4]
>
> I collect Old Master drawings. But I don't really hoard them. I have helped form exhibitions at [a major museum of Art]. Often, many of the drawings come from my collection. So I can enjoy them and other people can enjoy them, too. But I don't have my name put on them. In a quiet way, I am now a member of those amateurs whom the experts at the museum have accepted. It is a welcome from people I respect. [1]

Passive openness to connoisseurs; a "flash community": Some consumers of subtle luxuries feel a form of mild elation and a temporary feeling of 'closeness' when the consumption is identified. It is a weak signal to some people of like mind (c.f. Belk 1988; Belk and Pollay 1985; Lipovetsky 1994).

> ....some people know it when they see it. For instance, look at my watch. It is an IWC. It is a very plain, stainless watch but it feels right on me. It is expensive but I will have it for a long time. And, if any body notices it, it makes me feel good. A tiny, brief connection with that person for a second. [5]
>
> Yes, well I hate to have flashy things, won't be defined by them. But sometimes someone will notice my Pelikan pen (which is very plain but very good) and there will be something like a brief *snap* between us. 'Ha,' I would say, 'this person recognizes it and maybe how I do my life.' [6]

Active invitation to connoisseurs/appreciators: For some people, more organized forms of subtle luxury consumption are a clearer reference to perceived membership in a self-referred "club," such as the in-group who go to an 'undiscovered' Caribbean island (St. John and Wolfe 2005). This could be a group or not but goes beyond an ephemeral identification.

> Any serious collection of American clocks has some. I am considered an expert on [makers'] clocks in the small circle of clock collectors. I know how to identify and validate models and to discover fakes. I do correspond with other people who collect clocks. [14]

That diamond ring and its social setting: Some of the examples given above are of luxuries that hardly seem subtle to a middle-class reader; remember, however, that it is the social setting in which the luxuries fit. Take for example, [2] and his comments:

> My wife likes jewelry. ...I hit a home run [in the eighties].... My wife deserved something nice. So I bought her a ring at Sotheby's. A 12.65 carat diamond ring ...
>
> Now, times are different. Now my wife feels uncomfortable with the ring—too big. So, I [traded?] the ring; the diamond wasn't perfect anyway. I bought her instead a ring with a perfect, flawless, diamond. It is only 10.85 carats but a perfect and colorless diamond. I traded down to perfection.

[But isn't that still pretty big?] Sure, but in the group my wife goes with, that's not *very* large; it goes unnoticed. And I have the satisfaction of knowing it's perfect.

Passive Exclusion

Just as subtle luxury consumption can be a way of reaching out to *some parts* of the outer world, it can also be more inturning, keeping the outer world out to some extent. One aspect is hiding.

Hiding—Fear of thievery: Consumption of subtle luxuries is also designed to be inconspicuous, sort of one's attempt to blend in without being recognized, driven by fear of being attacked by criminals.

> This interview is really about the owner more than me. He now controls many properties in Singapore [hotels, publishing, fashionable stores, some media].... [H]e controlled the personal lifestyles of the eight directors who report to him and (trickling down) to all his managers. All of us dressed down. Little jewelry. Black suits. Not even fancy cars, although we were doing well. It was both for protection from envy and also a kind of inverted snobbery.
>
> Singapore is a society in which, after you ask somebody new the name and where he/she works, then you'd ask, "How much did you pay for your house?"
>
> But not for people in the company. Certainly not the owners. It was as if [the owners] wanted to [be in] a secret place, like a secret handshake. [Was it all about taste?] Under it all, it was mostly a way not to attract any attention. Singapore is pretty law-abiding but there is always the danger of a kidnapping. Or even a murder by the envious. *Best not to attract any attention.* [11]

A form of misanthropy: In one case, [7], a person of wealth, inflicted his somewhat Spartan consumption patterns on guests, forcing them in effect to consume as he does—a not-too-subtle expression of misanthropy. In fact, [7] said after the contact that he just wants to have free alone-time, without others.

> I have no particular attachments to objects. I never owned a wristwatch. I buy off-the-rack from J. Press or L.L. Bean. I still have the same luggage I had back in college. I bought my last wallet in 1978 and I very rarely carry it because I hardly ever need it.
>
> Concerning my liquor cabinet, I find extensive knowledge of dinner wines rather tacky... I would never select a specific wine for a specific meal—I consider most table wine drinkers sissies and I only drink and serve either hard liquor or Champagne, usually Veuve Cliquot. Anyone else can have tap water.
>
> I consider my greatest luxury is <u>having free time</u> [emphasis original]. I just do not want to be bothered by people.

At least two other participants said that free time was a hidden subtle luxury but neither said so in such an extreme form. For all three, however, "free time" meant the exclusion of others.

Religious/traditional reasons: Two participants indicated that they had subtle luxuries, quite different in content but for a similar reason: the preservation of a religious or family tradition. They were kept quite private and 'silent'. [1] believed that her husband's family's heirlooms were not his but were held quietly in safekeeping for future generations; his other consumption was not luxurious:

> We have all we need. Old, good family furniture, family silver, family portraits and jewelry. We haven't bought anything like a luxury of the kind other people mean in years. Jewels: Very little. Not ornate. Mainly gold and diamonds. All family gems. [Wife] never wears them. Clothes: Well, mainly wear loafers from L. L. Bean. Button-down shirts and khaki pants (from ditto). Same for modest dress-up plus tweed jacket (old) and a couple of bow ties (ditto). Watch: I don't care as long as it tells time and I can throw it away when it breaks.
>
> I know that some of our things are valuable. They won't be sold. Nothing of this is so attention-getting that anyone would pay much attention to it. But it is valuable.
>
> Think of that watch advertisement in the New Yorker. Well, we feel that we are just the guardians of these things for [daughter] and her children and their children. They are not to be shown or used much.
>
> Participant [10] is an independent architect, a Quaker:
>
> I am not interested in showing off to others—ever. There is no pleasure in that. Other people might *need* to do it but my needs are met. …Jewelry doesn't interest me. The family has learned not to get me fancy things. Oh yes, sometimes one of my daughters gets me something nice—a necklace. But they know that it should not be expensive. It [being a Quaker] is an inherent understanding that money is to be used appropriately, not squandered. It came through the blood. My mother got her special occasion dresses from the used clothing shop.
>
> The best luxury is just something that others take for granted, having the nuclear family together. Every summer we go camping. Ordinary to others but a special treat for all of us, not ordinary.
>
> I like naturalness, simplicity. I don't want to hide behind things. It is a mask between me and the world. Hiding me.

Not caring what others think or know: Liking and treasuring fine things for themselves; not caring if anyone else knows or sees them—this characterize these people. Quite unlike the social valuations put upon consumption items by people of high status (Bourdieu 1984), this can be also a 'rational' personal choice, not dependent on what others think (Boudon 2004).

> My shirts are made by Turnbull & Asser…; the shoes made by a guy in New Hampshire. These cost $900. But feel the leather. They are very comfortable…. I want to be totally satisfied. I'd rather spend $4,000 for a suit I feel good in rather than three suits I don't feel good in. I refuse to compromise on what I need to spend on things that give me great joy. I won't compromise.
>
> [Does anybody notice?]
>
> Probably not, that is completely immaterial. After all, who would notice an old, short guy with decent clothing? It's that joy, the joy of having just what I like. [3]

Protest (Usually Hidden)

Two participants used their subtle luxuries as a subversive weapon: quietly differentiating themselves from people whose behavior they disliked (see Trifonas and Balemenos 2003; (Davis 2003; De Rooy 2002; McCracken 1988, p.116). The first of these two was an associate in a law firm in New England:

> Most of the partners in my office wear Rolexes, gold ones. This one costs about the same; it's a GP. But it is plain. Looks like stainless but it's white gold. I couldn't spring for platinum. Those Rolexes are a kind of expensive uniform; not for me.

> We all need fountain pens at the office.... The partners, many of them, use Mont Blanc pens. Like the Rolexes, they are easily seen as very good, expensive. Not for me. I have a few pens but not Mont Blancs. A couple of Montegrappas, and a Visconti. Very quiet. That's just enough to give me an internal boost—-to use something really good but not to broadcast it. I want to be different from my partners but not too different. But I must fit in or seem to. I pick my ground and the way I show it. Or not. These things are a kind of kick for me and a very subtle kick in the ass for those flashy partners. [9]

The second was a woman whose husband was wealthy and who liked to be seen as a public benefactor. During the interview, she expressed a dislike for the kind of public charity that brought public attention to her husband.

> We give to charity. But my husband and I are different. He is on the Board of the [major cultural institution] and other things. We give these places a lot of money. But my giving is different. I have been involved with a number of homeless people. *I have saved people's lives.* It is not a big social thing but I can see how my money and work can make people's lives better. That's my kind of luxury. [1]

Commonality Among Users of Subtle Luxuries

At first glance, not only the luxuries but also the reasons for using and enjoying them differ. Some want to invite people in, some keep others out, while others say they do not care. All the participants in this research used their subtle luxuries (at least in part) as a way to deal with (or ignore) the outer world in a personal way.

This 'dealing with the outer world' has an even deeper commonality; this commonality explicates all these behaviors. Subtle luxuries *control access either to or from certain others.* Every participant in this research expressed, usually directly, that the very quietness of the luxury can (in different situations) either keeps people away as desired or else invite or preserve some connection. Thus, there is an element of perceived social control in the participants' consumption of subtle luxuries.

Of course, much of that perceived 'control' may be a hope and be relatively ineffectual; think of the person hoping that someone will recognize his watch and shoot him a monetary flash of shared understanding. Others might be misdirected, as for the lawyer secretly mocking his partners. But all seem to share that general common goal.

The theoretical model for such behavior is contained in *Bridges and Doors* (Simmel 1957 [1909]). Some behaviors can be bridges to connect with others with similar preferences while being doors closed against others with different preferences. Those doors might open slightly to admit beliefs, behaviors, or persons that are congruent. But those bridges or doors can either be illusory or ineffective, this-worldly or fantastic. Boudon (2001, 2004) would argue that these behaviors are rational in the sense similar to Weber's idea of *Wertrationalität.* This behavior is directed at socially shared goals; it aims to achieve certain shared values, reality-based or theological or imaginary, personal but shared. Whatever those values, people acting within them are acting as rationally as people acting rationally to achieve an instrumental goal, the more commonly accepted *Zweckrationalität* ("goal rationality").

Table 1 Profile of participants in the study

Identification	Gender	Age	Brief description
1	F	Early 70s	Spouse of a recently wealthy man; participant offended by his flashy style
2	M	Mid 60s	New York real estate lawyer
3	M	Early 80s	Retired production manager, advertising agency
4	F	Early 40s	Husband has prospered investing in telecommunications industry
5	M	50s	University professor
6	M	70s	Retired academic
7	M	50s	Inherited wealth; owns factory making valves
8	M	60s	Retired school teacher; downwardly mobile family
9	M	Late 30s	Partner in New Haven law firm
10	F	Early 40s	Architect; birthright Quaker
11	F	Mid 30s	Former PR officer for a Singapore trading firm
12	M	Mid 50s	Civil servant
13	F	Mid 50s	Owns a small gift shop
14	M	Late 60s	Retired; devotes time to studying clocks formerly made by small family firm

The use of subtle luxuries is one means to keep value-order in a world that is increasingly multi-valued and chaotic. In other times, order was exemplified by external control of luxury display: sumptuary laws (Hunt 1996), or even the quiet rules of the dandy's dress (Barbey d'Aurevilly 1887; Unknown 2005). Now the consumers of subtle luxuries may attempt to maintain personally some of that sort of order.

Much of the marketing literature touches the authenticity of the brand or product advertised (cf. Arnould et al. 2005, pp. 134, 149, 376). The perceived authenticity of the item (object or not) seems to shed light on the person to strengthen his or her self-image (see (Beverland et al. 2008). Subtle luxuries can be a way to protect personal integrity and authenticity; their very subtlety can hide (except to perceptive others) that the authenticity lies within and not with the luxury item. It may be a failing struggle, however; as Heidigger claims, authenticity merely suspends inauthenticity (Thiele 1995, p. 233).

Discussion

If one abides with the dream of classical scientific rigor, this study can only suggest next steps. It is based on a convenience sample and at best the conclusions are tentative. However, this research suggests something interesting in a corner of the world of consumption: that certain consumption might be an active striving for a certain kind of order.

This research also suggests some interesting questions: How do people become involved in the world of subtle luxuries? How and when do they recognize them in others? What are the clues for which they might look (think of the two-hole buttons in the suits of that Savile Row tailor)? And finally, how wide is this sub-world of consumption? Even if small, it could command a rather large share of spending either for things, or for that most subtle luxury, time.

References

Arnould, E. J., Piece, L., & Zhinkhan, G. (2005). Consumers, 2nd edition. New York: W. W. Norton.

Barbey d'Aurevilly, J. (1887), Du dandysme et de G. Brummel: memoranda. Paris: Alphonse Lemerre.

Bayley, S. (1992). Taste: The secret meaning of things (1st American ed.). New York: Pantheon Books.

Belk, R. W. (1988). Possessions and the extended self. Journal of Consumer Research, 15, 139-168.

Belk, R. W., & Pollay, R. W. (1985). Images of ourselves: The good life in twentieth century advertising. Journal of Consumer Research, 11(4), 887-897.

Berg, M. (2005). Luxury and pleasure in eighteenth-century Britain (First ed.). Oxford: Oxford University Press.

Beverland, M. B., Lindgreen, A., & Vink, M. W. (2008). Projecting authenticity through advertising: Consumer judgments of advertisers' claims. Journal of Advertising, 37(1), 5-15.

Boudon, R. (2001). The origin of values: Sociology and philosophy of beliefs. New Brunswick, NJ: Transaction Publishers.

Boudon, R. (2004). The poverty of relativism (Peter Hamilton, Trans.). Oxford: The Bardwell Press.

Bourdieu, P. (1984). Distinction: A social critique of the judgment of taste. Cambridge, MA: Harvard University Press.

Briggs, C. L. (1986). Learning how to ask: A sociolinguistic appraisal of the role of the interview in social science research. Cambridge: Cambridge University Press.

British Association for the Advancement of Science (1874). Notes and queries on anthropology for the use of travelers and residents in uncivilized lands. London: E. Stanford, Charing Cross.

Carlsson, F., Johannson-Stenman, O., & Martinsson, P. (2003). Do you enjoy having more than others? Survey evidence of positional goods. In Working Papers in Economics. Göteborg, Sweden: Göteborg University.

Cohen, D. (2006). Household gods: The British and their possessions. New Haven: Yale University Press.

Davis, J. E. (2003). The commodification of self. The Hedgehog Review, 5(2), 41-49.

De Rooy, P. (2002). Republiek van Rivaliteiten. Nederland sinds 1813 (First ed.). Amsterdam: Mewts en Schilt.

Dittmar, H. (1992). The social psychology of material possessions: To have is to be. Hemel Hempstead (UK) and New York: Harvester Wheatsheaf and St. Martin's Press.

The Economist (2005). Luxury: Inconspicuous consumption. In The Economist, December 24, pp. 66–67.

Hunt, A. (1996). Governance of the consuming passions: A history of sumptuary law. Houndmills, Basingstoke, Hampshire and New York: Macmillan. St. Martin's Press.

Kapner, S. (2015). Luxury handbags lose some cachet. In The Wall Street Journal, November 4, pp. B1, B6.

Lavallee, A. (2007). Inconspicuous consumption: Hiding the plasma TV. In The Wall Street Journal. New York.
Lehrer, B. (2006). Sharp dressed men. In The Brian Lehrer Show. United States: WNYC, New York.
Lipovetsky, G. (1994). The empire of fashion: Dressing modern democracy (Catherine Porter, Trans.). Princeton: Princeton University Press.
McCracken, G. (1988). Culture and consumption: New approaches to the symbolic character of consumer goods and activities. Bloomington, IN: Indiana University Press.
Postrel, V. (2008). Inconspicuous consumption. Atlantic, 302(1), July/August. 148, 150–151.
Schama, S. (1987). The embarrassment of riches: An interpretation of Dutch culture in the golden age (First ed.). New York: Alfred A. Knopf, Inc.
Simmel, G. (1957). Brücke und Tür. In M. Landmann (Ed.), Brücke und Tür: Essays des philosophen zur geschichte, religion, kunst, und gesellschaft (pp. 1-7). Stuttgart: K. F. Koehler Verlag.
Sirgy, M. J. (1982). Self-concept in consumer behavior: A critical review. Journal of Consumer Research, 9(3), 287-300.
St. John, W., & Wolfe, A. (2005). What do peacocks say? In The New York Times. New York.
Thiele, L. P. (1995). Timely meditations: Martin Heidigger and postmodern politics (Paperback ed.). Princeton, NJ: Princeton University Press.
Trifonas, P., & Balemenos, E. (2003). Good taste: How what you choose defines who you are. Cambridge: Icon Books.
Unknown (2005). The Dandy. In The Regency Collection, Vol. 2006.

The Relevancy and Perceived Quality of the Academy Awards to Millennials: An Abstract

Monica Fine, John T. Gironda, and Maria Petrescu

Abstract The Academy Awards (the Oscars) is recovering from criticisms regarding a lack of diversity among nominees, the show being overly long, incongruity between nominated movies and their popularity with the public, and poor host selections. Ratings for the broadcast have declined every year for the past five years. The Motion Picture Academy has taken steps in recent years to address previous criticisms and modernize the Academy Awards, such as reaching out to younger viewers, increasing its usage and integration of social media to promote electronic word-of-mouth, increasing the diversity of its membership, and electing the first African-American president of the Academy (Kalra 2016; Pond 2013).

Of particular interest are young adult moviegoers' perceptions of the Academy Awards. The millennial market of adults between the ages of 18–36 represents a key audience for motion pictures, as this segment embodies 38% of frequent moviegoers and contributes 40% of box office sales (MPAA 2018). If marketers can establish genuine connections with this group, millennials have shown themselves to be staunch supporters, co-promoters, and advocates of brands (Mancini 2014). Thus, determining the relevancy of the Academy Awards to millennials will be an immense asset to movie marketers and distributors as well as to the Academy itself.

This study investigates millennials' perceived quality of the Academy Awards and the relevancy of movie characteristics, consumer behavior, social media usage, eWOM. We will examine multiple generations in order to compare age group

M. Fine
Coastal Carolina University, Conway, SC, USA
e-mail: mfine@coastal.edu

J. T. Gironda (✉)
University of North Carolina Wilmington, Wilmington, NC, USA
e-mail: girondaj@uncw.edu

M. Petrescu
International University of Monaco, Les Moneghetti, Monaco
e-mail: mpetrescu@monaco.edu

F. Pantoja, S. Wu (eds.), *From Micro to Macro: Dealing with Uncertainties in the Global Marketplace*, Developments in Marketing Science: Proceedings of the Academy of Marketing Science, https://doi.org/10.1007/978-3-030-89883-0_64

differences in perceived quality of the Academy Awards. The Motion Picture Academy would benefit from a study like this by gaining insights on what age groups they should be targeting and how perceptions of the awards have changed from generation to generation. Additionally, as marketers have long used Academy Award nominations and winners as differentiators between movies, it will also be interesting to examine if this makes a difference to younger generations, i.e., are millennials more likely to watch Oscar-nominated/winning films over other films that have not received such accolades?

Given the millennial generation's proclivity for frequent movie attendance, a study such as the one proposed here should serve as a critical market analysis for the Oscars' future. Additionally, it should be an immense asset to movie marketers and distributors, as well as to the Academy itself, as it will provide insights into young adults' views and behaviors about the movie industry.

Keywords Academy Awards · Oscars · Millennials · Word of mouth · eWOM

References Available Upon Request

Social Media Effects on Human Brand Sampling: A Non-Linear Time Series Analysis: An Abstract

Navid Bahmani

Abstract Human brands, or well-known personas who are the subject of marketing communication efforts (Thomson 2006) have millions of fans who enjoy their offerings. However, extensive research has shown that these fans may in fact identify with human brands on a far deeper level, as doing so provides them with an opportunity to feel good about themselves (Chernev et al. 2011) and express and validate their identity by self-defining themselves as part of a group (Chernev et al. 2011). With the growing popularity of social media, group identification is easy to accomplish, as consumers can "follow" human brands and become part of their online brand communities. As this relationship is established, content sharing (i.e., word of mouth) begins to occur throughout a follower's own social network, which includes individuals who are not part of the human brand community. For these individuals, word of mouth can "clear the air" regarding a human brand and its offerings, and they likely trust it more than typical advertising sources (Faber and O'Guinn 1984). This can easily benefit human brands such as musical artists, who regularly post samples of their information/experience goods (e.g., YouTube music videos) to social media with the goal of consumers engaging with them and subsequently forming higher-order beliefs (Marks and Kamins 1988) and becoming less uncertain of the level of quality (Gopal et al., 2006). This process can lead to greater purchase intentions (Liebowitz 1985) and ultimately more sales (Bawa and Shoemaker 2004).

The goal of the current research is to study the time-varying dynamic between the aforementioned social media drivers and musical artist sampling behavior, a research gap, which differs from prior literature that has focused directly on sales (Saboo et al. 2016; Dewan and Ramaprasad 2012). The social media variables analyzed include the growth of a brand community (GBC) and the extent of content sharing (EOS), which impact sampling of a musical artist's YouTube music videos

N. Bahmani (✉)
University of Wisconsin-Milwaukee, Milwaukee, WI, USA
e-mail: nbahmani@uwm.edu

F. Pantoja, S. Wu (eds.), *From Micro to Macro: Dealing with Uncertainties in the Global Marketplace*, Developments in Marketing Science: Proceedings of the Academy of Marketing Science, https://doi.org/10.1007/978-3-030-89883-0_65

(Views). To account for endogeneity and stationarity concerns of these time series variables, an autoregressive distributed lag model is estimated, in addition to a non-linear model, which allows for potential asymmetric effects. Across a sample of 20 musical artists, this research finds that while most artists' Views is impacted by GBC and EOS in the short-run, only half of the artists receive a sustainable impact in the long-run. Asymmetric effects are found, which suggest that the impact of GBC or EOS on Views varies depending on whether an increase or decrease occurs.

Keywords Human brands · Sampling · Brand community · Word of mouth · Time series econometrics · Asymmetric effects

References Available Upon Request

Towards Abundant Sales Organizations: How Workplace Spirituality and Innovative Climate Foster Customer-Related Outcomes: An Abstract

Ashish Kalra, Vishag Badrinarayanan, Raj Agnihotri, Vinay Sharma, and Rajat Agrawal

Abstract Firms are rapidly acknowledging that employees seek meaning and purpose at work by developing a positive and nurturing work environment as well as a supportive organizational climate. Ulrich and Ulrich (2010) describe firms that have institutionalized this philosophy as "abundant organizations" and postulate that more fulfilling workplaces can ultimately engender better value for employees, customers, and shareholders.

Further, workplace spirituality refers to "the recognition that employees have an inner life that nourishes and is nourished by meaningful work that takes place in the context of community" (Ashmos and Duchon 2000, p. 137). That is, workplace spirituality encompasses three dimensions: *meaningful work*, *sense of community* and *alignment with organizational values* (Milliman et al. 2003).

Prior research has identified that the sales profession is characterized by high levels of stress, pressure, and workload (e.g., Jones et al. 2007), which consequently exert detrimental effects on salespersons' well-being and performance (e.g., Jaramillo et al. 2006). However, barring a few exploratory attempts to comprehensively import research on workplace spirituality and organizational climate to the

A. Kalra (✉)
LaSalle University, Philadelphia, PA, USA
e-mail: kalra@lasalle.edu

V. Badrinarayanan
Texas State University, San Marcos, TX, USA
e-mail: vb16@txstate.edu

R. Agnihotri
Iowa State University, Ames, IA, USA
e-mail: raj2@iastate.edu

V. Sharma · R. Agrawal
Indian Institute of Technology, Roorkee, India
e-mail: vinayfdm@iitr.ac.in; rajatfdm@iitr.ac.in

F. Pantoja, S. Wu (eds.), *From Micro to Macro: Dealing with Uncertainties in the Global Marketplace*, Developments in Marketing Science: Proceedings of the Academy of Marketing Science, https://doi.org/10.1007/978-3-030-89883-0_66

sales literature (e.g., Badrinarayanan and Madhavaram 2008), research gaps remain. Correspondingly, in this study, we develop and test a conceptual framework guided by the following research questions: (1) How does workplace spirituality transcend organizational boundaries to influence customer-related outcomes? In this regard, we focus on two customer-related outcomes, namely, salesperson diligence and customer engagement. (2) What role does organizational climate play in the relationship between workplace spirituality and customer-oriented outcomes? The results from a unique dyadic dataset of 162 B2B salesperson-customer matched responses show that workplace spirituality positively enhances salespersons' diligence and customer engagement. These relationships are strengthened when salespeople perform under high innovation climate than under low innovation climate.

Keywords Workplace spiritualty · Innovation climate · Diligence · Customer engagement

References Available Upon Request

Effect of Brand Compatibility on the Success of Entrepreneurial Campaigns: An Abstract

Masoud Moradi

Abstract Entrepreneurs are increasingly eschewing traditional funding processes, which rely on a small number of large investors. Instead, they are focusing more on online crowdfunding approaches, which rely on a large number of small funders. This paper examines the effects of brand compatibility of crowdfunding projects and entrepreneurial narratives on the success of crowdfunding campaigns. Drawing upon signaling theory and using data from 581 crowdfunding campaigns, this paper investigates the following research questions: (1) What is the effect of brand compatibility on the funding level of crowdfunding projects? (2) What are the effects of narrative language style (i.e., emotional language style and cognitive language style) and narrative length on funding level? (3) What is the moderating effect of brand compatibility on the relationship between narrative style/length and funding level?

Results suggest that funders expect an emotional tone from brand compatible projects rather than a cognitive language style. An explanation for this result pertains to the characteristics of brand compatible projects. Funders are already familiar with the analytical aspects of the known brands. Therefore, for those projects, they prefer an emotional narrative to improve their emotional bonds with brands. However, funders expect a more analytical language from non-branded projects because funders are not familiar with the analytical aspects of those unknown projects; therefore, creators should explain their ideas cognitively to provide funders with diagnostic information. Results also show a negative interaction between brand compatibility and narrative length. This finding suggests that potential funders expect a shorter description from branded products as they are already informed of those brands. However, funders need more details on non-branded projects as they don't have adequate information about those projects. Hence, creators should explain their ideas in detail to provide funders with adequate information.

M. Moradi (✉)
Texas State University, San Marcos, TX, USA
e-mail: masoud.moradi@txstate.edu

F. Pantoja, S. Wu (eds.), *From Micro to Macro: Dealing with Uncertainties in the Global Marketplace*, Developments in Marketing Science: Proceedings of the Academy of Marketing Science, https://doi.org/10.1007/978-3-030-89883-0_67

In general, project creators can use both emotional language style and cognitive language style as these narrative styles positively affect the funding level. However, brand compatible projects should use emotional language style in the descriptions rather than cognitive language style as there is no negative interaction between brand compatibility and emotional language style. Moreover, non-branded projects should use cognitive language style in the descriptions rather than emotional language style as there is a positive interaction between non-branded projects and cognitive language style. Also, brand compatible projects should provide shorter descriptions and details as there is a negative interaction between brand compatibility and narrative length. However, non-branded projects should provide longer project descriptions and details as there is a positive interaction between non-branded projects and narrative length.

Keywords Brand compatibility · Narrative language styles · Narrative length · Crowdfunding success

References Available Upon Request

Relationship of Mindfulness, Mindful Consumption and Life Satisfaction: An Abstract

Sharad Gupta and Harsh V. Verma

Abstract Mindfulness is paying attention non-judgmentally and in non-reactive manner to the present moment (Kabat-Zinn 2003). It keeps us sensitive to the present context and prevents us from getting overwhelmed by rules and routines (Langer 2014). Past research, in separate strands, showed that mindfulness leads to life satisfaction (Bajaj and Pande 2016) and mindful consumption (Gupta and Verma 2019) but these two strands remain disconnected due to the missing linkage between mindful consumption and life satisfaction. This missing link is the reason for limited research on mindfulness in consumer context despite ground-breaking research by renowned academician Prof. Jagdish Sheth (Sheth et al. 2011) and seminal investigation by noted practitioner Dr. Shalini Bahl (Bahl et al. 2016). We attempt to join these separate research strands by analyzing multiple models generated from an experimental study.

We establish the relationship between mindful consumption and life satisfaction by using difference-in-differences research design and intervention of guided short meditation (Kabat-Zinn 1982) after a regular class. Previously established scales for mindfulness (Brown and Ryan 2003), mindful consumption (Gupta and Verma 2019), and life satisfaction (Diener et al. 1985) were used for pre and post intervention measurements. We examined correlation, moderation, and moderated mediation relationships by employing models 2, 76, and 59 (Hayes 2018) using Process plugin.

The multi-model comparison shows that mindful consumption mediates the influence of mindfulness on life satisfaction. Post-hoc analysis shows that this mediation effect is not due to demographic variables. This research also shows that

S. Gupta (✉)
Delhi School of Business, Delhi, India
e-mail: sharad.gupta@dsb.edu.in

H. V. Verma
University of Delhi, Delhi, India
e-mail: harsh.verma@fms.edu

F. Pantoja, S. Wu (eds.), *From Micro to Macro: Dealing with Uncertainties in the Global Marketplace*, Developments in Marketing Science: Proceedings of the Academy of Marketing Science, https://doi.org/10.1007/978-3-030-89883-0_68

mindfulness, mindful consumption, and life satisfaction could change significantly within a short period of two months. There are academic, practical, and policy implications for establishing this linkage between mindful consumption and life satisfaction. This research opens important avenues for future research in the areas of mindfulness, mindful consumption, and life satisfaction. Sample size and attrition were the limitations of this study.

Keywords Mindfulness · Mindful consumption · Life satisfaction · Moderated mediation

References Available Upon Request

Antecedents of Mindful Consumption: An Abstract

Sharad Gupta and Harsh V. Verma

Abstract Mindful consumption includes awareness, caring and temperance (Sheth et al. 2011; Armstrong 2012; Bahl et al. 2016; Milne et al. 2019). Like mindfulness, there are different conceptualizations of mindful consumption. Some researchers conceptualized it within the context of mindfulness (Armstrong 2012; Bahl et al. 2016; De wet 2008; Milne et al. 2019; Rosenberg 2004) whereas others expounded it without referring to mindfulness (Assadourian 2009; Giri 2004; Maind 2014; Sheth et al. 2011; Sheth 2017). Prof. Jagdish Sheth (Sheth et al. 2011) conceptualized mindful consumption in a ground-breaking article in the Journal of the Academy of Marketing Science. Bahl and colleagues (2016) also explained mindful consumption in their seminal study on Mindful consumption. Despite such good theoretical support, there is very little research on Mindful consumption in last ten years. The reason lies in misperceptions about mindfulness, which is considered the antecedent of mindful consumption. For example, parents complain schools about roots of mindfulness and suspect mindfulness to indirectly promote Eastern religions (Gregoire 2013). To make the matters hazier, mindfulness finds its roots in different religions like Hinduism, Buddhism, Christianity, Islam, Judaism, and Taoism. Bahl and colleagues (2016) identified these misperceptions about linkage between mindfulness and religion as challenge to achieve Mindful consumption.

In this research, we aim to establish the antecedents of mindful consumption and to ascertain the linkage between mindfulness and religiousness. We conducted three studies and employed ANOVA, correlation analysis, regression analysis and structural equation modelling. The first study observed the causal effect of mindfulness on mindful consumption and the second study examined the direct and interaction

S. Gupta (✉)
Delhi School of Business, Delhi, India
e-mail: sharad.gupta@dsb.edu.in

H. V. Verma
University of Delhi, Delhi, India
e-mail: harsh.verma@fms.edu

F. Pantoja, S. Wu (eds.), *From Micro to Macro: Dealing with Uncertainties in the Global Marketplace*, Developments in Marketing Science: Proceedings of the Academy of Marketing Science, https://doi.org/10.1007/978-3-030-89883-0_69

effect of mindfulness and religious faith on mindful consumption. The final study validated the generalizability of the effect of mindfulness and religious faith on mindful consumption across gender, occupations, and household incomes using multi-group analysis.

Results show that both mindfulness and religiousness are indeed the antecedents of mindful consumption but mindfulness and religiousness do not interact with each other. Several demographic variables do not impact these relationships. The research has important academic and practical implications.

Keywords Mindful consumption · Mindfulness · Religiousness · Multi-group analysis

References: Available on request

What Aspects Drive the Success of a Low-Fit Extension Retailer? A Structural Topic Modeling Approach Using Product Reviews: An Abstract

Sungha Jang, Ji Hye Kang, Tian Liu, and Huichen Yang

Abstract A common motivation for firms' brand extension is to leverage the equity in established brands and enable the development of profitable products or increase sales in other categories. Higher-fit congruity between established brands and a new business easily produces spillover benefits and leads to more positive evaluations of brand extensions. However, firms sometimes extend their new business to new categories, a move associated with a low-fit extension. Considering Amazon, a retailer with a low fit to fashion, and Macy's, a retailer with a high fit to fashion, we examine the spillover effect of the retailers on consumers' evaluations of their fashion merchandise. Drawing on product reviews of identical products from both retailers' websites, we compare the topics discussed in the reviews as important product attributes of consumer evaluations and examine the effects of these topics on review ratings, which are potentially associated with success factors of low- and high-fashion-oriented retailers. We collected review information for two fashion product categories from 21 brand items in the men's and women's divisions carried by Amazon and Macy's. Our empirical findings show that the product topics mentioned for identical products are generally different between Amazon (the low-fashion-oriented retailer) and Macy's (the high-fashion-oriented retailer). In addition, the different topics discussed at the two retailers eventually lead to different ratings. These findings support a spillover effect of retailers on consumers' evaluations of products and the significance of fit congruency in a brand extension.

S. Jang (✉)
San Francisco State University, San Francisco, CA, USA
e-mail: shjang@sfsu.edu

J. H. Kang
University of Rhode Island, Kingston, RI, USA
e-mail: jhkang@uri.edu

T. Liu · H. Yang
Kansas State University, Manhattan, KS, USA
e-mail: tliu@ksu.edu; huichen@ksu.edu

F. Pantoja, S. Wu (eds.), *From Micro to Macro: Dealing with Uncertainties in the Global Marketplace*, Developments in Marketing Science: Proceedings of the Academy of Marketing Science, https://doi.org/10.1007/978-3-030-89883-0_70

We provide managers with insights on developing and maintaining competitive advantages for the low-fit extension company and existing company.

Keywords Online retailing · Retailer's spillover effect · Product reviews · Consumer evaluation · Structural topic model

References Available Upon Request

Mature Consumers and Smart Devices: How Do They Mitigate Future Vulnerability? An Abstract

Agnès Helme-Guizon, Maureen Bourassa, and Monica LaBarge

Abstract Do mature consumers (aged 50–65; Moschis et al. 2004) anticipate smart devices (defined in Hoffmann and Novak 2018) will simplify their activities of daily living and facilitate their vision of aging well? Or, do they forecast negative implications of using smart devices as they age? We find mature consumers perceive smart devices may make them more, not less, vulnerable—where vulnerability is characterized by powerlessness and dependence (Baker et al. 2005; Baker, LaBarge and Baker 2015).

Nineteen mature consumers in France participated in interviews and focus groups. Data were analyzed using a thematic approach (Braun and Clarke 2006). We identified two overarching themes: (1) perceived threats to future vulnerability related to smart device use—concerns about loss of competence (fear of losing cognitive and physical faculties replaced by smart devices and thus not continually used), autonomy (fear of giving up decision-making and goal-setting to smart devices), and relatedness (fear of losing quality social relationship to technology); and (2) a collection of four novel coping strategies to mitigate this threat.

Coping strategies identified include: **Dissociating**—particularly emotionally—meant that rather than talking about smart devices as possible representations of identity and image (Belk 1988; Fournier 1998; McCracken 1989), our participants spoke of smart devices largely in functional terms, focusing primarily on the intended practical benefits (e.g., tracking steps, performing cooking functions). **Minimizing** meant that in their efforts to reduce the importance of smart objects, participants shared stories about putting their smart devices under their beds or in drawers where they gathered dust. **Deprecating** smart devices meant that partici-

A. Helme-Guizon (✉)
Université Grenoble Alpes, Grenoble, France
e-mail: agnes.helme-guizon@univ-grenoble-alpes.fr

M. Bourassa
University of Saskatchewan, Saskatoon, SK, Canada
e-mail: bourassa@edwards.usask.ca

M. LaBarge
Queen's University, Kingston, ON, Canada
e-mail: monica.labarge@queensu.ca

F. Pantoja, S. Wu (eds.), *From Micro to Macro: Dealing with Uncertainties in the Global Marketplace*, Developments in Marketing Science: Proceedings of the Academy of Marketing Science, https://doi.org/10.1007/978-3-030-89883-0_71

pants reduced the benefits of smart devices in relation to their cost—for example, by harshly criticizing their unreliability or by condemning their planned obsolescence. **Projecting** meant that participants described the benefits of smart devices as best suited to other populations, namely much younger or much older consumers.

The four coping strategies we identify are directed primarily towards managing the individual's psychological positioning of smart devices in their lives, in an attempt to mitigate anticipated future vulnerability—a perceived loss of control that in turn generates negative feelings—and so the coping strategies are also attempts to reshape the emotional and psychological aspects of consumption experiences. Our research adds to our understanding of vulnerability theory by suggesting that mature consumers' potential future vulnerability is not only a result of structural or systemic variables, but also actively managed through consumption choices.

Keywords Vulnerability · Mature consumers · Smart devices · Coping strategies

References Available Upon Request

Consumer Preferences and Their Willingness to Pay for Local Products (by Means of Consumer Ethnocentrism): An Abstract

Vüsal Hasanzade, Ossama Elshiewy, and Waldemar Toporowski

Abstract Consumers are increasingly willing to opt for locally produced alternatives to counteract the downsides resulting from food that often travels all around the world. Along with the increased demand for local products, there is also an increased demand for greater transparency on the consumer side. Due to a lack of a standardized definition of the term 'local' (Meyerding et al. 2019), however, there is little known about consumer perception, preferences and their respective willingness to pay for local product attributes. While research suggests that both the geographical *and* the social proximity need to be taken into account when defining local products (Eriksen 2013), the majority of existing research solely focuses on one aspect. However, all these approaches make it difficult to assess the relative importance of different local product attributes that fit the expectations of consumers and drive their choice behavior. This study aims to fill this research gap by using a choice-based conjoint analysis.

Results indicate that 'fair prices for farmers' is of particularly high importance for respondents' choice behavior when it comes to consuming local dairy products (b = 1.118***, WTP = .98 EUR), followed by the distance to where the dairy good is being produced. The part-worth utility for the detailed distance information decreases with increasing radius of product origin and place of purchase, while dairy products which are produced within 100 km from the place of purchase are still favored (b ranging from 1.046*** to .254**, WTP ranging from .92 to .22 EUR). 'Securing jobs in the area' (b = .76***, WTP = .67 EUR) and 'the financial support of local producers' (b = .779***, WTP = .68 EUR) seem to be further drivers for local product purchase. Results of a linear regression, when taking consumer characteristics into account to explain the individual-level attribute importance, indicate that regardless of the consumer characteristics the majority of consumers seem to be very interested in local product features. Local ethnocentric consumers,

V. Hasanzade (✉) · O. Elshiewy · W. Toporowski
University of Göttingen, Göttingen, Germany
e-mail: vhasanz@uni-goettingen.de; oelshie@uni-goettingen.de; wtoporo@uni-goettingen.de

F. Pantoja, S. Wu (eds.), *From Micro to Macro: Dealing with Uncertainties in the Global Marketplace*, Developments in Marketing Science: Proceedings of the Academy of Marketing Science, https://doi.org/10.1007/978-3-030-89883-0_72

however, place a high importance in product origin declaration in general (b = .524***) and in information about the farm (b = .115***).

The results show that consumers are indeed willing to pay higher prices for local products, as long as the dairy product correspondents to their understanding of local, while providing important insights for food marketers and policy makers to increase market shares for environmentally friendly local products.

Keywords Local consumerism · Consumer choice · Preference · Willingness to pay

References Available Upon Request

"Does It Go Without Saying?" Implication of Electronic Word of Mouth in Luxury Branding: An Abstract

Harjordan Mander, Zixuan (Mia) Cheng, Anouk De Regt, Rayan Fawaz, and Matteo Montecchi

Abstract The rise of social media has provided firms with ample new opportunities to communicate their brands (Carlson et al. 2019; Zhang et al. 2018). Additionally, because textual and audio-visual data on social media platforms can be preserved, the medium has become a valuable tool for providing insights and informing strategic brand management (Kim et al. 2019; Greco and Polli 2019). Within the overall social media communication environment, brand communities specifically provide unique insights, as they can enhance understanding regarding changes in consumer's opinions and feeling and how they perceive and talk to each other about a brand (Kim and Lee 2019). Using automated text analysis and Berthon and his colleagues' (2009) framework to classify the user-generated brand content, this study investigates consumer attitudes towards luxury products based on the online communication within a Facebook brand community.

This study includes a sample size of 15,014 comments from 302 posts from a Facebook luxury fashion group. The analysis revealed several significant main and interaction effects. This included significant main effects of aesthetics on analytic thinking and tone. More importantly, a significant two-way interaction between aesthetic and ontology occurred on analytic thinking and tone.

The study provides useful and interesting insights into the theory and practice of luxury branding. For marketers bringing luxury to the masses could ensure higher sales, however, the perceived loss of exclusivity experienced by the high aesthetic customers could negatively impact the brand's image in the long run. Luxury brands could mitigate these negative feelings and fuel prolonged consumer engagement by providing other options that make this part of their target audience feel special. Since the high aesthetic consumers are generally well informed about a company's products or services, brands should consider selecting these individuals for co-creation and product innovation design purposes. This will not only help in re-

H. Mander · Z. (. Cheng (✉) · A. De Regt · R. Fawaz · M. Montecchi
King's College London, London, UK
e-mail: harjordan.mander@kcl.ac.uk; zixuan.cheng@kcl.ac.uk; anouk.de_regt@kcl.ac.uk; rayan.fawaz@kcl.ac.uk; matteo.montecchi@kcl.ac.uk

F. Pantoja, S. Wu (eds.), *From Micro to Macro: Dealing with Uncertainties in the Global Marketplace*, Developments in Marketing Science: Proceedings of the Academy of Marketing Science, https://doi.org/10.1007/978-3-030-89883-0_73

building the consumer-brand relationship but because of their status within the social group will likely add to enhanced positive social discourse. This work also adds to the luxury fashion literature by incorporating linguistic inquiry and word count as a research tool to investigating luxury brand discourse in online brand communities, confirming the influence of the social context and conclusions by Berthon et al. (2009) that multiple market segments for one luxury brand exist and that marketing strategies should be focused accordingly.

Keywords Luxury branding · eWOM · Social media · LIWC

References Available Upon Request

You Feed Me and I'll Feed You: Exploring the Relationship Between Sales Activity and Organizational Social Media Marketing Culture: An Abstract

Adam C. Merkle

Abstract Social selling, defined as a selling approach using principles of digital marketing such as content and social media marketing, is a topic at the forefront of business-to-business sales research (Ancillai et al. 2019). Does strategic social media marketing offer any value for salespersons when driving sales activities? Selling and buying in semi-complex firms may be better conceptualized as a dynamic value creation activity involving a plurality of decision-makers (Hartmann et al. 2018). The concept of institutions within institutional theory captures the up-to-date reality of the buying process. Organizational buying is based on 'how things actually get done' (according to institutional arrangements) and involves many entities within and outside the organization (Hartmann et al. 2018). In this view, salespeople should focus on institutional work that either creates and maintains beneficial institutions or disrupts competing institutions. Social media signaling is one form of institutional work (Banarjee et al. 2020). But how do organizational buyers and buying committees use social media for sales-related activities?

Another relevant topic regarding social media marketing within buyer-seller relationships is the complexity of transactions, otherwise known as "crossing points.“ The notion of crossing points originated in literature about modular design and subsystems (Baldwin and Clark 2000). Professional salespeople need tools to help create, maintain, and defend thin and thick crossing points. They also need tools aimed at disrupting rival firms' crossing points. Social media marketing may be one potential tool available to salespeople, depending on their organization's social media marketing culture.

At the interface of social media marketing (SMM) culture and sales activity, the evaluation in this study includes the effects of buyer SMM culture on sales activities, along with a component to assess buyers' ability to effectively use social media. Sellers can also affect a buyer's social platform, for example by pushing content

A. C. Merkle (✉)
University of South Alabama, Mobile, AL, USA
e-mail: acm1821@jagmail.southalabama.edu

F. Pantoja, S. Wu (eds.), *From Micro to Macro: Dealing with Uncertainties in the Global Marketplace*, Developments in Marketing Science: Proceedings of the Academy of Marketing Science, https://doi.org/10.1007/978-3-030-89883-0_74

into the social media feeds of the buyer. Three studies within a mixed-methods research design are proposed including responses from both buyers and sellers. Study one includes cross-sectional data from 102 buyers. Study two proposes similar data collection from salespersons. The results are analyzed using PLS-SEM. Study three proposes a content analysis of both sellers' and buyers' social media messaging and connections. Together these findings should (a) link organizational SMM culture with sales activity, (b) distinguish between SMM cultural influences on sales activity at thin and thick crossing points, and (c) provide understanding about the impact of SMM for organizational buyers and professional sellers.

Keywords B2B purchasing · Crossing points · Social selling · Institutional theory

References Available Upon Request

An Aspirational Definition of Marketing: An Abstract

Michael R. Hyman and Alena Kostyk

Abstract Marketing is the best-positioned discipline for orchestrating efforts to realize a desirable future because its internal theoretical shortcomings (i.e., lack of unifying theory and consensus definition) often compelled its scholars to borrow other disciplines' theories and constructs, which amplified its interdisciplinary status. As a result, marketing is not beholden to a single scholarly weltan-schauung. Hence, marketing is the apical social science for identifying, pondering, and effectuating alternative futures because it can serve as a nexus for futurology-related scholarship.

Moreover, marketers are uniquely positioned to shape the future because they are skilled in molding consumer consciousness and routinely track internal and external signals critical to foreseeing opportunities and threats (Bilgin 2010; Mendonça et al. 2012). Central to successful business-to-consumer marketing is ascertaining consumers' preferences accurately despite high uncertainty. Fortunately, the knowledge and tools needed to reveal those preferences also pertain to ascertaining humanity's preferences for a future world.

We suggest structuring marketing futurology around an aspirational definition of marketing and a set of related higher-order questions. Our proposed aspirational and futurology-concordant definition of marketing is as follows: *Marketing is the interdisciplinary normative social science addressing multi-party, volitional, and value-creating exchanges that promote personkind's sustained flourishing*. This definition is consistent with the late Robert Lusch's argument that marketing has evolved from a 'to market' philosophy to a 'marketing with' philosophy, which "views the customer as endogenous and as a partner in the co-creation of value" (Lusch 2007, p. 265).

M. R. Hyman
New Mexico State University, Las Cruces, NM, USA
e-mail: mhyman@nmsu.edu

A. Kostyk (✉)
University of Glasgow, Glasgow, Scotland, UK
e-mail: Alena.Kostyk@glasgow.ac.uk

F. Pantoja, S. Wu (eds.), *From Micro to Macro: Dealing with Uncertainties in the Global Marketplace*, Developments in Marketing Science: Proceedings of the Academy of Marketing Science, https://doi.org/10.1007/978-3-030-89883-0_75

The American Marketing Association (AMA) currently defines 'marketing' as "*the activity, set of institutions, and processes for creating, communicating, delivering, and exchanging offerings that have value for customers, clients, partners, and society at large*" (American Marketing Association, 2018). Unlike the current AMA definition, our definition implies morality and ethics (Mick 2007) by including the words *normative*, *volitional*, *sustained*, and *flourishing*.

To identify and then effectuate a future that promotes humanity's sustained flourishing, marketers must answer three higher-order questions, which in turn relate to groups of value-laden questions: *What is a person? What is a good life? Who is in charge, and how do they decide?* These questions, sequentially, can be re-imagined as lower-order research questions, such as *Should sentient machines be considered persons? Can persons live a 'good life' in a virtual world? To what extent should deontology or teleology (i.e., intention versus outcome) criteria be used to base and assess decisions and outcomes?*

Keywords Definition of marketing · Futurology · Theory · Ethics

References Available Upon Request

Improving Translation-Based Communication in Japanese Multinationals Using Internal Marketing

Yoko Aoyama and Takako Yamashita

Abstract This paper focuses on translation as a means of information transmission from Japanese corporate headquarters to their overseas subsidiaries. Means to minimize gaps in understanding between senders and receivers were examined by clarifying the cognitive mechanism by which information is transformed from Japanese into English. First, qualitative research was conducted to clarify communication issues in light of previous studies in the areas of *explicit versus tacit knowledge, relevance theory, communities of practice,* and *internal marketing*. Next, quantitative research was carried out using indexes from previous studies and factors identified in the qualitative research, and gaps in understanding between Japan headquarters and overseas subsidiaries were analyzed using covariance structure analysis. Based on the results of the qualitative and quantitative research, suggestions are made for improving organizational decision-making via reappraisal of the position of translation in the organization and adoption of more effective information transfer methods.

Keywords Global enterprises · Translation · Explicit knowledge · Tacit knowledge · Relevance · Communities of practice · Internal marketing

Introduction

In global enterprises, organizational decision-making with overseas affiliates located in countries with different cultures and languages is performed using translation, with information first being translated in written form. It is sometimes the case that the senders of information believe that their intentions are accurately

Y. Aoyama
Shimadzu International Inc., Kyoto, Japan
e-mail: aoyama@int.shimadzu.co.jp

T. Yamashita (✉)
Doshisha University, Kyoto, Japan
e-mail: tayamash@mail.doshisha.ac.jp

F. Pantoja, S. Wu (eds.), *From Micro to Macro: Dealing with Uncertainties in the Global Marketplace*, Developments in Marketing Science: Proceedings of the Academy of Marketing Science, https://doi.org/10.1007/978-3-030-89883-0_76

conveyed through the translation process, but later find out that their intentions were not well understood by receivers of the information. In this paper, we focus on translation as a means of transmitting information within a multinational company whose headquarters are located in Japan, a typical "high-context" country. A high-context country is one in which communication is carried out in ways that are implicit and rely heavily on context. Our research questions are two. First, in such a high-context country, what problems occur in using translated documents to transmit information from corporate headquarters to overseas subsidiaries that cause gaps in understanding between sender and receiver? Second, how can such gaps in understanding be minimized? More specifically, we examined what cognitive problems occur when transferring information from Japanese to English, and what measures and considerations are necessary in order to transmit information between different languages without creating gaps in understanding. Our investigation was carried out through empirical research conducted in Shimadzu Corporation and its subsidiaries.

Literature Review

When analyzing international communication in global enterprises, four fields of knowledge are particularly relevant: *explicit versus tacit knowledge*, *relevance theory*, *communities of practice*, and *internal marketing*.

Explicit Knowledge Versus Tacit Knowledge

According to knowledge management studies, communicated information consists of both *explicit knowledge* and *tacit knowledge* (Nonaka and Konno 1999; Nonaka and Takeuchi 1995). Thus, with regard to the subject of this study, effective communication between headquarters and overseas subsidiaries requires transmission of both explicit knowledge and tacit knowledge. However, the use of translated documents presents challenges with regard to the transmission of tacit knowledge.

Relevance Theory

Relevance theory is a framework for explaining the fact that communicators generally convey more information in an utterance than the literal meaning of their words. In addition to literal meaning, the receiver of an utterance infers what the speaker intends to convey based on what he/she already knows or believes (Sperber and Wilson 1995). There are two principles of relevance. The *cognitive principle of relevance* says that humans can process new information because it is relevant to them. The *communicative principle of relevance* says that every utterance is presumed by the communicator to have optimal relevance to the receiver. These principles highlight the significance of relevance in the successful communication of intended information and meaning, and apply to the research questions at hand as translation can be seen as a form of "utterance."

Communities of Practice

A community of practice is a group of people who share a craft or a profession. Communities of practice share three essential elements: (1) people are involved in an activity (a domain of knowledge), (2) they share a way of communicating in the activity (community), and (3) there is a specific focus around which the community develops, shares, and maintains its knowledge (practice) (Wenger et al. 2002). In communities of practice, there exists a state in which the utilization of resources is carried out without hesitation and the parties understand them tacitly (Tanabe 2003). That is to say, in communities of practice, it becomes possible for members to understand even information that is not clearly specified; the mere mention of "you-know-who," "you-know-what," or "you-know-where" suffices. This is because members of communities of practice possess a common body of experience- and intuition-based internalized knowledge which can be difficult to transfer in written or oral form.

Internal Marketing

The goal of internal marketing is to ensure that "everyone in the organization accept the concepts and goals of marketing and engage in choosing, providing, and communicating customer value" (Kotler and Keller 2012, *p. 645*). However, Sumihara et al. (2008) take the position that "When management philosophy is written in words, those words remain only text, and can only partially express the true essence of the management philosophy." The true essence of management philosophy, they argue, "lies in the interaction between the written text and the people who interpret and reinterpret the text in carrying out company business." The purpose of internal marketing is to align every aspect of company operations to ensure all organizational members, in carrying out those operations, share to the greatest extent possible the same values and understanding of the mission of the business. Effective internal marketing raises relevance, promotes learning in communities of practice, and helps make corporate philosophy well-understood and a common goal.

A Model of Corporate Philosophy Communication via Translated Documentation

Based on the literature cited above, we constructed a model of headquarters-to-subsidiary communication of corporate philosophy through translated documentation (Fig. 1). With regard to the process and stages by which a corporate philosophy permeates the organization, Matsuoka (1997) identifies four infiltration levels. The shallowest is "Know the existence of the words"; the deepest is "Be tied to behavior." Takao and Wang (2012), who studied the penetration of management principles in organizations, propose that "behavioral involvement" occurs when "cognitive understanding" and "emotional empathy" are obtained. For this paper, we have created a scale of penetration of corporate philosophy that includes measurement of "emotional empathy" toward the philosophy, "cognitive understanding" of the content of the philosophy, and "behavioral involvement" in putting the philosophy into action. It was assumed that common knowledge of the corporate philosophy is a goal of both Japanese and overseas employees, and that it enhances *relevance*, promotes accumulation of organizational knowledge in *communities of practice*, promotes understanding of *tacit knowledge*, and leads to better understanding and sharing of translated documents. *Relevance theory*, *communities of practice*, and *internal marketing* were verified to affect the penetration of corporate philosophy beyond the differences of language.

Figure 1 shows the process by which a document from headquarters in Japan, on the left-hand side, is transferred through translation to overseas subsidiaries, on the right-hand side. In this process, when a translator transforms a Japanese document into the words of a different language, the result contains both "codified" content (intent specified) and "uncodified" content (intent not specified). The codified part is read by the reader as *explicit knowledge* and then judged, in consideration of the context, as either relevant or not relevant. If it is judged by the receiver as being

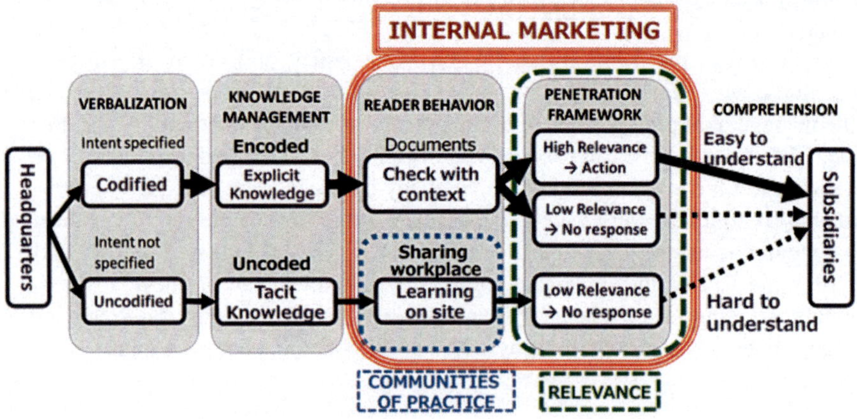

Fig. 1 Communication model through translated documentation

"highly relevant," the content becomes easily understood; if it is judged as "less relevant," the document ends up not being understood. The uncoded part, which does not explicitly appear in the translation, is *tacit knowledge*. If there exists a community of practice in which members "share a workplace," this knowledge can be inferred and understood by members of the community. In the absence of a community of practice, however, this tacit knowledge is difficult to understand. This is where internal marketing comes in. If internal marketing works effectively, it strengthens relevance and the accumulation of organizational knowledge in the community of practice, and understanding of corporate policy will be improved regardless of codification.

Qualitative Study and Hypotheses

Based on the model shown in Fig. 1, semi-structured interviews were designed and conducted with two employees in the Shimadzu's Information System Department, the unit responsible for translating from Japanese to English documents that transfer information to subsidiaries via translated documents. Next, language data from the semi-structured interviews were organized and coded with concept names, and hypothesis models were created and tested using covariance structure analysis. As a result of the analysis, three problems were identified: (1) "understood only on the basis of real experience," (2) "true meaning cannot be transferred," and (3) "simply distributing documents is not sufficient."

The first problem, "understood only on the basis of real experience," is related to the *cognitive principle of relevance* (recipients are able to receive information only if it is relevant to them) and to the *communicative principle of relevance* (the communicator's presumption that the information has optimal relevance to the receiver). In other words, optimal relevance—which Sperber and Wilson (1995) describe as "the addressee is entitled to expect a level of relevance high enough to warrant his attending to the stimulus, and which is, moreover, the highest level of relevance that the communicator was capable of achieving given her means and goals" (*pp. 270–271*)—is not achieved.

The second problem, "true meaning cannot be transferred," revealed gaps in the interpretation of sentences. This can be explained by the underdevelopment of communities of practice: when the condition of "sharing a workplace" is not realized, there is no field in which tacit knowledge can be shared, and employees do not fully understand how knowledge and information apply to actual activities.

The third problem is "simply distributing documents is not sufficient." In order for employees to work effectively, much more is required than the distribution of documents, especially when overseas subsidiaries face local conditions that are different from those in the corporation's home country. Efforts to influence employee behavior and values and to ensure that company policies and communications produce positive results in the workplace hinge upon a variety of factors, including the complexity of information and the utilization of internal marketing to promote cognitive understanding, emotional empathy, and behavioral involvement. Based on the above, the working hypotheses presented in Table 1 were derived.

Quantitative Study and Results

To test the working hypotheses, a questionnaire survey (web survey) was conducted of headquarters in Japan and overseas subsidiaries. Convenience sampling was used. Validated question items from Takao and Wang (2012), Shibata (2017), Foreman and Money (1995) were used in the empirical analysis. The questionnaire used for headquarters contained 57 items, while the questionnaire for overseas subsidiaries contained 64 items (including optional questions on internal marketing that could be skipped if the respondent ran out of time).

To analyze the questionnaire data, the first step was factor analysis of 15 internal marketing items using the maximum likelihood method. The first factor consisted of items related to measures taken to increase employee satisfaction; this factor was named "Employee Measures." The second factor was made up of items regarding in-house transmission of the corporate philosophy, and was judged to be shared knowledge that was not explicitly stated; this factor was named "Tacit Knowledge (Communication of Corporate Philosophy)."

Next, factor analysis using the maximum likelihood method was conducted in order to determine whether the score for "penetration of corporate philosophy" is divided into the three stages of "cognitive understanding," "emotional empathy," and "behavioral involvement." The analysis found that it was divided into three factors, unlike previous studies. The first factor was named "cognitive understanding

Table 1 Qualitative research results and hypotheses

Results of the qualitative research	Working hypotheses	Analytical concepts
Understood only on the basis of real experience	**H1.** Increased relevance enhances cognitive understanding, emotional empathy, and behavioral engagement.	Relevance theory
True meaning cannot be transferred	**H2.** Increased communities of practice enhance cognitive understanding, emotional empathy, and behavioral engagement.	Communities of practice
Simply distributing documents is not sufficient	**H3.** Increased tacit knowledge enhances cognitive understanding, emotional empathy, and behavioral engagement. **H4.** Improved internal marketing enhances cognitive understanding, emotional empathy, and behavioral engagement. **H6.** Measures to increase employee satisfaction enhance tacit knowledge.	Internal marketing

Note: An additional hypothesis about the dimensions of corporate philosophy penetration, "**H5**: As cognitive understanding and emotional empathy increase, behavioral engagement increases," is incorporated into the hypothetical structural models of three analytical concepts to be tested and emotional empathy," because it was composed of items related to understanding of and empathy toward the content of the corporate philosophy. The second factor was regarded as signifying the level of permeation of the corporate philosophy as it was composed of items of showing action taken based on the philosophy; it was named "Behavioral Involvement (High)." The third factor consisted of two items showing the corporate philosophy being quoted but not acted on; this factor was named "Behavioral Involvement (Low)."

Finally, three hypothetical structural models based on previous studies were constructed and covariance structure analysis was performed using a stepwise approach for the three factors of "Cognitive Understanding and Emotional Empathy" to "Behavioral Involvement (Low)" to "Behavioral Involvement (High)." Data used for the analysis were from 285 subjects: 190 in Japan and 95 overseas. The first hypothetical structural model, for "Relevance" and "Penetration of Corporate Philosophy," was made based on working hypotheses *H1* and *H5* (Fig. 2).

Table 2 shows the results for both overseas subsidiaries and Japan using the structure model in Fig. 2.

In the case of the overseas subsidiaries, as "Relevance" increased, "Cognitive Understanding and Emotional Empathy" also increased (*H1a*), and in addition, significant paths were created for *H5a* "Cognitive Understanding and Emotional Empathy" to "Behavioral Involvement (Low)" and for *H5b* "Behavioral Involvement (Low)" to "Behavioral Involvement (High)." The paths from "Relevance" to "Behavioral Involvement (High)" were statistically significant. That is to say, when "Relevance" increases in non-Japanese countries, the penetration of corporate philosophy also increases.

In Japan, when "Relevance" increases, "Cognitive Understanding and Emotional Empathy" increases (*H1a*), but there is no significant path from "Cognitive Understanding and Emotional Empathy" to "Behavioral Involvement." However, the *H5b* path was significant, indicating that the higher "Behavioral Involvement (Low)," the higher "Behavioral Involvement (High)," regardless of "Relevance."

In this research, the concept of "Relevance" is understood as "the effect of promoting recognition by 'inferring' the wording of the corporate philosophy in light of the receiver's own context." For overseas subsidiaries, it was found that

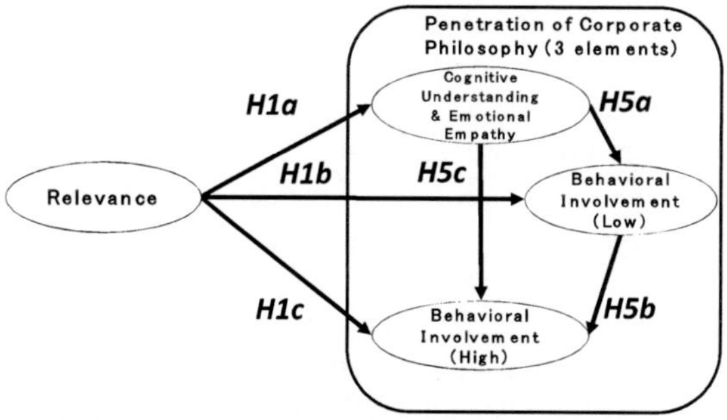

df=59,
CMIN=130.872,
P=0.000,
GFI=0.929,
AGFI=0.891,
CFI=0.766,
RMSEA=0.065,
(<*n*=285)

Fig. 2 Hypothetical structural model

Table 2 SEM results

				Overseas ($n = 95$)		Japan ($n = 190$)	
				β	p	β	p
H1a	Cognitive Understanding and Emotional Empathy	←	Relevance	0.930	***	0.952	***
H1b	Behavioral Involvement (Low)	←	Relevance	−0.412	*n.s.*	0.825	*n.s.*
H5a	Behavioral Involvement (Low)	←	Cognitive Understanding and Emotional Empathy	0.960	†	−0.198	*n.s.*
H5b	Behavioral Involvement (High)	←	Behavioral Involvement (Low)	0.895	***	0.434	***
H1c	Behavioral Involvement (High)	←	Relevance	0.528	*n.s.*	0.836	*n.s.*
H5c	Behavioral Involvement (High)	←	Cognitive Understanding and Emotional Empathy	−0.405	*n.s.*	−0.381	*n.s.*

***$p < 0.001$, **$p < 0.01$, *$p < 0.05$, †$p < 0.01$, *n.s*

increasing "Relevance" had a positive effect on penetration of the corporate philosophy, with "Cognitive Understanding and Emotional Empathy" leading to "Behavioral Involvement (Low)" and "Behavioral Involvement (High)." In Japan, on the other hand, "Relevance" had an effect on the first dimension of "Cognitive Understanding and Emotional Empathy," but was not directly related to "Behavioral Involvement" from that point onward.

Next, in order to verify "Communities of Practice" and "Penetration of Corporate Philosophy," a hypothetical structural model was made on the basis of working hypotheses *H2* and *H5* (Fig. 3).

Table 3 shows the results for overseas subsidiaries and Japan using the structure model in Fig. 3. The data used for this analysis were from 279 subjects: 184 in Japan and 95 overseas (six of the Japan questionnaires contained invalid answers).

The concept of "Communities of Practice" is understood as "the effect of situational learning in the sharing of practice, or the group itself," and the frequency of communication with overseas subsidiaries was adopted as an index. It was hypothesized that as the formation of "Communities of Practice" proceeds, the level of the three dimensions of "Penetration of Corporate Philosophy" would also rise.

The paths *H5a* and *H5b* were found to be significant for overseas subsidiaries, but the *H2a* path was not significant. This suggests that the formation of the "Communities of Practice" is not related to "Cognitive Understanding and Emotional Empathy," but strongly influences the "Behavioral Involvement" dimensions of penetration, by means such as quoting or thinking back to the corporate philosophy while conducting business. It is interesting to note that the paths from "Relevance" for the overseas subsidiaries in the Fig. 2 model are reinforced by the paths from "Communities of Practice" leading to "Behavioral Involvement (High)" in the Fig. 3 model.

For the Fig. 3 model, all paths were significant for Japan. A positive relationship was found for *H2a*, *H2b*, *H5a*, and *H5c*, with each variable of "Cognitive

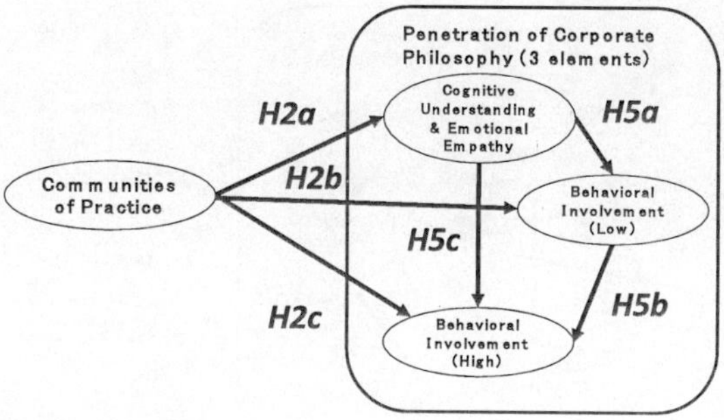

Fig. 3 Hypothetical structural model

Table 3 SEM results

				Overseas ($n = 95$)		Japan ($n = 184$)	
				β	p	β	p
H2a	Cognitive Understanding and Emotional Empathy	←	Communities of Practice	0.500	*n.s.*	0.330	**
H2b	Behavioral Involvement (Low)	←	Communities of Practice	0.016	*n.s.*	0.220	*
H5a	Behavioral Involvement (Low)	←	Cognitive Understanding and Emotional Empathy	0.631	***	0.499	***
H5b	Behavioral Involvement (High)	←	Behavioral Involvement (Low)	0.878	***	0.592	***
H2c	Behavioral Involvement (High)	←	Communities of Practice	0.117	*n.s.*	−0.155	†
H5c	Behavioral Involvement (High)	←	Cognitive Understanding and Emotional Empathy	−0.005	*n.s.*	0.377	***

***$p < 0.001$, **$p < 0.01$, *$p < 0.05$, †$p < 0.01$, *n.s*

Understanding and Emotional Empathy" and "Behavioral Involvement (Low)" increasing as "Communities of Practice" increases. A positive relationship was also found for *H5b*. The *H2c* path is significantly negative, however, showing that when the frequency of communication with overseas subsidiaries increases, Japanese feel a gap in the way of thinking, which hinders applying the philosophy in actual practice. It is notable that for Japan, "Communities of Practice" was confirmed to have a positive effect on paths *H5c*, *H5a*, and *H2b*, whereas "Relevance" (in the Fig. 2 model, above) showed no significant effect on these paths. The above suggests that raising the level of "Communities of Practice" may help to promote penetration of the philosophy when the relation between "Relevance" and the philosophy penetration dimensions is weak.

Next, in order to test the relationship between internal marketing and penetration of the philosophy, a hypothetical structural model incorporating the three hypotheses *H3*, *H4*, and *H6*, and which divides internal marketing into two factors ("Tacit Knowledge" and "Employee Measures"), was created (Fig. 4).

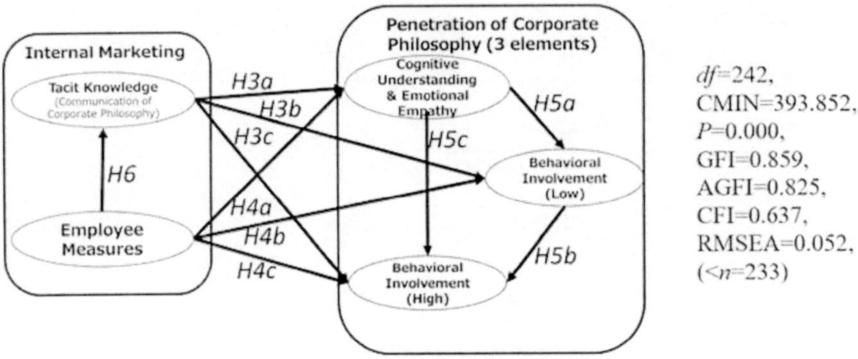

Fig. 4 Hypothetical structural model

First, analysis was carried out using combined data from Japan (183 subjects) and outside Japan (50 subjects). The following paths were found to be significant: *H6* "Employee Measures" to "Tacit Knowledge (0.709); *H3a* "Tacit Knowledge" to "Cognitive Understanding and Emotional Empathy" (0.708); *H5c* "Cognitive Understanding and Emotional Empathy" to "Behavioral Involvement (High)" (0.217); and *H3c* "Tacit Knowledge" to "Behavioral Involvement (High)" (0.293). Then separate analyses were conducted using only the data from Japan and only the data from outside Japan; these produced unstable results with low goodness of fit.

Discussion

In this paper, we postulate that even when internal communication is performed in a language other than the home-country language, the intention of corporate headquarters can be understood regardless of the difference in language if the texts can be understood in relation to the context of the receivers of the communication. Structural models of how *explicit and tacit knowledge*, *relevance theory*, *communities of practice*, and *internal marketing* influence three dimensions of *penetration of corporate philosophy* were constructed, based on a review of relevant literature. The concepts of the models were confirmed through qualitative investigation, and quantitative analysis was then conducted to test the models, using as a text the Japanese and English versions of the corporate philosophy of Shimadzu Corporation, which is presented to all Shimadzu employees.

It was found that in overseas subsidiaries, increasing "Relevance" had a stepwise effect on penetration of the three dimensions of corporate philosophy. In Japan, however, increasing "Relevance" affected penetration of the first dimension of corporate philosophy, "Cognitive Understanding and Emotional Empathy," but had no direct relationship to the other two dimensions, "Behavioral Involvement (Low)" and "Behavioral Involvement (High)."

In overseas subsidiaries, the formation of the "Communities of Practice" was not enhanced even if there were chances to communicate with Japan, and such formation was not found to be related to "Cognitive Understanding and Emotional Empathy." But it was found that stepwise penetration from "Cognitive Understanding and Emotional Empathy" to "Behavioral Involvement (Low)" and "Behavioral Involvement (High)" was achieved by quoting or thinking back to the corporate philosophy while conducting business. In Japan, a positive relationship was observed in which the variables "Cognitive Understanding and Emotional Empathy" and "Behavioral Involvement (Low)" increased as "Communities of Practice" increased. However, a negative relationship was found from "Communities of Practice" to "Behavioral Involvement (High)." When the frequency of communication exchange between Japan and overseas subsidiaries increased, a gap in the way of thinking arose between Japan and the overseas subsidiaries, which hindered putting the philosophy into practice. However, it seems that raising the level of "Communities of Practice" can help promote "Penetration of Corporate Philosophy" if the relation between "Relevance" and "Penetration of Corporate Philosophy" is weak.

Finally, the impact of "Internal Marketing," divided into the two factors of "Tacit Knowledge" and "Employee Measures," on the dimensions of "Penetration of Corporate Philosophy" was analyzed. The same tendency was found in both Japan and overseas subsidiaries. "Internal Marketing" did not create direct paths from "Employee Measures" to "Cognitive Understanding and Emotional Empathy" and "Behavioral Involvement." But executing "Employee Measures" was found to enhance "Tacit Knowledge," and this in turn led to enhanced "Cognitive Understanding and Emotional Empathy" and "Behavioral Involvement (High)." This suggests that appropriate execution of "Employee Measures" is important for the formation of "Tacit Knowledge," and that "Internal Marketing" should be incorporated into the organizational system to enhance the effectiveness of internal communications.

Implications for Business

The purpose of this study was to explore ways for company headquarters to more effectively convey their intentions in their communications with overseas subsidiaries. In this section we suggest how the learnings from our research can be applied in the company's translation operations from the standpoint of headquarters in Japan.

First, efforts should be made to make outgoing information more relevant to the receiver by including context into the contents and wording. The key to doing this is for the sender to be able to is accurately speculate about the contextual situation of the reader.

Second, it is important to utilize and develop *communities of practice* to complement explicit knowledge. Employees learn much of their tacit knowledge from their organizations and communities of practice. It is important for members to create an inclusive environment and to promote continued participation in the community. Doing so leads to the sharing of concerns, problems, and interests, and promotes working together to fulfill common goals.

To promote understanding of tacit knowledge, it is important to codify it into explicit knowledge, and to strengthen internal marketing. Creating shareable tacit knowledge through internal marketing is necessary to help receivers efficiently and fully interpret foreign language documents.

Finally, it is necessary for translators, in their practicing of cross-cultural communication, to read, understand, and explicitly express tacit knowledge that is contained in Japanese documents. Thus, the key lies with the translators. It is necessary for corporate headquarters and the senders of documents overseas to consider translators as members of the organization and to either incorporate them into *communities of practices* or treat them as targets of internal marketing. At present, there is a tendency to regard translation as a cost to be kept as low as possible, but investment in translation should not be spared in global enterprises that wish multinational employees to work together to achieve corporate growth. Establishment of the position of Chief Communications Officer (CCO) would help to eliminate language barriers that stand in the way of business success worldwide.

Shimadzu devotes considerable resources to its overseas subsidiaries to create international competitiveness in global markets as a cooperative partner in manufacturing, sales, and research and development. Translation of internal documents sent from headquarters in Japan plays a very important role in the company's operations, and should not be outsourced to an external party which lacks tacit knowledge and true understanding of the company's businesses, mission, and operating philosophy. The empirical analysis of this paper suggests that the effective application of *relevance theory, communities of practice*, and *internal marketing* in translation work, and the sharing of context between translators and employees at Japanese headquarters and personnel in overseas subsidiaries, can reduce gaps in understanding from documents in different languages and help integrate organizational knowledge across the company. Companies need to take language barriers seriously, and take appropriate measures that address geographical, cultural, and linguistic challenges.

References

Foreman, S. K. & Money, A. H. (1995). Internal marketing: Concepts, measurement and application. *Journal of Marketing Management, 11*, 755–768.

Kotler, P. & Keller, K. L. (2012). *Marketing management, global edition*. Harlow, Essex: Pearson Education.

Matsuoka, K. (1997). Keyim rinen no shintō reberu to shintō mekanizumu: Kōpu Kōbe ni okeru "ai to kyōdō" [Penetration levels and mechanisms of corporate credo in an organization: a case analysis of Co-op Kobe]. *Rokkodai Ronshū Keieigaku-hen, 44, 1*, 183–203. [published in Japanese].

Nonaka, I. & Takeuchi, H. (1995). *The knowledge-creating company: How Japanese companies create the dynamics of innovation*. New York: Oxford University Press.

Nonaka, I. & Konno, N. (1999). *Chishiki keiei no susume* [The advance of knowledge management]. Tokyo: Chikuma Shinsho. [published in Japanese].

Shibata, M. (2017). *Jissen no ba ni okeru keiei rinen no shintō: Kanren-sei riron to jissen komyuniti ni yoru intānaru māketingu komyunikēshon no kōsatsu* [Penetration of management philosophy in the field: Relevance theory and internal marketing communication by communities of practice]. Tokyo: Soseisha. [published in Japanese].

Sperber, D. & Wilson, D. (1995). *Relevance: communication and cognition*. Oxford, UK & Cambridge, MA: Blackwell Publishing.

Sumihara N., Mitsui, I., & Watatabe, Y. (2008). *Keiei rinen keishō to denpa no keiei jinruigakuteki kenkyū* [A management anthropological study of the succession and propagation of management philosophy]. Kyoto: PHP Institute. [published in Japanese].

Takao, Y. & Wang, Y. (2012*). Keiei rinen no shintō aidentiti purosesu kara no jisshō bunseki* [Management Philosophy and Individuals—Unpacking the Dynamics of Identity Processes]. Tokyo: Yuhikaku Publishing. [published in Japanese].

Tanabe, S. (2003). *Ikikata no jinrui-gaku jissen to wa nanika* [How to put the anthropology of living into practice]. Tokyo: Kodansha Gendai Shinsho. [published in Japanese].

Wenger, E., McDermott, R., & Snyder, W. M. (2002). *Cultivating communities of practice: A guide to managing knowledge*. Boston: Harvard Business School Press.

Should We Continue Using Intelligent Virtual Assistants? The Role of Uses Gratifications and Privacy Concerns: An Abstract

Hajer Kefi and Chiraz Aouina-Mejri

Abstract Intelligent Virtual Assistants (IVAs) are invading homes and workplaces all over the world. Continuance advancements and innovations with automation technologies such as Robotic Process Automation, Artificial Intelligence and Natural Language Processing have boosted the global market of these devices. After first adoption, which could be fostered due to marketing and promotional campaigns and also users' curiosity, the continuance usage of these tools is tremendously important to build a sustainable market and is therefore challenging for vendors. This article investigates the motivation to continue using these tools that could stem from the gratifications they afford to users. We are also interested in the constraints that hinder this behavior, especially privacy concerns, as IVAs are perceived as 'open-ended' and community-based devices (Ku et al. 2013).

Building on three areas of research: information technology and information systems (IS/IT) continuance usage (Al-maghrabi et al. 2011; Zhou 2013), uses and gratifications theory (UGT) (Dolan et al. 2016; Ifinedo 2016) and privacy concerns (Ku et al. 2013; LaRose and Eastin 2002), we develop an original research model of IVAs continuance usage intention. Our focus will be put on home usage of IVAs, which excludes usage at professional settings (Burns and Igou 2019; Todorov et al. 2018).

To test the model, an online survey is conducted within a sample of 258 IVAs' users in France. Part least squared structural equation modeling is applied to analyze data. Results show that privacy concerns strongly and negatively affect continuance intention. This dependent construct is also positively and directly determined by subjective norms, perceived critical mass, and uses gratifications, i.e. utilitarian gratifications (social interactions and information seeking) and more significantly hedonic gratifications (entertainment and fashion). Besides, only

H. Kefi (✉) · C. Aouina-Mejri
PSB Paris School of Business, Paris, France
e-mail: h.kefi@psbedu.paris; c.aouinamejri@psbedu.paris

F. Pantoja, S. Wu (eds.), *From Micro to Macro: Dealing with Uncertainties in the Global Marketplace*, Developments in Marketing Science: Proceedings of the Academy of Marketing Science, https://doi.org/10.1007/978-3-030-89883-0_77

subjective norms could be considered as antecedent factors to all our gratifications constructs.

This study contributes to the literature on IVAs, UGT and privacy concerns. It also provides IVAs' vendors with useful insights on how to retain their users.

Keywords Uses and gratifications theory · Intelligent virtual assistant · Privacy concerns · Continuance intention to use

References Available Upon Request

From B2C to P2P: A Marketing Driven Analysis of Peer-to-Peer Business Models in Shared Mobility Markets: An Abstract

Maximilian Schwing, Marc Kuhn, and Lars Meyer-Waarden

Abstract According to Bagozzi (1974) one core task of marketing is to facilitate exchange between buyers and sellers. In the recent past several drivers like technology developments and enhanced concern for sustainability have shaped new forms of exchange that challenge the classical way how marketing operated between buyers and sellers. The sharing economy and other terminologies used in this context represent a rapid growing part of our economies in which you can consume without having to buy and own. Shared mobility, the shared use of a mode for transportation, is one of the biggest and most important industry of the worldwide sharing economy (McKinsey and Company 2017).

Within the sharing economy the concept of peer-to-peer sharing and collaborative consumption (P2P SCC) is a subset and one specific form in where users can act as both as consumer as well as provider. Assets, goods and services are provided by the network of users itself and not by or many companies. Therefore, P2P SCC plays an essential part as, on the one hand, it offers many societal and environmental benefits (Perren and Kozinets 2018; Benjaafar et al. 2019), e.g. better usage of underutilized assets, and on the other hand, it has brought forth some well-known and successful companies, such as BlaBlaCar.

Marketing research in the last decade has seen the rise of the sharing economy as well as the implications for research on this topic (Eckhardt et al. 2019). In this context a lot of research has been done about B2C sharing that has increased our understanding in many respects, e.g. distinguishing between different classical and sharing forms of exchange. Since P2P SCC can still be considered a young

M. Schwing (✉) · L. Meyer-Waarden
University of Toulouse 1 Capitole, Toulouse, France
e-mail: maximilian.schwing@tsm-education.fr; lars.meyer-waarden@tsm-education.fr

M. Kuhn
Baden-Wuerttemberg Cooperative State University, Stuttgart, Germany
e-mail: marc.kuhn@dhbw-stuttgart.de

F. Pantoja, S. Wu (eds.), *From Micro to Macro: Dealing with Uncertainties in the Global Marketplace*, Developments in Marketing Science: Proceedings of the Academy of Marketing Science, https://doi.org/10.1007/978-3-030-89883-0_78

phenomenon, management research, particularly from a marketer's point of view, is still at its beginning, e.g. when it comes to understand distinctive features between and within these new form of exchange (Benoit et al. 2017; Lin et al. 2019).

Based on a systematic literature review (Tranfield et al. 2003) and an inductive qualitative analysis (Mayring 2014) we deduce a set of characteristics and attributes and propose a categorization for P2P SCC to contribute to this research gap.

Keywords Peer-to-peer sharing · Collaborative consumption · Shared mobility · Sharing economy

References Available Upon Request

The Impact of Medicaid and SNAP Program Participation on WIC Participants' Redemption Behavior Pattern: An Abstract

Junzhou Zhang, Chuanyi Tang, and Qi Zhang

Abstract The federal government spends a large amount of money on assistance programs such as the Special Supplemental Nutrition Assistance Program for Women, Infants, and Children (WIC), Supplemental Nutrition Assistance Program (SNAP), and Medicaid to address the food insecurity issue of low-income consumers (Au et al. 2016; Greenblatt et al. 2015; Zhang et al. 2020). However, there is a lacking of understanding regarding how these assistance programs interplay with each other, and little research has been conducted from the marketing and consumer behavior perspective.

Aiming to better understand the WIC participants' behavioral pattern and provide actionable implications to the WIC program, this study analyzed the profiles and shopping transaction records of over 59,000 WIC participants in Virginia and empirically examined how WIC participants' Medicaid and SNAP program participation influences their redemption behavior in terms of WIC food benefits. Specifically, we first identified a curvilinear redemption pattern during the participants' benefit cycle. This pattern suggests that the WIC participants in general redeemed more about their benefits in the beginning and the end of each benefit cycle. Further, such a curvilinear relationship was significantly moderated by Medicaid participation but not by SNAP participation. Family structure change such as adding a new baby was found to significantly influence this relationship.

This study contributes to the literature on the WIC program and the research on food insecurity of low-income consumers. The insights provided in this study help consumer researchers and public policymakers better understand the behaviors of

J. Zhang (✉)
Montclair State University, Montclair, NJ, USA
e-mail: zhangju@montclair.edu

C. Tang · Q. Zhang
Old Dominion University, Norfolk, VA, USA
e-mail: ctang@odu.edu; qzhang@odu.edu

F. Pantoja, S. Wu (eds.), *From Micro to Macro: Dealing with Uncertainties in the Global Marketplace*, Developments in Marketing Science: Proceedings of the Academy of Marketing Science, https://doi.org/10.1007/978-3-030-89883-0_79

low-income consumers and provide implications for WIC program managers to improve the WIC or other food assistance programs.

Keywords WIC program · Medicaid program · SNAP program · Redemption behavior pattern

References Available Upon Request

“We know everything about you…”: A Conceptual Model on the Acceptance of Smart Products

Marius Huber, Marc Kuhn, and Luca Petruzzellis

Abstract Technological advances make products increasingly smart. Such smart innovations seem to have certain characteristics. In this paper, we present different traits and take into account that these types of innovations differ in their future development stage from the current accessible form. In the case of autonomous vehicles, consumers already imagine the completely intelligent innovation whereby the car drives autonomously whilst the passenger is not involved in driving. However, this distinctive type is supposed to be available in the future, since at present only partially automated driving functions are developed. In general, it is expected that in the future development stage of smart innovations that include a high degree of autonomy, human interaction with the innovation itself will be reduced or even obsolete. These special characteristics of smart innovations led researchers to question the suitability of available acceptance models. With regard to the special future characteristics of smart innovations, we review previously used variables for the investigation of innovation acceptance and other related concepts to examine their suitability. The result is a conceptual model to be utilized for the investigation of Smart Product acceptance. This model will be tested and applied within a user experience study for fully autonomous cars.

Keywords Innovation acceptance · Smart Products · Product intelligence · Consumer behavior

M. Huber (✉) · L. Petruzzellis
University of Bari Aldo Moro, Bari, Italy
e-mail: marius.huber@lehre.dhbw-stuttgart.de; luca.petruzzellis@uniba.it

M. Kuhn
Baden-Wuerttemberg Cooperative State University Stuttgart, Stuttgart, Germany
e-mail: marc.kuhn@dhbw-stuttgart.de

F. Pantoja, S. Wu (eds.), *From Micro to Macro: Dealing with Uncertainties in the Global Marketplace*, Developments in Marketing Science: Proceedings of the Academy of Marketing Science, https://doi.org/10.1007/978-3-030-89883-0_80

Introduction

Through advancements in Artificial Intelligence, Internet of Things and Automation, products become increasingly smarter (Porter and Heppelmann 2014). Autonomous Cars, Smart Assistants (e.g. Apple's Siri, Amazon's Alexa, Microsoft's Cortana, Facebook's M and Google's Assistant) as well as Smart Homes (Cronin 2010; Ford 2016; European Commission 2018) are just a few examples of Smart Products. They are considered to gather, work with and produce information due to built-in sensors, microchips and software (Rijsdijk et al. 2007). Among the factors used to characterize Smart Products, Autonomy is important (Rijsdijk and Hultink 2009). It is seen as the ability of a product to deal with tasks completely on its own without interference of users. Therefore, it is assumed that the expected effort to use a Smart Product becomes less important or maybe even irrelevant depending on the level of autonomy (Porter and Heppelmann 2014, p. 73). Even though Smart Products are available today, we expect them to be even smarter in the future. For instance, Autonomous Cars are now available in a state called "Level 2" where the driver can take his hands off the steering wheel but has to be aware and prepared to take over control at any time. The future product development stage is "Level 5" where the driver does not have to interact at all since a steering wheel will be obsolete (SAE International 2014). Thus, the use of Smart Products might be linked to less effort in their current development stage. Moreover, effort will be less or even non-existent because of even smarter products in the future. Due to the expected effortless use of Smart Products in their future development stage it is assumed that variables which argue for or against the Ease of Use also become less important or irrelevant (Kuhn et al. 2018). Therefore, available models to measure innovation acceptance might not work for Smart Products because one key component is the measurement of Perceived Ease of Use (Davis 1989), also known as Effort Expectancy (Venkatesh et al. 2003). This leads to an important question concerning research in terms of Smart Products: *"Which factors affect consumers' adoption of smart [products] (...)?"* (Wuenderlich et al. 2015, p. 445).

Innovation acceptance research has been widely investigated. Within this field different variables are analyzed and various contexts as well as frameworks are used to test the models (Davis 1989; Venkatesh and Davis 2000; Venkatesh and Bala 2008; Venkatesh et al. 2003, 2012; Kulviwat et al. 2007). Models and their explanations are also dependent on the particular subject they are tested with and thus adaptions in those models have to be done or new models have to be formed (Kuhn and Marquardt 2019; Kuhn et al. 2018). Since all these previous models have considered Ease of Use as a variable, which may become more irrelevant in the future due to the special characteristics of Smart Products, we think that a tailored conceptual model is needed for Smart Products acceptance.

Some of the previous research investigated for instance the resistance towards Smart Products (Mani and Chouk 2017), the effect of perceived disempowerment towards Smart Products adoption (Schweitzer and van den Hende 2016), adoption of a smart kitchen environment (Mayer et al. 2011), adoption of Internet of Things

(Hsu and Lin 2016; Gao and Bai 2014), impact of Smart Products on customer satisfaction (Rijsdijk et al. 2007), characteristics of Smart Products (Rijsdijk and Hultink 2009) or the interaction with automated technologies (Kuhn et al. 2018). To the best of our knowledge there is no such tailored model respecting Smart Products adoption in general. Hence, we aim in this paper to propose a conceptual Smart Products acceptance model based on their specific characteristics.

Theoretical Background

IT components enable products to be smart. A product can only be enabled to be smart when those enabling characteristics can be affirmed (Dhebar 1996). Smart Products can also have several ability features, which show the smartness of a product. The higher the degree of each characteristic and the more of them are possessed, the smarter the product (Rijsdijk and Hultink 2009). Another feature is the embeddedness that represents how much a specific product is ingrained into the life of a user. An illustrative example of such a product is a cardiac pacemaker which is fully ingrained (Wuenderlich et al. 2015). Based on this, we argue that Smart Product features can be classified with the following three categories (See Table 1). The first category "Characteristics enabling Smart Products" groups the features that enable products to be smart, including IT components and associated abilities to process data, share information, initiate actions and their form. The second category "Characteristics of Smart Products abilities" contains ability features, enabled by the characteristics of the first category. Those characteristics are Autonomy, Adaptability, Reactivity, Multifunctionality, Ability to Cooperate, Humanlike Interaction and Personality. Lastly, there are "State characteristics of Smart Products" that represent a condition such as Embeddedness describing the nature of Smart Products.

To illustrate that current Smart Products are expected to become smarter, we describe the products Smart Home, Smart Assistant and Autonomous Car with some of their current and future abilities, representing their respective development stages. These innovations are chosen because they cover most of the three main Smart Products application fields "Smart Home", "Mobility" and "Communication and Entertainment" (Mani and Chouk 2017).

Smart Homes are currently able to take several tasks at the same time such as switch lights on or off, adjust temperature or move window shades but with predefined commands or on demand. Smart Homes become increasingly intelligent because they will not only act on predefined actions, but will operate independently and learn to react on the basis of circumstances and changes in the house or the needs of its inhabitants (Aldrich 2003). Such an increase in intelligence is also apparent to Smart Assistants. They interact with a rather robotic sounding voice today but will be able to sound humanlike, representing a credible character. At present, tasks must be assigned in the form of specific commands but in the future, users will be talking in their natural language as if they would talk to another person resulting in humanlike interaction (European Commission 2018). Lastly, Autonomous Cars are currently available at a Level 2 development stage, where the car can transport its passenger mostly independently depending on the circumstances. The human driver has to pay full attention, be able to interact and take over control whenever it is necessary. Future autonomous driving does not require any interference of a passenger because the car will fulfill all tasks on its own. This stage is called Level 5 (NHTSA n.d.). Some of these Smart Products can be interconnected (Müller et al. 2018). For example, it is possible that an Autonomous Car or a Smart Home is equipped with a Smart Assistant.

From these insights we conclude that Smart Products become even smarter in their future development stages. Either they possess more of the specific ability characteristics from Table 1 or the extents of the respective characteristics increase (Rijsdijk et al. 2007).

Table 1 Characteristics of Smart Products

Characteristics enabling Smart Products	
IT components	Hard- and software, connectivity-features. (e.g. sensors, actuators, WIFI, mobile network, microchips etc.) (Hoffman and Novak 2015; Mani and Chouk 2017; Miorandi et al. 2012; Rijsdijk and Hultink 2009)
Data processing	Collect, manage, process and produce data (Miorandi et al. 2012; Mani and Chouk 2017; Rijsdijk and Hultink 2009)
Information sharing	Sending and receiving processed data through ubiquitous connectivity (Hoffman and Novak 2015; Porter and Heppelmann 2014)
Action triggering	General ability to activate/start (tangible) actions (Mani and Chouk 2017; Miorandi et al. 2012)
Form	Physical embodiment with a set of associated physical features (Miorandi et al. 2012)
Characteristics of Smart Products abilities	
Autonomy	Ability to operate in independent and goal-directed way without interference of user. (Hoffman and Novak 2015; Porter and Heppelmann 2014; Rijsdijk and Hultink 2009)
Adaptability	Ability to improve match between its functioning and its environment (Nicoll 1999; Hoffman and Novak 2015; Rijsdijk and Hultink 2009)
Reactivity	Ability to react to changes in its environment (Bradshaw 1997; Hoffman and Novak 2015; Rijsdijk and Hultink 2009)
Multi-functionality	Ability to fulfill multiple functions (Poole and Simon 1997; Rijsdijk and Hultink 2009)
Ability to cooperate	Ability to cooperate with other devices to achieve common goal and to communicate not only with their users but also among themselves. (Hoffman and Novak 2015; Rijsdijk and Hultink 2009)
Humanlike interaction	Ability to communicate and interact with user in natural, human way. (Rijsdijk and Hultink 2009)
Personality	Ability to show the properties of a credible character. (Rijsdijk and Hultink 2009)
State characteristics of Smart Products	
Embeddedness	Extent to which a product is integrated into the life of a consumer. (Wuenderlich et al. 2015)

Method

To develop a conceptual Smart Product acceptance model, we respect previous research for innovation acceptance and review variables that might lead towards adoption. However, to the best of our knowledge previous studies have not delivered a universally applicable model yet (Wuenderlich et al. 2015).

For the evaluation of variables, we set the following basis. We investigate Smart Products utilization and adoption within the private domain. The variables as well as the resulting conceptual model should investigate Smart Products in their future development stages, where characteristics such as Autonomy, Adaptability, Reactivity, Multifunctionality, Humanlike Interaction and Personality are predominantly possessed to a high degree. Based on the characteristics from Table 1, we argue for or against the usage of a particular variable.

Evaluation of Acceptance Variables and Derivation of Conceptual Model

The Technology Acceptance Model (TAM) (Davis 1989) would be the most obvious choice to investigate Smart Products due to their IT components (Hoffman and Novak 2015; Mani and Chouk 2017; Miorandi et al. 2012; Rijsdijk and Hultink 2009). But previous research on the acceptance of Smart Products investigated, recommended and tested the applicability of the Unified Theory of Acceptance and Use of Technology (UTAUT) (Venkatesh et al. 2003; Mayer et al. 2011). It includes the relevant variable Social Influence. This variable is missing in TAM and thus limits its ability to explain the acceptance of Smart Products. The social context is seen as very important regarding the private domain the products are supposed to be used in (Mayer et al. 2011). UTAUT (Venkatesh et al. 2003) is built upon several other acceptance models or theories (e.g. TAM (Davis 1989), TAM2 (Venkatesh and Davis 2000), Theory of Planned Behavior (Ajzen 1991), Theory of Reasoned Action (Fishbein and Ajzen 1975), Innovation Diffusion Theory (Rogers 1995) and several others). Mayer et al. (2011) made several adaptions to examine their respected case of a smart kitchen environment. Although this adapted model has been found practicable for their specific investigation, we propose the usage of UTAUT2 (Venkatesh et al. 2012) as a framework for the investigation of Smart Products in general. Reasons are that UTAUT2 includes the relevant variable Price Value and it rejects the non-relevant variable Voluntariness of Use from UTAUT. The relevancy or non-relevancy for both of those variables is due to the investigation of Smart Products adoption within the private domain. Lastly UTAUT2 also includes Social Influence which is important for Smart Products with regard to the usage investigation in the private domain (Mayer et al. 2011). Therefore, we decided to use UTAUT2 as a framework model to review its variables and discuss the integration of other parameters for the investigation of Smart Products adoption based on their characteristics.

This paragraph reviews the variables proposed by the framework model UTAUT2 and argues either for or against their usage in the conceptual model. The determinant variable remains **Behavioral Intention** and its direct effect on Use Behavior as proposed in UTAUT2 (Venkatesh et al. 2012). This variable was also largely agreed on within the research of innovation acceptance (Ajzen 1991; Fishbein and Ajzen 1975; Davis 1989; Venkatesh and Davis 2000; Venkatesh et al. 2003, 2012; Venkatesh and Bala 2008). **Effort Expectancy**, also known as Perceived Ease of Use, represents the actual effort associated with the usage of an innovation (Venkatesh et al. 2012; Davis 1989). Due to the Smart Products' Autonomy, Adaptability, Reactivity and Multifunctionality characteristics (Hoffman and Novak 2015; Porter and Heppelmann 2014; Rijsdijk and Hultink 2009; Nicoll 1999; Bradshaw 1997; Poole and Simon 1997), we expect this variable to lose its relevancy since the effort to use a Smart Products decreases. This is because they fulfill their tasks completely on their own, improve their task solving based on learnings, react towards changes and can fulfill multiple functions. Consumers will use their own voice to tell the product what to do and based on the products' ability to interact humanlike it reduces potentially complex human machine interaction. Resulting in drastically reduced effort linked to the usage of a product. Its decreasing influence on Behavioral Intention has also been highlighted as the outcome of a study (Mayer et al. 2011). Thus, we reject this parameter for the conceptual model of Smart Products Acceptance. **Performance Expectancy**, also known as Perceived Usefulness, is defined as a degree to which using an innovation is beneficial to fulfill tasks (Venkatesh et al. 2012; Davis 1989). Based on the Autonomy, Adaptability, Reactivity, Multifunctionality and their Ability to Cooperate characteristics (Hoffman and Novak 2015; Porter and Heppelmann 2014; Rijsdijk and Hultink 2009; Nicoll 1999; Bradshaw 1997; Poole and Simon 1997), we expect this variable to stay relevant. The product performances increase because users do not need to invest time to fulfill tasks which is beneficial for users. Smart Products will do everything on their own or in cooperation with other Smart Products while being aware of their environments and the ability to react towards circumstances. Benefits are for instance an increase in free-time for the user. A smart lawn mower or smart vacuum cleaner will know when, where and how to do the work. In addition, users could use their time in an Autonomous Car to read a book, work, watch a movie or even sleep. Previously those tasks needed to be done with a user operating each one of the Non-Smart Products. In terms of highly developed Smart Products those tasks are omitted resulting in the benefit that users do not need to do anything for specific tasks. Hence, Performance Expectancy remains relevant and needs to be included into the model which was also confirmed by a study (Mayer et al. 2011). Performance Expectancy has a positive effect on Behavioral Intention (Davis 1989; Kulviwat et al. 2007; Venkatesh and Davis 2000; Venkatesh et al. 2003, 2012; Venkatesh and Bala 2008). **Social Influence** represents the urge to buy a product based on whether the consumer thinks that important others expect him to use this product (Venkatesh et al. 2003, 2012). The social context in which Smart Products are used is important because Smart Products target consumers in their private domain and may change their routines (Mayer et al. 2011). For this reason, we decide to include Social

Influence. Social Influence has an effect on behavioral intention (Ajzen 1991). **Facilitating Conditions** represent the users perception that all technological and infrastructural requirements are given for a product to function and solve a task properly (Venkatesh et al. 2012, 2003). We argue that this variable should be included since Smart Products send and receive information through ubiquitous connectivity with WIFI and mobile phone networks to cooperate among each other to solve tasks (Hoffman and Novak 2015; Mani and Chouk 2017; Rijsdijk and Hultink 2009; Porter and Heppelmann 2014). Without connectivity and increasing smartness their functions might be restricted resulting in not being able to cooperate and potentially not fulfilling the activities correctly. This might result in users potentially doubting their abilities or rejecting their usage. Therefore, the perception of Facilitating Conditions remains relevant within the adoption construct and needs to be included. We hypothesize that Facilitating Conditions positively affect Behavioral Intention (Venkatesh et al. 2012). **Hedonic Motivation** represents pleasure or fun while using an innovation (Venkatesh et al. 2012). We expect, that at first, Smart Products will induce excitement due to their novelty and their characteristics Humanlike Interaction, Personality as well as Autonomy, Adaptability, Reactivity, Multifunctionality and their Ability to Cooperate (Rijsdijk and Hultink 2009; Hoffman and Novak 2015; Porter and Heppelmann 2014). Users will be impressed that the Smart Product can interact like a human with an own character and that they are reliable in solving tasks. But after a period of time habituation occurs and it is expected that these hedonic motivation drivers will disappear. Moreover, hedonic motivation drivers, which are created by the agitation and dominance of the user himself (e.g. sportive driving in a Non-Autonomous Car instead of being transported autonomously or personality presentation through choosing the right music at an event instead of music selected by a Smart Assistant), are increasingly omitted with increasing smartness of the products because of increasing Autonomy, Adaptability, Reactivity and Multifunctionality. Therefore, we argue that Hedonic Motivation is not relevant for Smart Products in their future development stages and reject its usage within the conceptual model. **Price Value** is defined as the tradeoff between the price and the benefits resulting from buying a product (Venkatesh et al. 2012). We assume that this variable remains relevant. Due to the private domain in which we investigate acceptance, Consumers will have to pay for the product themselves and weigh up whether the benefit corresponds to or even exceeds the price. The further a Smart Product is developed, the higher its benefits are to be expected and the higher its price will be. We expect the price value to be crucial and hence integrate it into our concept. Price Value has a positive effect on Behavioral Intention (Venkatesh et al. 2012). **Habit** corresponds to the routine or automaticity with which a product is used (Venkatesh et al. 2012). As said before all abilities making a product smart (Hoffman and Novak 2015; Porter and Heppelmann 2014; Rijsdijk and Hultink 2009; Bradshaw 1997; Nicoll 1999; Poole and Simon 1997) might lead to excitement but after a certain time Habit will arrive and it will feel normal to use Smart Products. This is in line with the argument that increasing habit leads to greater acceptance. In the beginning, to command a product to fulfill a task with a humanlike interaction which a user would also say to a real person might feel unusual but we expect this only to be in the beginning. The better the characteristics Humanlike Interaction and Personality are developed and integrated into the Smart Product, the more natural the interaction with them will feel and the quicker a Habit will arrive. Thus, in this case, we advocate the use of Habit in the conceptual model. Habit has direct effects on Behavioral Intention and on Use Behavior (Venkatesh et al. 2012). The moderators **Age** and **Gender** correspond to consumer characteristics, which are perceived as important (Rijsdijk and Hultink 2009), because those variables can show how different Age and Gender groups react towards Smart Products (Rijsdijk et al. 2007). Their moderating effects and directions are based on the UTAUT2 framework (Venkatesh et al. 2012) including their influence on for example the relevant variables Performance Expectancy, Social Influence and Facilitating Conditions. All effects are visualized or named in the following conceptual model (see Fig. 1). Therefore, we include those moderators. We also propose to integrate the moderator **Experience** due to the difference between current and future development stages of Smart Products. The moderator "reflects an opportunity to use a target technology and is typically operationalized as the passage of time from the initial use of a technology by an individual" (Venkatesh et al. 2012, 2003). We assume that with more Experience gained through the various stages of development, acceptance increases. If consumers use currently available Smart Products with lower levels of the specific characteristics and accompany their

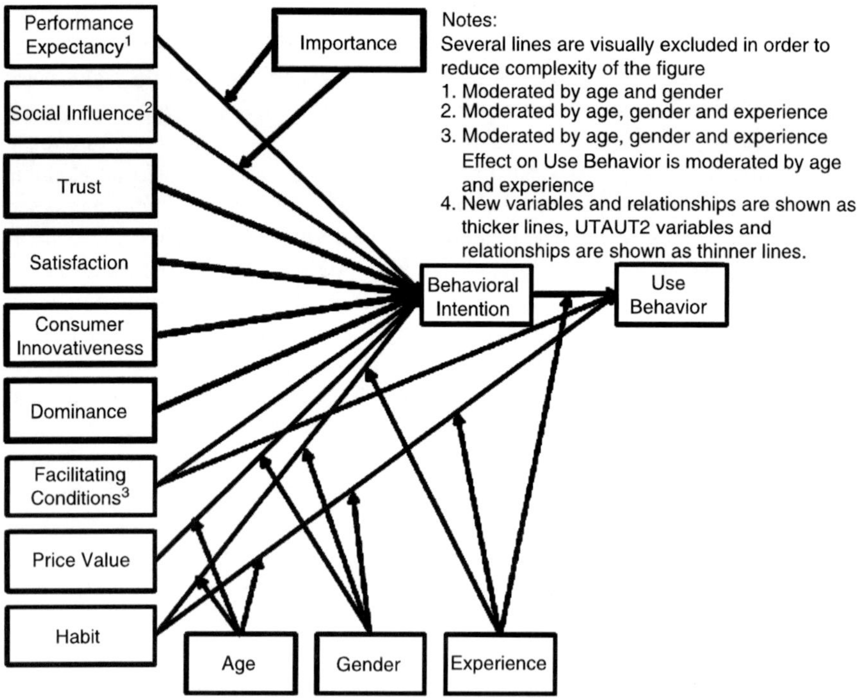

Fig. 1 Proposed conceptual model to investigate the acceptance of Smart Products

development step by step towards future development stages in which characteristics like Autonomy, Adaptability, Reactivity and others are available to a higher extent, the Experience that they have gained throughout the steps could lead them to accept the future stage of development. Hence, we include this moderator. Its several moderating effects are taken from the framework model UTAUT2 (Venkatesh et al. 2012) and are presented in the following conceptual model.

This section deals with variables that have not yet been considered in UTAUT2, but whose use is recommended or seen as beneficial for the investigation of Smart Products. **Trust** is defined as an individual's willingness to depend on another party because of the characteristic of the other party (Rousseau et al. 1998). It is a relevant construct within the research of Smart Products (Kuhn et al. 2018) due to the Autonomy, Adaptability and Reactivity of Smart Products (Hoffman and Novak 2015; Porter and Heppelmann 2014; Nicoll 1999; Bradshaw 1997; Rijsdijk and Hultink 2009). Users hand over control to them. So, consumers rely on the abilities of the Smart Product to complete tasks autonomously and therefore users need to trust them (Glancy 2012). The higher the level of autonomy, the more trust is needed (Rödel et al. 2014). Consumers have to trust the products that they react in an appropriate way and that they learned correct behaviors based on previous circumstances. Especially with regard to Smart Products which fulfill safety-critical tasks autonomously such as Autonomous Cars, consumer must have a high degree of Trust. But also, with regard to their Ability to Cooperate (Hoffman and Novak 2015; Rijsdijk and Hultink 2009), privacy concerns can be raised due to the sending and receiving of information (Hoffman and Novak 2015; Porter and Heppelmann 2014) necessary to solve a task with other Smart Products. Therefore, we rate Trust as an important variable for the investigation of Smart Products adoption. Trust will positively affect Behavioral Intention (Kaur and Rampersad 2018). **Satisfaction** refers to "the extent to which the chosen product meets or exceeds consumer expectations" (Rijsdijk et al. 2007; Oliver 1993). The different characteristics of Smart Products abilities (Hoffman and Novak 2015; Porter and Heppelmann 2014; Nicoll 1999; Bradshaw 1997; Poole and Simon 1997; Rijsdijk and Hultink 2009) have an effect on Customer Satisfaction (Rijsdijk et al. 2007). Satisfaction can be crucial in terms of the fact that people might expect too much from a currently available development stage of a Smart Product, e.g. a too high degree of Autonomy, Adaptability and/or Reactivity. In the case of Autonomous Cars, consumers already imagine the completely Smart Product in which the car drives autonomously (Level 5) while the passenger is not involved in driving. This stage is not yet available. Instead, users have to be aware that they must interact whenever there is a need for it (Level 2). This difference between current and future development stages of Smart Products and the user's general perception that those products are already available with all of the expected future features could lead to dissatisfaction and thus a lower acceptance rate. Therefore, Satisfaction has an important role because users have to be satisfied with the Smart Product to be able to accept those. We argue that this variable needs to be integrated into the conceptual model with its effect on Behavioral Intention (Mittal et al. 2001). **Dominance** represents the extent to which a user feels controlled by an innovation and was proposed to be integrated into acceptance models in general

(Kulviwat et al. 2007). We suggest to incorporate this variable because consumers use Smart Products by which they are controlled in a certain way due to their Autonomy characteristic (Hoffman and Novak 2015; Porter and Heppelmann 2014; Rijsdijk and Hultink 2009). In terms of Smart Products and more specifically for Autonomous Cars this variable can lead to interesting results because Dominance is outside of the consumer. Hence, we respect this variable in our concept with its effect on Behavioral Intention (Mehrabian and Russell 1974). **Importance** was proposed within the investigation of Smart Products acceptance (Mayer et al. 2011). Its usage is reasoned because it marks the extent of intrinsic motivation or personal need for support throughout the fulfillment of a task. The variable reflects the need to adopt a product. Because Smart Products will not only help in fulfilling tasks but take over whole working processes to fulfill tasks autonomously (Hoffman and Novak 2015; Porter and Heppelmann 2014; Rijsdijk and Hultink 2009), we argue that this moderator needs to be respected in our concept. Importance moderates Performance Expectancy and Social Influence. Another characteristic that we identify as potentially relevant for whether or not consumers accept Smart Products is **Consumer Innovativeness**. It represents the degree of interest a consumer has in knowing about new high-tech products as well as the desire to be among the first to buy them (Goldsmith and Hofacker 1991). It can be assumed that for novel or technically highly developed innovations (Porter and Heppelmann 2014), innovativeness plays an important role in acceptance. This is the case for Smart Products and hence we argue for the usage of this variable within our concept. Consumer Innovativeness has a positive effect on Behavioral Intention (Rogers 1995). Lastly, **Product Embeddedness** is recommended to be a part within the adoption investigation (Wuenderlich et al. 2015). But we cannot argue for the characteristics' relevancy for Smart Products acceptance. The herein investigated products can only be seen as slightly integrated into the users' life. We cannot affirm a high degree of integration. Therefore, this variable is not respected for the conceptual model.

Based on the above review and evaluation we can form the conceptual Smart Products acceptance model in Fig. 1. The effects of the different variables are based on the framework from UTAUT2 which explains most of the directions and moderating effects. The effects of the newly integrated variables are also stated above for each variable and visualized below.

Conclusion, Discussion and Future Research

The objective of this paper is to propose a conceptual acceptance model for Smart Products based on their specific characteristics. UTAUT2 serves as a basis to form this conceptual model. Out of the original model we rejected the variables Effort Expectancy and Hedonic Motivation because we argued against their suitability for the investigation of Smart Products acceptance based on their specific characteristics. We included and argued for the previously not in UTAUT2 respected variables Trust, Satisfaction, Consumer Innovativeness, Dominance and the moderator

Importance. This conceptual model should help us to conduct our first study on the acceptance of Smart Products. A first study should serve to test the model before we start our future research activities.

An advantageous aspect of this paper is that the model is built based on a widely accepted model. Whether a variable should be used in the context of Smart Products is justified. It might be critical that we do not respect the different stages which the innovations go through until they reach their future development stage. For example, Autonomous Cars will go through two more levels until they reach the Level 5 of full autonomy. The different levels of autonomy lead also to different levels of acceptance (Rödel et al. 2014). So, do the different steps need acceptance so that the final condition will be accepted by consumers as well or is it sufficient if only the future mature product state is accepted? Control perceptions (Wuenderlich et al. 2015) could have been further investigated and whether they are adequately represented through the variable Dominance.

Our future research activities within this field include studies to test and refine the model. We will examine the current and future development stages of Autonomous Cars more detailed. One of our studies will include Autonomous Cars in Level 2 during real traffic situations where the subject will be in the driver seat completing the tasks: lane keeping, lane switching and parking each one time manually and one time automated. This study represents the current development stage. Our further planned study will consist of a fully autonomous driving simulator in which we will utilize Virtual Reality glasses to be able to investigate the future development stage. Lastly, we plan to integrate neuroscience tools to investigate adoption with implicit measures. Electroencephalography (EEG) to measure frontal asymmetry (Davidson et al. 1979; Park et al. 2018), Eye-Tracking to analyze gaze behavior (Eyes on and off road) and Galvanic Skin Responses/Epidermal Activity (Walker et al. 2019) to measure Arousal. This plan is subject to the addition of further measurement methods and neurophysiological parameters to the herein presented conceptual model.

References

Ajzen, I. (1991). The theory of planned behavior. *Organizational Behavior and Human Decision Processes, 50*, 179–211.

Aldrich, F. K. (2003). Smart Homes: Past, Present and Future. In R. Harper (Ed.), *Inside the Smart Home*. London: Springer-Verlag London Limited.

Bradshaw, J. M. (1997). *Software agents*. Menlo Park, Calif.: American Association for Artificial Intelligence.

Cronin, M. J. (2010). *Smart products, smarter services: Strategies for embedded control*. Cambridge: Cambridge University Press.

Davidson, R. J., Taylor, N., & Saron, C. (1979). Hemisphericity and styles of information processing: Individual differences in EEG asymmetry and their relationship to cognitive performance. In *Abstracts of Papers Presented at the Eighteenth Annual Meeting of The Society for Psychophysiological Research* (Vol. 16).

Davis, F. D. (1989). Perceived Usefulness, Perceived Ease of Use, and User Acceptance of Information Technology. *MIS Quarterly, 13*, 319–340.

Dhebar, A. (1996). Information technology and product policy: 'Smart' products. *European Management Journal, 14*, 477–485.

European Commission. (2018). Digital Transformation Monitor: The rise of Virtual Personal Assistants. https://ec.europa.eu/growth/tools-databases/dem/monitor/sites/default/files/Virtual%20personal%20assistants_v1.pdf.

Fishbein, M., & Ajzen, I. (1975). *Belief, attitude, intention and behavior: An introduction to theory and research* (Addison-Wesley series in social psychology). Reading, Mass.: Addison-Wesley.

Ford, M. (2016). *Rise of the robots: Technology and the threat of a jobless future*. New York: Basic Books.

Gao, L., & Bai, X. (2014). A unified perspective on the factors influencing consumer acceptance of internet of things technology. *Asia Pacific Journal of Marketing and Logistics, 26*, 211–231.

Glancy, D. J. (2012). Privacy in Autonomous Vehicles. *Santa Clara Law Review, 52*(4), 1170–1239.

Goldsmith, R. E., & Hofacker, C. F. (1991). Measuring consumer innovativeness. *Journal of the Academy of Marketing Science, 19*, 209–221.

Hoffman, D. L., & Novak, T. P. (2015). Emergent Experience and the Connected Consumer in the Smart Home Assemblage and the Internet of Things. http://ssrn.com/abstract=2648786.

Hsu, C.-L., & Lin, J. C.-C. (2016). An empirical examination of consumer adoption of Internet of Things services: Network externalities and concern for information privacy perspectives. *Computers in Human Behavior, 62*, 516–527.

Kaur, K., & Rampersad, G. (2018). Trust in driverless cars: Investigating key factors influencing the adoption of driverless cars. *Journal of Engineering and Technology Management, 48*, 87–96.

Kuhn, M., & Marquardt, V. (2019). "What-are-you-looking-at?": Implicit Behavioral Measurement Indicating Technology Acceptance in the Field of Automated Driving. *AMS Annual Marketing Congress Vancouver 2019.*

Kuhn, M., Lowe, B., Bertrandias, L., Sadik-Rozsnyai, O., & Hubert, M. (2018). Consumer Interactions with Automated Technologies. *AMS World Marketing Congress Porto 2018.*

Kulviwat, S., Bruner II, G. C., Kumar, A., Nasco, S. A., & Clark, T. (2007). Toward a unified theory of consumer acceptance technology. *Psychology and Marketing, 24*, 1059–1084.

Mani, Z., & Chouk, I. (2017). Drivers of consumers' resistance to smart products. *Journal of Marketing Management, 33*, 76–97.

Mayer, P., Volland, D., Thiesse, F., & Fleisch, E. (2011). User Acceptance of 'Smart Products': An Empirical Investigation. In A. Bernstein (Ed.), *Proceedings of the 10th International Conference on Wirtschaftsinformatik: 16–18 February 2011 Zurich, Switzerland*. Zürich.

Mehrabian, A., & Russell, J. A. (1974). *An approach to environmental psychology*. Cambridge, Mass.: MIT Press.

Miorandi, D., Sicari, S., Pellegrini, F. de, & Chlamtac, I. (2012). Internet of things: Vision, applications and research challenges. *Ad Hoc Networks, 10*, 1497–1516.

Mittal, V., Katrichis, J. M., & Kumar, P. (2001). Attribute performance and customer satisfaction over time: Evidence from two field studies. *Journal of Services Marketing, 15*, 343–356.

Müller, R., Plapper, P., Brüls, O., Gerke, W., Abba, G., Vette-Steinkamp, M., et al. (Eds.). (2018). *Robotix-Academy Conference for Industrial Robotics (RACIR) 2018* (1st ed., Berichte aus der Robotik). Hydrogenate: Shaker.

NHTSA. (n.d.). Automated Vehicles for Safety. https://www.nhtsa.gov/technology-innovation/automated-vehicles-safety.

Nicoll, D. (1999). *Taxonomy of Information Intensive Products*. Working Paper. University of Edinburgh Management School.

Oliver, R. L. (1993). Cognitive, Affective, and Attribute Bases of the Satisfaction Response. *Journal of Consumer Research, 20*, 418.

Park, C., Shahrdar, S., & Nojoumian, M. (2018). EEG-Based Classification of Emotional State Using an Autonomous Vehicle Simulator. In *2018 IEEE 10th Sensor Array and Multichannel Signal Processing Workshop (SAM), Sheffield, 08.07.18–11.07.18* (pp. 297–300): IEEE.

Poole, S., & Simon, M. (1997). Technological trends, product design and the environment. *Design Studies, 18*, 237–248.

Porter, M. E., & Heppelmann, J. E. (2014). How smart, connected products are transforming competition. *Harvard Business Review, 92*(11), 64–88.

Rijsdijk, S. A., & Hultink, E. J. (2009). How Today's Consumers Perceive Tomorrow's Smart Products*. *Journal of Product Innovation Management, 26*, 24–42.

Rijsdijk, S. A., Hultink, E. J., & Diamantopoulos, A. (2007). Product intelligence: Its conceptualization, measurement and impact on consumer satisfaction. *Journal of the Academy of Marketing Science, 35*, 340–356.

Rödel, C., Stadler, S., Meschtscherjakov, A., & Tscheligi, M. (2014). Towards Autonomous Cars: The Effect of Autonomy Levels on Acceptance and User Experience. In L. N. Boyle (Ed.), *The 6th International Conference, Seattle, WA, USA, 17.09.14–19.09.14* (pp. 1–8). New York, New York, USA: ACM Press.

Rogers, E. M. (1995). *Diffusion of innovations* (4th ed.). New York, NY u. a.: Free Press.

Rousseau, D. M., Sitkin, S. B., Burt, R. S., & Camerer, C. (1998). Not So Different After All: A Cross-Discipline View Of Trust. *Academy of Management Review, 23*, 393–404.

SAE International. (2014). Automated Driving: LEVELS OF DRIVING AUTOMATION ARE DEFINED IN NEW SAE INTERNATIONAL STANDARD J3016. https://www.smmt.co.uk/wp-content/uploads/sites/2/automated_driving.pdf.

Schweitzer, F., & van den Hende, E. A. (2016). To Be or Not to Be in Thrall to the March of Smart Products. *Psychology & Marketing, 33*, 830–842.

Venkatesh, V., & Davis, F. D. (2000). A Theoretical Extension of the Technology Acceptance Model: Four Longitudinal Field Studies. *Management Science, 46*, 186–204.

Venkatesh, V., Morris, M. G., Davis, G. B., & Davis, F. D. (2003). User Acceptance of Information Technology: Toward a Unified View. *MIS Quarterly, 27*, 425-478.

Venkatesh, V., & Bala, H. (2008). Technology Acceptance Model 3 and a Research Agenda on Interventions. *Decision Sciences, 39*, 273–315.

Venkatesh, V., Thong, J. Y.L., & Xu, X. (2012). Consumer Acceptance and Use of Information Technology: Extending the Unified Theory of Acceptance and Use of Technology. *MIS Quarterly, 36*(1), 157–178.

Walker, F., Wang, J., Martens, M. H., & Verwey, W. B. (2019). Gaze behaviour and electrodermal activity: Objective measures of drivers' trust in automated vehicles. *Transportation Research Part F: Traffic Psychology and Behaviour, 64*, 401–412.

Wuenderlich, N. V., Heinonen, K., Ostrom, A. L., Patricio, L., Sousa, R., Voss, C., et al. (2015). "Futurizing" smart service: Implications for service researchers and managers. *Journal of Services Marketing, 29*, 442–447 (2015).

Finding the Right Price: Exploring an Implicit Price Meter

Steffen Schmidt, Sascha Langner, and Michael Schiessl

Abstract Customers hold an internal and external reference price, which gives them an idea about an appropriate price within a range of the actual price. Following this assumption, marketers are able to increase the price of a product within a specific zone of price indifference to their advantage when they accurately exploit customers' price knowledge. The knowledge about prices is stored in the implicit memory of customers, and thus processed in the non-/sub-conscious areas of customers' brain. Still, conventional research approaches on finding the "right" price mostly concentrate on customers' explicit reflected thoughts and opinions about prices and not the unconscious price knowledge. Our research introduces an Implicit Price Meter (IPM); a new approach from neuromarketing that is capable to explore implicit price knowledge. The results of a first study indicate a superior performance of the IPM to find an optimal price in contrast to conventional price measures.

Keywords Implicit measurement · Reaction time measurement · Pricing · Behavioral economics · Mental accounting · Mental budgeting

Introduction

The role of price in the marketing mix is obvious: "It is arguably the easiest element of a product to change and it has the largest direct effects on sales." (Sharp et al. 2010). Indeed, besides the brand of the product or service itself, the price of a

S. Schmidt · S. Langner (✉)
Leibniz University of Hanover, Hanover, Germany
e-mail: schmidt@m2.uni-hannover.de; langner@m2.uni-hannover.de

M. Schiessl
EYE SQUARE GMBH, Berlin, Germany
e-mail: schiessl@eye-square.de

F. Pantoja, S. Wu (eds.), *From Micro to Macro: Dealing with Uncertainties in the Global Marketplace*, Developments in Marketing Science: Proceedings of the Academy of Marketing Science, https://doi.org/10.1007/978-3-030-89883-0_81

product is another extrinsic (informational) cue in terms of value signal customers used most often when evaluating products during purchase decision-making (Dodds et al. 1991). Specifically, customers product evaluation incorporates a cost and perceived quality side, and both sides are affected by the price (Morgan 2011). While the role of price seems to be clear regarding the impact on companies' profitability, return and market competitiveness (Monroe 2003), how to set an appropriate price for a product remains less clear for the marketing management. In the past, many managers do not undertook serious efforts to set the right price customers are willing to pay (Hoffman et al. 2002), even though a slow change towards the usage of value-based pricing strategy as a more sophisticated pricing approach is recognizable, but so far only a minority of firms adopted it (Ingenbleek 2007; Liozu and Hinterhuber 2012). Instead a limited pricing approach is frequently applied that relies on the cost, physical features plus an added margin of return (Morris 1987; Cross and Dixit 2005). This conventional pricing technique with a product-centric focus is not only to be classified as simple, it also leads to a poor pricing capability which is inappropriate for developing an optimal pricing strategy and for avoiding profit sacrifice, respectively (Simon 1992). Or as Dutta et al. (2003) argues from a resource-based perspective: "If a firm sets prices too low, it may cede some of the value created to the customer. In contrast, if the firm sets prices too high, then the quantity sold will be too low. A firm's ability to set the right prices is an important means of appropriating value and therefore an important determinant of the ability of a firm to generate rents." (Dutta et al. 2003).

The lack of well-managed pricing decisions in business—with the exception of leading companies in the consumer goods industry such as Procter and Gamble—comes along with a lack of well-researched pricing decisions in science (Nagle and Holden 1995; Hinterhuber 2004). In the light of the elementary importance of pricing on firms' performance (Baker et al. 2010), only roughly 2% of all research articles in leading marketing journals are focusing explicitly on pricing as past literature reviews have indicated (e.g., Malhotra 1996; Reid and Plank 2000; Kienzler and Kowalkowski 2017).

However, not only practice and academia suffer from this kind of "blind spot" and low level of knowledge regarding pricing, even most customers are very inaccurate and unaware when it comes to recall or recognize the correct (actual) price of a product sold in a store as demonstrated by a study of Vanhuele and Drèze (2002). However, although customers do not know the exact price of a product, at least they are able to compare the known price level of a product (e.g., mid-price level) in comparison to the known product price level of other brands in the same segment, so the relative price is important and less the absolute price (Kohli and Suri 2011). Actually, customers hold an internal and external reference price, which gives them an idea about an appropriate price within a range of the actual price (Sharp et al. 2010). Following this assumption, marketers are able to increase the price of a product within a specific zone of price indifference to their advantage when they accurately exploit customers' price knowledge (Kohli and Suri 2011). But, of course, the right measurement instrument is needed to reveal the right price.

Theoretical Background

The Art of Price of Evaluation/Price Knowledge Measurement

Several studies showed that people often are not able to give an accurate answer regarding the actual price of a product. As revealed by the well-known study of Dickson and Sawyer (1990), less than half of the interviewed supermarket shoppers gave the right answer when asked for the price, even though they just grabbed the product and put it in their cart. The inaccuracy of customers guesses about the price is still regularly demonstrated in the famous television game show *The Price is Right* as hosted by CBS since 1972, with prices chosen by the TV contestants that are often more than 50% off the actual price (Anderson and Simester 2003). Given that great discrepancy of customers guessed prices and products real prices, someone might argue that "Consumers' knowledge of the market is so far from perfect that it hardly deserves to be called knowledge at all" (Anderson and Simester 2003). One reason for the high failure rates might be caused that price knowledge is stored and retrieved from customer's implicit memory (Anderson and Simester 2009). Concerning this matter, Monroe and Lee (1999) argue that what customers remember about a price (price recall) is different from what customers know about a price (price knowledge). With regard to the information processing of customers, Monroe and Lee (1999) state that "the distinction between remembering and knowing contrasts the capacity for conscious recollection about the occurrence of facts and events versus the capacity for non-conscious retrieval of the past event, as in priming, skill learning, habit formation, and classical conditioning." (Monroe and Lee 1999, p. 214).

Thus, the recall of a price is explicitly processed in the conscious mind, while the knowledge of a price is implicitly processed in the non-/sub-conscious mind. Furthermore, the implicit processing of environmental cues such as a brand logo or price information appears to be the primarily mode of information processing as stated by Bargh and Chartrand (1999): "Most of a person's everyday life is determined not by their conscious intentions and deliberate choices but by mental processes that are put into motion by features of the environment and that operate outside of conscious awareness and guidance." (Bargh and Chartrand 1999, p. 462). To explore the implicit knowledge customers hold about a brand or product, neuroscience and cognitive psychology developed several measures such as response time measures to study the underlying mechanism of the implicit mind (Mast and Zaltman 2005; Camerer et al. 2005).

Conventional pricing approaches disregard those findings and measures from psychology. Indeed, established direct and indirect methods frequently used in practice and research such as van Westendorp's Price Sensitivity Meter (PSM), Gabor-Granger technique (GGT) and the various types of conjoint analysis measure customer's willingness to pay (WTP) as stated preference (Wertenbroch and Skiera 2002; Breidert et al. 2006). Basically, those kind of methods apply explicit self-report measures such as ranking order and rating scale to assess the utility, with the underlying assumption that customers are choosing products with highest utility (Green and Srinivasan 1978; Kalish and Nelson 1991). In so doing, such stated preference techniques proclaim to predict at least an intended choice (Green and Srinivasan 1990), which is based on individual's analytic-deliberative decision making process and fits to the random utility theory with its assumption of the weighted additive (Louviere et al. 2007; Cunningham et al. 2010). That premise of deliberated utility maximization is an essential part of the standard theory in economics that portrays the average customer as self-interested (selfish), but principally a perfectly informed and strong rational agent, also known as homo economicus, who is able to make an optimal choice through maximizing one's individual utility (Lindenberg and Frey 1993; Mathis and Steffen 2015).

In the real world, the customer's behavior is often inconsistent with that normative model of the standard economic theory, which might only predict the right outcome in a very easy decision situation, but in more complicated situations, especially under uncertainty, judgement and decisions will not be in line with the predictions of the standard theory in reality (Thaler 1980). According to Simon (1957), the reason for the systematic difference between the predicted behavior and actual behavior relies on customer's bounded rationality: "The capacity of the human mind for formulating and solving complex problems is very small compared with the size of the problems whose solution is required for objectively rational behavior in the real world" (Simon 1957, p. 198). In this regard, Dijksterhuis and Nordgren (2006) presented the unconscious-thought theory postulating that simple issues can be better decided by conscious thought, but complex problems are expected to be better decided by unconscious thought. Dijksterhuis et al. (2006) found support for that postulate in a series of studies on consumer choice. Customers engaged in conscious thought chose the more favorable product under simple conditions, whereas customers of the unconscious thought condition chose the more desirable product under complex conditions, both in the laboratory and in a real shopping environment (Dijksterhuis et al. 2006). Additionally, taking into account that the conscious (explicit) information processing is limited and effortful, but the unconscious (implicit) information processing has no capacity limitations and operates also effortless (Dijksterhuis and Nordgren 2006), unconscious thought is the norm of decision-making (Kahneman 2003).

Another essential concept of customer decision-making is mental accounting. It is a theory from behavior economics and replaces the utility function from standard economic theory with the value function from Kahneman and Tversky's (1979) prospect theory (Thaler 1985). According to that concept, the value of a purchase is the sum of acquisition utility (perceived added value of an economic transaction) and transaction utility (perceived bargain of an economic transaction) (Thaler 1999). More precisely, the acquisition utility represents customer's perceived gain or loss associated with the purchased product (Lichtenstein et al. 1990), which again relates to the perceived price risk of that purchase (Novemsky and Kahneman 2005). The transaction utility incorporates the perceived worth of the purchase (Urbany et al. 1997) and depends on the perceived price fairness of that purchase (Boza and Diamond 1998). Furthermore, Heath (1995) argues that customer's decision making also relies on a special type of mental accounting labelled as mental budgeting. Specifically, that theory proposes that customers have set multiple monetary budgets for various mental accounts such as entertainment or food and monitor their spendings against the allocated budgets (Heath and Soll 1996). When the total spendings exceed the total expected benefits within a given mental account, customers will be less likely to purchase a product, since the perceived appropriateness of the price in relation to the expected value is not given and customers believe that their overall expenses will be too great at all (e.g., Fennema and Perkins 2008).

In the light of that findings and theories, business and research have to consider an advanced measurement approach to assess the unconscious price knowledge of customers that determines the price acceptance within a specific zone of price indifference. As shown in Fig. 1, such an approach needs to evaluate the implicit information processing of customers. Specifically, the mental accounting with regard to the perceived risk and perceived fairness of a product price from a customer perspective needs to be evaluated. In addition, the mental budgeting needs to be taken into account considering the perceived appropriateness of the product price. The effectiveness of such measurement approach labelled as Implicit Price Meter (IPM) compared to PSM and GGT as conventional approaches is demonstrated in the following case study.

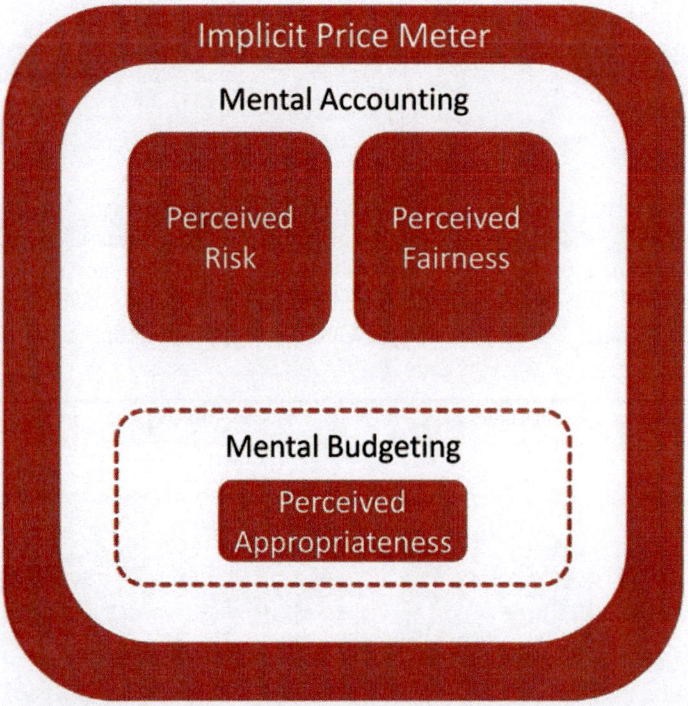

Fig. 1 The implicit price meter as a tool to evaluate customer's price knowledge

Methodology

An Application of the Implicit Price Meter in the E-Commerce: Study Background

The aim of the presented research was to apply various methods to elicit customer's WTP. Specifically, the performance of the developed Implicit Price Meter (IMP) as an advanced method was compared to the van Westendorp's Price Sensitivity Meter (PSM) and the Gabor-Granger technique (GGT) as well-known pricing methods often used in marketing research due to their quick and easy application (e.g., Lipovetsky et al. 2011; Desmet 2016). As investigation objects, two similar products from the gift online shop Monsterzeug (www.monsterzeug.de) were chosen: a gift box filled up with 9 beers and the other one filled up with 12 beers as shown in Fig. 2. Both gift boxes included beers from all over the world. Interestingly, the recommended retail price for the 12-beer gift box is lower (24.95 EUR) than the recommended retail price for the 9-beer gift box (29.29 EUR). Furthermore, Monsterzeug ignored the recommended retail prices and increased significantly the current shop prices for both gift boxes (12-beer box: 39.39 EUR; 9-beer box: 49.95 EUR) stepwise without recognizing any essential change in the volume of sales. However, Monsterzeug was interested in a more evidence-based and less trial and error approach to exploit customers' price knowledge and to identify an optimal price within a given range of acceptable prices (latitude of price acceptance).

Measurements

A variant of Gabor and Granger's (1966) price list procedure was used. Subjects rated the likelihood of buying on a 5-point Likert scale (1 = not all likely to 5 = extremely likely) regarding the exposed product at a variety of four different price points. The top 2 box scores of the GGT were used to define a subject as a

Fig. 2 Investigation objects

potential buyer. Based on that buyer segmentation, the demand curve was calculated and a revenue distribution was estimated, subsequently. With regard to the PSM, the four basic questions as introduced by van Westendorp (1976) and which are related to a scale of price (e.g., price too expensive) were answered by the subjects. Next, the cumulative distribution for each question was computed to receive the respective intersection points that indicate the indifference price point (price cheap and price expensive) and the optimal price point (price too cheap and price too expensive). That two intersection points reveal the latitude of price acceptance. Furthermore, a demand curve was generated by computing the cumulative distribution considering the subject's highest prices they are willing to pay (see Lipovetsky et al. 2011). Again, the revenue was estimated for each price point based on the computed customer demand and a revenue distribution derived.

The IPM was conducted using a reaction time measurement approach. Similar to Craddock et al. (2012), the reaction time measurement was used as an approach of human associative learning, here with regard to the implicit price knowledge of customers. Specifically, various price attributes were presented on the screen related to the perceived risk, perceived fairness and perceived appropriateness (appropriate price or inappropriate price) of the corresponding product price. In addition, attitude attributes were shown as an indicator of product preference in order to calculate the likelihood of buying. Each attribute was paired together with various product prices combined with the product itself in the range from 19.95 EUR to 65.95 EUR (increasing prices in five EUR steps) and presented on the screen in a randomized order. The subjects were forced to decide as quick as possible if the attribute shown on the screen fits together with the corresponding product price (key response: "yes" or "no"). Latencies outside 300 ms and 3000 ms, respectively, were recorded to the nearer boundary value in accordance to the conventional algorithm of the Implicit Association Test (IAT) (Greenwald et al. 2003). Based on the response time and response given, the association strength and association meaning was calculated into a single score using the formula of Craddock et al. (2012). Furthermore, the implicit scores were rescaled in the range from 0 to 100 to enhance the comparability with the PSM and GGT (e.g., Schmidt et al. 2017). The higher (lower) the implicit score, the greater (smaller) the level of approval. Similar to the PSM, two intersection points indicate the range of accepted prices: The indifference price point (fair price and risked price) and the optimal price point (appropriate price and inappropriate price). Also, an demand distribution was computed by the proportion of potential buyers who will buy the product at a certain price level in order to estimate an corresponding revenue curve. When the subject's implicit product preference score for a certain product price was above 50 as selected threshold, then the subject was categorized as potential buyer.

Sample and Procedure

In June 2017, an online survey among actual customers of the online shop Monsterzeug was conducted. Customers were recruited via a survey invitation in Monsterzeug's weekly email newsletter. In total, 198 customers completed the entire survey. If a customer confirmed not to know any relative or friend as a possible presentee of the exposed gift box, then this customer response was removed from the data set to ensure a high level of potential buying motivation. Also, responses were deleted if the customer agreed to have seen and/or bought this product already before to avoid any biased price knowledge. In total, 122 customer responses were used for the final analyses. Customers were mostly female (59.0%), on average 43.97 years old (SD = 12.73) and with an average customer order of 1.40 per year (SD = 1.22). That sample characteristics is relatively representative for Monsterzeug's customer base.

Subjects were randomly assigned either to evaluate the gift box with 9 beers (n = 60) or with 12 beers (n = 62). First, subjects answered questions with regard to their general online consumption and their familiarity with Monsterzeug. Next, the respective gift box was exposed to the subjects as a screenshot, whereby the information about the current price was removed. They were told to view the product presentation and to imagine that this product might be a gift for a relative or friend of them. After the product presentation, subjects conducted the IPM, followed by the PSM and GGM. Within each price measurement, the order of questions was randomized.

Results

The analysis incorporated three WTP estimations with regard to the GGT, PSM and IPM. The results of each method are shown in Fig. 3. Against that empirical analysis, the GGT reveals an optimal price of 34.95€ for the 9-beer gift box as indicated by the peak of the revenue curve. For the 12-beer gift box, the GGT shows a comparatively low revenue curve due to customer's small likelihood of buying, whereby the price should be set lower than 29.95€, presumably at 24.95€, according to the GGT estimation in order to reach a sufficient number of customers to ensure a profitable revenue stream. In contrast, the PSM reveals a range of acceptable prices from 19.95€ to 24.95€ for the 9-beer gift box. Within this range, the revenue is highest at a price level of 24.95€ which indicates the optimal price. For the 12-beer gift box, the optimum price is identified at a price level of 19.95€, since the indifference price point does not reach 24.95€. Both conventional WTP measures revealed a higher level of price acceptance for the 9-beer gift box compared to the 12-beer gift box.

The results of the IPM show a higher price level for both beer gift boxes than the estimates of the conventional measures. Considering the 9-beer gift box, an optimal

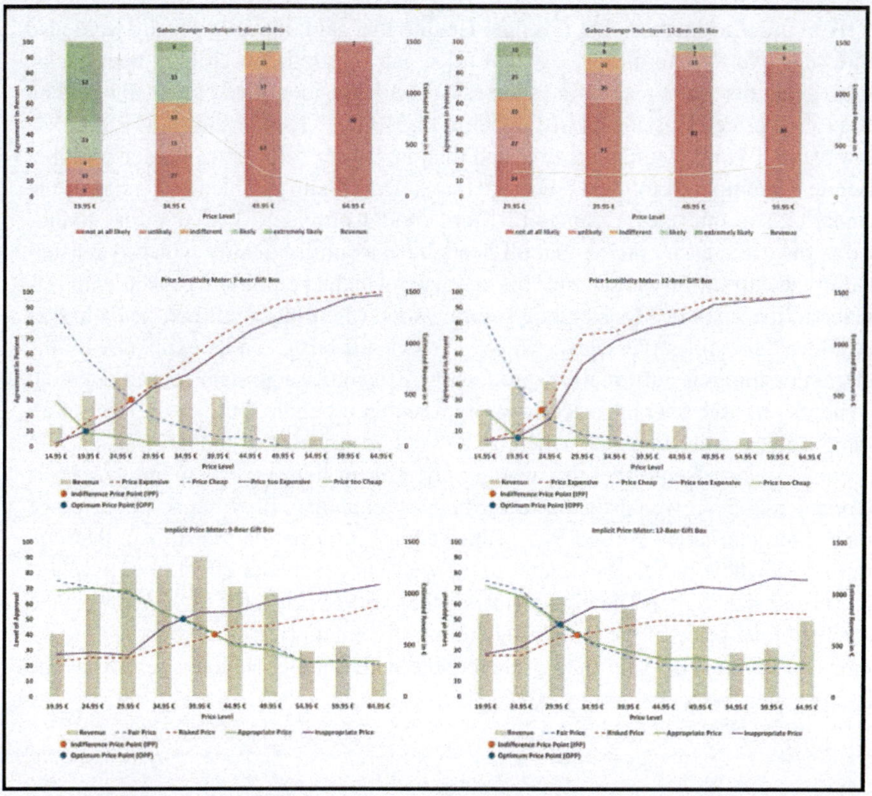

Fig. 3 Comparison of the results

price of 39.95€ is suggested by the IMP estimation. By analogy with the estimates of the conventional WTP measures, the IPM suggested a lower optimal price with a price level at 29.95€ for the 12-beer gift box compared to the 9-beer gift box.

General Discussion

The implicit WTP estimation based on the IPM suggests for both beer packs a higher level of price acceptance in comparison to the conventional WTP estimations referring to the GGT and PSM. Specifically, the IPM estimations of the optimal prices are closer to the current shop prices, while the GGT and PSM estimations are closer to the recommended retail prices. In the past, Monsterzeug increased the prices by a trial an error approach of both beer gift boxes without recognizing any essential change in the volume of sales. Therefore, the IPM suggests a higher level of external validity compared to both conventional WTP measures. However, according to the IPM results, Monsterzeug should slightly lower the current price levels in order to increase the revenue. Having that said, the IPM results were also more sensitive to determine the actual price gap of 10€ between both beer packs, which again fits to the real online shop sales, while the identified price gap based on the explicit price assessments was either to high (GGT: 15€) or to small (PSM: 5€). However, all WTP estimations revealed that the 9-beer gift box can reach a higher price level compared to the 12-beer gift box. That finding is inconsistent with the standard economic theory, since 12 beers should provide a higher utility than 9 beers, under the assumptions that all beers have a similar quality which is reasonable in the current investigation. This anomaly, which is empirical proven with reference to the sales in Monsterzeug's online shop (the 9-beer gift box has a higher price level and still more sales than the 12-beer gift box), can be explained by the automatic, implicit information processing. Customer's un-/subconscious mind considers only the average price of an item within a bundle, but not the sum of all items in the bundle together, whereby a standard price of a bundle is taken into account. As a consequence, the average price of an item of a 12 items bundle is automatically perceived as being lower than of a bundle with 9 items. The average price of an item again is used as an (misleading) information to estimate the total price of the whole bundle and relates to the well-known anchor effect from psychology (Kahneman 2011). The higher (lower) the average price, the higher (lower) the estimated total price of the bundle. Therefore, the total price of the bundle with 12 items is perceived as lower than of the bundle with 9 items, which is termed as the "less is better" phenomenon by Hsee (1998).

Pricing Beyond the Utility and Rationality Premise

Business and research still lacks of a deep knowledge regarding the capability of the available conventional WTP measures such as PSM and GGT to estimate an optimal price within a given range of acceptable prices from a customer perspective (Voelckner 2006). Also, customers often lack the knowledge about the actual price of a product (Sharp et al. 2010). To put it in an exaggerated nutshell: The one side does not know that the other side knows nothing et vice versa. One reason for this lack of valid knowledge is the traditional commitment of economics to the premises of utility maximization and rationality (Skouras et al. 2005). However, findings from neuroeconomics and behavioral economics clearly show that the mind of customers is by default more irrational and assesses the overall value of consuming a product within a given consumption context (e.g., Kahneman 2011; Thaler 2015). The main reason for this kind of evaluations and judgements is the automatic processing of information in the implicit mind, something that customers are not aware and which results in a heuristic instead of deliberated decision making in an adaptive way with more accurate decisions in customer's regular environmental world (Gigerenzer and Gaissmaier 2011).

In the light of that findings, it is less surprising that neuromarketing has gained an increasing popularity over the course of the last decade in the hope of providing marketing-relevant information beyond the homo economicus understanding that is not measurable with conventional marketing research methods (Ariely and Berns 2010). The introduced IPM in the presented research is an advanced pricing method from neuromarketing using a reaction time measurement that is capable to assess customer's implicit price knowledge. As the results revealed, the IPM demonstrated a greater capability to determine an optimal price level that reflected better the actual volume of sales. Specifically, the applied conventional WTP measures, here GGT and PSM, underestimated a realistic range of accepted prices, which in turn would come along with a lower revenue. In contrast, the IPM estimations indicated a higher price level with a greater revenue stream, that comes relatively close to the actual sales and revenue situation of the investigated product sold in a real online shopping environment. Indeed, it seems that the IPM is capable to figure the price is right in an authentic consumption context, that can be summarized shortly as: "An implicit penny saved is a real penny earned."

References

Anderson, E. T., Simester, D. (2003). Mind Your Pricing Cues. *Harvard Business Review*, 81 (9), 96–103.

Anderson, E. T., Simester, D. (2009). Price Cues and Customer Price Knowledge. in *Price Cues and Customer Price Knowledge*, V. Rao, ed., Northampton, MA: E. Elgar Publishing Ltd., 150–68.

Ariely, D., Berns, G. S. (2010). Neuromarketing: the hope and hype of neuroimaging in business. *Nature Reviews Neuroscience*, 11 (4), 284–92.

Baker, W. L., Marn, M. V., Zawada, C. C. (2010). *The Price Advantage*. Hoboken, NJ: Wiley.

Bargh, J. A., Chartrand, T. L. (1999). The unbearable automaticity of being. *American Psychologist*, 54 (7), 462–79.

Boza, M.-E., Diamond, W. (1998). The Social Context of Exchange: Transaction Utility, Relationships and Legitimacy. in *NA - Advances in Consumer Research*, J. W. Alba and J. W. Hutchinson, eds., Provo, UT: Association for Consumer Research, 557–62.

Breidert, C., Hahsler, M., Reutterer, T. (2006). A Review of Methods for Measuring Willingness-to-Pay. *Innovative Marketing*, 2 (4), 8–32.

Camerer, C., Loewenstein, G., Prelec, D. (2005). Neuroeconomics: How Neuroscience Can Inform Economics. *Journal of Economic Literature*, 43 (1), 9–64.

Craddock, P., Molet, M., Miller R. R. (2012). Reaction time as a measure of human associative learning. *Behavioural Processes*, 90 (2), 189–97.

Cross, R. G., Dixit, A. (2005). Customer-centric pricing: The surprising secret for profitability. *Business Horizons*, 48 (6), 483–91.

Cunningham, C. E., Deal, K., Chen, Y. (2010). Adaptive Choice-Based Conjoint Analysis. *The Patient: Patient-Centered Outcomes Research*, 3 (4), 257–73.

Desmet, P. (2016). Effectiveness of measures assessing response to price information. *Journal of Product & Brand Management*, 25 (7), 676–86.

Dickson, P. R., Sawyer, A. G. (1990). The Price Knowledge and Search of Supermarket Shoppers. *Journal of Marketing*, 54 (3), 42–53.

Dijksterhuis, A., Bos, M. W., Nordgren, L. F., van Baaren, R. B. (2006). On Making the Right Choice: The Deliberation-Without-Attention Effect. *Science*, 311 (5763), 1005–7.

Dijksterhuis, Ap., Nordgren, L. F. (2006). A Theory of Unconscious Thought. *Perspectives on Psychological Science*, 1 (2), 95–109.

Dodds, W. B., Monroe, K. B., Grewal, D. (1991). Effects of Price, Brand, and Store Information on Buyers Product Evaluations. *Journal of Marketing Research*, 28 (3), 307.

Dutta, S., Zbaracki, M. J., Bergen, M. (2003). Pricing process as a capability: a resource-based perspective. *Strategic Management Journal*, 24 (7), 615–30.

Fennema, M. G., Perkins, J. D. (2008). Mental budgeting versus marginal decision making: training, experience and justification effects on decisions involving sunk costs. *Journal of Behavioral Decision Making*, 21 (3), 225–39.

Gabor, A., & Granger, C. W. (1966). Price as an Indicator of Quality: Report on an Enquiry. Economica, 43–70.

Gigerenzer, G., Gaissmaier, W. (2011). Heuristic Decision Making. *Annual Review of Psychology*, 62, 451–82.

Green, P. E., Srinivasan, V. (1978). Conjoint Analysis in Consumer Research: Issues and Outlook. *Journal of Consumer Research*, 5 (2), 103–23.

Green, P. E., Srinivasan, V. (1990). Conjoint Analysis in Marketing: New Developments with Implications for Research and Practice. *Journal of Marketing*, 54 (4), 3–19.

Greenwald, A. G., Nosek, B. A., Banaji, M. R. (2003). Understanding and using the Implicit Association Test: I. An improved scoring algorithm. *Journal of Personality and Social Psychology*, 85 (2), 197–216.

Heath, C. (1995). Escalation and De-escalation of Commitment in Response to Sunk Costs: The Role of Budgeting in Mental Accounting. *Organizational Behavior and Human Decision Processes*, 62 (1), 38–54.

Heath, C., Soll, J. B. (1996). Mental Budgeting and Consumer Decisions. *Journal of Consumer Research*, 23 (1), 40–52.

Hinterhuber, A. (2004). Towards value-based pricing—An integrative framework for decision making. *Industrial Marketing Management*, 33 (8), 765–78.

Hoffman, K. D., Turley, L. W., Kelley, S. W. (2002). Pricing retail services. *Journal of Business Research*, 55 (12), 1015–23.

Hsee, C. K. (1998). Less is better: when low-value options are valued more highly than high-value options. *Journal of Behavioral Decision Making*, 11 (2), 107–21.

Ingenbleek, P. (2007). Value-informed pricing in its organizational context: literature review, conceptual framework, and directions for future research. *Journal of Product & Brand Management*, 16 (7), 441–58.

Kahneman, D. (2003). Maps of Bounded Rationality: Psychology for Behavioral Economics. *American Economic Review*, 93 (5), 1449–75.

Kahneman, D. (2011). *Thinking, fast and slow*, London: Penguin Books.

Kahneman, D., Tversky, A. (1979). Prospect Theory: An Analysis of Decision under Risk. *Econometrica*, 47 (2), 263–91.

Kalish, S., Nelson, P. (1991). A comparison of ranking, rating and reservation price measurement in conjoint analysis. *Marketing Letters*, 2 (4), 327–35.

Kienzler, M., Kowalkowski, C. (2017). Pricing strategy: A review of 22 years of marketing research. *Journal of Business Research*, 78, 101–10.

Kohli, C., Suri, R. (2011). The price is right? Guidelines for pricing to enhance profitability. *Business Horizons*, 54 (6), 563–73.

Lichtenstein, D. R., Netemeyer, R. G., Burton, S. (1990). Distinguishing Coupon Proneness from Value Consciousness: An Acquisition-Transaction Utility Theory Perspective. *Journal of Marketing*, 54 (3), 54–67.

Lindenberg, S., Frey, B. S. (1993). Alternatives, Frames, and Relative Prices: A Broader View of Rational Choice Theory. *Acta Sociologica*, 36 (3), 191–205.

Lipovetsky, S., Magnan, S., Zanetti-Polzi, A. (2011). Pricing Models in Marketing Research. *Intelligent Information Management*, 3 (05), 167–74.

Liozu, S. M., & Hinterhuber, A. (2012). Industrial product pricing: a value-based approach. Journal of Business Strategy.

Louviere, J., Hensher, D., Swait, J. (2007). Conjoint Preference Elicitation Methods in the Broader Context of Random Utility Theory Preference Elicitation Methods. in *Conjoint Measurement*, A. Gustafsson, A. Herrmann, and F. Huber, eds., Berlin: Springe, 167–197.

Malhotra, N. K. (1996). The Impact of the Academy of Marketing Science on Marketing Scholarship: An Analysis of the Research Published in JAMS. *Journal of the Academy of Marketing Science*, 24 (4), 291–98.

Mast, F. W., Zaltman, G. (2005). A behavioral window on the mind of the market: An application of the response time paradigm. *Brain Research Bulletin*, 67 (5), 422–27.

Mathis, K., Steffen, A. (2015). From Rational Choice to Behavioural Economics: Theoretical Foundations, Empirical Findings and Legal Implications. in *European Perspectives on Behavioural Law and Economics*, Economic Analysis of Law in European Legal Scholarship, K. Mathis, ed., Cham: Springer, 31–48.

Monroe, K. B. (2003). *Pricing: making profitable decisions*, Boston: McGraw-Hill/Irwin.

Monroe, K. B., Lee, A. Y. (1999). Remembering versus Knowing: Issues in Buyers Processing of Price Information. *Journal of the Academy of Marketing Science*, 27 (2), 207–25.

Morgan, N. A. (2011). Marketing and business performance. *Journal of the Academy of Marketing Science*, 40 (1), 102–19.

Morris, M. H. (1987). Separate prices as a marketing tool. *Industrial Marketing Management*, 16 (2), 79–86.

Nagle, T. T., Holden, R. K. (1995). *The Strategy and tactics of pricing: a guide to profitable decision making*, Englewood Cliffs, NJ: Prentice Hall.

Novemsky, N., Kahneman, D. (2005). The Boundaries of Loss Aversion. *Journal of Marketing Research*, 42 (2), 119–28.

Reid, D. A., Plank R. E. (2000). Business Marketing Comes of Age: A Comprehensive Review of the Literature. *Journal of Business-to-Business Marketing*, 7 (2-3), 9–186.

Schmidt, S., Langner, S., Hennigs, N., Wiedmann, K.-P., Karampournioti, E., Lischka, G. (2017). The green brand: Explicit and implicit framing effects of ecolabelling on brand knowledge. *Cogent Psychology*, 4 (1).

Sharp, B., Dawes, J., Scriven, J. (2010). What Price Promotions Really Do. in *How brands grow: what marketers dont know*, Melbourne: Oxford University Press, 153–70.

Simon, H. A. (1957). *Models of man: social and rational: mathematical essays on rational human behavior in a social setting*, New York, NY: Wiley.

Simon, H. (1992). Pricing opportunities—And How to Exploit Them. *Sloan Management Review*, 33 (2), 55–65.

Skouras, T., Avlonitis, G. J., Indounas, K. A. (2005). Economics and marketing on pricing: how and why do they differ? *Journal of Product & Brand Management*, 14 (6), 362–74.

Thaler, R. (1980). Toward a positive theory of consumer choice. *Journal of Economic Behavior & Organization*, 1 (1), 39–60.

Thaler, R. (1985). Mental Accounting and Consumer Choice. *Marketing Science*, 4 (3), 199–214.

Thaler, R. H. (1999). Mental accounting matters. *Journal of Behavioral Decision Making*, 12 (3), 183–206.

Thaler, R. H. (2015). *Misbehaving: The Making of Behavioural Economics*, London: Penguin Books.

Urbany, J. E., Bearden, W. O., Kaicker, A., Smith-De Borrero, M. (1997). Transaction Utility Effects when Quality is Uncertain. *Journal of the Academy of Marketing Science*, 25 (1), 45–55.

Vanhuele, M., Drèze, X. (2002). Measuring the Price Knowledge Shoppers Bring to the Store. *Journal of Marketing*, 66 (4), 72–85.

van Westendorp P. H. (1976). NSS-Price sensitivity meter: A new approach to study consumer perceptions of prices, ESOMAR (European Society for Opinion and Marketing Research) Congress, Venice, Italy. 139–167.

Voelckner, F. (2006). An empirical comparison of methods for measuring consumers' willingness to pay. *Marketing Letters*, 17 (2), 137–49.

Wertenbroch, K., Skiera, B. (2002). Measuring Consumers' Willingness to Pay at the Point of Purchase. *Journal of Marketing Research*, 39 (2), 228–41.

The Role of Trust in the Service Recovery Context and Its Subsequent Effect on the Repurchase Intention

Zonaib Tahir and Kiane Goudarzi

Abstract Trust is considered a central construct in the relationship marketing and despite appreciating the role of service recovery efforts in restoring trust, service recovery literature has not explored the phenomenon much. Moreover, the position of trust in the service recovery context is still ambiguous. This led to the examination of the antecedents that explain the role of trust in the service recovery model and its consequential effect on the repurchase intention. A 3 (compensation level: 20%, 50% or 100%) × 2 (compensation type: refund or coupon) between subjects experimental design, based on a clothing scenario was undertaken. The antecedents assessed to evaluate the role of trust were compensation level and type, and satisfaction with service recovery. The conceptual model integrated 'trust after recovery' as a serial mediator in the relationship between compensation level, satisfaction and repurchase intention. The results revealed that the inclusion of trust, generates a higher repurchase intention after service recovery. Our key finding of the role of trust as a serial mediator in the service recovery context implies that the companies should compensate for the failure as per customers' expectation to generate higher repurchase intention.

Keywords Service recovery · Compensation · Trust · Repurchase intention

Introduction

The organizations strive to deliver high quality and consistent services in order to gain and maintain competitive advantage but despite their best efforts, the inherent nature of services leads to failures in the delivery process (Kelley and Davis 1994). Service failures should be addressed with effective recovery, which is an essential element of the firm's overall quality (Smith et al. 1999). Importantly, satisfactory

Z. Tahir (✉) · K. Goudarzi
Université Jean Moulin Lyon 3, Lyon, France
e-mail: zonaib.tahir@univ-lyon3.fr; kiane.goudarzi@univ-lyon3.fr

F. Pantoja, S. Wu (eds.), *From Micro to Macro: Dealing with Uncertainties in the Global Marketplace*, Developments in Marketing Science: Proceedings of the Academy of Marketing Science, https://doi.org/10.1007/978-3-030-89883-0_82

recovery actions positively influence customers' evaluations, strengthen customer relationships and enhance customer trust (DeWitt et al. 2008).

Distributive justice is considered a key driver of satisfaction with service recovery because customers expect their tangible loss to be refunded (Orsingher et al. 2010). Gelbrich and Roschk's (2011) meta-analysis reveals that compensation is the most powerful determinant of distributive justice and its effect is greater than the interactional and procedural justice.

Service recovery efforts are also regarded as mechanisms by which trust can be rebuilt after violations caused by service failures (DeWitt et al. 2008; Smith et al. 1999; Tax et al. 1998). Customers expect their complaints to be resolved in a way that validates their decision to have opted for the service provider in the first place. Despite being considered the foundation of relationship marketing (Morgan and Hunt 1994), trust has not been a focus of service recovery studies and its position in the nomological network remains unclear (Gelbrich and Roschk 2011; Orsingher et al. 2010) because it has been studied as an attitudinal outcome of the customers' evaluations of the firm's recovery (Kau and Loh 2006; Tax et al. 1998; Weun et al. 2004) and also as a mediating variable (Choi and La 2013; DeWitt et al. 2008).

Kim (2014) considers trust to be a non-static construct that evolves with new experiences. Provision of appropriate service recovery is one such experience that reflects firm's ability and willingness to correct the problem (De Matos et al. 2009). Trust acts as a control mechanism that helps deal with the uncertainty concerning the firm's behavior. In case of a service failure, it is crucial that the pre-failure trust be restored through appropriate recovery actions in order to regress customer switching behavior and generate positive attitudes. Keeping in view the equivocal position of trust in the service recovery context, the overall aim of our research is:

To Understand the Antecedents That Explain the Role of Customer's Trust in the Service Recovery Context and the Subsequent Effect of Trust on Behavioral Intentions

The research will examine two research questions, grouped under the following theme:

Does the Relationship Between Satisfaction with Recovery and Trust Help Define Trust's Role in the Service Recovery Context?

1. How does satisfaction with recovery affect trust?
2. How does the relationship between satisfaction and trust affect the repurchase intention?

Background and Hypotheses Development

Firms should respond to service failures with effective recovery efforts in order to generate customer satisfaction, improve customer relationships and prevent defection (Bambauer-Sachse and Rabeson 2015; Orsingher et al. 2010). Employing service recovery process is even more crucial because customers are often more dissatisfied by a firm's failure to recover than by the service failure itself (Smith et al. 1999).

Compensation

Dissatisfied customers mostly want a replacement or compensation when they complain, as evident from most studies of post-complaint satisfaction, which show that distributive justice in the form of compensation has the greatest impact on customer satisfaction with recovery, repurchase intention and loyalty (Goodwin and Ross 1992; Kau and Loh 2006; Smith et al. 1999; Tax et al. 1998). The results of Orsingher et al.'s (2010) study further strengthen the premise that distributive justice has the strongest average correlation with satisfaction with complaint handling because customers expect the company to restore the service promise through a fair compensation. Moreover, Gelbrich and Roschk's (2011) relative effect size analysis revealed that compensation is the most powerful determinant of distributive justice.

In order to ensure satisfaction with the service recovery, the value of the compensation offered should equate the value of the loss experienced. Most of the service recovery studies have considered one or two levels of compensation to assess the causal relationships amongst their variables. For example, 20% discount (Mattila and Patterson 2004), $10 voucher, 50% coupon, 20% discount (Grewal et al. 2008), 100% refund, 100% voucher (Roschk and Gelbrich 2014).

We propose to test three levels: 20% as minimum or basic, 50% as moderate and 100% as full compensation to deduce the relative effect of compensation on satisfaction. Since overcompensation has low incremental effect (Gelbrich and Roschk 2011), we do not wish to test its effect. Hence we propose the following hypothesis:

H1: Compensation level will have a positive effect on satisfaction with service recovery.

Trust

In the context of service recovery, a customer's trust depicts his or her willingness to accept vulnerability on the basis of a positive expectation of the service failure resolution. Therefore, if a complainant receives a poor response from an organization, the customer is likely to perceive that organization as untrustworthy (DeWitt et al. 2008). Service failures negatively impact a service provider's perceived reliability and customer's confidence in a service firm (Weun et al. 2004). Therefore, trust needs to be recovered because the trusting beliefs influence buyers' intentions and behavior such as the repurchase intent or generating negative word of mouth (Wang and Huff 2007). However, Orsingher et al. (2010) reported trust to be an infrequent consequence of satisfaction with complaint handling and Gelbrich and Roschk (2011) excluded trust from their conceptual framework because it was only addressed in a few studies.

The unclear position of trust in the service recovery context and customers' expectation of their tangible loss being refunded prompts us to assess the direct effect of compensation on trust. Along with, similar to the previous researches (Tax et al. 1998; Kau and Loh 2006), we will test the indirect effect of compensation on trust through satisfaction in order to establish which effect is stronger, if both effects are possible. We therefore propose the following hypotheses:

H2: Compensation level will have a positive effect on trust in the company.
H3: Satisfaction with the service recovery will have a positive effect on trust in the company.

Repurchase Intention

Repurchase intention is the likelihood of making future purchases from the service provider involved in the failure and recovery scenario. Given that the cost of retaining an existing customer is less than prospecting for a new customer, purchase intention is a very important consideration for marketers. Complainants who feel satisfied with the way the company has handled their problem are likely to repurchase (Maxham 2001). The positive relationship between satisfaction with complaint handling and return intent is consistent across studies (Orsingher et al. 2010). In view of the equity theory, firms can positively restore low purchase intentions following a service failure by effectively resolving a perceived inequity, thereby preserving a customer's intent to repurchase from the firm in the future (Goodwin and Ross 1992).

In line with the previous service recovery studies (Grewal et al. 2008; Wirtz and Mattila 2004), we wish to examine the indirect effect of compensation on repurchase intention through satisfaction. Furthermore, the studies that incorporated trust as a mediator in their studies (DeWitt et al. 2008; Choi and La 2013) had loyalty as their dependent variable. We, on the other hand, want to inspect the mediating role of trust in the relationship between compensation and repurchase intention. Along with, we want to examine the direct effect of compensation on repurchase intention so as to establish which effect is stronger, if all the effects are possible. Therefore we propose the following hypotheses:

H4: Compensation level will have a positive effect on repurchase intention.
H5: Satisfaction with the service recovery will have a positive effect on repurchase intention.
H6: Trust in the company will have a positive effect on repurchase intention.

Methodology

In order to test the hypotheses, a between subjects experimental study, based on a clothing scenario was undertaken. The experimental design was 3 (compensation level: 20%, 50% or 100%) × 2 (compensation type: refund or coupon). Since our study is based on the activities associated with service failure and recovery which might unfold over days or weeks, experimental research design will enable the compression of time (Hess Jr. et al. 2003). The service context selected for our study is the buying of clothes as it will provide a familiar context to our respondents. The service failure described draws inspiration from the scenario of Gelbrich et al. (2014) and outlines a post-purchase failure involving a jacket, which is viewed as a service device (Vargo and Lusch 2004, cited in Gelbrich et al. 2014).

The respondents were first asked to think about a clothing brand from where they will consider to buy a jacket for themselves. This allowed us to establish that the respondents are familiar with the brand and have a certain level of trust in it. The respondents then answered questions that measured their trust (T1) and repurchase intention (RI1) before buying. The respondents then read the service failure and answered questions that measured their trust (T2) and repurchase intention (RI2) after failure. They also answered 1 question each for failure severity and failure responsibility. Each respondent then randomly received 1 of the 6 compensation manipulations i.e. 20%, 50% or 100% refund or coupon and answered questions that measured their satisfaction with service recovery, trust (T3) and repurchase intention (RI3) after recovery.

Sample

The questionnaire was distributed through surveymonkey and a total of 1573 complete responses were received. A rigorous screening process, based on responses to the manipulation check questions, identification of mahalanobis distance based multivariate outliers and response pattern checks, led to a usable sample of 461. The respondents had a mean age of 23.98 years (S.D. = 6.024) and 49% were female. 32% respondents were French and 58% belonged to Pakistan. 46% respondents had a Bachelor's degree and 42% had a Master's degree.

Measures and Manipulation Check

Realism (The scenario presented to you is realistic) and believability (It is easy for me to imagine myself in this situation) of the scenario were recorded on a 7 point likert type scale (1 = strongly disagree, 7 = strongly agree). The results of one-sample t-tests show that the respondents considered the scenario to be realistic (M = 5.13, S.D. = 1.45, $t = 75.85$, $p < 0.001$) and were able to imagine themselves in the situation described in the scenario (M = 5.43, S.D. = 1.30, $t = 89.50$, $p < 0.001$). A one-way analysis of variance revealed that the satisfaction was significantly different across the 20% (M = 3.75, N = 149), 50% (M = 4.37, N = 138), and 100% (M = 5.57, N = 174) conditions, $F (2, 458) = 57.73$, $p < 0.001$, which is portrayed in the figure below (Fig. 1).

Trust was operationalized through six items adapted from Garbarino and Johnson (1999), Chaudhuri and Holbrook (2001) and Sirdeshmukh et al. (2002) and the responses were recorded on a seven point likert type scale (1 = strongly disagree, 7 = strongly agree). KMO and Bartlett's test confirm the adequacy of sample. The developed scales for trust before buying (T1) ($\alpha = 0.827$), trust after failure (T2) ($\alpha = 0.944$) and trust after recovery (T3) ($\alpha = 0.959$) are reliable.

Repurchase intention was measured through the scale, adapted from Maxham and Netemeyer (2002). The responses were recorded on a 7 point likert type scale (1 = strongly disagree, 7 = strongly agree; 1 = very unlikely, 7 = very likely). KMO and Bartlett's test confirm the adequacy of sample. The developed scales for repurchase intention before buying (RI1) ($\alpha = 0.837$), repurchase intention after failure (RI2) ($\alpha = 0.911$) and repurchase intention after recovery (RI3) ($\alpha = 0.948$) are reliable.

In order to assess the satisfaction with service recovery of the respondents, the scale of Maxham and Netemeyer (2002) was adapted. The responses were recorded on a 7 point likert type scale (1 = strongly disagree, 7 = strongly agree; 1 = very unsatisfied, 7 = very satisfied). KMO and Bartlett's test confirm the adequacy of sample and the developed scale is reliable ($\alpha = 0.970$).

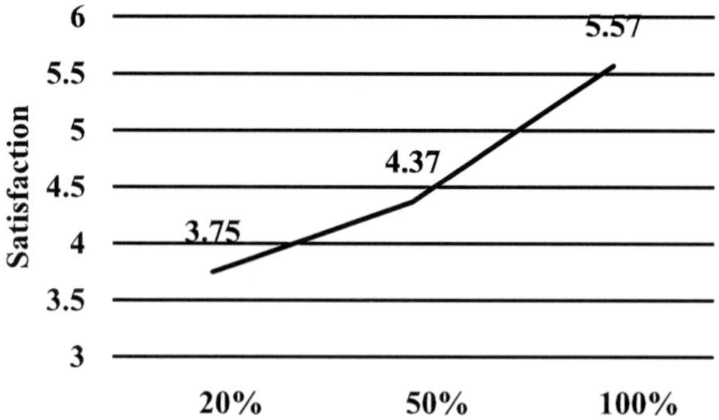

Fig. 1 Satisfaction across compensation conditions

We controlled for the compensation type, failure severity, failure responsibility, T1 and RI1. Failure severity and failure responsibility were each measured by a single item (I consider this failure to be very severe; I feel responsible for this failure), both on a seven point likert-type scale (1 = strongly disagree, 7 = strongly agree). One sample t-test showed that the failure severity mean = 4.64 (S.D. = 1.43, $t = 69.49$) is significantly above the midpoint ($p < 0.001$) which shows that the failure narrated in the scenario is considered severe. The failure responsibility mean = 2.84 (S.D. = 1.59, $t = 38.27$) is significantly below the midpoint ($p < 0.001$) which implies that the respondents feel that the brand is responsible for the failure.

A confirmatory factor analysis (CFA) showed an acceptable fit with the data, including minimum discrepancy (x^2/df) = 3.04, comparative fit index (CFI) = 0.97, root mean square residual (RMR) = 0.08, goodness of fit index (GFI) = 0.91, adjusted goodness of fit index (AGFI) = 0.89 and root mean square error of approximation (RMSEA) = 0.05. The composite reliability (CR) values ranged from 0.832 to 0.965.

Analysis and Discussion

In order to test the hypotheses, we estimated the mediation model template 6 (Fig. 2) of Hayes' (2013) PROCESS macro with 5000 bootstrapped samples.

Compensation level is the independent variable X, repurchase intention after recovery (RI3) is the dependent variable Y, satisfaction with the service recovery is the mediator M1 and Trust after recovery (T3) is the mediator M2.

The significant positive effect of compensation level on satisfaction with service recovery, shown in Table 1 lends support to hypothesis 1.

Table 2 shows that the 'compensation level' has a non-significant effect on 'trust after recovery', therefore hypothesis 2 is not supported. However, the evolution of trust for each of the compensation levels, presented in Fig. 3, exhibits that more the compensation level, more is the trust after recovery. Satisfaction with service recovery has a strong positive effect on trust after recovery (T3), thereby lending support to hypothesis 3.

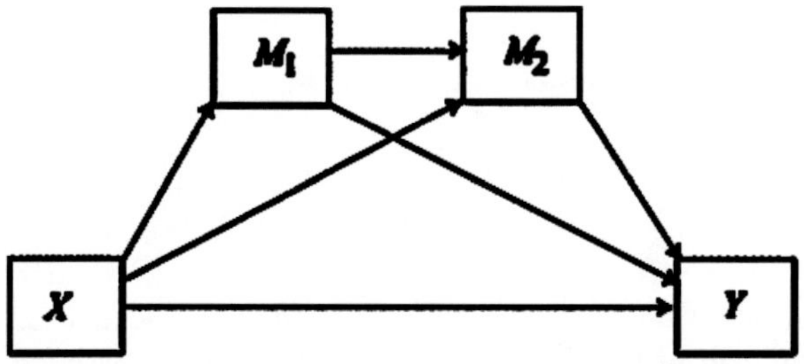

Fig. 2 Mediation model 6 (Hayes 2013)

Table 1 Effects on satisfaction with service recovery, $R^2 = 0.28$

	Effect	Standardized effect	s.e.	t (454)	p
Compensation level	0.87	0.42	0.08	10.41	<0.001
Compensation type	−0.09	−0.03	0.14	−0.64	0.52 ns
Failure severity	−0.24	−0.20	0.05	−4.97	<0.001
Failure responsibility	0.16	0.14	0.04	3.60	<0.001
Initial trust	0.33	0.14	0.11	2.90	0.004
Initial repurchase intention	−0.06	−0.03	0.10	−0.61	0.54 ns

Table 2 Effects on trust after recovery (T3), $R^2 = 0.67$

	Effect	Standardized effect	s.e.	t (453)	p
Compensation level	−0.05	−0.03	0.05	−1.04	0.30 ns
Satisfaction	0.63	0.74	0.03	23.52	<0.001
Compensation type	0.01	0.003	0.08	0.10	0.92 ns
Failure severity	−0.07	−0.07	0.03	−2.64	0.01
Failure responsibility	0.03	0.03	0.03	1.26	0.21 ns
Initial trust	0.30	0.15	0.07	4.59	<0.001
Initial repurchase intention	0.20	0.11	0.06	3.41	<0.001

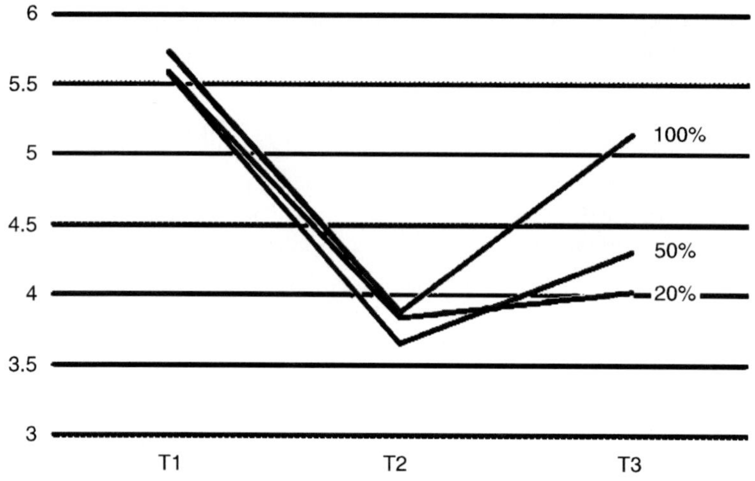

Fig. 3 Evolution of trust per compensation level

Table 3 shows that the compensation level and satisfaction with service recovery have a non-significant effect on repurchase intention after recovery (RI3), which implies that hypotheses 4 and 5 are not supported. The rejection of hypothesis 5 negates the argument of Grewal et al. (2008) and Writz and Mattila (2004) who advocated the positive effect of satisfaction with service recovery on repurchase

Table 3 Effects on repurchase intention after recovery (RI3), $R^2 = 0.78$

	Effect	Standardized effect	s.e.	t (452)	p
Compensation level	−0.03	−0.01	0.04	−0.59	0.56 ns
Satisfaction	0.03	0.03	0.03	0.81	0.42 ns
Trust after recovery	0.80	0.80	0.04	20.62	<0.001
Compensation type	0.15	0.05	0.07	2.26	0.02
Failure severity	−0.07	−0.06	0.02	−2.76	0.01
Failure responsibility	0.04	0.04	0.02	1.86	0.06 ns
Initial trust	−0.05	−0.02	0.06	−0.82	0.41 ns
Initial repurchase intention	0.29	0.16	0.05	5.90	<0.001

intention. The strong positive effect of trust after recovery (T3) on repurchase intention after recovery (RI3) provides evidence in support of hypothesis 6. Moreover, in view of the findings of DeWitt et al. (2008) and Kim (2014), it may be inferred that fulfillment of customers' recovery expectation leads to positive repurchase intention. In other words, repurchase intention after a failure cannot be generated unless the recovery expectation of the customers is met.

The non-significant direct effect of compensation level on repurchase intention after recovery (RI3) and the significant indirect effect of compensation level on repurchase intention after recovery through satisfaction and trust after recovery (**COMLEV → SAT → T3 → RI3**) supports full serial mediation. It can be argued that the only way of generating the repurchase intention in the event of a service failure is when satisfaction with service recovery and trust after recovery (T3) act as serial mediators. Our results confirm the mediating effect of trust after recovery (T3) on repurchase intention, which has not been studied before. We can conclude that trust after recovery (T3) as a serial mediator with satisfaction leads to positive repurchase intention after recovery (RI3), hence signifying the role of trust as a serial mediator. The following figure shows the standardized effect values of only the signifcant relations amongst the varibles (Fig. 4).

Implications for Theory and Practice

Theoretical Implications

The main aim of this research was to assess the role of trust in the service recovery context. The results show that the only way of generating the repurchase intention in the event of a service failure is when satisfaction with service recovery and trust after recovery (T3) act as serial mediators (Table 4). Thereby, signifying the role of trust as a serial mediator in the service recovery context.

The results appear to have negated an established relationship between 'satisfaction with service recovery' and 'repurchase intention' (Grewal et al. 2008; Writz and Mattila 2004) but it should be noted that the previous studies did not take trust

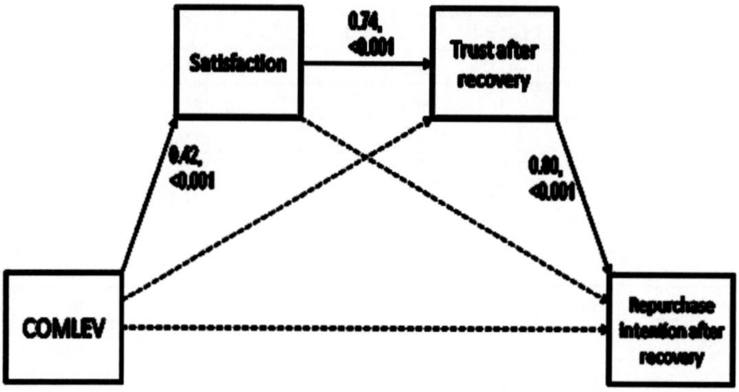

Fig. 4 Relations amongst the variables. Where COMLEV = compensation level, Satisfaction = satisfaction with service recovery

Table 4 Indirect effects of compensation level on repurchase intention after recovery

COMLEV → SAT → RI3	COMLEV → T3 → RI3	COMLEV → SAT → T3 → RI3
0.01 ns	−0.03 ns	0.25

Where COMLEV = compensation level, SAT = satisfaction with service recovery, T3 = trust after recovery and RI3 = repurchase intention after recovery

into account in their models. Unlike the previous studies, which used fictitious brands in their scenarios, we asked the respondents of our experimental study to state a brand of their choice and record their trust in the brand before proceeding to the failure and recovery scenario. This led to the inference that once the customers establish a certain level of trust in the firm, 'trust after recovery' and not 'satisfaction' dictates 'repurchase intention after recovery'.

The studies that incorporated trust as a mediator in their studies (DeWitt et al. 2008; Choi and La 2013) had loyalty as their dependent variable. We on the other hand examined the mediating role of trust in the relationship between compensation level and repurchase intention. The mediating effect of trust on repurchase intention has not been assessed before and hence adds to the existing literature.

The positive significant effect of trust before buying (T1) on satisfaction with service recovery suggests that more the trust before buying (T1), more will be the satisfaction with the compensation level (Table 1). This effect, which has not been studied before, appears to act as a safeguard to the relationship, similar to loyalty (Hess et al. 2003).

The positive effect of initial trust on trust after recovery adds to the service recovery literature by tracking the evolution of trust (Fig. 3) to highlight how the trust before failure transforms into post-recovery trust as a result of compensation. Customers' evaluation of the firm's recovery efforts are vital in re-evaluating the firm's trustworthiness and rebuilding post failure customer trust (La and Choi, 2012).

Managerial Implications

Our results reveal that the repurchase intention cannot be ensured merely through satisfaction with the service recovery. The fulfillment of the customers' recovery expectation, that is trust, plays a key role such that unless their recovery expectations are met, repurchase intention cannot be guaranteed. Hence, it is vital for the companies to provide remedy to the failure which minimizes their perception of loss. The firms should have procedures in place to assess the perception of customers' loss in various situations so that they can act accordingly in real time. Depending on the type of the service, firms can hold interviews or focus groups with their customers to understand how they feel about certain failures and what do they expect in return. The customers can also be asked to fill the satisfaction surveys after they have received the compensation and the feedback can be used by the firms to shape their compensation policies.

The trust of the customers when they enter in a relationship with a firm is based on calculation or reasoning but over the time it evolves based on new experiences and confirmation of expectations (Kim 2014; Wang and Huff 2007). It is important for the firms to perform well the first time and manage their reputation so that the customer enters early transactions with as high a level of initial trust as possible. Our results reveal that a higher initial trust appears to safeguard a relationship in the similar manner as loyalty i.e. higher the initial trust, more will be the satisfaction with the service recovery. Importantly, this means that the customers with a low initial trust must specially be taken care off in the case of a service failure because they are more prone to defection.

Limitations and Future Research Directions

The first limitation of our research is the cross-sectional nature of data collection. The respondents answered the survey questions based on the brand of their choice and there is a possibility that they never experienced failure with the brand they stated or the failure portrayed in the scenario was never faced. The real intentions and attitudes might differ from the ones stated in the questionnaire. Therefore, the replication of the study with a longitudinal data is encouraged to assess if the attitudes and intentions revealed over time generate the same results as obtained in our study.

The second limitation of our study is the measurement of only repurchase intention as a behavioral intention after the recovery. The future research can benefit from the inclusion of word of mouth intention, especially when the customers nowadays can take to social media and appraise the services even before they actually repurchase.

The third limitation is the use of only three compensation levels (20%, 50% and 100%). Since the compensation level used in our scenario did not restore the trust to the pre-failure levels, the future research can benefit from the use of overcompensation to see if it can restore the trust to the pre-failure levels.

The fourth limitation is the use of only one service context in our scenario based study. The customers usually have industry or product specific knowledge that influences their failure and recovery expectations (Hess et al. 2003). The future research should examine the causes and effects studied in this research to see if they hold true for other service contexts.

References

Bambauer-Sachse, S., & Rabeson, L. E. (2015). Service recovery for moderate and high involvement services. *Journal of Services Marketing, 29*, 331–343.

Chaudhuri, A., & Holbrook, M. B. (2001). The chain of effects from brand trust and brand affect to brand performance: The role of brand loyalty. *Journal of Marketing, 65*, 81–93.

Choi, B., & La, S. (2013). The impact of corporate social responsibility (CSR) and customer trust on the restoration of loyalty after service failure and recovery. *Journal of Services Marketing, 27*, 223–233.

De Matos, C. A., Rossi, C. A. V., Veiga, R. T., & Vieira, V. A. (2009). Consumer reaction to service failure and recovery: The moderating role of attitude toward complaining. *Journal of Services Marketing, 23*, 462–475.

DeWitt, T., Nguyen, D. T., & Marshall, R. (2008). Exploring customer loyalty following service recovery: The mediating effects of trust and emotions. *Journal of Service Research, 10*, 269–281.

Garbarino, E., & Johnson, M. S. (1999). The different roles of satisfaction, trust and commitment in customer relationships. *Journal of Marketing, 63*, 70–87.

Gelbrich, K., Gathke, J., & Gregoire, Y. (2014). How much compensation should a firm offer for a flawed service? An examination of the nonlinear effects of compensation on satisfaction. *Journal of Service Research, 18*, 107–123.

Gelbrich, K., & Roschk, H. (2011). A meta-analysis of organizational complaint handling and customer responses. *Journal of Services Research, 14*, 24–43.

Goodwin, C., & Ross, I. (1992). Consumer responses to service failures: influence of procedural and interactional fairness perception. *Journal of Business Research, 25*, 149–63.

Grewal, D., Roggeveen, A. L., & Tsiros, M. (2008). The effect of compensation on repurchase intentions in service recovery. *Journal of Retailing, 84*, 424–434.

Hayes, A. F. (2013). *Introduction to mediation, moderation, and conditional process analysis: A regression-based approach*. The Guilford Press.

Hess, R. L. Jr., Ganesan, S., & Klein, N. M. (2003). Service failure and recovery: the impact of relationship factors on customer satisfaction. *Journal of the Academy of Marketing Science, 31*, 127–46.

Kau, A., & Loh, E. W. (2006). The effects of service recovery on consumer satisfaction: A comparison between complainants and non-complainants. *Journal of Services Marketing, 20*, 101–111.

Kelley, S. W., & Davis, M. A. (1994). Antecedents to customer expectations for service recovery. *Journal of the Academy of Marketing Science, 22*, 52–61.

Kim, D. J. (2014). A study of the multilevel and dynamic nature of trust in e-commerce from a cross-stage perspective. *International Journal of Electronic Commerce, 19*, 11–64.

Mattila, A. S., & Patterson, P. G. (2004). The impact of culture on consumers' perceptions of service recovery efforts. *Journal of Retailing, 80*, 196–206.

Maxham, J. G. (2001). Service recovery's influence on consumer satisfaction, positive word-of-mouth, and purchase intentions. *Journal of Business Research, 54*, 11–24.

Maxham, J. G., & Netemeyer, R. G. (2002). A longitudinal study of complaining customers' evaluations of multiple service failures and recovery efforts. *Journal of Marketing, 66*, 57–71.

Morgan, R. M., & Hunt, S. D. (1994). The commitment-trust theory of relationship marketing. *Journal of Marketing, 58*, 20–38.

Orsingher, C., Valentini, S., & De Angelis, M. (2010). A meta-analysis of satisfaction with complaint handling in services. *Journal of the Academy of Marketing Science, 38*, 169–186.

Roschk, H., & Gelbrich, K. (2014). Identifying appropriate compensation types for service failures: a meta-analytic and experimental analysis. *Journal of Service Research, 17*, 195–210.

Sirdeshmukh, D., Singh, J., & Sabol, B. (2002). Consumer trust, value, and loyalty in relational exchanges. *Journal of Marketing, 66*, 15–37.

Smith, A. K., Bolton, R. N., & Wagner, J. (1999). A model of customer satisfaction with service encounters involving failure and recovery. *Journal of Marketing Research, 36*, 356–372.

Tax, S. S., Brown, S. W., & Chandrashekaran, M. (1998). Customer evaluations of service complaint experiences: Implications for relationship marketing. *Journal of Marketing, 62*, 60–76.

Wang, S., & Huff, L. C. (2007). Explaining buyers' responses to sellers' violation of trust. *European Journal of Marketing, 41*, 1033–1052.

Weun, S., Beatty, S. E., & Jones, M. A. (2004). The impact of service failure severity on service recovery evaluations and post-recovery relationships. *Journal of Services Marketing, 18*, 133–146.

Wirtz, J., & Mattila, A. S. (2004). Consumer responses to compensation, speed of recovery and apology after a service failure. *International Journal of Service Industry Management, 15*, 150–166.

Do You Love Open Kitchen Restaurants? Exploring Visitors' Motivators of Restaurant Visit for Sustainable Growth of Tourism' Industry: An Abstract

Vikas Arya, Deepa Sethi, Anshuman Sharma, Atul Shiva, and Tahir Islam

Abstract This study examines how restaurants' concern shifted towards visitors' motivating factors and their impact on visitors' attachment with the restaurants which leads restaurants to have loyalty from visitors. Authors investigate whether attitude towards restaurants and digital relationship experience is mediating the established relationship or not. We also explored the role of open kitchen service in a restaurant as a moderator.

An empirical investigation was carried out on a total of 745 respondents from India, where primary data was collected through an online survey method. Items drawn for the current study are based on an exhaustive literature review. This study has utilised symmetric as well as asymmetric methods to test and validate the data analysis results. For symmetric model assessment, this study has used SmartPLS, Process Micro, and Artificial Neural Network and for asymmetric modelling, fuzzy set qualitative comparative analysis (fsQCA) has been applied.

The empirical study outcomes confirm that visitors' attachment with restaurants is high when restaurants are taking care of motivating factors such as: engaging

V. Arya (✉)
Rajalakshmi School of Business, Chennai, India
e-mail: vikas.arya@rsb.edu.in

D. Sethi
Indian Institute of Management, Kozhikode, India
e-mail: deepa@iimk.ac.in

A. Sharma
CBA Ajman University, Dubai, UAE
e-mail: a.sharma@ajman.ac.ae

A. Shiva
Chandigarh University, Mohali, India
e-mail: atul.e8105@cumail.in

T. Islam
Tongji University, Shanghai, China
e-mail: tahir@tongji.edu.cn

F. Pantoja, S. Wu (eds.), *From Micro to Macro: Dealing with Uncertainties in the Global Marketplace*, Developments in Marketing Science: Proceedings of the Academy of Marketing Science, https://doi.org/10.1007/978-3-030-89883-0_83

their visitors in online communities, aspire to inspire, customized billboards, VIP gestures, quality of hygienic food, user-generated content in the form of reviews. Also, building a relationship with visitors helps to build their experience in favour of restaurants which turns them into loyal visitors. And, most important, the concept called the open kitchen is quite appreciated by the young generation.

The concept explored in the current study is innovative since it gives the new direction to the restaurants to build their loyalty and get connected with the visitors with more advanced motivating factors that help them to build visitors' attachment towards the restaurants.

Keywords Open kitchen · Sustainable growth · Tourism · Restaurants · Visitors

References Available Upon Request

Personalized Online Customer Experience: The Effect of Information Transparency: An Abstract

Laetitia Lambillotte, Yakov Bart, and Ingrid Poncin

Abstract Companies increasingly personalize their website content to offer an optimal online experience to their customers. Personalization enables them to automatically adapt their content based on customers' data. Although customers may value personalization, they may also have negative responses to it, such as privacy concerns. In this context, companies expect that information transparency about data collection and use will help mitigate negative responses to personalization (Kim et al. 2018).

Prior studies investigating the role of information transparency in the personalization process were mainly conducted in the advertising context. While some prior research found that information transparency may improve click-through rates of personalized ads (Aguirre et al. 2015) a recent research found that it may also decrease behavioral intentions depending on the type of data being collected to personalize content (Kim et al. 2018). We still have limited knowledge about how information transparency influences the effect of personalization on online customer experience. In addition, we still have limited knowledge about the influence of customer characteristics in the processing of transparency message.

This research aims at investigating the backfire effects of personalization on online customer experience. It also aims at examining the role of information transparency and need for cognition in this process. Need for cognition has been identified as an important personality trait in the processing of messages (Cacioppo and Petty 1982; Sicilia and Ruiz 2010). The results of two experiments show that perceived control is lower on personalized websites and that this perceived loss of control triggers privacy concerns. However, the presence of information transparency can reduce these backfire effects depending on customer need for cognition.

This research contributes to prior research on personalization and customer experience by further investigating the backfire effects of personalization and by

L. Lambillotte (✉) · I. Poncin
UCLouvain, Louvain, Belgium
e-mail: laetitia.lambillotte@uclouvain.be; ingrid.poncin@uclouvain.be

Y. Bart
Northeastern University, Boston, MA, USA
e-mail: y.bart@northeastern.edu

F. Pantoja, S. Wu (eds.), *From Micro to Macro: Dealing with Uncertainties in the Global Marketplace*, Developments in Marketing Science: Proceedings of the Academy of Marketing Science, https://doi.org/10.1007/978-3-030-89883-0_84

providing a better understanding of the role of information and need for cognition in this process.

Keywords Information transparency · Need for cognition · Online customer experience · Personalization

References Available Upon Request

How to Counter the Reasons for Rejecting Insects as Food? An Abstract

Céline Gallen, Gaëlle Pantin-Sohier, and Dominique Peyrat-Guillard

Abstract Although insects are nutritional and their consumption plays an economic and environmental role globally, they are viewed as inedible within French culture. The aim of this research is to study to what extent strategies for regulating people's ambivalence (Health-Illness, Pleasure-Displeasure, Life-Death) would make it possible to counter the reasons for rejecting insects as food—danger, aversion and disgust—and to promote their acceptance. Using an original interdisciplinary theoretical framework, we examine whether linking studies on food behaviour in sociology on the one hand and in psychology on the other can resolve a marketing issue with regard to the culturally defined consumption of insects. A qualitative study conducted with 37 participants validates this theoretical approach and puts forward marketing suggestions for producers.

To answer the objectives of the research, we conducted a qualitative study in two French cities (Nantes and Angers). 21 individual interviews were carried out together with two focus groups (2 × 8 participants: focus group 1 = Angers, focus group 2 = Nantes), the advantage of these being that more varied or even innovative responses could be obtained than in the individual interviews. Interview guides are subdivided into five stages. Stage 1 explores the world evoked (or the mental representations) by insects and entomophagy. Stages 2, 3 and 4 are concerned with the participants' acceptance of different types of insects or insect products. Stage 5 addresses the motivations, reluctance and circumstances of target consumers and levers for acceptance. The participants were selected from an adult and urban student population—since such a population is less neophobic (Tuorila et al. 2001; Verbeke 2015)—on a voluntary basis, making sure that none of them suffered from

C. Gallen
University of Nantes, Nantes, France
e-mail: celine.gallen@univ-nantes.fr

G. Pantin-Sohier (✉) · D. Peyrat-Guillard
University of Angers, Angers, France
e-mail: gaelle.pantin-sohier@univ-angers.fr; dominique.peyrat-guillard@univ-angers.fr

F. Pantoja, S. Wu (eds.), *From Micro to Macro: Dealing with Uncertainties in the Global Marketplace*, Developments in Marketing Science: Proceedings of the Academy of Marketing Science, https://doi.org/10.1007/978-3-030-89883-0_85

food allergies or had a specific diet for reasons of health or religious belief. All the discourses collected were subjected to a thematic manual content analysis and a lexicometric analysis carried out with IRaMuTeQ software.

This study shows that the perception of danger associated with entomophagy could be reduced by providing information on the nutritional benefits, provenance, and methods of production, slaughter and harvesting of insects. Health-related messages may, on the other hand, increase people's interest in consuming insects. Familiarization could overcome aversion and could help to regulate pleasure-displeasure ambivalence. Finally, our study shows that the transformation (into granular or ground form) and concealment of insects overcomes disgust on the part of respondents. So, insects combined with or incorporated into familiar foods are less likely to activate mental representations preventing their consumption.

Keywords Entomophagy · Taste · Disgust · Culture · Acceptability

References Available Upon Request

The Effectiveness of Anthropomorphic Brand Characters Versus Spokespeople in Collaborative Consumption: An Abstract

Abigail H. Edwards and Pia A. Albinsson

Abstract We examine advertising effectiveness of anthropomorphic brand characters versus spokespeople. While some research has focused on how anthropomorphism works in various marketing schemes and contexts (Huang et al. 2011), limited research has compared the effectiveness of brands using a person (spokesperson) versus an anthropomorphized brand character (Heiser et al. 2008). In a time of brand parity, where the marketplace is inundated with brands offering similar product features and benefits, especially services use spokespeople or brand characters to better differentiate their brands. To illustrate, in the auto insurance industry Geico's gecko, Liberty Mutual's LiMu Emu and Doug, and Farmer's Billy goat are used for differentiation. Research show that brand impression and advertising effectiveness increases when animated spokes characters are used (Huang et al. 2011). Additionally, anthropomorphic characters in advertisements may result in increased positive emotions, positive attributions of brand personality, and brand liking (Delbaere et al. 2011). Brand characters often create a desirable product image by linking the personality and cultural meaning of the character to the product (Callcott and Phillips 1996). Ad stimuli featuring an animated/ anthropomorphic horse versus a male endorser was used in a mock-ad for a fictitious home sharing brand to test the hypotheses:

H1: The use of an anthropomorphic brand character compared to a human spokesperson will increase advertising effectiveness for (a) attitude towards the Ad, (b) attitude towards the brand, (c) attitude towards the endorser, and (d) brand personality appeal.

Results showed no differences for Hypotheses H1a and H1b. However, respondents (convenience sample N = 98) favored the human spokesperson in terms of attitude towards the endorser ($M_{spokesperson} = 3.19$, $M_{brandcharacter} = 2.67$, t-value = 2.09, p = 0.005) and in brand personality appeal ($M_{spokesperson} = 3.69$, $M_{brandcharacter} = 3.07$,

A. H. Edwards (✉) · P. A. Albinsson
Appalachian State University, Boone, NC, USA
e-mail: edwardsah1@appstate.edu; albinssonpa@appstate.edu

F. Pantoja, S. Wu (eds.), *From Micro to Macro: Dealing with Uncertainties in the Global Marketplace*, Developments in Marketing Science: Proceedings of the Academy of Marketing Science, https://doi.org/10.1007/978-3-030-89883-0_86

t-value 1.983, $p = 0.05$), opposite of the hypothesized direction in H1c and H1d. Our findings are novel as research on anthropomorphic spokes characters suggest that they should increase brand impressions and advertising effectiveness (Heiser et al. 2008; Huang et al. 2011). Additional research comparing the effectiveness of brand mascots versus human endorsers is warranted as both continue to be used and the former bring additional benefits as they work for free, don't complain, and rarely go of the rails (Pringle 2004).

Keywords Anthropomorphic brand characters · Spokespeople · Ad effectiveness · Brand image · Advertising

References Available Upon Request

How UGC Advertising Parody Drives Negative WOM: The Mediating Role of CSR Consumer Beliefs: An Abstract

Diletta Acuti and Valentina Pitardi

Abstract A parody is a form of creative art that reimagines a serious, copyrighted work as a comic form through the use of ironic, humorous, or satiric imitation (Johnson and Spilger 2000). Being an effective type of communication (Chattopadhyay and Basu 1990; Chung and Zhao 2003), parodies and humorous messages have been widely used in advertising strategies (Strick et al. 2013). Although such messages were previously prerogative of professionals, today any user with a computer and some creativity may produce a user generated advertising parody, so much that both positive and negative ad parodies populate the social media sphere. While several studies have analyzed the effect of positive ad parodies undertaken by brand loyalists on behalf of the brand (Berthon et al. 2008), very few research have investigated the influence of consumer-created negative ad parodies on both users and the parodied brand (Jean 2011; Sabri and Michel 2014; Vanden Bergh et al. 2011), and still no studies, to our knowledge, have focused on consumers-created negative ad parodies of brand misconduct. To this aim, the present research focuses on UGC negative ad parodies that seek to entertain consumers while spoofing a brand irresponsible behavior. Specifically, the study investigates the effect of such consumer-created contents in fostering negative word-of-mouth, while exploring the mediating role of users' corporate social responsibility (CSR) beliefs. Moreover, the paper examines whether the display of a corporate/brand comment may mitigate this effect.

The study adopts a mixed methodology including a content analysis and an experimental design (Ihantola and Kihn 2011; Bellucci et al. 2019). The first study analyses users' comments of a total of 8 user generated YouTube videos parodies about British Petroleum and it shows how consumer-created ad parodies spur negative users' engagement, which result in the expression of negative feelings, opinions and willingness to share the video. The second experimental study tests the hypothesized relationships and it demonstrates that negative parodic videos influence the users' willingness to engage in negative WOM because of the activation of (nega-

D. Acuti · V. Pitardi (✉)
University of Portsmouth, Portsmouth, UK
e-mail: diletta.acuti@port.ac.uk; valentina.pitardi@port.ac.uk

F. Pantoja, S. Wu (eds.), *From Micro to Macro: Dealing with Uncertainties in the Global Marketplace*, Developments in Marketing Science: Proceedings of the Academy of Marketing Science, https://doi.org/10.1007/978-3-030-89883-0_87

tive) CSR beliefs. Moreover, results show how this effect can be attenuated by the display of a company's comment.

While previous research focused on positive consumer-created ad parodies, this study investigates negative ad parodies effects on sharing intentions and negative WOM and it sheds lights into the underlying mechanism under which negative ad parodies influences users' sharing behavior. Moreover, the study provides valuable insight for practitioners as it highlights the need for the parodied brand to develop detailed responses strategy to negative parodies (Sabri and Michel 2014).

Keywords Parody advertising · CSR · CSR belief · Humor · Mixed-method

References Available Upon Request

Feeling Watched: The Impact of Tip Visibility on Customer Engagement and Firms' Financial Outcomes: An Abstract

Nathan Warren, Sara Hanson, and Hong Yuan

Abstract Tips have traditionally been requested in restaurants via a line on a paper bill, which was handed to the customer in a discreet billfold at the end of the service encounter. New digital point-of-sale technologies, such as Square, are changing the visibility of tips, reducing customer's tipping privacy. With increasing frequency, employees and other patrons are physically present while customers are deciding on a tip amount. Popular press accounts indicate that the changing visibility of tipping may encourage customers to tip as a public display of generosity, but may also put unwanted social pressure on customers who wish to keep their tipping decisions private (Elejalde-Ruiz 2018; Kim 2018; Levitz 2018). Some service workers report averting their eyes or walking away while the customer selects a tip amount to avoid "begging" or "pushing" customers to tip (Levitz 2018). Do customers tip more or less when being watched by others (i.e., service employees or other patrons)? We find that when customers feel watched by employees, they tip less and report lower customer engagement (i.e., word-of-mouth and repatronage intentions). These negative impacts occur because customers' perceived control is reduced. Interestingly, when another patron is nearby, the effect of visibility on tips reverses, such that customers tip more when other patrons can see their tip selection due to an increased desire to signal generosity. However, in this case of other patron visibility, customer engagement does not follow the increase in tips, but results in the surprising instance where customers tip more but are less likely to patron the business or report positive word-of-mouth. Demonstrating the differential effects of employee and other patron tip visibility suggests that managers should first ensure that tip selection screens are visible to other patrons (but not employees), and second, should minimize the

N. Warren · H. Yuan
University of Oregon, Eugene, OR, USA
e-mail: nwarren7@uoregon.edu; hongy@uoregon.edu

S. Hanson (✉)
University of Richmond, Richmond, VA, USA
e-mail: skhanson@richmond.edu

F. Pantoja, S. Wu (eds.), *From Micro to Macro: Dealing with Uncertainties in the Global Marketplace*, Developments in Marketing Science: Proceedings of the Academy of Marketing Science, https://doi.org/10.1007/978-3-030-89883-0_88

degree to which customers feel a lack of control when making a tip selection, perhaps by assuring customers that their tip selections are private and anonymous.

Keywords Tipping · Visibility · Customer engagement · Generosity · Perceived control

References Available Upon Request

Tell Me About It: Narrativity Perceptions in Product Packaging Influence Consumer Word of Mouth: An Abstract

Haley Hardman, Christian Barney, Brett Kazandjian, Jutong Wen, and Tyler Hancock

Abstract Stories are perhaps one of the most influential tools brands have to engage with consumers. Some researchers even suggest that brands may be considered a type of story (Twitchell 2004). Companies tell stories over their websites, social media pages, and even post them on the walls of their retail establishments (Hollenbeck et al. 2008). However, little research has been devoted to relaying a brand story through product packaging.

While research suggests that the inclusion of a brand story on product packaging may result in a myriad of positive brand associations (Solja et al. 2018), the process through which this occurs, and the relationships between the variables impacted, remains to be discovered. Therefore, this study uses narrative transportation theory to examine how brand stories included on product packaging impact perceptions of a brand, such as brand uniqueness and brand sincerity, and how it ultimately leads to consumer word of mouth intentions. In accordance with narrative transportation theory, when individuals are presented with a narrative, they can become immersed with a story, and even "mentally enter a world that a story evokes" (Van Laer et al. 2013, p. 797). Narrative transportation has been shown to influence affective responses to a product, beliefs, attitudes, and intentions (Van Laer et al. 2013). The idea of what a narrative constitutes has been a matter of debate, however, and some narratologists suggest that rather than considering "narrative" and "non-narrative" as a dichotomy, there may be a spectrum of "narrativity" (Ryan 2006). Applying this idea to brand narratives on product packaging, we suggest that perceptions of a brand story's "narrativity" will have a positive relationship with word of mouth when mediated through narrative transportation, uniqueness, and sincerity.

H. Hardman (✉) · C. Barney · B. Kazandjian · J. Wen
Mississippi State University, Starkville, MS, USA
e-mail: heh189@msstate.edu; cb3496@msstate.edu; bjk209@msstate.edu; jw3901@msstate.edu

T. Hancock
The University of Toledo, Toledo, OH, USA
e-mail: tyler.hancock@utoledo.edu

F. Pantoja, S. Wu (eds.), *From Micro to Macro: Dealing with Uncertainties in the Global Marketplace*, Developments in Marketing Science: Proceedings of the Academy of Marketing Science, https://doi.org/10.1007/978-3-030-89883-0_89

While most research on narrative transportation looks at narratives as a dichotomous variable, this study shows that narratives may be regarded as a continuum. Additionally, this study shows that narrativity influences word-of-mouth intentions through perceptions of uniqueness and brand sincerity, and thus by incorporating a brand story on their product packaging, consumer packaged goods companies may increase their positive consumer word-of-mouth. Overall, this shows that the use of brand stories on product packaging can have multiple positive outcomes for the brand.

Keywords Narrative transportation · Product packaging · Brand stories · Word-of-mouth

References Available Upon Request

Propensity to Assimilate: A Grounded Theory Development of the Consumer Acculturation Process: An Abstract

Kristina Harrison, John B. Ford, Kiran Karande, and Altaf Merchant

Abstract The United States is becoming increasingly multi-cultural and there are various new immigrant consumer groups that businesses try to reach through ethnic-based segmentation and targeting. However, there is evidence that acculturation may be a better predictor of consumer behavior such as preferences for brand, services, and/or marketing communications. Acculturation is an important measurement tool for understanding consumer behavior and for segmenting and targeting multi-cultural consumers appropriately (Poulis et al. 2013; Ogden et al. 2004). Acculturation is defined as a process, but it has not been treated as a process, and the literature calls for a desire to assimilate first before an individual is able to do so. Past research has suggested that first an individual has a desire to acculturate and this desire influences the acculturation process and outcomes (van den Berghe 1981; Bun and Kiong 1992). Acculturation is defined as all the changes that arise following contact between groups and individuals of different cultural backgrounds as well as the adoption by a person or group of the culture of another social group or the process leading to this adoption (Berry 1997). Assimilation is the adoption by a person or a group of the culture of another social group to such a complete extent that the person or group no longer has any characteristics identifying him or her with their former culture and no longer has any particular loyalties to the former culture, or the process leading to the adoption (Berry and Sam 2016). The findings from extant literature suggests that acculturation is a multi-process variable that starts with first a desire or a propensity to assimilate, which then influences acculturation behavioral outcomes. We conducted an in-depth literature review and two qualitative studies in order to uncover the acculturation process and establish the

K. Harrison (✉)
University of Southern Mississippi, Hattiesburg, MS, USA
e-mail: kristina.m.harrison@usm.edu

J. B. Ford · K. Karande
Old Dominion University, Norfolk, VA, USA
e-mail: jbford@odu.edu; kkarande@odu.edu

A. Merchant
University of Washington Tacoma, Tacoma, WA, USA
e-mail: altafm@uw.edu

F. Pantoja, S. Wu (eds.), *From Micro to Macro: Dealing with Uncertainties in the Global Marketplace*, Developments in Marketing Science: Proceedings of the Academy of Marketing Science, https://doi.org/10.1007/978-3-030-89883-0_90

Propensity to Assimilate construct. To control for possible cultural confounding, this study focuses on the Chinese American cultural demographic and through conducting two qualitative studies with 57 participants on both the east and west coasts of the country (Virginia, New York, and California), we found that in order to effectively examine acculturation, there must first be a desire or propensity to assimilate and then that propensity in turn will influence actual acculturation behaviors. Thus, through a combination of deduction and induction methods, we contributed to the theoretical understanding of the acculturation process and offered a new construct in that process.

Keywords Consumer acculturation · Propensity to assimilate · Grounded Theory · Cross-cultural consumers

References Available Upon Request

The Power of Knowledge: Driving Sustainable Hotel Choices Through Decision Trade-Offs: An Abstract

Weng-Kei Loke, Brishna Nader, and Meng-Hsien Lin

Abstract The effects of climate change as reflected in the increased intensity and frequency of extreme weather events are raising concerns about the social and economic wellbeing. Therefore, the United Nations World Tourism Organization (UNWTO) created the 2030 Agenda for Sustainable Development in 2017 in efforts to mitigate the negative impacts the tourism industry has onto the environment. Increasing public scrutiny and pressure from governments have also influenced companies to act in a more socially responsible manner. One way hotels can support this initiative is by being Leadership in Energy and Environmental Design (LEED) or Green certified. In this study, we aim to understand how such certifications influence consumer's decision to stay at a sustainable hotel. We used a revised version of Ajzen's Theory of Planned Behaviour and predict that consumers with higher knowledge of the LEED or Green certifications will perceive sustainable hotel practices as more important. Therefore, more willing to trade-off non-environmental factors (e.g., cost, location, ease of booking, convenience) to stay at a sustainable hotel. A survey was administered in the field, resulting in 324 responses, with a majority of US tourists. A series of Chi-square and t-tests were conducted to test the relationship between knowledge and willingness to stay and other dependent variables. Additionally, a mediation model was tested to explain the relationship between knowledge and willingness to stay at a sustainable hotel. We found that guests with green knowledge indeed weigh non-sustainable related factors as less important compared to guests without this knowledge, and are therefore more willing to trade-off non-environmental factors for sustainable factors. Results from the mediation model suggests that willingness to trade-off explains the relationship between knowledge of certification and willingness to stay at a sustainable hotel. These findings emphasize the importance of creating consumer awareness about such green certifications, whether through the hotel's website or advertisements, to

W.-K. Loke (✉) · M.-H. Lin
California State University, Monterey Bay, CA, USA
e-mail: wloke@csumb.edu; jelin@csumb.edu

B. Nader
Fontys University of Applied Science, Noord-Brabant, Netherlands
e-mail: b.nader@fontys.nl

F. Pantoja, S. Wu (eds.), *From Micro to Macro: Dealing with Uncertainties in the Global Marketplace*, Developments in Marketing Science: Proceedings of the Academy of Marketing Science, https://doi.org/10.1007/978-3-030-89883-0_91

ensure potential guests are able to make informed decisions when choosing which hotel to stay in.

Keywords Decision-making · Sustainable hospitality · Information processing · Knowledge · Sustainable consumer behavior

References Available Upon Request

Ad Eroticism from A Distance: Scuba Diving into Male and Female Buyers' Reactions whilst Seeking for Moral Cues in their Lives: An Abstract

Ioannis G. Theodorakis and Grigorios Painesis

Abstract The erotic ad appeal is one of the most frequently used appeals in marketing communications. However, scientific scrutiny focused on its performance has produced mixed findings so far (LaTour and Henthorne 1994; Pope et al. 2004). Based on construal-level theory (a paradigm presenting how people construe an entity based on the level of psychological distance they experience from such an entity) (Trope and Liberman 2010) and the concept of psychological distance (the extent to which an entity pertains to an individual's here and now experience) (Trope et al. 2007), the present research concentrates on erotic appeal ads' impact in terms of consumers' moral, attitudinal and behavioral reactions. Also, demographic as well as psychographic factors, such as gender and moral attentiveness (pertaining to the extent to which an individual chronically perceives and considers morality and moral elements in his/her experiences) (Reynolds 2008; Van Gils et al. 2014) are examined. Additionally, further relevant erotic-driven traits such as that of sexual liberalism as well as behavioral traits such as that of product involvement are captured in order to further demystify the network of effects.

Findings from two online experimental studies with US-based MTurkers as participants each focused on a different type of psychological distance inducing variant construal levels while promoting a different product category across different ad eroticism intensity levels, show that as psychological distance or construal level increases (decreases) consumers' reactions become less (more) unfavorable especially, when the ad's eroticism intensity level varies from moderate to high. Also, reactions vary based on gender and moral attentiveness such that in general, females and high morally attentive individuals denote stronger objections. Last, sexual

I. G. Theodorakis (✉)
INSEEC Grande École, Paris, France
e-mail: itheodorakis@inseec.com

G. Painesis
Athens University of Economics and Business, Athens, Greece
e-mail: gregpain@aueb.gr

F. Pantoja, S. Wu (eds.), *From Micro to Macro: Dealing with Uncertainties in the Global Marketplace*, Developments in Marketing Science: Proceedings of the Academy of Marketing Science, https://doi.org/10.1007/978-3-030-89883-0_92

liberalism and product involvement exert a strong positive influence on consumer reactions.

Next, there are important implications stemming from the paper including the importance of applying psychological distance/construal level cues in marketing communications; the caution in using the erotic ad appeal such that it does not produce unfavorable outcomes; and the significance of both gender and moral attentiveness in determining consumers' reactions to erotic ads.

Finally, the paper concludes by referring to its limitations as well as by providing suggestions for future research such as the need to study the phenomenon at hand on a cross-cultural basis and by considering additional individual difference variables in such a research endeavor.

Keywords Psychological distance · Construal level theory · Eroticism · Gender · Moral attentiveness · Moral judgments · Attitudes · Moderated mediation

References Available Upon Request

To Trust or Not to Trust My AI Based Voice Assistant: Dealing with Consumer Uncertainties: An Abstract

Valentina Pitardi and Hannah Marriott

Abstract Despite the increasing adoption rate of AI-based technologies, as well as their estimated future growth, very few research has explored the factors that influence the usage of Voice Activated assistants (VAs) in daily life (McLean and Osei-Frimpong 2019; Moriuchi 2019), and the factors affecting users' trust with VAs interactions remain underexplored (Foehr and Germelmann 2020). To this aim, this study integrates Human-Computer Interaction literature on the functional and hedonic attributes of the system and individual's perceived privacy risks, by adopting a Para-Social Relationship Theory perspective (Turner 1993) and it investigates the drivers of users' trust toward VAs.

According to Wirtz et al (2018), when interacting with an AI-based personal assistants, functional elements, such as usefulness and perceived ease of use, will appear to be given in most cases, but would be a barrier if not provided at a level expected by consumers. However, the peculiarities of AI agents, and their ability to engage in conversational-based communication with users, go beyond a functional approach and require a more social-relationship perspective (Foehr and Germelmann 2020). A large body of research has outlined how individuals apply social roles and treat computes like a social entity (Nass and Brave 2005; Nass and Moon 2000). This is especially true when technology mimics human-like attributes (Li 2015). As VAs use natural language, interact with users in real-time, and are characterised by human- like attributes such as voice, it is possible to expect that interactions with VAs may elicit social responses, such as a sense of social presence (Chattaramn et al. 2018). Moreover, being an AI-based technology, VAs are more likely to be perceived as intelligent and skilful (van Doorn et al 2016). While these social elements can foster trust building, the process may be affected by the perceived risks surrounding privacy and security (Lei et al. 2018).

V. Pitardi (✉)
University of Portsmouth, Portsmouth, UK
e-mail: valentina.pitardi@port.ac.uk

H. Marriott
University of Winchester, Winchester, UK
e-mail: hannah.marriott@winchester.ac.uk

F. Pantoja, S. Wu (eds.), *From Micro to Macro: Dealing with Uncertainties in the Global Marketplace*, Developments in Marketing Science: Proceedings of the Academy of Marketing Science, https://doi.org/10.1007/978-3-030-89883-0_93

Building on the above, the research develops and tests a comprehensive model of theory-drivers of users' trust, attitude and intentions to use VAs on a sample of 547 VA-users. In addition, a qualitative study, involving in-depth interviews, is conducted to further investigate trust developing mechanisms with smart technology. The study identifies social presence and social cognition to be the main drivers of user trust towards VAs. Further, it shows the existence of different sources of trustworthiness (Foher and Germelmann 2020) that allow individuals to direct their privacy concerns toward VA producers rather than toward the AI agent (Belanche et al. 2020). Finally, the research confirms the role of functional and hedonic elements in the acceptance of advanced smart technology (Wirtz et al. 2018, 2019), while highlighting the role of emotional reactions in driving users' attitudes towards human-AI agents' interactions (van Pinxteren et al. 2019).

Keywords AI · Voice-based assistant · Trust · Artificial intelligence · Social cognition · Privacy

References Available Upon Request

Entrepreneurial Ecosystems: A 25-Year Bibliographic Overview: An Abstract

Jeandri Robertson, Caitlin Ferreira, Leyland Pitt, and Christine Pitt

Abstract Interest in entrepreneurial ecosystems—the geographically-bound social networks of institutions and cultural values that give rise to and sustain entrepreneurial activity—have intensified in recent years (Roundy 2016; Spigel 2016). This growing attraction is driven by a need to better understand the concentration of high growth ventures in regions with thriving entrepreneurial ecosystems (Roundy and Fayard 2019). Despite the evolving discussions, few studies have conducted a critical analysis of the entrepreneurial ecosystems literature, with a surge in recent calls to do so (Audretsch et al. 2019). To address this gap, this study presents a bibliographic analysis of extant literature on entrepreneurial ecosystems in academic journal articles, spanning the last 25 years. The aim is to identify the most relevant authors, countries, and institutions in the field and to analyze who has contributed to the growth of the concept since its emergence.

The Web of Science Core Collection is used as the repository for the bibliometric information, and bibliographic network mapping is developed using the visualization of similarities, VOSviewer, software tool. The most cited paper was published in Research Policy in 2014, by authors Autio et al. (2014), titled "Entrepreneurial innovation: the importance of context". A citation count over the past twenty-five years shows that the authors who have influenced the field of entrepreneurial ecosystems the most are Wright, Autio, and Kenney. Other notable scholars who have also made significant contributions to the field are the economists Ács, Audretsch, and Etzkowitz, and the entrepreneurship scholars Isenberg, Spigel, and Stam. The

J. Robertson (✉) · C. Ferreira
University of Cape Town, Cape Town, South Africa
e-mail: jeandri.robertson@uct.ac.za; caitlin.ferreira@uct.ac.za

L. Pitt
Simon Fraser University, Vancouver, BC, Canada
e-mail: leyland_pitt@sfu.ca

C. Pitt
Royal Institute of Technology, Stockholm, Sweden
e-mail: christine.pitt@indek.kth.se

F. Pantoja, S. Wu (eds.), *From Micro to Macro: Dealing with Uncertainties in the Global Marketplace*, Developments in Marketing Science: Proceedings of the Academy of Marketing Science, https://doi.org/10.1007/978-3-030-89883-0_94

most prolific journals on the topic are Small Business Economics, Journal of Technology Transfer, and European Planning Studies, while country-level impact and research productivity is concentrated in the USA and England. Using citations as a proxy, the most influential and prolific academic literature on entrepreneurial ecosystems is produced in countries, institutions, and co-author networks mostly situated in the USA, UK, and the Netherlands. Most commonly co-occurring keywords are innovation, entrepreneurship, performance, knowledge, and entrepreneurial ecosystems. Three key themes are also identified: innovation (linked to performance, technology, university, and industry), entrepreneurship (with a focus on an ecosystem, management, and business), and knowledge (with an emphasis on growth, policy, and networks).

The findings of the bibliographic analysis highlight the intensified multidisciplinary interest in entrepreneurial ecosystem research, underlining the diverse international attention that it has amassed over the last quarter-century.

Keywords Entrepreneurial ecosystem · Bibliographic analysis · VOSviewer · Literature review

References Available Upon Request

Can You Hear the Tension? Musical Tension-Release Effect on Affect and Recall in Advertising: An Abstract

Shawn P. Scott, Lauren I. Labrecque, Christy Ashley, and Ian Reyes

Abstract Tension and resolution exist as a universal structure in all music. It can increase a listener's attention, even change a consumer's cognitive state. Yet this powerful musical tool has not been studied in the context of how it shapes consumers' attitudes towards advertising and brands. Through four experiments, we aim to understand these effects in more detail and outline the properties of this phenomenon. In addition, we aim to show how this effect is due to an underlying curiosity caused by the anticipation of the tension-resolution structure which in turn causes excitement. We also explore potential boundary conditions associated with consumer curiosity. Through four experiments and two pretests, we uncover evidence to support our six hypotheses.

In our first experiment, we show how advertising with a tension-resolution musical structure (versus no resolution) has a net positive consumer attitude for the advertisement and induces higher curiosity and satisfaction levels in participants. Our second experiment explores how the placement of the tension-resolution structure in the ad changes advertising likeability. For this experiment we use a different musical stimuli (developed from the second pretest) which had two versions of the same song, one with the tension build and resolution structure in the first half of the experiment and the second with the same musical structure in the second half of the advertisement. In our third experiment, we show how the individual difference variable Need for Cognitive Closure (NFCC) explains this phenomenon of consumer attitudes towards musical tension resolution structure in music.

These findings contribute to the music, consumer, branding, and advertising literatures in many ways. This research adds to the existing theories on music in advertising by highlighting positive effects from elements previously seen as negative in advertising, musical tension. In addition, this research adds to the musical literature by outlining boundary effects inherent in consumer individual difference variables and teases out the specifics of tension-resolution structures in music as in the duration, placement, and mediating factors that drive consumer attitudes.

S. P. Scott (✉) · L. I. Labrecque · C. Ashley · I. Reyes
University of Rhode Island, Kingston, RI, USA
e-mail: sscott@uri.edu; lauren33@uri.edu; christyashley@uri.edu; ianreyes@uri.edu

F. Pantoja, S. Wu (eds.), *From Micro to Macro: Dealing with Uncertainties in the Global Marketplace*, Developments in Marketing Science: Proceedings of the Academy of Marketing Science, https://doi.org/10.1007/978-3-030-89883-0_95

Keywords Sensory marketing · Musical tension · Music · Consumers · Curiosity · Uncertainty

References Available Upon Request

A Star Was Born: The Professional Trajectory of Brazilian Digital Influencers

Ana Cristina Munaro, Renato Hübner Barcelos, and Eliane Cristine Francisco Maffezzolli

Abstract This study analyzed the professional trajectory of Brazilian digital influencers by identifying the milestones in their career from anonymity to stardom. To this end, we adopted an interpretative exploratory approach based on the observation and analysis of digital influencers' self-presentation videos on YouTube. As a result, five important moments emerged from data representing the main stepstones in the influencer career: (1) the initial stage, when they start a career as content creator; (2) the professionalization decision; (3) the image development, which includes career milestones such as the endorsement from traditional media, product development, partnerships and increased revenue; (4) the positioning review, comprising a crisis period and the subsequent image repositioning; (5) and finally, maturity and experience. These five stages describe the main events at the trajectory of professional influencers who evolve from ordinary YouTubers to become human brands. Finally, we conclude with managerial implications and suggestions for future studies.

Keywords Digital influencer · Professional trajectory · Human brands · YouTube · Social media

A. C. Munaro (✉) · E. C. F. Maffezzolli
Pontifícia Universidade Católica do Paraná, Curitiba, Brazil
e-mail: ana.munaro@pucpr.edu.br; eliane.francisco@pucpr.br

R. H. Barcelos
Université du Québec à Montréal, Montreal, QC, Canada
e-mail: hubner_barcelos.renato@uqam.ca

F. Pantoja, S. Wu (eds.), *From Micro to Macro: Dealing with Uncertainties in the Global Marketplace*, Developments in Marketing Science: Proceedings of the Academy of Marketing Science, https://doi.org/10.1007/978-3-030-89883-0_96

Introduction

As companies move increasingly toward digital means of communication to promote their products and brands, understanding how to leverage social media and influencer marketing when defining marketing strategies becomes almost unavoidable (Sokolova and Kefi 2020). In particular, there is great interest to understand more about digital influencers and other classifications for which they are known, such as microcelebrities or non-tradition celebrities (Djafarova and Rushworth 2017; Jerslev 2016), YouTubers (Jerslev 2016; Lovelock 2017), bloggers (Agarwal et al. 2008; Uzunoğlu and Misci Kip 2014) or opinion leaders (Li and Du 2011).

Research about this phenomenon is still scarce and has been focusing on models to identify digital influencers (Agarwal et al. 2008; Fang and Hu 2016; Uzunoğlu and Misci Kip 2014) and attempts to understand how they relate to customer digital engagement (Djafarova and Rushworth 2017; Kupfer et al. 2018). On social media, digital influencers have differing information-spreading power and perceived credibility than other sources (Kim and Song 2018). At the same time, the "always-on" nature of social media encourages celebrities and those aspiring to be famous to share constant details of their day-to-day lives. This high exposure ensures influencers' proximity and identification with their audience. Moreover, as many traditional jobs are disappearing, achieving some kind of celebrity status has come to seem as reasonable a life goal as any other for many people (Hearn and Schoenhoff 2016).

From a managerial perspective, the visible and easily comparable metrics of social media performance encourage the active inculcation of an audience (Marwick 2015). The popularity and power of influence of digital influencers provide brands with a new platform for building relationships with fans by offering a glimpse into their lives and addressing them directly (Kupfer et al. 2018). Nevertheless, it is essential for brands to consider what type of celebrity would be the most effective in appealing to a particular target group (Djafarova and Rushworth 2017). Businesses need to understand the 'influencer' phenomenon in order to make the right decisions and investments in influencer marketing (Sokolova and Kefi 2020). To this end, it is essential for managers to understand how the influencer's trajectory begins and develops itself on social media.

Hence, the main objective of this study is to investigate the professional trajectory of digital influencers. Specifically, we aim to identify the turning points in the career of a digital influencer and understand how they develop it to a business model. In this sense, we also want to identify if there are common characteristics in the trajectory of successful influencers. To achieve these goals, we adopted an exploratory interpretative approach to analyze secondary data derived from the YouTube channels of five Brazilian digital influencers.

The results of this study contribute to the literature on social media and influencer marketing, since studies on digital influencers are still incipient and focused mostly on identifying and measuring their influence on consumer digital engagement. Hence, the question of how an ordinary social media user becomes a digital influencer remains unexplored (Carrillat and Ilicic 2019). This study also contributes to managerial practice by informing marketing managers on the milestones in the professional career of Brazilian digital influencers and the strategies they use to increase and/or maintain engagement with customers, hence providing insights into future investments with influencers to build enduring and effective relationships.

Digital Influencers

An influencer is someone who has credibility in the group, persists in attempting to convince others, and introduces topics/ideas that others pick up on or support. An influencer can alter the opinions of their audience, resolve disagreements where no one else can, be recognized by others as someone who makes significant contributions, and can exert an influence even when not present (Rosenthal and Mckeown 2017).

Specifically, "YouTube celebrity" denotes an individual whose celebrity status stems directly from their activities on the site. The term "YouTubers" refers to video bloggers (vloggers) who regularly post videos on their personal YouTube channels (Jerslev 2016). Many of these videos are recorded by individuals in domestic settings, talking in confessional style into a static camera, with seemingly minimal editing (Lovelock 2017). The success of the "micro-celebrities" (as named by Jerslev 2016) typically involves three elements: constant activity, immediacy, and a perception of authenticity based on the loss of their privacy (Lovelock 2017).

The influencers can help users with customer support and troubleshooting, and their solutions are often seen as trustworthy because of their perception as authorities and the strong social connections established, guiding the decision-making process of their followers (Agarwal et al. 2008; Djafarova and Rushworth 2017).

Digital Influencers as Human Brands

According to Hearn and Schoenhoff (2016), the digital influencer works to generate a form of celebrity capital by cultivating as much attention as possible and crafting an authentic personal brand via social networks. The influencer is "produced", not born; he/she is identified and constituted by a variety of social media intelligence analytics and social scoring companies (Hearn and Schoenhoff 2016). It typically involves self-conscious, carefully constructed personas, which may be primarily textual, visual, or in video. Influencers see their audience as fans rather than friends or family, and share information strategically with this audience to boost their popularity (Marwick 2015). Furthermore, an influencer is also a content producer, identified and arguably constituted by the variety of measurement mechanisms that serve to both bestow and extract value from a wide array of "selves". Then, the influencer is an economic condition rather than a singular "stellar" individual (Hearn and

Schoenhoff 2016). In this sense, digital influencers may be considered as human brands.

"Human brands", to Thomson (2006), refer to any well-known persona who is the subject of marketing communications efforts. Digital influencers can also be considered brands because they can be professionally managed and because they have additional associations and features of a brand. Erz and Christensen (2018) argue that the digital influencer can be understood as a human brand from a brand-as-process perspective, as they actively negotiate, re-interpret and adapt their identity within a multiple-stakeholder system. Their performances off- and on-line, public or private, are marketing and branding exercises. Their everyday life choices and values are intrinsically private, but performed in public (Marwick 2015; Centeno and Wang 2017).

Human brand identities form through an orchestrated co-creation that emerge as stories and conversations about the celebrity collide (Centeno and Wang 2017). Through social media as an avenue of co-creation, human brand identities develop via a function of media experiences, second-hand information (gossips, hand-me-down historical accounts), and even personal encounters (Centeno and Wang 2017). Consequently, brand identities are reflexive and contextual; however, they are pliable only to the extent that they fit the individual's range of constructed human identities (Centeno and Wang 2017; Hearn and Schoenhoff 2016; Marwick 2015).

Human brands make consumers feel appreciated, empowered, and understood to succeed in creating feelings of autonomy (Loroz and Braig 2015; Thomson 2006). When consumers view the human brand as accessible, there is an opportunity for feelings of autonomy and relatedness to be promoted. Then, repeated interactions between consumers and the human brand reduce uncertainty and provide the basis for an attachment to grow (Thomson 2006). These interactions are powerful because human brands convey a level of authenticity and potent cultural meaning that non-human brands cannot match. This grants the resonance, differentiation and personal connections required for brands to thrive in today's commoditized world.

In the other hand, Fournier and Eckhardt (2018) argue that the human brands' very humanness—the physical and social realities, mental biases and limitations of being human—introduces risk while at the same time generating the ability for enhanced returns. Four human tenets can create imbalance or inconsistency across the human brand's: mortality, hubris, unpredictability and social embeddedness. The human being inadvertently leaks meanings every day and these meanings do not always align with the brand's positioning (Fournier and Eckhardt 2018). Indeed, this very quality lends authenticity in a powerful way that non-human brands can never match. A large part of the cultural meaning of a human brand stems from what others reveal about the brand to the public. This lends an intimacy to the consumer-brand connection, as consumers feel they know the "real" person behind the brand (Fournier and Eckhardt 2018; Thomson 2006).

Methodology

The study adopted an interpretative, exploratory approach with the main premise of observing and analyzing digital influencers' presentations of themselves on YouTube. From the collection and analysis of the contents and milestones of influencers' career over time, we aimed to identify the different stages of their professional trajectory. We collected data from the channels of real digital influencers with the objective of identifying patterns that would allow to describe the trajectory stages of these individuals. Our perspective was that the accumulation of evidence pointing to empirical regularities would provide a much broader and more generalized understanding of the world (Helfat 2007).

Selection of Digital Influencer Profiles

When selecting profiles for the study, we looked for active digital influencers born in the digital environment, established and recognized publicly as important in their fields. Our study focused on the Brazil digital market has a digital market, where social media is the category with the highest time spent online per user among the population (Comscore Media Metrix Multi-Platform 2019). Influencer marketing is very strong in the country—a recent survey found that 41% of Brazilians have purchased a product or service recommended by digital influencers and 46% of them rely on influencers' opinion (Mathias 2019).

We were interested in influencers in the consolidation stage of the celebrity capital life cycle (Carrillat and Ilicic 2019). For this reason, we selected profiles in different rankings of influencers from Brazilian specialized websites such as Social Blade (https://socialblade.com), ID Creators (http://criadoresid.com), Prêmio Influenciadores (http://premioinfluenciadores.com.br) and QualiBest Institute (https://www.institutoqualibest.com). To increase the validity of the study, we chose to address different content categories—fashion and beauty, food and travel, parenting, science and humor. We initially selected 10 digital influencers who met these criteria. However, after the analysis of 5 top-ranked influencers, we found that the information provided by the other profiles would not reveal new theoretical insights, neither change the categories of analysis. Thus, having achieved the criteria of data saturation (Charmaz 2006), we considered the five top-ranked influencers enough for analysis (see Table 1).

Table 1 Data from the selected digital influencers profiles

Digital Influencer	Channel Name	Category	On YouTube since	Total subscribers (thousands)[a]	Total views (millions)[a]	Total videos[a]
Bianca Andrade	Boca Rosa	Fashion and beauty	2011	5243	370	594
Danielle Noce	Danielle Noce	Food and travel	2011	2799	344	1023
Felipe Castanhari	Canal Nostagia	Science	2011	12,352	1045	321
Flavia Calina	Flavia Calina	Parenting	2009	6787	2220	1566
Whindersson Nunes	Whindersson Nunes	Humor	2013	36,589	3019	364

[a] Data obtained on the August 2019 on YouTube platform

Data Collection and Analysis

For each influencer channel, we selected all video titles published since the beginning of his/her career on YouTube (average of 51 videos for each one, corresponding to a total of 773 min). We watched all the videos representative of distinct periods in the influencer's life, the channel's history and development. In this sense, the videos selected show information such as: personal news, significant changes in the channel (content, frequency) or in their careers, new product launches, celebrations of achievements, frustrations and problems faced by the influencer, retrospectives of the year, and finally, videos in which they narrate their own trajectory themselves.

For all selected videos, we took notes and extracted the descriptions of the videos and parts of the transcriptions of speech. Then, these data and the video posts consisted the primary data sources for the analysis. Following the recommendations of Erz and Christensen (2018), the researchers did not actively participate as commenters (co-creators) but remained at a distance to the Youtubers and its channels. The collection was made independently at one channel at a time. In order to be sure of the correct dates of events and other information, we also looked for supplementary data in the influencer's other media, such as blogs, Instagram, Facebook, and Twitter.

During data analysis, we employed the qualitative data manipulation operation recommended by Spiggle (1994) to extract meaning, elaborate conclusions, and create conceptual schemes. This operation consists of an iterative process including the steps of categorization, abstraction, comparison, dimensionalization, and integration/interpretation. Categorization/coding was proceeded inductively, i.e., from emergent categories of data. The essence of categorization is identifying and naming segments of chunk/unit of data as belonging to, representing, or being an example of some more general phenomenon (Spiggle 1994; Charmaz 2006). Abstraction encompasses several more concrete instances found in the data that share certain common features. The theoretical significance of a construct springs from its connection to a broader meaning of an individual's experiences (Spiggle 1994). We created preliminary codes for the data of each channel, and the iterative process allowed us to generate new codes emerging, thus renewing the ones already created.

The following step, the comparison between channels, explores differences and similarities across incidents within the data collected (Spiggle 1994). We employed a constant comparative method of analysis, where the initial findings of one channel were re-interpreted in the light of the findings of the subsequent channels. This made it possible to better understand the attributes or characteristics along influencers dimensions and integrate the relationships between conceptual elements. Dimensionalization involves identifying properties, attributes or characteristics in the created categories. Finally, the integration step requires the mapping of relationships between conceptual elements and the interpretation represents a synthetic and holistic grasp of meaning, as in deciphering a code (Spiggle 1994). We identified patterns in the created categories and mapped the relationships among the digital influencers.

Findings

Some common stages in the trajectory of the five successful digital influencers emerged from data analysis. Each phase change in their careers is marked by turning points defined as major transitions that involve a variety of small, but significant changes in their actions and interactions. The influencers start adopting a new social role that is connected to newly defined relations to a set of stakeholders and a new self-conception (Erz and Christensen 2018).

First Stage: Starting a Career

The beginning of a digital content creator's career is uncertain. The decision to open a YouTube channel to share to the public some content/knowledge/experience about a subject is unpretentious at first and begins as a secondary priority. The new YouTubers are still unsure of their success and financial return, as in any new venture. In a similar way as the bloggers in the study of Martensen et al. (2018), the YouTubers report boredom and desire for fun and self-expression as their main driving factors to start posting. Some of them seek inspiration from already well-established YouTubers to create their content, and produce videos such as makeup tutorials, or translate contents from other countries about gastronomy and geek life.

> My channel started as a joke and it worked. I watched some Americans doing makeup and was blown away. I asked my mother and sister if they wanted me to do a video for them to teach what I have learned, as they did not speak English. I was already married and had my permanent job (preschool teacher). (Flavia Calina)

The first videos are recorded and uploaded by amateurs, and, from their perspective, without any commercial objectives. These new YouTubers set up with ordinary cameras and ignore most usual features of professional film making (Schwemmer and Ziewiecki 2018).

> I walked 3 km to a friend's house that had a good camera, came back, filmed, edited and walked another 2 km to post the video in a lan house, since I had no internet connection at home. (Whindersson Nunes)

The content is presented in a personal diary-style, using unprofessional pictures and an informal tone of voice, thus creating an intimate and personal storyline that allow followers to feel closer to the YouTubers' lives. At this point, some posts are characterized by informative accounts of brands and interesting events, and, similarly to the findings of Erz and Christensen (2018), they more often reproduce and adapt existing contents than present original ones.

Second Stage: Professionalization Decision

From the moment the channel is able to attract thousands of followers, the creator will begin to play the role of influencer, and such activity increasingly dominates his/her life. As the YouTubers gain popularity and their videos become popular, they transform an initially fun-motivated hobby into a serious activity. Hence, they are driven to improve the quality of content in their channels, for instance, by buying digital cameras and filming equipment, minding the lighting, looking for specific locations for filming, and learning how to properly edit videos. At the same time, their videos become more personal, and they disclose more information about themselves. In this way, the new influencers can be seen as human brands (Erz and Christensen 2018).

> For 3 years I continued to work in kindergarten and made the videos whenever I could, but with the increasing number of hits I realized that I could create my own online classroom and reach many more students. I made the decision to make YouTube my classroom full time. (Flavia Calina)

At this stage, the digital influencers begin to disconnect from their traditional jobs to focus exclusively on creating content for their channel/blog and other social media. They also seek to specialize at their new profession—for example, the influencer Bianca Andrade decided to take a makeup course and the influencer Dani Noce moved to Paris to take classes in gastronomy.

Third Stage: Career Milestones

After the professionalization decision, begins a stage of great personal and professional transformations for the influencers. In their study about bloggers, Erz and Christensen (2018) named this phase as "collective identity," which is decisive for negotiation and development as an organizational field. Digital influencers aim to professionalize their content without losing the essence and authenticity of themselves. It is a challenge to innovate and maintain the authenticity image by which they became famous. On the one hand, the vertical distance between the influencers and their followers increases, marking their transformation towards a new possible self. The tone of their posts becomes more professional: vacations become travels, events turn into meetings, other bloggers become colleagues (Erz and Christensen 2018). On the other hand, the influencers disclose more personal information in their posts, which keeps the narrative going. Despite their growing popularity, they are still seen as authentic and trustworthy within their communities. As they actively engage in discussions held by their fellowship and share major parts of their private lives, the influencers give the impression of being approachable persons (Schwemmer and Ziewiecki 2018).

During this phase of collective image development, we can highlight some important milestones in the trajectory of the digital influencers:

Endorsement from traditional media: Despite the rise of consumer engagement in digital media, influencers still welcome the attention of traditional mass media. As they become increasingly popular, they are invited to participate in TV shows, magazine and newspaper reports, radio programs, which greatly increases their reach by allowing them to catch up with a different audience. For this reason, the influencers may work to develop new skills such as acting and interpersonal communication. The influencers achieve a new level of transmedia storytelling, an important strategy for their career advancement and to raise the interest of business partners.

> The television's power puts me in touch with an audience that goes beyond my followers. It's a challenge. As much as the internet is universal, TV speaks for all ages at the same time. And being able to share a little bit of knowledge about what I love, to millions of people, it's magic. The responsibility is even greater. (Bianca Andrade)

Product development: Product development is an important issue for the influencers' career, as it provides new sources of income and allows them to develop a diversified business model. Based on the success of their main channel, the influencers may expand their content to new platforms and create by-products to increase monetization. These products are directly linked to their personality, image, and target market. For example, the influencer Bianca Andrade (fashion and beauty) launched her own collection of nail polishing, makeup, clothing, handbags, jewelry, and online makeup courses. The influencer Danielle Noce (gastronomy) launched her own cookbooks, kitchenware, online bakery courses. Whindersson Nunes (humor) focused on stand-up comedy tours, in addition to selling the content of his shows on DVDs and streaming.

Partnerships: At this stage in their career, the influencers further broaden their presence on digital media and begin to produce content in partnership with other influencers. For instance, they are invited to participate in competitions, activities, tags, and invite partners to their programs. By doing a "collab" (i.e., participating in videos of another YouTuber), they also expand their own reach to the audience of other influencers. Other partnerships include joining a media network to receive mentoring and commercial support or partnering with an agency to benefit of professional career management and new business opportunities. YouTube is also a crucial partner, organizing meetings where creators can learn about video production and connect to each other.

Increased revenue: Their popularity brings opportunities for other income sources and exposure. The digital influencers in this study have several different income sources beyond the monetization of YouTube videos (AdSense): sponsored contents, product placement, advertising campaigns, licensed products aligned to their business segment, magazine articles, presentations in TV shows or commercial events, online courses, consulting and coach programs. Some influencers even benefit of guest roles in movies, theatre productions, soap operas, and music albums.

> We exist outside of YouTube. (…) We always talk to you about business and you need to, regardless of where you work in life, you need to diversify the portfolio; It is very, very important that you do not leave your eggs in one place. Then people ask: Do you only work with YouTube? No, we increasingly want to work with more things. (Danielle Noce)

While enjoying their new earned success, influencers also experience the bad side of fame and exposure. Dealing with haters, criticisms, and controversies becomes a significant part of their lives. For example, as the influencers' personal image is intrinsic to their brand image, they often undergo changes such as weight loss, plastic surgery, dental whitening, etc. These changes can raise controversies on excessive commercialism and loss of identity. In our analysis, we noticed that the way each influencer deals with these criticisms depends mostly on his/her personal style. Usually, they opt for a strategy of transparency to maintain the intimacy with their audience, i.e., they may accept even greater exposure to mitigate the criticism, such as explaining their point of view to the public and trying to get even closer to their followers.

> I knew it was normal to change, but I didn't assume that change. And why? Because these changes of mine were exposed, my girl-to-adult phase was fully filmed on YouTube. But the downside is that I've always had a before and after, a comparative. And many people have always said they preferred the 'me' from before… but guys, to me this is very obvious, life is made of changes. (…) The changes are amazing, what you can't let is change the best in you. (Bianca Andrade)

Fourth Stage: Positioning Review

The influencers' investment into their channels and their partnerships professionalized their identity projects and provided them with new opportunities. As such, a common strategy among top influencers is the creation of a parallel channel with more flexible content (e.g., vlog style) to remain up to date, increase exposure, and increase closeness to their audience. This new, second channel can also a way for creators to escape the rigidity and structure of their main channel. The new opportunities lead the digital influencers to question themselves and review their positioning. We identified two common situations associated with the trajectory of the evaluated profiles: (a) a period of crisis, and/or (b) the decision to reposition their image and innovate the channel content.

Crisis: There are times in the influencer's career when he/she must face a crisis and rethink their brand strategy as well as his/her career. For example, the influencer may experience fatigue, stress, and more serious psychological problems like anxiety and depression. The crisis moment can happen at any given moment in one's trajectory. Whindersson Nunes, revealed an experience of psychological crisis and decided to interrupt his work temporarily to deal with depression.

> In spite of all the good that has been happening to me, with all that I have achieved, I feel sad for some years. I feel anguish every day, every day, some laughs, some jokes and then there I am again with this bad feeling. I feel bad for not being able to help me, even though I sometimes help someone, I seek help from friends, family, but I feel so sad, so sad. (Whindersson Nunes)

Crises may also advent from the channel's specific context and the difficulty to create quality content and achieve a financial return from it. For example, Canal Nostalgia, a YouTube channel focused on longer videos about science topics, faces itself sometimes with challenges such as controversial themes requiring greater intellectual and technical effort.

> I'm sacrificing visualization, subscribers, engagement and money for quality (...) It's very hard to do what I'm doing here on YouTube, and why am I saying that? With each passing month, the number of bad things that are pumping on YouTube almost triples. (...) My goal is to keep doing the hard in a place where the easy prevails. (Felipe Castanhari)

Image repositioning: The channel of each digital influencer experiences several changes over time. The strategies adopted during these changes include the creation of secondary channels or new series, an increase or decrease in the periodicity of the posts, the insertion of new contents, and name alterations. The influencers feel a constant pressure on their careers to reinvent themselves, which is intensified by the high exposure of their private/public lives. Moreover, as human brands, when their personal opinions and perceptions change, their careers and media channels also reflect these changes. As reported by the influencers themselves in their videos, they are human beings who undergo changes as any other; hence, it is impossible for their channels to remain the same from the beginning until the end of their careers.

> We didn't want to be branded as a 'how-to' channel because it leads to stagnation. Not only do we offer cooking tips, but also a lifestyle, which I would call a somewhat unpretentious chic, a way to lightly demystify some things in life without judging who doesn't know or who doesn't have. In the end, we are our product. (Paulo Cuenca)

> We are always reinventing ourselves. We cannot stop. We always think of new and different things to bring to the channel. (Danielle Noce)

The image repositioning can happen after a crisis or gradually over time. In the channels of the influencers of the study, we noticed small and constant changes, followed by major transformations normally related to search of personal realization and dreams.

Fifth Stage: Maturity and Experience

After experiencing crises, the burden of fame and high exposure, the criticism of followers or from the media, and also learning how to deal with their own personal demands and expectations, the influencers reach a moment of professional maturity. In their study of bloggers, Erz and Christensen (2018) called this stage as the brand identity phase. The influencers embark on a process of reconnection with their selves, while actively and continuously negotiating, adapting and reinterpreting internally and externally created meanings. As human brands, they start to choose more strategically with whom to collaborate, whether in the short- or long-term. It is a time of greater personal and professional balance, and even though their professional career is intertwined with their personal lives, they already know how to discern and partially separate the professional side from the personal one. Also, they are aware of the bonuses and burdens of their actions, what they speak, write, and the life they have chosen for themselves.

> At first it bothered me a lot. If I had 20,000 good comments and one bad one, I read the bad and I was wondering all the time what I did for this person not to like. Today I'm like not even there. (Whindersson Nunes)

This maturity stage may still be marked by new crises, major changes, and repositioning. Despite their maturity and experience, the digital influencers are aware of the little chance of stability in their careers.

Discussion and Implications

Through the analysis of the profiles of digital influencers and the content collected from their channels on YouTube, we could distinguish a common pattern of events in their trajectory to success. The results of our findings reveal five important moments in the influencers' career: (1) the initial stage, when they start a career as content creator; (2) the professionalization decision; (3) the image development, which includes career milestones such as the endorsement from traditional media, product development, partnerships and increased revenue; (4) the positioning review, comprising a crisis period and the subsequent image repositioning; (5) and finally, maturity and experience.

The beginning of a YouTuber's activity is uncertain, as they cannot foresee achieving the "digital influencer" status. All had initial motivations and a unique style of creating content and interact with the public. This initial phase is marked by the constant transformation of the influencer's identity and learning. As the channel grows in engagement and monetization metrics, business partnerships emerge, and the influencer decides to make this activity their profession. With professionalism, they experience important milestones and identity consolidation, driven by high exposure and the constant pressure to be engage the audience. Them there comes a time when they need to review their positioning, which can happen during personal or professional crises. The burden of fame, excess work, and criticism can shake their self-images and even lead to periods of "withdrawal" from digital media. Finally, the influencers achieve some balance regarding their profession and the level of self-disclosure they are willing to use in their communication. However, they remain aware of the inherent ephemerality of their profession and the need of constant learning and innovation.

It is important to note that these stages in the career of a digital influencer are not necessarily linear, neither follow a strict sequence; some can repeat or happen simultaneously. Also, the influencer's maturity determines his/her role in an authentic, profitable, and highly engaged business model with the audience.

In line with Thomson (2006), the influencers in this study are human brands but also satisfy their human needs on their daily interactions, such as autonomy, relatedness, and competence. Moreover, endorsing Loroz and Braig (2015), the analysis show that they create a strong attachment in their niche communities. In the other hand, the study provides insights so far unexplored in previous studies. For instance, the different education levels and backgrounds of the digital influencers seem to matter little in face of the challenges they face in their trajectory; instead, the level of self-taught professionalism has a greater influence on how they conduct their careers, deal with times of difficulty, and profit of business opportunities. The human being behind the brand lends authenticity in a powerful way, and the cultural meaning of a human brand is co-created from what stakeholders reveal about the brand to the public (Centeno and Wang 2017). To Fournier and Eckhardt (2018), this lends an intimacy to the consumer-brand connection and brand managers do not have control over this.

The results contribute to the decision-making of marketing managers and advertising professionals in their communication strategies by providing a better understanding of the digital influencers' personal characteristics and their power of influence on the decision makings. Companies operate in a challenging consumer landscape, in which populations are demographically and behaviorally diverse, and customer needs and expectations are demanding more connection and authenticity. In this sense, digital influencers are human brands in constant transformation, continually creating and connect with a similar ever-changing audience.

Acknowledgments This study was financed in part by the Coordenação de Aperfeiçoamento de Pessoal de Nível Superior - Brasil (CAPES).

References

Agarwal, N., Liu, H., Tang, L., and Yu, P. S. (2008). Identifying the influential bloggers in a community. *Proceedings of the 2008 international conference on web search and data mining* 207-218.

Carrillat, F. A., and Ilicic, J. (2019). The Celebrity Capital Life Cycle: A Framework for Future Research Directions on Celebrity Endorsement. *Journal of Advertising*, *48*(1), 61-71.

Centeno, D., and Wang, J. J. (2017). Celebrities as human brands: An inquiry on stakeholder-actor co-creation of brand identities. *Journal of Business research*, *74* 133-138.

Charmaz, K. (2006). *Constructing grounded theory: A practical guide through qualitative analysis*. Sage.
Comscore Media Metrix Multi-Platform. Average Minutes per visitor by day, Jun 2019, Brasil. https://www.comscore.com/por/Insights/Infographics/Onde-o-brasileiro-esta-passando-seu-tempo-online. Accessed October 2019.
Djafarova, E., and Rushworth, C. (2017). Exploring the credibility of online celebrities' Instagram profiles in influencing the purchase decisions of young female users. *Computers in Human Behavior, 68* 1–7.
Erz, A., and Christensen, A. B. H. (2018). Transforming consumers into brands: tracing transformation processes of the practice of blogging. *Journal of Interactive Marketing, 43*, 69-82.
Fang, X. and Hu, P. J. (2016). Top Persuader Prediction for Social Networks. MIS Quarterly.
Fournier, S., and Eckhardt, G. (2018). Managing the human in human brands. *GfK Marketing Intelligence Review 10*(1), 30-33.
Hearn, A., and Schoenhoff, S. (2016). From celebrity to influencer. In: Marshall, P. D., and Redmond, S. (Eds.). (2016). *A companion to celebrity*. Hoboken, NJ: Wiley Blackwell: London, p. 194-212.
Helfat, C. E. (2007). Stylized facts, empirical research and theory development in management. *Strategic Organization*, 5(2) 185–192
Jerslev, A. (2016). In The Time of the Microcelebrity: Celebrification and the YouTuber Zoella. International Journal of Communication 10, 5233-5251.
Kim, M., and Song, D. (2018). When brand-related UGC induces effectiveness on social media: the role of content sponsorship and content type. *International Journal of Advertising, 37*(1) 105-124.
Kupfer, A. K., Pähler vor der Holte, N., Kübler, R. V., and Hennig-Thurau, T. (2018). The Role of the Partner Brand's Social Media Power in Brand Alliances. *Journal of Marketing, 82*(3) 25-44.
Li, F., and Du, T. C. (2011). Who is talking? An ontology-based opinion leader identification framework for word-of-mouth marketing in online social blogs. *Decision Support Systems, 51*(1) 190-197.
Loroz, P. S., and Braig, B. M. (2015). Consumer attachments to human brands: The "Oprah effect". *Psychology and Marketing, 32*(7), 751-763.
Lovelock, M. (2017). 'Is every YouTuber going to make a coming out video eventually?': YouTube celebrity video bloggers and lesbian and gay identity. *Celebrity Studies, 8*(1), 87-103.
Martensen, A., Brockenhuus-Schack, S., and Zahid, A. L. (2018). How citizen influencers persuade their followers. *Journal of Fashion Marketing and Management: An International Journal 22*(3), 335-353.
Marwick, A. (2015). You may know me from YouTube. In: Marshall, P. D., and Redmond, S. (Eds.). (2016). *A companion to celebrity*. Hoboken, NJ: Wiley Blackwell*: London*, p. *333*.
Mathias, Lucas. Quem são os principais influenciadores digitais de 2019? MindMiners. https://mindminers.com/blog/influenciadores-digitais-2019/. Accessed October 2019.
Rosenthal, S., and Mckeown, K. (2017). Detecting influencers in multiple online genres. *ACM Transactions on Internet Technology (TOIT) 17*(2) 12.
Schwemmer, C., and Ziewiecki, S. (2018). Social media sellout: The increasing role of product promotion on YouTube. *Social Media + Society, 4*(3) 1-20.
Sokolova, K., and Kefi, H. (2020). Instagram and YouTube bloggers promote it, why should I buy? How credibility and parasocial interaction influence purchase intentions. *Journal of Retailing and Consumer Services, 53*.
Spiggle, S. (1994). Analysis and interpretation of qualitative data in consumer research. *Journal of Consumer Research 21*(3), 491-503.
Thomson, M. (2006). Human brands: Investigating antecedents to consumers' strong attachments to celebrities. *Journal of marketing, 70*(3), 104-119.
Uzunoğlu, E., and Misci Kip, S. (2014). Brand communication through digital influencers: Leveraging blogger engagement. *International Journal of Information Management, 34*(5), 592–602.

Heterogeneity of Online Review Readers in Evaluating Helpfulness: A Finite Mixture Model Approach: An Abstract

Iman Raoofpanah, César Zamudio, and Christopher Groening

Abstract The advent of online stores and platforms has offered fertile ground for consumers to share their purchase experiences with each other. For instance, Yelp hosts over 210 million reviews for 4.6 million local business locations. Given the importance of online reviews to both consumers and firms, researchers have investigated what makes review readers perceive online reviews to be helpful. Although these studies have advanced our understanding of consumers' reaction to online reviews, they generally treat online review readers as a homogeneous group. That is, the effect of a given review or reviewer characteristic on review helpfulness is the same for the whole population.

Using a sample of 544,640 online U.S. restaurant reviews from Yelp.com, this study examines helpful voting behavior of online review readers and challenges the assumption of earlier studies that online review readers exhibit homogeneity when determining the helpfulness of an online review. The results obtained using a finite mixture model (FMM) to allow for inferential statistical analysis, reveal three segments of online review readers who utilize the *review* characteristics (*content*) in different manners to determine review helpfulness. We show that segments of review readers take review characteristics into consideration in a different manner and that *reviewer* characteristics (*context*) moderates the effects of review characteristics. This study describes each segment using zip-code level demographic data.

Since the paper used publicly available demographic data as the bases of segmentation, managers can determine which segment of review readers they are serving and accordingly review platforms can display reviews that review readers in that segment are more likely to perceive helpful. In addition, review platform managers can maximize review helpfulness by differently displaying review information on a segment-by-segment basis. Helpful online reviews attract more consumers to share or read reviews, enabling review-hosting platforms to monetize their user base.

I. Raoofpanah (✉) · C. Groening
Kent State University, Kent, OH, USA
e-mail: iraoofpa@kent.edu; cgroenin@kent.edu

C. Zamudio
Virginia Commonwealth University, Richmond, VA, USA
e-mail: zamudiomc@vcu.edu

F. Pantoja, S. Wu (eds.), *From Micro to Macro: Dealing with Uncertainties in the Global Marketplace*, Developments in Marketing Science: Proceedings of the Academy of Marketing Science, https://doi.org/10.1007/978-3-030-89883-0_97

Keywords Online reviews · Helpfulness · FMM · Segmentation

References Available Upon Request

Self-Construal and Willingness to Participation in Sharing Economy: An Abstract

Ashok Bhattarai, Maryam Farhang, José Saavedra Torres, Ramin Bagherzadeh, and Monika Rawal

Abstract The emergence of sharing economy has opened up several research avenues in the Marketing field.

One such research area is exploring how individuals' self-construal affects their participation motives on sharing economy. This research will thus examine the difference in participation motives among independent and interdependent individuals and explain why such difference exists. Further, the study proposes different incentive techniques that can be used to attract individuals with both independent and interdependent individuals to participate in the sharing economy.

Consumers' engagement in any form of exchange is affected by their own self-construct (Escalas and Bettman 2005) and it is no different in the case of the sharing economy. The independent self-construal is characterized as being autonomous, unique and bounded (Singelis 1994) whereas the interdependent self is viewed as collectivistic, communal and relational (Markus and Kitayama 1991). Individuals with independent self-construal tend to focus on fulfilling individual-level goals (Heine and Lehman 1995), while those with interdependent self-construal focus on establishing strong social bonds within their social group (Trafimow et al. 1991). Stepping on these findings, we argue that the willingness to participate in sharing economy differs by individual's self-construal.

A. Bhattarai (✉) · M. Farhang
Southern Illinois University, Carbondale, IL, USA
e-mail: ashok.bhattarai@siu.edu; maryam.farhang@siu.edu

J. S. Torres
Northern Kentucky University, Highland Heights, KY, USA
e-mail: saavedraj1@nku.edu

R. Bagherzadeh
Ithaca College, Ithaca, NY, USA
e-mail: rbagherzadeh@ithaca.edu

M. Rawal
Millsaps College, Jackson, MS, USA
e-mail: rawalm@millsaps.edu

F. Pantoja, S. Wu (eds.), *From Micro to Macro: Dealing with Uncertainties in the Global Marketplace*, Developments in Marketing Science: Proceedings of the Academy of Marketing Science, https://doi.org/10.1007/978-3-030-89883-0_98

Additionally, sharing motives are not only formed by functional benefits like financial incentives and convenience, but also by social and normative benefits (Möhlmann 2015). According to the cognitive evaluation theory (CET) (Deci and Ryan 2010), external incentives or events have different effect on individuals with different internal motivation. Individuals with a dominant interdependent self-construal are more likely to hold attitudes that demonstrate points of similarity with their peers (Aaker and Schmitt 2001) and hence the recognition and identification by others (social rewards) may drive their behaviors to be consistent with those of the community (Markus and Kitayama 1991). Individuals with a dominant independent self-construal on the other hand hold attitudes that allow them to express that they are distinct from others (Singelis 1994). These individuals put much emphasis on leisure and exploration and expression of emotions (Oyserman et al. 2002). Thus, normative benefits like sustainability might work better for them because these benefits are more consistent with their self-belief.

The contribution of these findings will be beneficial to companies operating in sharing economy, as they will have a clear understanding of what benefit strategy will work for a particular self-construal and segment and target these groups accordingly.

Keywords Sharing economy · Self-construal · Rewards · Benefits

References Available Upon Request

Exploring the Effect of the Pharmacy Benefit Manager (PBM) on Pricing in Pharmaceutical Distribution Channels

Guanyu Geng and Lou E. Pelton

Abstract Pharmacy benefit managers (PBMs) play an essential role set in pharmaceutical pricing and distribution channels. This article focuses on discussing the functions of PBMs in the pharmaceutical distribution channel and how they influence drug pricing. Moreover, this research also examines the impact of PBMs' revenue and power on the National Average Drug Acquisition Cost at the retail level in the pharmaceutical distribution channel. This research sheds light on the importance of the PBMs on pharmaceutical pricing and distribution channel but also challenges the imbalance of power and dependency between PBMs, channel members and third-party payers in pharmaceutical distribution. The authors also seek to explain the complex relationship between PBMs and the multitude of stakeholders in the pharmaceutical distribution channel.

Keywords PBMs · Pharmacy benefit manager · Pharmaceutical channel pricing · Pharmaceutical distribution channels

Introduction

As pharmaceutical prices have risen significantly during the last two decades and continue to rise at a rate that outpaces inflation, prescription drug costs continue to attract media scrutiny as a prominent political issue. In fact, U.S. President Donald Trump campaigned on the promise of allowing the government to negotiate drug prices. Virtually every presidential candidate in the Year 2020 election has offered ways to potentially reduce prescription costs for consumers. Despite extensive regulatory initiatives to control pharmaceutical pricing, the cost of pharmaceuticals continues to rise at an unprecedented rate. There is a very complex pharmaceutical channel related to the flow of products, services, and payments for the drugs. Figure 1 shows the pharmaceutical pricing and distribution channel. However, one

G. Geng (✉) · L. E. Pelton
University of North Texas, Denton, TX, USA
e-mail: guanyu.geng@unt.edu; pelton@unt.edu

F. Pantoja, S. Wu (eds.), *From Micro to Macro: Dealing with Uncertainties in the Global Marketplace*, Developments in Marketing Science: Proceedings of the Academy of Marketing Science, https://doi.org/10.1007/978-3-030-89883-0_99

of the most influential arbiters of drug pricing is the pharmacy benefit manager (PBM), which is a third- party administrator (TPA) or extramediary (Pelton et al. 2005) that negotiates the pricing between manufacturers and retailers, ultimately impacting the final product prices to consumers. In addition to the negotiation of the pricing, PBMs are also responsible for developing and maintaining the formulary, contracting with pharmacies, and processing and paying prescription drug claims.

A great deal of literature has explored the role and effect of pharmaceutical manufacturers in the pharmaceutical distribution channel. However, the predominance of the previous research focused on discussing pharmaceutical retail pricing. There also is extensive research on price competition among multiple branded drug manufacturers when their drugs are distributed through common pharmacy benefit managers (PBMs) (Kouvelis et al. 2018). A major research gap is the role of channel power and dependency between pharmaceutical channel members and PBMs, and the ensuing impact on retail pharmaceutical prices. Our proposed research addresses this gap and investigates the power of PBMs through the lens of inter-organizational dependence theory. Most pharmaceutical manufacturers, wholesalers, and pharmacies have a high dependency on PBMs.

According to power dependence theory (Kelley and Thibaut 1978; Lusch and Brown 1982), one's dependency on another is a critical resource of interorganizational power, even when there is a mutual dependence between them. Power dependency structure among intermediaries and extramediaries can influence their performance (Lusch and Brown 1996). Because the pharmaceutical channel in the U.S. has relied on PBMs for more than 50 years (Garrett and Garis 2007), many cases of inefficiency exist in the industry. For example, although the drug list prices have grown sharply from 2010 to 2014, manufacturers have experienced limited growth in net revenues.

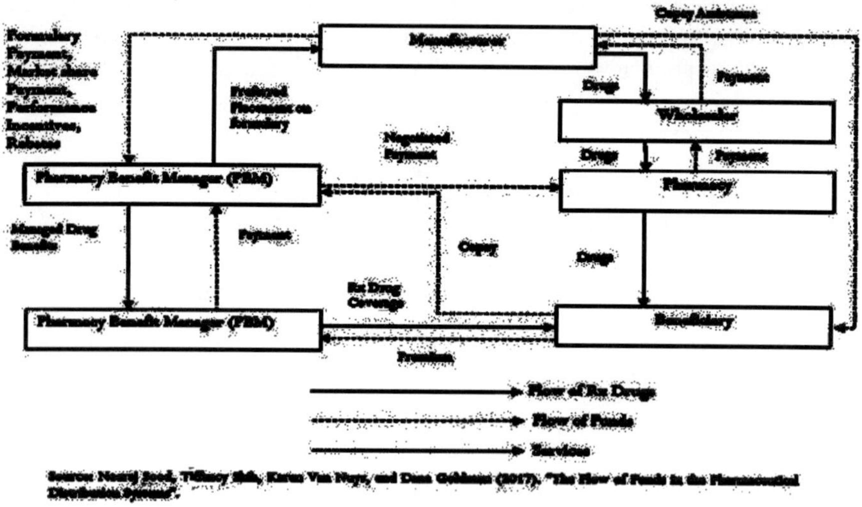

Fig. 1 The Flows of Products Services and Funds for Non-specialty Drugs

During that period, the invoice prices rose by $26.3 billion (13.5%), while manufacturers' sales rose by only $10.3 billion (5.5%) (Drug Channels 2020). We postulate that this growing gross- to-net disparity is largely due to the high dependency on PBMs. Therefore, our basic proposition is that the revenue and power of PBMs can influence the National Average Drug Acquisition Cost at retail level. In this research, the objective is to proffer a model that may provide insights into managerial mechanisms for understanding the role of PBMs in pharmaceutical pricing in the distribution channel. Because of the role of the PBMs, a theory- driven approach to understand the effect of the revenue and power of PBMs on pricing in pharmaceutical distribution and pricing channel can illustrate why PBMs are important in this complicated distribution channel. Previous literature has already illustrated that only U.S. pharmaceutical distribution channel has PBMs. The traditional marketing channel is shown in Fig. 2. Specifically, this paper seeks to critically explore the following questions:

R1: What is the role of PBMs on pricing in the pharmaceutical channels?

R2: How do PBM's power and revenues influence the National Average Drug Acquisition Cost (NADAC) of pharmaceutical retailers?

The pharmaceutical distribution channels and the pricing margins are complex. Many environmental factors can not only influence the relationship between each intermediary, but it can also intensify the conflict between intermediaries and

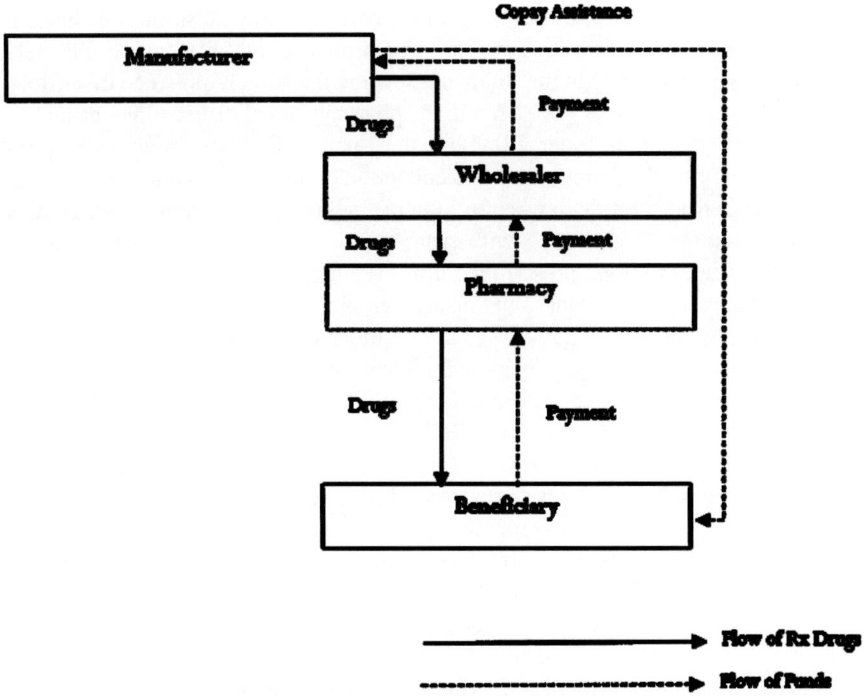

Fig. 2 The Traditional Market Channel For Non-Specialty Drugs

extramediaries. These conflicts not only increase the transaction costs at each level of the distribution channel; they also intensify the imbalance of power of the particular extramediary in the distribution and pricing channel.

Conceptual Foundation

Power dependence theory is the name commonly given to the social exchange theory originally formulated by Richard Emerson (1962, 1976). As the name suggests, the dynamics of the theory revolve around power, power use, and power balancing operations, and rests on the central concept of dependence. Mutual dependence brings people together; that is, to the extent that people are mutually dependent, they are more likely to form exchange relations and groups and to continue these channel relationships. Inequalities power dependence theory has been applied to multiple disciplines such as psychology, sociology, and organizational behavior. For the marketing channel paradigm, the literature focused on discussing how the imbalance of power between intermediaries in marketing channels influenced conflict and organizational performance. Based on the previous literature, power dependence theory not only highlights the importance of the power imbalance between channel members but also illustrates the consequences of the power dependence and the imbalanced power status. PBMs play a vital role set in the pharmaceutical distribution channel. When did PBMs become a "player" in the pharmaceutical distribution channel? Why are PBMs important? In the following section, the authors illustrate the history of the PBMs and the role of the PBMs in the pharmaceutical distribution channel.

A pharmacy benefit manager (PBM) is a third-party administrator who is responsible for developing the formulary (i.e., a collection of medications that are approved to be prescribed in a particular health system), negotiating discounts and rebates with manufacturers, contracting with pharmacies, and enabling beneficiaries to obtain lower prices for their prescription drugs (Feldman 2016). PBMs administrate many commercial health plans, self- insured employer plans, and the Federal and State Employees Health Programs. There are more than 414 PBMs in the United States. Over the past 5 years, they grew by 9.6% with its revenue of $453 billion in 2018. The three largest public PBMs include CVS Health, Express Scripts, and United Health/OptumRx/Catamaran (IBIS World 2018). PBMs originated when Pharmaceutical Card Systems (PCS) developed the plastic benefit card in 1968 (Garrett and Garis 2007). PBMs started with the idea that their buying power would reduce health care costs and pass the savings on to consumers. The role of the PBMs is like the giant buying networks for drugs, representing consumers from multiple employers and insurers. In economic terms, they aggregate demand which gives them leverage in the market. PBMs use their buying power, combined with utilization management strategies, to lower the total cost of pharmaceuticals (Arnold 2018). The complicated pricing in distribution channels not only intensifies the conflict between each intermediary but also amplifies the imbalance of power between intermediaries and extramediaries.

Literature Review

PBMs are now playing an increasingly important role set in establishing access to pharmaceutical products for patients. The topics of the previous literature focused on discussing the role of the PBMs in the pharmaceutical channel pricing and how PBMs manage the different generic drugs simultaneously. For example, Schulman and Dabora (2018) illustrated the relationship between PBMs and the cost of therapies in the U.S. pharmaceutical market. They found that net revenues for the sample firms grew by an average of 2.7% annually between 2011 and 2016, whereas rebates and other payments increased by 15% annually over the same period. The huge increase of the rebate intensifies the power of PBMs in the whole pharmaceutical pricing and distribution channel. Kouvelis et al. (2015) modeled the competition among multiple PBMs for the patronage of a client organization. This research used the quantitative methodology to illustrate the importance of the role of the PBMs in pharmaceutical channel pricing. Kouvelis et al. (2018) also studied the price competition among multiple branded drug manufacturers when their drugs are distributed through a common PBM. This research not only revealed the power of PBMs in the dyadic relationship between PBMs and manufacturers but also illustrated how the effect of the PBMs influences the marketing strategies of the manufacturers.

Pharmaceutical Distribution and Pricing Channel

In the pharmaceutical channel, it is important to differentiate the role sets of consumers, providers, and payers. The providers refer to "the entities that actually purchase and take both title and physical possession of pharmaceutical products, either directly or indirectly providing them to consumers" (Berndt and Newhouse 2010, p. 7). Providers not only include the retailers, such as CVS or Walgreens and mail-order pharmacies, but also contain various wholesalers, hospitals, and physician offices that administer medicines (Berndt and Newhouse 2010). In contrast, payers are the third parties in the pharmaceutical channels, such as health care plans, PBMs, and most group purchasing organizations and employers. They typically "do not take title to and physical possession of drug products, but instead reimburse providers for the purchase they or their beneficiaries have made" (Berndt and Newhouse 2010, p. 7). Because the payers do not actually purchase the drugs from manufacturers or wholesalers, the prices involved in the transactions in which the payers engage are not the purchase prices of drugs from manufacturers or wholesalers (Berndt and Newhouse 2010). Manufacturers sell their drugs primarily to certain providers which include wholesalers, retail drug chains, and warehouse clubs (e.g., Sam's, Costco). Pharmaceutical distributors purchase prescription drugs and other medical products directly from pharmaceutical manufacturers for storage in warehouses and distribution centers across the country (HDA.org). Pharmacies, hospitals, and healthcare providers place orders with distributors for the medicines and products they need, and the distributors process and deliver the orders daily (HAD.org).

Pharmaceutical wholesalers do not produce, prescribe, or promote medicines. Wholesalers also do not make clinical decisions as to who should or should not receive drugs or what drugs are best for a particular patient (HAD.org). The main responsibility of wholesalers is to make sure that whatever the healthcare provider prescribes gets to the hospital, pharmacy or other healthcare facilities safely, securely and reliably. The price at which manufacturers sell to wholesalers and chain warehouses is generally described as the Wholesale Acquisition Cost (WAC), which is a published list price minus a trivial discount for prompt payment and other incentives. Then, wholesalers sell the drugs to retail and mail-order pharmacies. Usually, the price is a few percent above the WAC. Accordingly, the margins for wholesalers are generally very low in comparison to all other channel members. Generally, services provided by PBMs include benefit design and contracting with manufacturers for third-party payers (i.e., insurance company, employers, and government); pharmacy network formation; real-time prescription benefit eligibility certification and claims processing; formulary management and rebate negotiations with manufacturers, payers and pharmacies; drug utilization screening and review; operation of mail order pharmacies, and other functions (Berndt and Newhouse 2010). Specifically, PBMs negotiate the pricing between manufacturers and retailers, ultimately impacting the final product prices to consumers. So, the role of the PBMs is like the negotiation agent among manufacturers, retailers, and insurance companies.

PBMs have a significant influence on pharmaceutical pricing channel. Berndt and Newhouse (2010) illustrated that there are several ways for third-parties in the pharmaceutical distribution channel to earn the benefits. One of these is the clawback. The pharmacy benefit manager sets the copay for patients filling a prescription at a pharmacy. If that copay is higher than the reimbursement cost of the drug, the pharmacy benefit manager can "claw back" that difference from the pharmacy that collected the copay. Besides the clawback, various rebates also exist in pharmaceutical transactions. Manufacturers contract with PBMs and then give them absolute number/dollar provisions that provide financial incentives for PBMs to meet certain sales targets for the drugs. This is extremely important because they are not reflected in the profit margins for the drug; they are service provisions that are essentially transparent in tracing the actual margins at each level of the distribution channel. Depending on the extent to which targets are attained or exceeded, manufacturers pay different levels of rebates to these organizations. Finally, prescription drug insurance benefit services are typically purchased from a PBM by the underlying health insurance company. The drug insurance benefit services include the specific drug list for the health plan of clients. PBMs negotiate lower prices with drug manufacturers but mark up the price when they charge insurance companies for individual prescription claims. Table 1 illustrates the financial flow of the PBMs.

PBMs are a knowledge reservoir. They need to balance the benefits among manufacturers, insurance companies, and pharmacies, and (despite the fact that they are a third-party operating outside the actual pharmaceutical channel), they singularly

Table 1 Financial flow of the PBMs

Financial flow	Explanation
Administrative functions	Managing and paying for prescription drugs of enrollees is the foundation of pharmacy benefit manager revenue. The insurers pay a fee to the pharmacy benefit managers for this work
Drug manufacturer rebates	In exchange for including drugs in their formulary—a list of approved drugs—drug manufacturers provide pharmacy benefit managers with rebates. Critics say this practice sometimes pushes patients toward higher-rebate drugs, which tend to cost more. It can also push pharmacy benefit manager margins higher
Price spreading	Pharmacy benefit managers also make money through a strategy called price spreading. PBMs negotiate lower prices with drug manufacturers but mark up the price when they charge insurance companies for individual prescription claims. This makes up about 10–15% of a pharmacy benefit manager's revenue
Clawbacks	The pharmacy benefit manager sets the copay for patients filling a prescription at a pharmacy. If that copay is higher than the reimbursement cost of the drug, the pharmacy benefit manager can "claw back" that difference from the pharmacy that collected the copay

Source: Colorado Health Institute (2018). "Understanding Pharmacy Benefit Managers". Retrieved from: *https://www.coloradohealthinstitute.org/research/understanding-pharmacy-benefit-managers*

have insights into each channel member's acquisition costs. During the communication process, they gather a massive amount of knowledge from the manufacturers, insurance companies, and pharmacies, and subsequently have proprietary information that is not shared between these channel members directly. The responsibilities of the PBMs intensify their importance in the whole distribution and pricing channel. In the following section, the authors will discuss the reasons why PBMs have acquired so much channel power in the pharmaceutical distribution channel and reinforced the dependency of channel members on PBMs.

The Power of the PBMs

Power and dependency have received widespread attention from marketing and management scholars. French and Raven (1959) have categorized the sources of the power or bases of the power into five types: reward, coercive, expert, referent, and legitimate. The five sources of power not only also illustrate how channel members perceive the power of others.

In the pharmaceutical channel, PBMs not only have the right to negotiate the price with the manufacturer and retailer but also can maintain the formulary. It can also develop a drug benefit plan for its clients, which includes a formulary list that specifies the copayment for each branded drug and a list of prices to be charged to the clients for each of the branded and generic drugs. PBMs not only have the pricing and formulary information from the manufacturers but also occupy the clients' demand information. The abundant information highlights the importance of PBMs in the pharmaceutical channel and also intensifies the PBMs' expert power in the channel. PBMs also have legitimate power. In 2003, the Medicare Modernization Act was passed. As Medicare expanded to pay for prescription drugs through Part D Program in this legislation, PBMs were given a role in implementing this new federal drug program. The Part D program is "an optional United States federal government program to help Medicare beneficiaries pay for self-administered prescription drugs through prescription drug insurance premiums" (Kirchhoff, 2018, p. 2). The coverage in Medicare Part D is available only through insurance companies, and the insurance companies have to purchase the formulary list from PBMs. In this transaction, this legitimate passage indirectly enhances the legitimate power of PBMs.

Depending on the characteristics of the pharmaceutical industry and the highly competitive business environment, initially there were many different PBMs; however, consolidation has left just three companies (CVS/Caremark, OptumRx, and Express Scripts) that control the pharmaceutical distribution channel. These three giant PBMs controlled nearly 85% of the market (IBISworld.com). This oligopoly gives these companies enough power and leverage to extract big discounts from drug manufacturers. Previous literature also revealed the profits margin of PBMs. These articles highlighted the high-profit margins of PBMs and also demonstrated the conflict between PBMs and intermediaries in the pharmaceutical distribution channel, finally implicitly revealing the power of PBMs (Sood et al. 2017). Additionally, such margins do not account for service payments and consultancy services paid from third-party payers and drug manufacturers that are reflected in earnings reports for PBMs.

As such, the profit margins of PBMs are not equal to the actual profit margins on any particular category of drug. The actual payments and profits from manufacturers, third-party payers, and retail pharmacies are much greater and not fully transparent; thereby this stimulates both perceptions of power and dependency on PBMs in the pharmaceutical distribution channel. Evidence of the impact of PBMs is the enormous operating costs per annum associated with the largest PBMs. This may be likened to lobbyists because the PBMs are regularly interacting with both public policymakers and private companies on a continuous basis. These investments help PBMs to build good relationships with third-party payers, insurance companies, and other channel members; but, they also keep them "connected to" the legislators who decide on regulations in the industry. These investments in "influence" actually dilute PBMs reported profit margins, which to some degree may veil the actual power of PBMs in the pharmaceutical distribution channel.

The big difference between large amounts of money paid from manufacturers and pharmacies and the profits margins of PBMs reveals that the high power of PBMs obfuscates the reported profits of PBMs. The lack of transparency of their profits intensifies the conflict between PBMs and other intermediaries in the pharmaceutical distribution channel. Previous literature has illustrated the undocumented sources of PBMs' revenue. Siracuse et al. (2008) defined spread pricing in the pharmaceutical industry and demonstrated that wide variations in spread pricing existed between two PBMs and between brand-name and generic medications.

Specifically, "spread" is defined as "the difference between the amount billed to the employer by the PBM, and the amount paid to the dispensing pharmacy for that line item" (Siracuse et al. 2008).

Spread pricing for PBMs not only refers to the difference between the discount price from manufacturers and the negotiated payment from PBMs but also includes the differential pricing afforded to different retailers. For example, Walmart pharmacies were expected to leave CVS Caremark pharmacy networks over a dispute about reimbursement rates. Because CVS owns CVS Caremark, which is among the largest PBMs in the U.S., CVS Caremark differentiates the negotiated price to Walmart and CVS. In other words, CVS can get better pricing from PBMs than Walmart. The differential pricing reveals both coercive and reward power of PBMs. PBMs are essentially third-party "power brokers" who signal pricing cues at all levels of the pharmaceutical channel. The unique role of PBMs intensifies their referent power. So, it is reasonable to assume that within the two relationships (PBMs to manufacturers, PBMs to retailers), PBMs have more power than the pharmaceutical manufacturers and retailers.

Because of the high power of PBMs, some giant pharmacies not only focus on their retailing business but also expanded their business to PBMs field. For example, CVS merged with Caremark to create CVS Caremark. Caremark was founded in 1993 in Birmingham, Alabama as Medpartners, Inc. (FundingUniverse.com). After going public in 1995, MedPartners quickly became the largest physician practice management (PPM) company (FundingUniverse.com). On 1996, Caremark International announced it would be acquired by MedPartners with MedPartners ending up with Caremark's PPM division and prescription benefit management (PBM) division and disposing of Caremark's rehabilitation Business to HealthSouth (FundingUniverse.com). The merger between giant pharmacies and PBMs intensify the "spread" price in the pharmaceutical distribution channel, finally intensifying the coercive and reward power of PBMs. PBMs not only have enough pricing and formulary knowledge from the manufacturers but also hold an abundant amount of patient information. The oligopoly market and the passage of the Medicare Modernization Act also enhance the importance and power of PBMs in the pharmaceutical pricing and distribution channels, finally increasing the evaluation of the importance of the assistance from the drug manufacturers and insurance companies. Lusch and Brown (1982) illustrated that in the dyadic relationship between two channel members, and the evaluation of the importance of the assistance from one channel member intensifies its perception of power from another channel member. It is reasonable to assume that the channel members of the pharmaceutical distribution channel can perceive the power of PBMs.

Previous sections have already discussed the financial flow of PBMs. The profits of PBMs highly depends on two types of power. Three main sources of their profits such as rebates, price spreading, and clawbacks directly relate to their legitimate power in an oligopoly. Their administrative profits highly depend on their knowledge power. It is reasonable to assume that their revenues can partly reflect their power in the pharmaceutical distribution channel. Figure 3 shows the PBMs' annual revenue from 2009 to 2018. Based on this figure, the annual revenue of PBMs from

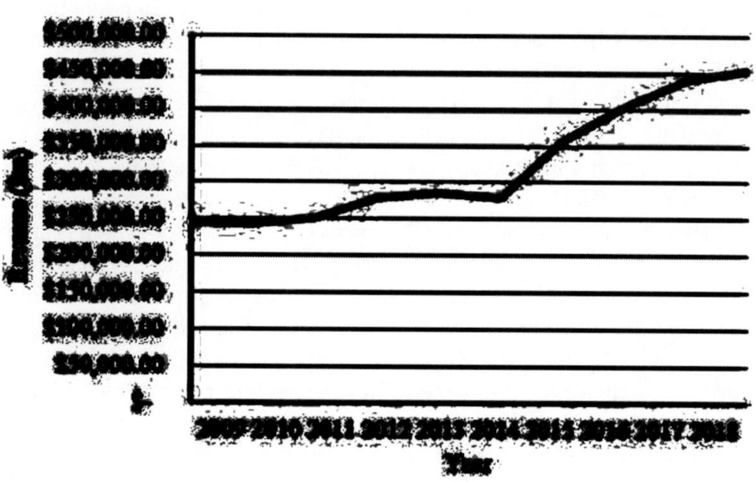

Fig. 3 The Annual Revenue of PBMS from 2009 to 2018

2009 to 2018 still increased. A series of U.S. House of Representatives resolutions to the Affordable Care Act (a.k.a., Obamacare) were introduced in Year 2010 and likely impacted PBMs' profitability. The resolutions provided PBMs with greater leverage to negotiate manufacturer drug pricing and insurance paybacks to retailers in an attempt to lower the patients' actual cost of drugs. It also increased Medicare reimbursements. This may have resulted in the exponential increase in PBM reported revenues since Year 2014.

The use of channel power can stimulate opportunism. Some researchers have already demonstrated the effect of power dependence on the relationship between the supplier's opportunism and outsourcing implementation (Morgan et al. 2018). Based on power dependence theory, the imbalance of power will create a conflict between PBMs, manufacturers, and retailers, stimulating the opportunism of the PBMs. For example, because of the huge purchasing power of PBMs, PBMs can get more discounts from manufacturers, creating more conflict with manufacturers. Hemphill (2017) illustrated two additional profits of PBMs beyond their client-negotiated prescription drug program management fees. There are instances where PBMs negotiate generic drug prices that are lower than the copay deductible paid by the patient (an industry practice referred to as a "clawback"). The PBM has discounted a portion of that payment from the pharmacy after determining what it will actually pay the retail pharmacy for the drug. Why would the retail pharmacy agree to such a business arrangement? The PBM offers the pharmacy access to the PBM's subscribers, a financial incentive that retailers are loathed to refuse. Contrarily, PBMs (depending on their level of buying power) can threaten to drop otherwise qualified retail pharmacies to leverage further price concessions from those vendors (Hemphill, 2017). Another PBM "profit center" involves negotiating with pharmaceutical manufacturers for rebates in exchange for a prescription program plan promise of an increased volume of pharmaceutical sales. As a result, neither the patient nor the retail pharmacy financially benefits from these incentives, only the PBM (Hemphill 2017). In general, in the pharmaceutical distribution and pricing channel, the role of PBMs is like a big valve, blocking the information flow between each intermediary. Because of the unique role of PBMs, they can sometimes sacrifice the benefits of other intermediaries or extramediaries in the pharmaceutical distribution channel to strengthen their own benefits. So, it is reasonable to assume that the existence of PBMs increases the pharmaceutical price.

National Average Drug Acquisition Cost (NADAC) estimates the national average drug invoice price paid by independent and retail chain pharmacies (Pierce and Sheldon 2018). NADAC excludes specialty and mail-order pharmacies and does not reflect rebates, price concessions, or off-invoice discounts (Pierce and Sheldon 2018). NADAC dataset at the retail level has been available on the government website (Data.Medicaid.gov). PBMs revenue is also available on publicly-available data on the 401 k. Based on the previous section, the authors illustrated the three main profit sources of PBMs: clawbacks, price spreading, and manufacturers' rebates. So, the authors will use spread pricing, clawbacks, and manufacturers rebate to measure the power of PBMs to demonstrate how these three main profits influence the NADAC. Specifically, the authors choose revenue, profit margins, and clawbacks as independent variables. The authors also choose retailer's NADAC, spread price between generic and branded NADAC, and retailers' redemption of manufacturer rebates as dependent variables. Thus:

P1: PBMs' revenues from health insurance companies positively influence retailer's NADAC for prescription drugs.

P2: PBMs' revenues from manufacturers positively influence retailer's NADAC for prescription drugs.

P3: PBMs' profit margins positively influence retailer's NADAC for prescription drugs.

P4: PBMs' clawbacks positively influence retailer's NADAC for prescription drugs.

P5: PBMs' profit margins positively influence the spread between generic and branded NADAC.

P6: PBMs' profit margins positively influence the retailers' redemption of manufacturer rebates.

General Discussion

This research discusses the role of the PBMs in the pharmaceutical distribution and pricing channel. Based on the unique role of the PBM, the authors highlight the impact of channel power and dependency on the PBM's role in NADAC. As such, it extends the power dependence theory to the pricing in the pharmaceutical distribution channel. Specifically, the authors illustrate that because of the imbalance power between PBMs and intermediaries in the pharmaceutical distribution channel, manufacturers, wholesalers, retailers highly depend on the PBMs. Moreover, this research reveals one reason that may illustrate why the pharmaceutical prices are high. This research reveals that PBMs not only have an abundant knowledge of the formulary from manufacturers but also can develop the drug list for the health plan of clients. More important after 2003, they have more legitimate power. The knowledge and legitimate power intensifies the importance of PBMs, raising the drug prices. At last, the authors also reveal the relationships between profit sources of PBMs and NADAC at the retail level. These relationships also demonstrate the power of PBMs in the pharmaceutical distribution channel. Specifically, the structure of dependency in the pharmaceutical distribution channel does have an impact on the relationship between intermediaries and PBMs. In this research, the authors reveal that high dependency on PBMs leads to a conflict between PBMs and retail pharmacies. The pharmacies may exert countervailing power to decline the power dependency of PBMs.

References

Arnold, J. (2018). *Are pharmacy benefit managers the good guys or bad guys of drug pricing?* STAT. Retrieved Dec 28, 2020 from https://www.statnews.com/2018/08/27/pharmacy-benefit-managers-good-or-bad/.

Berndt, E. R. & Newhouse, J. P. (2010). Pricing and reimbursement in U.S. pharmaceutical markets. Working Paper.

Colorado Health Institute (2018). *Understanding pharmacy benefit managers.* Retrieved Dec 28, 2020 from https://www.coloradohealthinstitute.org/research/understanding-pharmacy-benefit-managers.

Drug Channels (2020). *Drug prices, manufacturer rebates, and the risk to channel economics.* Retrieved Dec 28, 2020 from https://www.drugchannels.net/2015/11/drug-prices-manufacturer-rebates-and.html.

Emerson, R. (1962). Power-Dependence relations. *American Sociological Review*, 27(1), 31-41. Retrieved Dec 28, 2020 from http://www.jstor.org/stable/2089716.

Emerson, R. (1976). Social exchange theory. *Annual Review of Sociology*, 2, 335-362.

Feldman, B. S. (2016). Big pharmacies are dismantling the industry that keeps U.S. drug costs even sort-of under control. Quartz. Retrieved Dec 28, 2020 from https://qz.com/636823/big-pharmacies-are-dismantling-the-industry-that-keeps-us-drug-costs-even-sort-of-under-control/

French, J. R. & Raven, B. (1959). The bases of social power. Studies in Social Power. Ann Arbor: University of Michigan Press, 150-167.

Garrett, A. D. & Garis, R. (2007). Leveling the playing field in the pharmacy benefit management industry. *Valparaiso University Law Review*, 42(1), 33–80.

Hemphill, T. A. (2017). The "Troubles" with pharmacy benefit managers. *Regulation*, 14-17.

Kelley, H. H. & Thibaut, J. W. (1978). Interpersonal relations: A theory of interdependence. New York: Wiley-Interscience.

Kouvelis, P., Xiao, Y., & Yang, N. (2015). PBM competition in pharmaceutical supply chain: formulary design and drug pricing. *Manufacturing & Service Operations Management*, 17(4), 511-526.

Kouvelis, P., Xiao, Y., & Yang, N. (2018). Drug pricing for competing pharmaceutical manufacturers distributing through a common PBM. *Production and Operations Management*, 27(8), 1399-1419.

Kirchhoff, S. M. (2018). Medicare Part D prescription drug benefit. Congressional Research Service.

Lusch, R. F., & Brown, J. R. (1982). A modified model of power in the marketing channel. *Journal of Marketing Research*, 19(3), 312-323.

Lusch, R. F., & Brown, J. R. (1996). Interdependency, contracting, and relational behavior in marketing channels. *Journal of Marketing*, 60(4), 19-38.

Morgan, R., Doran, D., & Morgan, S. J. (2018). Strong contracts: the relationship between power and action. *Internal Journal of Operations & Production Management*, 38(1), 272-294.

Pelton, L. E., Cooper, M., Strutton, D., & Lumpkin, J. R. (2005). *Marketing Channels: Managing Supply Chain Relationships*. Burr Ridge, IL: McGraw Hill Irwin.

Pierce, K. & Sheldon, A. (2018). NADAC-plus: An emerging paradigm in pharmacy pricing? MILLIMAN WHITE PAPER. Retrieved Dec 28, 2020 from http://www.milliman.com/insight/2018/NADAC-plus-An-emerging-paradigm-in-pharmacy-pricing/.

Schulman, K. A. & Dabora, M. (2018). The relationship between pharmacy benefit managers (PBMs) and the cost of therapies in the U.S. pharmaceutical market: A policy primer for clinicians. *American Heart Journal*, 206, 113-122.

Siracuse, M. V., Clark, B. E., & Garis, R. I. (2008). Undocumented source of pharmacy benefit manager revenue. *American Journal of Health-System Pharmacy*, 65(6), 552-557.

Sood, N., Shih, T., Nuys, K. V., & Goldman, D. P. (2017). Follow the money: The flow of funds in the pharmaceutical distribution system. Retrieved Dec 28, 2020 from https://www.healthaffairs.org/do/10.1377/hblog20170613.060557/full/.

Motivations Behind Consumer Online Shopping Cart Use and Abandonment: An Abstract

Larry Olanrewaju Orimoloye, Monika Kukar-Kinney, Jeffrey R. Carlson, Angeline Close Scheinbaum, and Heping He

Abstract Worldwide, approximately 70% of online shopping carts are abandoned (Statista 2019) leading to potentially billions of unrealized sales dollars. Such statistics make one contemplate—what motivates online shoppers to place an item in an online shopping cart to begin with? Whereas past work has investigated the motivations for online shopping cart use (e.g., Close and Kukar-Kinney 2010; Close et al. 2012) and determinants of online shopping cart abandonment (e.g., Albrecht et al. 2017) individually, there is a need for a model that jointly examines both cart use and abandonment. Despite the established managerial and economic importance, the marketing literature lacks a framework of consumer behavior with respect to online shopping carts that considers both use and abandonment, and the relationship between use and abandonment. Further, extant research has not examined cart use and abandonment with field data; Close and Kukar-Kinney (2010) called for scholars to examine the topic with e-commerce click-stream data.

Thus, based on the managerial problem surrounding online shopping cart abandonment, and the void in the literature, the purpose of this research is to extend research on online shopping carts. Specifically, the objectives are threefold: (1) to provide and empirically test a theory-based conceptual model of how online consumer motivations influence shopping cart use and shopping cart abandonment, (2)

L. O. Orimoloye
University of Southampton, Southampton, UK
e-mail: o.orimoloye@soton.ac.uk

M. Kukar-Kinney · J. R. Carlson (✉)
University of Richmond, Richmond, VA, USA
e-mail: mkukarki@richmond.edu; jcarlso2@richmond.edu

A. C. Scheinbaum (✉)
Clemson University, Clemson, SC, USA
e-mail: aschein@clemson.edu

H. He
Shenzhen University, Shenzhen, China
e-mail: jeremyhe@szu.edu.cn

F. Pantoja, S. Wu (eds.), *From Micro to Macro: Dealing with Uncertainties in the Global Marketplace*, Developments in Marketing Science: Proceedings of the Academy of Marketing Science, https://doi.org/10.1007/978-3-030-89883-0_100

to examine the relationship between online shopping cart use and online shopping cart abandonment, and (3) to address the call to examine online shopping cart research with behavioral data, and provide a theoretical framework linking online shopping motivations with actual shopping behaviors.

We used a field study to obtain consumer shopping click-stream data from a large British multinational retailer specialized in clothing, footwear and home products. The company has over 500 stores globally with large presence in the UK. The total number of observations used for analysis is one million, spanning session visits from 07/28/2018 till 08/08/2018. Overall, the research demonstrates that both goal-driven and hedonic motivations are reasons for consumers to add items to their online shopping cart. At the same time, these motivations may also be reasons for abandoning the cart when the final purchase decision needs to be made.

Keywords Online shopping cart use · Online shopping cart abandonment · Click-stream data · Online shopping

References Available Upon Request

Effects of Different Types of Endorser in Social Media: An Abstract

Woojong Sim, Nicolas Jankuhn, and Brad D. Carlson

Abstract Are influencers just cheaper version of celebrities in social media endorsement (Forbes 2018)? Therefore, based on Attribution Theory, this study's objective is to examine whether consumers perceive celebrities and influencers as distinct categories and if such perceived differences in turn influence consumers' endorsement responses.

This research follows categorizations these different types of endorsers according to two criteria: "source of fame" and "source of income." (e.g., Evans 2019). Following Attribution theory, since people are aware that influencers' source of fame and income depend on social media, they will associate influencers' endorsements on social media with "extrinsic motive" compared to traditional celebrities' endorsements. Thus, this study argues that while influencers' endorsement leads to higher perceived fit (Schouten et al. 2020), when previous attitude is controlled, sincerity is the most important predictor to endorsement response or PI, leading higher purchase intention from celebrity's endorsement.

This research conducted three studies to investigates the effects of two different endorsers. Both utilized hypothetical scenario to control previous awareness and attitudes. All studies showed similar results as we predicted. Hierarchical Regression from Study 2 showed sincerity ($\beta = 0.28$, $t = 3.3$, $p = 0.001$) has stronger impacts on PI than PF ($\beta = 0.20$, $t = 2.4$, $p < 0.05$). Study 3's results from mediation analysis of Haye's (2013) PROCESS v. 3.3. show that while direct effect of endorser type to PI is not significant, indirect effect through sincerity to PI was significant ($F(7,102) = 26.757$, $p = 0.000$, $R2 = 0.666$; $\beta = 0.14$, 95% CI: 0.055–0.258), while PF didn't have significant effect.

W. Sim (✉)
Emporia State University, Emporia, KS, USA
e-mail: wsim@emporia.edu

N. Jankuhn · B. D. Carlson
Saint Louis University, Saint Louis, MO, USA
e-mail: nicolas.jankuhn@slu.edu; brad.carlson@slu.edu

F. Pantoja, S. Wu (eds.), *From Micro to Macro: Dealing with Uncertainties in the Global Marketplace*, Developments in Marketing Science: Proceedings of the Academy of Marketing Science, https://doi.org/10.1007/978-3-030-89883-0_101

This research's contribution is to differentiate between the two different types of endorsers on social media and their impact on consumers' endorsement responses, based on "source of popularity" and "source of income." Following three studies, the research argues, based on Attribution Theory, that people discount other attracting factors of endorsers (perceived fit/PF) when they attribute extrinsic motives of endorsers (sincerity/"source of income") to endorsements. Therefore, this research provides support for the claim that that people have different perceptions of social media influencers compared to traditional celebrities and different endorsement responses in social media due to endorsers' source of income. For managerial implications, this study hopes to provide guidance on which endorsers companies should sponsor in social media. To provide more justifications of theory and implication, this study proposes to test effects of sincerity when an influencer has other primary or secondary sources of income.

Keywords Attribution theory · Discounting principle · Influencer · Endorsement

References Available Upon Request

Commercialization in Professional Sports: Understanding Consumers' Perceptions and Responses: An Abstract

Vanessa O'Neill, David M. Woisetschläger, Christof Backhaus, and T. Bettina Cornwell

Abstract Growing levels of commercialization in the sports industry bring forward an increasing amount of negative reactions from sports fans. Those reactions span from the formation of a negative attitude towards the involved businesses or clubs to a complete boycott of the sport itself (e.g., Crompton 2014; Howard 1999), which ultimately widens the gap between the sports fans on the one side and business partners, sports organizations, clubs or athletes on the other side.

While existing studies have looked at individual drivers or consequences of commercialization there is little research on how consumers perceive commercialization in professional sports. In particular, no study has made a more comprehensive attempt to capture the nature of commercialization alongside the fans' attitudes in sports. In order to gain a deeper understanding of consumers' perceptions of commercialization, semi-structured interviews with socio-demographic diverse sports fans from different countries were conducted and analyzed through the application of an inductive and deductive content analysis (Mayring 2010).

Although commercialization in sports is often referred to as a negative concept in professional sports (Lobmeyer and Weidinger 1992; Slack 2014), our findings from the consumer interviews show that the phenomena associated with commercialization range from negative (e.g., exploitation), neutral (e.g., profit orientation) to positive associations (e.g., professionalization) in which commercialization manifests itself for consumers. Depending on the extent to which those phenomena are present, consumers' commercialization perception varies, resulting in different

V. O'Neill (✉) · D. M. Woisetschläger
Technische Universität Braunschweig, Braunschweig, Germany
e-mail: v.oneill@tu-braunschweig.de; d.woisetschlaeger@tu-braunschweig.de

C. Backhaus
Edinburgh Napier University, Edinburgh, UK
e-mail: c.backhaus@napier.ac.uk

T. B. Cornwell
University of Oregon, Eugene, OR, USA
e-mail: tbc@uoregon.edu

F. Pantoja, S. Wu (eds.), *From Micro to Macro: Dealing with Uncertainties in the Global Marketplace*, Developments in Marketing Science: Proceedings of the Academy of Marketing Science, https://doi.org/10.1007/978-3-030-89883-0_102

internal responses. The internal responses are of a cognitive or emotional nature and translate into either an acceptance, resignation, or opposition mindset, thereby triggering different behavioral consequences.

The consumer-based conceptualization of commercialization and the resulting nomological network developed contribute to the literature by providing insights into the phenomenon of commercialization as seen from a consumers' viewpoint. With regard to management practice, the study derives implications for sponsors, clubs, athletes and sports organizations on how to adjust their behaviors to lower consumers' commercialization perceptions.

Keywords Commercialization · Professionalization · Exploitation · Sports marketing

References Available Upon Request

The Charming Appeal of Brand Heritage and Its Suitors

Alessandra Vecchi

Abstract Outward Foreign Direct Investments (OFDI) from emerging economies have begun to increase significantly and have been growing at a faster pace than FDI from the developed world. The research seeks to assess the impact of Chinese acquisitions and their implications for the Made in Italy luxury sector and its firms. This paper presents the preliminary results stemming from a single case study on a Chinese acquisition in order to provide some in-depth insights over the influences and the motives driving Chinese firms to invest in the luxury Made in Italy, the patterns and modes of the Chinese acquisitions as well as the competitive strategies and the distinctive challenges that both investors and acquired firms have to face. From the findings, it emerges that both the investor and the acquired firm need to overcome several key challenges if they want to mutually benefit from the acquisition.

Keywords Brand heritage · Chinese acquisition · Made in Italy · Luxury firm

Introduction

While traditionally Foreign Direct Investments (FDI) have flowed from the advanced developed economies into developed and developing countries, more recently, a new trend has emerged in the pattern of FDI. Outward FDI (OFDI) from emerging economies have begun to increase significantly and have been growing at a faster pace than FDI from the advanced developed world. Increasingly nowadays

This research was supported by a Marie Curie FP7 Integration Grant within the 7th European Union Framework Programme.

A. Vecchi (✉)
University of Bologna, Bologna, Italy
e-mail: alessandra.vecchi@unibo.it

F. Pantoja, S. Wu (eds.), *From Micro to Macro: Dealing with Uncertainties in the Global Marketplace*, Developments in Marketing Science: Proceedings of the Academy of Marketing Science, https://doi.org/10.1007/978-3-030-89883-0_103

Multinational Corporations (MNCs) from Newly Industrialised Countries (NICs) are buying business assets and capabilities in the luxury sector all over Europe. Italy has a traditional competitive advantage in the production of luxury products (Vecchi 2008, 2013). The Italian luxury market has been long been regarded as the origin of mainstream luxury goods and includes brands like Ferragamo, Prada, Gucci just to name a few. With a rich cultural heritage embedded within their brands, these firms have captured loyal customers and remarkable profits from all over the world. In Italy, luxury brands are deeply rooted in their design, quality, artisanship and service and it has often taken decades to build their reputation. These features often appeal to those who want to instantly build a luxury brand such as the Chinese investors. This paper presents some preliminary results of a case study of a Chinese acquisition to provide some in-depth insights over the influences and the motives driving Chinese firms to invest beyond their borders and in particular into the luxury Made in Italy. The case explores the distinctive challenges that both the Chinese investor and the acquired firm inevitably have to face. The paper comprises six sections. The first section provides an introduction covering the background of the research and outlines its rationale. While the second section reviews the relevant literature, the third section provides a description of the methodology. The fourth and the fifth section respectively deal with the findings and the conclusion. The original contribution of the research, the managerial implications of its findings, limitations and directions for further research are also discussed in the concluding section of the paper.

Chinese Acquisitions in the Made in Italy Luxury Sector

The scenario between Italy and China is particularly interesting due to the peculiarity of the Italian economic system which shares some features with the Chinese one. These are namely the strong presence of Small and Medium-sized Enterprises (SMEs) that are specialized in traditional industries (Rabellotti and Sanfilippo 2008; Amighini et al. 2010). A recent study (Pietrobelli et al. 2010) shows that Chinese firms often regard Italy as a particularly informative European market since the consumers' taste is often regarded as a very demanding and very sophisticated. Moreover, in mainland China, Italy's reputation for high quality and prestige products remains strong and the market for luxury goods has experienced remarkable growth (The Economist 17/03/2012). According to Filippov and Saebi (2008), Chinese investments in Italy reflect the effort to enter competitive European markets and obtain access to superior technologies, know-how and capabilities. The high level of specialization in sectors such as the automotive, textile and clothing, machinery and home appliances represents a very appealing factor for China wishing to upgrade its production and technological capabilities and build its own global champions in these industries (Mariotti and Mutinelli 2009). According to a report conducted by Rhodium Group (2012), the first Chinese investment in Italy took place in 1986 when Air China opened a commercial office in Rome and until the end of the 1990s the number of investments registered was very negligible. However, since 2000 the number of Chinese acquistions in Italy has increased significantly as a confirmation of the importance of the strategic asset seeking motivation. Pietrobelli et al. (2010) affirm that what is happening today in Italy resembles the "*Marco Polo effect*" that happened in China centuries ago but in the opposite direction. At that time, Marco Polo was impressed by the level of civilization achieved in China and brought back to Italy some important scientific and technological discoveries. The same is happening today, since Chinese companies seem to be interested in gaining the knowledge and the expertise developed in Italy, in particular in design-intensive and in high-quality productions. For these reasons, Chinese MNEs are increasingly targeting the acquisition of technological skills, design capabilities and brands to acquire those local competences that are available in the Italian specialized manufacturing clusters (Pietrobelli et al. 2010) as illustrated in the Table 1 below.

Table 1 Main acquisitions by Chinese firms in Italy by sector

Year	Target	Acquirer	Sector	Stake %
2001	Meneghetti	Haier	White goods	100
2004	Wilson	Wenzhou Hazan	Textile	90
2005	Benelli	Qianjiang Ltd	Motorbikes (luxury)	100
2006	Elios	Feidiao Electrics	White goods	NA
2007	HPM Europe Spa	Hunan Sunward Intelligent Machinery	Machinery	51
2007	Omas srl	Xynyu Hengdeli Holdings	Textile	90
2008	Cifa	Changsha Zoomlion	White goods	60
2008	Tacchini Group	Hembling International Holdings Limited	Fashion (luxury)	100
2009	Elba	Haier	White goods	20
2010	Volvo Italia	Zhejiang Geely Holding	Automotive	NA
2011	Sirton	Shanghai First Pharmaceuticals	Pharmaceutical	NA
2012	Ferretti Group	Shandong Heavy Industries-Weichai Group	Boats (luxury)	75
2012	De Tomaso	Hotyork Group	Automotive (luxury)	80
2012	Miss Sixty	Crescent Hyde Park	Fashion (luxury)	50
2012	Ferragamo	Peter Woo	Fashion (luxury)	8
2012	Hony Capital	Mr&Mrs Italy	Fashion	30
2014	Pinco Pallino	Lunar Capital	Fashion—Children ware	70
2014	Krizia	Marisfrolg Fashion Co. Ltd	Fashion	NA
2014	Roberta di Camerino	United Trademark Group	Fashion	100
2014	Caruso	Fosun	Luxury Fashion	35
2014	Salov	Yimin	Food	NA
2016	Curiel	RedStone Group	Fashion	NA
2017	Buccellati Gioielli	Gangsu Gangtai Holding	Jewellery	85

Source: Data collected by the author

Rather than building home-grown brands that would require a long time to become established Chinese firms seek to invest in Italian brands that possess a rich heritage but have fallen on hard times or gone out of fashion to consolidate their position in the global market. An emblematic example is the acquisition of Omas, a company specialized in the production of luxury fountain pens since 1925, which was acquired in 2007 by the group Xinyu Hengdeli. Other cases are the Hembly International Holdings, leading Asian clothing retailing group that acquired Sergio Tacchini, well-known but declined luxury clothing brand in 2007 and Trendy International, Hong Kong clothing distributor who recently bought a minority stake in Miss Sixty, a popular luxury clothing manufacturer for teens. Overall, the widespread anxiety concerning China's international expansion calls for a better understanding and knowledge of the strategies of Chinese companies entering the Italian market to better inform what is becoming an increasingly relevant debate. Although this topic is becoming fashionable in international business studies, the empirical evidence on Chinese FDI in European countries is quite limited and mainly relates to the UK (Burghart and Rossi 2009; Cross and Voss 2008; Liu and Tian 2008) and Germany (Schüller and Turner 2005). This evidence is even scarcer if we consider Italy and to large extent the luxury sector. As such, there is a valuable opportunity to conduct further research.

Methodology

This paper presents the preliminary results of a single case study of a Chinese acquisition that was conducted to provide some in-depth insights over the influences and the motives driving these firms to invest into the luxury Made in Italy. The paper relies on one in-depth case study (Yin 2008) that was purposefully chosen to illustrate some distinctive organizational challenges that were faced by both the target and the acquirer firms before, during and after the acquisition. OMAS was selected as a suitable case study. The firm was acquired by the Chinese investor Xinyu Hendeli Holding (XHH) in 2007. OMAS operates in a niche luxury sector and enjoys a long history and tradition and can be considered as being representative of the luxury Made in Italy due to its design-intensive nature and the premium quality of its products. To enhance the rigour of the findings, the case study followed a very structured research protocol that included one in-depth interview with the company CEO and six interviews with key-informants to better contextualize and validate the findings. Firstly, OMAS's CEO was interviewed to investigate some aspects of the acquisition that would not emerged with other data collection methods. The CEO has been working in the company for many years and played an extensive role both during and after the acquisition. The interviewee also provided useful material such as company reports along with secondary data that were useful to corroborate the findings. Additionally, to overcome the limitations that conducting a single case study entails (Yin 2008), five key informants possessing some relevant expertise in the field were also interviewed to further increase the robustness of the findings (Tellis 1997).

Findings

The target OMAS (Officina Meccanica Armondo Simoni) is one of the most important Italian luxury fountain-pen manufacturers. The company was founded by Armando Simoni in 1925 and has a very rich history and its products are entirely manufactured in their factory located in Bologna, Italy. While the company started as a small workshop it has grown into an internationally recognized pen company. Armando was a skilled technician with strong interest in Greek culture. The founder was nominated *Cavaliere della Corona d'Italia*—Knight of the Italian Crown—and the noble status of Simoni was extended to his firm as the company soon become an important player on its market due to its rich history and soon developed a strong international presence with about 75% of its revenues outside of Italy. However, OMAS remains a family business. After the founder death in 1958, his daughter, Raffaella and her husband, Angelo Malaguti took over the leadership of the company. In 1983, their son Gianluca continued in the role. In May 2000, OMAS became part of the LVMH Group (Moët Hennessy Louis Vuitton), that was able to recognize in OMAS a great know-how and underdeveloped potential (LVMH website). This partnership allows OMAS access to the benefits of the large commercial network of LVMH Group while maintaining its operations in Bologna. In 2007, Xinyu Hengdeli Holdings Limited (XHH), luxury watch distribution and retail in Asia and strategic partner of LVMH Watches and Jewelry Division announce the acquisition of a 90.1% equity stake in OMAS.

The acquirer Xinyu Hengdeli Holding Limited (XHH), founded in Beijing in 1957, is the world's largest watch retailer of internationally renowned brands.[1] The Company operates in two segments the retail segment, which engages retail business in Mainland China, Taiwan and Hong Kong, and wholesale segment, which distributes numerous world renowned brand watches in Mainland China and Hong Kong. XHH has been listed on the Main Board of the Hong Kong Stock Exchange since 2005.[2] Hengdeli Group employed a total of 7015 employees in Mainland China, Hong Kong and Taiwan. The group's core business is the retail of middle-to high-end internationally renowned watch brands and it primarily focuses on building-up of the retail network in the Greater China region with a core presence in

[1] Its strategic shareholders include: The Swatch Group Limited, which increased its shareholdings in XHH to over 7% in July 2006; LVMH, the world's largest luxury goods conglomerate, which holds more than 7% of XHH shares; and Temasek, the investment arm of the Singapore Government, which holds over 6% of XHH shares.

[2] As at 31 December 2011, the group recorded sales of RMB11,375,280,000, representing a growth of 38.5% over the corresponding period last year. Retail sales amounted to RMB 8,589,323,000, representing an increase of 34.7% over the corresponding period in 2010 and accounted for 75.5% of the total sales. In 2011, the group recorded net profit of RMB 918,276,000, representing a substantial increase of 48.7% over the corresponding period in 2010.

Mainland China.[3] With internationally renowned watches serving as a core focus, the retail of a portfolio comprising middle-to-high end products, such as jewellery, leather goods and writing instruments, remains the strategic direction of the group. XHH has an extensive sales network of 428 retail outlets in Mainland China, Hong Kong, Taiwan and Macau, through which it distributes over 50 internationally renowned watch brands (Hengdeli Group interim report 2012).[4] The group is engaged in the distribution of numerous internationally watch brands on both exclusive and non-exclusive basis. Across its entire wholesale business, XHH serves approximately 400 wholesale customers in nearly 100 major cities. The group distributes over 50 internationally renowned brands. XHH has developed a comprehensive network of retail outlets in Mainland China, with heavy presence in key regions including Shanghai, Beijing, Northeast China, Zhejiang, Jiangsu, Henan, Shanxi and Hubei, which facilitated the consolidation of its market share. Meanwhile, the group is also strengthening its retail network by expanding into Southwest and Central China. The retail business of the group in Taiwan is currently in the network-building stage while it operates a total of 15 retail outlets located in prime districts in Hong Kong.

The acquisition On October 28th 2007, XHH acquired 90.1% equity stake in OMAS from the LVHM Group with whom has a strategic partnership. The remaining 9.9% stake in OMAS is still held by LVMH Group. "*The opportunity of acquiring OMAS comes from the proposal of the LVHM group which had been our partner since a long time. The group decided to seize this opportunity by having a clear purpose: to enter the domestic market by leveraging on the prestige of the Made in Italy brand. Thus, we have decided to invest in its creativity, design and brand power*" (Interview with the OMAS CEO). The acquisition is in line with the group business expansion in the sector of luxury consumer goods. The rationale for the acquisition has been twofold. First, XHH was highly interested into acquisitions of Italian luxury brands in order to diversify their core business that is the distribution of European watch luxury brands in the Chinese market. Second, XHH wished to acquire a better understanding of the know-how in both production and brand marketing in order to increase XHH's market share in China by taking advantage of the great market potential. OMAS has been one of the very first luxury brands they bought in Europe and having a very traditional brand like OMAS in their portfolio the group can better understand the strategy of other European luxury brands.

[3] In March 2012, Hengdeli chairman and chief executive Zhang Yuping said in an interview that the group is adhering to the principle of '*Be strong and be big, stable yet progressive*' by "*expanding the retail network in line with market trends and focusing on strengthening the management of existing retail outlets, enhancing the quality of retail outlets adjusting the brand portfolio, optimizing inventory composition and effectively controlling costs to achieve a steady business growth*" (WatchPro, March 2012).

[4] The group owns an extensive retail network that includes Elegant (for top-grade internationally renowned brand watches), Prime Time/Hengdeli (for middle-to-high-end renowned brand watches), With Time (for high-end fashion watches) and single-brand boutiques.

The post-acquisition "The aim I had once I become OMAS CEO was to restore the organizational and operational structure of the company that led OMAS underperforming despite of its great potential" (Interview with OMAS CEO). According to the CEO, this improved performance comes from a better management both of the short-term liquidity and of the post-sales service. XHH is a leader in the distribution of luxury goods, but it has no experience in the manufacturing sector. The Chinese MNEs has therefore decided to maintain the Italian production in Bologna recognizing that the value of OMAS lies in its handcraft products coming from a long tradition and know-how "*Our market positioning is a niche one, so we have to offer high quality standards and those can be assured only by maintaining the Italy based production with the historical Italian technicians*" (Interview with OMAS CEO). Moreover, after the acquisition, many suppliers have ended their relationship with OMAS since they feared the fact that the Chinese group could move the production to China thus decreasing the quality and the prestige of its products. Therefore, the Chinese management did not want to nourish this thinking. For the same reason no Chinese technicians were hired. As a result, OMAS production was kept in Bologna and the company has kept the Italian technical team in his current capacity in order to transmit an authentic image of Made in Italy which justifies the higher prices of its products in China. This has allowed the firm to increase its control over its supply chain giving Omas an higher degree of flexibility. Before the acquisition, one of the main difficulties faced by Omas was to collect the account receivables (OMAS financial statements 2002–2012). LVHM strategy was to push for high volume sales by often granting long deferred payments. As a result, this strategy led to generate a high need for cash that forced the company to increasingly rely on financial debt (OMAS financial statements 2002–2012). After the acquisition, in order to solve this issue, a "no payment, no shipment" strict policy has been adopted. Another objective of the new Chinese management has been to recover the relationship and reacquire an image of reliability with former customers that previously faced inefficiencies linked to the post-sale assistance service. Accordingly, a great part of investments were aimed to improve the customer service—"*Our product is a luxury one and, in order to create a customer loyalty marketing, it is fundamental to offer an efficient and reactive service. We aim at three objectives in this service: speed, higher standards, satisfaction*" (Interview with OMAS CEO). For this reason, a new internal policy states that within 12 h since the enquiry, the OMAS team has to email back the customer with a detailed analysis of the problems and the costs and time for fixing. "*I could summarize the new business approach in two words: standardization and continuity*" (Interview with OMAS CEO). As far as the standardization of processes concerned, the CEO has implemented a strict internal regulation regarding working hours and working procedures aimed at a proper cost control while further developing the company's production facilities. The second point is related to the vision and strategy of the company. "*I think it is fundamental to always bear in mind the direction and follow it. I expect that once given the rules, there will be a total continuity, consistency and consolidation*" asserted OMAS CEO. Therefore, the managerial structure of the company was significantly reduced. The complete sales team of OMAS decided to leave the company as they were unconvinced about the changes implemented by the new management. They complained that the process was managed from top down and about the fact that the team was left unclear about the strategy in the first few months. While the new XHH management team blamed the OMAS sales team for the unsound financial situation of the company. As a result of this issue the first few months after the acquisition were characterized by mistrust and criticism against each other. Finally, a lot of inside knowledge and reputation was lost when the former Vice-President and nephew of the OMAS founder decided to step out of the company. Managers in marketing, sales, operations and purchase management were reduced from 11 to 4. According to the CEO, by centralizing all the activities in the same position the aim was to increase the efficiency and the effectiveness of the management, the promotion of a more cohesive team spirit and increase the productivity. A strict monitoring system has been implemented through several dedicated meetings that weekly take place in OMAS. The CEO aim is to continuously motivate, control and correct his team in order to better allow them to follow the company's strategic vision. To this purpose, training programs and several dedicated meetings were introduced in order to align employees' expectations with the company strategic vision.

The integration phase During the integration process many difficulties were faced by the new Chinese management. "*In the Italian system, the main problem is the bureaucracy. Too many procedures and too long waiting times*" (Interview with OMAS CEO). The Italian legislative and bureaucratic system often discourages Chinese investors. Moreover, the Chinese CEO stressed the fact that the Government does not give any incentive or support to balance a so complex system—"*It does nothing for make foreign companies comfortable to invest here. No English, no service, no support*" (Interview with OMAS CEO). Another main obstacle is represented by the high taxation. Yet, to provide another example of inefficiency the CEO explained that he has to wait more than a year to get his Visa and that when he finally obtained his Visa and went to collect it the employee threw it to hi—"*Things like these would never happen in other countries*" commented the CEO. Due to such difficulties the CEO explained that many times thought of moving the production in countries like Slovenia offering great incentives and to maintain, in Italy, just the R&D, the choice of style and design, a warehouse, a marketing office and to change the label from "made in Italy" to "designed in Italy". According the CEO, this approach is allowed by the high degree of discretion of some informal conventions adopted by the firm prior the acquisition and that often caused technical problems. For this reason, the Chinese management has implemented a strict set of informal rules to standardise the work procedures—"*OMAS has 85 year-history and also people working inside this firm have their habits and want to keep doing what they were used to. However, everyone has to start and finish work at the same time. We are a team and if there are some delays everyone will have pay for it*" added the CEO. To explain the Chinese management approach the CEO used the metaphor of the boat and the skipper. "*As CEO I am the skipper who chooses the direction. The sailors are the employees who have the task to give me the right information and I give them the guidelines. They should trust me and follow me. I do not have time to* *hear their complaints. Those who do not share my idea can get off the boat*" (Interview with OMAS CEO). Yet, the CEO stressed the importance to have a highly hierarchic structure since each employee has to be afraid of the boss as this is the only way to increase efficiency. "*A good manager has to know how to share the tasks with the right people, control them and give them the right direction but the confidence is gained in time only by the achievement of some positive results*" (Interview with OMAS CEO).

Conclusion

Despite the topic is gaining importance, research on the internationalization of Chinese MNEs is quite limited to studies that attempt to provide an overall overview of the trends with a limited focus on specific sectors and on the drivers of the acquisitions' choices (Pietrobelli et al. 2010; Amighini et al. 2010). Therefore, this research has been an attempt to provide some anecdotal evidence by highlighting the strategic drivers behind the acquisition and the main difficulties arisen during the integration process between the target and the acquirer. As for the strategic drivers behind the acquisition, the findings confirm that the ongoing increase of acquisitions carried out by Chinese MNEs in the luxury Made in Italy is a signal of the strategic-asset seeking motivations where the intent is to absorb new knowledge and know-how from the target company (Child and Rodrigues 2005). Within this context XHH pursued the acquisition route for securing international differentiation and brand advantage. The findings also support Rui and Yip's view (2008) who suggests that Chinese firms strategically use cross-border acquisitions to achieve goals, such as acquiring strategic capabilities to offset their competitive disadvantages and leveraging their unique ownership advantages. In particular, XHH seems to be driven by the increased fierce competition in its backyard that impelled the group to choose quick solutions to enhance their competitive advantages. Such a feature is often described as one common push factor for emerging market investors and the case study presents itself as an emblematic example. The analysis of the acquisition confirms that design and the prestige of a long-established brand are the main drivers. In particular, the research shows that the acquirer seeks to strengthen its competitiveness on the international market by leveraging the design and the heritage behind the brand. In relation to the main difficulties arisen during the integration process between the target and the acquirer, the findings support Child and Rodriguez's argument (2005) that post-acquisition integration and management challenges can have a significant impact on Chinese acquisitions. The findings over the impact of the acquisition on the target are in line with Hofstede's cultural distance hypothesis (1980) that suggests that the difficulties, costs, and risks associated with cross-cultural contact increase with growing cultural differences between two firms (Morosini et al. 1998; Nahavandi and Malekzadeh 1988; Johnson et al. 2006). The research thus provides additional insights by highlighting how the two different management styles might cause significant misunderstandings that created a rift between management and employees, impeding or delaying the strategy implementation. The findings thus confirm that acquisitions are difficult to implement because they require a "double layered acculturation" (Barkema et al. 1996), whereby not only corporate cultures, but also national cultures have to be aligned. Different values, goals and beliefs concerning what constitute appropriate organizational and daily practices may lead to conflicts and limit the potential for trust to emerge between the parties. As far as the post-acquisition phase, the literature suggests that, in most cases, the acquirer follows a structural integration approach by replacing senior managers and erasing the target identity (Yamin and Forsgren 2006). However, the findings highlight that this approach was not followed by XHH. On the contrary, XHH tried to keep the target's identity by retaining its executives, its workforce and its suppliers. This seems to be in line with the identification of strategic asset seeking as the main motivation of the Dragon multinationals (Pietrobelli et al. 2010). The findings also highlight how the success of an acquisition is strictly related to the management of the post-acquisition phase. As today's business decisions and choices are increasingly influenced by the diverse cultural backgrounds and by the perspectives of various corporate stakeholders, it becomes an imperative for managers to acquire some multicultural understanding. As partially developed by XHH, it would be therefore advisable to develop an education program both for the executives and for the employees. Yet, seminars and cultural initiatives could be established to enable a fuller multicultural appreciation of the mutual differences. The limited number of Chinese acquisitions in Italy in the luxury sector prevents the conduction of a more generalizable econometric assessment. A case study approach has been therefore deemed as an appropriate methodological choice. Even if this approach can provide in-depth insights, the issue of generalizability looms larger here than with other approaches. The research focused only on a single case study, conducting multiple studies within different sectors of the Made in Italy luxury industry would be surely desirable. Moreover, despite the case study relied on multiple sources of evidence, it heavily relied on the view provided by the CEO, who is Chinese. This has inevitably led to some bias in the findings and hearing the view from the Italian counterpart would have provided a more faithful representation of the acquisition. Nonetheless, due to the increasing number of Chinese acquisitions in Italy and their important implications for the luxury industry, there is the hope that the study may spark a wider interest over the issue and stimulate further research to generate a cumulative body of knowledge on the topic. This scenario represents a great learning opportunity for both the Italian and the Chinese firms and it is becoming crucial to gain a fuller appreciation of how this phenomenon can be turned into a mutually beneficial opportunity. Therefore, additional studies may help to investigate further problems arising in the integration process and thus suggest corrective actions that can be implemented to ease the success of the acquisitions. Due to the increasing intensification of Chinese acquisitions activities and of the related fears and expectations regarding Chinese expansion into the luxury Made in Italy sector a fuller understanding of the phenomenon is not only desirable but also indeed necessary. This is critically important given the degree of anxiety that stems from the sensitivity of this novel topic. The provision of concrete research results can assist governments in supporting the sector with responding to this phenomenon by adjusting their policies so that local economies are able to capitalise on the advantages to be derived while minimising the negative impacts.

References

Amighini, A., Rabellotti, R., and Sanfilippo, M. (2010). The Outward FDI from Developing Country MNEs as a Channel for Technological Catch-Up, *Working Papers Print 012*, Dipartimento Scienze Economiche, Universita' di Bologna.

Barkema, H. G., Bell, J. H., & Pennings, J. M. E. (1996). Foreign entry, cultural barriers and learning. *Strategic Management Journal*, 3(1):151-166.

Burghart, N., & Rossi, V. (2009). *China's overseas direct investment in the UK*. Chatham House Programme Paper IE 2009.

Child, J., and Rodrigues, B.S. (2005) The Internationalization of Chinese Firms: A Case for Theoretical Extension? *Management and Organization Review* 1(3): 381-410.

Cross, A.R. and Voss, H. (2008), Chinese direct investment in the United Kingdom: An assessment of motivations and competitiveness, presented at *Corporate Strategies in the New Asia*, University of Bremen 1-2 February 2008.

Filippov, S., & Saebi, T. (2008). *Europeanisation strategy of Chinese companies: Its perils and promises*. UNU-MERIT.

Hofstede, G., (1980). Culture's Consequences: International Differences in Work-related Values, Sage, London.

Johnson, J. P., Lenartowicz, T., & Apud, S. (2006). Cross-cultural competence in international business: Toward a definition and a model. *Journal of International Business Studies*, 37(4): 525-543.

Liu, L. and Tian, Y. (2008) The internationalisation of Chinese enterprises: the analysis of the UK case. *International Journal of Technology and Globalization*, 4 (1): 87-102.

Mariotti, S., & Mutinelli, M. (2009). *Italia multinazionale 2008. Le partecipazioni italiane all'estero ed estere in Italia*. Rubbettino, Soveria Mannelli.

Morosini, P., Shane, S., & Singh, H. (1998). National cultural distance and cross-border acquisition performance. *Journal of International Business Studies* 137-158.

Nahavandi, A., & Malekzadeh, A. R. (1988). Acculturation in mergers and acquisitions. Academy of management review 13(1): 79-90.

Pietrobelli, C., Rabellotti, R., & Sanfilippo, M. (2010). The 'Marco Polo' Effect: Chinese FDI in Italy. *International Economics Programme Paper*, 4.

Rabellotti, R., and Sanfilippo, M. (2008). Chinese FDI in Italy. Proceedings of the Conference *Emerging Multinationals: Outward Foreign Direct Investment from Emerging and Developing Economies*, Copenhagen Business School, Copenhagen, 9-10 October 2008.

Rhodium Group (2012). *China invests in Europe*. Available at: http://rhgroup.net/wp-content/uploads/2012/06/RHG_ChinaInvestsInEurope_June2012.pdf

Rui, H., Yip, G.S. (2008). Foreign acquisitions by Chinese firms: A strategic intent perspective. *Journal of World Business*, 43(2):213-226.

Schüller, M., and Turner, A., (2005) Global ambitions: Chinese companies spread their wings. *Journal of Current Chinese Affairs* - China Aktuell, Institute of Asian Studies, GIGA German Institute of Global and Area Studies, Hamburg, 34(4):3-14.

Tellis, W. (1997). Application of a case study methodology. The qualitative report, 3(3): 1-17.

The Economist, (17/3/2012). *Luxury on the cheap. Chinese and other buyers snap up Italian brands*. Available at http://www.economist.com/node/21550285.

Yamin, M., & Forsgren, M. (2006). Hymer's analysis of the multinational organization: Power retention and the demise of the federative MNE. *International Business Review* 15(2): 166-179.

Yin, R.K. (2008). *Applications of case study research* (Applied Social Research Methods Series Volume 34). Sage: Newbury Park.

Vecchi, A. (2008). *Globalisation and the Viability of Industrial Districts.* Verlag Dr Muller: Saarbrucken, Germany.

Vecchi, A. (2013). Chinese acquisitions and their impact on the Made in Italy luxury sector. *Journal of International Finance and Economics* 13 (2): 75-82.

Consumers' Perception of Product Information and Its Effect on Product Evaluation and Behavioral Intention: An Abstract

Klaus-Peter Wiedmann and Levke Walten

Abstract The constant change in consumer lifestyle is also reflected in their eating habits, which is consequently leading to changes in the food industry (Romano et al. 2015). Consumers are increasingly demanding products that are less processed and free from ingredients that are perceived negatively in various ways, such as food additives (Aschemann-Witzel et al. 2019). Although additives play an important role in food supply and their safety is extensively tested, some consumers are skeptical about the use of food additives, especially artificial ones (Bearth et al. 2014). However, studies have shown that information about the product has a fundamental role in consumer perception and product evaluation (e.g., Pereira et al. 2019). Additionally, consumers become increasingly interested in non-sensory food qualities, especially in the methods of production (Deliza et al. 2003; Torjusen et al. 2001). Furthermore, consumers' perception of product properties may be markedly affected by information about the product itself or about the manufacturing process (Caporale and Monteleone 2004; Napolitano et al. 2010). The acceptance tends to be greater when consumers understand what they are consuming and get a feeling for the product quality (Deliza et al. 2003).

Therefore, the present study aims to understand consumers' perception and behavior towards food additives in processed foods and how it is affected by different quantities of information regarding the food additive. For this purpose, an online survey in Germany with a natural smoke flavoring used in a smoked ham as the object of investigation and three different information conditions (low, intermediate, high level of information) was conducted. Based on previous literature, the variables product quality, naturalness, risk and benefit perception, attitude towards the product, intention to buy, and willingness to pay a premium were chosen as measures for the consumers' outcome judgment.

K.-P. Wiedmann · L. Walten (✉)
Leibniz University Hannover, Hannover, Germany
e-mail: wiedmann@m2.uni-hannover.de; walten@m2.uni-hannover.de

F. Pantoja, S. Wu (eds.), *From Micro to Macro: Dealing with Uncertainties in the Global Marketplace*, Developments in Marketing Science: Proceedings of the Academy of Marketing Science, https://doi.org/10.1007/978-3-030-89883-0_104

The empirical results showed significant differences for the variables risk perception, attitude towards the product, and willingness to pay a premium. In terms of descriptive statistics, it was generally shown that the evaluation of the product-related perception, as well as the behavioral intention, is the worst at the high information condition. These findings are contrary to the results of many other studies. One possible explanation might lay in the information used in the stimulus, mentioning a production process that is still quite unknown in Germany, probably causing confusion rather than understanding, which is in turn, an important aspect when it comes to the evaluation of (novel) food products (Deliza et al. 2003).

Keywords Consumer perception · Product information · Product evaluation · Behavioral intention · Food additives

References Available Upon Request

"You Vote. We Donate." An Investigation of the Efficacy of Empowerment to Select Strategies Implemented in CRM Campaigns: An Abstract

Hajer Bachouche, Ouidade Sabri, and Ekin Pehlivan

Abstract Scholars have paid particular attention to cause-related business efforts with choice, as an emerging co-created cause-related marketing (CRM (CRM abbreviation will be used throughout the document)) strategy (Krishna 2011; Grolleau et al. 2016). Within CRM persuasion literature (Bergkvist and Zhou 2018), effects of choice of cause on brand evaluations have been addressed by two pioneering references (Robinson, Irmak and Jayachandran 2012; Kull and Heath 2016). Results advanced by Robinson, Irmak, and Jayachandran (2012) have shown that CM campaigns that allow consumers to choose the cause that receives the donation lead to greater consumer support than those in which the company determines the cause. The authors have highlighted that empowering the consumers to select the cause in a CRM campaign is more likely to enhance consumers' perception of their personal role in helping the cause and, thus, purchase intentions (1) for those consumers who are high (vs. low) in collectivism and (2) when the company and causes have low (vs. high) perceptual fit.

Building on these results, Kull and Heath (2016) have emphasized that empowering consumers to select the cause to be supported strengthens brand attachment via the mediating roles of empowerment and engagement; their findings also support that brand image (positive vs. negative) can act as a boundary condition of positive effects of prosocial cocreation contests. Moreover, it appears that risks associated with choice overload increases decision difficulties but it isn't actually moderating efficacy of CM with choice settings. Indeed, while recent evidence has

H. Bachouche (✉)
IPAG Business School, Paris, France
e-mail: h.bachouche@ipag.fr

O. Sabri
IAE Paris, Paris, France
e-mail: ouidade.sabri@univ-paris1.fr

E. Pehlivan
Martin V. Smith School of Business and Economics, Camarillo, CA, USA
e-mail: ekin.pehlivan@csuci.edu

F. Pantoja, S. Wu (eds.), *From Micro to Macro: Dealing with Uncertainties in the Global Marketplace*, Developments in Marketing Science: Proceedings of the Academy of Marketing Science, https://doi.org/10.1007/978-3-030-89883-0_105

documented positive effects of CM with choice campaigns to be supported on consumers' evaluations, we still lack a proper understanding of other situational and individual conditions of the design of CRM campaigns that will enhance their effectiveness. Important theoretical questions are remaining: How do psychological empowerment affect consumer-brand relationship? In what circumstances employing empowerment to select strategies in CRM can backfire? Extending Robison et al. (2012) and Kull and Heath (2016) line of research, this project aims at providing evidence about boundary conditions of empowerment to select in CRM campaigns and impact of such practices on brand equity indicators. As a matter of fact, we can assume that empowerment to select in CRM does not always enhance consumers' perception of their role and may even negatively affect their reactions to such campaigns.

Keywords CSR campaigns · Backfire effects · Choice overload · Empowerment to select · Brand equity

References Available Upon Request

Incivility Among Employees as the Driver of Customer Unethical Behavior and Customer Citizenship Behavior: The Role of Customers' Perceived Ethicality: An Abstract

Yu-Shan (Sandy) Huang, Shuqin (Monica) Wei, and Tyson Ang

Abstract In the workplace, employees encounter incivility on a regular basis (Pearson and Porath 2005). The prevalence of incivility among employees increases the chance of customers witnessing employee-to-employee incivility during front-line encounters (Porath et al. 2010). Such incivility can lead customers to appraise the situation as unpleasant and blameworthy, resulting in their desire to seek revenge against the employees' organization (Porath et al. 2011). Because incivility violates the generally accepted moral norm that every person ought to be treated with respect, we contend that one important, yet overlooked, question is whether witnessing employee-to-employee incivility encounter can influence customers' perceived ethicality of an organization and their subsequent behaviors (e.g., unethical behavior targeting the organization).

To answer this question, we draw upon the Stimulus-Organism-Response paradigm (Mehrabian and Russell 1974) and the person-situation interactionist model (Trevino 1986) to propose a theoretical model. The results of our experimental study provide general support for the hypothesized model such that witnessing incivility among employees exerts a negative effect on customers' perceived ethicality of these employees' organization while this effect is amplified when customers perceive the organization as competent prior to being exposed to employee incivility. As customer perceived ethicality decreases, witnessing customers are likely to respond negatively by engaging in customer unethical behavior and reducing customer citizenship behavior. This research offers meaningful theoretical

Y.-S. Huang (✉)
Texas A&M University-Corpus Christi, Bryan, TX, USA
e-mail: sandy.huang@tamucc.edu

S. Wei · T. Ang
Marshall University, Huntington, WV, USA
e-mail: weish@marshall.edu; ang@marshall.edu

F. Pantoja, S. Wu (eds.), *From Micro to Macro: Dealing with Uncertainties in the Global Marketplace*, Developments in Marketing Science: Proceedings of the Academy of Marketing Science, https://doi.org/10.1007/978-3-030-89883-0_106

contributions and practice implications for managing frontline encounters that involve employee-to-employee incivility.

Keywords Employee incivility · Customer perceived ethicality · Competence · Customer unethical behavior · Customer citizenship behavior

References Available Upon Request

Co-creating CSR Value Between Firms and Employees: An Abstract

Olga Pereira and Cláudia Simões

Abstract This study investigates the extent of CSR value co-creation from the employees' perspective and further develops and tests hypotheses of CSR value co-creation antecedents and outcomes. In this study CSR is considered from an internal perspective as a co-created reality. An interactional approach to the concept of CSR is adopted, based on the concept of VCC. The reconceptualization of CSR as a shared phenomenon can benefit from deepening the analysis about how CSR co-creation occurs. Since CSR is conceived as a shared phenomenon between the firms and employees, the aim of the study is to investigate in what extent CSR is co-created between firms and its employees. In particular, we address the following research question "To what extent is CSR value co-created between firms and employees?". The empirical study is predominantly quantitative. Data collection entailed an online questionnaire administered to employees of domestic and international companies operating in Portugal. Findings support the idea of CSR as a co-created experience between the company and the employees entailing three dimensions: dialogue, access and risk assessment (DAR). Findings further revealed that: (1) there is a positive relationship between the employees' perceptions as an antecedent of CSR value co-creation; (2) there is a positive relationship between the CSR value co-creation experience and the participation of employees' in CSR initiatives; (3) there is a positive relationship between the CSR value co-creation experience and the participation enjoyment of employees in CSR initiatives. Challenging the conceptual view of responsible business and how it is perpetuated throughout the firm allow organizational actors to reorganize CSR strategies and policies. At the same time, it is predictable that addressing CSR in these terms leads to different discussions on social and environmental issues, its provenance and solution. The discussion is also opened to policy makers who can benefit from rethinking the CSR dynamics.

O. Pereira · C. Simões (✉)
University of Minho, Braga, Portugal
e-mail: opereira@eeg.uminho.pt; csimoes@eeg.uminho.pt

F. Pantoja, S. Wu (eds.), *From Micro to Macro: Dealing with Uncertainties in the Global Marketplace*, Developments in Marketing Science: Proceedings of the Academy of Marketing Science, https://doi.org/10.1007/978-3-030-89883-0_107

Keywords Corporate social responsibility · Value co-creation · Internal marketing · Employee perceptions

References Available Upon Request

The Nature of Cross-Cultural Research Problems: An Abstract

John B. Ford, Douglas C. West, Mohammadali Koorank Beheshti, and Vin Luong

Abstract A number of studies over the years have addressed various issues relating to best methodological practice in cross-cultural research (Malhotra, Agarwal and Peterson 1996; Samiee and Jeong 1994). Many of the problems have been shown to re-occur despite such studies suggesting alternative and better approaches (Douglas and Craig 2006; Douglas and Nijssen 2003). The underlying problem appears to be that cross-cultural/cross-national research is often highly complex and challenging to set up (Steenkamp and Baumgartner 1998). This study sets out to ascertain the position since Samiee and Jeong's seminal work over 24 years ago, and to identify a set of protocols that cross-cultural/cross-national researchers should apply.

To do so, the study (1) identified relevant articles published in leading marketing journals since 1995 and (2) had four trained PhD students code the content. The analyses identified 17 problem areas that are currently under further investigation. To put these issues into some perspective, a panel of experts were approached to determine the ranking and importance of each item. Thirteen scholars known for their publications in cross-cultural/cross-national business research were contacted and responded to our survey. The 13 judges coded each statement as either "a problem" or "not a problem".

Overall, three grouping of problems can be discerned: problems with the sample, method or anal. Sample issues proved the most serious with an average score of 5.05 (SD 1.02), followed by method at 4.61 (SD 0.38) and analysis at 3.72 (SD 0.23) using a seven-point scale from 1 (not serious) to 7 (fatal flaw).

Cross-cultural research is difficult given the need for special quality controls that are not necessarily inherent in domestic studies. There is a need to avoid confounding problems to ensure that the study results are sound and that the conclusions

J. B. Ford (✉) · M. K. Beheshti · V. Luong
Old Dominion University, Norfolk, VA, USA
e-mail: jbford@odu.edu; mkoor001@odu.edu; vloun001@odu.edu

D. C. West
King's Business School, London, UK
e-mail: douglas.west@kcl.ac.uk

F. Pantoja, S. Wu (eds.), *From Micro to Macro: Dealing with Uncertainties in the Global Marketplace*, Developments in Marketing Science: Proceedings of the Academy of Marketing Science, https://doi.org/10.1007/978-3-030-89883-0_108

drawn are really warranted by the data involved. As part of a larger study, this important first step aimed to develop a list of potential problems and assess the level of severity of the problems through the examination by a panel of top cross-cultural scholars. The main problems revolved around issues involving the sample, followed by the methods undertaken and then the analyses applied.

Keywords Cross-cultural research · Cross-national research · Methodology · Survey research

References Available Upon Request

Generational Differences in Brand Hate: An Abstract

Oula Bayarassou, Pierre Valette-Florence, and Imene Becheur

Abstract Consumer-brand relationships researchers are manifesting an increased interest in investigating the concept of brand hate (e.g., Fetscherin 2019; Kucuk 2019; Zarantonello 2016). In line with this research mainstream, this paper aims to further discern the mechanism of brand hate by studying the trajectories of brand hate across generations. More specifically, we test a model integrating brand hate antecedents and consequences and investigate the moderating role of consumer narcissism on the relationships between brand hate and its consequences. Furthermore, we determine the similarities and differences in brand hate activation and regulation processes between generation Y and generation Z.

We posit the following hypotheses:

H1: The fallacious character of the brand positively influences active brand hate
H2: The fallacious character of the brand has a positive impact on passive brand hate
H3: Active brand hate has a positive impact on desire for revenge.
H4: Passive hate positively influences the desire for avoidance.
H5: Consumer's narcissism positively moderates the relationship between active brand hate and desire for revenge
H6: Consumer's narcissism positively moderates the relationship between passive brand hate and desire for avoidance

O. Bayarassou (✉)
South Champagne Business School, Troyes, France
e-mail: oula.bayaa-rassou@yschools.fr

P. Valette-Florence
Grenoble Alpes University, Grenoble, France
e-mail: pvalette@grenoble-iae.fr

I. Becheur
Qatar University, Doha, Qatar
e-mail: imene.becheur@qu.edu.qa

F. Pantoja, S. Wu (eds.), *From Micro to Macro: Dealing with Uncertainties in the Global Marketplace*, Developments in Marketing Science: Proceedings of the Academy of Marketing Science, https://doi.org/10.1007/978-3-030-89883-0_109

We also propose that the relationship between passive brand hate and desire for avoidance is stronger among generation Y consumers (versus generation z consumers). In addition, we argue that the relationship between active brand hate and revenge is stronger among generation Z consumers (versus generation Y consumers).

Our model was tested with data collected from a French representative consumer (N = 361). Data was analyzed via PLS structural equation modeling. All measures are adapted from previous work and were based on six-point Likert scales.

Results show that: for the generation Y, all hypotheses were validated except H6 and for the generation Z, all hypotheses were validated except H5 and H6 linked to the moderating role of consumer narcissism. Moreover, in contrast with the desire for avoidance, the desire for revenge is stronger among haters belonging to Generation Z. However, the impact of passive hate on the desire to avoid the brand is more important among Generation Y members. This result could be explained by the incongruent relationships between generation Y consumers and brands, mainly for reasons related to ethics and CSR. Moreover, the narcissistic character of Y consumers seems to accentuate the link between active hate and the desire for revenge. This could be explained by the high sense of entitlement among this generation Twenge (2006). Finally, in accordance with the results of the global model test, consumer narcissism has no significant effect on the relationship between passive hate and desire for avoidance among both generations.

Keywords Brand hate · Desire for revenge · Desire of avoidance · Generations · Narcissism

References Available Upon Request

Customer Participation in Health Care Services: A Proposed Framework for Enhancing Chronic Illness Management

Muhammad Junaid and Kiane Goudarzi

Abstract Customer participation (CP) is a major research area in services marketing. The focus remains on outcomes of CP, mainly in want-based services. The existing literature is limited to answer; what is meaning of CP in need-based services like health care? how CP itself is being affected? and what is role of psychological forces on CP. The mix method research is used to answer these questions. Seventy-five semi structured interviews were conducted with doctors, patients and paramedical staff to conceptualize patient participation and patient education as study constructs besides identifying certain psychological factors in building a conceptual model. Structural equation modeling (SEM) is used to test the model by analyzing survey data of 690 patients of chronic diseases like diabetes, hypertension and cancer. Findings show that patient education has a significant positive impact on participation, patient perceived control and satisfaction. Conceptual fluency mediates relationship between patient education and participation. Doctor's psychological considerations strengthen positive relationship between patient education and conceptual fluency. The study concludes with research directions and policy implications for professionals.

Keywords Patient participation · Conceptual fluency · Perceived control · Psychological considerations · Health care services

M. Junaid (✉)
Aix Marseille Université, Marseille, France
e-mail: muhammad.junaid@iae-aix.com

K. Goudarzi
Université Jean Moulin Lyon 3, Lyon, France
e-mail: kiane.goudarzi@univ-lyon3.fr

F. Pantoja, S. Wu (eds.), *From Micro to Macro: Dealing with Uncertainties in the Global Marketplace*, Developments in Marketing Science: Proceedings of the Academy of Marketing Science, https://doi.org/10.1007/978-3-030-89883-0_110

Introduction

The importance of customer participation is well recognized in services literature (Chan et al. 2010; Dellande et al. 2004; Dong and Sivakumar 2017) and also endorsed by health care professional in clinical studies (e.g., Cahill 1995, 1998; Guadagnoli and Ward 1998; McColl-Kennedy et al. 2012, 2017). Although a growing body of literature (Chan et al. 2010; Dong and Sivakumar 2017) highlights the importance of customer participation in services marketing but the understanding of the factors that facilitate participation is not well developed. In the debate of customer participation, a larger focus is found on the outcomes of customer participation and lesser attention is paid on the antecedent of customer participation (Dong and Sivakumar 2017). The role of customer education as an antecedent to customer participation in high credence services like health care is yet to be explored. According to Ostrom et al. (2015) health care provides to scholars an important context for services research. Berry and Bendapudi (2007) also acknowledged health care as a "fertile field for service research".

The purpose of the study is to present a comprehensive understanding of the concept of "patient participation" and "patient education" in health care services and to explore the impact of psychological patient factors modifying the patient education, patient participation and patient satisfaction chain for health care customers under prolonged treatment. The next section gives a brief review of literature on customer participation.

Customer Participation

"Customer participation refers to the degree to which the customer is involved in producing and delivering the service" (Dabholkar 1990). The growing potential of customer participation has grasped the attention of many researchers from multiple disciplines. The initial work stressed the benefits of involving customers as co-producers or partial employees mostly for customization, productivity gains, quality improvements and so on (e.g., Lovelock and Young 1979; Mills and Morris 1986). On the customer side it was attempted to know when and why customers are motivated to participate (Bateson 1985) and means of facilitating customer participation (Goodwin 1988). The research progressed also from conceptual to empirical investigation to see the effect of customer participation on service outcomes, like satisfaction and loyalty (Auh et al. 2007; Bendapudi and Leone 2003). The scope of research in the last decade even reaches new product development (Fang 2008; Fang et al. 2008), service failure and recovery (Dong et al. 2008).

The Customer participation is a major focus of interest in service research (Chan et al. 2010; Dong and Sivakumar 2017). Service management and marketing scholars have much to offer to a critically important, intellectually challenging, but deeply troubled health care service sector (Berry and Bendapudi 2007). In past few years, customer participation has emerged as major research subject in health care services (e.g., Berry and Bendapudi 2007; Dellande et al. 2004; Gallan et al. 2013; McColl-Kennedy et al. 2017). The customer participation outside of service organization, which is considered a key requirement of many health services is largely an ignored area in service marketing literature (Dellande et al. 2004). Health care being a complexed service needs higher level of customer participation. Successful management of health particularly in chronic diseases like diabetes, hypertension and cancer is very much dependent on participation of heath care customers rather than health care providers. The question arises how the appropriate participation can be made by the customers particularly in complexed services like health care? Although a growing body of literature highlights the importance of customer participation in services marketing but the understanding of the factors that facilitate participation like customer education is less well developed particularly in high credence services like health care. Therefore, this study focus on the role of customer education for desired outcomes in health care services. The literature helped us to identify the following knowledge gaps to be focused:

Research Gaps Customer participation and customer education not comprehensively conceptualized in high credence services like health care.

Customer education as an antecedent of customer participation is not well focused in the services marketing literature particularly in health care services.

The understanding of the psychological factors to facilitate participation is missing in discourse of customer participation.

The later part of the paper is organized in a way that firstly we present the methodology and key findings of our qualitative study to conceptualize patient participation and patient education as the major study constructs. Secondly, we give the conceptual framework and hypotheses developed for empirical testing. Later, methodology and results of quantitative study are presented. The last section discusses the study contributions and limitations followed by future research directions and policy implications for health care professionals and policy makers.

Qualitative Study

The review of literature on customer participation and customer education in services marketing and health care journals revealed that the concepts of customer participation and customer education are complexed and multifactorial and furthermore the literature is very much fragmented. These concepts were defined and operationalized mostly in certain specific contexts or pertaining to only one single encounter or involving a specific stage in service delivery process. This clearly indicates that that efforts are needed to formulate standardized definitions of the concept of patient participation and patient education to build consistent understanding of the concepts and developing reliable and valid measures. The purpose of qualitative study is to get deep down insights on patient participation and to conceptualize in a comprehensive way the concept of patient education and patient participation in health care services and to identify potential psychological factors playing key role in relationship between patient education and patient participation.

Methodology

The study was conducted using 75 semi structured interviews with doctors (33), patients (30) and paramedical staff (12). An interview guide was prepared following guidelines given by McCracken (1988), literature on customer participation and customer education and incorporating the recommendations from researchers and senior doctors and hospital administration staff. The face to face interviews were mostly conducted in the hospitals and clinics to get more factual data in natural settings. To ensure the diversification and richness of data special efforts were made to interview doctors with different specialization, patient with different diseases and experienced paramedical staff performing diversified tasks in the health care operations at different clinics and hospitals. The hospital includes both from public and private sectors. The doctors were also having experience of serving in different geographical location of Pakistan including urban and rural areas, small and big cities. The patients interviewed were also having diversified diseases with different educational background and professions. Interviews were recorded using an electronic device with the permission of participants. Recoding time range was 15–37 min. Later, interviews were transcribed producing 184 single spaced pages of textual data with 93,021 words. The data was analyzed on the basis of objective of the study and the guidelines for analysis of qualitative data by Bryman (2012). The codes/themes were developed to conceptualize patient participation and patient education using content analysis with mix method approach. The results and finding of the study are presented in next section.

Findings of Qualitative Study

We got lot of interesting findings and results through our qualitative study here we will restrict to our study objectives i.e. the conceptualization of patient participation and patient education along with the potential variable identified for our conceptual model. Patient participation emerged as three-dimensional construct (Table 1) which indicates that patient can participate firstly, by providing and sharing informations to the health care providers, secondly by actively involving in the decision making process and thirdly by ensuring compliance to many of the things required by the health care providers.

Patient education also emerged as three-dimensional construct (Table 2) which indicates that patient education is basically the communication by the doctor focused on the disease and treatment information. *Secondly*, communication

Table 1 Three dimensions of patient participation emerged through qualitative data analysis

Patient participation dimensions	Selected quotes
1. Sharing informations	"In my opinion, patient participation means to help the doctors in explaining the conditions and to convey the history" (RPT30) "First of all, they should give us all the details about their disease including all the signs and symptoms" (RDR18)
2. Involvement in decision making	"So, in the modern practice patient is always involved in decision-making and patient has the right to discuss about her problems in detail and about her management" (RDR25) "These days many surgical procedures could be applied like laparoscopic or open surgery .... patient decides the final option" (ROT12)
3. Ensuring compliance	"By participation mean patient have to Follow the schedule of visits recommended by doctor" (RDR22) "The patient should have availability on follow-ups visit as advised like visits after certain days or weekly or monthly basis" (RDR31)

Table 2 Three dimensions of patient education emerged through qualitative data analysis

Patient education dimensions	Selected quotes
1. Communication focused on disease and treatment information	"For me it is very important if the patient knows what he is suffering from why he or she is sick, and how the sickness can be handled" (RPT01) "In simple words by educating the patient mean telling the patient about the disease, that what exactly is the disease?" (RDR18)
2. Communication focused on diet and life style modification	"We expect they should be following the diet, certain lifestyle modifications and doing some exercises as well." (RDR25) "Many diseases which are related to your diet and are related with your lifestyle; we advise patients on lifestyle modification." (RDR27)
3. Communication focused on negative consequences	"We also tell him about the mishaps with the people who didn't take their medicine regularly, as per schedule." (RPT03) "In educating patient, you should tell the patient for example in case of chronic disease what could be the side or bad effects." (RDR29)

focused on diet and life style modifications and *thirdly* communication focused on negative consequences.

We also identified some potential variables including conceptual fluency, psychological consideration and patient control on illness for inclusion in our empirical model (This paper is brief of PhD dissertation and discussion of these results is beyond the scope of this paper). Our results also show that the chronic diseases need comparatively higher level of patient participation. The 61% (46/75) participants used the words indicating higher participation in their discussion and out of these 46 patients, 96% (44/46) participants related the need of higher participation in case of chronic diseases like diabetes, hypertension and cancers. This helped us to focus on chronic illnesses only for empirical testing of our model. In the next section we conceptualize our model along with hypothesis development.

Conceptual Framework and Hypotheses

Patient Education and Patient Participation The literature shows that customer education has been considered an important antecedent of active customer participation in service process (Bateson 2002; Lovelock 2011). Patient education improves the participation through better compliance in a broad range of conditions and severity of disease (Gold and McClung 2006). Customer receiving knowledge and skills through education in turn, are willing to reciprocate with participation, so customer education is likely to have a significant effect on customer participation (Eisingerich and Bell 2006). Thus, we hypothesize as:

H1. Patient education will positively impact patient participation.

Conceptual Fluency Conceptual fluency is the ease of processing the meaning of a stimulus, or the fluency of conceptually driven processing (Whittlesea 1993). The conceptual fluency for the current study is described as "the ease with which patients process and understands the instructions given by the health care professionals". "The Conceptual fluency describes the ease with which customers can process and understand information (Lee and Labroo 2004; Sirianni et al. 2013)". The patient education in the form of communication by doctor is expected to enhance the conceptual fluency of patients. Thus, we hypothesize as:

H2. Patient education will have significant positive impact on conceptual fluency.

A better comprehension of information developed by the patient relates to higher compliance with the advice given by doctor (Kincey et al. 1975). The increased conceptual fluency of patients will facilitate them in understanding better the instructions and follow them subsequently in an effective way. Thus, we hypothesize as:

H3. Conceptual fluency will mediate the impact of patient education on patient participation.

Patient Control on Illness The nature of chronic diseases is that these cannot be cured completely rather need to be managed or controlled. The chronic illness patients have to control their signs and symptoms and keep track of certain parameters. The patient control is "the patient's psychosocial adjustment to the illness and perceived competence and control over symptoms, the future course of the disease and medical care" (Ouschan et al. 2006). Health care being a complexed service needs higher level of participation. The patient participation is associated with better health outcomes by empowering the patients to take control of the chronic illness (Michie et al. 2003). Thus:

H4. Patient participation will mediate the impact of patient education on patient control on illness.

Satisfaction with Doctor The treatment of chronic illness mostly involves the services of a medical expert like diabetologist, medical specialist, dermatologist, urologist, oncologist etc. Accordingly, satisfaction is derived from the services provided by the treating doctor. The active customer participation in service process has an impact on the customer satisfaction (Bitner et al. 1997). The patients involved in health care decisions usually get realistic and more appropriate treatments, lesser complaints and, enjoy better sustainable health outcomes and ultimately experience higher satisfaction (Trede and Higgs 2003). Similarly, Dellande et al. (2004) demonstrated that customer compliance (participation) significantly relates to customer satisfaction. Accordingly, we hypothesized as follows:

H5. Patient participation will mediate the impact of patient education on satisfaction with doctor.

Satisfaction with Life Chronic illness conditions create difficulties and limitations for the patients in their daily life. When patients start participating actively in the treatment of these diseases, they find the ways to adjust in their daily life. They live with these chronic conditions and could be satisfied too with the ongoing life. Satisfaction with life is not objective rather it is subjective and vary from person to person. Life satisfaction is based on a cognitive judgmental process (Diener et al. 1985). This shows that perhaps there is no single criteria of life satisfaction. According to Shin and Johnson (1978) life satisfaction is "a global assessment of a person's quality of life according to his own chosen criteria". The patients with chronic illness conditions take care of themselves by actively participating in the treatment process. This act of participation gives the patients feeling of performing the activities like persons not handicapped with these chronic illnesses. These patients could find new meaning in their life. This resultantly give them a feeling of leading a satisfied life even with chronic illnesses. Therefore, we hypothesized.

H6. Patient participation will mediate the impact of patient education on satisfaction with life

Doctors Psychological Considerations The health psychology literature highlights the importance of biopsychosocial model to be pursued by the doctor in dealing with the patients. The current biopsychosocial perspective in contrary to biomedical perspective (which considered the disease only a biological disorder) puts more emphasis on doctors to treat the patients with greater empathy, respect and psychological adherence (Sarafino and Smith 2014). If doctors while educating the patients pay greater physiological consideration it will enhance the impact of patient education on their ease of processing the educational input in the form of verbal or oral content. Therefore, we hypothesize as:

H7. Psychological considerations strengths the positive relationship between patient education and conceptual fluency

The next section gives the detail of quantitative study.

Methodology

Measures The measures for satisfaction with doctor (Hausman 2004) and satisfaction with life (Diener et al. 1985) were adopted and measure for conceptual fluency was expanded and rephrased to fit our context as used in Journal of marketing by Sirianni et al. (2013). The measures for Psychological considerations, patient perceived control on illness were developed particularly for the current study based on qualitative findings and existing literature. The measures for patient participation was developed as three-dimensional second order construct with the help of 10 items from existing literature (Chan et al. 2010; Gallan et al. 2013; Hausman 2004) and 13 items are developed through exploration of qualitative work. The measures for patient education was developed as three dimensional second order construct with the help of 11 items from existing literature (Auh et al. 2007; Ouschan et al. 2006; Seiders et al. 2015) and 10 items are developed through exploration of qualitative work (the development of measures was part of PhD thesis and is beyond the scope of current paper).

Data collection Data was collected using survey form circulated through survey monkey and self-administered questionnaires given to patients by visiting different hospital's waiting area in major cities of Pakistan. The patients who were under treatment of a chronic disease for at least more than 6 months were chosen through purposive sampling. Firstly, the researcher got the approval from the senior administration of hospital and specialized clinic of chronic disease through written correspondence or power point presentation in order to recruit the participants. Later, consent was obtained from the individual respondents to participate in the survey. 1150 questionnaires in total were distributed (500 through survey Monkey and 650 self-administered paper printed). Out of these 744 filled surveys were received; 54 incomplete forms were excluded, and 690 responses were available for the data analysis. The distribution is given in Table 3.

Data Analysis Initially data cleaning was performed on SPSS 25 for checking the normality of data. After removing 57 respondents identified as outliers, the remaining normally distributed data of 633 respondents was used to run the final analysis in AMOS 24. Firstly, a measurement model was run using all the study variables of first order and then by adding second order constructs of patient participation and patient education. Trough successive deletion of weak and cross loading of observed variables (items) the model was improved. The final measurement model achieved the maximum fit indices of global criteria (χ^2/df = 2.193, TLI = .946, CFI = .951, RMESA = .043, SRMR = .0429, PCLOSE = 1). The reliability and validity test achieve the threshold values of Cronbach alpha, convergent and discriminant validity (AVE > .5, MSV < AVE) as shown in Table 4. All the HTMT ratios are also less than .85 as shown in Table 5.

Table 3 Disease and gender details of research participants

Demographics	Total	%age
	690	100%
Gender:		
Male	393	56.96%
Female	295	42.75%
Other (Transgender)	2	0.29%
Disease:		
Diabetes	109	15.80%
Hypertension (blood pressure)	88	12.75%
Asthma/COPD	39	5.65%
Hepatitis B/C	23	3.33%
Cancer	53	7.68%
Tuberculosis (TB)	7	1.01%
Skin Disease	73	10.58%
Arthritis/joint pain	63	9.13%
Heart problems	61	8.84%
Stroke	8	1.16%
AIDS (HIV)	2	0.29%
Chronic kidney disease (CKD)	59	8.55%
Allergies	17	2.46%
Others (migraine, disorders, chronic pains)	88	12.75%

Structural Model Later the measurement model in AMOS was converted into structural model by removing all the covariance and connecting the variables using single head arrows as per our hypotheses. Gender impact on patient perceived control on illness was controlled. The final structure model fit also achieved the local and global fit indices (χ^2/df = 2.350, TLI = .937, CFI = .942, RMESA = .046, SRMR = .0489, PCLOSE = .988) (Fig. 1).

Results and Discussion

The effect of patient education on patient participation ($\beta = .20$, $\rho < .001$) and conceptual fluency ($\beta = .51$, $\rho < .001$) is positive and significant, validating H1 and H2. The mediations test was performed in AMOS using Bootstrap sample 5000 with CI 95%. Table 6 shows all the mediations hypotheses (H3, H4, H5, H6) are validated whereas the impact of patient education on satisfaction with life is fully mediated through patient participation.

Table 4 Reliability and validity table

Variable	CB Alpha	CR	AVE	MSV	MaxR(H)	Sat_Dr	Pat_Contrl	C_Fluency	Sat_Life	Pyc_Consid	Pat_Edu	Pat_Part
Sat_Dr	0.954	0.955	0.808	0.527	0.956	0.899						
Pat_Contrl	0.89	0.892	0.673	0.428	0.895	0.573***	0.821					
C_Fluency	0.845	0.859	0.605	0.484	0.868	0.637***	0.562***	0.778				
Sat_Life	0.901	0.903	0.7	0.254	0.912	0.433***	0.441***	0.400***	0.836			
Pyc_Consid	0.911	0.914	0.729	0.61	0.928	0.698***	0.533***	0.547***	0.282***	0.854		
Pat_Edu	0.913	0.903	0.757	0.61	0.946	0.656***	0.514***	0.589***	0.261***	0.781***	0.87	
Pat_Part	0.864	0.815	0.595	0.484	0.818	0.541***	0.526***	0.696***	0.403***	0.492***	0.567***	0.771

*** ($p < 0.001$)

Table 5 HTMT ratios showing discriminant validity (Threshold for individual values <.85)

	Sat_Dr	Pat_Contrl	C_Fluency	Sat_Life	Pyc_Consid	Com_F_DT	Com_F_DL	Invl_DM	Com_F_NC	Info_Sharing	P_Compl
Sat_Dr											
Pat_Contrl	0.581										
C_Fluency	0.641	0.576									
Sat_Life	0.427	0.444	0.405								
Pyc_Consid	0.724	0.543	0.573	0.291							
Com_F_DT	0.645	0.483	0.572	0.274	0.715						
Com_F_DL	0.607	0.484	0.585	0.24	0.759	0.806					
Invl_DM	0.416	0.438	0.518	0.337	0.452	0.525	0.454				
Com_F_NC	0.482	0.38	0.415	0.167	0.612	0.652	0.808	0.343			
Info_Sharing	0.422	0.35	0.543	0.288	0.367	0.468	0.385	0.671	0.227		
P_Compl	0.447	0.481	0.558	0.323	0.399	0.444	0.404	0.51	0.259	0.631	

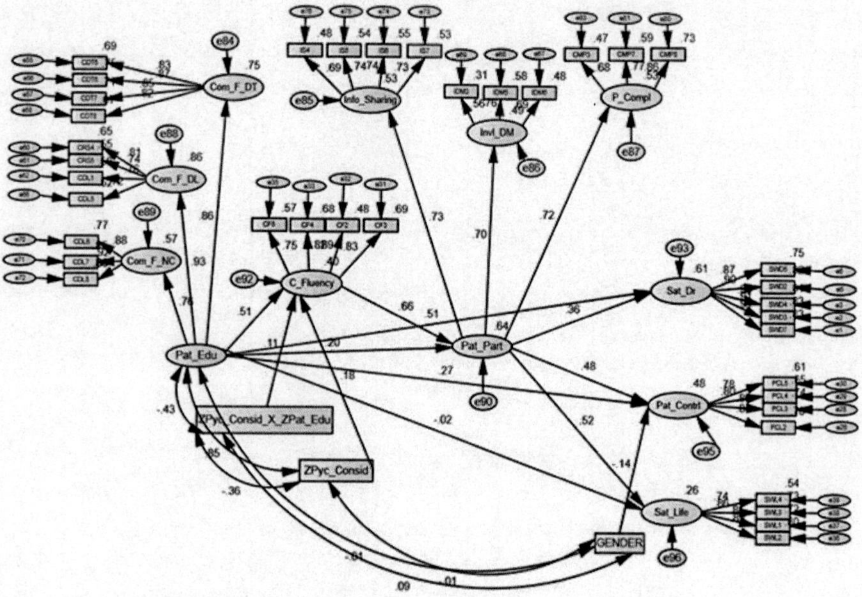

Fig. 1 Structural model using AMOS 25

Table 6 Mediations results using Bootstrapping in AMOS 25

	Total effect	Direct effect	Indirect effect	Observation
Pat_Edu ==> Pat_Part (*via C_Fluency*)	.538*** [.342; .714]	.204** [.074; .350]	.334*** [.185; .527]	Partial mediation
Pat_Edu ==> Sat_Dr (*via Pat_Part*)	.701*** [.572; .803]	.510** [.281; .677]	.191*** [.105; .350]	Partial mediation
Pat_Edu ==> Pat_Contrl (*via Pat_Part*)	.529*** [.373; .662]	.270* [.041; .443]	.259*** [.164; .423]	Partial mediation
Pat_Edu ==> Sat_Life (*via Pat_Part*)	.264*** [.117; .413]	−.016NS [−.243; .159]	.281*** [.168; .468]	Full mediation

*($p < 0.05$)
**($p < 0.01$)
***($p < 0.001$)

The result of moderation shows that impact of all the three variables i.e. independent variable (Pat_Edu, $\beta = .50$***), moderator (Pyc_Consid, $\beta = .18$*) and Interaction term (Pat_Edu_X_Pyc_Consid, $\beta = .11$**) is positive and significant which shows that Psychological considerations strengthen the relationship between patient education and conceptual fluency as shown also in Fig. 2.

Theoretical Contributions Two scales "Patient control on illness" and "Psychological consideration" were developed particularly for this study. Patient education and patient participation was conceptualized as three-dimensional higher order constructs. Refinement and extension were made in measurement scale used for "Conceptual Fluency." Customer participation studies previously are mostly conducted in want-based services the current study gives the insights of need based services like health care.

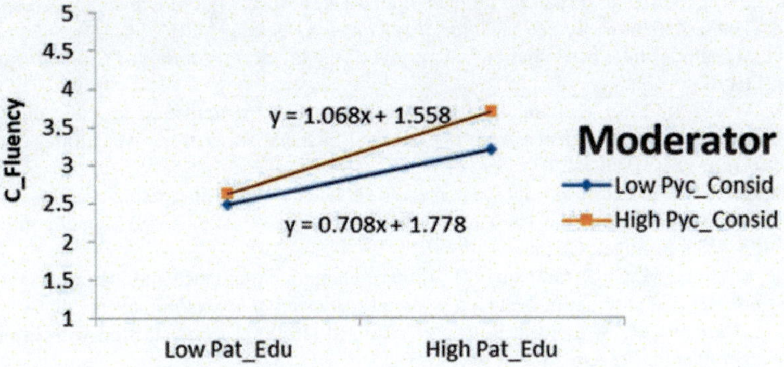

Fig. 2 Moderation effect of Psy_Consideration

Managerial Implications Health care organizations could use the present research in developing training programs for doctors, paramedical and front-line staff for patient education. Irreversible impact of non-participation or wrong participation could be minimized, through proper patient education efforts leading to enhanced patient participation. The mediations results have practical implications for doctors and health care professionals in building satisfaction and patient control on illness.

Limitations and Future Research recommendations Cross sectional data was collected; research should be repeated with longitudinal studies. There could be common method bias as quantitative data was collected for all the variables from same respondent. Objective measures (e.g. biomarkers like blood pressure readings, blood glucose, MRI Image etc.) could be used in experimental studies to investigate the impact of Patient education on patient participation. Some variable like religiosity and emotional support could be included in in future studies as antecedent of patient participation for disease like cancer and kidney failure patients.

References

Auh, S., Bell, S. J., McLeod, C. S., & Shih, E. (2007). Co-production and customer loyalty in financial services. *Journal of Retailing*, *83*(3), 359–370.

Bateson, J. (2002). Are your customers good enough for your service business? *The Academy of Management Executive*, *16*(4), 110–120.

Bateson, J. E. (1985). Self-service consumer: An exploratory study. *Journal of Retailing*, 49-76.

Bendapudi, N., & Leone, R. P. (2003). Psychological implications of customer participation in co-production. *Journal of Marketing*, *67*(1), 14–28.

Berry, L. L., & Bendapudi, N. (2007). Health care: A fertile field for service research. *Journal of Service Research*, *10*(2), 111–122.

Bitner, M. J., Faranda, W. T., Hubbert, A. R., & Zeithaml, V. A. (1997). Customer contributions and roles in service delivery. *International Journal of Service Industry Management*, *8*(3), 193–205.

Bryman, A. (2012). Social Research Methods (4th ed.) New York: Oxford University Press.
Cahill, J. (1995). Patient participation. *Journal of Advanced Nursing*, *22*(5), 561–571.
Cahill, JO. (1998). Patient participation—A review of the literature. *Journal of Clinical Nursing*, *7*(2), 119–128.
Chan, K. W., Yim, C. K., & Lam, S. S. (2010). Is customer participation in value creation a double-edged sword? Evidence from professional financial services across cultures. *Journal of Marketing*, *74*(3), 48–64.
Dabholkar, P. A. (1990). How to improve perceived service quality by increasing customer participation. In Proceedings of the 1990 academy of marketing science (AMS) annual conference (pp. 483–487). Springer, Cham.
Dellande, S., Gilly, M. C., & Graham, J. L. (2004). Gaining compliance and losing weight: The role of the service provider in health care services. *Journal of Marketing*, *68*(3), 78–91.
Diener, E., Emmons, R. A., Larsen, R. J., & Griffin, S. (1985). The satisfaction with life scale. *Journal of Personality Assessment*, *49*(1), 71–75.
Dong, B., Evans, K. R., & Zou, S. (2008). The effects of customer participation in co-created service recovery. *Journal of the Academy of Marketing Science*, *36*(1), 123–137.
Dong, B., & Sivakumar, K. (2017). Customer participation in services: Domain, scope, and boundaries. *Journal of the Academy of Marketing Science*, *45*(6), 944–965.
Eisingerich, A. B., & Bell, S. J. (2006). Relationship marketing in the financial services industry: The importance of customer education, participation and problem management for customer loyalty. *Journal of Financial Services Marketing*, *10*(4), 86–97.
Fang, E. (2008). Customer participation and the trade-off between new product innovativeness and speed to market. *Journal of Marketing*, *72*(4), 90–104.
Fang, E., Palmatier, R. W., & Evans, K. R. (2008). Influence of customer participation on creating and sharing of new product value. *Journal of the Academy of Marketing Science*, *36*(3), 322–336.
Gallan, A. S., Jarvis, C. B., Brown, S. W., & Bitner, M. J. (2013). Customer positivity and participation in services: An empirical test in a health care context. *Journal of the Academy of Marketing Science*, *41*(3), 338–356.
Gold, D. T., & McClung, B. (2006). Approaches to patient education: Emphasizing the long-term value of compliance and persistence. *The American Journal of Medicine*, *119*(4), S32–S37.
Goodwin, C. (1988). "I can do it myself:" training the service consumer to contribute to service productivity. *Journal of Services Marketing*, *2*(4), 71–78.
Guadagnoli, E., & Ward, P. (1998). Patient participation in decision-making. *Social Science & Medicine*, *47*(3), 329–339.
Hausman, A. (2004). Modeling the patient-physician service encounter: Improving patient outcomes. *Journal of the Academy of Marketing Science*, *32*(4), 403–417.
Kincey, J., Bradshaw, P., & Ley, P. (1975). Patients' satisfaction and reported acceptance of advice in general practice. *JR Coll Gen Pract*, *25*(157), 558–566.
Lee, M. P., Yoon, C., & Mitchell, A. A. (2004). *Perceptual and conceptual fluency as antecedents of the mere exposure effect*. School of Business, Singapore Management University.
Lovelock, C. (2011). *Services Marketing, 7/e*. Pearson Education India.
Lovelock, C. H., & Young, R. F. (1979). Look to consumers to increase productivity. *Harvard Business Review*, *57*(3), 168–178.
McColl-Kennedy, J. R., Snyder, H., Elg, M., Witell, L., Helkkula, A., Hogan, S. J., & Anderson, L. (2017). The changing role of the health care customer: Review, synthesis and research agenda. *Journal of Service Management*, *28*(1), 2–33.
McColl-Kennedy, J. R., Vargo, S. L., Dagger, T. S., Sweeney, J. C., & van Kasteren, Y. (2012). Health care customer value cocreation practice styles. *Journal of Service Research*, *15*(4), 370–389.
McCracken, G. (1988). *The long interview* (Vol. 13). Sage.
Michie, S., Miles, J., & Weinman, J. (2003). Patient-centredness in chronic illness: What is it and does it matter? *Patient Education and Counseling*, *51*(3), 197–206.

Mills, P. K., & Morris, J. H. (1986). Clients as "partial" employees of service organizations: Role development in client participation. *Academy of Management Review*, *11*(4), 726–735.

Ostrom, A. L., Parasuraman, A., Bowen, D. E., Patricio, L., & Voss, C. A. (2015). Service research priorities in a rapidly changing context. *Journal of Service Research*, *18*(2), 127–159.

Ouschan, R., Sweeney, J., & Johnson, L. (2006). Customer empowerment and relationship outcomes in healthcare consultations. *European Journal of Marketing*, *40*(9/10), 1068–1086.

Sarafino, E. P., & Smith, T. W. (2014). *Health psychology: Biopsychosocial interactions*. John Wiley & Sons.

Seiders, K., Flynn, A. G., Berry, L. L., & Haws, K. L. (2015). Motivating customers to adhere to expert advice in professional services: A medical service context. *Journal of Service Research*, *18*(1), 39–58.

Shin, D. C., & Johnson, D. M. (1978). Avowed happiness as an overall assessment of the quality of life. *Social Indicators Research*, *5*(1–4), 475–492.

Sirianni, N. J., Bitner, M. J., Brown, S. W., & Mandel, N. (2013). Branded service encounters: Strategically aligning employee behavior with the brand positioning. *Journal of Marketing*, *77*(6), 108–123.

Trede, F., & Higgs, J. (2003). Re-framing the clinician's role in collaborative clinical decision making Re-thinking practice knowledge and the notion of clinician–patient relationships. *Learning in Health and Social Care*, *2*(2), 66–73.

Whittlesea, B. W. (1993). Illusions of familiarity. *Journal of Experimental Psychology: Learning, Memory, and Cognition*, *19*(6), 1235.

The Moderating Roles of Time Pressure and Individualism for Retail Event Sponsorship: An Abstract

Buduo Wang, Angeline Close Scheinbaum, Siyan Li, and Anjala Krishen

Abstract Event sponsorship is a form of promotion where the underwriting of a special event supports corporate objectives, such as stimulating sales of products (Javalgi et al. 1994). It has become an increasingly popular marketing strategy for retailers and other brands to provide an enjoyable experience and stimulate more purchasing. Although scholars have examined the general effects of event marketing and sponsorship on consumers' purchase intentions, studies have not been conducted to investigate whether or not the effects of event marketing and retail sponsorship vary for: (1) shoppers in a hurry (vs. those with time available while shopping) or (2) shoppers from collectivist cultures (vs. those from individualist cultures). These questions are worth asking given that retail events, by nature, consist of some attributes (e.g., sensational or emotional) that are likely to be more appealing to some consumers depending on these two considerations.

Therefore, this study examines the impact of shopping enjoyment (as a personality trait) on purchase intentions for retail sponsors as mediated by event entertainment. More importantly, time pressure while shopping (an individual difference—Model 1) and the individualism level of international tourist's country-of-origin (a cultural difference—Model 2) are examined as moderators of the relationship between shopping enjoyment and event entertainment.

The method is a set of field studies for a prominent retailer at a high-end shopping mall. This weekend-long filed study collects data from 21 fashion shows sponsored by the retailer (n = 583). The results show that shopping enjoyment positively affects event entertainment, which then leads to enhanced purchase intentions for the retail sponsor. Moreover, time pressure while shopping and individualism each

B. Wang (✉) · S. Li
The University of Texas at Austin, Austin, TX, USA
e-mail: buduo.wang@utexas.edu; siyan_li@utexas.edu

A. C. Scheinbaum
Clemson University, Clemson, SC, USA
e-mail: aschein@clemson.edu

A. Krishen
University of Nevada, Las Vegas, NV, USA
e-mail: anjala.krishen@unlv.edu

F. Pantoja, S. Wu (eds.), *From Micro to Macro: Dealing with Uncertainties in the Global Marketplace*, Developments in Marketing Science: Proceedings of the Academy of Marketing Science, https://doi.org/10.1007/978-3-030-89883-0_111

moderates the role of shopping enjoyment on event entertainment. The effect of shopping enjoyment on event entertainment is found to be stronger for shoppers with more available time (vs. shoppers in a hurry). Meanwhile, the positive relationship between shopping enjoyment and event entertainment only exists for shoppers from collectivist cultures with low individualism scores. Both theoretical and practical implications are provided.

Keywords Retailing · Shopping enjoyment · Shopping time · Event marketing · Sponsorship

References Available Upon Request

Determinants and Process of Negative Customer Engagement Behaviors

Diem Khac Xuan Do, Kaleel Rahman, and Linda Robinson

Abstract Understanding negative customer engagement is as important as positive customer engagement. This study aims to investigate determinants and process of negative customer engagement behaviors. Negative service quality disconfirmation and justice are proposed to be determinants of negative customer engagement behaviors that are examined in a process, including complaining, negatively engaged complaining, disengaged behavior, switching and negative word-of-mouth. Survey data collected from 404 respondents experiencing negative critical incidents in a service context was used to test the conceptual model. The data was analyzed using Structural Equation Modeling. Bootstrapping approach in SPSS Macro PROCESS was employed to test the process of negative customer engagement behaviors. The results show that negative disconfirmation positively affects complaining while perceived injustice does not result in complaining. The findings support two processes of negative customer engagement behaviors: (1) Complaining → Negatively Engaged Complaining → Switching → Negative word-of-mouth; and (2) Complaining → Disengaged behavior → Switching → Negative word-of-mouth. This result provides empirical evidence of the dynamic nature of customer engagement. Understanding how negative customer engagement behaviors occur enables management to have appropriate strategies to prevent the development of negative customer engagement behaviors.

Keywords Negative engagement · Disengagement · Negative disconfirmation · Justice

D. K. X. Do (✉) · K. Rahman · L. Robinson
RMIT University, Melbourne, VIC, Australia
e-mail: diem.do@rmit.edu.au; kaleel.rahman@rmit.edu.au; linda.robinson2@rmit.edu.au

F. Pantoja, S. Wu (eds.), *From Micro to Macro: Dealing with Uncertainties in the Global Marketplace*, Developments in Marketing Science: Proceedings of the Academy of Marketing Science, https://doi.org/10.1007/978-3-030-89883-0_112

Introduction

Customer engagement (CE) has transpired as a new metric of customer management in the current decade (Verhoef et al. 2010). Different from traditional marketing focusing on customer purchase, engagement marketing utilizes customer resources that bring value to the firm beyond financial contribution (Harmeling et al. 2018). However, CE can be positive or negative (Van Doorn et al. 2010), engaged or disengaged (Kumar and Pansari 2016). While positive engagement adds significant value to the firm, negative engagement or disengagement has adverse effects on the firm's reputation, customer equity, financial performance (Bowden et al. 2015; Juric et al. 2016). It is posited that negative information (e.g. negative word-of-mouth) has stronger influences on a customer's brand evaluation or purchase decision than positive information (Oliver 1997). In practice, negative customer engagement (NCE) appears as negative comments on Facebook (Hollebeek and Chen 2014), blog writing (Juric et al. 2016). Given that, research on NCE has remained scant to date. There is inconsistency in NCE conceptualization and drivers. Hollebeek and Chen (2014) view NCE as the opposite form of positive CE and suggest the same antecedents for both positive engagement and negative engagement, whilst Juric et al. (2016) argue that NCE is not merely the reverse form of positive engagement. It is a distinctive and complex construct that is triggered by perceived threats to self and dissonance resulting from negative critical events. Other authors view negative engagement and disengagement as a negative valence of CE that customers have negative orientation towards the firm; but they are distinguished based on the intensity level and activeness of negative expressions (Dolan et al. 2016; Naumann et al. 2017). Given research on NCE is exploratory in nature and specific drivers of NCE are not known, this study examines determinants of NCE in a quantitative study. Based on Expectancy Disconfirmation theory (EDT) (Oliver 1980) and Justice/Inequity theory (Adams 1965; Homans 1961), we specify negative service quality disconfirmation and justice as determinants of NCE behaviors, including disengaged and negatively engaged behaviors. Further, it is argued that CE is a dynamic process depending on context; however, this characteristic has not been empirically investigated. Based on negative critical incidents experienced by customers in a service consumption context and literature review, the process of NCE behaviors is suggested and examined in this study. Understanding how NCE behaviors occur is useful for management to prevent NCE development. Specifically, this study aims to address the following research questions: *(1) What determines NCE behaviors? and (2) How do NCE behaviors occur?*

Theoretical Background

Negative Customer Engagement

NCE is viewed as the opposite form of positive CE and defined as a customer's unfavorable thoughts, emotions and behaviors towards a brand during brand interactions (Hollebeek and Chen 2014). Contrast to this view, Juric et al. (2016) distinguish NCE with CE with negative valence. Specifically, NCE is viewed as a psychological process catalyzed by perceived threats to self. To reduce dissonance associated with threats, customers premeditatedly adopt coping behaviors with the intention of causing harms to the brand. However, CE with negative valence may result from personal motivation of enhancing individual prestige with friends. In this sense, CE with negative valence does not aim to cause harms to the brand but still focuses on value cocreation. Other authors view disengagement and negative engagement as a negative valence of CE (Bowden et al. 2016; Naumann et al. 2017). While negatively engaged customers actively and dedicatedly expresses strong negative thoughts, emotions and behaviors, disengaged customers adopt a passive, slightly negative orientation towards a brand or service provider (Bowden et al. 2016; Dolan et al. 2016). Consistent with this view, NCE behaviors in this study include disengaged and negatively behaviors. We define NCE behaviors as actions that have negative consequences (financial or non-financial) for the service provider in a short or long run. Adopting dimensions found by Naumann et al. (2017), 'neglect' represents disengaged behavior and 'complaining', 'negative word-of-mouth' (negative WOM) and 'switching' indicate negatively engaged behaviors. Complaining in this study is categorized as complaining and negatively engaged complaining indicating the intensity level of negativity of the actions. Specifically, complaining refers to a complaint made to the service provider seeking redress for the problem. Negatively engaged complaining includes *vindictive complaining*, *online complaining* and *third-party complaining* that indicate a stronger negative level of customer response to the unfavorable service experience.

Antecedents of Negative Customer Engagement

Research on NCE is underdeveloped to date, particularly its drivers. Hollebeek and Chen (2014) suggest the same antecedents for both positive and negative engagement. As such, the key tenets and drivers of NCE are not fully understood. The low level or absence of antecedents of positive engagement may not result in negative engagement. Juric et al. (2016) explain NCE triggered by perceived threats to self. However, the threats are not discussed in detail. Similarly, Bowden et al. (2015) explain disengagement based on service category (utilitarian/participative services) that is too broad to understand the underlying reasons of customer disengagement.

Common to these studies is exploratory in nature. Therefore, it is necessary for further research to investigate determinants of NCE.

Conceptual Framework

Expectancy Disconfirmation theory (EDT) (Oliver 1980) and Justice theory (Adams 1965; Homans 1961) are used to explain determinants of NCE behaviors in this study. These two theories are foundational and trusted theories that are well applied to explain customer satisfaction and customer reactions in conflict situations (Grégoire et al. 2010; Smith et al. 1999; Sweeney et al. 2005; Verma 2003). EDT hold that customer satisfaction is dependent on customer expectation of product performance before purchase and disconfirmation after purchase. Disconfirmation refers to a comparison of product performance and customer expectation. Product performance higher or lower than customer expectation results in positive or negative disconfirmation, respectively. Negative disconfirmation attributed to the service provider results in customer distrust (Darke et al. 2010) and negative emotions (Oliver 1993) that motivate customers react against the offending service provider (Plé and Cáceres 2010; Smith 2013). Justice theory implies a comparison of inputs and outcomes within an individual or a comparison of the ratio inputs/outcomes of an individual with others who have a direct exchange relationship or have the same exchange relationship with a third-party. A perception of injustice occurs when the outcomes are not perceived to be comparative with the inputs or the ratio of inputs/outcomes perceived not equal to that of others. In such case, 'tension' resulting from perceived unfairness motivates individuals act to reduce inequity or regain equity (Adams 1965). We suggest negative service quality disconfirmation, distributive injustice, procedural injustice and interactional injustice as determinants of NCE, including disengaged and negatively engaged behaviors (see Fig. 1).

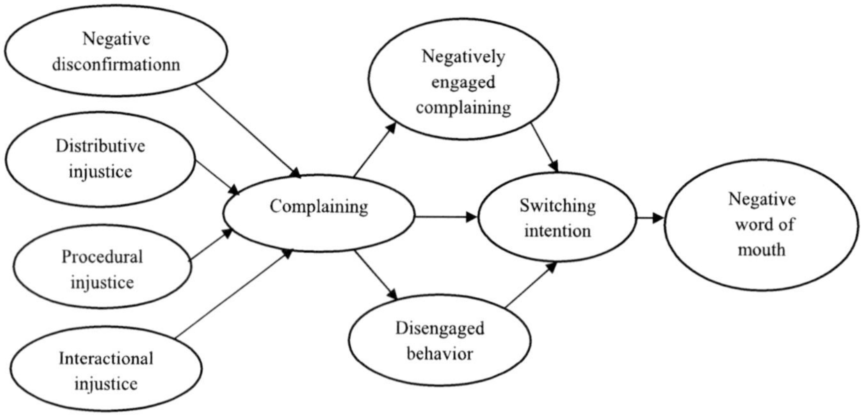

Fig. 1 Conceptual framework

CE is well recognized as a context-dependent construct that generates different levels of CE (Brodie et al. 2011). In addition, CE is viewed as a dynamic process (Brodie et al. 2011; Van Doorn et al. 2010) that develops over time. It is argued that CE behaviors would be changed depending on the quality of service experience (Van Doorn et al. 2010). Therefore, we suggest disengaged and negatively engaged behaviors experienced by respondents in this study occur in a process that are contingent on the context during the service experience. It is argued that complaining is a dynamic process. Depending on the context, complaining can be expressed in different forms (Blodgett et al. 1993; Tronvoll 2012). For instance, if customer complaint is handled well, it would reduce the likelihood of third-party complaining, negative WOM and increase the tendency of customer repatronage (Blodgett et al. 1993). Tronvoll (2012) posits complaining as a process resulted from negative incidents that trigger unfavorable service experience. This emphasizes that complaining does not just occur after purchase related to the outcome, but it can happen during service provision. Based on these arguments, we suggest complaining to the service provider seeking for redress as the initial action taken by customers when they experience negative disconfirmation or injustice during service process (see Fig. 1).

To examine the interrelationship between NCE behaviors, we suggest and examine the following serial mediations. *First,* the effect of complaining on switching through negatively engaged complaining (Complaining → Negatively Engaged Complaining → Switching) or disengaged behavior (Complaining → Disengaged behavior → Switching). *Second,* the effect of complaining on negative WOM through negatively engaged complaining, disengaged behavior and switching (**1.** Complaining → Negatively Engaged Complaining → Switching → Negative WOM; **2.** Complaining → Disengaged behavior → Switching → Negative WOM; **3.** Complaining → Negatively Engaged Complaining → Negative WOM; **4.** Complaining → Disengaged behavior → Negative WOM; **5.** Complaining → Switching → Negative WOM) (see Fig. 1).

Methodology

We use Critical Incident Technique (CIT) method (Flanagan 1954; Gremler 2004) integrated with Survey approach to investigate determinants of NCE behaviors and understand the interrelationship of these behaviors. Respondents were required to tell their negative critical service experiences and provide information regarding (1) the specific circumstances related to the negative event, (2) what they thought, feel and act during and after the event. Then, based on their own stories, respondents were required to complete a survey questionnaire that is developed to test the relationships between constructs. Face to face interview at shopping mall centers in Ho Chi Minh City, Vietnam and self-administered online survey were conducted to collect data. The usable sample for data analysis is 404. The sample is dominated with female (69.8%), age range 26–35 (38.4%), graduated and full-time employed (65%, 77.5%; respectively). The reported negative critical events are related to a wide range of service industry, including retailing, telecommunication, banking, hospital, tourist, hospitality, repair and warranty service.

Measurement instrument was developed based on existing scales borrowed from previous studies with seven-point Likert scale (1: strongly disagree, 7: strongly agree). Negative Service Quality Disconfirmation was measured by three items adopted from Oliver (1980) and Dabholkar et al. (2000). The items measured Distributive/Procedural/Interactional Justice were borrowed from Tax et al. (1998) and Smith et al. (1999). We measured Complaining with four items borrowed from Swan and Oliver (1989). Disengaged behavior was measured by Neglect found by Naumann et al. (2017). The scale for Neglect was adopted from Ping (1993) with five items. Negatively Engaged Complaining was considered a second-order construct measured by Vindictive Complaining, Online Complaining and Third-party Complaining. The scale three items measured Vindictive Complaining was borrowed from Grégoire and Fisher (2008). Online Complaining was measured with three items taken from Grégoire et al. (2010). We measured Third-party Complaining with four items adopted from Singh (1988). The scale for Switching Intention was borrowed from Burnham et al. (2003) with five items. Negative WOM was measured with three items adopted from Zeithaml et al. (1996). The questionnaire was originally developed in English, then translated into Vietnamese. A back-translation approach was used to ensure the validity and understanding of the Vietnamese questionnaire.

Data Analysis and Results

Measurement Model

The measurement model was tested using Confirmatory Factor Analysis approach. Several items were eliminated to fit with the data. The adjusted model achieved a good fit with the observed data (x^2 = 696.149, df = 423, p = .000, x^2/df = 1.646, Comparative Fit Index (CFI) = .955, Root Mean Square Error of Approximation (RMSEA) = .040 (.035–.045, 90% CI), Standardized Root Mean Square Residual (SRMR) = .051) (Hair et al. 2010). The convergent validity of all constructs was satisfied with all factor loadings above 0.5, averaged variance extracted (AVE) greater than 0.5 and composite reliability (CR) above 0.7, except CR of negative disconfirmation (ND) (0.675) (Hair et al. 2010). Discriminant validity among constructs were also achieved with the square root values of the constructs higher than the absolute correlation values between the construct and other constructs (Fornell and Larcker 1981; Hair et al. 2010) (see Table 1).

Table 1 Means, standard deviations and correlations

	Mean	SD	SWI	ND	DJ	IJ	PJ	DB	NEC	COB	NWOM
SWI	5.80	0.98	**0.751**								
ND	6.29	0.64	0.430	**0.714**							
DJ	6.12	0.72	0.380	0.688	**0.713**						
IJ	5.45	1.17	0.300	0.360	0.501	**0.779**					
PJ	5.27	1.29	0.218	0.332	0.459	0.547	**0.711**				
DB	4.12	1.48	0.356	0.208	0.203	0.171	0.253	**0.710**			
NEC	3.31	1.32	0.163	0.102	0.136	0.052	0.109	−0.222	**0.740**		
COB	5.43	1.49	0.034	0.199	0.066	−0.110	−0.007	−0.258	0.303	**0.802**	
NWOM	6.10	0.87	0.636	0.558	0.560	0.416	0.271	0.270	0.201	0.087	**0.751**

SWI Switching, *ND* Negative disconfirmation, *DJ* Distributive injustice, *IJ* Interactional injustice, *PJ* Procedural injustice, *DB* Disengaged behavior, *NEC* Negatively engaged complaining, *COB* Complaining behavior, *NWOM* Negative word-of-mouth

Common Method Variance (CMV)

CMV would bias the findings of this study as cross-sectional survey data was used (Podsakoff et al. 2003). Therefore, we applied procedural remedies to mitigate the effects of CMV, such as items checked by marketing experts, back-translation approach employed, pilot test to ensure the questionnaire understandable by respondents. In addition, the items were intentionally dispersed through the survey mixing both positive and negative items to prevent and identify ungagged responses. Respondents were also advised the anonymity and confidentiality of their responses. In addition to procedural remedies, we employed full collinearity test (Kock and Lynn 2012) testing collinearity among variables in the conceptual model and marker variable technique (Lindell and Whitney 2001) based on correlations between variables to test CMV. Risk takers construct that is not theoretically related to other constructs in the conceptual model was used as a marker variable. The results indicate that CMV was not a significant issue in this study (VIF < 3.3) (Kock and Lynn 2012) and the correlations between substantive variables were still statistically significant (t-value >1.96, two tailed t-test) after controlling CMV (Lindell and Whitney 2001; Malhotra et al. 2017).

Hypothesis Testing

Structural Equation Modeling (SEM) in AMOS was used to test hypotheses. The model including both measurement and relationships between constructs showed a good fit with the observed data (x^2 = 849.054, df = 443, x^2/df = 1.917, CFI = .933, RMSEA = .048 (.043–.053, 90% CI), SRMR = .098) (Hair et al. 2010). The findings indicate negative disconfirmation positively related to complaining (β = .294, $p < 0.01$) while distributive injustice and procedural injustice show no statistically significant relationships with complaining. Interactional injustice has a negative impact on complaining (β = −.208, $p < 0.05$). Complaining is positively related to negatively engaged complaining (β = .307, $p < 0.001$) and negatively associated with disengaged behavior (β = −.257, $p < 0.001$). Negatively engaged complaining and disengaged behavior have positive influences on switching intention (β = .225, $p < 0.001$; β = .416, $p < 0.001$). The relationship between complaining and switching intention is not supported. Switching intention has a positive impact on negative word-of-mouth (β = .642, $p < 0.001$) (see Table 2).

To examine the process of negative customer engagement behaviors under the effects of negative disconfirmation and injustice, we further conducted a series of mediation analysis using macro PROCESS in SPSS (Hayes 2018). Percentile bootstrapping approach with 5000 samples was performed to construct confidence intervals (CI) at 95% significant level. If the confidence interval straddles zero, we cannot certainly claim that the indirect effect is supported (Hayes 2018). First, we test the indirect effect of complaining on switching intention through negatively engaged complaining/disengaged behavior. The findings show that the effect of complaining on switching intention is mediated by negatively engaged complaining (.031, CI [.012, .052]), disengaged behavior (−.049, CI [−.076, −.025]). Second, we examine the indirect effect of complaining on negative word-of-mouth through negatively engaged complaining, disengaged behavior and switching intention. The results indicate the indirect of complaining of negative word-of-mouth is mediated by (1) disengaged behavior (−.014, CI [−.029, −.001]), (2) a serial mediation of

Table 2 Results for structural equation modeling

Independent variable	Dependent variable				
	Complaining	Negatively engaged complaining	Disengaged behavior	Switching intention	Negative word-of-mouth
Negative disconfirmaiton	.294 **				
Distributive injustice	−.043 (ns)				
Procedural injustice	.027 (ns)				
Interactional injustice	−.208 *				
Complaining		.307 ***	−.257 ***	.085 (ns)	
Negatively engaged complaining				.225 ***	
Disengaged behavior				.416 ***	
Switching intention					.642 ***
R-squared	0.078	0.094	0.066	0.210	0.413

N = 404, * $p < 0.05$, ** $p < 0.01$, *** $p < 0.001$, ns: non-significant negatively engaged complaining—switching intention (.012, CI [.005, .021]), (3) disengaged behavior—switching intention (−.019, [−.033, −.009]). Hence, the findings support the proposed process of NCE behaviors.

Discussion and Implications

Theoretical Implications

This study suggests a process of NCE behaviors and empirically investigate this process under determinants of negative service quality disconfirmation and justice perception. The findings reveal that negative disconfirmation is positively related to complaining while perception of injustice shows no relation with complaining. These findings support previous studies that negative disconfirmation is more related to complaining while perceived injustice is more likely to result in stronger actions after complaining (Oliver and Swan 1989; Schneider and Bowen 1999). The findings can be explained by the mechanism of comparison of negative disconfirmation and justice. Negative disconfirmation is a comparison of service performance with customer expectations. The expectations in the context of this study were created by the service provider through advertising or promises before purchase. These promises establish standards of service quality/performance in the minds of customers. Therefore, when service quality is not performed as the standards, customers have strong evidence to make complaints to the offending service provider. Alternatively, the comparison standards in fairness judgement are passively associated with interpersonal relationship within society (Oliver and Swan 1989). In other words, the expectation standards of justice are based on individuals' social experiences. They observe a reference person or group and make comparisons. As such, the comparison standards are more subjective depending on every person. This might inhibit customers to make complaints to service providers when they perceive injustice.

Complaining is found to have positive impact on negatively engaged complaining. This is consistent with the literature on CE that the intensity of NCE would be increased when customers experience multiple negative events (Juric et al. 2016; Van Doorn et al. 2010). When customer complaint is not addressed, customers are likely to adopt negatively engaged complaining, such as shouting, forcefully arguing, making complaint online or to a third-party. The negative relationship between complaining and disengaged behavior supports the different nature between the two concepts. While complaining illustrates customer approach to the service provider seeking for redress; disengaged behavior describes customers separate themselves from involving in the problems or the provider (Bowden et al. 2016; Dolan et al. 2016). Negatively engaged complaining and disengaged behavior have positive effects on switching intention. This is consistent with the arguments that negative engagement and disengagement may lead to customer switching (Bowden et al.

2015; Juric et al. 2016). Switching in this case is also explained by the Inequity theory (Adams 1965) that individuals will leave the field when they perceive no means to cope with unfairness. Switching is positively related to negative word-of-mouth. This supports the finding that customers are more likely spread negative word-of-mouth about the service/service provider if the reason for switching is due to customer dissatisfaction with the service/offending provider (de Matos and Rossi 2008; Wangenheim 2005).

The present study provides empirical evidence of dynamic nature of CE behaviors depending on context (Brodie et al. 2011; Van Doorn et al. 2010). The results reveal complaining does not directly lead to switching or negative word-of-mouth. Indeed, the effect of complaining on switching/negative word-of-mouth is explained through negatively engaged complaining or disengaged behavior. After complaining, customers may take negatively engaged complaining such as vindictive complaining, online complaining or third-party complaining to react against the offending service provider and then finish using the service. Alternatively, customers may become disengaged, but they will change to another service provider and spread negative word-of-mouth.

Managerial Implications

Service firms firstly should ensure core services rightly delivered to customers as what was promised. Customers may feel cheated and leave the service when service performance is not as the promises. In addition, customers should be treated fairly during service provision not just after complaining as customers are not likely to make complaints when they perceive unfairness. However, they become disengaged or negatively engaged; then switching and spreading negative word-of-mouth.

This study sheds light on the process of NCE behaviors to management. Understanding how NCE behaviors emerge enables managers develop marketing strategies to prevent them. For instance, negatively engaged complaining, disengaged behavior, switching or negative word-of-mouth arisen after customers make complaint to seek for redress. Hence, it is necessary for service providers to address customer complaints in the first instance. Customers should be made satisfied after complaining to prevent complaining evolve to negatively engaged complaining or disengaged behavior. When negatively engaged complaining and disengaged behavior are well monitored, switching and negative word-of-mouth are less likely to happen.

Limitation and Future Research

Although we rely on theories and respondent interviews to propose the process of NCE behaviors, cross sectional survey data of this study may not strong enough to convince the findings. Hence, other research approaches should be employed to investigate the process of NCE behaviors, such as experimental or longitudinal study. In addition to service context, NCE behaviors are argued to be contingent on customer resources (Brodie et al. 2011; Juric et al. 2016). Hence, it is useful for future research to examine how disengaged/negatively engaged behaviors are related to costs/benefits (e.g., time, effort), personality traits (e.g., self-confidence/efficacy), customer relationship with service providers.

References

Adams, J. S. (1965). Inequity In Social Exchange. In B. Leonard (Ed.), *Advances in Experimental Social Psychology* (Vol. 2, pp. 267-299): Academic Press.

Blodgett, J. G., Granbois, D. H., & Walters, R. G. (1993). The effects of perceived justice on complainants' negative word-of-mouth behavior and repatronage intentions. *Journal of Retailing, 69*(4), 399-428.

Bowden, J. L.-H., Gabbott, M., & Naumann, K. (2015). Service relationships and the customer disengagement – engagement conundrum. *Journal of Marketing Management, 31*(7-8), 774-806. doi:https://doi.org/10.1080/0267257X.2014.983143

Bowden, J. L.-H., Luoma-Aho, V., & Naumann, K. (2016). Developing a spectrum of positive to negative citizen engagement. In R. J. Brodie, L. D. Hollebeek, & J. Conduit (Eds.), Customer Engagement: Contemporary Issues and Challenges: Taylor & Francis.

Brodie, R. J., Hollebeek, L. D., Jurić, B., & Ilić, A. (2011). Customer Engagement: Conceptual Domain, Fundamental Propositions, and Implications for Research. *Journal of Service Research, 14*(3), 252-271. doi:https://doi.org/10.1177/1094670511411703

Burnham, T. A., Frels, J. K., & Mahajan, V. (2003). Consumer switching costs: A typology, antecedents, and consequences. *Journal of the Academy of Marketing Science, 31*(2), 109. doi:https://doi.org/10.1177/0092070302250897

Dabholkar, P. A., Shepherd, C. D., & Thorpe, D. I. (2000). A comprehensive framework for service quality: an investigation of critical conceptual and measurement issues through a longitudinal study. *Journal of Retailing, 76*(2), 139-173. https://doi.org/10.1016/S0022-4359(00)00029-4

Darke, P. R., Ashworth, L., & Main, K. J. (2010). Great expectations and broken promises: misleading claims, product failure, expectancy disconfirmation and consumer distrust. *Journal of the Academy of Marketing Science, 38*(3), 347-362. doi:https://doi.org/10.1007/s11747-009-0168-7

de Matos, C. A., & Rossi, C. A. V. (2008). Word-of-mouth communications in marketing: a meta-analytic review of the antecedents and moderators. *Journal of the Academy of Marketing Science, 36*(4), 578-596. doi:https://doi.org/10.1007/s11747-008-0121-1

Dolan, R., Conduit, J., & Fahy, J. (2016). Social media engagement: A construct of positively and negatively valenced engagement behaviours. In L. D. H. R. J. Brodie, J. Conduit (Ed.), Customer Engagement: Contemporary Issues and Challenges (pp. 102-123). London: Routledge.

Flanagan, J. C. (1954). The critical incident technique. *Psychological Bulletin, 51*(4), 327-358. https://doi.org/10.1037/h0061470

Fornell, C., & Larcker, D. F. (1981). Evaluating structural equation models with unobserved variables and measurement error. *Journal of Marketing Research, 28*(1), 39-50.

Grégoire, Y., & Fisher, R. J. (2008). Customer betrayal and retaliation: when your best customers become your worst enemies. *Journal of the Academy of Marketing Science, 36*(2), 247-261. doi:https://doi.org/10.1007/s11747-007-0054-0

Grégoire, Y., Laufer, D., & Tripp, T. M. (2010). A comprehensive model of customer direct and indirect revenge: understanding the effects of perceived greed and customer power. *Journal of the Academy of Marketing Science, 38*(6), 738-758. doi:https://doi.org/10.1007/s11747-009-0186-5

Gremler, D. D. (2004). The Critical Incident Technique in Service Research. *Journal of Service Research, 7*(1), 65-89. doi:https://doi.org/10.1177/1094670504266138

Hair, J. J. F., Black, W. C., Babin, B. J., & Anderson, R. E. (2010). *Multivariate Data Analysis: A global perspective* (7th ed.). Upper Saddle River, New Jersey: Pearson Prentice Hall.

Harmeling, C. M., Moeffett, J. W., & Palmatier, R. W. (2018). Conclusion: Informing Customer Engagement Marketing and Future Research. In R. W. Palmatier, V. Kumar, & C. M. Harmeling (Eds.), *Customer Engagement Marketing*. Cham, Switzerland: Palgrave Macmillan US.

Hayes, A. F. A. (2018). *Introduction to mediation, moderation, and conditional process analysis : a regression-based approach* (2nd edition). New York, New York London, [England]: The Guilford Press.

Hollebeek, L. D., & Chen, T. (2014). Exploring positively- versus negatively-valenced brand engagement: a conceptual model. *Journal of Product & Brand Management, 23*(1), 62-74. doi:https://doi.org/10.1108/JPBM-06-2013-0332

Homans, G. G. (1961). *Social Behavior: Its Elementary Forms*. New York, NY: Harcourt Brace.

Juric, B., Smith, S., Wilks, G. (2016). Negative customer brand engagement: an overview of conceptual and blog-based findings. In R. J. Brodie, L. D. Hollebeek, J. Conduit (Eds.), Customer Engagement : Contemporary issues and challenges (pp. 278-294). London: Routledge.

Kock, N., & Lynn, G. (2012). Lateral Collinearity and Misleading Results in Variance-Based SEM: An Illustration and Recommendations. *Journal of the Association for Information Systems, 13*(7), 546-580. doi:https://doi.org/10.17705/1jais.00302

Kumar, V., & Pansari, A. (2016). Competitive Advantage Through Engagement. *Journal of Marketing Research (JMR), 53*(4), 497-514. doi:https://doi.org/10.1509/jmr.15.0044

Lindell, M. K., & Whitney, D. J. (2001). Accounting for common method variance in cross-sectional research designs. *Journal of Applied Psychology, 86*(1), 114.

Malhotra, N. K., Schaller, T. K., & Patil, A. (2017). Common Method Variance in Advertising Research: When to Be Concerned and How to Control for It. *Journal of Advertising, 46*(1), 193-212. doi:https://doi.org/10.1080/00913367.2016.1252287

Naumann, K., Bowden, J. L.-H., & Gabbott, M. (2017). A Multi-Valenced Perspective on Consumer Engagement Within a Social Service. *Journal of Marketing Theory and Practice, 25*(2), 171-188. doi:https://doi.org/10.1080/10696679.2016.1270772

Oliver, R. L. (1980). A Cognitive Model of the Antecedents and Consequences of Satisfaction Decisions. *Journal of Marketing Research, 17*(4), 460-469. doi:https://doi.org/10.2307/3150499

Oliver, R. L. (1993). Cognitive, Affective, and Attribute Bases of the Satisfaction Response. *Journal of Consumer Research, 20*(3), 418-430.

Oliver, R. L. (1997). *Satisfaction: A Behavioral Perspective on the Consumer*. New York, NY: McGraw-Hill.

Oliver, R. L., & Swan, J. E. (1989). Equity and Disconfirmation Perceptions as Influences on Merchant and Product Satisfaction. *Journal of Consumer Research, 16*(3), 372-383.

Ping, R. A. (1993). The effects of satisfaction and structural constraints on retailer exiting, voice, loyalty, opportunism, and neglect. *Journal of Retailing, 69*(3), 320-352. https://doi.org/10.1016/0022-4359(93)90010-G

Plé, L., & Cáceres, R. C. (2010). Not always co-creation: introducing interactional co-destruction of value in service-dominant logic. *The Journal of Services Marketing, 24*(6), 430-437. https://doi.org/10.1108/08876041011072546

Podsakoff, P. M., MacKenzie, S. B., Lee, J. Y., & Podsakoff, N. P. (2003). Common method biases in behavioral research: a critical review of the literature and recommended remedies. *Journal of Applied Psychology, 88*(5), 879.

Schneider, B., & Bowen, D. E. (1999). Understanding Customer Delight and Outrage. *Sloan Management Review, 41*(1), 35-45.

Singh, J. (1988). Consumer Complaint Intentions and Behavior: Definitional and Taxonomical Issues. *Journal of Marketing, 52*(1), 93-107. doi:https://doi.org/10.2307/1251688

Smith, A. K., Bolton, R. N., & Wagner, J. (1999). A model of customer satisfaction with service encounters involving failure and recovery. *Journal of Marketing Research, 36*(3), 356-372. https://doi.org/10.2307/3152082

Smith, A. M. (2013). The value co-destruction process: a customer resource perspective. *European Journal of Marketing, 47*(11/12), 1889-1909. https://doi.org/10.1108/EJM-08-2011-0420

Swan, J. E., & Oliver, R. L. (1989). Postpurchase Communications By Consumers. *Journal of Retailing, 65*(4), 516.

Sweeney, J. C., Soutar, G. N., & Mazzarol, T. (2005). *The difference between positive and negative word-of-mouth—emotion as a differentiator. Proceedings of the ANZMAC 2005 Conference: Broadening the Boundaries* (pp. 331-337).

Tax, S. S., Brown, S. W., & Chandrashekaran, M. (1998). Customer Evaluations of Service Complaint Experiences: Implications for Relationship Marketing. *Journal of Marketing, 62*(2), 60-76. doi:https://doi.org/10.2307/1252161

Tronvoll, B. (2012). A dynamic model of customer complaining behaviour from the perspective of service-dominant logic. *European Journal of Marketing, 46*(1/2), 284-305. doi:https://doi.org/10.1108/03090561211189338

Van Doorn, J., Lemon, K. N., Mittal, V., Nass, S., Pick, D., Pirner, P., & Verhoef, P. C. (2010). Customer Engagement Behavior: Theoretical Foundations and Research Directions. *Journal of Service Research, 13*(3), 253-266. doi:https://doi.org/10.1177/1094670510375599

Verhoef, P. C., Reinartz, W. J., & Krafft, M. (2010). Customer Engagement as a New Perspective in Customer Management. *Journal of Service Research, 13*(3), 247-252. doi:https://doi.org/10.1177/1094670510375461

Verma, H. V. (2003). CUSTOMER OUTRAGE AND DELIGHT. *Journal of Services Research, 3*(1), 119-133.

Wangenheim, F. V. (2005). Postswitching Negative Word of Mouth. *Journal of Service Research : JSR, 8*(1), 67-78.

Zeithaml, V. A., Berry, L. L., & Parasuraman, A. (1996). The Behavioral Consequences of Service Quality. *Journal of Marketing, 60*(2), 31-46. doi:https://doi.org/10.2307/1251929

The Moderating Effect of Failure Severity, Failure Stability and Self-Construal in Perceptions of Group Versus Individual Service Failure and Their Effects on Outcomes: An Abstract

Maryam Farhang, Ashok Bhattarai, Jose Saavedra Torres, Ramin Bagherzadeh, and Monika Rawal

Abstract Customers can have a significant influence on each other in the context of service delivery and service failure. Group service failures (GSF)—which is defined as, failure to satisfy the expectations of a group of service users—are pervasive. Despite the difference in the underlying psychological mechanisms of the failure perceptions as well as customer's behavioral outcomes in GSF versus individual service failure (ISF), little is known about how customers in group service failure setting would react to failure severity, failure stability and how the effect of failure setting would differ based on customer identity. Therefore, drawn upon blame attribution theory, this study aims to examine the moderating effect of severity, failure stability and self-construal in GSF versus ISF setting. Three different scenario-based studies will be used to test our hypothesis which are the moderating effect of failure severity, failure stability, and self-construal on outcomes.

Findings of this research will help managers to effectively craft their communications with customers in GSF (vs. ISF) setting. Research in this context had sug-

M. Farhang (✉) · A. Bhattarai
Southern Illinois University, Carbondale, IL, USA
e-mail: maryam.farhang@siu.edu; ashok.bhattarai@siu.edu

J. S. Torres
Northern Kentucky University, Highland Heights, KY, USA
e-mail: saavedratj1@nku.edu

R. Bagherzadeh
Ithaca College, Ithaca, NY, USA
e-mail: rbagherzadeh@ithaca.edu

M. Rawal
Millsaps College, Jackson, MS, USA
e-mail: rawalm@millsaps.edu

F. Pantoja, S. Wu (eds.), *From Micro to Macro: Dealing with Uncertainties in the Global Marketplace*, Developments in Marketing Science: Proceedings of the Academy of Marketing Science, https://doi.org/10.1007/978-3-030-89883-0_113

gested that in case of service failure managers are better to notify customers individually or separating customers to prevent intensifying negative outcomes due to customer's interactions in GSF. However, based on our expected results, if the service failure is severe or is predicted to be stable, separation and individual notification of the failure is a waste of effort and resource as there is no difference in ISF and GSF in negative outcomes since the customers are temporarily occupied with taking action to control the failure situation. In this case, focusing on resolving the issue in a timely manner is more critical than spending time on notifying them individually. However, if service failures happen in societies that people dominantly have interdependent characteristics (i.e. countries in eastern Asia), it is better to communicate with customers individually regarding a failure and try not to make them feel that many others are involved.

Keywords Group service failure · Failure stability · Failure severity · Self construal

References Available Upon Request

Exploring the Impact of Entrepreneurial Orientation and Sense of Belongingness on Consumers' Purchase Intentions from Direct Selling Agents and Warehouse Clubs

Guanyu Geng and Lou E. Pelton

Abstract This research extends research on the intrinsic and extrinsic motivation by examining how different marketing channels stimulate the different motivations of consumers, influencing their purchase intention from different channels. Depending on the research from self-determination theory, this research reveals that direct selling and warehouse club can intensify the effect of entrepreneurial orientation and sense of belongingness of consumers on their purchase intention from these two channels. This research contributes to the research in self-determination theory by revealing the influence of the direct selling channel and warehouse club on the intrinsic and extrinsic motivation of consumers, stimulating them to purchase products from these two channels.

Keywords Entrepreneurial orientation · Sense of belongingness · Direct selling channel · Warehouse club · Self-determination theory

Introduction

Consumers' retail patronage and purchase intention are inextricably connected by intrinsic factors such as emotional feelings or extrinsic situations such as social recognition. These intrinsic and extrinsic factors directly relate to people's desired goals. Within the context of the goal orientation, perhaps the most powerful source of influence is to satisfy people's basic needs. Based on Maslow's hierarchy of needs (1943), the self-actualization and sense of belongingness can be treated as two powerful

G. Geng (✉) · L. E. Pelton
University of North Texas, Denton, TX, USA
e-mail: guanyu.geng@unt.edu; pelton@unt.edu

F. Pantoja, S. Wu (eds.), *From Micro to Macro: Dealing with Uncertainties in the Global Marketplace*, Developments in Marketing Science: Proceedings of the Academy of Marketing Science, https://doi.org/10.1007/978-3-030-89883-0_114

intrinsic factors to motivate people to pursue a certain goal. Conversely, if the context can motivate people to feel that their self-actualization and sense of belongingness is satisfied, people are more willing to build a strong attachment to this context, influencing their behavior. With a growing number of Millennials participating in the "Gig Economy," a labor market characterized by the prevalence of short-term contracts or freelancers rather than more conventional permanent jobs. In this situation, being an independent entrepreneur can be a good way to satisfy the self-actualization need. The retail environment plays an important role set in consumers' purchase intention. The factors such as atmospherics, service, and tenant variety contributed to consumers' perceived pleasurable shopping experiences. The social dimensions of the shopping environment are important because they fulfilled consumers' basic social needs. This social need originally comes from one of the basic human needs: sense of belongingness. In this research, we focus on discussing how the warehouse club influences the effect of sense of belongingness on consumers' purchase intention.

Because of the economic instability and increasingly competitive environment, organizations need to differentiate themselves and increase their competitive edge (Escamilla-Fajardo et al. 2018). Entrepreneurial orientation (EO) is increasingly attracted to the attention of the organizations to improve the performance of the organizations. Understanding the effect of individual entrepreneurial orientation can shed light on why people choose the short-term and more challenging direct selling channel. Previous research articles have already illustrated that the individual entrepreneurial orientation can be one of the extrinsic factors, which can influence consumers' choice and their job performance (Khedhaouria et al. 2015). Actually, individual entrepreneurial orientation can be influenced by the personal value and psychological characteristics (Lumpkin and Erdogan 2004).

There has been extensive research exploring the factors which affect the consumers' entrepreneurial orientation, such as personal network, personalities, creativity, self-efficacy, proactiveness, and risk-taking propensity (Khedhaouria et al. 2015; Alam et al. 2015). There is a lack of research attention afforded to discuss the impact of different channels on the relationship between motivations and consumers' purchase intention. In this paper, we choose the direct selling channel and warehouse club to illustrate how these two channels intensify the effect of the intrinsic and extrinsic motivations of consumers on their purchase intention.

Today, direct selling and warehouse club play an essential role in retails sales in the U.S. In 2019, direct selling generated $35.2 billion in retail sales in the United States, and it is estimated to engage 36.9 million people (Direct Selling Association 2020). Relative to the warehouse club, in 2016, the revenue of the warehouse club and supercenter in the U.S. was $481.7 billion dollars (IBISWorld.com). The market share of the Costco Whole Sale Corp was 19.4%, which is the second-largest marketing share relative to the marketing share of Walmart (70.2%) (IBISWorld.com). Because of the huge economic impact of these two channels, it is worth for the scholars to conduct deep research to understand how these two channels influence consumers' purchase behavior.

Relative to the traditional channel selling, the direct selling channel is unique for several reasons. Direct selling transaction highly depends on the high interpersonal closeness. The high interpersonal closeness can not only cultivate the positive word of mouth but also can increase the trust between the direct sales agents and consumers. Besides boosting the sales transaction, direct selling agents can also develop their own sales networking association. The trust can intensify the persuasion effect, attracting consumers to join their sales networking association. Today, the direct marketing may include various selling approaches: party plans, personal demonstrations as well as internet sales.

Depending on the membership format, warehouse club retail stores provide low prices on consumables, such as fresh foods, health and beauty care items, high-quality apparel, electronics, hardware, jewelry, and other general merchandise. The warehouse club operates under a club model that encourages members to visit regularly to achieve savings. The membership format can not only solidify a recurring revenue stream but also can promote the loyalty customer.

Because of the high economic impact of the direct selling industry and warehouse club retailing business, understanding why consumers choose these two channels to purchase the products can give the companies a guideline to select the appropriate channels. Furthermore, examining the effect of different channels on the motivations of consumers may provide crucial insights on how different motivations influence the purchase intention of consumers and why choosing the different marketing channel are essential. Specifically, in this article, we analyze the impact of entrepreneurial orientation (extrinsic motivation) and sense of belongingness (intrinsic motivation) on consumers' purchase intentions from different channels. The marketing channel is a conduit to transfer the intangible value to customers. One of the effective strategies for companies to deliver their value to consumers is to stimulate their motivations. But, how different motivations influence consumers' purchase intention from different channels? How can different marketing channels stimulate the different motivations of customers? Can different marketing channels influence consumers' purchase intention from different channels?

In this research, we address these questions by examining how direct selling channel and warehouse club motivate consumers' entrepreneurial orientation and sense of belongingness, finally influencing their purchase intention from these two channels. Using self-determination theory, we propose that the direct selling channel can intensify the effect of entrepreneurial orientation on consumers' purchase intention from the direct selling channel. Conversely, the warehouse club can strengthen the impact of sense of belongingness on the purchase intention from the warehouse club. We test these propositions in three studies. Together, our research contributes to the motivation literature by demonstrating how different marketing channels influence the consumers' purchase intention from particular channels.

Theoretical Background

Self-Determination Theory

Motivation can be categorized as either intrinsic or extrinsic (Ryan and Deci 2000). When an individual experiences intrinsic motivation, he or she performs "an activity for itself, and the pleasure and satisfaction derived from participation" (Shillingford and Karlin 2013, p. 92). Conversely, when an individual experiences extrinsic motivation, he or she is "engaging in an activity as a means to an end and not for its own sake" (Jovanovic and Matejevic 2014, p. 457).

Following many studies analyzing intrinsic and extrinsic motivation, Ryan and Deci (2000) developed the self-determination theory. Self-determination theory focuses on discussing the degree to which an individual's behavior is self-motivated and self-determined. Self-determination theory systematically demonstrates why people act this behavior and builds the relationship between motivation and behavioral intention. As long as the outside stimuli increase the motivation of customers, they are more likely to have the behavior which can satisfy their motivation.

Purchase Intention of Consumers

Purchase intention has already received considerable attention from marketing and management scholars. Previous literature has illustrated that purchase intention can be influenced by many factors. These factors not only include the extrinsic elements, such as culture, shopping environment, and online customer review, but also directly related to basic human needs. Consumers intrinsically motivate themselves to purchase products to satisfy their basic needs or increase their satisfaction. Or, the extrinsic goal can also raise the purchase intention of consumers. For example, Truong et al. (2010) illustrated that extrinsic aspiration positively related to the consumption of luxury foods because people would like to maintain their social recognition. Extrinsic motivation also determines shopping activity. Consumers with a high compulsive buying propensity showed a life aspiration system characterized by high scores in extrinsic personal aspiration (Otero-Lopez and Villardefrancos 2015).

In general, the purchase intention of consumers can be influenced by intrinsic and extrinsic motivation. Environmental stimulus can be catalysts, which can intensify the effect of the intrinsic and extrinsic motivations of consumers on their purchase intention. In this research, we define the purchase intention as the degree to which the consumers would like to purchase certain products from a particular marketing channel (Korgaonkar et al. 1985).

Entrepreneurial Orientation and Purchase Intention

Entrepreneurial orientation (EO) can be defined as "an entrepreneurial process promoted by business owners and triggered by their individual creativity and self-efficacy" (Khedhaouria et al. 2015, p. 486). EO originally developed by Mintzberg (1973) and Khandwalla (1977). The two research articles find that entrepreneurial firms take more risks and are more proactive in searching for new business opportunities. Although EO is considered a complex organizational-level process, some scholars revealed that EO has a strong connection with individual behaviors (Khedhaouria et al. 2015). Khedhaouria et al. (2015) illustrated that self-efficacy and creativity could positively influence individual EO. Alam et al. (2015) demonstrated that personal values could influence individual entrepreneurial orientation. So, entrepreneurial orientation can be treated as a construct including multiple dimensions and as a personal trait that influences the decision making and final choices.

Consistent with self-determination theory, extrinsically motivated actions are performed not for the pleasure they give but for the results they bring. Previous literature has already revealed that extrinsic goals include financial success and social recognition (Razmus et al. 2017). High EO can motivate people to be more involved in their careers, influencing their job performance. When people feel that they can get social recognition, they are more likely to engage in this action.

In the direct selling channel, the direct sales agents not only try to build a good relationship with the customers but, simultaneously, can also develop their own sales networking association. During the whole sales transaction, they try to stress the extrinsic benefits of the direct selling business. The direct selling channel is not only a marketing channel to deliver the products to the consumers but also a good opportunity for people to start their own business. Because the sales transaction of the direct selling channel depends on high interpersonal closeness, the high interpersonal closeness can increase trust and decrease the communication barrier between the direct sales agent and their consumers. More importantly, consumers with high entrepreneurial orientation are more likely to join sales teams of direct sales agents. Although the high extrinsic motivation cannot increase the satisfaction of the whole sales transaction (Razmus et al. 2017), it can stimulate consumers' entrepreneurial orientation, attracting them to purchase the products from direct selling channel.

Moreover, high interpersonal closeness in the direct selling sales transaction will also stimulate the sense of belongingness of the consumers, attracting them to purchase the products from the direct selling channel. It is reasonable to assume that the sense of belongingness intensifies the effect of the entrepreneurial orientation. In other words, consumers who have both high entrepreneurial orientation and sense of belongingness will be more likely to purchase products from direct selling channels. Thus,

H1: High entrepreneurial orientation positively influences consumers' purchase intention from the direct selling channel.

H2: Direct selling channels intensify the effect of entrepreneurial orientation on the purchase intention of consumers from the direct selling channels.

H3: The consumers with a high sense of belongingness and entrepreneurial orientation are more likely to purchase the products from the direct selling channel.

Definition of Belongingness

In the previous sections, we discussed the effect of entrepreneurial orientation on consumers' purchase intention and also illustrate how the interaction effect between these two constructs on purchase intention. In the following section, we will illustrate the effect of sense of belongingness on consumers' purchase intention from the warehouse club and how the warehouse club intensifies this effect.

Belongingness

Many researchers have revealed that "the human drive for social relationship such that forming and maintaining social bonds reflects an innate tendency that is adaptive and crucial for survival" (Lambert et al. 2014, p. 1418). Maintaining a good social relationship not only can satisfy people's adaptive feelings to society but also can enhance the people's satisfaction level. People will intrinsically motivate themselves to pursue the sense of belongingness. However, satisfying the general for a positive social relationship does not guarantee that people can experience sense of belongingness. In this research, the definition of the sense of belongingness goes beyond whether one has positive relationships and extends to the subjective experience of having relationships that bring about a secure sense of fitting in. We refer to this as having a sense of belongingness.

Sense of Belongingness and Its Effect on Purchase Intention of Consumers

Korgaonkar et al. (1985) illustrated that the attitudes which influenced the purchase intention from a particular channel include four functions: Utilitarian function, Ego-defensive function, Value-expressive function, and Knowledge function. Value-expressive attitudes directly related to basic human needs: need to relatedness, need to competence, and need to autonomy. When one of the basic human needs is satisfied by the particular marketing channel, consumers are more likely to have a positive attitude toward that channel, motivating them to purchase the products from that channel. Moreover, Huang et al. (2018) suggest that crowded shopping environment can sometimes have a positive impact on consumer behavior. Specifically, the feeling crowded leads the consumers to become more attached to brands as an alternative way of maintaining their basic need for belongingness. This research not only highlights the effect of the crowded environment of the retail store on consumers' brand attitudes but also revealed that the crowded shopping environment can stimulate the sense of belongingness of the consumers.

Warehouse clubs are a retail store that has been strategically designed to look like a warehouse. Relative to the direct selling channel, the warehouse club has several unique characteristics. First, before shopping at the club store, consumers should pay the annual membership fees to become a member of the club store. Based on the membership information, the club store periodically sends the brochure, which includes new product information and the coupon to the consumers.

Sending the product brochure and coupon to consumers can not only attract the consumers to shop at the club store but also can activate the sense of belongingness of the consumers. It is because the new product information and the coupon are the membership benefits of the club store. These membership benefits can not only attract the consumers to continue to be the member of the club store but can motivate the consumers to understand that all the benefits come from the membership status of the club store. The whole motivation process and the membership benefits might activate the sense of belongingness of the consumers. Thus, we hypothesize;

H4: Sense of belongingness positively influences the purchase intention of consumers from the warehouse club.

H5: Warehouse club intensifies the effect of the sense of belongingness of the consumers on their purchase intention, finally attracting them to purchase the product from the warehouse club.

In general, the whole model was shown in Fig. 1.

Study Design

Three studies were developed to illustrate the effect of entrepreneurial orientation and the sense of belongingness on consumers' purchase intention from particular channels. Specifically, study 1 tests the causality relationship between entrepreneurial orientation and purchase intention from the direct selling channel. Study 2 tests the causality relationship between the sense of belongingness and purchase intention from the warehouse club. Study 1 and 2 reveal that when the entrepreneurial orientation or sense of belongingness of consumers become salience, consumers are more willing to purchase the products from the direct selling channel or warehouse club. In study 3, we manipulate the channel types and motivations simultaneously to test whether the interaction between the sense of belongingness and entrepreneurial orientation can influence the purchase intention of consumers.

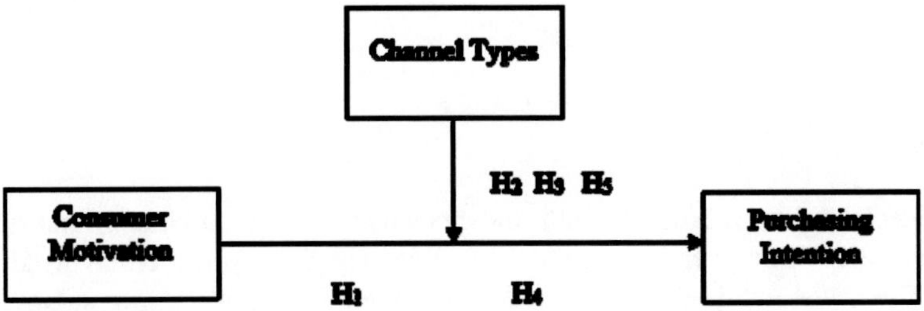

Fig. 1 Research model

Study 1

Study 1 was designed to initially test the effect of entrepreneurial orientation on the purchase intention and also to illustrate how direct selling channel intensify this effect.

Measures

Sense of Belongingness To measure the sense of belongingness of the consumers, we choose the Sense of Belongingness Instrument (SOBI) (Hagerty and Patusky 1995). SOBI instrument consists of a total of 27-items but is broken into two separate tests which assess belongingness in two separate areas, psychological sense of belongingness as assessed by the SOBI-P, and antecedents to the sense of belongingness, people's motivation (desire and ability) for the sense of belongingness, as assessed by the SOBI-A. Previous sections have already illustrated that the membership benefits and psychological reaction of consumers to the crowded environment in the warehouse club can stimulate the sense of belongingness of consumers. The membership benefits and the psychological reaction can represent the two separate aspects of the Sense of Belongingness Instrument (SOBI).

Entrepreneurial Orientation Entrepreneurial orientation was measured by using the scale developed by Bolton and Lane (2011). This scale is focused on measuring the individual entrepreneurial orientation and includes five entrepreneurial orientation dimensions presented by Lumpkin and Dess (1996). These five dimensions include several factors of individual differences, such as personalities, risk-taking propensity, innovativeness, and creativity. These factors capture the main characteristics of entrepreneurial orientation.

Purchase Intention Purchase intention of consumers is measured using a scale modified from the research of Maichum et al. (2016). This research also tests the moderation effect of different channels on the causality relationship between motivations and purchase intention. Then, we combine the scales of channel patronage developed by Korgaonkar et al. (1985) to establish the measures of purchase intention.

Method

We collect the data by working with students who have different majors and studied at one of the U.S. universities in the south area. The data collection involved three steps. First, we email 80 students requesting their participation in a survey. This research uses nutrition bars to finish all experiments because consumers can purchase nutrition bars from the direct selling channel and warehouse club. So, all participants will be asked whether they always eat nutrition bars. We exclude the participants who don't always eat the nutritional bar. At last, all participants will be asked to finish a survey to measure their entrepreneurial orientation. After these three steps, all participants will be asked to do two unrelated tasks.

First, all participants will read a short vignette. The vignette describes that a new brand of the nutritional bar has been introduced. The vignette is available in Appendix 1. After reading the short vignette, all participants see a nutrition bar picture, which is also available in Appendix 1. Then, all participants will be randomly assigned to two conditions: direct selling channel and warehouse club. In the direct selling condition, participants asked to imagine that a direct sales agent is now selling the nutrition bar to them. Simultaneously, he/she is now inviting them to join the sales networking association to start their own business. Conversely, in the warehouse club condition, participants will be asked to imagine that the nutrition bar will be available in a warehouse club retailing store. When all participants finished the two tasks, they will finish the purchase intention questionnaires.

Study 2

Study 2 is designed to test the causality relationship between the sense of belongingness and purchase intention of consumers from the warehouse club. Specifically, we manipulate the sense of belongingness and channel types to test whether the high sense of belongingness can motivate consumers to purchase the products from the warehouse club. A 2 (Sense of Belongingness: high vs. low) × 2 (Channels: direct selling channel vs. warehouse club) between-subject design will be conducted.

Method

Two hundred undergraduate students were randomly assigned to two conditions: high sense of belongingness and low sense of belongingness. Like study1, study 2 excludes the students who don't always eat nutrition bars. The manipulation processes include three steps. First, all participants read the same vignette and see the same nutrition bar picture as those in study 1. After the reading task, participants then completed an imagination task, which is related to the manipulation of the sense of belongingness.

Adapting procedures from Lambert et al. (2014), the participants in the high sense of belongingness condition are asked to think of two people or groups of people with whom they feel that they really belong. Then, they will be asked to write the names of the individuals or groups and the type of relationship you have with them. They are then asked to describe each individual (or group), why they felt like they belonged, and how it made them feel. Finally, they will be asked to write a paragraph describing a specific instance when they felt a strong sense of belongingness with this person/group. The participants in the low sense of belongingness condition will be asked to do an imagination, which is unrelated to this manipulation. The manipulation scenarios of the sense of belongingness are available in Appendix 1.

When all participants finished the tasks, all participants are randomly assigned to two groups: direct selling channel vs. warehouse club. In the direct selling channel, to rule out the effect of the entrepreneurial orientation on the purchase intention of consumers, participants will be only asked to imagine that a direct sales agent is now selling the nutrition bar to them. In the warehouse club, participants will be asked to imagine that the nutrition bar is now available at the warehouse club where they always purchase the products. After finishing the imagination task, all participants will finish the purchase intention survey.

Study 3

Study 3 was designed to examine the interaction effect of the sense of belongingness and entrepreneurial orientation on consumers' purchase intention.

Method

One hundred and sixty undergraduate students who come from one of the U.S. universities in the south area were randomly assigned to a 2 (Channel: direct selling channel vs. warehouse club) × 2 (Motivations: entrepreneurial orientation vs. sense of belongingness) between-subject design. For the entrepreneurial orientation condition, in study 1, we measure the entrepreneurial orientation of participants before the imagination task. To exclude the effect of the sequence of taking the survey, in study 3, we ask the participant to finish the reading and imagination tasks first and then measure their entrepreneurial orientation. The channel manipulation process is the same as those in study 1. The manipulation process of sense of belonging is the same as that in study 2. After finishing the two tasks, all participants will be required to finish the questionnaires of the purchase intention.

General Discussion

The current research makes several theoretical contributions to research on consumer motivation, purchase intention, and marketing channels. First, we extend the self-determination theory to different marketing channels: direct selling channel and warehouse club. Specifically, we illustrate that different channels can intensify the effect of consumers' different motivations on their purchase intention from a particular channel. Furthermore, we specifically demonstrate how different motivations influence their purchase intention. Moreover, marketing channels are efficient tunnels for the company to build a strong connection to the consumers. But, seldom researches illustrated how different marketing channels attract consumers to purchase the products. In this research, we address this research gap based on the self-determination theory.

The current research also offers a variety of implications that can help the company to find out appropriate channels. For example, if the company chooses a direct selling channel to deliver their products to the consumers, their sales representatives can try to motivate the entrepreneurial orientation of consumers. Specifically, they can highlight the unique characteristics of the direct selling industry, such as excellent financial benefits and the opportunity to be an independent entrepreneur, increasing their willingness to buy the products through direct selling channels. For the warehouse club, the club store can highlight the membership benefits, stimulating the sense of belongingness of the consumers and ultimately increasing their purchase intention.

Appendix 1

Direct Selling Condition

Reading Task

Please read the following vignette.

A new brand of the nutritional bar called "Energy" has been introduced. The "Energy" bar serves whole food protein bars made with organic nut, butter, honey, cereal, and clean ingredients. "Energy" bar is a convenient dose of vitamin and mineral-dense nutrition thanks to the 20 organic superfoods like kale, spinach, and lemon, found in every bar. For the taste, gone are the days of struggling with your protein bar, the "Energy" bar is a creamy bite with crunchy bits of real fruit, nuts, or chocolate. It's loaded with all the goodness you want, plus a cookie-dough texture worth writing home about.

Imagination Task

Direct Selling Channel

Please close your eyes and imagine that a sales representative is now selling the "Energy" nutrition bar to you. Simultaneously, he/she also tells you that if you can join his or her sales team, you can start your own business immediately. The sales job is very flexible. And the entrance barrier is very low. No need for you to invest a large amount of money at the beginning stage. Then, please write a paragraph describing the shopping experience and why or why not you would like to purchase the nutrition bar from this sales representative.

Warehouse Club Condition

Please close your eyes and imagine that you can purchase the "Energy" nutrition bar is now available in the warehouse club where you always purchase the products. Then, please write a paragraph describing the shopping experience and why or why not you would like to purchase the nutrition bar from this warehouse club.

Picture of Nutrition Bars

The picture of the nutrition bar is shown below.

Study 2 Manipulation Scenarios

High Sense of Belongingness Condition

Please close your eyes and think of two people or groups of people with whom you feel that you really belong. Now, please describe each individual (or group), why you felt like you belonged, and how it made them feel. Then, please write a paragraph describing a specific instance when you felt a strong sense of belongingness with this person/group.

Low Sense of Belongingness Condition

Please close your eyes and imagine a book that you recently read. Then, please write a paragraph describing your reading experience.

Channel Manipulation

Direct Selling Channel

Please close your eyes and imagine that a sales representative is selling the nutrition bar in front of you.

Warehouse Club Condition

The warehouse club condition is the same as that in study 1.

Picture of Nutrition Bars

The picture of nutrition bars is the same as that in study 1.

Study 3 Manipulation Scenarios

In study 3, we manipulate the channel types and motivation simultaneously. The channel manipulation process is the same as those in study 1. The manipulation of the sense of belonging is the same as that in study 2. The picture of the nutrition bar is the same as that in study 1 and 2.

References

Alam, S. S., Mohd R., Kamaruddin, B. H., & Nor, N. G. M. (2015). Personal values and entrepreneurial orientations in Malay entrepreneurs in Malaysia mediating role of self-efficacy. *International Journal of Commerce*, 25(4), 385-401.

Bolton, D. L. & Lane, M. D. (2011). Individual entrepreneurial orientation: development of a measurement instrument. *Education + Training*, 54(2/3), 219-233.

Direct Selling Association (2020). Direct Selling in the United States: 2019 Industry Overview Retrieved Dec 28, 2020 from https://www.dsa.org/statistics-insights.

Escamilla-Fajardo, P., Nunez-Pomar, J. M., & Prado-Gasco, V. (2018). Does the level of competition influence the relationship between entrepreneurial orientation and service quality? *Journal of Physical Education and Sport*, 18(3), 1306-1315.

Hagerty, B. M. K. & Patusky, K. L. (1995). Developing a measure of sense of belongingness. *Nursing Research*, 44, 9-13.

Huang, X., Huang, Z. Q., & Wyer R. S. Jr (2018). The influence of social crowding on brand attachment. *Journal of Consumer Research*, 44, 1068-1084.

IBISWorld.com. Retrieved from https://clients1.ibisworld.com/reports/us/industry/majorcompanies.aspx?entid=499 and https://clients1.ibisworld.com/reports/us/industry/majorcompanies.aspx?entid=1119.

Jovanovic, D. & Matejevic, M. (2014). Relationship between rewards and intrinsic motivation for learning - researches review. *Procedia-Social and Behavioral Science*, 149(5), 456-460.

Khandwalla, P. N. (1977). Some top management styles, their context and performance. *Organization & Administrative Sciences*, 7(4), 21–51.

Khedhaouria, A., Gurau, C., & Torres, O. (2015). Creativity, self-efficacy, and small-firm performance: the mediating role of entrepreneurial orientation. *Small Business Economy*, 44, 485-504.

Korgaonkar, P. K., Lund, D., & Price, B. (1985). A structural equations approach toward examination of store attitude and store patronage behavior. *Journal of Retailing*, 61(2), 39-60.

Lambert, N. M., Stillman, T. F., Hicks, J. A., Kamble, S., Baumeister, R. F., & Fincham, F. D. (2014). To belong is to matter: Sense of belongingness enhances meaning in life. *Personality and Social Psychology Bulletin*, 39(11), 1418-1427.

Lumpkin, G. T. & Erdogan, B. (2004). If not entrepreneurship, can psychological characteristic predict entrepreneurial orientation? – A pilot study. USASBE, San Diego, CA: United States Association for Small Business Entrepreneurship.

Lumpkin, G. T., & Dess, G. G. (1996). Clarifying the entrepreneurial orientation construct and linking it to performance. *Academy of management Review*, 21(1), 135-172.

Maichum, K., Parichatnon, S., & Peng, K. C. (2016). Application of the extended theory of planned behavior model to investigate purchase intention of green products among Thai consumers. *Sustainability*, 8(10), 1077.

Maslow, A. H. (1943). A theory of human motivation. *Psychological Review*, 50(4), 370-390.

Mintzberg, H. (1973). Strategy-making in three modes. *California Management Review*, 16(2), 44–53.

Otero-Lopez, J. M. & Villardefrancos, E. (2015). Compulsive buying and life aspirations: An analysis of intrinsic and extrinsic goals. *Personality and Individual Difference*, 76, 166-170.

Razmus, W., Jaroszynska, M., & Palega, M. (2017). Personal aspirations and brand engagement in self-concept. *Personality and Individual Difference*, 105(15), 294-299.

Ryan, R. M. & Deci, E. L. (2000). Intrinsic and extrinsic motivations: Classic definitions and new directions. *Contemporary Educational Psychology*, 25(1), 54-67.

Shillingford, S. & Karlin, N. J. (2013). The role of intrinsic motivation in the academic pursuits of nontraditional students. *New Horizons in Adult Education & Human Resource Development*, 25(3), 91-102.

Truong, Y., McColl, R., & Kitchen, P. J. (2010). Uncovering the relationships between aspirations and luxury brand preference. *Journal of Product & Brand Management*, 19(5), 346-353.

Virtual Reality as a Tool in the Classroom and Integrating Technology into Higher Ed Curriculum: An Abstract

Gerardo Moreira, Cuauhtemoc Luna-Nevarez, and Enda McGovern

Abstract The use of digital technologies has exponentially grown across all academic levels. This has opened more opportunities for educators to embrace these digital technologies and use them in marketing curriculum. In an ability to also enhance students' learning experience, the use of Virtual Reality (VR) has become a growing digital technology. VR can be defined as "a medium composed of interactive computer simulation that sense the participant's position and actions and replace or augment the feedback to one or more senses, giving the feeling of being mentally immersed or present in the simulations (a virtual world)" (Sherman and Craig 2002, p. 16). This mixed methods study investigates adoption of VR applications. VR applications are software that enhances an educational experience.

In Study 1, two 1-h long focus groups (n = 20) were conducted. Participants had previously experienced Ovation VR, a VR application used to enhance presentation skills. Five major themes emerged: immersion, engagement, enjoyment, satisfaction, and perceived learning effectiveness. These five major themes were integrated with the Technology Acceptance Model (TAM) for Study 2. Students will have a brief presentation introducing themselves and giving interests. Participants will log-in using their account profile, start their presentation recording, complete their presentation, and evaluate their grading. Upon completing these steps, participants will finish and exit the VR lab. They will then participate in an online survey including construct-related items and demographic questions. Data will be analyzed using Structural Equation Modeling (SEM).

Study 1 has identified major themes when adopting VR applications which adds to the digital technologies' literature. It has also further developed the literature on student learning experiences through gamification. Study 2 will then expand TAM literature with an adaptation to the model that integrates the five major themes identified in Study 1. Marketing educators will also have a blueprint to integrating VR

G. Moreira (✉) · E. McGovern
Sacred Heart University, Fairfield, CT, USA
e-mail: moreirag@sacredheart.edu; mcgoverne@sacredheart.edu

C. Luna-Nevarez
Texas A&M University—San Antonio, San Antonio, TX, USA
e-mail: cnevarez@tamusa.edu

F. Pantoja, S. Wu (eds.), *From Micro to Macro: Dealing with Uncertainties in the Global Marketplace*, Developments in Marketing Science: Proceedings of the Academy of Marketing Science, https://doi.org/10.1007/978-3-030-89883-0_115

applications into their marketing courses. And finally, this study expands the VR literature in marketing education.

Keywords Virtual reality · Digital technologies · Technology acceptance model · Higher education

References Available Upon Request

Quelling the Fires: A Case Study in Progress of an Extended RBV Process: An Abstract

Kavitha A. Meredith, Frank G. Adams, Peter M. Ralston, and Christina O'Connor

Abstract Competition and cooperation among industrial network members are central concerns of supply chain research (Huemer 2014). Supply chains may exhibit cases where the interests of network members do not perfectly align (Lambert and Enz 2016; Williamson 2008). There is a need to explore how firms and networks identify and address functional deficiencies within and between supply chain members to develop capabilities that support the implementation and ongoing management of better supply chain processes (Lambert and Enz 2016).

A case study method examines conversion of a steel processing firm's extant shipping procedures to an automated scheduling system (portal), with which the focal firm seeks to both better cooperate with their supply chain partners and preserve focal firm resources otherwise appropriated by customer firms. Extended Resource-based View theory (ERBV) explains this "outbound spillover rent" that occurs when focal firm resources unintentionally leak out to benefit alliance partners or marketing channel members (Lavie 2006). Such appropriation can lead to erosion of operational efficiency and effectiveness, constituting a problem worth investigating that has implications for managing resource sharing and appropriation in industrial supply chains.

The researchers conducted nine interviews, ranging from 15 to 120 min with employees of various levels of the toll-processor, a customer firm service procurement manager, and the fleet manager of the transportation carrier most commonly

K. A. Meredith (✉) · F. G. Adams
Mississippi State University, Starkville, MS, USA
e-mail: kan229@msstate.edu; fadams@business.msstate.edu

P. M. Ralston
Iowa State University, Ames, IA, USA
e-mail: pralston@iastate.edu

C. O'Connor
Maynooth University, Maynooth, Ireland
e-mail: christina.oconnor@mu.ie

F. Pantoja, S. Wu (eds.), *From Micro to Macro: Dealing with Uncertainties in the Global Marketplace*, Developments in Marketing Science: Proceedings of the Academy of Marketing Science, https://doi.org/10.1007/978-3-030-89883-0_116

recommended to customers by the toll-processor. Researchers additionally reviewed secondary data on focal firm performance metrics, procedures, and culture.

Initial findings lend themselves to an ERBV interpretation. ERBV extends Resource-based View (Barney 1996) by noting that competitive advantage derives from assembling the most important resources and by groups of firms combining their unique resources to generate greater rents than their individual resources in isolation (Lavie 2006). This case displays multiple actors coordinating their efforts to execute shipping tasks, consistent with ERBV. Members of a supply chain may share a partner's resources, as well as appropriating their partner's resources and the accompanying rents they derived (Lavie 2006). The tendency of partners to influence schedule adjustments suggests appropriation of partner resources in the form of knowledge of processes and control over scheduling. Implementation of the portal will require process redesign and development of new capabilities by users to operate the portal, thus, reducing the resource demand on the toll-processor, and increasing the resource contribution of the other stakeholders.

Keywords Extended resource-based view · Supply chain · Case study · Competition · Cooperation · Resource appropriation

References Available Upon Request

Brand Vulgarity: The Impact on Reputation, Image and Corporate Social Responsibility: An Abstract

Merlyn Griffiths, Sarah Lefebvre, Laurel Aynne Cook, Channelle James, and Andrea Scott

Abstract Expletives and derogatory terminology are increasingly being used in the naming structure for companies, products and brands as a marketing strategy. As a growing practice across numerous industries, it is intended to garner attention of the target audience, break through the proverbial clutter and create distinction within the competitive landscape. We identify this strategy as *brand vulgarity,* which refers to the use of sexual, derogatory, insults and scatology referents in branding. This comprises referents socially determined as profanity, obscenity, or indecent terminology as elements (i.e., name, taglines, logos/symbols, URL's, etc.) used to identify a company, its products and brands (Griffiths 2018).

Much research exists on the impact and importance of names (corporate, product, brand), yet minimal attention has been given to brand vulgarity as a marketing strategy, that affects a company's reputation, image and corporate social responsibility initiatives. Corporate reputation is the "observer's collective judgments of a corporation based on assessment of the financial, social and environmental impacts attributed to the corporation over time" (Barnett et al. 2006, p. 34). Gray and Balmer (1998, 696) defines corporate image as "the mental picture of the company held by its audiences—what comes to mind when one sees or hears the corporate name or sees its logo". CSR is a growing means for enhancing goodwill and building brand

M. Griffiths (✉) · C. James
University of North Carolina, Greensboro, NC, USA
e-mail: magriff3@uncg.edu; cdjames2@uncg.edu

S. Lefebvre
Murray State University, Murray, KY, USA
e-mail: slefebvre@murraystate.edu

L. A. Cook
West Virginia University, Morgantown, VI, USA
e-mail: laurel.cook@mail.wvu.edu

A. Scott
George Fox University, Newberg, OR, USA
e-mail: scotta@georgefox.edu

F. Pantoja, S. Wu (eds.), *From Micro to Macro: Dealing with Uncertainties in the Global Marketplace*, Developments in Marketing Science: Proceedings of the Academy of Marketing Science, https://doi.org/10.1007/978-3-030-89883-0_117

equity, and many companies have created and implanted formalized CSR programs and initiatives aimed at creating favorable associations from customers, employees and other stakeholders, and helping to build a sustainable advantage (Bernstein 1984; Brown and Dacin 1997; Davies and Miles 1998; Worcester 1972).

A key component of CSR is corporate reputation. Research has shown corporate reputation mediates the relationship between corporate social responsibility and several outcomes including brand performance (Lai et al. 2010), customer satisfaction and market value (He and Li 2011), brand satisfaction and customer loyalty. Given that a company's reputation and image are intimately tied to the outcome of its CSR activities, what would be the effect of brand vulgarity on reputation and image? Subsequently, what might be the impact on CSR activities when brand vulgarity is present? We explore these research questions here as we conceptualize the effects brand vulgarity has on the CSR → reputation → image relationship.

Keywords Brand vulgarity · Corporate reputation · Corporate image · Risqué marketing · Corporate social responsibility

References Available Upon Request

Consumer's Regulatory Foci and Construal Levels as Determinants of the Effectiveness of Online Marketing Messages: An Abstract

Yunmei Kuang and Meichen Dong

Abstract The proliferation of the internet and the development of communication technology have hastened the internationalization process of business. As such, firms or individuals that use the internet to pursue opportunities, whether they market their offerings domestically or internationally, have the potential to become instant born-globals that derive significant competitive advantages from the use of resources and the sales of offerings in multiple countries (Oviatt and McDougall 1994, 2005; Yamin and Sinkovics 2006; Chandra and Coviello 2010).

Previous research argues that born-globals compete by their strengths in mobilizing and utilizing different resources instead of by the amount of resources owned (Knight and Cavusgil 2004; Cavusgil and Knight 2015). It is through the internet-enabled market that, regardless of the location and the actual amount of resources, individual sellers compete with their firm counterparts, and small, unknown sellers compete with more famous brands. For sellers who lack resources, capitalizing on the knowledge of their consumers is often the most effective way to remain in business, because interactions with consumers are limited due to the online nature. Therefore, if limited-resource companies can correctly interpret their consumers' behaviors, they can remain in competition with much larger firms.

Extant consumer research has investigated consumers' regulatory foci and their construal levels extensively; yet a dearth of studies examine their interaction, especially in the context of internet-enabled markets. With more research conducted in this stream, sellers can acquire more updated knowledge about their consumers. They can also allocate their limited resources effectively by developing appropriate

Y. Kuang (✉)
Saint Louis University, Saint Louis, MO, USA
e-mail: yunmei.kuang@slu.edu

M. Dong
Valparaiso University, Valparaiso, IN, USA
e-mail: meichen.dong@valpo.edu

F. Pantoja, S. Wu (eds.), *From Micro to Macro: Dealing with Uncertainties in the Global Marketplace*, Developments in Marketing Science: Proceedings of the Academy of Marketing Science, https://doi.org/10.1007/978-3-030-89883-0_118

marketing messages that enhance consumer engagement, which could eventually contribute to their profitability and sustainability (Harmeling et al. 2017).

Drawing on Regulatory Focus Theory and Construal Level Theory, we develop testable propositions to fill the gap in the literature and managerial strategy. It is our interest to generate strategic marketing implications stemming from the interaction between the regulatory foci and construal levels of consumers in the context of internet-enabled markets. Notably, the premises of this paper are as follows. (1) Consumers with different regulatory foci are likely to buy from different sellers. (2) Consumers with different construal levels process information of sellers, products, and marketing messages differently. (3) Sellers, who successfully manipulate their marketing messages that are contingent on their consumers' characteristics, are more likely to out-compete their counterparts in the global market.

Keywords Regulatory Focus Theory (RFT) · Construal Level Theory (CLT) · Internet-enabled market · Perceived risk · Online marketing messages

References Available Upon Request

The Effects of Loneliness on Consumers' Attitudes Towards Brands' Social Media Strategies

Ruby Saine, Geraldo Matos, and Miao Zhao

Abstract There are two popular digital media strategies that marketers use: one that relies on posting brand experience and brand moments, and the other that relies on receiving product updates and promotional offers. The major challenge over time is to determine which one is more attractive to consumers who are lonely. To date, the relationship between consumers' loneliness and digital media strategies has not been established and empirically tested in marketing. We hope to fill this gap in literature and to offer valuable managerial implications to the domains of digital marketing and social media.

Keywords Loneliness · Digital media · User-generated content · Marketer-generated content

Introduction

Companies are increasingly shifting their marketing dollars from traditional media to digital media, and are under increasing pressure from stakeholders to demonstrate an increased ROI as a result of this shift. The total digital advertising spending in the United States is expected to grow 19%, reaching $129.34 billion in 2019, and surpass traditional media spending (EMarketer 2019). Despite this exponential growth, digital media still misses an opportunity to effectively reach online consumers, representing at least $30 billion worth of lost revenue, considering the potential from the consumers' digital consumption time (KPCB 2014). This challenge for brands persists and negatively impacts the bottom line of companies; for example, just the mobile marketing segment alone within digital marketing represents $7 billion worth of lost sales in 2018 (Kleiner Perkins 2018).

The challenge suggests that marketers are still in the process of figuring out how to effectively integrate digital media into their marketing strategies. To achieve this

R. Saine (✉) · G. Matos · M. Zhao
Roger Williams University, Bristol, RI, USA
e-mail: rsaine@rwu.edu; gmatos@rwu.edu; mzhao@rwu.edu

F. Pantoja, S. Wu (eds.), *From Micro to Macro: Dealing with Uncertainties in the Global Marketplace*, Developments in Marketing Science: Proceedings of the Academy of Marketing Science, https://doi.org/10.1007/978-3-030-89883-0_119

goal, marketers need to better understand the unique needs and motivations of different online user segments and, more importantly, the strategies that they can use to attract the digital consumer segments to become brand fans. The focus in the present research is to explore and provide initial empirical evidence to how the different approaches might impact individuals with varying levels of loneliness.

With consumers facing a wide array of digital content options, it is important for marketers to know which digital marketing campaigns are appealing to the lonely consumers versus the connected consumers. Strategically, marketers may decide whether to promote on social media through the use of marketer-generated content (MGC) such as product updates and promotional offers, or user-generated content (UGC) such as consumer reviews and comments about their brand experience and brand moments.

One brand actively using both strategies is Adobe. Many of its Facebook posts for the Adobe Creative Cloud simply promote a specific feature of the software, and invite consumers to click on a video or go to a website to learn more. A second strategy employed by Adobe focuses on inviting expressive posting of user-generated content (UGC). One such example involved inviting consumers to enter the "Trailer Remix Challenge" by creating and submitting a trailer remix for the launch of Terminator: Dark Fate (Facebook 2019). Similarly, while many Starbucks Facebook and Instagram posts simply highlight seasonal product launches and promotions, the brand has invited consumers to share their creativity with such programs as the #whitecupcontest (Starbucks 2014).

Given the two general paths to connecting with online consumers, we investigate the following research question: Will certain consumer segments be more attracted to either of the digital marketing strategies? Our focus narrows down to two consumer segments: the connected versus the lonely consumers. Feeling lonely or disconnected motivates greater digital usage among individuals as a coping strategy (Burke et al. 2010; Kim et al. 2009; Kraut et al. 1998; Kross et al. 2013; Stepanikova et al. 2010). In a study examining the relationship between young adults' subjective well-being and their use of Facebook, researchers find that the lonelier people feel, the more they use Facebook over time; more Facebook use leads to lower life-satisfaction and self-perceived emotional well-being (Kross et al. 2013). Further, lonely individuals are found to develop compulsive online behaviors, which further isolates them from face-to-face social interactions (Kim et al. 2009) and spend more time on online communication (Hood et al. 2018). This negative feedback loop could subsequently ensnare the lonely into a deeper sense of loneliness.

It is unknown what type of digital media content (MGC or UGC) is preferred under the circumstance. The objective of this study is to study whether lonely consumers (vs. connected consumers) prefer the brands and products that are promoted through a pro-active digital marketing strategy featuring user-generated content (such as having consumers sharing their brand experiences and moments), or prefer the brands and products that are promoted through a passive digital marketing strategy featuring marketer-generated content (such as distributing product updates and promotional offers).

In the following sections, we begin by reviewing relevant research in this domain. Drawing on the literature on avoidance coping (Duhachek 2008; Duhachek and Iacobucci 2005; Lazarus and Folkman 1984; Weiten and Lloyd 2008), we introduce a conceptual framework in which lonely consumers display a preference for those products and brands that are promoted via MGC, whereas connected consumer favor those products and brands that are promoted via UGC. Broadly, our research on the effects of loneliness on compensatory digital consumption yields the important finding that the level of digital connectivity may render different marketing strategies (marketer-generated owned content vs. user-generated earned content) more effective than another.

Hypotheses Development

Loneliness is an aversive self-threat (e.g.: Cacioppo and Patrick 2008; Peplau and Perlman 1982; Weiss 1973), and will prompt consumers to react or cope (Baumeister and Leary 1995; Cacioppo et al. 2011; Higgins 1987; Ryan and Deci 2008). Coping involves the process that one undergoes to manage a psychological stressor (Duhachek 2008).

Common coping strategies include active coping and avoidance coping (Duhachek and Iacobucci 2005; Holahan and Moos 1987; Lazarus and Folkman 1984; Weiten and Lloyd 2008). Active coping or problem-focused coping focuses on directly addressing and eliminating the cause of the self-threat. For example, Joe realizes he needs a new car. With inadequate knowledge about cars, if Joe chose to utilize an active coping mechanism, he could proactively look up information about cars online and seek advice from friends before visiting an auto dealership. On the other hand, avoidance coping prefers shunning direct dealing with the root of the problem and passively managing one's emotional response to the self-threat. In this instance, Joe might choose to put off buying a new car, perhaps even if it meant paying for expense repairs that were unwarranted given the age of his current vehicle, all in order to avoid the discomfort of having to face up to his lack of car knowledge. In a different example, after having a paper rejected by a prestigious journal, which creates a threat to one's intelligence and competence, a scholar could choose to use avoidance coping—by burying the rejected paper and instead working on less important projects, or active coping—by focusing closely on addressing the concerns raised by the reviewers and ultimately resubmitting the work to another journal.

To cope, lonely people on social media may become posters (those who create content) or lurkers (those who consume online content; Hollenbeck and Kaikati 2012; Hoffman et al. 2016). Posters directly connect with one another online via expressive posting, sharing product experiences, photos, and videos, whereas lurkers passively consume the online content such as receiving and reading product updates, following trending topics, and upcoming offerings, others' status updates, photos, and friends' conversations with other friends (Burke et al. 2010; Hoffman et al. 2012).

Most Facebook users search for people with whom they already have an offline connection more than they browse for complete strangers to meet (Ellison et al. 2007), and online social relationships are weaker than those formed and maintained off-line (Cummings et al. 2002). Ross et al. (2009) called this an offline-to-online trend: Facebook friends meet offline and then add each other online later. Therefore, those lacking social networks in offline settings will have a small online circle, thus giving them less motivation to share online. Therefore, it is plausible that they are lurkers, as compared to the connected consumers who have a larger social network. In other words, there is a congruence between a brand's digital marketing strategic promoted via MGC and lonely people's lurking tendency. Lonely consumers are less motivated to share online because there is little prospect of establishing the desired connectivity through online sharing. In the same vein, when companies and brands ask consumers to share their brand moments and experiences, lonely consumers will be reluctant to share, relative to the connected consumers who have more satisfying offline and online relationships.

Based on the reasoning presented above, we therefore propose the following hypotheses:

H1—Lonely consumers (vs. connected consumers) are less likely to favor a brand digital strategy requiring user-generated content (UGC).

H2—Lonely consumers (vs. connected consumers) are more likely to favor a brand digital strategy featuring marketer-generated content (MGC).

In the present paper, we focus on consumers' attitudes towards products and brands presented on Facebook to form brand connections. We examine three main reasons for using a brand's social media site Facebook: sharing personal brand experience, receiving product updates and news, and receiving discounts and coupons. The importance of the social and economic benefits for forging and maintaining a relationship between customers and service providers has been noted in prior literature (Gwinner et al. 1998). Indeed, among the top reasons that consumers visit a brand's social media sites are getting deals and product information, and sharing their product experiences. In a study examining reasons for connecting with brands on social media, among 1176 consumers who followed brands on social media, 56% of the respondents reported getting regular coupons and promotions, 48% reported their interests in buying products, and 44% reported an incentive such as sweepstakes, discount, or a gift card as their top reasons (MarektingSherpa 2015). In another study conducted by Yes Marketing in June of 2018, 63% of consumers indicated that they followed brands on social media in order to receive sales information and 36% engaged with content to receive discounts from brands (Southern 2019).

We contextualize our study in companies' digital media strategies of using user-generated content (UGC) versus marketer-generated content (MGC). We expect to find that lonely consumers (vs. connected consumers) tend to have a significantly lower tendency to share their product experiences on the social media platform Facebook. Instead, lonely consumers are more likely to adopt a passive coping strategy of compensatory digital consumption by passively receiving information about the brand and information with financial benefits. On the other hand, connected consumers are more likely to get connected with a brand by sharing their personal brand experiences and moments on Facebook.

Methodology

Our study uses a 2 (perceived connectivity: loneliness, connectedness) × 3 (Facebook connecting strategy: share experiences, receive updates, receive promotions) mixed design. Perceived connectivity was a between-subject factor. Facebook connecting strategy was a within-subject factor. We used a balanced Latin Square design to arrange the order in which the three Facebook connecting strategies were displayed to participants. We recruited 133 participants from Amazon MTurk and compensated them with a small monetary reward.

Following an established procedure as used in manipulating self-threats (Han et al. 2015; Pickett et al. 2004), participants were first asked to recall a past personal experience when they felt lonelier (in the loneliness condition) than they should be or desired to be in that situation versus when they felt connected (in the connectedness condition). Using a cover story of a writing test in which researchers were interested in how vividly people could write about their past experiences, they were told to use vivid descriptions about what exactly happened to them and how it made them feel at the moment. They had to write at least eight detailed sentences. Next, participants filled out two manipulation check questions (How lonely did writing about your past experience make you feel? How connected did writing about your past experience make you feel?) on a seven-point scale (1 = feeling very connected; 7 = feeling very lonely). We averaged the ratings from the two questions to form a composite score. Seven participants in the loneliness condition and one participant in the connectedness condition failed the manipulation check and were excluded from analyses. After two additional incomplete submissions were removed, there remained a total of 123 participants ($M_{age} = 33.6$, 57.5% female).

Participants then read three Facebook ads for a brand Fitbit, each followed by a set of three questions to assess participants' ad attitudes on a seven-point scale (1 = bad, negative, unfavorable; 7 = good, positive, favorable; Burnkrant and Unnava 1995). The three Facebook ads differed in their connecting strategies: feel connected by sharing your Fitbit experiences and moments on the Fitbit Facebook page (coded as E); feel connected by getting the latest Fitbit updates and news on the Fitbit Facebook page (coded as U); and feel connected by getting the exclusive Fitbit discounts and coupons on the Fitbit Facebook page (coded as D). Getting connected by E is a form of expressive posting, and getting connected by U or D represent passive compensatory digital consumption wherein people cope with their lack of connectivity through passively receiving information from external sources. We used a balanced Latin Square design to counterbalance the order of treatment

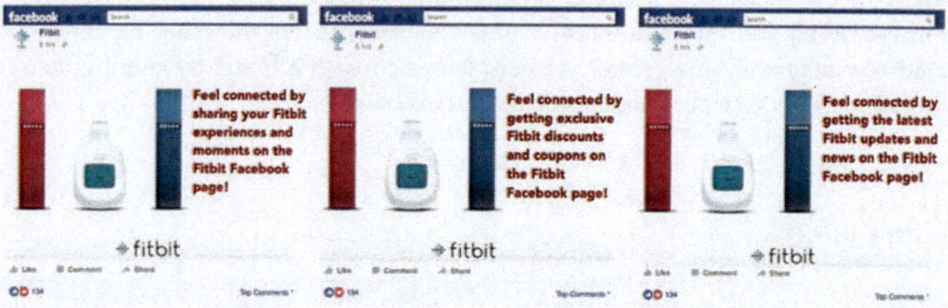

Fig. 1 Stimuli on Facebook connectivity strategy used in the study

presentation, thus avoiding the within-subject confounds potentially introduced by order effects. Participants saw one of the three Facebook connecting strategies, randomly picked from the E-U-D, U-D-E, or D-E-U sequence. Lastly, participants indicated their age and gender, and whether or not they owned or had owned a Fitbit (1 = yes; 2 = no) (Fig. 1).

We performed a manipulation check on the efficacy of the perceived connectivity manipulations, using the response that indicated the extent to which participants felt lonely or disconnected (1 = feeling very connected/not lonely; 7 = feeling very lonely/disconnected.) Participants in the loneliness condition reported significantly higher ratings than those in the connectedness condition (F (1, 121) = 156.1, $p < .001$, $M_{loneliness} = 5.19$, $M_{connectedness} = 2.52$). The ANOVA testing indicated that the manipulations were successful.

Results

We performed an ANCOVA to compare the mean differences between groups that differ on the between-subject factor of perceived connectivity and the within-subject factor of Facebook connecting strategy. We used prior ownership with Fitbit as a covariate. Age and gender were not significant covariates. An interaction between the two factors emerged, suggesting that the effect of various Facebook connecting strategies (E, U, D) on ad attitudes depended on participants' perceived connectivity (loneliness, connectedness), F (2, 240) = 4.25, $p < .05$. There was a significant main effect for Facebook connecting strategy (F (2, 240) = 4.32, $p < .05$) but a non-significant main effect for perceived connectivity (F (1, 120) = 1.53, p = n.s.).

Additional simple main effect tests indicated that participants in the loneliness condition had a less favorable attitude than those in the connectedness condition towards the Facebook ad featuring getting connected via sharing the experiences and moments using the product Fitbit (F (1, 121) = 5.83, $p < .05$, $M_{loneliness} = 4.77$, $M_{connected} = 5.35$). No differences were found between the two groups in terms of their attitudes towards the Facebook ads featuring either getting connected via receiving Fitbit updates and news (F (1, 121) = 1.25, p = n.s., $M_{loneliness} = 5.14$, M

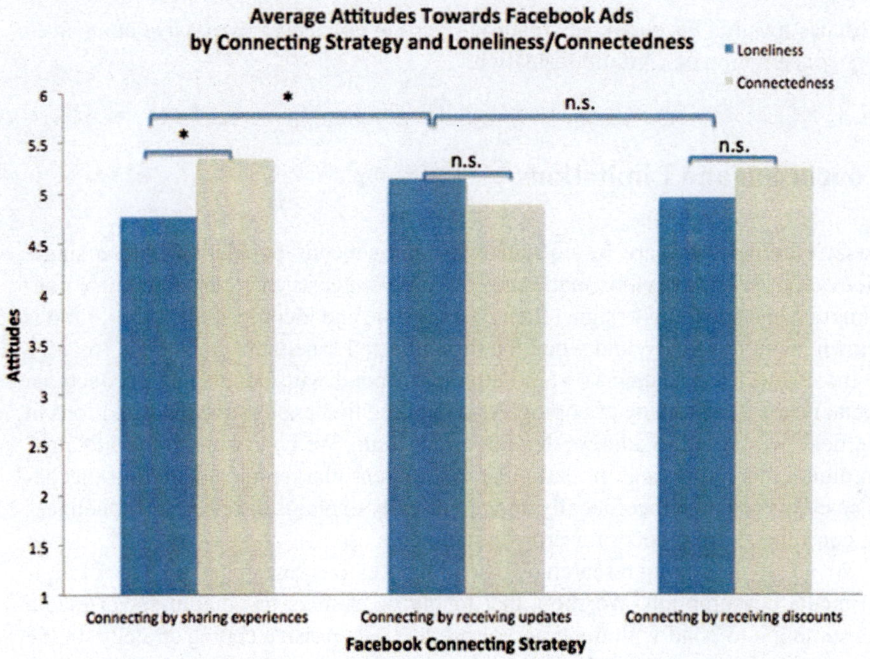

Fig. 2 Average attitudes towards Facebook ads by connecting strategy and loneliness/connectedness

$_{connected}$ = 4.89), or getting connected via receiving Fitbit discounts and deals (F (1, 121) = 1.41, p = n.s., $M_{loneliness} = 4.95$, $M_{connected} = 5.25$). For lonely participants, they have a much more positive attitude towards those Fitbit Facebook ads featuring getting connected by passively receiving product information or promotional offers (t = −1.65, p = n.s., $M_U = 5.14$, $M_D = 4.95$) than the ads featuring getting connected by actively sharing their experiences and moments of using the product (t = −1.49, $p < .05$, $M_E = 4.77$, $M_U = 5.14$; t = .82, $p < .05$, $M_E = 4.77$, $M_D = 4.95$) (Fig. 2).

Discussion

In support of our hypotheses, we find that lonely consumers (vs. connected consumers) tend to have a significantly lower tendency to share their product experience on the social media platform Facebook. Instead, lonely consumers are more likely to adopt a passive coping strategy of compensatory digital consumption by passively receiving information about the brand and information with financial benefits. On the other hand, connected consumers are more likely to get connected with a brand by sharing their personal brand experiences and moments on Facebook. Further, the connected consumers are equally likely as the lonely consumers to hold positive attitudes towards Facebook ads featuring getting connected by passive compensatory consumption of digital information.

Conclusion and Limitations

Today's digital users are by no means a homogeneous population with a single motivation. While previous marketing research suggests that consumers use consumption and spending to signal their desired state and identity (Belk 1988), little is known about how, why, and when the disconnected loneliness consumers (relative to the connected consumers) would attempt to bond with brands and products on social media as a strategy of coping. As one of the first explorative investigations in the field, we started to address this important issue. We contribute to the literature on digital marketing, and, in particular, on content marketing and sharing mechanisms. This research theoretically and empirically explains the effects of loneliness on consumers' preferences towards digital media use.

We add to the coping research by extending previous research to the area of digital media consumption. We show that lonely consumers use digital social media consumption to bond with the brand or product as a passive coping strategy. In the process, they repair the self-threats that arise from the perceived discrepancy between their desired level of connectivity and the status quo. The research provides managerial recommendations to marketers when they are designing digital marketing campaigns targeting certain consumer segments. Thus, the study offers managerial insights regarding how to leverage digital marketing for better brand and product connections. It is interesting to note that the now-trendy user-generated content marketing strategy is not equally appealing to everybody in terms of building consumer-brand connections.

One limitation of this research is that it is possible that the current finding may only generalizable to brands and products that are promoted on Facebook. It would be worthwhile studying other social networks and digital channels such as Instagram, Snapchat, and Twitter. Another limitation is the use of Amazon MTurk as the sole method to test the hypotheses. Future research could involve the use of other experimental methods.

References

Baumeister, R. F., & Leary, M. R. (1995). The need to belong: desire for interpersonal attachments as a fundamental human motivation. *Psychological Bulletin*, 117 (3), 497–529.

Belk, R. W. (1988). Possessions and the extended self. *Journal of Consumer Research*, 15 (September).

Burke, M., Marlow, C. & Lento, T. (2010). Social network activity and social well-being. *ACM CHI 2010: Conference on Human Factors in Computing Systems* (pp. 1909–1912). New York, NY: Association for Computing Machinery.

Burnkrant, R., & Unnava, H. (1995). Effects of self-referencing on persuasion. *Journal of Consumer Research, 22*(1), 17-26.

Cacioppo, J. T., Hawkley, L. C, & Patrick, W. (2011). Lonely planet. *RSA Journal*, 157 (Autumn), 10-15.

Cacioppo, J. T., & Patrick, W. (2008). *Loneliness: Human Nature and the Need for Social Connection*, New York: Norton.

Cummings, J. N., Butler, B. & Kraut, B. (2002). The quality of online social relationships. *Communications of the ACM,* 45(7), 103-108.

Duhachek, A. (2008). Summing up the state of coping research: prescriptions and prospects for consumer research. In Curt P. Haugtvedt, P. M. Herr, & F. R. Kardes (eds.), *Handbook of Consumer Psychology*, New York, NY: Psychology Press, pp. 1057-1077.

Duhachek, A. & Iacobucci, D. (2005). Consumer personality and coping: testing rival theories of process. *Journal of Consumer Psychology*, 15(1), 52-63.

Ellison, N. B., Steinfield, C., & Lampe, C. (2007). The benefits of Facebook "friends:" Social capital and college students' use of online social network sites. *Journal of Computer-Mediated Communication, 12*, 1143–1168.

Emarketer (2019). *US digital ad spending will surpass traditional in 2019*. Retrieved October 13, 2019 from https://www.emarketer.com/content/us-digital-ad-spending-will-surpass-traditional-in-2019.

Facebook (2019). *Adobe Brand Page*. Retrieved October 12, 2019 from https://www.facebook.com/adobecreativecloud.

Gwinner, K. P., Gremler, D. D. & Bitner, M. J. (1998). Relational benefits in services industries: The customer's perspective. *Journal of the Academy of Marketing Science*, 26(2), 101-114.

Han, D., Duhachek, A. & Rucker, D. D. (2015). Research article: Distinct threats, common remedies: How consumers cope with psychological threat. *Journal of Consumer Psychology*, 25, 531-45.

Higgins, E. T. (1987). Self-Discrepancy: A theory relating self and affect. *Psychological Review*, 94 (July), 319–40.

Hoffman, D. L. Novak, T. P. & Kang, H. (2016). Let's get closer: Feelings of connectedness from using social media with implications for brand outcomes. Available at SSRN: http://ssrn.com/abstract=2728281.

Hoffman, D. L., Novak, T. P. & Stein, R. (2012). The digital consumer. In *The Routledge Companion to Digital Consumption* ed. R. W. Belk & R. Llamas (Abingdon: Routledge).

Holahan, C. J., & Moos, R. H. (1987). Personal and contextual determinants of coping strategies. *Journal of Personality and Social Psychology*, 52(5), 946.

Hollenbeck, C. R., & Kaikati, A. M. (2012). Consumers' use of brands to reflect their actual and ideal selves on Facebook. *International Journal of Research in Marketing, Special Issue on Consumer Identities,* 29, 395-405.

Hood, M., Creed, P. A., & Mills, B. J. (2018). Loneliness and online friendships in emerging adults. *Personality and Individual Differences*, 133, 96-102.

Kim, J., Robert, L. & Wei, P. (2009). Loneliness as the cause and the effect of problematic internet use: The relationship between internet use and psychological well-being, *Cyberpsychology and Behavior*, 12, 451–455.

Kleiner Perkins (2018). *Internet Trends 2018*. Retrieved October 15, 2019 from https://www.kleinerperkins.com.

Kraut, R., Patterson, M., Lundmark, V., Kiesler, S., Mukophadhyay, T. & Scherlis, W. (1998). Internet paradox: A social technology that reduces social involvement and psychological well-being? *American Psychologist, 53*, 1017–1031.

Kross, E., Verduyn, P., Demiralp, E., Park, J., Lee, D. S., Lin, N., Shablack, H., Jonides, J. & Ybarra, O. (2013). Facebook use predicts declines in subjective well-being in young adults. *PLoS ONE,* 8(8), 1-6.

KPCB (2014). https://www.kleinerperkins.com.

Lazarus, R. S., & Folkman, S. (1984). *Stress, appraisal, and coping.* New York: Springer.

MarektingSherpa (2015). MarketingSherpa consumer purchase preference survey: Why customers follow brands' social accounts. Retrieved October 13, 2019 from https://www.marketingsherpa.com/article/chart/why-customers-follow-brands'-social-accounts.
Peplau, L. A., & Perlman, D. (1982). *Loneliness: A Sourcebook of Current Theory Research, And Therapy*, eds, New York: Wiley Interscience.
Pickett, C. L., Gardner, W. L., & Knowles, M. (2004). Getting a cue: The need to belong and enhanced sensitivity to social cues. *Personality and Social Psychology Bulletin*, 30(9), 1095-1107.
Ross, C., Orr, E. S., Sisic, M., Arseneault, J. M., Simmering, M. G., & Orr, R. R. (2009). Personality and motivations associated with Facebook use. *Computers in Human Behavior*, *25*(2), 578-586.
Ryan, R. M., & Deci, E. L. (2008). Self-determination theory and the role of basic psychological needs in personality and the organization of behavior. In O. P. John, R. W. Robins, & L. A. Pervin (Eds.), *Handbook of personality psychology: Theory and research* (3rd ed., pp. 654–678). New York, NY: Guilford Press.
Southern, M. (2019). *The top reasons consumers follow and engage with brand on social media*. Retrieved on October 13, 2019 from https://www.searchenginejournal.com/the-top-reasons-consumers-follow-and-engage-with-brands-on-social-media/293233/#close.
Starbucks (2014). *Starbucks invites you to decorate its iconic white cup*. Retrieved on October 12, 2019 from https://stories.starbucks.com/stories/2014/starbucks-invites-you-to-decorate-its-iconic-white-cup.
Stepanikova, I., Nie, N. H., & He, X. (2010). Time on the Internet at home, loneliness, and life satisfaction: Evidence from panel time-diary data. *Computers in Human Behavior, 26*(3), 329-338.
Weiss, R. S. (1973), *Loneliness: The Experience of Emotional and Social Isolation*. Cambridge, MA: MIT Press.
Weiten, W., & Lloyd, M. A. (2008). *Psychology applied to modern life: Adjustment in the 21st century*, 9th Edition. Belmont, CA: Wadsworth/Cengage.

Consumer-Based Brand Equity as Predictor of Three Behavioral Intention Outcomes on a Coastal Tourism Destination: An Abstract

Oliver Cruz-Milan

Abstract Several studies in the marketing literature have been conducted utilizing consumer-based brand equity (CBBE) in tourism destinations settings. However, there is scant research on the predictive effects of the CBBE dimensions on various marketing outcomes that are relevant for tourism destinations. Therefore, this research examines the effects of various dimensions of Keller's (2013) Brand Resonance Model on three behavioral intentions outcomes in the context of tourism destination: visit intentions, word-of-mouth (WOM) recommendation, and willingness to spend money. Using a coastal tourism destination as a case study, survey data from a sample of 210 consumers in the United States is analyzed to provide initial evidence for the hierarchy of effects in a CBBE model by comparing the relative impact of different brand equity dimensions on behavioral intentions. Additionally, the predicting effects of CBBE dimensions are compared with those of overall consumer-based brand equity (OCBBE), an established scale of brand equity drawn from the marketing literature, as a way to evaluate their predicting power on the three behavioral intention variables. The analysis is conducted using partial least squares structural equation modeling (PLS-SEM) with SmartPLS. The investigated model consists of four levels of constructs and factors based on Keller's (2013) Brand Resonance Model (awareness, meanings, judgements, relationships) adapted the particular context of tourism destination brand dimensions. The study findings demonstrate that lower-level factors in the Brand Resonance Model have an impact on the higher-level factors that ultimately constitute tourism destination CBBE. However, contrary to the hypothesized effects, the higher-level dimensions of the CBBE do not always yield stronger effects on the model's dependent variables. Thus, results provide general support to the role of the building blocks (constructs) in the CBBE model, although not always in the hierarchy of effects proposed by Keller (2013). From a managerial standpoint, practitioners should pay attention

O. Cruz-Milan (✉)
Texas A&M University-Corpus Christi, Corpus Christi, TX, USA
e-mail: Oliver.CruzMilan@tamucc.edu

F. Pantoja, S. Wu (eds.), *From Micro to Macro: Dealing with Uncertainties in the Global Marketplace*, Developments in Marketing Science: Proceedings of the Academy of Marketing Science, https://doi.org/10.1007/978-3-030-89883-0_120

to the entire set of factors in the full Brand Resonance Model, and monitor their contribution to marketing indicators that are linked to the mechanisms for creating brand equity.

Keywords Consumer-based brand equity · Tourism destinations · Behavioral intention outcomes · Visit intentions · WOM · Willingness to spend · Coastal destination

References Available Upon Request

Trade Policy and International Marketing Under Reagan and Trump: An Abstract

Michael Czinkota and Gary Knight

Abstract We investigate the international marketing implications of the international trade policies of US Presidents Ronald Reagan ('Reagan') and Donald Trump ('Trump'). Today, in international trade, tariffs are low, averaging about 3% in the advanced economies and 10–15% in the emerging markets. Average tariff across all goods worldwide is about 6%, down from 18% in 1990. Meanwhile, world trade has increased consistently. China is the most important trading partner of the US. China is a huge supplier of many products, and a huge market.

In the 1970s, a goods trade deficit emerged in the US, and persists to the present day. In our research, we found that the administrations of both presidents sought to reduce the US trade deficit, and defend and enhance the international marketing performance of US firms. In the early phase of his administration, trade policy under Reagan was restrained but became more assertive. Reagan focused on the trade deficit with Japan and on enhancing international market opportunities for US firms. But Reagan's policies fell short of their goals. Today, the US faces a much larger trade deficit, primarily with China. Trump adopted policy goals similar to those of Reagan. Trump's approach has been more assertive. Like Reagan, however, Trump's policies have fallen short of achieving the intended goals.

In this paper, we provided empirical background, and discussed the policies and outcomes of the policies of Reagan and Trump. We highlighted implications for firms' international marketing efforts and performance, and as well as directions for future research. We pointed to research opportunities for scholars. Research might investigate better, smarter trade policy, and examine benchmarking by reviewing various trade policy approaches, of the US and other nations, and then examining

M. Czinkota
Georgetown University, Washington, DC, USA

G. Knight (✉)
Willamette University, Salem, OR, USA
e-mail: gknight@willamette.edu

F. Pantoja, S. Wu (eds.), *From Micro to Macro: Dealing with Uncertainties in the Global Marketplace*, Developments in Marketing Science: Proceedings of the Academy of Marketing Science, https://doi.org/10.1007/978-3-030-89883-0_121

those successful in achieving intended goals. Scholars might seek to identify appropriate strategy and tactics for enhancing performance, of nations and of firms.

Implications suggest that companies need to increase their competitive advantages in global trade. The US needs to increase it national competitive advantages by improving national factors of production and implementing smarter economic policies that promote US business. Public policy makers should emphasize investing in infrastructure, for example, in communications technologies that can increase the effectiveness of the management of firms' value chain operations. Broadly, firm strategy and public policy should aim to improve performance on in the areas of entrepreneurship, innovation, and productivity, in order to make US companies more competitive in the global marketplace.

Keywords International trade policy · International marketing · Tariffs · Protectionism · Public policy

References Available Upon Request

Pushing Boundaries in Marketing Concepts and Research: An Abstract

Martin Key, Terry Clark, O. C. Ferrell, Leyland Pitt, and David Stewart

Abstract The discipline of marketing is undergoing a significant transition that seems to have both positive and negative effects in the type and pace of knowledge it creates (Eisend 2015). Specifically, scholarly research has become more specialized and fragmented and potentially meaningful to industry but not necessarily producing forward-thinking relevance as methodological sophistication has trumped other valuable contributions, such as theoretical and conceptual development, straightforwardness, and communicability (Yadav 2010; Lehmann et al. 2011). As a result of this tension, it is worth spending time exploring whether or not marketing provides the answers and informational groundwork needed in areas of innovation such as changing social, technological, and global-growth oriented realities of the twenty-first century (Webster and Lusch 2013; Ferrell and Ferrell 2016). Perhaps there are areas of our past that can serve as avenues for our future (see Brown 2014). Despite the current state of marketing scholarship, there are significant contributions to the business academy and practice that have come from our journals. Regardless, there will continue to be significant changes and development for

M. Key (✉)
University of Colorado, Colorado Springs, CO, USA
e-mail: tkey@uccs.edu

T. Clark
Southern Illinois University, Carbondale, IL, USA
e-mail: tclark@business.siu.edu

O. C. Ferrell
Auburn University, Auburn, AL, USA

L. Pitt
Simon Fraser University, Vancouver, BC, Canada
e-mail: lpitt@sfu.ca

D. Stewart
Loyola Marymount, Los Angeles, CA, USA
e-mail: David.Stewart@lmu.edu

F. Pantoja, S. Wu (eds.), *From Micro to Macro: Dealing with Uncertainties in the Global Marketplace*, Developments in Marketing Science: Proceedings of the Academy of Marketing Science, https://doi.org/10.1007/978-3-030-89883-0_122

business models, growth strategies, marketing channels, customer relationship management, AI, as well as the domain of mainstream marketing research, its methodology, and relevance (Clark et al. 2014).

The purpose of this Special Session is to stimulate critical, forward (backward)-looking (scrutinizing) conversation on the nature of marketing concepts and research, how and in what areas we do and should produce knowledge, and whether or not we are actually pushing any boundaries at all.

Keywords Future of marketing · Marketing influence · Marketing theory · Marketing knowledge

References Available Upon Request

Relationship Building Between Marketing and IT: The Impact of Information Governance and Collaboration: An Abstract

Stefan Sleep and Dana Harrison

Abstract Marketers are increasingly using data and information to drive decision making and as a result becoming more engaging in information management activities. To address the increasing role of information and technology in marketing strategy, the focus of this research is twofold. First, the study investigates the impact of information governance on the quality of information available: How are firms managing information (strategy, structure, process) to provide high quality information? The second research question is: How do relational (e.g., collaboration) elements impact the role of information use on information quality and firm performance? Through the lens of strategy, structure, process (SSP) theory this research utilizes a survey of 298 marketing and Information Technology (IT) managers to evaluate the impact of information governance and marketing IT collaboration on information quality and firm performance.

The research results show that all three components of information governance, structure, strategy and process, positively impact information quality which has a positive effect on business results. When specifically exploring the relationship between marketing and IT, we find that differences in functional power and difference in knowledge of marketing and IT at the executive level can negatively affect collaboration between the two functions. This is critical because marketing/IT collaboration enhances the effects of information processes on information quality.

For managers, this research demonstrates the importance of having a well-defined information governance strategy that promotes individual decision making

This research was funded by the Harold and Muriel Berkman Charitable Foundation.

S. Sleep (✉)
Kennesaw State University, Kennesaw, GA, USA
e-mail: ssleep@kennesaw.edu

D. Harrison
East Tennessee State University, Johnson City, TN, USA
e-mail: harrisondl@mail.etsu.edu

F. Pantoja, S. Wu (eds.), *From Micro to Macro: Dealing with Uncertainties in the Global Marketplace*, Developments in Marketing Science: Proceedings of the Academy of Marketing Science, https://doi.org/10.1007/978-3-030-89883-0_123

and a focus on cross-function information sharing to improve information quality. Managers can then use accessible, integrated, high quality data to improve overall business results. Additionally, managers should improve collaboration between the marketing and IT functions, which enhances information quality, by reducing power differences between the departments and enhancing knowledge of both marketing and IT by executives.

Keywords Marketing and IT · Collaboration · Information governance · Information quality

References Available Upon Request

Organizational Innovativeness and Firm Performance: Does Sales Management Matter?: An Abstract

Louis J. Zmich, Mya P. Groza, and Mark D. Groza

Abstract The sales manager sets the tone for the salesforce operations. An intellectually stimulating sales manager can create a ripple effect of innovation down the line of salespeople in an organization. Salespeople then interact with individual customers to drive revenues by identifying and finding solutions to customer needs.

To successfully execute this role, salespeople must acquire information external to the firm, including market trends, changing customer tastes, preferences, and customer perception of competition. Salespeople then use this knowledge and work with other units within their firm to develop innovative solutions for individual customers. The motivation received from intellectually stimulating sales managers, and external knowledge salespeople acquire in conjunction with the network position they hold within their firm, suggest the salesforce may have great value in facilitating firm innovation.

It is argued here that sales managers can harness the sales unit's knowledge and insights to ensure firm innovativeness. Specifically, we propose that organizational innovativeness is enhanced when sales managers offer intellectual stimulation; that is when sales managers encourage salespeople "to challenge existing assumptions, to reframe problems, and to approach old situations in new ways" (Eisenbeiss et al. 2008, p. 1439). This enhanced organizational innovativeness then leads to improved firm performance.

Survey data were collected from a cross-industry sample (n = 264) of companies. Results support the notion that sales manager intellectual stimulation leads to firm innovation, which in turn, enhances firm performance. However, intellectual stimulation is needed through the whole sales process to prevent the "dark sides" of over-innovative firms.

L. J. Zmich (✉)
Louisiana Tech University, Ruston, LA, USA
e-mail: ljz001@latech.edu

M. P. Groza · M. D. Groza
Northern Illinois University, DeKalb, IL, USA
e-mail: mya@niu.edu; mgroza@niu.edu

F. Pantoja, S. Wu (eds.), *From Micro to Macro: Dealing with Uncertainties in the Global Marketplace*, Developments in Marketing Science: Proceedings of the Academy of Marketing Science, https://doi.org/10.1007/978-3-030-89883-0_124

Keywords Intellectual stimulation · Sales-firm integration · Organizational innovativeness · Sales performance

References Available Upon Request

Assessing Video Ad Performance Through Observation of Facial Expressions: An Abstract

Alexandre Tellier, Sandrine Prom Tep, and Sylvain Sénécal

Abstract Facial expressions can be used to assess emotional response to a stimulus such as an advertisement video. Facial recognition technology can now reliably and remotely assess emotions in real-time using a webcam. To explore the potential of the technology to evaluate ad performance, we compared it with traditional survey-based ad evaluation.

We used *FaceReader*, facial analysis software by *Noldus*, which classifies expressions into basic emotional categories—happy, sad, angry, surprised, scared, disgusted, and neutral. Each basic emotion reported by *FaceReader* consists of a family of emotions varying in intensity and form. We relied on valence as the best way to measure the relative 'positiveness' of respondents' emotional reactions to ads. The valence of each basic emotion expressed at a given moment is calculated as the intensity of 'Happy' minus the intensity of the negative emotion with the highest intensity with values between −1 and +1. We produced an 'emotional journey' of the ad, consisting of the real-time variation in valence throughout the ad. By locating positive and negative emotional peaks we could identify their causes through corresponding timestamps in the ad.

The study comprised ten video ads, between 15 and 30 s long, from Canadian B2C companies across industries such as banking, insurance, and apparel. A sample of 200 Canadian consumers aged 18+ participated in the study, split into two groups, each viewing five of the ten ads. While viewing ads, facial expressions of respondents were captured with a webcam for analysis by *FaceReader*. To assess the potential for facial analysis technology to measure ad performance, we compared emotional data with responses to standard survey questions administered after the ad viewing to measure appreciation of the ad. Data analysis demonstrated that emo-

A. Tellier · S. Sénécal
HEC Montréal, Montreal, QC, Canada
e-mail: alexandre.tellier@hec.ca; sylvain.senecal@hec.ca

S. P. Tep (✉)
University of Quebec in Montreal, Montreal, QC, Canada
e-mail: Promtep.sandrine@uqam.ca

F. Pantoja, S. Wu (eds.), *From Micro to Macro: Dealing with Uncertainties in the Global Marketplace*, Developments in Marketing Science: Proceedings of the Academy of Marketing Science, https://doi.org/10.1007/978-3-030-89883-0_125

tional valence data is a great predictor of ad preference, with top performing ads showing a definite peak of positive emotion in the last 5 s.

Our results demonstrate that facial analysis shows objective and accurate progression of emotions in real-time, generating insights for better ads that would otherwise be unobtainable. Identifying precisely what generates positive and negative peaks enables formulation of best practices for advertisers in designing video ads, such as generating a positive surge in emotion throughout the ad and avoiding a marked decrease in emotional valence at the end by integrating the ad and its tagline within the ad's story.

Keywords Facial expression · Emotion measurement technology · Advertising performance · Research methods evaluation

References Available Upon Request

Innovation for Economically Disadvantaged Customers and Shareholder Value: Exploring the Role of Marketing, Corporate Governance, and Corporate Citizenship: An Abstract

Muhammad Musharuf Hossain Mollah, Saim Kashmiri, and Brad D. Carlson

Abstract Each year, thousands of firms introduce new products to target economically disadvantaged customers (EDC). Extant research reveals significant heterogeneity in the stock market response to such introduction of new products. The current research addresses the following questions: (a) Do EDC innovations, on average, increase shareholder value?, (b) Do some companies get rewarded more for their EDC innovations?, (c) If so, do certain factors such as high market orientation, strong marketing capability, large pay gap between chief executive officer (CEO) and top management team (TMT) members, high corporate social performance (CSP), and greater number of new product introductions (NPIs) impact shareholder value? This study proposes that the above mentioned four factors are likely to moderate the impact of EDC innovations on shareholder value. The authors conducted an *event study* of company announcements on EDC innovations for 241 publicly listed U.S. firms during the period 2007–2015. The study is expected to show that marketing factors such as market orientation and marketing capability, and corporate governance factor influence how EDC innovations affect shareholder value. The market model (Brown and Warner 1985) reveals a mean cumulative abnormal return (CAR) of 0.30% for the sample firms. The result demonstrated that EDC innovations have positive and significant relationship with shareholder value of firms. The authors also used an alternative measures of cumulative average abnormal return (CAAR) for robustness checks. This result is consistent with the original empirical analysis. However, we did not find support for moderation effect of CSP

M. M. H. Mollah (✉) · B. D. Carlson
Saint Louis University, St. Louis, MO, USA
e-mail: muhammad.mollah@slu.edu; brad.carlson@slu.edu

S. Kashmiri
University of Mississippi, Oxford, MS, USA
e-mail: skashmiri@bus.olemiss.edu

F. Pantoja, S. Wu (eds.), *From Micro to Macro: Dealing with Uncertainties in the Global Marketplace*, Developments in Marketing Science: Proceedings of the Academy of Marketing Science, https://doi.org/10.1007/978-3-030-89883-0_126

on the relationship between EDC innovations and shareholder value of firms. Using both *signaling theory* and *resource-based view (RBV)*, the paper posits that firms with high market orientation, strong marketing capability, and new product introductions which are radical (radical vs. incremental) are likely to accrue greater stock market returns from EDC innovations. However, the large pay gap between CEO and TMT members will attenuate this relationship. The paper concludes with implications of this research and suggests future research agenda.

Keywords Economically disadvantaged customers · Shareholder value · Corporate social performance · Top management team · New product introduction

References Available Upon Request

Sharing a Laugh: The Moderating Role of Need for Humor on the Sharing of Online Advertisements: An Abstract

Catherine Hessick

Abstract Consumers spend an ever-increasing amount of time online each day, thus prompting marketers to devote more of their efforts to generating online advertising. Once viewed, these advertisements can be "liked," shared with social networks on various platforms, and appear on subsequent feeds through amplification. To encourage sharing, one tactic often implemented is the inclusion of humor within the advertisement. However, what individuals find humorous in advertisements depends on the individual's need for humor (NFH).

Divided into two components, NFH refers to an individual's inclination to create (i.e. internal) and consume (i.e. external) humor. This paper examines the moderating role an individual's external and internal NFH plays on the relationship between how humorous an advertisement is and the online sharing of that advertisement. Previous literature has revealed individuals express their uniqueness and identity by what they share. Furthermore, individuals whose self-esteem depends on public evaluation are more vigilant in managing their online image. Therefore, those who considered themselves having a humorous personality (i.e. internal NFH) may share an advertisement only if it is congruent to their image. On the other hand, individuals who simply enjoy humorous content and situations (i.e. external humor) may share humorous advertisements without regard to their image.

Prior to conducting the study, advertisements were pre-tested for familiarity as previous research has shown perceived humor decreases after the first viewing. Participants (N = 160; 43.8% male; average age = 35.5 years old) viewed one randomly selected advertisement and then answered questions on how humorous the advertisement was, their intention of sharing, and their need for humor. As hypothesized, our results reveal opposite effects for internal NFH and external NFH on the sharing of humorous advertisements. When internal NFH increased, individuals were 38.2% less likely to share whereas an increase in external NFH showed an

C. Hessick (✉)
James Madison University, Harrisonburg, VA, USA
e-mail: hessicce@jmu.edu

F. Pantoja, S. Wu (eds.), *From Micro to Macro: Dealing with Uncertainties in the Global Marketplace*, Developments in Marketing Science: Proceedings of the Academy of Marketing Science, https://doi.org/10.1007/978-3-030-89883-0_127

individual was 56.5% more likely to share the advertisements. These findings contribute to both the humor and advertising literature by expanding the research on NFH. To our knowledge, this paper is the first to show the effect of humor on sharing can be moderated by the consumer's personality as well as the first that separately examines the two dimensions of the NFH scale.

Keywords Advertising · Humor · Digital marketing · Moderation

References Available Upon Request

Pleasure Versus Meaning: Differences in Elevation and Psychological Well-Being for Hedonic and Eudaimonic Purchases: An Abstract

Aditya Gupta and James W. Gentry

Abstract As scholars continue to unearth novel insights regarding happiness from consumption (Mogilner et al. 2011, 2012), many experts in the discipline are calling for a move beyond the hedonic paradigm, which equates happiness with pleasure, toward a eudaimonic paradigm, which equates happiness with meaningfulness (Alba and Williams 2013; Schmitt et al. 2015). Extant work on this topic within consumer behavior, however, continues to be sparse (e.g., Gupta 2018; Percival Carter and Williams 2014). Thus, the present research aims to illustrate how consumers experience hedonic and eudaimonic purchases differently.

To this effect, a study was conducted by randomly allocating a sample of 100 MTurk respondents to either a hedonic purchase condition (associated with a strong sense of pleasure) or a eudaimonic purchase condition (associated with a strong sense of meaningfulness). Following a prompt to describe the purchase in detail, respondents then completed measures for elevation, PWB, and hedonic well-being. Finally, they provided information regarding purchase details and demographics. Manipulation checks confirmed that the recall task was successful in making respondents think of different types of purchases.

A MANCOVA analysis found significant group differences (Wilk's Lambda = 0.83, $p < 0.05$) between hedonic and eudaimonic purchases. Specifically, respondents in the eudaimonic condition reported higher levels of purpose ($M = 5.60$, $SE = 0.18$) than those in the hedonic condition ($M = 4.71$, $SE = 0.16$; $F(1, 91) = 12.55$, $p < 0.05$); higher levels of self-acceptance ($M = 5.41$, $SE = 0.14$) than those in the hedonic condition ($M = 5.00$, $SE = 0.13$; $F(1, 91) = 4.32$, $p < 0.05$); and marginally higher levels of introspection ($M = 4.74$, $SE = 0.44$) than those in the

A. Gupta (✉)
Illinois State University, Normal, IL, USA
e-mail: agupt16@ilstu.edu

J. W. Gentry
University of Nebraska-Lincoln, Lincoln, NE, USA
e-mail: jgentry@unl.edu

F. Pantoja, S. Wu (eds.), *From Micro to Macro: Dealing with Uncertainties in the Global Marketplace*, Developments in Marketing Science: Proceedings of the Academy of Marketing Science, https://doi.org/10.1007/978-3-030-89883-0_128

hedonic condition (M = 4.21, SE = 0.20; F(1, 91) = 2.96, $p < 0.10$). While average values for other dimensions of the dependent variables were directionally higher for the eudaimonic purchase condition than for the hedonic purchase condition, group differences did not reach significance (all ps > 0.05). Finally, a multiple mediation analysis conducted with experimental group as the antecedent, introspection as the dependent variable, and all PWB dimensions entered simultaneously as potential mediators using the bootstrap mediation technique (Preacher and Hayes 2008), revealed a significant indirect effect through purpose (indirect effect = 0.294, standard error = 0.157, 95% CI [0.0323, 0.6515]).

Findings from this study, therefore, provide emergent proof that hedonic and eudaimonic purchases differ in terms of affective experience and well-being dimensions. We also find that eudaimonic purchases engender a sense of purpose which, in turn, is linked to an eventual feeling of introspection that can help consumers reflect on their choices and make them want to be better people.

Keywords Eudaimonic consumption · Hedonic consumption · Well-being · Elevation

References Available Upon Request

Brand Narratives in a World of Fragmented Digital Media: An Abstract

David A. Gilliam, Steven W. Rayburn, and Mayoor Mohan

Abstract Narratives are deeply embedded elements of human cognition and social being and widely recognized across psychology, management, and the humanities as such (e.g. Bruner 1986; Gergen and Gergen 1988; McAdams 1993, 2010; Polkinghorne 1988; Wyer 1995). Narratives and storytelling are increasingly recognized in marketing as powerful drivers of consumer behavior (e.g., Ardelet et al. 2015; Bertele et al. 2020; Gilliam and Zablah 2013; Gilliam and Flaherty 2015; Gilliam et al. 2017, 2018; Godin 2012; Kozinets et al. 2010; Van Laer et al. 2018).

Brand narratives can impact buyers' self-identity and facilitate sense-making during purchase and consumption journeys (Cooper et al. 2010).

Narrative transportation into a story world can affect consumers' beliefs, attitudes, intentions, and behaviors (Escalas 2007; Van Laer et al. 2014). This can occur with just a short story or photo without regard to age or culture (Escalas 2004; Kim et al. 2016).

Research questions

RQ1—what are brand narratives?
RQ2—how do brand narratives originate and evolve?
RQ3—how are brand narratives used in purchasing?
RQ4—what framework could be used for analyzing brand narratives in a digital world?

D. A. Gilliam (✉)
University of Arkansas at Little Rock, Little Rock, AR, USA
e-mail: dagilliam@ualr.edu

S. W. Rayburn
Texas State University, San Marcos, TX, USA
e-mail: steven.rayburn@txstate.edu

M. Mohan
Virginia Commonwealth University, Richmond, VA, USA
e-mail: mmohan@vcu.edu

F. Pantoja, S. Wu (eds.), *From Micro to Macro: Dealing with Uncertainties in the Global Marketplace*, Developments in Marketing Science: Proceedings of the Academy of Marketing Science, https://doi.org/10.1007/978-3-030-89883-0_129

Following the 6-step process of Gilliam and Voss (2013) for developing definitions of marketing constructs, the contributions from extant literature were distilled into the following definition of brand narratives: "a consumer's evolving, co-created narrative formed via a sensemaking amalgamation of brand meanings and consumer self-identity."

The origin, evolution, and use in purchasing of brand narratives is dynamic and complex. The consumer develops a brand narrative for each brand in a product category by using information from the market. In a purchase, this brand narrative interacts with the deal and the promise sought. The consumer chooses the desired state which then provides feedback to future purchases.

Keywords Branding · Story · Storytelling · Digital marketing · Social media

References Available Upon Request

Reexamining the Perceived Quality-Market Share Relationship: The Moderating Role of the Quality Perception Gap: An Abstract

Billur Akdeniz and Berk Talay

Abstract Quality is a critical factor in explaining brand strategy and performance. Extant marketing research has examined quality with two of its most prominent dimensions as objective and perceived quality. Objective quality refers to the aggregate performance of all product attributes whereas perceived quality refers to a consumer's subjective judgment of the aggregate performance. Relatively scarce research in marketing has examined the discrepancy between the two quality dimensions. In this study, we treat the difference between the perceived and objective quality of a brand as the quality perception gap.

This study follows closely the footsteps of Helloffs and Jacobson (1990) and Rego et al. (2013) in re-examining the perceived quality-market share relationship. It contributes to the branding and quality literature in two ways. First, similar to Rego et al. (2013), we re-examine a famous relationship in the branding literature by analyzing the time-varying effects of perceived quality-market share relationship. Second, this study introduces the concept of comparative perceived quality, which measures the perceived quality of a car brand with respect to the competitive product segment it belongs. Instead of the absolute perceived quality score, we think that the comparative score can explain the variance in market share of a brand more clearly.

Drawing upon signaling theory and previous research, we propose four hypotheses and test them using dynamic panel generalized method of moments (GMM) estimation (Arellano and Bover 1995; Blundell and Bond 1998; Roodman 2009) on a unique dataset comprised annual observation of 45 car brands (i.e., makes) and 196 products (i.e., models) in the U.S. automotive industry between 2000 and 2010.

B. Akdeniz (✉)
University of New Hampshire, Durham, NH, USA
e-mail: billur.akdeniz@unh.edu

B. Talay
University of Massachusetts Lowell, Lowell, MA, USA
e-mail: berk_talay@uml.edu

F. Pantoja, S. Wu (eds.), *From Micro to Macro: Dealing with Uncertainties in the Global Marketplace*, Developments in Marketing Science: Proceedings of the Academy of Marketing Science, https://doi.org/10.1007/978-3-030-89883-0_130

Overall, this study provides a more detailed analysis of the relationship between two important brand management related variables as previously discussed in the literature. We find support for Helloffs and Jacobson's (1990) negative relationship between market share and perceived quality. But interestingly, we find no support for a positive impact of current perceived quality on future market share when perceived quality is treated as an absolute measure. Yet, when a car brand's perceived quality is comparatively higher than the average perceived quality in its own product category, it may affect the future market share positively. In addition, our findings not only show that consumers' over-appreciation for a car brand can have a positive impact on its future market performance but also the positive main effect of comparative perceived quality on market share is further enhanced for over-appreciated brands.

Keywords Perceived quality · Automotive industry · Brand management · Quality perception gap

References Available Upon Request

Interactivity, Engagement, Value Co-creation and e-WOM in Virtual Educational Environments in Colombia

Cielo Esperanza Mahecha-Duarte, Mónica Andrea Álvarez-Marín, and Juan Fernando Tavera-Mesías

Abstract Theoretical and empirical marketing studies related to virtual education in Latin America and Colombia are scarce. For this reason, this research proposes a hypothesis model integrating variables such as interactivity, customer engagement, value co-creation and Electronic Word of Mouth or e-WOM, in order to identify how to promote effective strategies to improve online learning experience. The model has been tested through a structural equations analysis with a convenience sample of 324 users of virtual educational platforms. The results evidence the model's adjustments and the positive relationship between the studied dimensions in virtual educational platforms.

Keywords Interactivity · Customer engagement · e-WOM · Value co-creation · e-Learning · Online education · Virtual education · Digital marketing

Introduction

The increase in people's use of the internet has also fostered the creation of new interactivity-based virtual communication environments and experiences. The user ceases to have a passive role in the relationship and takes control of the medium to create and share with others on platforms that are characterized by their visual appeal, easy-to-navigate design and offer of various co-creation tools (Vargo et al. 2008), such as forums, chats, tutorials, content platforms, access to digital libraries, a specialized tutor who provides support and assistance, among others.

In the virtual education setting, the internet broadens the learning styles used in traditional education and offers the advantage of unlimited space and time, thus

C. E. Mahecha-Duarte (✉) · M. A. Álvarez-Marín · J. F. Tavera-Mesías
University of Antioquia, Medellin, Colombia
e-mail: cielo.mahecha@udea.edu.co; mandrea.alvarez@udea.edu.co; juan.tavera@udea.edu.co

F. Pantoja, S. Wu (eds.), *From Micro to Macro: Dealing with Uncertainties in the Global Marketplace*, Developments in Marketing Science: Proceedings of the Academy of Marketing Science, https://doi.org/10.1007/978-3-030-89883-0_131

enhancing learning opportunities and facilitating communication in online education (Wang and Bagaka 2003).

However, there are no studies dealing with interactivity, engagement, value co-creation and e-WOM in the learning experience in the context of virtual education. In this light, and given the scarcity of marketing research literature on virtual education concerning the use, technology and methodological program design factors, which is all but non-existent in the case of the constructs addressed in this article, attention is drawn to the need of finding out how they take place in users' experience and permanence in educational platforms and the connection with brands, as well as shedding light on the elements that influence the generation of value co-creation and e-WOM.

Consequently, this work aims to determine the relationship between interactivity, customer engagement, value co-creation and e-WOM in virtual education platforms in order to contribute to better marketing management in the education sector.

Theoretical Background

Interactivity

In this research, website interactivity is understood as an essential high-tech capability for a company attempting to establish a long-term relationship with its consumers [and users] through high technology and a central determinant for building online brands to the extent that it allows reciprocal communication between system and users (Neelotpaul 2011; Voorveld et al. 2013).

Three main dimensions have been found in the literature. The first dimension is two-way communication and refers to the possibility of reciprocal communication between the organization and the web user as well as among web users, whereby resources such as discussion forums and links to email addresses facilitate bilateral communication. The second dimension is active control and alludes to the extent to which the website user can influence the communication process; features such as the choice of language, downloads and delivery tracking systems allow active control over brands' websites. The third dimension is synchronicity and refers to the degree to which two-way communication is a simultaneous process occurring in real time. Synchronicity depends on the speed and reliability of the internet connection (Van Noort et al. 2012).

Studies have identified interactivity in e-learners as a critical success factor in virtual learning environments (Selim 2007; Johnson et al. 2008; Paechter et al. 2010) because e-learners do not interact face-to-face with instructors, university administrative staff or peers (Mahle 2007; Peltier et al. 2007).

Customer Engagement (CE)

This study draws from the proposals of Vivek et al. (2014) and So et al. (2014) to view CE as the degree of identification and connection that consumers establish with the brand's offerings and activities initiated by either themselves or the organization, thus assessing users' affective dimension regarding their brand experience on virtual education platforms.

In the case of virtual education, the literature regarding the subject matter is scarce, barely cited, and focused on the direct influence of engagement (understood as participation or commitment) on perceived quality and student retention levels in massive open online courses or MOOC (de Freitas et al. 2015; Hew 2016). Conversely, the value co-creation experience was found to be positively influenced by student engagement in the face-to-face university scene, as long as the learner has an interest in participating both dialogically and collaboratively in the learning experience and interacting with the elements deployed for it (goods, people, activities, platforms, etc.) thus developing skills and attributes important for employment and post-university life (Dean et al. 2016).

Value Co-creation

In this research study, value co-creation is defined as the set of activities among those involved in direct interactions, whose purpose is to contribute to the creation of value that emerges from one or both parties (Grönroos 2012).

Most value co-creation studies use a multidimensional approach to capture customers' co-creation behavior, arguing it is comprised of distinctive components which involve cognition, emotion and behavior (Storbacka et al. 2016; Vargo and Lusch 2016; Merz et al. 2018; Wong and Lai 2018). The interaction is a fundamental aspect (Vargo and Lusch 2016; Yi and Gong 2013) that occurs through dialogue, participation and engagement among service actors (beneficiaries and providers), enabling an active exchange that results in the creation of beneficial solutions (Yi and Gong 2013; Ranjan and Read 2016; Finsterwalder 2018).

Early research identifies some types of customer co-creation dimensions such as: creativity, connectedness and commitment (Merz et al. 2018), information, responsible behavior, feedback, helping (Yi et al. 2011; Yi and Gong 2013).

e-WOM

In this paper, e-WOM is understood as a statement made by a potential, current or former customer about a product or company and which is made available to a multitude of people and institutions via the internet (Hennig-Thurau et al. 2013).

In the online education sphere, research indicates the education industry is a service akin to that of travel and tourism, where students are customers and make purchasing decisions based on the information available (Shanka et al. 2006). Many researchers have identified this resource as more credible than the information published by institutions on their websites (Crotts 1999).

Several studies have revealed different antecedents of e-WOM, such as credibility of both the information and the source from which it comes (Chang and Wu 2014; Erkan and Evans 2016; Yan et al. 2016); intrinsic motivations (concern for others, self-enhancement, social benefits) and extrinsic motivations (economic incentives), with the former kind being the most powerful in promoting e-WOM systems (Yoo et al. 2013). Other antecedents found are customer satisfaction and engagement (Purnasari and Yuliando 2015; Duarte et al. 2018) in addition to loyalty and satisfaction in the case of WOM in the education sector (Özdemir et al. 2016).

Methodology

From the bibliographical and empirical review exhibited in Fig. 1 the hypothesis model proposed for this study is presented, with interactivity as the independent variable, and engagement, e-WOM and value co-creation as the dependent variables.

Hypotheses

Brodie et al. (2011) and Hollebeek (2011) found that interactivity between customers and companies is the main variable for the generation of customer engagement, especially in digital environments where the consumer can play an active

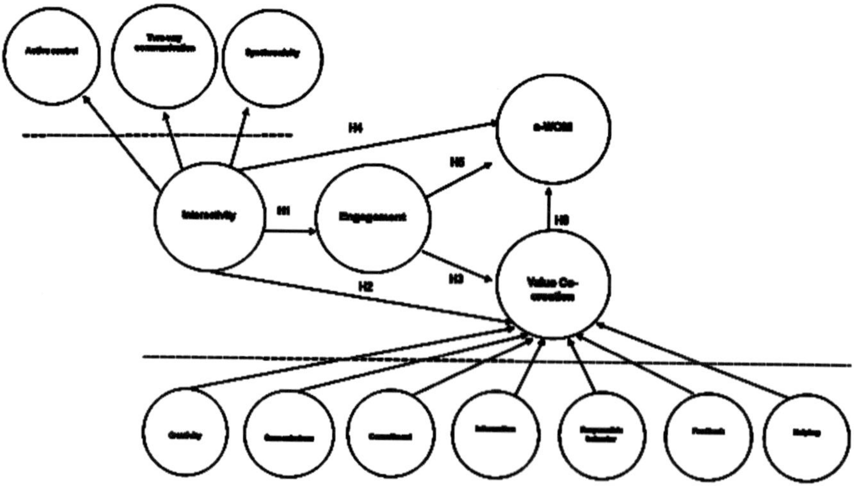

Fig. 1 Hypothesis model proposed

participation role associated, for instance, with actions related to content download, video/podcast playback, as well as publication of opinions and subscription derived from the identification and connection with the brand values (Vivek et al. 2014; So et al. 2014). This promotes the joint creation of value (communities, new uses of the service, etc.) supported by a win-win relationship (Vargo et al. 2008). Based on the above, it can be stated that: H1: Interactivity positively affects customer engagement.

Reciprocal interaction between customers and suppliers facilitates value co-creation (Frow et al. 2008; Grönroos 2012; Aarikka-Stenroos and Jaakkola 2012) and in the university setting, interaction among students, teachers, administrative staff and peers has positive results on process design and knowledge generation (Bowden and D'Alessandro 2011; Pinar et al. 2011; Seraj 2012; Bovill 2014; Rodríguez-Ardura and Meseguer-Artola 2016; Ribes-Giner et al. 2016). From the above it can be stated that: H2: Interactivity positively affects value co-creation.

In turn, CE is one of the most profitable marketing activities since its management favors positioning and the attraction of customers, who deliver elements to an organization beyond purchase (Brodie et al. 2011; Cambra et al. 2012), which are voluntary and important behaviors for the brand, such as collaboration with other customers, after-sales service (they help other customers about product use) and new product and/or service development (with other customers or the company). And the organization supports its relation on win-win situations such as providing valuable information, reducing service gaps and creating communities and networks, which are strengthened and increase in value in the long term (Hudson et al. 2015; Storbacka et al. 2016; Serna et al. 2017; Zhang et al. 2017; Finsterwalder 2018). For the above it can be said that: H3: Customer engagement positively affects value co-creation.

e-WOM is considered an interactive process among consumers (Park et al. 2012; Cheung et al. 2011; Yan et al. 2016); therefore, high interactivity levels on the web site stimulate the production of e-WOM (Van Noort et al. 2012; Yoo et al. 2013). Considering the above it can be stated that: H4: Interactivity positively affects e-WOM.

CE also favors voluntary behaviors that go beyond purchase such as online generation of opinions and comments on the brand (Brodie et al. 2011; Cambra et al. 2012; Chu and Kim 2011). Thus, it can be claimed that: H5: Customer engagement positively affects e-WOM.

Other studies confirm communication among customers about a firm is considered one of the key variables in the co-creation process (Frow et al. 2008; Grönroos 2012; Jaakkola and Alexander 2014). Therefore, it can be stated that: H6: Co-creation positively affects e-WOM.

Data Collection and Analysis

The survey was applied to 324 individuals with the aim of explaining the study phenomenon.

The questionnaire was applied through the Survey Monkey platform, organically shared and paid for its completion in virtual communities related with online education and digital marketing. Mass emails were also sent to personal and virtual education student databases (through contacts in some selected institutions, Ude@ and Unad). The data analysis was performed with the SmartPLS 3.0 software. When analyzing the data, reliability and validity were verified through confirmatory factor analysis and the hypotheses were subsequently contrasted with partial least squares (PLS) regression and structural equations techniques (Chin 1998; Hair et al. 2012).

Results

Cronbach's alpha obtained scores above 0.7 (Nunnally and Bernstein 1994), that is, reliability of the dimensions is confirmed. Additionally, the results evidence respondents' co-creation behaviors on virtual educational platforms, since the mean yielded values greater than 0.718, except for Responsible Behavior (P = 0.639). Next the validity of the measurement instrument for the reflective constructs was analyzed to verify its internal consistency, reliability and convergent and divergent validity (Hair et al. 2017). The same was done for the formative construct measurement instrument, through the indicator's weight and significance and multicollinearity. Finally, the structural model was measured, checking the determination coefficient values, the significance of the structural values and their predictive relevance.

Measurement Model

Cronbach's alpha (CA) and Composite Reliability (CR) values were valid for all the constructs. Likewise, meeting convergent validity requirements is evidenced from the Variance Extracted Index (VEI) values, since the loadings of the variables were above 0.5 (Fornell and Larker 1981) so they adequately measure the factors.

Discriminant validity of each construct was demonstrated based on the arguments by Hair Jr et al. (2014) and Fornell and Larker (1981). With the SmartPLS software, diagonal values were identified as well as the square root of the average variance extracted (AVE) (Chin 1998), and it was subsequently evaluated that the variances exceeded the highest quadratic correlation of the factors placed below the diagonal.

Measurement Instrument for Second-Order Formative Construct

To model the formative second-order construct, value co-creation, the two-stage model was used. First the second-order construct was not included in the model and each original relationship proposed was directly modeled to and from each dimension. Then the scores of the latent variables were used to build the original dimensions as co-creation indicators (Hair Jr et al. 2014). Although not all dimensions have significant weights ($p > 0.001$), loadings do, so it was decided to keep all the dimensions to ensure the construct's content validity. Regarding multicollinearity, the Variance Inflation Factor (VIF) was estimated for each dimension, whose results were adequate for co-creation validity ($0.2 < VIF < 5$) (Hair Jr et al. 2014).

Structural Model

The dependent variables of the model meet Hair Jr et al.'s (2014) indicator criteria for the determination coefficients ($R^2 \leq 0.75$ and ≥ 0.51, relevant; ≤ 0.50 and ≥ 0.26, moderate; and <0.25, weak), as well as predictive relevance ($Q^2 > 0$ of Stone 1974; Geisser 1975; Tenenhaus et al. 2005). The hypotheses were validated from calculating the standardized coefficients, the t values and the significance of each hypothesis. The analysis evidenced five (5) significant hypotheses ($p < 0.001$) and one that was not significant ($p > 0.001$). The study confirmed the direct and positive impact of Interactivity on Customer engagement (H1: $\beta = 0.592$) and of the latter on Value co-creation and e-WOM (H3: $\beta = 0.723$; H5: $\beta = 0.403$), reinforcing the findings of other works (Brodie et al. 2011; Cambra et al. 2012; Hudson et al. 2015; Rodríguez-Ardura and Meseguer-Artola 2016). It was also demonstrated that Interactivity affects Value co-creation (H2; $\beta = 0.164$), and the latter affects e-WOM (H6; $\beta = 0.380$), confirming the reviewed literature (Frow et al. 2008; Hoyer et al. 2010; Pinar et al. 2011; Bowden and D'Alessandro 2011; Aarikka-Stenroos and Jaakkola 2012; Grönroos 2012; Bovill 2014; Jaakkola and Alexander 2014; Ribes-Giner et al. 2016).

On the other hand, the relationship between Interactivity and e-WOM (H4: $\beta = 0{,}072$) was not supported, which may be due to the fact that the perceived experience of interactivity that students have in Colombia's digital platforms is not enough to encourage the production of opinions and comments on the internet. Although the hypothesis on the relationship of the rest of the constructs with e-WOM was rejected, this may be explained because the model proposes an indirect relationship between the latter and Interactivity through Customer engagement.

General Discussion

The present study on virtual education in Colombia shows that Interactivity has a positive direct influence on the development of Customer engagement and the Value co-creation behavior among digital environment learners. Although argued in the literature, the same does not occur in the case of the relationship between Interactivity and e-WOM, where it was possible to ascertain that the relationship was not supported in the model. That is, the perceived experience of interactivity that students have in Colombia's digital platforms is not enough to encourage the production of opinions and comments on the internet.

In addition, Customer engagement was also found to significantly influence Value co-creation among virtual education students; in other words, it motivates their commitment, creativity, feedback, production of information, and responsible behavior towards the brand and their educational process. Similarly, Engagement has a high positive impact on e-WOM in comparison with other constructs, which is why the production of information by virtual education users in different digital channels is promoted by it.

Regarding Interactivity and Customer engagement in online learning environments in Colombia, Value co-creation is mainly influenced by the latter, as the greater the enjoyment of the experience and the identification with the brand (educational institution or organization) are, the more Value co-creation behaviors can take place. Moreover, the study confirms Co-creation has a positive impact on sharing, commenting and recommending the brand among virtual education users.

Hence, in the virtual education context, it is important for organizations to start work on experiential marketing strategies that create value for users in such a way that attaining high levels of commitment to brands, positive emotions towards them, and brand recognition in their communities, is supported by those strategies. This will guarantee students will remain present until courses have been completed, with the organization achieving a higher position and reach among possible users, whose decisions are based on other students' experiences, as a competitive advantage.

References

Aarikka-Stenroos, L., and Jaakkola, E. (2012). Value co-creation in knowledge intensive business services: A dyadic perspective on the joint problem solving process. *Industrial Marketing Management, 41*(1), 15–26.

Bovill, C. (2014). An investigation of co-created curricula within higher education in the UK, Ireland and the USA. *Teaching International, 51(1)*, 15–25.

Bowden, J. L. H., and D'Alessandro, S. (2011). Co-creating value in higher education: The role of interactive classroom response technologies. *Asian Social Science, 7(11)*, 35.

Brodie, R. J., Hollebeek, L. D., Jurić, B., and Ilić, A. (2011). Customer engagement: Conceptual domain, fundamental propositions, and implications for research. *Journal of Service Research, 14*(3), 252–271.

Cambra, J., Melero, I., and Sese, F. (2012). Customer engagement: An exploratory study in the mobile communications industry. *Universia Business Review, 33*, 84–103.

Chang, H. H., and Wu, L. H. (2014). An examination of negative e-WOM adoption: Brand commitment as a moderator. *Decision Support Systems, 59*(1), 206–218.

Cheung, C., Lee, M., and Jin, X. (2011). Customer Engagement in an Online Social Platform: A Conceptual Model and Scale Development. *ICIS 2011 Proceedings*.

Chin, W. W. (1998). The partial least squares approach to structural equation modeling. *Modern Methods for Business Research, 295*(2), 295–336.

Chu, S. C., and Kim, Y. (2011). Determinants of consumer engagement in electronic Word-Of-Mouth in social networking sites. *International Journal of Advertising, 30*(1), 37–41.

Crotts, J. C. (1999). Consumer decision making and prepurchase information search. *Consumer Behavior in Travel and Tourism, Edited by A. Pizam and Y. Masfeld. New York: The Haworth Hospitality Press*, 149–168.

De Freitas, S. I., Morgan, J., and Gibson, D. (2015). Will MOOCs transform learning and teaching in higher education? Engagement and course retention in online learning provision. *British Journal of Educational Technology*, *46*(3), 455–471.

Dean, A. M., Griffin, M., and Kulczynski, A. (2016). Applying Service Logic to Education: The Co-creation Experience and Value Outcomes. *Procedia - Social and Behavioral Sciences*, *224*(August 2015), 325–331.

Duarte, P., Costa, S., and Bernardo, M. (2018). How convenient is it? Delivering online shopping convenience to enhance customer satisfaction and encourage e-WOM. *Journal of Retailing and Consumer Services*, *44*(June), 161–169.

Erkan, I., and Evans, C. (2016). The influence of eWOM in social media on consumers' purchase intentions: An extended approach to information adoption. *Computers in Human Behavior*, *61*, 47–55.

Finsterwalder, J. (2018). A 360-degree view of actor engagement in service co-creation. *Journal of Retailing and Consumer Services*, *40*, 276-278.

Fornell, C., and Larker, D. (1981). Evaluating Structural Equation Models With Unobservable Variable Sand Measurement Error. *Journal of Marketing Research*, *18*(1), 39–50.

Frow, P., Payne, A. F., Storbacka, K., and Frow, P. (2008). Managing the Co-Creation of Value. *Journal of the Academy of Marketing Science*, (March 2008).

Geisser, S. (1975). The predictive sample reuse method with applications. *Journal of the American Statistical Association*, *70*(350), 320–328.

Grönroos, C. (2012). Conceptualising value co-creation: A journey to the 1970s and back to the future. *Journal of Marketing Management*, *28*(13–14), 1520–1534.

Hair Jr, J. F., Sarstedt, M., Hopkins, L., and Kuppelwieser, V. G. (2014). Partial least squares structural equation modeling (PLS-SEM). *European Business Review*, *26*(2), 106–121.

Hair, J. F., Sarstedt, M., Ringle, C. M., & Mena, J. A. (2012). An assessment of the use of partial least squares structural equation modeling in marketing research. *Journal of the Academy of Marketing Science*, 40(3), 414–433.

Hair, J., Hollingsworth, C. L., Randolph, A. B., and Chong, A. Y. L. (2017). An updated and expanded assessment of PLS-SEM in information systems research. *Industrial Management & Data Systems*, *117*(3), 442–458.

Hennig-Thurau, T., Hofacker, C. F., and Bloching, B. (2013). Marketing the Pinball Way: Understanding How Social Media Change the Generation of Value for Consumers and Companies. *Journal of Interactive Marketing*, *27*(4), 237–241.

Hew, K. F. (2016). Promoting engagement in online courses: What strategies can we learn from three highly rated MOOCS. *British Journal of Educational Technology*, *47*(2), 320–341.

Hollebeek, L. D. (2011). Demystifying customer brand engagement: Exploring the loyalty nexus. *Journal of Marketing Management*, *27*(7–8), 785–807.

Hoyer, W. D., Chandy, R., Dorotic, M., Krafft, M., and Singh, S. S. (2010). Consumer Cocreation in New Product Development. *Journal of Service Research*, *13 (3)*, 283–296.

Hudson, S., Roth, M. S., Madden, T. J., and Hudson, R. (2015). The effects of social media on emotions, brand relationship quality, and word of mouth: An empirical study of music festival attendees. *Tourism Management*, *47*, 68–76.

Jaakkola, E., and Alexander, M. (2014). The Role of Customer Engagement Behavior in Value Co-Creation: A Service System Perspective. *Journal of Service Research*, (April), 10–11.

Johnson, R.D., Hornik, S. and Salas, E. (2008). An empirical examination of factors contributing to the creation of successful e-learning environments. *Int. J. Hum. Comput. Stud.*, *66*, 356–369.

Mahle, M. (2007). Interactivity in distance education. *Distance Educ.*, *4*, 47–51.

Merz, M. A., Zarantonello, L., and Grappi, S. (2018). How valuable are your customers in the brand value co-creation process? The development of a Customer Co-Creation Value (CCCV) scale. *Journal of Business Research*, *82*(August 2017), 79–89.

Neelotpaul, B. (2011). A study on interactivity and online branding. Advances in Management.

Nunnally, J. C., and Bernstein, I. H. (1994). Psychometric Theory (McGraw-Hill Series in Psychology). McGraw-Hill New York.

Özdemir, A., Tozlu, E., Şen, E., and Ateşoğlu, H. (2016). Analyses of word-of-mouth communication and Its effect on students' university preferences. *Procedia - Social and Behavioral Sciences*, *235*(October), 22–35.

Paechter, M, Maier, B., and Macher (2010). Students' expectations of, and experiences in e-learning: their relation to learning achievements and course satisfaction. *Comput. Educ.*, *54*, 222–229.

Park, J., Gu, B., and Lee, H. (2012). The relationship between retailer-hosted and third-party hosted WOM sources and their influence on retailer sales. *Electronic Commerce Research and Applications*, *11*(3), 253–261.

Peltier, J.W., Schibrowsky, J.A. and Drago, W. (2007). The interdependence of the factors influencing the perceived quality of the online learning experience: a causal model. *J. Mark. Educ.*, *29*, 140–153.

Pinar, M., Trapp, P., Girard, T., and Boyt, T. E. (2011). Utilizing the brand ecosystem framework in designing branding strategies for higher education. *International Journal of Educational Management*, *25(7)*, 724–739.

Purnasari, H., and Yuliando, H. (2015). How Relationship Quality on Customer Commitment Influences Positive e-WOM. *Agriculture and Agricultural Science Procedia*, *3*, 149–153.

Ranjan, K. R., & Read, S. (2016). Value co-creation: concept and measurement. *Journal of the Academy of Marketing Science*, 44(3), 290–315.

Rodríguez-Ardura, I. and Meseguer-Artola, A. (2016). E-learning continuance: The impact of interactivity and the mediating role of imagery, presence and flow. *Information & Management*, 53, 504–516.

Ribes-giner, G., Perello-marín, M. R., and Pantoja, O. (2016). Co-creation impacts on student behavior. *Procedia - Social and Behavioral Sciences*, *228*(June), 72–77.

Selim, H. M. (2007). Critical success factors for e-learning acceptance: confirmatory factor models. *Comput. Educ.*, *49*, 396–413.

Seraj, M. (2012). We Create, We Connect, We Respect, Therefore We Are: Intellectual, Social, and Cultural Value in Online Communities. *Journal of Interactive Marketing*, *26*(4), 209–222.

Serna, Daniela Castaño, Balvín, Daniela Rico and Mesías, J. F. T. (2017). Perspectiva de marketing para comprender la innovación de servicios tecnológicos en un país emergente. In *XXI Congreso Internacional de Contaduría, Administración e Informática* (p. 17). México: Universidad Nacional Autónoma de México. Retrieved from http://congreso.investiga.fca.unam.mx/docs/xxii/docs/13.09.pdf

Shanka, D. T., Quintal, V., and Taylor, R. (2006). Factors Influencing International Students' Choice of an Education Destination–A Correspondence Analysis. *Journal of Marketing for Higher Education*, *15(2)*, 31–46.

So, K. K. F., King, C., and Sparks, B. (2014). Customer Engagement With Tourism Brands: Scale Development and Validation. *Journal of Hospitality and Tourism Research*, *38*(3), 304–329.

Stone, M. (1974). Cross-validatory choice and assessment of statistical predictions. *Journal of the Royal Statistical Society. Series B (Methodological)*, 111–147.

Storbacka, K., Brodie, R. J., Böhmann, T., Maglio, P. P., and Nenonen, S. (2016). Actor engagement as a microfoundation for value co-creation. *Journal of Business Research*, *69*(8), 3008–3017.

Tenenhaus, M., Vinzi, V. E., Chatelin, Y.-M., and Lauro, C. (2005). PLS path modeling. *Computational Statistics & Data Analysis*, *48*(1), 159–205.

Van Noort, G., Voorveld, H. A. M., and van Reijmersdal, E. A. (2012). Interactivity in Brand Web Sites: Cognitive, Affective, and Behavioral Responses Explained by Consumers' Online Flow Experience. *Journal of Interactive Marketing*, *26*(4), 223–234.

Vargo, S. L., and Lusch, R. F. (2016). Institutions and axioms: An extension and update of service-dominant logic. *Journal of the Academy of Marketing Science*, *44*, 5–23.

Vargo, S. L., Maglio, P. P., and Akaka, M. A. (2008). On value and value co-creation: A service systems and service logic perspective. *European Management Journal*, *26*(3), 145–152.

Vivek, S. D., Beatty, S. E., Dalela, V., and Morgan, R. M. (2014). A Generalized Multidimensional Scale for Measuring Customer Engagement. *The Journal of Marketing Theory and Practice*, *22*(4), 401–420.

Voorveld, H. A., Van Noort, G., and Duijn, M. (2013). Building brands with interactivity: The role of prior brand usage in the relation between perceived website interactivity and brand responses. *Journal of Brand Management*, *20(7)*, 608–622.

Wang, L. C. C., and Bagaka, J. G. (2003). Understanding the dimensions of self exploration in Web-based learning environments. *Journal of Research on Technology in Education*, *34(3)*, 364–373.

Wong, J. W. C., and Lai, I. K. W. (2018). Evaluating value co-creation activities in exhibitions: An impact-asymmetry analysis. *International Journal of Hospitality Management*, *72*, 118–131.

Yan, Q., Wu, S., Wang, L., Wu, P., Chen, H., and Wei, G. (2016). E-WOM from e-commerce websites and social media: Which will consumers adopt? *Electronic Commerce Research and Applications*, *17*, 62–73.

Yi, Y., and Gong, T. (2013). Customer value co-creation behavior: Scale development and validation. *Journal of Business Research*, *66*(9), 1279–1284.

Yi, Y., Nataraajan, R., and Gong, T. (2011). Customer participation and citizenship behavioral influences on employee performance, satisfaction, commitment, and turnover intention. *Journal of Business Research*, *64*(1), 87–95.

Yoo, C. W., Sanders, G. L., and Moon, J. (2013). Exploring the effect of e-WOM participation on e-Loyalty in e-commerce. *Decision Support Systems*, *55*(3), 669–678.

Zhang, M., Guo, L., Hu, M., and Liu, W. (2017). Influence of customer engagement with company social networks on stickiness: Mediating effect of customer value creation. *International Journal of Information Management*, *37*(3), 229–240.

Two Faces of Brand Hate: Corporate vs. Human Brands: An Abstract

Kenneth W. Graham, Mark J. Pelletier, and Kelly Wilder

Abstract In rapidly evolving online environments, brands must meaningfully engage consumers to foster consumer-brand relationships and to communicate brand values that permeate consumer self-identity and culture. Recent research into negative consumer-brand relationships explores *brand hate*. Much of the brand hate literature examines the brand hate construct in the context of corporate brands, while little research explores brand hate in the context of human brands. Given the increasing reliance on human brands among marketers, it is important to better understand differences in how brand hate is manifested toward corporate and human brands.

Building upon the psychological literature and Sternberg's Triangular Theory of Hate (2003), research finds three primary drivers of brand hate including: negative consumer experiences with the brand, the consumer's perceptions of the organization and its values, and negative perceptions of the brand as a social entity. Consistent with the brand hate literature, consumer behavior in response to these drivers included brand avoidance or reduction of patronage (exit), mild negative WOM behaviors (voice), and more extreme reactions of active complaining and protesting about the brand (revenge). Therefore, we turn to the Huefner and Hunt's (2000) adaptation of Hirshman's exit voice framework (1970), which they expand to include retaliation.

K. W. Graham (✉)
University of Wisconsin—La Crosse, La Crosse, WI, USA
e-mail: kgraham2@uwlax.edu

M. J. Pelletier
University of North Carolina Wilmington, Wilmington, NC, USA
e-mail: pelletierm@uncw.edu

K. Wilder
Meredith College, Raleigh, NC, USA
e-mail: kwilder@meredith.edu

F. Pantoja, S. Wu (eds.), *From Micro to Macro: Dealing with Uncertainties in the Global Marketplace*, Developments in Marketing Science: Proceedings of the Academy of Marketing Science, https://doi.org/10.1007/978-3-030-89883-0_132

To explore the drivers of brand hate as it relates to human and corporate brands, a critical incident technique survey was constructed. Respondents were randomly assigned to one of two conditions—identifying either a corporate brand or human brand that they hate. After identifying a specific brand, respondents were asked to describe why they hated that brand and then to describe any actions they had taken towards that brand as a result of their hatred toward the brand. Responses included a total of 124 usable responses from the corporate brands survey and 86 usable responses from the human brands survey.

Based on the results of the qualitative study and our review of the brand hate literature, we find support for a theoretic model of brand hate consistent with Sternberg's Triangular Theory of Hate (2003), where consumer response to negative brand experiences is mediated by the degree to which they experience hate toward the brand. We also find support for the notion that these relationships are moderated by the type of brand (corporate or human) that is the object of the consumer's hate, with human brands having a stronger moderating effect.

Keywords Brand hate · Human brands · Exit-voice · Triangular theory of hate

References Available Upon Request

Competing Through Compelling FLOW Experiences: Examining the Antecedents and Consequences of Chinese Video Gamers: An Abstract

Mohammad Rahman, Jamie Carlson, William Powell, and Jiehua Chen

Abstract The importance of the video game atmospheric cues is critical for explaining consumer attitudes and behaviors towards the game developers. Therefore, understanding the psychological and cognitive-based aspects of gamers' experiences in a video game environment is important for devising strategies to gain gamers' loyalty, purchase intentions, and active interaction. Research has focused on understanding the psychological assessment of Flow Experiences, its drivers, and loyalty outcomes. However, more needs to be known on the role of collaboration in the Flow dimensionality and presence of future customer engagement behaviors (CEB) within the game environment.

By integrating Flow theoretical basis, this study contributes to the marketing and information systems literature by examining the impact of video gamer experiences such as concentration, interactivity, telepresence, collaboration, challenge, and goals on the dimensionality of flow experience and their subsequent impact on key behavioral response outcomes such as repeat purchase and continues interaction intentions.

Data were collected from 201 Chinese video gamers' where we used Structural Equation Modeling (SEM) to analyze our data and demonstrates the determinants of a compelling gaming experience on video game environments as represented by flow experiences that drive positive customer engagement behaviors and game loyalty. The results validate flow modeled as a higher-order construct, which unlocks

M. Rahman (✉) · W. Powell
Shippensburg University, Shippensburg, PA, USA
e-mail: MMRahman@ship.edu; WAPowell@ship.edu

J. Carlson
University of Newcastle, Newcastle, NSW, Australia
e-mail: Jamie.carlson@newcastle.edu.au

J. Chen
University of Melbourne, Parkville, VIC, Australia
e-mail: jiehuac@student.unimelb.edu.au

F. Pantoja, S. Wu (eds.), *From Micro to Macro: Dealing with Uncertainties in the Global Marketplace*, Developments in Marketing Science: Proceedings of the Academy of Marketing Science, https://doi.org/10.1007/978-3-030-89883-0_133

and positively influences perceptions of flow experiences in a video gaming environment. Our results offer interesting insights for video game development strategy, especially video game developers to create closer player-game relationships, higher skills level games, and collaborations amongst players to provide lasting enjoyment.

Game developers can deliver enhanced flow experiences amongst players by implementing in-game collaboration tools (such as Text and Voice chat), skilled based matchmaking, and third-party customization module. Game developers can also create multi-platforms compatible games where gamers can compete in multiplayer and tournament settings while live streaming to social media platforms to increase awareness, trust, and loyalty amongst players towards the developer which drives CEB. Future research can include customer in-game purchases/cross-game purchase. The theoretical model could be extended by including moderating factors such as addiction, device preference, time spent on gaming, and platform compatible games to determine the appropriate segment to deliver optimum flow experiences.

Keywords Video game · Flow experience · Collaboration · Consumer engagement behaviors

References Available Upon Request

Stakeholders and Science, Communication and Coping: An Abstract

Natalie Bolen and Maureen Bourassa

Abstract When industry, government, and community actors join to address complex issues that impact them all, this is a multi-stakeholder system (Roloff 2008)—a type of marketing system that exchanges value in terms of ideas and information, as well as social and economic capital. The complex issues they address are often contentious and science-intensive (e.g., climate change, GMOs, global health, energy). Stakeholder engagement in these settings is especially challenging because productive communication around science—which privileges specialized education, knowledge, and/or jargon—can be complicated.

In this research, we ask: what are the experiences of one group of stakeholders—women—as they navigate interpersonal conversations around contentious and science-intensive issues? Our context is nuclear sector developments, which are generally perceived as high risk (Geng et al. 2018); previous research suggests women perceive risks, including nuclear risks, differently than men (Barke et al. 1997; Berdahl et al. 2014), react to interpersonal conflict differently (Portello and Long 2001), and are under-represented in science sectors (Wall 2019; Dionne-Simard et al. 2016). We conducted 17 interviews with women representing government, industry, and community, and engaged as stakeholders in nuclear sector developments.

We found that contentious nuclear conversations spurred interpersonal conflict, which prompted five different forms of coping strategies to minimize the negative social and emotional impact of conflict. The types of coping strategies ranged not only from problem- to emotion-focused coping (Lazarus and Folkman 1984), but also from disengagement to engagement: more problem-focused coping was accom-

N. Bolen (✉)
University of Alberta, Edmonton, AB, Canada
e-mail: nbolen@ualberta.ca

M. Bourassa
University of Saskatchewan, Saskatoon, SK, Canada
e-mail: bourassa@edwards.usask.ca

F. Pantoja, S. Wu (eds.), *From Micro to Macro: Dealing with Uncertainties in the Global Marketplace*, Developments in Marketing Science: Proceedings of the Academy of Marketing Science, https://doi.org/10.1007/978-3-030-89883-0_134

panied by disengagement, and more emotion-focused coping by engagement. The problem-focused/disengaged coping strategies are: (1) *avoiding* (physical or mental removal from a conversation), (2) *placating* (soothe or mollify to make a conversation less hostile), and (3) *qualifying* (sustain dialogue by softening aggressiveness of a statement). The emotion-focused/engaged coping strategies are: (4) *rationalizing* (justify or give reasonable explanations for own or another's behavior) and (5) *relating* (find commonalities, nurture relationships).

Our findings point to *relating*, and potentially *rationalizing*, as the coping strategies that best align with the goals of stakeholder engagement. These coping strategies can be helpful for individual stakeholders who are seeking to minimize negative social and emotional impact from difficult conversations, but who aim to remain engaged in stakeholder engagement processes. These findings have implications for understanding multi-stakeholder networks and marketing systems, as well as the role of stakeholder engagement within science-based sectors.

Keywords Marketing systems · Science · Stakeholders · Coping · Nuclear · Women · Conflict

References Available Upon Request

Shifting Brick-and-Mortar Retailing to the Next Level: Exploring the Quality of Digital Services: An Abstract

Amela Dizdarevic, Heiner Evanschitzky, and Christof Backhaus

Abstract Although the offer of digital services via mobile or fixed devices to visitors of inner-city shopping areas can be considered at an early stage, the usage of innovative technologies is gaining ground in retail practice. Surprisingly, within marketing science, little is known about customers' perception of the quality of digital services offered by traditional retailing.

This article reviews prior conceptualizations of the role of technologies in retail and service marketing, management and information systems. The quality of digital services is introduced as the extent to which a consumer believes that the digital service offered by a retail destination performs well. A digital service is conceptualized as e.g. an availability check of products offered via a shopping center's website or app.

In the framework of a mixed-methods approach, a measurement tool is developed by means of four qualitative studies compromising a face-to-face survey with shoppers, an online panel and expert judges. Empirical findings demonstrate that the application of two scale parts reflecting a second-order construct is reasonable.

The scale is validated by means of three quantitative studies, a student survey, a consumer panel and an online experiment. The position of the developed construct within the nomological network of related marketing constructs is empirically supported. Further, using an online experiment, we find that the quality of digital services can explain variance in consumer outcome behaviors and perceptions.

The conceptualization and validation of the measure shifts the retail agglomeration literature from a traditional offline view to an up-to-date digital perspective. Recent studies in marketing science present initial approaches of capturing

A. Dizdarevic (✉)
Aston University, Birmingham, UK
e-mail: dizdarea@aston.ac.uk

H. Evanschitzky
University of Manchester, Manchester, UK
e-mail: heiner.evanschitzky@manchester.ac.uk

C. Backhaus
Edinburgh Napier University, Edinburgh, UK
e-mail: c.backhaus@napier.ac.uk

F. Pantoja, S. Wu (eds.), *From Micro to Macro: Dealing with Uncertainties in the Global Marketplace*, Developments in Marketing Science: Proceedings of the Academy of Marketing Science, https://doi.org/10.1007/978-3-030-89883-0_135

consumer-perceived applications of digital technologies within retail agglomerations, but due to sole explorative research approaches and lacking coherent definitions of the investigated construct, the development of a reliable and easy-to-administer scale had yet to emerge. Applying the scale in marketing practice enables retail destinations to assess the performance of offered digital services, evoking in turn an overall attractive evaluation of the retail destination.

Keywords Service quality · Digital services · Scale development · Retail agglomerations

References Available Upon Request

"We Shall Not Remain Passive": TSR Implications in the Sharing Economy Context: An Abstract

Mohamed Sobhy Temerak and Nora Ramadan

Abstract TSR promises the transformation of the service experience for all the involved stakeholders; taking into account the wellbeing and the interests of the service provider, the service user and the wider service community. While TSR logic can appear to contradict with the profit maximisation logic, TSR aims to improve the quality of life of the involved service community; which should, on the long term, be reflected on the sustainability of that service community. With the growing interest in the TSR, the question that seems pressing is to what extent one can find implications of TSR evident in the challenging practice. This paper takes this question to the evolving area of the sharing economy services in the context of developing countries.

Sharing economy service models have three main actors; the platform providing firm, the peer service provider, and the service user. These service models offer several benefits to the involved service actors including financial, psychological, and social benefits. While the word "sharing" implies some equivalence among the service actors, several questions arise when linking the TSR to the sharing economy services. First, does the participation in the sharing economy service models result in the creation of some vulnerable service actors? If so, how do these vulnerable actors respond in relation to their vulnerabilities; passively or actively? Second, how can their response affect the sustainability of these sharing economy services? We aim to answer these questions in the ride-sharing services in the context of a developing country. Developing countries are characterized by several voids and therefore the vulnerabilities of the service actors are expected to be more apparent compared to a developed country context.

We undertake a qualitative research approach by interviewing 75 ridesharing drivers and then, we conduct a content analysis of their largest Facebook groups. Our results suggest that while the peer-service providers gain financial benefits from

M. S. Temerak (✉)
University of Kent, Medway, UK
e-mail: m.s.a.hassan@kent.ac.uk

N. Ramadan
Cairo University, Giza, Egypt
e-mail: nora.ramadan@foc.cu.edu.eg

F. Pantoja, S. Wu (eds.), *From Micro to Macro: Dealing with Uncertainties in the Global Marketplace*, Developments in Marketing Science: Proceedings of the Academy of Marketing Science, https://doi.org/10.1007/978-3-030-89883-0_136

participating in the sharing economy services, their benefit comes with a high price both psychologically and physically (such as personal or property safety). Yet, these peer service providers do not remain passive toward their vulnerabilities as suggested in the TSR literature in case of vulnerable users. They take an active role by engaging in different coping and offsetting strategies and educate other peers about these strategies via their online community. Such strategies are, in many cases, detrimental to the sustainability of the sharing economy service as it lowers its quality and hence its value.

Keywords Transformative service research · Sharing economy · Emerging market · Wellbeing

References Available Upon Request

Special Session: How International Scholars Maneuver Doctoral and Early Career Obstacles in new Environments beyond Academic Walls: An Abstract

Nina Krey, Shuang Wu, Sabinah Wanjugu, and Jihane Ait Samo

Abstract While all young academics and doctoral candidates face difficulties acclimating to new surroundings, international scholars often manage additional uncertainties beyond the academic walls. Some of these obstacles that are unique to faculty members and doctoral students shifting their lives to the USA range from adjusting to the US education system and social life, navigating a foreign job market, to teaching in an environment that might embrace different cultural and social norms. This special session focuses on how to manage these difficulties and to succeed in a career that transforms not only the professional but also the personal elements of the individual.

A lot of times there are limited resources available to international students on how to maneuver the doctoral and early career journey. Faced by these challenges, international students find themselves inclining towards some unfortunate stereotypes of sticking together for comfort. While working together with peers might help provide a comfort zone, in the end it results to negative consequences that may hurt a student during job search, dissertation committees and getting tenure. It is essential for international students to participates in activities that are going to help them expand their network early enough in their career journey. Some of the things they can do include, joining organizations, going to conferences, and participating in conferences by either reviewing, presenting, or acting as session chairs. Moreover, international students should consider their personal goals when navigating the job market, for example, research preferences, workload threshold, and geographic

N. Krey (✉) · S. Wu
Rowan University, Glassboro, NJ, USA
e-mail: krey@rowan.edu; wus@rowan.edu

S. Wanjugu
University of Southern Indiana, Evansville, IN, USA
e-mail: swanjugu@usi.edu

J. A. Samo
University of Mississippi, Oxford, MS, USA
e-mail: jsamo@bus.olemiss.edu

F. Pantoja, S. Wu (eds.), *From Micro to Macro: Dealing with Uncertainties in the Global Marketplace*, Developments in Marketing Science: Proceedings of the Academy of Marketing Science, https://doi.org/10.1007/978-3-030-89883-0_137

locations. Lastly, young academicians need to keep in mind the weight of each of the three pillars of academic life: research, teaching and service. International scholars are encouraged to reach out to researchers in their areas for collaboration, to seek advice and feedback from colleagues in teaching, and to be actively involved in conferences for networking and collaboration opportunities.

Keywords International scholar · Stereotypes · Job market · Tenure · International doctoral candidate

References Available Upon Request

What Happens When Social Media Influencers Lie? Authenticity and Human Brands: An Abstract

Louis J. Zmich, Breanne Mertz, Cameron Sumlin, and Julie Moulard

Abstract Social media influencers (SMIs) represent a "new type of independent third-party endorser who shapes audience attitudes through blogs, tweets, and the use of other social media" (Freberg et al. 2011, p. 90). SMIs use various social media platforms to portray their online persona and, as such, can be considered human brands (Thompson 2006). Given the increase in the numbers of SMIs as well as their ever-growing audiences, it is no wonder that in 2019, the money traditional brands have spent sponsoring SMIs topped $8 billion in net worth and is projected to reach $15 billion in net worth by 2022 (Schomer 2019). This new phenomenon is referred to as influencer marketing (Audrezet et al. 2018), a strategy traditional brands use in which they promote their products via SMIs (i.e., human brands).

While being passionate and transparent are identified as two aspects associated with how SMIs manage their authenticity (Audrezet et al. 2019), prior research has not empirically examined whether these authenticity types affect consumer responses. Recently, research has identified three authenticity types that may help explain consumer responses. The specific types of authenticity that were developed are True-to-Self (TTS), True-to-Ideal (TTI), and True-to-Fact (TTF) (Moulard et al. 2020). For the purposes of this study, these three types of authenticity will be applied to the SMI.

These three authenticity types can be conceptualized within the context of SMIs. TTS authenticity of an SMI entails that the SMI loves what he/she does and the brands he/she promotes (intrinsic motivation). TTI authenticity entails that the SMI's content within his/her stories consistently reflects his/her brand essence (i.e., the ideal). TTF authenticity in the SMI context refers to consumers' perceptions of their honesty, forthrightness, and transparency within their online stories. We use these three types of authenticity to assess their effect on attitudes toward the social media influencer.

Thus, this manuscript addresses the following questions: Do influencer "stories," which attempt to showcase authentic behavior, positively affect viewer attitudes? Further, what if the stories portrayed by SMIs are not true? Do the lies actually

---

L. J. Zmich (✉) · B. Mertz · C. Sumlin · J. Moulard
Louisiana Tech University, Ruston, LA, USA
e-mail: ljz001@latech.edu; baw030@latech.edu; csu006@latech.edu; jmoulard@latech.edu

F. Pantoja, S. Wu (eds.), *From Micro to Macro: Dealing with Uncertainties in the Global Marketplace*, Developments in Marketing Science: Proceedings of the Academy of Marketing Science, https://doi.org/10.1007/978-3-030-89883-0_138

matter? This manuscript examines the relationship of SMI storytelling, authenticity, and attitudes toward the SMIs.

Keywords Authenticity · Social media influencers · Human brands · Transparency

References Available Upon Request

Entertainment Value in Pop-up Retailing: An Abstract

Ebru Ulusoy, Roberto Saldivar, and Arne Baruca

Abstract Retailing field is increasingly a competitive one. Brand differentiation through offering unique physical products and services is becoming more challenging in such a fierce competitive environment. Retailing field is going through the most radical shifts (Kahn et al. 2018). Competition is based primarily on price/convenience or experience in this field. Yet, for brick and mortar stores, the entertainment value that is based on unique, authentic, and relatable experiences has become a dominant theme in differentiation (Pine and Gilmore 1999; Kozinets et al. 2002).

This research focuses on a specific form on retailing, pop-up retailing, to investigate what retailers can do to offer entertainment value to consumers, and the implications of such value. More specifically, it analyzes the social media buzz created and supported by consumers to understand the consumer discourses of the entertainment value consumers drive from them. This study is exploratory in nature. It follows a qualitative analysis of social media buzz created and supported by consumers of several different pop-up stores. We systematically looked at how consumers talk about these pop-up stores, how they express their experience with them on social media. We collected and analyzed both the verbal posts and comments, and pictures.

Initial data analysis shows that pop-up stores satisfy three important characteristics of consumers: participation, personalization, and experientialism. All three characteristics, are reflected in the entertainment aspects of pop-up stores. In this

E. Ulusoy (✉)
Farmingdale State College, Farmingdale, NY, USA
e-mail: ebru.ulusoy@farmingdale.edu

R. Saldivar
University of Incarnate Word, San Antonio, TX, USA
e-mail: rosaldiv@uiwtx.edu

A. Baruca
Texas A&M University – San Antonio, San Antonio, TX, USA
e-mail: arne.baruca@tamusa.edu

F. Pantoja, S. Wu (eds.), *From Micro to Macro: Dealing with Uncertainties in the Global Marketplace*, Developments in Marketing Science: Proceedings of the Academy of Marketing Science, https://doi.org/10.1007/978-3-030-89883-0_139

research we attempt to understand how is this entertainment viewed in consumers' minds. The most common themes that emerged in the data analysis explaining the entertainment value are Interactivity, Exclusivity and deeper connection with the brand.

Even though pop-up stores are becoming popular among consumers, they are not free of flaws. There are still some consumers whose primary entertainment in these stores evolves around posing for pictures, and taking selfies. Others, believe that these stores often "look cheap and grimy" in person. Clearly, as with every innovative idea, pop-up stores as they are, will not be sufficient to satisfy all consumers unless they are designed as more substantial entertainment contexts, focused on more interactivity, exclusivity, and the very connection with the brand. As of now, the entertainment value is mainly created through sensory stimulation. But, the key to their future success would be to make these spaces social occasions of interaction that do not only evolve around sensations, but go beyond them, and create deeper experiences.

Keywords Pop-up stores · Retailing · Entertainment value · Qualitative

References Available Upon Request

Stressed and Relaxed Behavior and Impact on Purchase Intentions through Menu Labeling: An Abstract

Rani Hecht and Prachi Gala

Abstract According to the American Psychological Association (APA), chronic stress is becoming a public health crisis. We define stress as a state of emotional strain resulting from demanding circumstances. A characteristic of stress is that it can lead people to perceive that they currently lack control over their environment. Since one constant in everyone's daily life is food, it becomes important to know how daily stress can play a role in the choices made for food. As of July 2018, the US government and the FDA passed a law requiring restaurants (typically larger chain restaurants) to provide nutritional information for standard menu items. This recent trend of calorie counting, and advertising nutritional information sparked an interest of how influential this information really is. Despite the time and money that has been put in to implement new rules and regulations, there is little research uncovering how beneficial these changes may be with the new constant of stress.

In order to fill this gap, we will answer the question: to what extent does the consumer's level of stress influence their purchase intentions when food images and menu labeling are present? To answer this question, we will conduct an experiment using MTurk that will study the differences in consumer decision-making for food choices under stressed versus relaxed conditions. One group of participants will be "stressed" using a five-question timed logical test while a second group of participants will be "relaxed" using a nature-guided therapy technique. After measurement to confirm their stress levels, participants will examine menus with either food images or caloric labeling and then answer a series of questions about their purchase intentions. We expect that in the presence of both images and calories, an individual under stress is more likely to make unhealthy food choices, because of the overwhelming level of information. Completing this research will not only demonstrate how great of an impact stress has on our lives, but it will also allow managers to understand stressed consumers and cater to these new needs.

R. Hecht (✉) · P. Gala
Elon University, Elon, NC, USA
e-mail: rhecht@elon.edu; pgala@elon.edu

F. Pantoja, S. Wu (eds.), *From Micro to Macro: Dealing with Uncertainties in the Global Marketplace*, Developments in Marketing Science: Proceedings of the Academy of Marketing Science, https://doi.org/10.1007/978-3-030-89883-0_140

Keywords Purchase intentions · Food choices · Stressed behavior · Relaxed behavior · Chronic stress · Menu labeling · Healthy eating habits · Unhealthy eating habits

References Available Upon Request

What If? A Robot Challenge in a Marketing Course: An Abstract

Carlos Mario Uribe-Saldarriaga, Tatiana Ortiz-Pradilla, and Simón Echeverry-Gómez

Abstract Marketing education faces numerous challenges arising from digital disruption. Currently, the world of marketing is digital. Therefore, it is imperative that training in the field also be, despite the difficulties of keeping up with these dynamics. A new wave digital innovation (artificial intelligence, blockchain, robots, among others) are beginning to alter companies' relationships with consumers even more. EAFIT University's marketing program is no stranger to this reality, which is why it has worked hard since the program's introduction in 2011 in the insertion of digital marketing in its curriculum and the use of cutting-edge technologies through a specialized laboratory (MercaLAB, 2020). The University has even entered into the experiential learning of new technologies through project-based learning and challenges (Aguilar-Barrientos et al., 2019), involving students in real situations that encourage critical thinking, creativity, conceptual strength, teamwork, and learning skills.

The authors developed a design experiment with robotics implemented in EAFIT's marketing program in its course of Innovation and New Product Development (NPD). This experiment was carried out with the design-based research methodology (Bakker, 2018). A characteristic the design team considered fundamental to the design experiments of this methodology was its iterative nature, which allows refinement through prototypes of the initial idea (or design), and, therefore, the desired innovation purposes. The robotic design experiment has been fulfilled through three iterations since 2017.

In the *first iteration, a limited challenge prototype* was implemented. This prototype aimed to assess the scope of the robotic challenge, its relevance in a marketing course, and the students' performance in it. In a *second iteration, we developed a complete challenge prototype* in whose design both the course professors and experts in the field of educational robotics participated. This second prototype aimed to develop a complete challenge integrated into the course's dynamics. In a

C. M. Uribe-Saldarriaga (✉) · T. Ortiz-Pradilla · S. Echeverry-Gómez
Universidad EAFIT, Medellín, Colombia
e-mail: cmuribe@eafit.edu.co; tortizpr@eafit.edu.co; secheve8@eafit.edu.co

F. Pantoja, S. Wu (eds.), *From Micro to Macro: Dealing with Uncertainties in the Global Marketplace*, Developments in Marketing Science: Proceedings of the Academy of Marketing Science, https://doi.org/10.1007/978-3-030-89883-0_141

third iteration, the full challenge prototype was implemented in all the new product development courses. This third prototype aimed to implement a robotic challenge with a broader scope, both in terms of the development of computational thinking, the programming and use of the robot, and a more detailed fusion regarding the course's dynamics.

The importance of educational robotics as a starting point for the introduction of new technologies in the undergraduate marketing curriculum was validated. Likewise, the authors proved that the robotic system framed in a narrative and a serious game is valuable for the Innovation and NPD course; This pilot was a relevant, valuable, fun, and creativity enhancer.

Keywords Digital disruption · Marketing education · Robotics competitions · Design-based research

References Available Upon Request

The Effect of Ingredient Images on Baby Food Packaging on Healthiness Perception, Tastiness, Attitude, and Purchase Intention: An Abstract

Fanny Thomas, Betina Piqueras-Fiszman, and Gaëlle Pantin-Sohier

Abstract Early childhood is a very sensitive area; health professionals are alerting the most vulnerable young people about what to eat. All European parents are looking for healthy baby food products and rely on facing packaging to assess the healthiness level and quality of products. Visual elements are more memorized than textual, for example, ingredient images depiction are very often used by baby food designers in order to better characterize the product's composition. Nevertheless, regulations are very poor and this depiction is not framed. Parents can use ingredient images as a heuristic to evaluate their quantity in the product recipe and can be misled because of perception bias. Therefore, the biased perception on baby food product triggered by the format in which ingredients depicted in the front of pack are represented (namely cut vs. whole) is investigated. Our research is in the field of consumer behavior, sensory marketing and young children's health, and considers the effects of graphic depiction bias on packaging on baby food product evaluation in several countries. To study the effect of ingredients images design, we conducted an experiment in 3 European countries within parents of babies 10-36 months old assessed the format of ingredient on front-of-pack of a fruit and cereal bar on perceived fruit quantity in the recipe, healthiness, tastiness, attitude towards the product, and then purchase intention. Our results highlight that Front of pack depicting cut ingredient images increases purchase intention via the increase of attitude

We acknowledge Enjeu(x), RFI Food for Tomorrow, MSH Ange Guépin, Fondation of university of Angers through Diana Food partnership, which have participated to funding this research from the BBSAIN project

F. Thomas (✉) · G. Pantin-Sohier
University of Angers, Angers, France
e-mail: fanny.thomas@univ-angers.fr; gaelle.pantin-sohier@univ-angers.fr

B. Piqueras-Fiszman
University of Wageningen, Wageningen, Netherlands
e-mail: betina.piquerasfiszman@wur.nl

F. Pantoja, S. Wu (eds.), *From Micro to Macro: Dealing with Uncertainties in the Global Marketplace*, Developments in Marketing Science: Proceedings of the Academy of Marketing Science, https://doi.org/10.1007/978-3-030-89883-0_142

towards the product and via the increase of perceived product healthiness and tastiness induced by more perceived fruit proportion in the product recipe. This research highlights the effect of format of ingredient depiction on product evaluation and the bias perception. We propose a standards suggestion for public policy on food labelling and on ethic positioning of baby food manufacturers.

Keywords Ingredient design · Baby food · Perception bias · Packaging

References Available Upon Request

How Does Personalization Affect Brand Relationship in Social Commerce? A Mediation Perspective: An Abstract

Trang P. Tran, Michelle van Solt, and James E. Zemanek Jr.

Abstract Growing literature has examined the effects of personalized ads in traditional media. Nonetheless, the effects of personalized ads on social media are scarce. This research paper has bridged the gap by developing a theory-driven model illustrating the impact of personalized ads on customer perceptions of brands advertised on social media. More specifically, this research identifies the relationship between perceived personalization in advertisements found on social media to the outcomes of brand relationship, purchase intention and brand loyalty. The model also proposes two mediators: consumer brand identification and consumer brand engagement.

Two studies are implemented to test the model, using PLS-SEM. All hypotheses are supported in study 1 studies, except for H4—there is a positive relationship between consumer brand engagement and brand relationship. All nine hypotheses are supported in Study 2 which includes control variables (i.e., past brand purchases of the brand, past positive or negative experiences with the brand, and whether participants "like" the brand on Facebook or not). The results also illustrate that consumer brand engagement and consumer brand identification partially mediate the influence of personalized ads on brand relationship.

Another contribution of this research takes into consideration consumers' attitudes toward perceived personalization gathered from their past online activity with brands. Some consumers enjoy ad personalization and find it convenient and exciting while others find ad personalization off-putting and have privacy concerns. This work identifies three market segments via discriminant analysis: (a) Ad Lovers, (b) Ad Adjusters, and Ad Haters. Customers in each market segment demonstrate typical customer attitudes toward personalized ads that are consistent with members in each segment, but different across the segments.

T. P. Tran · J. E. Zemanek Jr.
East Carolina University, Greenville, NC, USA
e-mail: trantra17@ecu.edu; zemanekj@ecu.edu

M. van Solt (✉)
Valparaiso University, Valparaiso, IN, USA
e-mail: michelle.vansolt@valpo.edu

F. Pantoja, S. Wu (eds.), *From Micro to Macro: Dealing with Uncertainties in the Global Marketplace*, Developments in Marketing Science: Proceedings of the Academy of Marketing Science, https://doi.org/10.1007/978-3-030-89883-0_143

The paper sheds lights into better understanding of the impact of personalized ads on the most dominant social media platform—Facebook, and suggests that if personalized ads are customized properly, this could be used as a marketing solution, creating competitive advantage for online marketers.

Keywords Personalized advertising · Facebook · PLS-SEM · Cluster analysis · Mediation

References Available Upon Request

Overcoming Big as Bad: Brand Dominance and the Authenticity Deficit of Sustainable Products: An Abstract

Karen Anne Wallach

Abstract Brands are responding to the increasing importance that consumers and society have placed on sustainable practices and products. The present work is designed as the first academic research to examine the attributions consumers make towards dominant brands and their sustainability initiatives. This research demonstrates a negative bias that exists with consumer perceptions of brand size and sustainability related to perceptions of authenticity. Thus, this work examines consumer perceptions of brand size and sustainability, and its impact on purchase intent. Across seven studies, including a field experiment on Facebook, this work identifies a negativity bias that exists with consumers towards large brands and sustainability efforts. This is rooted in a perceived incongruence between profitability, which strong dominant brands represent, and societal good, which sustainability is focused on. This work builds on previous research asserting that critical to achieving authenticity is being linked to a commitment motivated beyond profits. As such, an authenticity deficit that arises out of the paradox between sustainability which is focused on "taking less" (i.e. less energy, chemicals, materials) and the prevailing measure of success in business which is focused on "making more" (i.e. more profit, production). Moreover, the challenge of a brand becomes further amplified as the brand is perceived as bigger and more profit centric. Importantly, while this authenticity deficit significantly impacts purchase intent, it can be attenuated with increased commitment or third-party certification. Thus, the objective of this paper is to further enhance the understanding of how consumers perceive sustainability initiatives, and more specifically, to establish a negativity bias towards large brands. However, overcoming the negative bias surrounding large brands is not only important to further understand consumers, but also has big implications for society and the planet. This work proposes recommendations for practionners and hopefully leads

K. A. Wallach (✉)
Emory University, Atlanta, GA, USA
e-mail: kwallach@emory.edu

F. Pantoja, S. Wu (eds.), *From Micro to Macro: Dealing with Uncertainties in the Global Marketplace*, Developments in Marketing Science: Proceedings of the Academy of Marketing Science, https://doi.org/10.1007/978-3-030-89883-0_144

to impactful sustainability commitments by brands. This research incorporates an interdisciplinary viewpoint (i.e. marketing, economics, management, psychology) to contribute to the literatures on authenticity, branding and sustainability.

Keywords Sustainability · Branding · Corporate social responsibility · Authenticity

References Available Upon Request

Love Me or Hate Me! This is Who I am: The Use of Instagram to Create Shared Ethnic Identity Practices: An Abstract

B. Yasanthi Perera, Sarita Ray Chaudhury, Lubna Nafees, and Pia A. Albinsson

Abstract Western media depictions of South Asians (SAs) are tinged with stereotypes (Madhawi 2017; Hirji 2019). Given their underrepresentation and misrepresentation, using Web 2.0 technologies, young SAs are circumventing traditional media gatekeepers to create and share content (Madhawi 2019; Shah 2019). This exploratory research uses a thick data approach to examine how young western women of SA heritage use Instagram, specifically the account @browngirlgang, to promote their collective wellbeing by expressing their ethnic identity in face of societal and intra-community pressures. We liken this setting to an online counterspace (Mwangi et al. 2018), a communal venue where those experiencing discrimination (e.g., racist, sexist, ableist narratives) can find reprieve by promoting positive self-concepts that enhance their well-being (Case and Hunter 2012). Ethnic identity, in turn, is a part of an individual's self-concept that stems from "that part of an individual's self-concept which derives from knowledge of membership of a social group (or groups) together with the value and emotional significance attached to that membership" (Tajfel 1984, 255). Based on interpretive qualitative research tenets (Geertz 1973), the thick data approach comprises three-stage layering process of contextualization, description, and signification (Latzko-Toth et al. 2016). Preliminary findings consist of four emergent themes. *Sharing the challenges of mainstream narratives of beauty and glamour* pertains to celebrating varied skin tones, and body shapes that counter lived experiences of feeling not beautiful enough while growing up in western societies. *Celebrating entrepreneurial and*

B. Yasanthi Perera (✉)
Brock University, St. Catharines, ON, Canada
e-mail: bperera@brocku.ca

S. R. Chaudhury
Humboldt State University, Arcata, CA, USA
e-mail: sarita@humboldt.edu

L. Nafees · P. A. Albinsson
Appalachian State University, Boone, NC, USA
e-mail: nafeesl@appstate.edu; albinssonpa@appstate.edu

F. Pantoja, S. Wu (eds.), *From Micro to Macro: Dealing with Uncertainties in the Global Marketplace*, Developments in Marketing Science: Proceedings of the Academy of Marketing Science, https://doi.org/10.1007/978-3-030-89883-0_145

business efforts of South Asian women highlight SA celebrities and non-celebrity artists, writers, business owners/ executives, entrepreneurs, and activists for empowerment purposes. *Laughing together in shared "fusion" culture* consist of content, including pop-culture based memes, utilizing SA languages and cultural elements for humor and community building purposes. *Seeking comfort when challenged by socio-cultural norms* comprises images that counter both western mainstream prejudices (e.g., stereotypes of being meek and compliant), and intra-ethnic community gender and sexual orientation-based discrimination. The @browngirlgang situates SA culture within the context of mainstream western culture and thereby bridge two (or more) cultures. Moreover, the research highlights the diversity of SAs, their accomplishments, and provides support for those traditionally marginalized within SA communities all of which serves to influence others and their own self-perceptions.

Keywords Brown Girl Movement · Ethnic identities · South Asian women · Instagram · Social Media Self-branding

References Available Upon Request

Bingewatching and Streaming Platforms: Brand Priming Influence on Behavior Intention and the Role of Social Distancing: An Abstract

Irina T. Toteva

Abstract Consumer consumption of video streaming services continues to evolve with new platforms such as Apple TV+, Disney+ and Peacock entering the $36-billion market and 60% of adults watching a few episodes of shows on demand, an activity known as bingewatching. At the onset of the 2020 pandemic people increasingly turned to bingewatching, cooking, or creative activities such as crafting. Prior research has shown that a creative brand such as Apple can prime a goal to be creative, resulting in better performance on a creative task. No research has explored the priming effects of video streaming platforms on consumer behavior.

The present research explores the priming effects of streaming platform brand on consumers' likelihood to engage in a creative task or in watching video episodes during social distancing. In Study 1, after participants were exposed to Netflix (vs. Apple TV+) logo, there was a main positive effect of social distancing tv watching habits on likelihood to participate in a creative task and number of video program episodes intended to watch. The more people changed their tv watching habits due to social distancing, the higher their behavior intention for creativity and for bingewatching.

In Study 2, participants were presented with Netflix logo (vs. control no-logo) and their productivity orientation, trait bingewatching, social distancing habits change were measured. Analyses with Hayes' Process Model 2 demonstrated a main effect of streaming platform brand such that in the Netflix condition (vs. the control no-logo) people were less likely to participate in the creative task. Productivity orientation moderates this relationship such that, in the Netflix condition, people with high productivity orientation were more likely to participate in the creative task. Counterintuitively, people who were high on bingewatching trait were more likely to engage in the creative task. Also, the more people changed their tv watching behavior due to social distancing, the higher the likelihood to participate

I. T. Toteva (✉)
Georgia Southwestern State University, Americus, GA, USA
e-mail: irina.toteva@gsw.edu

F. Pantoja, S. Wu (eds.), *From Micro to Macro: Dealing with Uncertainties in the Global Marketplace*, Developments in Marketing Science: Proceedings of the Academy of Marketing Science, https://doi.org/10.1007/978-3-030-89883-0_146

in the creative task. While streaming platform brands may be associated with creativity, they are less likely to prime a goal to engage in a creative task (compared to a control no-brand). This effect is attenuated for consumers with high productivity orientation. Thus, brand priming may be more consistent with the purpose of the service provided rather than with a brand personality association such as creativity. The practical implications of this research for companies that offer creative experiences – they should target consumers with high productivity orientation.

Keywords Brand Priming · Bingewatching · Creativity · Social Distancing

References Available Upon Request

Do You Need More Committed Volunteers for Your Nonprofit? Support their Brand Community: An Abstract

Janna M. Parker, Doreen Sams, and Kevin W. James

Abstract The brand community literature has shown that a brand community's existence leads to greater loyalty and positive outcomes for manufacturer's brands and higher education. This study explored whether social media engagement and in-person social activities for volunteers foster a brand community leading to more committed volunteers.

Nonprofit volunteers were recruited on M-Turk for the survey on Qualtrics. Respondents were asked to name the nonprofit for which they volunteered the most and to think of it while answering questions beginning with how frequently they volunteered. They were removed if the response was less than a year. The final sample was $n = 301$ (Female = 52.8%). All measures used a six-point scale anchored with strongly disagree to strongly agree. Algesheimer et al. (2006) developed a multi-dimensional Brand Community scale. The subscales of Brand Community Identification (BCI) (0.87), Brand Community Engagement (BCE) (0.80), and Brand Community Relationship Quality (BCRQ) (0.86) and the Wiertz and Ruyter (2006) Interaction Preference (IP) (0.90) were included as covariates. For the DVs, the Organizational Commitment (OC) (0.81) by Maltz and Kohli (1996) and one item from Membership Continuance Intentions (MCI) (Algesheimer et al. 2006) were adapted. For the 2 × 3 MANCOVA design, Hi/Low groups were formed using the single item of Community Participation Intentions (CPI), for in-person social activities, with none selecting strongly disagree (1) to somewhat disagree (3). Respondents who selected somewhat agree (4) formed the low group ($n = 83$) and agree (5) or strongly agree (6) formed the high group ($n = 218$). An index Social Media Engagement (SME) (low = 1 or less, 2 = 2, high = 3 or more) was measured

J. M. Parker (✉)
James Madison University, Harrisonburg, VA, USA
e-mail: parke4jm@jmu.edu

D. Sams
Georgia College and State University, Milledgeville, GA, USA
e-mail: doreen.sams@gcsu.edu

K. W. James
The University of Texas at Tyler, Tyler, TX, USA
e-mail: kjames@uttyler.edu

F. Pantoja, S. Wu (eds.), *From Micro to Macro: Dealing with Uncertainties in the Global Marketplace*, Developments in Marketing Science: Proceedings of the Academy of Marketing Science, https://doi.org/10.1007/978-3-030-89883-0_147

by the number of social media accounts followed. Sample size and differences in group sizes are not problematic since this was not a randomized assignment (Hair et al. 2010).

No covariate was significant for both dependent variables. For MCI, only BCE and IP were significant. For OC, only BCRQ and BCI were significant. The interaction (CPI x SME) was significant for OC but not MCI. The main effect of CPI was only significant for MCI, and SME was only significant for OC. The adjusted R2s were MCI (0.121) and OC (0.307).

Results suggest that nonprofit organizations can benefit from supporting the growth and development of an online brand community more than in-person social activities. MTurk samples are not representative which is a limitation of the study.

Keywords Brand communities · Nonprofits · Volunteers · Social media · Organizational commitment

References Available Upon Request

Typography of Commercial Websites: The Effects of the Interline Spacing on Internet Users' Reactions

Jean-François Lemoine and Raouf Zafri

Abstract As long as the text on commercial websites is omnipresent, managers are brought to make decisions concerning the typography in terms of typeface characteristics, spacing and layout. This research is particularly interested in the effect of text's interline spacing of commercial websites. The results of an experimental study, conducted on 122 buyers, show that Internet users who visited a site with a wide spacing experience felt a stronger sensation of well-being than those who visited it with narrowed spacing. The wide interline spacing also allows to arouse better perceived aesthetics of the website. However, the effect of interline spacing on behavioral intentions is not direct. These intentions depend, on the one hand, on the simple mediation of well-being and, on the other hand, on the multiple mediation of the perceived aesthetics and then on the perceived ease of use of the website.

Keywords Typography · Interline spacing · Emotions · Perceived ease of use · Perceived aesthetics · Online store atmospherics

Introduction

Faced with the competitive intensification of online commerce and thus the need for differentiation that results from it, websites are increasingly relying on textual content to improve their search engine optimization (SEO) and enhance their online attractiveness (Canivet-Bourgaux 2017). However, while it is true that the presence of text offers a myriad of advantages in terms of site visibility and persuasion, the

---

J.-F. Lemoine · R. Zafri (✉)
Université Paris 1 Panthéon-Sorbonne, Paris, France
e-mail: jean-francois.lemoine@univ-paris1.fr; raouf.zafri@univ-paris1.fr

F. Pantoja, S. Wu (eds.), *From Micro to Macro: Dealing with Uncertainties in the Global Marketplace*, Developments in Marketing Science: Proceedings of the Academy of Marketing Science, https://doi.org/10.1007/978-3-030-89883-0_148

fact remains that its typography[1] is a top priority for managers in search of visual staging of the interfaces and continuous improvement of the browsing experience.

Many studies have focused on typography in several disciplines such as semiotics, linguistics, cognitive psychology, design or art history. In this vein, particular attention was paid to the typeface and the character size and much less to interline spacing, defined as « the existing distance between lines of text » (McCarthy and Mothersbaugh 2002). However, everything suggests that it is a stimulus that can affect the reactions of individuals by guiding the reader in the treatment of information (Lemarié et al. 2008) and by inducing mental associations during visual exploration of the webpage (McCarthy and Mothersbaugh 2002). Similarly, Lemoine and Zafri (2017) specify, in a preliminary qualitative study, that spacing is the typographic component that is most likely to generate emotional and behavioral reactions to the website. Although earlier research, made in the context of human-machine interaction and psycholinguistics, shows that interline spacing can affect the readability of the text and the reading behavior of the individual (Bentley 1921; Campbell 1995; Chung 2004; Van Overschelde and Healy 2005; Bernard et al. 2007; Lee et al. 2011; Sergeev and Tarasov 2013), it seems then useful to study, from a marketing point of view, the influence of this typographic factor on the reactions of Internet users in an online shopping context.

In digital marketing, interline spacing is an environmental component of the « ambient » dimension of the web atmosphere, as much as color, images and sound (Lemoine 2008).[2] In order to examine its influence on the responses of Internet users, we use the Stimulus-Organism-Response (SOR) model (Mehrabian and Russell 1974; Eroglu et al. 2001) according to which atmospheric factors are likely to influence, as a first step, the internal reactions (emotions, cognitions) of the individual and then his behavior. In this logic, we made the choice to adopt this model, which is commonly used to report the effects of a website's atmosphere on the Internet users' reactions (Chang et al. 2014; Koo and Ju 2010; Mummalaneni 2005). At the emotional level, this article proposes to study the influence of the interline spacing on the well-being defined as "a pleasant emotional state, of weak activation which mixes sensations of calm and well-being"[3] (Lichtlé and Plichon 2014). On the cognitive level, this research attempts to examine the impact of interline spacing, on the one hand, on the perceived aesthetics that refers to the evaluation of the site's beauty and seemliness (Yeh et al. 2015), and on the other hand, on the perception of its ease of use reflecting the degree to which a person believes that the use of

[1] Typography deals with the form, spacing, and layout of words and sentences. It is a function of three factors: (1) Typeface characteristics (style, size, x-height, weight, slant, stress, color and movement). (2) Spacing characteristics (distance between words, between letters within words, and between lines of text). (3) Layout characteristics (number of columns, length of the line of text, text justification, and contrast among text units) (McCarthy and Mothersbaugh 2002).

[2] The other two dimensions of the web atmosphere are design (navigability of the site, accessibility of the offer) and social factors (virtual assistants, forums, customer reviews) (Lemoine 2008).

[3] Following an exploratory study conducted with 28 Internet users, it has been shown that the main emotions generated by the typography of commercial websites are: well-being (34% of citations), pleasure (23% of citations), constriction (18% of citations), nervousness (11% of citations), confusion (8% of citations) and finally relaxation (6% of citations) (Lemoine and Zafri 2017).

the site would be without physical and mental efforts (Visinescu et al. 2015; Davis et al. 1989). At the conative level, this paper aims to test the direct effect of the interline spacing on the behavioral intentions of the user.

Through this research, we would like to enrich the literature in typography marketing, that has not, until now, been interested in the influence of interline spacing in an online sales context. From a managerial point of view, this research aims to inform the professionals on the type of spacing to privilege, given the emotional and behavioral responses they want to arouse in their customers. It also aims to make them more aware of the consequences of their choice in typographic matters, in particular by examining the impact of interline spacing on the well-being felt, the perceived ease of use of the site, the perceived aesthetics of the site and the behavioral intentions.

Research Model and Hypotheses

The physiology of reading suggests that reduced interline spacing would lead to overlaps between successive lines (McCarthy and Mothersbaugh 2002) which may be confusing for the reader and make recognition quite difficult because it requires longer and/or repeated fixations on the same letters and words (Pollatsek and Rayner 1982; Rayner et al. 1998). However, even if the effects of very large spacing on the speed of reading are controversial, researchers agree that, given the interline scale used in general for the text of electronic interfaces, the increase in interlining level creates a feeling of ease, well-being and visual comfort when reading (Sergeev and Tarasov 2013; Lee et al. 2011; Chung 2004). In line with these studies, we formulate hypothesis H1a according to which the well-being felt during the visit of the commercial sites will be higher when the spacing is wide than when it is narrowed. Moreover, in view of considering the well-known mediating effects of emotions on behavioral intentions in the literature on the web atmosphere (Eroglu et al. 2003; Mummalaneni 2005), we hypothesize that well-being mediates the effects of interline spacing on behavioral intentions (H1b).

Previous research has shown that the perceptual fluency with which consumers can identify and process the information of an object significantly improves individuals' attitudes and gives the impression of an easier understanding and interaction with this object (Reber et al. 2004; Labroo et al. 2008; Hart et al. 2013). Based on the literature available in reading physiology, we can expect that a wider line will increase the perceptual fluency, the understanding of the information and will reduce the effort involved in the research. This can be inferred by an easier interaction with the site and a better perception of its ease of use. We therefore make the following hypothesis: the perceived ease of use of the site will be judged more favorably when the line spacing is wider than when it is narrowed (H2a). Several researches in human-machine interaction using the technology acceptance model have demonstrated the mediating effect of ease of use in explaining Internet users' behaviors (Davis et al. 1989; Visinescu et al. 2015). Based on this literature, we formulate Hypothesis H2b according to which the perceived ease of use of the site mediates the influence of interline spacing on behavioral intentions.

Interlining can also influence judgments about the aesthetics of the site by affecting the physical appearance of the web page. Studies in design and semiotics emphasize that wide spacing is often associated with simplicity and purity and de facto reduces the visual complexity of the page (McCarthy and Mothersbaugh 2002). According to Pandir and Knight (2006) this would result in a better perception of aesthetics. In fact, several studies support the idea that the aesthetic judgments made by individuals are all the more favorable when the visual complexity is less important (Bauerly and Liu 2008; Pandir and Knight 2006). Thus, we hypothesize that the perceived aesthetics of the site will be more favorable when the interline spacing is wide than when it is narrowed (H3a).

Additionally, some studies have already established that the perception of aesthetics is an antecedent of intention to revisit by Internet users (Yoo and Donthu 2001). Similarly, in design, some research has highlighted the determining role of aesthetics in consumer buying behavior (Celhay and Trinquecoste 2015). We thus formulate the hypothesis according to which the perceived aesthetics of the site mediates the influence of the interline spacing on the behavioral intentions (H3b).

Furthermore, it seems useful to ask ourselves about the mediating role of the variables that could enrich the understanding of the relationship « interline spacing—behavioral intentions », including the perception of aesthetics of the site and that of its ease of use. Existing relationships between the aesthetics of systems and their ease of use are generating more and more studies (Hassenzahl 2004; Tuch et al. 2012; Lee 2013). Several studies have found a strong correlation between perception of aesthetics and perceived ease of use (Hartmann et al. 2008; Lavie and Tractinsky 2004). Some authors believe that "what is usable is beautiful" (Ben-Bassat et al. 2006; Lee and Koubek 2010). Others, instead, argue that "what is beautiful is usable" referring to the study by Tractinsky et al. (2000) whose evocative title was "what is beautiful is usable". We propose to jointly analyze the effect of these two variables and present them in a multiple mediation relationship in series. Hence our hypothesis H4: the effect of interline spacing on behavioral intentions is mediated by the perceived aesthetics of the site and then by the perception of its ease of use.

Finally, in line with the studies on the atmosphere of websites that have identified direct links between atmospheric factors and behavioral intentions (Bonnardel et al. 2011; Cherif and Lemoine 2019), we suggest to test the validity of the following hypothesis: the behavioral intentions will be more favorable on the site with a large interline spacing than on the site with a narrowed interline spacing (H5).

Research Methodology

Experimental Procedure

In order to test the validity of our hypotheses, an inter-subject online experiment was conducted with 122 Internet users. Interline spacing was handled on two levels: narrowed and wide. To define more precisely and realistically the values of these two methods, we conducted a benchmark with 42 French commercial sites across all business sectors. The results of this benchmark established that the median line spacing is 127%. Using the median-split method, the values of 100% (narrowed) and 140% (wide) were selected. Two versions of a commercial website selling electric toothbrushes with fictitious brands were designed (see Appendix 1). Following a pre-test conducted with 96 respondents, the realism of the sites and their speed of download were considered satisfactory. The same is true for the perceived congruence between the typography of the site and the category of product. In addition, we have selected the electric toothbrush as a product category because it is a product that can be purchased via the Internet and by many individuals, regardless of age, income and gender. Moreover, it is a product that is both utilitarian and hedonic, which is appropriate for our study given the affective and cognitive nature of the variables of our model. Finally, given the diversity of web access tools used by the consumer, we limited our investigation to the case of the computer because it remains the device most used by Internet users to make a purchase on the Internet (79% sales) (FEVAD 2018).

Data Collection, Sample

To compose our sample and administer our online questionnaire, we used the Cint (Sphinx Online) panel. The mood before visiting the site was measured as well as the involvement towards the product category and price perception. Each participant was randomly assigned to one of the two versions of the site to simulate an online shopping act. At the end of the visit, the Internet user was subjected to the scales of measurement of the variables studied. To be eligible for this study, the respondent must have already made at least one purchase on the Internet in the last 12 months and be connected via a computer when administering our survey. To participate in the study, it was also necessary that the Internet user did not set special preferences on his browser such as zoom and that he did not have a vision problem. A person who did not meet these criteria could not continue to respond to the survey. Control filter questions were therefore used from the beginning of the questionnaire. Similarly, we have implemented a strict database clean-up procedure, retaining only those participants who surfed at least three pages with reference to Bucklin and Sismeiro (2003), and discarding observations with extreme values on several items. This collection allowed us to collect 122 valid responses (60 respondents for the narrowed line spacing version and 62 for the wide line version). These two samples were representative of the buyers of electric toothbrushes on the Internet.

Manipulation Check and Homogeneity of the Samples

The comparison of averages shows that there are statistically significant differences between the two experimental conditions ($M_{\text{narrowed spacing perception}} = 3.04$ et $M_{\text{wide spacing perception}} = 4.61$; $t = -0.827$; $p = 0.000$). It is therefore possible to conclude that the two types of line spacing are perceived as different by the two groups of respondents. In addition, using the Chi-square test, it was verified that the two samples made were matched in terms of gender ($\chi^2 = 0.036$; $p = 0.849$), age ($\chi^2 = 2950$; $p = 0.566$), and the frequency of purchase on the Internet ($\chi^2 = 0.355$; $p = 0.551$).

Measurement Scales

Well-being was measured via the Lichtle and Plichon scale (2014), the perceived ease of use and the perceived aesthetics of the site using the Bressolles scale (2006) and the behavioral intentions thanks to the Keeling et al. (2007) scale. For other control variables, product category involvement was measured with the Strazzieri scale (1994), mood before the site's visit with the Peterson and Sauber (1983) scale, and finally the price perception using the Gonzalez single-item scale (2005). All items were measured by 7-step Likert scales (see Appendix 2).

Data Analysis Method

To test our research model, we favored the PLS structural equation modeling method because of its requirements in terms of sample size, multivariate normality and its ability to integrate any type of scale (nominal, ordinal or metric) (Hair Jr et al. 2014). The reliability and convergent validity of the measurements were first studied and proved satisfactory following the exploratory and confirmatory factorial analyzes (Appendix 2). In the same way, the discriminant validity between the constructs has been established (Appendix 3).

Research Results

Preliminary Analyses

Before testing the hypotheses, we made sure of the similarity of the people assigned to each of the experimental conditions. No significant difference was found for mood before site visit ($p = 0.443$), product involvement ($p = 0.896$) and price perception ($p = 0.701$).

Direct Effects

The level of the interline spacing has been coded as follows: 1 = narrowed; 2 = wide. The model indicates a satisfactory GoF of 0.433 (>0.36). The direct effects of interline spacing on the well-being and perceived aesthetics of the site are significant (H1a and H3a supported). Wide line spacing leads to more favorable reactions than narrowed line spacing. On the other hand, no significant effect was found with regard to the direct influence of line spacing on ease of use (H2a not supported) and on behavioral intentions (H5 not supported) (Appendix 4).

Mediation Effects

The tests associated with bootstrap (n = 5000 samples) allow to directly examine mediation effects. The results show that well-being is an indirect mediator of the effect of line spacing on behavioral intentions [0,090; (0,029; 0,152)] (H1b supported). Regarding the simple mediating role of the perceived ease of use and perceived aesthetics of the site, the statistical analyzes revealed no significant indirect effects (H2b and H3b not supported). However, the study of multiple mediation in series corresponding to the effect of interline spacing on behavioral intentions, including perceived aesthetics and perception of ease of use of site is significant. [0.008; (0.004; 0.016)] (H4 supported). A favorable perception of the aesthetics of the site resulting from wide line spacing results in a positive perception of the ease of use of the site, which, in turn, will positively influence behavioral intentions (see Appendix 5) (Fig. 1).

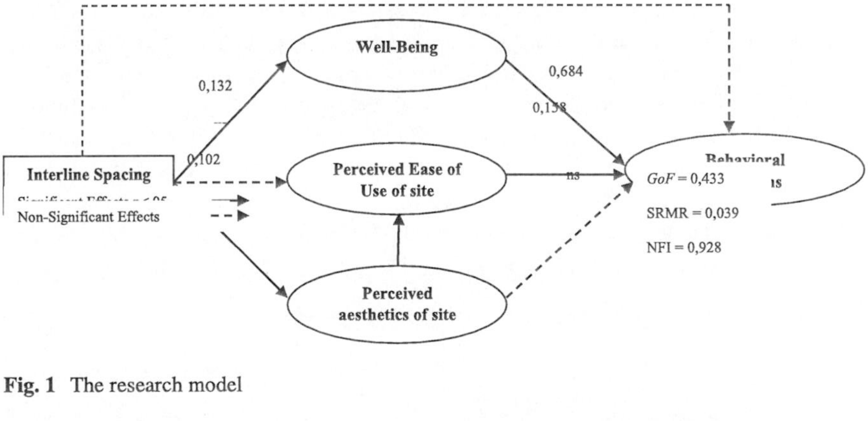

Fig. 1 The research model

Contributions, Limitations and Future Research

On the theoretical level, this research presents four main contributions. The first is to look at the effects of the interline spacing of a website in a market context. This study comes to enrich the literature in marketing and more particularly that dealing with the impact of environmental factors on the behavior of Internet users. The second contribution of this article is to confirm the relevance of using the S-O-R model to account for the effects of line spacing on the reactions of Internet users. This thus overcomes the limits of the existing literature by going beyond the vision based on the readability and the cognitive processing of the information to propose another more global approach taking into account the affects and the behaviors of approach during the typographical choices. The third contribution of this research lies in the study of theoretical links that have never been studied until now in a digital market context. Thus, this research has demonstrated the existence of links between the interline spacing of a website and the well-being, perceived aesthetics, perceived ease of use and behavioral intentions. The last contribution of this paper is the demonstration of simple mediation effects of well-being and multiple mediation in series of the perceived aesthetics of the site and the perceived ease of use in the relation: interline spacing - behavioral intentions.

At the managerial level, we would recommend professionals to favor a rather wide line spacing. By making this choice, managers can increase the well-being of users, generate better judgment on the aesthetics of the site and its ease of use. Moreover, when they rely on this type of interlining, they are able to indirectly influence the behavioral intentions towards the site even more. In other words, by its effects on the internal and behavioral state of the visitor, line spacing is presented as a mechanism by which a website can create an interesting differentiation in a context of high competitive intensity.

Our research has limitations that should be emphasized. It has reduced external validity given the particularities of the device used (computer) and the category of products selected. In the future, similar experiments on other devices should be undertaken to take into account the adaptive nature of the current design of the websites (responsive design) and on sites selling other categories of products. In addition, our work has been reduced to the study of the effects of the type of interlining. We did not take into account other typographic features such as font and character size. It would therefore be relevant to look at the interaction effects between the typographic components of the site. Finally, to better understand the effects of interline spacing, it seems desirable to enrich our model with some moderating variables such as the purpose of the visit and the need for cognition or other dependent variables measuring the actual behavior of Internet users like the length of visit, the number of pages consulted and the nature of the shopping cart.

Appendix 1: The Stimuli Used for the Experiment

Screenshot of the experimental website: narrowed line spacing

Screenshot of the experimental website: wide line spacing

Liphis HX6512/02 – Programme blancheur -Rechargeable

102,05€

Brossage : sonique

Alimentation : rechargeable

Pulsations : 31000/min

Accessoires : 2 manches EasyClean et 2 brossettes

Ajouter au panier

Liphis HX6711/02 – 2 modes de brossage – 31 000 pulsations/min

102,12€

Brossage : sonique

Modes de brossage : standart et blancheur

Alimentation : rechargeable

Accessoires : 1 brossette

Ajouter au panier

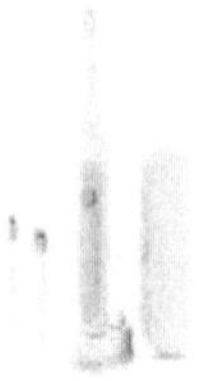

Liphis HX6713 – Programme blancheur – 3 brossettes – 31000/min

99,99€

Brossage : sonique en 2 modes Clean et Clean White

Alimentation : rechargeable

Pulsations : 31000/min

Accessoires : 3 brossettes fournies

Appendix 2: The Measures and their Psychometric Properties

Scales	Items	Loadings	Cronbach's Alpha	CR	AVE
Well-being (Lichtlé and Plichon 2014)	It's warm	0.880	0.935	0.950	0.792
	You feel a sense of harmony	0.893			
	I get a nice feeling	0.886			
	You feel Zen	0.890			
	You feel chilled	0.902			
Perceived Ease of Use (Bressolles 2006)	The site is easy to use	0.890	0.954	0.965	0.845
	It is easy to move around and find what I am looking for on the site	0.916			
	The organization and the layout of the site make information research easy	0.939			
	The site is laid out in a clear and simple way	0.931			
	It is easy to look for information on the site	0.920			
Perceived aesthetics (Bressolles 2006)	The site is visually attractive	0.971	0.967	0.979	0.939
	The site looks good	0.970			
	The site is creative	0.966			
Behavioral Intentions (Keeling et al. 2007)	likely to buy	0.890	0.885	0.929	0.813
	likely to revisit	0.920			
	likely to recommend	0.895			
Product Involvement (Strazzieri 1994)	I am particularly attracted by this product	0.926	0.967	0.974	0.860
	The simple fact of learning about this product is a pleasure	0.938			
	I particularly like to talk about this product	0.913			
	You can say that is a product that interests me	0.933			
	It's a product that really matters to me	0.944			
	It's a product to which I attach special importance	0.908			

Scales	Items	Loadings	Cronbach's Alpha	CR	AVE
Mood before the site's visit (Peterson and Sauber 1983)	Currently I am in a good mood	0.837	0.902	0.931	0.771
	As I answer these questions, I feel very cheerful	0.904			
	For some reason, I am not very comfortable right now	0.884			
	At this moment, I feel edgy or irritable	0.886			
P rice perception (Gonzalez 2005)	Cheap/expensive	–	–	–	–

Appendix 3: Discriminant Validity: Matrix of Correlations between Constructs

	Well-being	Ease of use	Perceived aesthetics	Behavioral intentions	Involvement	Mood
Well-being	**0.890**[a]					
Ease of use	0.481	**0.919**[a]				
Perceived aesthetics	0.813	0.509	**0.969**[a]			
Behavioral Intentions	0.761	0.487	0.637	**0.902**[a]		
Involvement	0.621	0.227	0.545	0.582	**0.927**[a]	
Mood	0.223	0.060	0.167	0.234	0.190	**0.878**[a]

aSquare root of the AVE

Appendix 4. Results of the Direct Effects

		Path coefficient	*t*	*p*
H1a	Interline spacing -> Well-being	0.132	2999	0.003
H2a	Interline spacing -> Ease of use	−0.010	0.245	0.807
H3a	Interline spacing -> Perceived aesthetics	0.102	2281	0.023
H5	Interline spacing -> Behavioral Intentions	0.005	0.179	0.858

		Path coefficient	*t*	*p*
Other direct effects	Well-being -> Behavioral Intentions	0.684	13.103	0.000
	Ease of use -> Behavioral Intentions	0.158	4470	0.000
	Perceived aesthetics -> Behavioral Intentions	−0.001	0.009	0.993
	Perceived aesthetics -> Ease of use	0.511	14.660	0.000

Appendix 5. Results of the Mediating Effects

		Indirect effect	*t*	*p*	Confidence interval
H1b	Interline spacing -> Well-being -> Behavioral Intentions	0.090	2892	0.004	[0.029; 0.152]
H2b	Interline spacing -> Ease of use -> Behavioral Intentions	−0.002	0.237	0.813	[−0.014; 0.011]
H3b	Interline spacing -> Perceived aesthetics -> Behavioral Intentions	−0.001	0.008	0.994	[−0.013; 0.013]
H4	Interline spacing -> Perceived aesthetics -> Ease of use -> Behavioral Intentions	0.008	1982	0.048	[0.004; 0.016]
Other mediating effect	Interline spacing -> Perceived aesthetics -> Ease of use	0.052	2225	0.026	[0.007; 0.099]

References

Bauerly, M., and Liu, Y. (2008). Effects of symmetry and number of compositional elements on interface and design aesthetics. *International Journal of Human-Computer Interaction* 24(3) 275–287.

Ben-Bassat, T., Meyer, J., and Tractinsky, N. (2006). Economic and subjective measures of the perceived value of aesthetics and usability. *ACM Transactions on Computer–Human Interaction* 13(2) 210–234.

Bentley, M. (1921). Leading and legibility. *Psychological Monographs,* 30, 48-61.

Bernard, J. B., Anne-Catherine, S., and Eric, C. (2007). Page mode reading with simulated scotomas: A modest effect of interline spacing on reading speed. *Vision research*, 47 (28), 3447–3459.

Bonnardel, N., Piolat, A., and Le Bigot, L. (2011). The impact of colour on Website appeal and users' cognitive processes. *Displays*, 32 (2), 69–80.

Bressolles, G. (2006). La Qualité de service électronique : NetQu@l, proposition d'une échelle de mesure appliquée aux sites marchands et effets modérateurs. *Recherche et Applications en Marketing* 21(3) 19–45.

Bucklin, R. E., and Sismeiro, C. (2003). A model of web site browsing behavior estimated on clickstream data. *Journal of Marketing Research*, 40(3) 249–267.

Campbell, K. S. (1995). *Coherence, continuity, and cohesion: theoretical foundations for document design*, Hillsdale, NJ: Lawrence Erlbaum Associates.

Canivet-Bourgaux, I. (2017). *Bien rédiger pour le web : Stratégie de contenu pour améliorer son référencement naturel.* Paris. Ed. 4. Éditions Eyrolles.

Celhay, F., and Trinquecoste, J. F. (2015). Package graphic design: Investigating the variables that moderate consumer response to atypical designs. *Journal of Product Innovation Management*, 32(6) 1014–1032.

Chang, S. H., Chih, W. H., Liou, D. K., and Hwang, L. R. (2014). The influence of web aesthetics on customers' PAD. *Computers in Human Behavior*, 36 168–178.

Cherif, E., and Lemoine, J. F. (2019). Anthropomorphic virtual assistants and the reactions of Internet users: An experiment on the assistant's voice. *Recherche et Applications en Marketing*, 34(1) 29–49.

Chung, S. T. (2004). Reading speed benefits from increased vertical word spacing in normal peripheral vision. *Optometry and vision science: official publication of the American Academy of Optometry*, 81(7), 525–535.

Davis, F. D., Bagozzi, R. P., and Warshaw, P. R. (1989). User acceptance of computer technology: a comparison of two theoretical models. *Management Science*, 35(8), 982–1003.

Eroglu, S. A., Machleit, K. A., and Davis, L. M. (2001). Atmospheric qualities of online retailing: A conceptual model and implications. *Journal of Business Research*, 54(2) 177–184.

Eroglu, S. A., Machleit, K. A., and Davis, L. M. (2003). Empirical testing of a model of online store atmospherics and shopper responses. *Psychology and Marketing* 20(2) 139–150.

FEVAD (Fédération du e-commerce et de la vente à distance) (2018). Les chiffres clés : cartographie du e-commerce en 2017, www.journaldunet.com/ebusiness/commerce/.

Gonzalez, C. (2005). Satisfaction du consommateur suite à la visite du catalogue électronique: impact de la lisibilité perçue et de la stimulation perçue. *Revue Française du Marketing* 205(5), 91–110.

Hair, Jr J. F., Hult, G. T. M., Ringle, C., and Sarstedt, M. (2014). *A primer on partial least squares structural equation modeling (PLS-SEM).* Sage Publications.

Hart, P. M., Jones, S. R., and Royne, M. B. (2013). The human lens: how anthropomorphic reasoning varies by product complexity and enhances personal value. *Journal of Marketing Management* 29 (1-2) 105–121.

Hartmann, J., Sutcliffe, A., and Angel, A. D. (2008). Towards a theory of user judgment of aesthetics and user interface quality. *ACM Transactions on Computer-Human Interaction* 15(4) 15–44.

Hassenzahl, M. (2004). The interplay of beauty, goodness, and usability in interactive products. *Human and Computer Interaction* 19(4), 319–349.

Keeling, K., McGoldrick, P., and Beatty, S. (2007). Virtual on screen assistants: A viable strategy to support online customer relationship building?. *Advances in Consumer Research*, 34 138–144.

Koo, D. M., and Ju, S. H. (2010). The interactional effects of atmospherics and perceptual curiosity on emotions and online shopping intention. *Computers in Human Behavior* 26(3), 377–388.

Labroo, A. A., Dhar, R., and Schwarz, N. (2008). Of frog wines and frowning watches: semantic priming, perceptual fluency, and brand evaluation. *Journal of Consumer Research*, 34(6), 819–831.

Lavie, T., and Tractinsky, N. (2004). Assessing dimensions of perceived visual aesthetics of web sites. *International Journal of Human-Computer Studies*, 60(3) 269–298.

Lee, D. S., Ko, Y. H., Shen, I. H., and Chao, C. Y. (2011). Effect of light source, ambient illumination, character size and interline spacing on visual performance and visual fatigue with electronic paper displays. *Displays*, 32(1) 1–7.

Lee, S. (2013). Understanding user experience with computer-based applications with different use purposes. *International Journal of Human-Computer Interaction* 29(11), 689–701.

Lee, S., and Koubek, R. J. (2010). Understanding user preferences based on usability and aesthetics before and after actual use. *Interacting with Computers* 22(6), 530–543.

Lemarié, J., Lorch, R. F., Eyrolle, H., and Virbel, J. (2008). SARA: a text-based and reader-based theory of text signaling. *Educational Psychologist*, 43(1) 1–23.

Lemoine, J. F. (2008). Atmosphère des sites web marchands et réactions des internautes. *Revue Française du Marketing* 217, 45–61.

Lemoine, J. F., and Zafri, R. (2017). Influence of the typography of commercial website on surfers' reactions: an explanatory study. *33ème Congrès International de l'Association Française de Marketing*. Tours.

Lichtlé, M. C., and Plichon, V. (2014). Emotions experienced in retail outlets: A proposed measurement scale. *Recherche et Applications en Marketing* 29(1), 3–26.

McCarthy, M. S., and Mothersbaugh, D. L. (2002). Effects of typographic factors in advertising-based persuasion: A general model and initial empirical tests. *Psychology and Marketing* 19(7-8), 663–691.

Mehrabian, A., and Russell, J. A. (1974). *An Approach to Environmental Psychology*, Cambridge. MA, MIT Press.

Mummalaneni, V. (2005). An empirical investigation of web site characteristics, consumer emotional states and on-line shopping behaviours. *Journal of Business Research*, 58(4), 526–532.

Pandir, M., and Knight, J. (2006). Homepage aesthetics: The search for preference factors and the challenges of subjectivity. *Interacting with Computers* 18(6) 1351–1370.

Peterson, R., and Sauber, M. (1983). A mood scale for survey research, American Marketing Association Educators Proceedings. Chicago. *American Marketing Association*, 409–414.

Pollatsek, A., and Rayner, K. (1982). Eye movement control in reading : the role of word boundaries. *Journal of Experimental Psychology : Human Perception and Performance*, 8, 817–833.

Rayner, K., Fischer, M. H., and Pollatsek, A. (1998). Unspaced text interferes with both word indentification and eye movement control. *Vision Research*, 38, 829–837.

Reber, R., Schwarz, N., and Winkielman, P. (2004). Processing fluency and aesthetic pleasure: Is beauty in the perceiver's processing experience? *Personality and Social psychology review*, 8(4), 364–382.

Sergeev, A. P., and Tarasov, D.A. (2013). High school paper textbooks' usability: leading and satisfaction. *Social and Behavioral Sciences* 106 1278–1291.

Strazzieri, A. (1994). Mesurer l'implication durable vis-à-vis d'un produit indépendamment du risque perçu. *Recherche et Applications en Marketing*, 9(1), 73–91.

Tractinsky, N., Katz, A. S., and Ikar, D. (2000). What is beautiful is usable. *Interacting with computers* 13(2) 127–145.

Tuch, A., Roth, S., Hornbaek, K., Opwis, K., and Bargas-Avila, J. (2012). Is beautiful really usable? Toward understanding the relation between usability, aesthetics, and affect in HCI. *Computers in Human Behavior*. 28(5) 1596–1607.

Van Overschelde, J. P., and Healy, A. F. (2005). A blank look in reading: The effect of blank space on the identification of letters and words during reading. *Experimental Psychology*, 52 213–223.

Visinescu, L. L., Sidorova, A., Jones, M. C., and Prybutok, V. R. (2015). The influence of website dimensionality on customer experiences, perceptions and behavioral intentions: An exploration of 2D vs. 3D web design. *Information and Management*, 52(1) 1–17.

Yeh, Y. C., Lin, C.W., Hsu, W. C., Kuo, W. J., and Chan, Y. C. (2015). Associated and dissociated neural substrates of aesthetic judgment and aesthetic emotion during the appreciation of everyday designed products. *Neuropsychologia*, 73 151–160.

Yoo, B., and Donthu, N. (2001). Developing a scale to measure the perceived quality of internet shopping sites (SITEQUAL). *Quarterly Journal of Electronic Commerce* 2(1), 31–47.

"Live Big, Eat Small"! Advertising for Entomophagy by Kids' Awareness Raising: An Exploratory Study on Children in France: An Abstract

Khaoula Jellouli and Joël Brée

Abstract Insects 'consumption, called "entomophagy" is a food practice advocated by the United Nations Food and Agriculture Organization, to address a projected risk of food shortage by 2050. Entomophagy is a food habit that has a specific cultural character, common for 2.5 billion people in Southeast Asia, Central Africa, and parts of South America (Van Huis et al. 2013). Although, this practice is still experiential and underdeveloped (Fischler 1990). Despite all its nutritional, economic and ecological benefits, for many of Western consumers, this food practice is often associated with a primitive and disgusting behavior. The exploratory studies conducted on adult European consumers, reveal many obstacles for this type of consumption (Séré de Lanauze 2015; Gallen et al. 2018). However, we still lack information regarding younger consumers such as kids. Very few studies have explored the acceptability of this practice among children in the world. In this paper, we studied the acceptability of entomophagy among children by highlighting the psychological barriers and motivations, in order to extract advertising factors that could help promoting entomophagy.

We tried to understand children's perception through a qualitative study conducted on 50 French children aged between 6 and 12 and that took place between November 2018 and September 2019, in France. Our study aims to help understanding kids' psychological barriers and motivations for insect consumption, in order to highlight the discourse that the public authorities must emphasize in their persuasive communication for promoting this food practice. The results show that, disgust, attachment and fear are the main inhibitors. Besides, the French culture is much embedded in the kid's mind and makes appear important cultural and psychological barriers. Even if children spontaneously manifest negative feelings about eating insects, they declare themselves ready to try at least once as soon as they become aware that this mode of feeding can be positive for the protection of the planet.

K. Jellouli (✉) · J. Brée
University of Caen Normandy, Caen, France
e-mail: khaoula.jellouli@unicaen.fr; joel.bree@unicaen.fr

F. Pantoja, S. Wu (eds.), *From Micro to Macro: Dealing with Uncertainties in the Global Marketplace*, Developments in Marketing Science: Proceedings of the Academy of Marketing Science, https://doi.org/10.1007/978-3-030-89883-0_149

Some individual motivations such as discovery, challenge, fun and reward had also been expressed by children as encouraging reasons to insects ‘consumption. These motivations are relevant elements of marketing, on which, advertising actions could be concretized.

It is likely that there is a significant difference between children's statements and their real actions. Therefore, it is necessary to commit them in a real consumer experience. This can help them overcome some misperceptions and thus lead them to introduce edible insects as a healthy, sustainable novel food.

Keywords Entomophagy · Edible insects · Children · Awareness · Motivations · Psychological barriers · Advertising

References Available Upon Request

The Interplay between Sensory Emojis and Background Color of an Email: A Construal Level Approach: An Abstract

Mohamed Didi Alaoui, Catherine Papetti, Mathieu Kacha, and Jean-François Lemoine

Abstract This research investigates the effect of interaction between sensory emojis and background color of an email on consumers' responses. More particularly, would emojis related to our senses (e.g. ✋ or 👂) be able to activate sensory imagery such as touch or auditory imagery? If sensory emojis produce sensory imagery into which appropriate background color (e.g. red vs blue) they have to be inserted in order to enhance consumers' responses? Indeed, atmospheric variables such as color are important marketing tools that attract and shape consumers' perceptions (Labrecque and Milne 2012).We leverage Construal level theory (CLT) that provides a theoretical framework to predict in which appropriate background color specific sensory emojis have to be inserted. We suggest that sensory emojis related to proximal (distal) senses such as touch (hear) have to be integrated in red (blue) background color. We explain these combinations through the fit between psychological distance associated with senses and the construal level activated by red or blue color. We run an experiment, in a real situation, that tests the interplay between sensory emojis (touch vs hearing) and background colors (red vs blue) inserted into a starter email of a chatbot. A residual means analysis (Umesh et al. 1996) suggest that inserted proximal (distal) sensory emoji into red (blue) background is the optimal combination that enhances consumers' responses. These first results contribute to literature on emoji by showing that color background play an important role in the use of emoji into an email. Moreover, we contribute to CLT by showing that this framework could predict the effect of interplay between sensorial elements such as

M. Didi Alaoui (✉) · C. Papetti
Université Côte d'Azur, Nice, France
e-mail: mohamed.didi-alaoui@univ-cotedazur.fr; catherine.papetti@univ-cotedazur.fr

M. Kacha
Université de Lorraine, Metz, France
e-mail: mathieu.kacha@univ-lorraine.fr

J.-F. Lemoine
Université Paris 1 Panthéon Sorbonne, Paris, France
e-mail: jean-francois.lemoine@univ-paris1.fr

F. Pantoja, S. Wu (eds.), *From Micro to Macro: Dealing with Uncertainties in the Global Marketplace*, Developments in Marketing Science: Proceedings of the Academy of Marketing Science, https://doi.org/10.1007/978-3-030-89883-0_150

sensory emojis and color. Regarding implications managerial, this research aims to provide concrete suggestions for marketers who use emoji and color in their digital content. There are several applications for different contexts such as email marketing or online websites.

Keywords Sensory emojis · Color · Psychological distance · Construal level theory

References Available Upon Request

Positive Interruptions in the Commercial Interaction: When Sellers Receive Unexpected Help: An Abstract

Aaron D. Arndt, Juliet F. Poujol, and Béatrice Siadou-Martin

Abstract Retailing is changing profoundly because of digitalization (Cascio and Montealegre 2016; Hagberg et al. 2016). Grewal and al. (2009) suggest that "*retailers must assess every location; if it does not produce profit, the store will not be viable*" (p. 1). Thus, it is important for retailers to improve the customer experience in order to promote loyalty and long-term relationships (Jones et al. 2006; Verhoef et al. 2009). However, because most retailers are open to the public, retailers do not have control over many aspects of the retail environment. In particular, customers interact with one another. There are a number of high-profile new stories in which customer-to-customer (C2C) interactions may be negative, such as the woman in a U.K. grocery store who attacked employees and other customers over a disagreement about social distancing. While negative interactions are more likely to generate news stories, there are also instances of positive C2C interactions.

Oftentimes customers interrupt one another to make nice comments or help each other. The literature on shopping task interruptions shows that interruptions vary in the extent to which they generate negative feelings (Niculescu et al. 2014). We propose that customer interruptions can benefit other customers in two ways. First, a customer can receive advice from another client. For example, one customer might explain how a product works or give an impromptu product review. It is likely that providing advice to other customers improves customer trust in the retailer and product, which then improves their customer satisfaction. Second, customers can make each other feel good by giving compliments, reducing cognitive dissonance or socializing with other customers. For instance, one customer might tell another that they look nice. This positive expression of emotions is likely to improve customer

A. D. Arndt
Old Dominion University, Norfolk, VA, USA
e-mail: AArndt@odu.edu

J. F. Poujol
University of Nanterre, Nanterre, France
e-mail: fpoujol@parisnanterre.fr

B. Siadou-Martin (✉)
University of Montpellier, Montpellier, France
e-mail: beatrice.siadou-martin@umontpellier.fr

F. Pantoja, S. Wu (eds.), *From Micro to Macro: Dealing with Uncertainties in the Global Marketplace*, Developments in Marketing Science: Proceedings of the Academy of Marketing Science, https://doi.org/10.1007/978-3-030-89883-0_151

satisfaction via the process of emotional contagion, in which one person's emotions spread to others (Hatfield et al. 1993).

This research aims to provide a better understanding of whether interruptions from other customers during a commercial interaction can have a positive impact on a focus customer's retail satisfaction. In theory, customer-to-customer interruptions can impart useful information and positively impact customers' emotional state. The findings show that imparting useful information does not lead to better satisfaction, but positive emotional messages improve customer satisfaction via emotional contagion. Interestingly, opposite gender interruptions that impart useful information appear to be viewed negatively and increase likelihood of leaving without making a purchase.

Keywords Positive Interruption · Gender · Customer experience · Customer-to-customer · Emotional contagion

References Available Upon Request

A Text Mining Approach to Assessing Company Ratings via User-Generated and Company-Generated Content: An Abstract

Nina Krey, Shuang Wu, and Shih-Hui Hsiao

Abstract Retailing and third-party websites serve as online platforms for customers to gather information and interact with other users as well as companies. User-generated content is available through different online platforms, with online reviews being one of the most common type of user-generated content. While previous research has primarily focused on influential characteristics of reviews or on perceived usefulness or helpfulness of reviews from the user perceptive, the current research expands the literature on company-customer online relationship building by investigating the influence of user reviews and manager responses on the overall rating of the corresponding company. User reviews is an important format of user-generated content, while manager responses is a strategically used form of company-generated content. This research implements a text mining approach and sentiment analysis to assess how emotional versus rational user reviews and manager responses impact overall company ratings. Specifically, Linguistic Inquiry and Word Count (LIWC) dictionary is used for the language processing tasks, including sentence segmentation, word tokenization, and lemmatization. Data collection implements a Python-based web crawler to gather a consistent panel of user-level activity from TripAdvisor.com. The final data includes a three-year period from 2016 to 2018 of hotel reviews featuring user information, text reviews, and ratings given by the reviewers. Manager responses and corresponding hotel ratings complete the data set. Current findings provide further insights into how companies can utilize public manager responses as a business strategy to increase online ratings of their firm. Managerial implications include that companies can improve online ratings if managers incorporate emotional responses with long sentences.

Future studies should incorporate additional cities beyond the US to enhance generalizability of findings. Furthermore, this research examines online rating data for one service category, namely hotels. Additional industries, service categories,

N. Krey · S. Wu (✉) · S.-H. Hsiao
Rowan University, Glassboro, NJ, USA
e-mail: krey@rowan.edu; wus@rowan.edu; hsiao@rowan.edu

F. Pantoja, S. Wu (eds.), *From Micro to Macro: Dealing with Uncertainties in the Global Marketplace*, Developments in Marketing Science: Proceedings of the Academy of Marketing Science, https://doi.org/10.1007/978-3-030-89883-0_152

and reviewer characteristics can enhance contributions of future research endeavors. Incorporating additional service categories would allow the robustness assessment of the negative influence of rational online content on company ratings. Lastly, the current time lag variable remains limited due to the three-year period. Assessing how repeated interaction between reviewer and manager influences company ratings over time would provide additional guidance for firms in addressing online content and maintaining positive online reputations.

Keywords User-generated content · Text mining · Online reviews · Rationality · Company rating · Sentiment analysis

References Available Upon Request

Similarity: A Conceptual Clarification and Examination of the Influence on Cognitive Processes from a Grounded Perspective: An Abstract

Margot Racat, Mathieu Kacha, Brad D. Carlson, and Sonia Capelli

Abstract To deal with uncertainty when purchasing over the internet, online shoppers use their experiences with offline purchases as a point of comparison between the virtual and physical representation of the targeted product. Therefore, the perceived similarity between these two experiences is likely to influence online shopping outcomes (Racat and Capelli 2016; Xu et al. 2013). Thus, our study aims to further develop the concept of similarity and investigate its influences on cognitive processes such as mental imagery and memorization. Research has investigated similarity from two differing perspectives, namely as either a global phenomenon or as a component of cognitive processes (i.e. categorizations, memory process, decision-making, etc.) (Bezes and Mercanti-Guerin 2016; Sagi et al. 2012). Another stream of research in psychology has emerged focused on cognitive processes, considering the senses and perception as well as the situation (i.e. Tversky's context) as initiating mental activities leading to behaviors (Barsalou 1999; Borghi and Pecher 2012; Erle and Topolinski 2017; Fischer 2012; Meier et al. 2012). Indeed, psychologists have dug into information processing through perception of objects with the use of senses and determined that each sense is an expert system, in particular tactile and visual senses, for acknowledging different elements of an object and tend to be

M. Racat (✉)
IDRAC Business School, Lyon, France
e-mail: margot.racat@idraclyon.com

M. Kacha
University of Lorraine, Metz, France
e-mail: mathieu.kacha@univ-lorraine.fr

B. D. Carlson
Saint Louis University, Saint Louis, MO, USA
e-mail: brad.carlson@slu.edu

S. Capelli
University of Lyon, Lyon, France
e-mail: sonia.capelli@unvi-lyon3.fr

F. Pantoja, S. Wu (eds.), *From Micro to Macro: Dealing with Uncertainties in the Global Marketplace*, Developments in Marketing Science: Proceedings of the Academy of Marketing Science, https://doi.org/10.1007/978-3-030-89883-0_153

more accurate and faster when used consistently (e.g. texture for touch, shape for vision) (Klatzky et al. 1985; Lederman and Klatzky 1987).

Based on these findings, the concept of similarity might also be reconsidered as the attention depends on the accuracy of the sense to consider the object, for which the attention is driven by the stimuli properties. Thus, we extent the current understanding of similarity by considering the effect of sensory similarity on mental imagery and memorization. We define sensory similarity as the extent to which an indirect sensory experience of a product mimics a direct sensory experience of it. Based on grounded cognition theories, the concept of sensory similarity considers the overall process of similarity judgement including literal and relational similarity during information acquisition such as the relational and literal similarities require mental analysis to make a differentiation between two objects while the sensations of a product perceived through one environment or another has already been "categorized" by one's sensory perception.

Keywords Similarity · Interface · Touch · Cognition · Grounded Theory

References Available Upon Request

Lonely Consumer's Brand Relationships: An Abstract

Eunyoung Jang

Abstract How are lonely individuals related to brands? Are they more loyal to brands? Concerning this research question, prior studies showed inconsistent findings—some suggests stronger loyalty of lonely individuals while others suggests weaker loyalty and more switching behavior of lonely individuals.

The present research proposes that loneliness can sometimes make consumers feel more loyal toward brands and other times appear less loyal, and the difference depends on the dimensions of loneliness. Although most consumer research treats loneliness as a unidimensional construct, loneliness involves two dimensions – emotional and social. *Emotional loneliness* is due to inadequate relationship quality (e.g., a lack of intimate relationships) whereas *social loneliness* is due to inadequate relationship quantity (e.g., a lack of group of friends). Since these dimensions of loneliness are not completely compensatory (Weiss 1983), feelings of emotional loneliness are resolved by developing intimate relationships with one individual, while feelings of social loneliness are resolved by developing new relationships with many individuals (Weiss 1973).

When consumers are deficient in their relationships with people, they often compensate through their relationships with brands. Present research proposes that unsatisfied social needs of lonely consumers would affect their brand relationships. Specifically, we suggest that consumers feeling emotional loneliness, characterized by inadequate intimacy, will prefer intimate brand relationships. Similar to building a loyal and devoted relationship with a few select people (e.g., spouse, best friend), people will build intimate relationships with a few select brands, creating a desire for strong brand loyalty. On the other hand, consumers feeling social loneliness, characterized by insufficient number of relationships with people, will compensate by developing a greater number of relationships with brands. In this situation, consumers will prefer to choose as many brands as possible. In sum, by synthesizing

E. Jang (✉)
Oklahoma State University, Stillwater, OK, USA
e-mail: eunyoung.jang@okstate.edu

F. Pantoja, S. Wu (eds.), *From Micro to Macro: Dealing with Uncertainties in the Global Marketplace*, Developments in Marketing Science: Proceedings of the Academy of Marketing Science, https://doi.org/10.1007/978-3-030-89883-0_154

the multidimensional loneliness and brand relationship and assuming that they can be compensated each other, the present research investigate how emotional and social loneliness differently affect brand loyalty and brand assortment.

Keywords Brand loyalty · Brand assortment · Loneliness · Social relationship

References Available Upon Request

Predicting NFL Ticket Sales with Social Media Data: An Abstract

Rae Yule Kim

Abstract Three billion people access their social media accounts every month (Tariq 2019). Social media had transformed marketing as managers focus on interacting with customers on this real-time channel rather than giving out brand messages and waiting for the customer response. Social media facilitates customer relationship management by enabling real-time interactions with a wider demographic of customers, which often trigger positive Word of Mouth and user-generated brand contents, maximizing brand marketing potentials (Kapoor et al. 2018). Thus, how managers exploit this online communication channel and engage customers on new media increasingly determine future business success (Shahzad et al. 2019). In this study, we utilize social capital theory and long-tail theory to rationalize how the followers on brand social media influence brand performances, and how the follower effect is varied by brand characteristics.

We examined 31 National Football League (NFL) teams on the number of followers on their social media and ticket sales. Consumer motives for attending sports events are as heterogeneous as their motives for product adoption, where social influence, experiential, or hedonic benefits all influence new purchases of sports tickets (James and Ross 2004). We utilized panel data models to investigate the effect and K-mean clustering to classify team characteristics. The findings of this study suggest that one unit increase in the number of social media followers can contribute to 3.43 USD in ticket revenues. However, the marginal effect of followers is negative. The early followers make more substantial contributions to brand performances compared to followers who inflowed as a team gains popularity. The follower effect on ticket sales is also varied by social media channels and team types between niche and mass teams. One unit increase in the number of followers for niche teams increased .47 USD more in ticket revenues compared to mass teams.

R. Y. Kim (✉)
Montclair State University, Montclair, NJ, USA
e-mail: kimr@montclair.edu

F. Pantoja, S. Wu (eds.), *From Micro to Macro: Dealing with Uncertainties in the Global Marketplace*, Developments in Marketing Science: Proceedings of the Academy of Marketing Science, https://doi.org/10.1007/978-3-030-89883-0_155

We suggest that the managers (1) identify the target audience, and (2) select the right social media channel to maximize potential brand support activities of the followers. Future research might explore content strategy about which type of brand-customer interaction on social media leads to increased brand support activities of followers and a greater contribution of social media marketing to sales performance.

Keywords Social media · Social media marketing · Digital marketing · Social media metrics · Social capital · Clustering

References Available Upon Request

Made by Mistake? The Co-creation Paradox: An Abstract

Vinícius Nardi, Wagner Ladeira, Diego Costa Pinto, and Márcia Maurer Herter

Abstract Visual attention is a key variable when consumers choose a product (in the store or online) and might be able to demonstrate consumers' engagement in the buying process using eye-tracking. It is possible that the negative effects of co-creation may derive from a common factor: consumers—after exposed to co-creation activities—may reduce their engagement to the outcomes of the process (i.e., new co-created product) that can be measured by the visual attention.

In four experimental studies using eye-tracking and online panels, we investigate the effects of co-creation on visual attention and buying intentions. Study 1 explores the effects of co-creation (vs. control) on consumers' visual attention and on buying intentions revealing that while consumers have higher buying intentions towards co-created products, it leads to reduced visual attention. We call this effect the co-creation paradox. Study 2 explores the moderating role of construal level on the co-creation effects. In particular, it establishes that visual attention depends not only on co-creation but also on consumers' salient construal level showing that concrete (vs. abstract) construal can mitigate the negative effects on visual attention. That is because people in abstract (vs. concrete) construal form representations of an object that retain only central aspects, omitting specific and detailed information (Liberman and Trope 1998), reducing consumers' visual attention. Study 3 suggests the moderating role of deindividuation on the cocreation-visual attention relationship. Deindividuation theory proposes that people act as if they immersed in the group, reducing self-perception and adhering to the community (Postmes and Spears 1998). Specifically, Study 3 findings reveal that low deindividuation states increase

V. Nardi · W. Ladeira
UNISINOS Universidade do Vale dos Sinos, Porto Alegre, Brazil
e-mail: vnardi@unisinos.br; wladeira@unisinos.br

D. C. Pinto
NOVA IMS – Universidade NOVA de Lisboa, Lisbon, Portugal
e-mail: dpinto@novaims.unl.pt

M. M. Herter (✉)
Universidade Europeia, Lisbon, Portugal
e-mail: marcia.herter@universidadeeuropeia.pt

F. Pantoja, S. Wu (eds.), *From Micro to Macro: Dealing with Uncertainties in the Global Marketplace*, Developments in Marketing Science: Proceedings of the Academy of Marketing Science, https://doi.org/10.1007/978-3-030-89883-0_156

the personal responsibility of co-creators and mitigate the negative on visual attention. Study 4 evaluate the interaction effects of deindividuation and construal level on the cocreation-buying intentions relationship. Study 4 shed light on the negative aspect of concrete (vs. abstract) construal, revealing the "neutralization" of co-creation positive effects on buying intentions. At the same time, Study 4 reinforces the positive effects of deindividuation in this context.

Keywords Visual attention · Eye-tracking · Co-creation · Deindividuation · Buying intentions

References Available Upon Request

The Crowdsourcing Effect: How Crowdsourcing Shapes Customer Engagement: An Abstract

Márcia Maurer Herter, Diego Costa Pinto, Paola Pontin, and Walter Nique

Abstract Consumers collaboration in companies' daily innovations has become a new path for business. Crowdsourcing refers to the phenomenon of company's outsourcing tasks using collective intelligence (Howe 2006). Crowdsourcing initiatives are usually efficient because the resulting ideas meet consumers expectations (Fuchs et al. 2013). However, Thompson and Malaviya (2013) suggest that consumers demonstrate two opposing responses to crowdsourcing: skepticism about the competence and identification with the creator. Yet, whether and how crowdsourcing can provide value for consumers and favor customer engagement remains unclear. To fill this research gap, this study aims to investigate the influence of crowdsourcing on customer engagement and purchase intentions.

In four experimental studies, we propose and test that purchase intentions and customer engagement depend on crowdsourcing initiatives. Study 1 show that the crowdsourcing presence (vs. absence) increase consumers purchase intentions. Study 2 examines the mediating role of customer engagement in the relationship between crowdsourcing and purchase intentions. Customer engagement is the perceived personal relevance or importance of the company for the engaged consumer (Greenwald and Leavitt 1984; Mittal 1995). Goh et al. (2017) suggest that crowdsourcing foster engagement and participation. Study 2 results show customer engagement mediation effect that is significantly higher for crowdsourcing (vs. absence). That because crowdsourcing provides significant inclusive and sharing values to consumers, building a sense of customer engagement, which in turn will

M. M. Herter (✉)
Universidade Europeia, Lisbon, Portugal
e-mail: marcia.herter@universidadeeuropeia.pt

D. C. Pinto
NOVA IMS - Universidade NOVA de Lisboa, Lisbon, Portugal
e-mail: dpinto@isegi.unl.pt

P. Pontin
ESPM, Porto Alegre, Brazil

W. Nique
UFRGS, Porto Alegre, Brazil
e-mail: walter.nique@ufrgs.br

F. Pantoja, S. Wu (eds.), *From Micro to Macro: Dealing with Uncertainties in the Global Marketplace*, Developments in Marketing Science: Proceedings of the Academy of Marketing Science, https://doi.org/10.1007/978-3-030-89883-0_157

increase purchase intentions. Study 3 and 4 further refines our theory by examining the moderating role of community belonging to the relationship between crowdsourcing and purchase intentions. Community belonging reflects the essential facets of company-consumer social sharing value (Simon and Tossan 2018). These authors state that community belonging represents the social gratifications derived from company-consumer virtually mediated interactions, which are likely to motivate the development of company relationships and, therefore, trigger an active engagement of consumers in virtual company communities. In the context of crowdsourcing, consumers can easily interact not only with their company but also with the company's other customers, thus extending their opportunities to acquire relational knowledge about the company. Study 3 and 4 results suggest that crowdsourcing can be less influential for companies with high (vs. low) community belonging.

Crowdsourcing emerges as a profitable format of product innovation. Companies are increasingly using crowdsourcing to achieve promising ideas for new products, which are commercialized later as consumer-designed products. Our results attest crowdsourcing initiatives as capable of positively affect consumers' customer engagement, which has positive downstream effects on purchase intentions (Nishikawa et al. 2017; Schreier et al. 2012, 2016). In addition, we reveal the moderating role of community belonging on the crowdsourcing effects (Brodie et al. 2013; Schau et al. 2009; Schembri and Latimer 2016; Zaglia 2013).

Keywords Crowdsourcing · Customer engagement · Community belonging · Purchase intentions

References Available Upon Request

Fighting Over-Indebtedness: An Artificial Intelligence Approach: An Abstract

Mário Ferreira, Diego Costa Pinto, Márcia Maurer Herter, Jerônimo Soro, Leonardo Vanneschi, Mauro Castelli, and Fernando Peres

Abstract This research focuses attention on over-indebtedness (i.e., recurrent incapability to repaying credits) and its risk factors, among Portuguese households in the context of the recent European sovereign debt crisis. Different theoretical accounts of consumers decision behavior and risk of becoming over-indebted vary (among other aspects) on the emphasis they put on situational (socio-economic) versus individual (psychological) factors (Angel et al. 2009; Berthoud and Kempson 1992; Kamleitner and Kirchler 2007; van Staveren 2002). Although several of the identified factors have been shown to be associated with over-indebtedness, actual cases of over-indebted households are likely to be multifactorial. Remarkably, how these different risk factors combine in producing concrete situations of over-indebtedness is a highly important issue to avoid poverty that has received less research attention.

This paper examines how artificial intelligence may contribute to better understanding and overcome over-indebtedness in contexts of severe economic austerity. We analyze a field database of over-indebted households with a high risk of poverty. Artificial intelligence algorithms are used to identify distinguishable over-indebtedness clusters and to predict over-indebtedness risk factors within each cluster. First, unsupervised machine learning generated three over-indebtedness clusters of families affected by abrupt economic crisis. Second, supervised machine learning with exhaustive grid search hyperparameters suggest algorithms that best predict families' over-indebtedness risk factors. These findings extend previous

M. Ferreira · J. Soro
Universidade de Lisboa, Lisbon, Portugal
e-mail: mferreira@psicologia.ulisboa.pt; jsoro@psicologia.ulisboa.pt

D. C. Pinto (✉) · L. Vanneschi · M. Castelli · F. Peres
NOVA IMS - Universidade NOVA de Lisboa, Lisbon, Portugal
e-mail: dpinto@isegi.unl.pt; lvanneschi@novaims.unl.pt; mcastelli@novaims.unl.pt; fperes@novaims.unl.pt

M. M. Herter
Universidade Europeia, Lisbon, Portugal
e-mail: marcia.herter@universidadeeuropeia.pt

F. Pantoja, S. Wu (eds.), *From Micro to Macro: Dealing with Uncertainties in the Global Marketplace*, Developments in Marketing Science: Proceedings of the Academy of Marketing Science, https://doi.org/10.1007/978-3-030-89883-0_158

research by proposing a multifaced and yet organized bottom-up approach to over-indebtedness and poverty risk.

Keywords Over-indebtedness · Poverty risk · Economic austerity · Credit control · Artificial intelligence · Machine learning

References Available Upon Request

The Role of Emotions in Sales Promotions: Influences of Anxiety and Sadness on Product Evaluations: An Abstract

Berna Basar

Abstract Consumers are being bombarded by sales promotions aimed at persuading them to purchase and purchase now. Since promotions are costly, marketers aim to design effective and persuasive promotional tools. Promotions vary on multiple dimensions in an attempt to stand out and entice consumers to make a purchase. However, providing high value in one dimension might mean sacrifices in other dimensions. For instance, promotions high in transaction value might cause negative quality inferences. On the other hand, other promotions such as money-back guarantee can provide reliability and lack instant rewards at the time of purchase. Research shows that emotions trigger changes in cognition, physiology, and action which guide subsequent behavior and perceptions in goal-directed ways, even in response to objects or events that are unrelated to the original cause of the emotion. The current study examines how sadness and anxiety influence the inferential knowledge derived from exposure to promotions. This study focused on these two specific negative emotions because of multiple reasons. First, anxiety and sadness are among the most widespread forms of emotional distress. Second, anxiety and sadness have highly differentiated appraisal profiles. Finally, there is lack of research examining the role of different negative emotions in sales promotions. Deriving from prior research, this study suggests that for products that come with rewarding promotions, individuals experiencing sadness might have higher product evaluations than individuals experiencing anxiety. On the other hand, for products that come with risk-reducing promotions, individuals experiencing anxiety might have higher product evaluations than individuals experiencing sadness.

Keywords Negative emotions · Anxiety · Sadness · Sales promotions

References Available Upon Request

B. Basar (✉)
Baruch College, New York, NY, USA
e-mail: bbasar@gradcenter.cuny.edu

F. Pantoja, S. Wu (eds.), *From Micro to Macro: Dealing with Uncertainties in the Global Marketplace*, Developments in Marketing Science: Proceedings of the Academy of Marketing Science, https://doi.org/10.1007/978-3-030-89883-0_159

How Sales Competitions Enhance Students' Interest and Prepare Them for a Career in International Sales: An Abstract

Ursula Haas-Kotzegger, Johannes Reiterer, Vivien Unger, and Alexander Bauer

Abstract "To sell is human" (Pink 2013). But not every human wants to sell. On the contrary, too few people pursue a career in sales. According to a study carried out by LinkedIn (2017), sales is the highest priority role to fill at companies worldwide. This has to do with the fact that sales jobs still have a negative image among students (e.g. Waldeck et al. 2010).

This supply/demand gap (Nielson and Cummins 2019) is not the only challenge that companies are currently facing. Firms are also confronted with a shift in the requirements and skills needed to perform a sales job. Sales managers are increasingly exposed globally. Markets are constantly growing closer together, and many countries heavily depend on export sales (export of goods and services in % of GDP: Germany 47%, UK 30%, US 12%, Worldbank 2020). Consequently, pursuing a career in sales for many means working in an international surrounding. This requires sales managers who are experienced in dealing with foreign cultures, in different languages, and particularly in different ways to build and sustain relationships.

So far, universities around the globe have responded to the shortage of sales people by increasing the number of their sales programs (Deeter-Schmelz and Kennedy 2011). However, the questions remain, (1) what can universities and sales programs do to make sales more attractive and increase students' interest, and (2), how to prepare students for the international und multicultural exposure of a sales position.

Based on the findings of qualitative interviews with teachers and students participating in a sales competition, the authors argue that the teaching method of sales competitions could be an excellent approach to fill this void by (1) increasing the

U. Haas-Kotzegger (✉) · J. Reiterer · V. Unger · A. Bauer
University of Applied Sciences, Wiener Neustadt, Austria
e-mail: ursula.haas-kotzegger@fhwn.ac.at; johannes.reiterer@fhwn.ac.at; vivien.unger@fhwn.ac.at; alexander.bauer@fhwn.ac.at

F. Pantoja, S. Wu (eds.), *From Micro to Macro: Dealing with Uncertainties in the Global Marketplace*, Developments in Marketing Science: Proceedings of the Academy of Marketing Science, https://doi.org/10.1007/978-3-030-89883-0_160

image of sales among students and (2) preparing them for an international position in sales.

Sales competition is an experimental learning method with origin in the USA, which today can be found in various formats. It consists of role plays that involve a certain level of pressure and motivation and encourage students to maximize their performance. The findings provide evidence that through transnational sales competitions students will be better prepared for international challenges. Furthermore, it appears that students who had the chance to train and participate in a sales competition changed their negative attitude towards the subject.

Keywords Sales competition · Marketing and sales education · International sales · Attitude towards sales

References Available Upon Request

The Technology Acceptance Model as a Predictor of Using a Disruptive Technology of Online Supermarkets: An Abstract

Doris Morales-Solana, Alejandro Alegret Cotas, and Irene Esteban-Millat

Abstract This research aims to improve the understanding of the consumer behavior in the use of a disruptive technology such as online supermarkets. The process governing the acceptance and use of virtual environments has a direct bearing on consumer behavior when using digital shopping platforms. By understanding this process, we can gain further insight into consumer behavior in terms of attitude toward online shopping as well as online shopping intentions. To address the lack of empirical data on the adoption of this type of shopping environment, we present and validate a model of the phenomenon. The study considers not only the utilitarian aspects included in the technology acceptance model (TAM) for the adoption of online supermarkets, but also an aspect of intrinsic motivation for an individual, flow, with a view to enhancing the explanatory power of the models presented.

An online questionnaire was used to gather the data. The final sample size of 651 consumers is appropriate for the aims of the investigation. The latent variables used in the model were measured using Likert-type scales. The model was verified by assessing the reliability and validity of the measurements and by evaluating the entire structural model. Exploratory factor analysis (EFA) was applied to the principal components variant. The results of the EFA were validated through confirmatory factor analysis (CFA) using structural equation modeling (SEM), which allows for stricter scale refinement. The fit of the analytical model was evaluated. The combined confirmatory factor analysis of all measurement scales provided satisfactory results.

The results obtained verify the direct effect of flow on perceived usefulness, perceived ease of use, and actual use. They also confirm the correlations between

D. Morales-Solana (✉) · I. Esteban-Millat
Universitat Oberta de Catalunya, Barcelona, Spain
e-mail: dmoralesso@uoc.edu; iestebanm@uoc.edu

A. A. Cotas
EAE Business School, Barcelona, Spain
e-mail: alejandro.alegret@campus.eae.es

F. Pantoja, S. Wu (eds.), *From Micro to Macro: Dealing with Uncertainties in the Global Marketplace*, Developments in Marketing Science: Proceedings of the Academy of Marketing Science, https://doi.org/10.1007/978-3-030-89883-0_161

perceived usefulness and attitude toward use and behavioral intention to use, and between perceived ease of use and attitude toward using. The results also demonstrate the effect of attitude toward use on behavioral intention to use and of the intention to use on actual system use. However, the results do not support that flow has a direct effect on attitude toward use and behavioral intention to use. The results therefore show for the first time in the literature the utility of flow as an element of intrinsic motivation helping to explain the use of online supermarkets. This conclusion could be useful to the strategies of mass consumption companies wishing to improve their customers' consumer and shopping experience.

Keywords TAM · Flow · Online supermarkets · Consumer behavior

References Available Upon Request

First Impressions of Foreign-Born Frontline Employees: Impact on Customer Participation: An Abstract

David Bourdin and Christina Sichtmann

Abstract In intercultural service encounters, customers use an employee's accent as a cue to infer their ethnicity, which may unconsciously trigger cultural stereotypes. However, it is still unclear how an employee's accent affects customer behavior. We address this research gap in three studies by examining the influence of employee accent on one important type of behavior, namely customer participation, that is, the degree to which customers are involved in the service process by contributing effort, knowledge, information, and other tangible or intangible resources.

Our findings from Study 1 show that a foreign accent weakens customer participation indirectly through reduced intelligibility, but that cultural distance does not play a role. Consistent with a negativity bias, Study 2 revealed that only an unfavorable employee accent negatively affects customer participation, partially because the service provider is viewed as less attractive and dynamic. In contrast, the effect of a positively valenced accent is non-significant. In Study 3, we found that an unfavorable accent has a negative effect on voluntary customer participation, whereas it increases replaceable participation indirectly through reduced trust. The relationship between trust and replaceable participation is moderated by customers' need for interaction.

Our research, which is among the first to examine an antecedent rather than a consequence of customer participation, leads to important managerial implications for service and retails firms. First, since it is virtually impossible for adult foreigners to ever sound like a native speaker anyway (Flege et al. 1995), the effectiveness of language training with the purpose of eliminating accents is questionable. Instead, service providers should invest in training that increases employees' ability to instill trust and to consistently deliver superior performance in order to maximize customers' service quality perceptions. Second, in order to increase customer evaluations

D. Bourdin (✉)
FHWien der WKW, Vienna, Austria
e-mail: david.bourdin@fh-wien.ac.at

C. Sichtmann
University of Vienna, Vienna, Austria
e-mail: christina.sichtmann@univie.ac.at

F. Pantoja, S. Wu (eds.), *From Micro to Macro: Dealing with Uncertainties in the Global Marketplace*, Developments in Marketing Science: Proceedings of the Academy of Marketing Science, https://doi.org/10.1007/978-3-030-89883-0_162

of an accented employee's competence, firms could get rid of scripted responses as an acknowledgment to the uniqueness of each service encounter. Third, if a frontline employee with a negatively connoted accent is involved in service delivery, additional information might be given e.g. by handing out a printed checklist with clear instructions in order to increase customer task clarity. Fourth, an accent appears to have detrimental repercussions mainly when it is partly unintelligible. This suggests that speech quality is far more important than whether or not someone speaks with a noticeable accent. Hence, rather than pressurizing employees to get rid of their accent quickly, firms should first encourage them to focus on speech quality in more general terms (voice volume, hesitations, enunciation, and clarity of arguments). Training in this direction could be offered to both native- and foreign-born employees. Finally, training can teach foreign-accented employees how to effectively respond to negative initial impressions due to cultural stereotyping.

Keywords Customer participation · Stereotypes · Accent · Intercultural service encounters

References Available Upon Request

Prompting Sustainable Consumption Choices: Exploring the Role of Construal Level Theory: An Abstract

Saray Garcia, Crystal Loke, Angeline Nariswari, and Jenny Lin

Abstract With rising awareness of the need to implement sustainability practices to decelerate climate change, environmentally-conscious businesses continue to explore means to encourage responsible consumption. We apply the construal level theory (CLT) to examine how marketers can encourage more sustainable consumption behaviors through message framing. Construal Level Theory (CLT) suggests that people construe the same persuasive information differently depending on the construal level or psychological distance (Trope and Liberman 2010). Actions can be viewed at varying levels of abstraction, from low levels (concrete), specifying how the action is performed, to high levels (abstract), specifying why it is performed (Freitas et al. 2004). Previous studies have found that consumers process information more efficiently when there is congruence between the portrayed distance and the message (Stewart and Nandkeolyar 2006). We report experiments situated in two distinct consumption contexts, namely green hotel decision making and sustainable food choices.

In the green hotel decision making study, we implemented a 2 (temporal distance: impending hotel stay vs. future hotel stay) × 2 (benefits: low/high construal level) between-subjects experimental research design. Participants imagined a future out-of-town trip that required booking a green hotel room. Temporal distance manipulation was implemented by having participants consider a trip for the upcoming spring break (near; concrete) or the following year (far; abstract). Participants then viewed an advertisement for a green hotel, which contained one of two advertising messages: first focusing on personal benefit, sleeping on organic and biodegradable mattresses (concrete), and another emphasizing an environmental benefit framed as helping reduce climate change (abstract). Initial findings indicate that when the consumption event is far (i.e., future hotel stay), expected satisfaction is higher when the attributes of the service are presented as abstract (i.e., an environmental benefit; high construal) rather than a concrete (i.e., a personal benefit; low construal).

S. Garcia (✉) · C. Loke · A. Nariswari · J. Lin
California State University Monterey Bay, Seaside, CA, USA
e-mail: saragarcia@csumb.edu; wloke@csumb.edu; anariswari@csumb.edu; jelin@csumb.edu

F. Pantoja, S. Wu (eds.), *From Micro to Macro: Dealing with Uncertainties in the Global Marketplace*, Developments in Marketing Science: Proceedings of the Academy of Marketing Science, https://doi.org/10.1007/978-3-030-89883-0_163

To further investigate the impact of construal levels in messaging, we extend construal levels in terms of social distance and implement experiments in the context of sustainable food decisions. A similar between-subject study will investigate how consumption decisions are influenced when respondents think about their immediate family (concrete; low construal) or society (abstract; high construal) and sustainable consumption benefits are framed in terms of personal health (concrete; low construal) or environmental benefits (abstract; high construal).

Keywords Sustainable consumption · Green marketing · Construal level theory · Message framing

References Available Upon Request

Addressing a Shift in Students' Perceptions of Value in Higher Education: An Abstract

Wendy Gillis, Justin Scott, and Kim Bynum

Abstract More than previous generations, the contemporary generation of students possess technological skills, yet they prefer face-to-face/personal touch (Twenge 2017). Today's students likely watched their parents lose jobs during the Great Recession. They enjoy unfettered technological access, allowing them to access world-wide events in real-time. Contemporary students can see and feel global issues. Now they are preparing to create solutions for those global issues. However, stuck between recognizing the need for value (Magda et al. 2020) and avoiding "catching feelings"—like feelings are a disease (Twenge 2017)—contemporary students seem frustrated. Essentially, they can access information *about* problems, but struggle to see how they find solutions *to* those problems. As a result, today's student-assessments of value might not mirror recent perceptions.

In recent years, a perception has evolved implying that students prefer to receive only positive feedback, as if addressing one's shortcomings might influence a person to feel personally attacked. Over thirty years ago, Martin (1986) explained that quality customer service involved one person cooperating with another to give the other person what they want. However, business executives specifically address handling feedback as a weakness for most college graduates. Because the authors regularly interact with students and executives, we sought to determine if students *really* want only positive feedback. If students want value from their education and executives want promotable graduates, then universities are primed to meet both

W. Gillis (✉)
Jacksonville University, Jacksonville, FL, USA
e-mail: wgillis@ju.edu

J. Scott
Pensacola Christian College, Pensacola, FL, USA
e-mail: jscott@faculty.pcci.edu

K. Bynum
Christian Brothers University, Memphis, TN, USA
e-mail: kbynum1@cbu.edu

F. Pantoja, S. Wu (eds.), *From Micro to Macro: Dealing with Uncertainties in the Global Marketplace*, Developments in Marketing Science: Proceedings of the Academy of Marketing Science, https://doi.org/10.1007/978-3-030-89883-0_164

parties' needs, particularly through the leader-like behaviors of teachers (Xiao and Wilkins 2015).

Behavior in the classroom space, much like other environments, can be delineated into trait and relational behaviors (DeRue et al. 2011). Since students want valuable preparation for their future (Daun-Barnett and Das 2013), the authors followed Yukl's (2012) assertions that relational behaviors were more positively linked with change-oriented opportunities. Using Behrendt et al.'s (2017) more parsimonious representation of relations-oriented behavior, it was assumed that contemporary students will appreciate when their teachers utilize behaviors consistent with Behrendt et al.'s (2017) model (i.e. coordination, cooperation, and the activation of resources).

Although data are still being gathered to support the authors' propositions, initial data indicate that students crave a relational component of their education, even if that relationship involves discomfort. Contrary to perceptions discussed earlier, contemporary students seem to recognize that growth stems from addressing their shortcomings. If a shift in students-perceptions exists, failing to address students' expectations might negatively affect university outcomes such as university reputation and retention.

Keywords Higher education value · Student perceptions · Relationship · Leader

References Available Upon Request

Improving Effectiveness of Food Waste Prevention Messages: An Abstract

Pinar Yildirim and Asli Elif Aydin

Abstract Many initiatives are now attempting to reduce consumer food waste around the globe by creating awareness about food waste. In the EU alone more than 100 programs and policies against food waste were developed (Monier et al. 2011). This study intends to help designing effective food waste prevention campaign communications. For this purpose, different message appeals with varying motives and frames will be compared for their persuasiveness. Specifically, the effects of motive appeal and regulatory focus of food waste prevention messages on perceived argument quality, attitudes towards the message and issue attitude will be analyzed.

An experimental study examined effects of ads promoting different motives to reduce food waste on consumer responses. Moreover, the impact of regulatory focus of the message conveyed in the ad on consumer evaluations of the ad was investigated. Therefore, a 2 (message motive: financial versus moral) × 2 (regulatory focus of the message: promotion versus prevention) between-subjects design was employed.

The sample consisted of one hundred and fifty-two graduate and undergraduate students. Participants were randomly assigned to one of four groups and asked to evaluate one of four types of ads. Half of the ads promoted food waste reduction by addressing the financial motives, namely monetary consequences of wasting food while the other half addressed the ethical motives, namely moral consequences of "doing the right thing". Moreover, half of the ads employed a promotion focus, which emphasizes the gains of not wasting food whereas the other half employed a prevention focus, which highlights the losses incurred as a result of food waste.

The results of the analysis presented no significant differences in consumer responses between messages conveying a financial or a moral motive to avoid food waste. Consumers perceived saving money and salving conscience as equally

P. Yildirim · A. E. Aydin (✉)
Istanbul Bilgi University, Istanbul, Turkey
e-mail: pinar.yildirim@bilgi.edu.tr; aslielif.aydin@bilgi.edu.tr

F. Pantoja, S. Wu (eds.), *From Micro to Macro: Dealing with Uncertainties in the Global Marketplace*, Developments in Marketing Science: Proceedings of the Academy of Marketing Science, https://doi.org/10.1007/978-3-030-89883-0_165

important. On the other hand, regarding the regulatory focus of the ads, consumer responses differ significantly. When the losses of food waste are emphasized with a prevention focused message consumers' issue attitude, perceived argument quality and attitude toward the ad were more favorable compared to when the gains of avoiding food waste are emphasized with a promotion focused ad. Consequently, it can be deduced that effectiveness of food waste prevention campaigns can be improved by employing prevention focused messages.

Keywords Food waste prevention · Financial motive · Moral motive · Prevention focus · Promotion focus

References Available Upon Request

Revisiting the Neglected Role of Targeting Strategy in Firm's Performance: An Abstract

Marina Kyriakou and Markos Tsogas

Abstract The aim of this study is to shed ample light to the concept of targeting within the boundaries of the overall marketing strategy and to investigate the actual targeting alternatives of firms. To the best of the authors' knowledge, it is the first effort to isolate targeting from its siblings in the STP strategic process.

After an exhaustive search of the strategic marketing literature, the authors identified two dimensions along which targeting alternatives can be developed i.e. (a) the number of products which a firm offers and (b) the number of segments which the firm targets. The international marketing literature suggests a third dimension of expansion into new segments (in this case countries): the time (or the speed) of expansion. The authors posit that the combination of these three dimensions offers a potentially richer matrix for the proposed market targeting alternative strategies. The research aims also to investigate at the same time the antecedents and performance consequences of the selected targeting strategy.

For the purposes of the research a structured questionnaire has been developed consisting of (a) questions about the company's product and environmental characteristics, such as product quality, price advantage, product innovativeness, product complexity, competitive environment, competitive intensity, market turbulence and technological turbulence, (b) questions measuring the adopted targeting strategy along three distinct dimensions, i.e. the number of products being offered, the number of segments being served and the speed of entrance to these segments and (c) questions on firm's capabilities and performance, as the main dependent variables. Using this questionnaire, a web-based survey took place among firms in a single European country and 265 usable questionnaires were collected.

The normative managerial 2 × 2 model of products offered and segments served, after being enriched with the dimension of speed or timing of entry, was proved to describe adequately the strategic alternatives of marketing managers. Having lifted the constrains of linearity, results indicate that the selected targeting strategies help in developing relevant marketing capabilities which in turn improve firm's perfor-

M. Kyriakou (✉) · M. Tsogas
University of Piraeus, Piraeus, Greece
e-mail: mkyriakou@unipi.gr; mtsogas@unipi.gr

F. Pantoja, S. Wu (eds.), *From Micro to Macro: Dealing with Uncertainties in the Global Marketplace*, Developments in Marketing Science: Proceedings of the Academy of Marketing Science, https://doi.org/10.1007/978-3-030-89883-0_166

mance. The speed or timing of entry into the market segments was found to act as a pure moderator or a booster for the deployment of marketing capabilities on performance, revealing also the true nature of the relationships between the complexity of product/markets served and the results achieved.

Keywords Targeting · Strategy · Capabilities · Segments

References Available Upon Request

Artificial Intelligence Analysis of Marketing Scientific Literature: An Abstract

Antonio Hyder and Ronjon Nag

Abstract We discuss the development of a machine-based research literature reading methodology for marketing science based on artificial intelligence (AI) developments made in other fields. Marketing science would benefit from adopting AI-based technologies for text mining, analysis and predictive writing. This could automate literature review and formulation of hypotheses.

Scientific progress is disseminated in scientific publications, which are growing exponentially. Thousands of papers are published each year. Research overload is a bottleneck for scientific development. Keeping up is untenable for researchers even within specialised fields. Recognising new questions or hypotheses will be increasingly challenging. The rapid increase in the rate of research points out the need for techniques that can simplify its use. AI techniques such as text mining and natural language processing (NLP) can assist in removing the bottleneck. Text mining is the use of algorithms for extracting information from text documents such as scientific articles. In AI, NLP is used to analyse large amounts of natural language data. The combination of NLP and text mining techniques enables scientific literature text mining with NLP. In this regard, the most advanced developments have been made in the disciplines of chemistry and materials (e.g. Kim et al. 2017; Tshitoyan et al. 2019). In these fields, knowledge extraction and relationships are made using massive bodies of scientific literature using CrossRef Application Programming Interface (API) to retrieve large lists of article Digital Object Identifiers (DOIs).

Our suggested method for marketing science will be based on the developments made in chemicals and materials. Word embeddings will be trained with marketing science abstracts retrieved from scientific databases (e.g. Elsevier and Science Direct). After removing irrelevant abstracts, the remaining relevant ones will be tokenised. This will result in a vocabulary formed by the extracted contents. We shall

A. Hyder (✉)
Hackers and Founders Research, Palo Alto, CA, USA
e-mail: ah@hf.cx

R. Nag
Stanford University, Stanford, CA, USA
e-mail: ronjon@dci.stanford.edu

F. Pantoja, S. Wu (eds.), *From Micro to Macro: Dealing with Uncertainties in the Global Marketplace*, Developments in Marketing Science: Proceedings of the Academy of Marketing Science, https://doi.org/10.1007/978-3-030-89883-0_167

then conduct a three-step process adopted from Tshitoyan et al. (2019). First, the compilation of consolidated bodies of offline marketing science research such as retail or advertising. Second, the embeddings will be trained with scientific abstracts from each topic. The abstracts will then be tokenised to produce individual words. Third, we shall repeat the first two integrating the offline topics with the equivalent online topics (i.e. online retail or advertising). Lessons learned when dealing with the offline research may help inform analyses made with the online research. Our method could eventually facilitate transfer of research knowledge to marketing practice, especially to startups, due to the increasing need for applying research to practice (Kumar 2017; Lilien 2011).

Keywords Marketing science · Artificial intelligence · Machine reading · Natural language processing

References Available Upon Request

Attachment Style and Loneliness as Determinants of Self-Gifting: An Abstract

Cindy B. Rippé, Carolina Werle, and Amanda Pruski Yamim

Abstract While there is extensive research on loneliness and its global burden affecting health and well-being, we have little understanding of how loneliness affects consumer purchases. Specifically, the consumer purchase of a self-gift is of interest because feeling loneliness may make one more susceptible to self-oriented shopping behavior. Drawing from attachment theory, three studies demonstrate that consumers are more likely to self-gift when feeling lonely. This effect, however, is related to attachment style with securely attached individuals self-gifting more when feeling lonely in comparison to insecurely attached individuals. This research followed a quantitative, experimental design using three studies with respective sample sizes of 161, 244, and 236 respondents. Analysis techniques included ANOVA and spot light analysis. In Study 1, we investigate if loneliness influences intentions to self-gift. In Study 2, we explore how attachment style moderates the relationship between loneliness and self-gifting. In Study 3, we examine the mediating role of negative emotions. Importantly, we show that the impact of loneliness is stronger (solely significant) for securely attached individuals because they cope with negative emotions by self-gifting. The present research, thus, contributes to our understanding of how loneliness influences consumer behavior. This research also adds to the understanding of how an individual's attachment style influences behavior and reactions to the environment. The first study confirms that loneliness leads to self-gifting behavior while the second study highlights that only for secure attachment styles does the experience of loneliness drive self-gifting behavior. The final study examines the process and uncovers that loneliness leads to self-gifting because of the negative emotions. Specifically, the findings display a difference in coping styles when dealing with the negative emotions associated with loneliness whereby the coping of secure styles translates into shopping behavior. With the prevalence of

C. B. Rippé (✉)
University of North Georgia, Dahlonega, GA, USA
e-mail: cindy.rippe@ung.edu

C. Werle · A. P. Yamim
Grenoble Ecole de Management, Grenoble, France
e-mail: carolina.werle@grenoble-em.com; amanda.pruskiyamim@grenoble-em.com

F. Pantoja, S. Wu (eds.), *From Micro to Macro: Dealing with Uncertainties in the Global Marketplace*, Developments in Marketing Science: Proceedings of the Academy of Marketing Science, https://doi.org/10.1007/978-3-030-89883-0_168

loneliness in today's society, our findings provide insight into the purchase decisions of lonely consumers while complementing prior work that notes that materialism is an outlet for lonely consumers.

Keywords Attachment style · Loneliness · Self-gifting · Negative emotions

References Available Upon Request

Special Session SIM-AMS: How Does Price Bundling Affect Tourists' Extra Spending? An Abstract

Claudia Cozzio, Oksana Tokarchuk, and Oswin Maurer

Abstract This is a preliminary study that investigates the effect of the expansion of a bundled holiday package on tourists' extra spending. From a theoretical perspective, much research has been conducted on how bundled pricing affects the perceived value of the products or services included in the bundle (Arora 2011; Shaddy and Fishbach 2016). However, the impact of price bundling on tourists' extra spending at the destination, which includes complimentary items that are not part of the bundle, has not been explored previously.

When the purchase is made in bundling conditions, consumers are less likely to clearly identify the cost-benefit connection and, in turn, they seem more likely to under-consume an already paid-for service (Soman and Gourville 2001). Furthermore, in the case of bundled offers in the service industry, that are typically broad in scope and in duration, the costs of a transaction significantly precede the benefits, thus having little sunk cost impact on the consumption of the pending benefits (Soman and Ahn 2010). The low likelihood of consuming all the items in the bundle and the tendency to forgo a pending benefit within the bundle might exert a beneficial effect on tourists' extra spending at the destination.

Tourists' extra expenses are perceived as exceptional expenditures that are of smaller magnitude compared to the overall holiday budget, and, for that reason, they are more likely be left unnoticed. To prevent overspending, consumers tend to set mental budgets that limit their spending within specific categories (Thaler 1985). The designation of the budget for extra expenses is done after paying for the whole holiday package (Legohérel and Wong 2006).

Although it is rational to expect that tourists' extra spending should decrease by the appeal and the completeness of the bundle on offer, our study, through a quasi-experiment focused on guests' extra expenses at the resort bar, provides empirical evidence that tourists do not behave rationally. Tourists dedicate similar budgets for extra spending regardless of what it is included and what they paid for the bundled holiday package. Resort managers aiming to increase their revenues should care-

C. Cozzio (✉) · O. Tokarchuk · O. Maurer
Free University of Bozen-Bolzano, Bolzano, Italy
e-mail: claudia.cozzio@unibz.it; oksana.tokarchuk@unibz.it; oswin.maurer@unibz.it

F. Pantoja, S. Wu (eds.), *From Micro to Macro: Dealing with Uncertainties in the Global Marketplace*, Developments in Marketing Science: Proceedings of the Academy of Marketing Science, https://doi.org/10.1007/978-3-030-89883-0_169

fully design mixed-product bundled holiday packages, paying attention to the appeal and the completeness of the offer beside the bundle.

Keywords Price bundling · Transaction decoupling · Mental budgeting · Tourists' spending

References Available Upon Request

Special Session SIM-AMS: We Are the Champions! The Role of Conversational Marketing on Fan Engagement: An Abstract

Letizia Lo Presti, Giulio Maggiore, Vittoria Marino, and Riccardo Resciniti

Abstract Despite the opportunities of conversational marketing, today little has been investigated regarding the role of the fan/team conversation in sport management through the use of digital engagement platforms (such as instant messaging apps) and regarding the impact generated by their involvement on fan engagement and loyalty. The literature on sport management has investigated the role of social media in the behavior of supporters (Na et al. 2019; Li et al. 2019; Filo et al. 2015; Stavros et al. 2013) but to date little is known about the role of conversation in service production processes in contexts of digital engagement platforms that lead the consumer from involvement to loyalty to a brand team: therefore, understanding the role that these have in the transition from lead generation actions to satisfaction and loyalty is a priority for those sports companies who wish to ride the wave of innovation in customer relations. This paper proposes a research model for investigating the effect on customer satisfaction and customer loyalty of the three dimensions of the customer engagement construct on Mobile Instant Messaging Apps when they are used as Engagement Platforms in a conversational marketing approach. In addition, the aim of this paper is to verify the mediating role of fan engagement and satisfaction on loyalty to the sports team. A survey was conducted on fans of a famous football team in Italy that recently, has decided to use WhatsApp (Mobile Instant Messaging App) to allow fans to communicate directly with football players. To test the hypotheses, a regression sequence was performed to evaluate the relationships between engagement and involvement and the mediating effect of fan engagement and satisfaction, checking for gender, instruction level and age. The results highlight the importance of emotional engagement on fan satisfaction and the role of behavioral engagement through the use of WhatsApp for enhancing fan

L. L. Presti (✉) · G. Maggiore
University of Rome Unitelma Sapienza, Rome, Italy
e-mail: letizia.lopresti@unitelmasapienza.it; giulio.maggiore@unitelmasapienza.it

V. Marino · R. Resciniti
University of Sannio, Benevento, Italy
e-mail: vmarino@unisannio.it; resciniti@unisannio.it

F. Pantoja, S. Wu (eds.), *From Micro to Macro: Dealing with Uncertainties in the Global Marketplace*, Developments in Marketing Science: Proceedings of the Academy of Marketing Science, https://doi.org/10.1007/978-3-030-89883-0_170

commitment. The results also reveal that involvement and fan engagement are determining for the loyalty to the sports team and for the continued use of the MIM apps in the future. In particular, this is true for young people who are particularly satisfied when using WhatsApp with players. It means that WhatsApp, also in sports management, is capable of giving young fans a more active role, increasing the fan engagement by means of emotional and behavioural engagement. Fans who are engaged and more satisfied thanks to the use of MIM apps can be ambassadors for the sport brand thus affecting the WoM and the support to the team. For this reason, sports team managers have to consider the MIM app as a tool that can increase fan engagement.

Keywords Conversational marketing · Customer engagement · Fan engagement · Mobile instant messaging · Sport management · Customer relationship management

References Available Upon Request